GOVERNMENTS, GLOBALIZATION, AND INTERNATIONAL BUSINESS

Governments, Globalization, and International Business

Edited by

JOHN H. DUNNING

UNIVERSITY PRESS

OXFORD
UNIVERSITY PRESS

Great Clarendon Street, Oxford OX2 6DP
Oxford University Press is a department of the University of Oxford.
It furthers the University's objective of excellence in research, scholarship,
and education by publishing worldwide in

Oxford New York

Athens Auckland Bangkok Bogotá Buenos Aires Calcutta
Cape Town Chennai Dar es Salaam Delhi Florence Hong Kong Istanbul
Karachi Kuala Lumpur Madrid Melbourne Mexico City Mumbai
Nairobi Paris São Paulo Singapore Taipei Tokyo Toronto Warsaw

and associated companies in Berlin Ibadan

Oxford is a registered trade mark of Oxford University Press
in the UK and certain other countries

Published in the United States
by Oxford University Press Inc., New York

First published 1997
Reprinted new as paperback 1999

British Library Cataloguing in Publication Data
Data available

Library of Congress Cataloging in Publication Data
Governments, globalization, and international business / edited by
John H. Dunning.
Includes bibliographical references.
1. International business enterprises—Government policy—Case
studies. 2. Competition, International—Case Studies. 3. Economic
policy—Case studies. I. Dunning, John H.
HD2755.5.G688 1997 338.8′8—dc21 96–52308

ISBN 0–19–829068–3 (hbk.)
ISBN 0–19–829605–3 (pbk.)

1 3 5 7 9 10 8 6 4 2

Printed in Great Britain
on acid-free paper by
Biddles Ltd., Guildford & King's Lynn

ACKNOWLEDGEMENTS

I wish, first, to thank the Carnegie Bosch Institute, Carnegie Mellon University, for providing me with a grant to commission contributions for this volume and to prepare it for publication; and also for sponsoring a conference at Georgetown University Conference Center, Washington DC, in June 1995, at which the drafts of the chapters were discussed. I am particularly indebted to Professor Bruce McKern, the erstwhile Director of the Institute, for his encouragement and support; and to Cathy Burstein, also of the Center, for so efficiently and cheerfully organizing the Conference.

I would also like to express my gratitude to a number of scholars, who kindly agreed to comment on the draft chapters presented at the Conference. These included Charles Wolf of Rand School of Public Policy, Raymond Vernon of Harvard University, Tom Brewer of Georgetown University, Colin Bradford of the US Agency for International Development, and Gary Hufbauer of the Institute for International Economics in Washington.

In preparing this volume for publication, I was fortunate to have the editorial assistance of one of my Ph.D. students at Rutgers—Alison McKaig Berliner; while my secretary, Mrs Phyllis Miller did her usual excellent job both in typing my own chapters and in finalizing the manuscript for the publishers. Two other doctoral students, Lorna Wallace and Cliff Wymbs, provided me with some notes from Professor Michael Porter's talk at Georgetown, which helped form the basis of Chapter 3 of this book. I much appreciate the contribution of all these individuals—not to mention the authors of the chapters of this volume—towards the successful completion of this project.

Rutgers and Reading Universities
September 1996

CONTENTS

LIST OF FIGURES

LIST OF TABLES

ABBREVIATIONS

AAAS	American Association for the Advancement of Science
AD	anti-dumping
AGPS	Australian Government Publishing Service
AGW	*Aussenwirtschaftsgesetz*
AMC	Australian Manufacturing Council
ASEAN	Association of South-East Asian Nations
APEC	Asia Pacific Economic Cooperation
ATP	Advanced Technology Program
BETRO	British Export Trade Research Organization
BFCE	Banque Française du Commerce Extérieure
BIAC	Business and Industry Advisory Committee
BIE	Bureau of Industry Economics
BMWi	Bundesministerium für Wirtschaft [German Ministry of Economics]
BNAC	British North American Council
CAFC	Court of Appeals for the Federal Circuit
CD	certificate of deposit
CEC	Commission of the European Communities/Countries
CEPR	Centre for Economic Policy Research
CER	Closer Economic Relations
CIME	Committee on International Investment and Multinational Enterprise
CMA	Canadian Manufacturers' Association
CMIT	Capital Movements and Invisible Transactions
CNPF	Centre National du Patronat Français
CRADA	cooperative research and development agreement
CTI	Committee on Trade and Investment
CVD	countervailing duty
DATAR	Délégation à l'Aménagement du Térritoire
DEG	*Deutsche Investitions- und Entwicklungsgesellschaft mbH*
DG	Directorate General
DIHT	Deutsche Industrie- und Handelstag
DNEA	Developing North-East Asia
DREE	Direction des Relations Économiques Extérieures
DSA	deep structural adjustment
EAAU	East Asian Analytical Unit

EPAC	Economic Planning Advisory Commission
EBRD	European Bank for Reconstruction and Development
EC	European Community
EDI	electronic data interchange
EEC	European Economic Community
EMU	Economic and Monetary Union
EPAC	Economic Planning Advisory Commission
ERM	exchange-rate mechanism
ERSO	Electronics Research and Service Organization
ETM	elaborately transformed manufactures
EU	European Union
FDI	foreign direct investment
FG	flying geese
FIAS	Foreign Investment Advisory Service
FIFI	physical-financial
FIRA	Foreign Investment Review Agency
FIRE	finance, insurance, real estate
FTA	Free Trade Agreement
GATS	General Agreementon Trade in Services
GATT	General Agreement on Tariffs and Trade
GDP	gross domestic product
GNP	gross national product
HDTV	High Definition Television
IBB	Invest in Britain Bureau
IC	integrated circuit
IC	international corporation
ICSID	International Centre for the Settlement of Investment Disputes
ICT	information and communications technologies
ID	inner-dependent
IEDB	International Economic Data Bank
ILO	International Labour Office
IMCB	Institute of Molecular and Cell Biology
IMF	International Monetary Fund
IMP	Internal Market Programme
INSEE	Institut National de la Statistique et des Études Économiques
IP	intellectual property
IPE	international political economy
IPR	intellectual property rights

IRAP	Industrial Research Assistance Program
ITAC	International Trade Advisory Committee
ITC	International Trade Commission
ITO	International Trade Organization
ITRI	Industrial Technology Research Institute
ITT	International Telegraph and Telephone
JETRO	Japan External Trade Organization
JTPA	Job Training Partnership Act
JV	joint venture
LO	Landsorganisationen
M&As	mergers and acquisitions
MAI	Multilateral Agreement on Investment
MERCOSUR	Southern Core Common Market
MES	minimum efficient size
MFN	most-favoured nation
MES	medium-sized enterprise
MIGA	Multilateral Investment Guarantee Agency
MITI	Ministry of Industry and Trade
MNE	multinational enterprise
NACA	National Advisory Committee on Aeronautics
NAFTA	North American Free Trade Agreement/Area
NBER	National Bureau of Economic Research
NCMS	National Center [sic] for Manufacturing Sciences
NEC	non-equity forms of international cooperation
NGO	non-governmental organization
NIC	newly industrialized country
NIE	newly industrializing economy
NIST	National Institute for Standards and Technology
NTB	National Technology Board
NTI	National Treatment Instrument
NUTEK	[Swedish National Board for Industrial and Technical Development]
OECD	Organization for Economic Cooperation and Development
OED	Operations Evaluation Department
OEM	original equipment manufacturer
OF	outer-focused
OPEC	Organization of Petroleum Exporting Countries
OPIC	Overseas Private Investment Corporation

PEEC	Pacific Economic Cooperation Council
PIER	politics of international economic relations
QR	quantitative restrictions
R&D	research and development
RSA	Regional Selective Assistance
S&T	science and technology
SBI	Singapore Bio-Innovation
SCAP	Supreme Commander for Allied Powers
SESSI	[French Ministry of Industry]
SIC	Standard Industrial Code
SMEs	small and medium-sized enterprises
SOU	Statens Offentlige Utredningar [Swedish Official Government Report]
STU	[National Board of Technical Development]
TAA	Trade Adjustment Assistance
TCF	textile, clothing, footwear
TDC	Technology Development Centre
TFRG	total factor productivity growth
TEP	techno-economic paradigm
TGV	*train grande vitesse* [high-speed train]
TNC	transnational corporation
TRIM	trade-related investment measure
TTK	Tokyo Tsushin Kogyo
UN	United Nations
UNCITRAL	UN Commission on International Trade Law
UNCTAD	UN Conference on Trade and Development
UNCTC	UN Centre on Transnational Corporations
USTR	US Trade Representation
USSR	Union of Soviet Socialism Republics
VCI	Association of the Chemical Industry
VCR	video-cassette recorder
VER	voluntary export restrictions
VSLI	very large-scale integrated circuits
WTO	World Trade Organization

LIST OF CONTRIBUTORS

MAGNUS BLOMSTRÖM, Professor of Economics, Stockholm School of Economics, Sweden.

JOHN H. DUNNING, Professor of International Business, Graduate School of Management, Rutgers University, USA and Economics Department, University of Reading, UK.

CLAUDIO R. FRISCHTAK, Consultant, World Bank, Brazil.

EDWARD M. (Monty) GRAHAM, Senior Fellow, Institute for International Economics, USA.

ROSE MARIE HAM, Ph.D. student, Walter A. Haas School of Business, University of California at Berkeley, USA.

HAL HILL, Head of the Indonesian Project and Senior Fellow in Economics at the Research School of Pacific and Asian Studies, the Australian National University, Australia.

DIRK HOLTBRÜGGE, Dr., Universität Dortmund, Germany.

NEIL HOOD, Professor of Business Policy, University of Strathclyde, Glasgow, UK.

STEPHEN J. KOBRIN, William H. Wurster Professor of Multinational Management, The Wharton School, University of Pennsylvania, USA.

ARI KOKKO, Assistant Professor, Stockholm School of Economics, Sweden.

SANJAYA LALL, University Lecturer in Development Economics, Queen Elizabeth House, University of Oxford, UK.

RICHARD G. LIPSEY, Professor of Economics and Fellow, Canadian Institute for Advanced Research, Simon Fraser University, Canada.

BRUCE MCKERN, President and Chief Executive Officer, Monash Mt Eliza Business School, Australia.

CHARLES-ALBERT MICHALET, Professor of International Business, University of Paris-Dauphine, France.

DAVID C. MOWERY, Professor of Business and Public Policy, Walter A. Haas School of Business, University of California at Berkeley, USA.

TERUTOMO OZAWA, Professor of Economics, Department of Economics, Colorado State University, USA.

ALAN M. RUGMAN, Professor of International Business, Faculty of Management, University of Toronto, Canada.

JOHN M. STOPFORD, Professor of International Business, London Business School, England.

SUSAN STRANGE, Professor of Political Economy, University of Warwick, UK.

MARTIN K. WELGE, Professor Dr, Academic Director, Universitätsseminar der Wirtschaaft, Schloss Gracht, Germany.

STEPHEN YOUNG, Professor of International Business, University of Strathclyde, Glasgow, UK.

Introduction

John H. Dunning

1

The role of the nation state in the contemporary world economy continues to fascinate scholars,[1] and is likely to do so well into the next century. Over the last decade, in particular, three major events have challenged much of received wisdom about the extent and form of the involvement of national governments in the organization of both domestic and international economic activity. These are, first, the widespread renaissance of the market economy as the dominant socio-institutional system of resource allocation—as is being most dramatically illustrated by contemporary events in Central and Eastern Europe and in China; second, the emergence of several new economies as powerful industrial players on the world economic stage; and, third, the evolving globalization of production and markets,[2] which is encapsulating, and reconfiguring the nature of, economic space.

These events are, of course, closely interlinked; and underpinning each, as Richard Lipsey persuasively argues in Chapter 2 of this volume, are the dramatic and far-reaching technological and organizational advances of the past two or more decades. While some of the events may be irreversible, others, including the response to them of individuals, firms, and governments, are not. Already, we are experiencing a backlash to the breakdown of Communism and the revival of marked forces, while some of the downsides of the new technologies and globalization are now gaining increasing attention.[3] The East Asian (or at least the Japanese) 'miracle' does not seem to be quite as awe-inspiring as was first perceived;[4] and, most certainly, analysts are much more cautious in recommending that Western societies should embrace the Far Eastern models of capitalism than once they were.

The purpose of this volume is to take the debate about the role of national administrations[5] in economic affairs a step further. More particularly, it seeks to describe and analyse the implications of the deepening structural interdependence of the world economy—which is, perhaps, the unique characteristic of globalization[6]—for the governance of economic activity of nation states. How, for example, does the increasing mobility of many intangible created assets, notably knowledge and information, influence the ability of governments to manage their internal affairs? What is the role of the main creator and transferor of these assets—namely, the multinational enterprise (MNE) in this process? What can, and should, national governments do to ensure that the location-bound assets within their jurisdiction are of sufficient quality to attract and retain the mobile assets of corporations, which the former need to advance their economic and social goals? What exactly are the kinds of policies—and particularly macro-organizational policies[7]—which demand re-evaluation as governments seek to use such policies as competitive devices for obtaining and retaining mobile assets? Do the liberalization and globalization of markets lessen the role, or do they require a different role, of governments; and, if the latter, in what ways? What are the tasks which governments performed prior to globalization which are now better undertaken by markets? To what extent is it more appropriate, in the closing years of the twentieth century, to consider the role of the state as complementary to, rather than substitutable for, other organizational modalities? Is the emergence of complex cross-border networks of economic activity requiring a more systemic and supranational approach to governance? How far are the forces of globalization changing the optimum size of national government—and how is this likely to vary by function? To what extent is Kenichi Ohmae's claim that the sovereignty of the nation state is being eroded by the emergence of sub-national regional states, on the one hand, and by supra-national regimes on the other, a correct one? (Ohmae 1995)

It is questions such as these which this book seeks to address. In acknowledging that the answers are likely to be contingent on the methodologies and ideologies of the authors—not to mention the historical and geographical perspective from which they are being viewed—the first five chapters set out the views of scholars of different intellectual backgrounds and persuasions on how they perceive globalization to be changing the role of the state in economic affairs.

In devising the second part of this volume, I was acutely aware that the interface between governments, globalization, and international business activity was (and is) likely to vary between countries according, for example, to their size, economic structures, stages of development, openness, and institutional frameworks; and also to their cultural and ideological heritages. Chapters 6 through 15, which present case studies of eight developed countries and two developing regions of the world, confirm that this interface is, in fact, highly country specific. Does this mean that one cannot draw any general conclusions about the appropriate governance of nation states? No, but it does mean that it is dangerous to conclude that the factors leading to the successes of one governance regime can be easily transferred to another regime where the political and legal systems, social values, economic mores, and commercial infrastructure are totally different.

In Part Three of the volume, John Stopford and Monty Graham try to draw some generalizations from the country case studies for national government policies. One such generalization relates to the notion of competing governments. At one time, governments used to compete with each other largely through their international trade policies; it was to set the rules of the game for that competition that GATT was initiated in 1945. Today, the areas of competition between governments are many and varied. To attract foreign direct investment (FDI) into their areas of jurisdiction,[8] states may use not only a battery of fiscal initiatives, but a gamut of macro-organizational policies—for example, with respect to education, the environment, transport, and communication, and so on—each of which may substantially effect the costs of doing business. To ensure that such policies facilitate the efficient workings of markets, rather than distort them, many scholars have argued that there is need for some kind of supranational governance; and it is with this issue that the final chapter of the book deals.

2

Although the first chapter of the book traces the evolutionary thought of economists and other scholars towards the perceived role of government, it does not attempt to identify the key themes of this volume. This introductory chapter seeks to do just this, albeit in an extremely abbreviated form. In particular, it examines four aspects of the governance of modern states, which, we believe, need reappraising in the light of the globalization of economic activity. These are, first, the distinction between the *systemic* and the *operational* roles of governments; secondly, the country specific factors most likely to affect this role, and especially now these change as countries move along their development paths; thirdly, the kinds of responses of governments to globalization; and, fourthly, the appropriate territorial jurisdiction of governments—for example, is it supranational, national, or sub-national. We shall deal with these issues in turn.

2.1. The Systemic and Operational Roles of the State

The distinction between the role of the state as (i) a setter-up, monitor, and manager of an economic system, and the ultimate resolver of disputes arising from it, and (ii) that of an organizational entity which operates within that system, is a critical one. Although, as Chapter 2 will show, there are many historical examples of analysts emphasizing the *systemic* role of the state (indeed, Adam Smith regarded this as its pre-eminent function), much of the post-Second World War debate has been about its *operational* functions, and especially about when and how governments should intervene in the functioning of particular markets. Only very recently, as the merits of alternative capitalistic systems have become increasingly debated, have scholars begun to re-emphasize the social architectural role of governments, which identifies the way in which economic relationships and processes are organized. And even today, practising politicians—particularly in Western industrialized economies—still focus on the question of 'more' or 'less' government, rather than on the kind of actions governments need to take to ensure the economic system for which they are responsible is best achieving its purpose. Here, it is useful to distinguish between the idea of *strong and efficient* governments and that of *strongly interventionist* governments. Here, too, as we shall see later, there is a useful parallel to be drawn between that of large multi-activity firms and the governance of non-market institutions.

Along with technological change, the globalization or regionalization of economic activity is the principal contemporary event which is challenging the traditional systemic role of capitalistic states. In essence, this role is to minimize the extra-market coordinating and transaction costs of economic activity. It follows that anything which causes that activity to become more specialized, complex, and interdependent, or for markets to become more uncertain and volatile, or characterized by externalities, information asymmetries, and opportunism, is likely to impose additional institutional and surveillance responsibilities on governments. Almost by definition, then, an information-intensive and innovating economy will require the participation of non-market institutions if it is to perform effectively.

It will be recognized that the above costs are also examples of the kind of transaction costs which firms incur in the use of particular intermediate product markets; and it is to avoid or reduce these costs that they internalize these markets. However, in addition to these *specific* transaction costs, there are general or societal transaction costs associated with the creation and management of an economic system *in toto*. Obvious examples are establishing and enforcing law and order, the protection of property rights, the enforcement of contracts and the management of conflicts, not to mention the costs of mitigating the adverse social affects of, and the adjustment of, non-market institutions, to economic change. As Douglass North (1993) and Wallis and North (1986) have demonstrated, the transaction sector of the US economy has escalated over the last century, and particularly so since the advent of the current generation of technological advances. These advances have both hastened the demise of the Fordist economy, based on mass production, and led to the emergence of the innovation-led economy.[9]

The evolution of an innovation-led economy, in which frequent and turbulent technological change is an endemic feature, is, perhaps, the main reason for the increased organizational costs of governance; and they arise independently of the brand of market-based capitalism practised. Indeed, they represent the fixed costs of such a system. And, although firms are responding to the demands of the innovating and competitive economy by decentralizing or downsizing their headquarters operations, at the same time there can be little doubt that their senior management has just as vital a role to play as it ever did. The same must surely be true of governments. However much they may disengage themselves from operational interventionism, their part in ensuring that the economic system runs effectively is at least as critical as it has ever been, if not more so.

Globalization introduces a new dimension to the systemic costs of an innovation-led economy by adding new spatially related transaction and coordination costs of doing business. From the perspective of firms, such costs range from those of surmounting natural and artificial barriers to trade and FDI, to the less easily measurable or 'tacit' costs of setting up, organizing, and administering a group of value-added activities in very diverse economic, political, and cultural environments;

and in maintaining a satisfactory communication both between headquarters and the operating units, and between the operating units. From the perspective of national governments, the costs essentially arise from understanding, monitoring, and, where appropriate, adapting to the institutional frameworks of other countries. Where such frameworks are broadly similar, or where governments agree to cede their authority to some form of supra-national governance (e.g. as in the case of trade matters), their systemic costs would be unaffected or even fall. But, more usually, national governments are reluctant to surrender any part of their sovereignty; and the price of this is the additional cost of interfacing with other economic systems. This is particularly the case in those areas where the systemic costs of governance affect the efficiency of locationally mobile industrial activity, and where critical technological changes impact on these systems differently. Much of the debate about the respective macro-organizational roles of the US and Japanese governments is not about their intervention within the market system; it is rather about how they can best manage the system as a whole.

It is a fundamental tenet of this volume that globalization is requiring national governments to re-evaluate various facets of their systemic governance. Sometimes, their efforts need to be directed to obtaining and enforcing common internationally accepted laws and regulations—for example, with respect to intellectual property rights. Sometimes, they need to be directed to ensuring that their institutional frameworks and governance systems do not disadvantage their own firms and citizens relative to those of other countries—for example, with respect to environmental regulations, competition policies, tax regimes, and so on. Sometimes, they need to be directed to reducing cross-border non-tariff barriers, discriminatory procurement policies, technical standards, and border controls; and sometimes to creating new regimes for encouraging entrepreneurship and/or resolving conflict management (Chang and Rowthorn 1995). Whatever their form, we are suggesting that, as the structural interdependence between nations deepens, so does the systemic role of domestic governments need re-examining; and particularly so in economies which, in all other respects, are similar to each other. In a very real sense, the systemic role of states must undergo continuous creative destruction, if the social net benefits of technological change and spatial economic interdependence are to be fully exploited.

The concept of the creative destruction of governments has even more validity when applied to their *operational* functions. For, whereas the establishment of an institutional framework for economic activity is a *unique* responsibility of governments, how much and in what form it participates in the workings of the system is primarily dependent on how cost efficient it is, relative to some alternative institutional modality in achieving societal objectives. Here, both technological advances and increasing globalization are affecting the balance of advantages between the organizational options. Sometimes, the balance favours the unaided market; sometimes, large hierarchies; and sometimes, state involvement. However, more often than not, it favours a plurality of complementary arrangements. In the nineteenth century even the most *laissez-faire* economists accepted the idea

TABLE 0.1. Some situations in which governments might successfully contain organizational costs

Intervention or form of government intervention	Consequences for the reduction of government-related transaction costs
• The enhancement of national competitiveness by market facilitating measures; and publicly promoting this objective.	• Reduces the effectiveness of rent seeking by special interest groups. • Increases work effort of public agents. • Makes policy trade-offs easier to identify and solve.
• The containment of interventionist policies to activities severely hampered by market failures.	• Clarifies policy-makers' task and reduces problem of bounded rationality.
• A holistic approach to the coordination of complementary policies and institutional mechanisms.	• Reduces likelihood of sub-optimization. • Captures economies of scope in governance and increases intra-organizational information flows and learning.
• An ethos of consensus and cooperation between private and public policy-markers, e.g. with respect to mutually beneficial goals and the means by which goals can best be achieved.	• Reduces transaction costs of interaction between representatives of private and public sector. • Increases knowledge of public decision-takers. • Reduces chance of uninformed or biased media coverage in forcing governments into ill-advised or hasty decisions.
• The recruitment of the most talented and well-motivated individuals for public-sector employment, e.g. by offering competitive working conditions and encouraging initiative and entrepreneurship.	• Likely to inhibit the pursuance of sub-optimal goals and to reduce bounded rationality and opportunism and use of inefficient production technologies.
• The insulation of the policy-making process from the strongest (and most undesirable) pressure groups.	• Reduces the effectiveness of rent seeking by special interest groups, and relieves the policy-making process from the pressure of day-to-day politics.
• The presence of a national ethos or mentality of the need to be competitive and create wealth. This embraces both a 'commutarian' culture and a social climate which encourages personal initiative, entrepreneurship, scientific specialization, and competition.	• Favours coordination of strategies and policies of public and private organizations and reduces the sub-optimization problem in the public sector.
• The absence of strong sectoral interest groups, e.g. farmers and left-wing labour groups, which might press for interventionist measures by governments other than those which are market facilitating.	• Reduces possibility of ideological conflicts and undue emphasis being placed on the redistribution of incomes as a (short-term) social good.

Sources: Wade (1989); Stiglitz (1989); Grestchmann (1991); Hämäläinen (1994).

of the state operating public utilities; and for years few questioned the desirability of a state postal or telecommunications monopoly. Yet, today, mainly because of technological developments, many of these functions are best provided by the private sector. Similarly, many of the initial reasons for regulating services—and particularly FDI in services—no longer hold good.

By contrast, there are other areas where technological change and globalization are encouraging either more direct non-market interventionism, or the formation of joint ventures between public and private interests. Foremost among these are idiosyncratic markets in which transaction and coordinating costs of free markets or hierarchies are increasing relative to those of extra-market governance. Several capital products are increasingly taking on the characteristics of public goods and require enormous fixed costs which may take an exceptionally long time to recoup; examples include a new rail link from London to the Channel Tunnel at Dover and the world's largest hydroelectric project in the Tumen region of North China. The market, for these and similar projects, also usually involves substantial externalities which increase the divergence of social and private net benefits.

The opening-up of cross-border markets is likely to have mixed results. On the one hand, such regional integration schemes (e.g. the Internal Market Programme (IMP) of the European Union (EU)[10] and the North American Free Trade Agreement (NAFTA), by outlawing nationally imposed structural market distortions, are reducing the role of national governments; on the other, as seen most clearly in the trade negotiations between the EU over agricultural products, and between the USA and Japan over a range of high-technology products, the internationalization of markets only increases the need of governments to counteract, or minimize the damage of, the actions of other governments, which, for one reason or another, they perceive to work against the interests of their own constituents. National governments may also increase their intervention in particular markets for environmental, strategic, or social reasons. All of these are examples of need for strong and efficient national administrations, even though, paradoxically, at the end of the day, this might result in the abrogation of their responsibilities to market or other non-market forces.

The literature is replete with examples of situations in which government intervention in the organization of particular markets is most likely to be cost effective. It is not our purpose, or that of other authors in this volume, to consider these in any great detail. However, Table 0.1, which draws upon some ideas of a number of scholars, sets out some kinds of government intervention which may be expected to reduce transaction or coordinating costs.[11] In considering how globalization affects these costs, we would argue that more operational interventionism by government *may* be justified wherever cross-border markets are more structurally distorted than domestic markets; and where traders or producers from the home country are faced with foreign-related non-commercial risks, information asymmetries, and opportunism. Such additional market failures are likely to be both country and transaction specific; and to be particularly felt by small or medium-size firms. Home governments may then intervene, and this intervention may discriminate between individual markets (or participants in the markets) (*a*) to provide cost-effective information about foreign markets, (*b*) to insure firms against political risks, and (*c*) to negotiate with foreign governments on such matters as the removal or reduction of trading and investment barriers, discriminatory treatment of their own, MNEs, and protection of their territorial or property rights.

With the rapid growth of cross-border business activity and the increased role of regional blocs and supra-national agencies or 'clubs' of one kind or another, the need for a firm and intelligent government voice in the international debating chambers should not be minimized. Indeed, we would probably rate this as the single most important implication of globalization for the operational interventionism by governments; and, as several contributors to this volume observe, it is particularly critical in the domain of high-technology sectors and in those in which globalization is having the most impact on job security and human-resource development.[12]

2.2. Country-Specific Characteristics and the Governmental Responses to the Globalizing Economy

It will be a recurring theme of this volume that there is no universal 'best' prescription of the ways national governments should respond to globalization. So much, it will be argued, depends on the existing institutional and economic infrastructure; and on the social and cultural fabric of the countries in question. Even among the most similar of industrial nations, educational and national innovatory systems, anti-trust legislation, environmental regulations, agricultural and regional policies—not to mention fiscal and social security systems—differ widely from each other. It is no wonder, then, that, although the current generation of technological advances and globalization *is* deeply affecting the polity of all countries, it is affecting them differently; and it is the objective of Part Two of this volume to describe these differences and how they affect the responses of national governments. In Chapter 16 John Stopford attempts to see whether, in spite of these differences, there are common consequences of globalization. Is it, for example, leading to a greater convergence of national macro-organizational policies? Is it leading to more or less centralization of governance within nation states? Is it forcing all governments to reappraise the institutional framework for effective governance? Is it making intra-national conflict management—for example, with respect to the rent-seeking activities of special interest groups or the distribution of the costs and benefits of globalization—more or less easy to deal with? Is it aiding or frustrating the attainment of specifically national economic and social goals?

National administrations have, of course, sought to answer these and similar questions for many generations; but contemporary events are intensifying the need for effective answers, if for no other reason than that the competence of governments to reconcile (or encourage the reconciliation of) the paradoxes posed by globalization[13] will critically affect their wider responsibilities to advance the economic and social well-being of their citizens. Once again, whether by systemic or operational interventionism, we see globalization as underlining the need for more, rather than less, effective national governance.

Of course, any serious study of the past or current economic development of any country cannot but acknowledge the decisive role of its national government in affecting that development. Nowhere is this better demonstrated in the country whose constituents are most suspicious of government intervention—namely, the USA. Throughout the nineteenth century, there was a panoply of measures introduced by the US federal and state governments to foster economic development.[14] Whether *ex post* these were market facilitating or market distorting is not really the point;[15] what is the point is that, without pro-active government measures, US economic development would have proceeded less rapidly, and probably on a different trajectory than it did. And, that they continue to have a critical role—particularly in the case of developing economies—is best exemplified in a plea articulated by the arch-priest of the market place—the World Bank—that governments and the private sector have a complementary—indeed a synergistic—role to play in economic development (World Bank 1991).

The importance of the role of the state in ameliorating market failures during the early stages of economic development is, in fact, well acknowledged by several scholars, notably Stiglitz (1989), Wade (1989), and Bardham (1990), although it is no less widely accepted that the record of the cost-effectiveness of governments in reducing market failure—both systemic and operational—is unimpressive (Datta-Chaudhuni 1990; Krueger 1990). It is also generally agreed that, as market economies become more mature, the systemic role of government is likely to become less intrusive, while its operational role is likely to be less specific and direct (e.g. with respect to targeting industrial sectors for development) and more general and indirect. The changing functions of the Japanese government in the post-war period is a classic case in point.

What, perhaps, most economists are less prepared to accept is the idea that, as and when a country reaches the stage of development now being experienced by the most advanced economies—and particularly those dependent on a continual upgrading of their created assets for their prosperity—the role of national administrations may begin to become more important once again. This U-shaped relationship between the extent and form of state involvement and economic development applies independently of the particular form of market-based capitalism practised by countries. Neither should it be measured by the proportion of the GNP for which governments are responsible. Rather—as we have already argued—it should reflect the increasing organizational complexity and dynamism of economic activity, and the rising transaction and coordination costs associated with its management and consequences. This suggests the need for increased government action to ensure that the social externalities of the markets for dynamic goods are fully exploited; and that the social assets necessary for the efficient upgrading and exploitation of the core competences of firms and individuals are adequately provided.[16]

It will come as no surprise that some governments have been much better at meeting the economic challenges of the late twentieth century than others. Partly, as later chapters in this volume will show, it is a question of how easily both individuals and institutions are able and willing to embrace economic change; and in this respect, at least, until the late 1980s, the East Asian countries had a better record than the rest of the world.[17] Partly, too, it is a matter of the power of well-entrenched customs, institutional rigidities, and vested interests to block or impede change. Moreover, most domestic governments are in office only four or five years; and few have the opportunities of Margaret Thatcher's Conservative government through the 1980s, or the broad consensus of successive Japanese and German post-war governments, to implement and initiate major programmes of systemic change. It is, perhaps, noteworthy that foremost among the governments of countries which have recorded the most economic success in the post-war period have been those which had the least institutional baggage to offload.

One of the features of the contemporary world economy is the encapsulation of time and space. After the Second World War, it took Japan forty years to reach a much more sophisticated level of development than it took the USA and Europe to accomplish in the century before the First World War. Yet, Hong Kong, Korea, Taiwan, Malaysia, and Singapore have moved from being in the bottom third of the world's economies in the 1960s to that of being in the top 20 per cent in the space of a single generation. Technological advances begin to obsolesce the moment they are made. One of the clues to successful and continuous product innovation is the speed at which this can be accomplished.

Likewise, the physical boundaries of the market place and production possibilities are being extended all the time. As Stephen Kobrin points out in Chapter 5, and in Kobrin (1995), we live in a world in which many transactions are undertaken by electronic networks; and many spatial constraints are irrelevant. All the same, as other contributors to this volume emphasize, the geography of production still matters; in spite of the increasing mobility of many resources, there is still much 'spatial stickiness in slippery space'.[18]

We make these points simply to illustrate that globalization is accelerating the pace at which country-specific variables affecting the interaction between governments and markets may change. Whether this leads to the economic convergence between countries is another matter; but, if it does, then the response of competing governments to economic change and globalization will have a lot to do with it.

2.3. Differing Responses of Nation States to Globalization

The third aspect of globalization examined by several authors in this volume concerns the various policy reactions to it by governments. Historically, the main awareness by governments that the deepening of cross-border economic interdependence was affecting their national goals and policies was through the impact of outward and inward FDI. Looking back two decades—as is particularly well illustrated in the contributions of Hood and Young, Blomstrom, and Frischtak—the main reaction of national governments to FDI was to ensure that it conformed to their *existing* macro-economic and development policies. The literature of the 1970s and 1980s is replete with illustrations of attempts by governments to regulate the extent and pattern of MNE activity, while offering fiscal and other incentives to attract the 'right' kind of FDI.[19] During this period, too, efforts were made to devise internationally acceptable guidelines of behaviour,[20] which were either addressed to MNEs, or to governments in their dealings with MNEs. While FDI policy remains an important macro-organizational instrument of governments, it is now more generally recognized that, rather than trying to mould the activities and conduct of the chief vehicles of globalization to *existing* governmental policies, the policies themselves should be re-evaluated. This is not to deny that specific action towards FDI and MNE activity may not sometimes be required; but in general, we would argue that globalization is demanding changes of the actions of national administrations quite independently of the ownership of the firms which produce within their jurisdiction.

In acknowledging this change in the focus of governments, most of the chapters in this volume deal with the ways in which different national administrations and organizational policies are accommodating themselves to global changes. Susan Strange sets the scene well by identifying some of the main challenges of globalization to both the macro-economic and macro-organizational policies of government; and most of the particular aspects of such policies are examined in some depth by the authors of most country studies.

2.4. The Spatial Context of State Involvement

The optimum size of nation state has long been discussed in the literature. As Charles Kindleberger (1974) pointed out over two decades ago, much depends on the particular functions of governance one is considering. Is it governance over the currency areas, labour markets, technical standards, the environment, fiscal policy, and so on; or is it, indeed, the ability to coordinate the needs and aspirations of people of different cultures, languages, and ideologies?

What impact are technological advances and globalization having on appropriate territorial areas of political jurisdiction? More particularly, to what extent is this affecting the efficient functioning of national governments as they existed prior to the dramatic events of the 1980s. To contain our discussion to manageable proportions, we shall consider three broad levels of spatial governance—namely, the micro-regional or sub-national, the national, and the macro-regional or supra-national.

Our basic contention is that, both in the private sector and the public sector, globalization is affecting the appropriate size of decision-taking units and the locus of decision-taking. Several apparently conflicting forces are at work. In the private sector, for example, the recent wave of mergers and acquisitions (M&As) has produced a host of mega-firms, or groups of firms, particularly in international industries. At the same time, the disinternalization of non-core activities by large firms, the emergence of a new breed of entrepreneurs, and the widening opportunities for inter-organizational networking have led to a renaissance in the small or medium-sized firm. Moreover, while firms are surrendering some of their individual sovereignty to gain the benefits of alliances with other firms, they are also becoming more heterarchical in their organizational structures, and devolving more responsibility to their localized production units. Globalization is then changing both the nature and the modality of the governance of private wealth, creating sectors in national economies.

Exactly the same challenges are facing national governments; but, for the most part, their response has been sluggish. Since the First World War, at least, most national governments have been the dominant vehicle for the organization and management of economic activity within their jurisdiction.[21] Exceptions include nation states which have become part of regional free trade areas or customs unions, and those subject to the discipline of such supra-national institutions as the World Bank. And, of course, in the trading area, governments have been subject to the rules and conventions of GATT, even though, sometimes, their interpretations of these have widely differed.

Globalization, however, is making new demands on the spatial organization of public governance. On the one hand, as Chapter 17 will describe, it would seem likely that macro-regional and supra-national regimes will widen their supervisory functions to cover a wide range of issues germane to promote a level playing field for the cross-border movement of all kinds of assets, goods, and services. On the other hand, as elaborated in Chapters 4 and 16, there are suggestions that sub-national spatial units (which may, in fact, traverse national borders) are becoming important economic entities in their own right; and that, far from particular intra-national economic activities becoming more evenly distributed, the agglomeration (or clustering) economies of related industries—and particularly those with high transaction costs of distance—is likely to lead to more spatial concentration.

While not all analysts would go as far as Kenichi Ohmae in his assertion that the nation state will give way to the regional state, it is difficult to argue that the territorial jurisdiction of national polities have much relevance to the operation of global industries; while, at the same time, much of the efforts of governments to attract these industries to their borders comes not from national governments, but from sub-national regimes. In the USA, for example, individual states compete more vigorously for in-bound investment than does the federal government; while, in Europe and Asia, the main efforts to attract footloose FDI[22] come not from the national administrations of large countries (e.g. Germany, India and China), but from regional authorities within those countries, or from small countries (e.g. Belgium, Ireland and Singapore). Increasingly, too, it would seem that, in a locational choice between countries offering broadly similar factor endowments and markets—say between Germany and the UK—it is the advantages of the concentration of related supply capabilities in particular areas of these countries—e.g. the Ruhr Valley compared with the north-east of England —that will determine the final decision of firms. In so far as demand-related variables are of any influence at all, they are likely to be contained in the ease of access from the micro-region to the macro-region surrounding it. Indeed, the Shenzhen special economic zone in Southern China, the immigrant city state of Dalian on the Liadong peninsula, and the Tumen delta project of North China, are linked much more closely with countries outside China—both for many of their inputs and their markets—than with the rest of China.

As many economies flourish, they develop into mini-countries in their own right. More than this, they often form couplings with regions in adjacent countries; in other words, they span national borders, and, in so doing, they form new allegiances and reduce some of their dependences on national governments. Nevertheless, central administrations are likely to continue to exercise a critical influence in setting standards and in formulating a whole range of macro-organizational policies.

Several authors, and especially John Stopford in Chapter 16 of this volume, explore these and related issues. In the light of their analysis—and those of other commentators (e.g. Ohmae 1995)—it is not surprising that they conclude that some of the sovereignty national governments enjoyed for so many years is now being seriously challenged. However, it would be premature to conclude that the days of the nation state are numbered. It is, of course, quite possible, as John Naisbitt (1994) forecasts, that there will be further fragmentation of existing nation states (as has occurred in the erstwhile USSR and Yugoslavia); but, in essence, this simply means that one or more larger nation states are replaced by a larger number of smaller nation states. Whether this comes about is likely to rest on the competence of existing national regimes to act as a sympathetic and effective coalescing force for the wishes and aspirations of many diverse cultures and interest groups within their borders; the more profound is this intra-national diversity and the stronger the economic links of the micro-regions with the rest of the world, the more the forces of fragmentation, rather than unification, will prevail.

A more plausible scenario is that, following the lead of the corporate sector, the functions of the national governments will become more streamlined and differently directed than in the past. This does not, however, mean it will become less important. On the one hand, national governments will continue to exercise a decisive role at the negotiating tables of regional authorities and supra-national regimes. On the other hand, they have the tasks of encouraging and empowering their constituents to upgrade and utilize the assets available to them to the fullest extent; and of ensuring that the intra-national distribution of economic activity is best suited to the needs of both the domestic and international market place. Beyond this, national governments will continue to bear the major responsibility for steering their economies through the waters of economic change with minimum social hardship and the maximum support for resource restructuring and manpower retraining. *Inter alia*, this requires a fine tuning of generally accepted macro-economic and macro-organizational policies in ways suitable to the particular and special needs of their constituents.

We have paid especial attention to four aspects of the role of national governments in the emerging global economy—namely, the distinction between the systemic and operational functions of governments; some country-specific characteristics influencing that role; the alternative options open to governments in their response to globalization; and issues related to the spatial dimension of governance. As we have indicated, these issues are, perhaps, the ones most frequently addressed in later chapters of this book, in either a general or a specific context.[23]

But, of course, they are not the only ones. Others, which are given some attention by contributors, include the organizational structure of national administrations; the relations between particular sectoral interests and governments; the interface between macro-economic and macro-organizational policies; the alternative approaches to systems management by governments; the changing attitudes of national regimes to being part of a more structurally integrated regional or world economy; the asymmetrical relationship which sometimes occurs between governments; and the particular problems which arise from countries or regions whose economic prosperity rests, or has previously rested, on the possession of non-renewable resources.[24]

3

The remainder of this introduction briefly highlights the main features of each chapter in this volume.

Chapter 1 takes a historical and geographical perspective of the changing role of national governments. It describes the evolution of scholarly thought about the appropriate economic and social functions of the state in capitalist economies; and, in doing so, it contends that the differing opinions of scholars principally reflects the particular issues they are addressing, their own ideological perspectives and—perhaps most important of all—the economic structure and developmental stage of the country they are writing about. Adam Smith, Frederick List, Karl Marx, Joseph Schumpeter, and John Maynard Keynes were all creatures of their time and space; and it is by no means certain that, had they been writing in a different era or country, their views and prescriptions would have been the same. The general conclusion of this chapter is that, even if it were possible to frame a general theory of government involvement, in practice, the extent and content of such involvement is strongly conditional on the political and economic circumstances at the time and on the spatial dimension in which it is embedded.

Chapter 2 sets out an economist's view of the role of government. In his contribution, Richard Lipsey argues that, as with other events now occurring in the world economy, globalization is best thought of as an outcome of a new generation of technological advances which came on stream in the 1980s. Just as over the past two centuries innovations such as the steam engine, the telephone, the automobile, electricity, and the aeroplane have widened geographical markets from the local to the regional and then to the national and international, so contemporary telecommunication advances are further encapsulating the costs and time of traversing space. In the 1990s it is easier and cheaper to communicate between New York and Bangkok, or to travel from Zurich to Sydney than it was to do the same between London and Birmingham or Paris and Marseilles 200 years ago. At the same time, technological change has been the most important factor influencing the way economic activity is organized;[25] and the costs and benefits of using one or other of a triad of organizations—namely, the market, hierarchies and governments. As we have described elsewhere (see, e.g., Dunning 1993), in the early stages of the modern industrial economy the dominant form of organization economic activity was the unfettered market. In the later nineteenth century, managerial capitalism emerged, and hierarchies and markets came to be the dominant organizational modes, although governments began to play a more active role. In the inter-war years, the role of governments further increased, partly as a result of technological forces bringing about unstable economic conditions and structural market failures; while in our contemporary age, globalization and the emergence of a new range of technologies are again demanding a reappraisal of the effectiveness of the three modes of governance.

In Chapter 3 I draw upon and extend some of Michael Porter's ideas and writings[26] on the interface between governments and the competitiveness of resources and capabilities within their territorial jurisdiction. In this chapter we consider, first, the strategic response of firms to globalization, and then proceed to draw parallels between this response and that of non-market institutions. We suggest that one of the consequences of globalization is to underscore the role of national governments as vision-setters and institution-builders; as ensurers of availability of high-quality locationally bound inputs; as smoothers of the course of economic change; and as creators of the right ethos for entrepreneurship innovation, learning, and high-quality standards. Their operational role, however, is viewed more critically. Although, in some instances, the costs of government failure may be less than those of market or hierarchical failure, in others, governments would do better to try to reduce the latter failures than to circumvent them.[27]

Chapter 3 also suggests that there is likely to be some dilution of the authority of national regimes as economic activity becomes more regio-centric, while, at the same time, supra-national agencies will increasingly harmonize the rules of the game for national policies designed to influence the location of economic activity, and particularly that of MNEs. In this respect, the chapter argues, governments should set the seeds for their own creative destruction; for, in order to meet their main economic and social objectives, they may need to support both the positive restructuring of regional economies and the evolvement of new and efficient supra-national regimes—not to mention any cost-effective measures to improve the functioning of private markets.

In her chapter—written from the perspective of an international political economist—Susan Strange embraces a broad canvas of issues. First, she offers a timely reminder that, in our attempts to assess the consequences of globalization on the role of *national* governments, we should not neglect its wider implications for the global economic system. Secondly, in her discussion of the notion of power—which she prefers to think of in terms of outcomes—Strange argues that, although economic wealth has become less concentrated in the hegemonies of the nineteenth and early twentieth centuries, this does not mean that the power which remains is of no consequence.[28] On the other hand, Strange does envisage—as do other contributors to this volume—that the structural sovereignty of the nation state is likely to be eroded as a result of deepening cross-border integration. In particular, she illustrates her contention by referring to three areas of macro-economic management (namely, counter-cyclical policy, monetary stability, and the financing of state budgets), and three of macro-organizational management (industrial and competition policy, labour relations, and crime protection). In each of these areas, she believes that the freedom of national governments to pursue independent lines of action is being curtailed. Strange then goes on to assert that, although most consequences of globalization are favourably viewed by *firms* (and particularly by MNEs), others (notably the instability of the international finance system and exchange rates) are not—although, as the author points out, how far such instabilities affect the performance of firms is an under-researched area. To most *people*, Strange suggests, the effects of globalization are more ambiguous than those facing firms or governments, as they embrace a range of social and ethical, as well as economic, issues. Strange outlines—but does not attempt to resolve—three such issues often neglected by scholars—namely, family life and flexible working systems, consumer protection, and provision for retirement and old age.

In Chapter 5 Stephen Kobrin looks directly at the impact of globalization on the sovereignty of nation states. He, along with Richard Lipsey, sees globalization as the structural fusion of economic activity across national boundaries; and argues that it is qualitatively different from previous forms of internationalization which linked discrete economic activities by a series of arm's-length market transactions. He views technological advances as providing both the rationale and the impetus for this integration; MNEs, cross-border alliances, and the networking of firms as the vehicles by which it is achieved; and governments as the creators or facilitators of the institutional framework in which production and exchange can be effectively organized. Kobrin believes that the sovereignty of nation states is being compromised—if not undermined—by globalization, and particularly by the emergence of electronic networks. He believes that this is leading to an asymmetry between political and economic space, and between the structural power of firms and national governments, both of which may be difficult to resolve without the establishment of some sort of supra-national order.

Part Two of the volume starts with two case studies of countries, both of which are usually classified as resource-rich countries, and both of which have, for many years, been highly dependent on foreign ownership for their economic prosperity. In Chapter 6 Alan Rugman argues that it is not so much globalization, but regionalization, which is affecting the changing governance of economic activity in Canada. He suggests that, although the NAFTA will increase the economic interdependence and corporate linkages between Canada, the USA, and Mexico, the rule-based regime of NAFTA is, in many ways, preferable to Canadian firms and citizens than the former US-dominated power-based system. While he accepts that the macro-organizational policies of Canadian government are increasingly correlated with those of US government, he believes that the opportunities offered by NAFTA to be drawn into the regional network of the USA, together with the built-in safeguards of the agreement-for example, the provision for national treatment, rather than reciprocity—offers Canadian administrators a more robust geographical context in which to design their policies than that they previously enjoyed.

Chapter 8, by Hal Hill and Bruce McKern, follows on nicely from the Canadian case study, as, not only are foreign MNEs also major actors in the Australian economy, but their strategies, and those of the Australian government towards globalization, are being increasingly fashioned by developments in the neighbouring (i.e. East Asia and Pacific) region. Hill and McKern begin their chapter by describing the changing role of Australia in the global economy; and the federal government's reactions to these changes. These reactions have partly taken the form of the removal of many impediments to structural change—with trade and exchange-rate policies, the liberalization of financial and labour markets, and an overhaul of the tax system being the main targets; partly a refashioning of macro-economic policy; and partly a deliberate effort by the government to provide a better link for the country to the dynamism of the East Asian economy. Hill and McKern argue that, apart from the reforms of the labour market and federal fiscal relations, most macro-organizational policies have been successfully implemented—as have the attempts to reorient Australia's trade, technology, and FDI flows to East Asia. However, the record elsewhere has been less commendable; indeed, the authors claim that macro-economic management has been one of the casualties of globalization. They—like Claudio Frischtak in Chapter 15 in his case study of Brazil and Argentina—believe that the failure of the Australian authorities to resolve its rising current-account deficit and accumulation of external debt could well jeopardize its programme of structural reforms.

The following four countries offer profiles of large industrial nations. Each author has a distinctive story to tell. Neil Hood and Stephen Young in Chapter 8 zero down to the interface between UK government policies and FDI—especially in the light of the domestic political changes of the 1980s and the UK's membership of the EU. Yet, although the UK is—and always has been—the most liberal of countries in its attitude and policies towards FDI, it is only recently that the UK government has begun to appreciate the importance of its general macro-organizational policies—and particularly those designed to upgrade the quality of location-bound infrastructure—in affecting the investment decisions of foreign MNEs. Hood and Young further suggest that economic integration and increased competition between the member states of the EU are forcing the UK government to pay more attention to these policies, particularly in the light of the European Commission's own efforts to formulate a competitiveness policy in which FDI plays a rather less important role. Hood and Young also draw attention to some conflicts of interest between the UK government's interests in maximizing the benefits of globalization (*inter alia* arising from its Commonwealth and North America linkages) and those of the European Commission, which are more *directly* focused on fully exploiting the advantages of regionalization.

In Chapter 9 Rose Marie Ham and David Mowery suggest that the response of the US federal government to globalization has been extremely piecemeal and directed more to the creation of firm specific mobile competitive assets than to the upgrading of country specific location-bound assets (which, *inter alia*, influence the ability of a country properly to exploit the benefits of the mobile assets). To this extent, there are certain parallels with the UK situation. Ham and Mowery illustrate their argument with reference to US policies towards technology, intellectual property rights, and human-resource development. They suggest that, in response to the increasing internationalization of intangible assets, and the growing competition between governments for these assets, the US government has evolved what it perceives to be 'the best of both worlds' strategy', which, while supporting the creation and upgrading of the former assets (notably technology), tries to restrict their cross-border mobility.

In fact, Ham and Mowery believe the outcome may be a 'worst of both worlds'. Better, they contend, that attention should be directed towards 'the development of a more effective and feasible strategy of strengthening the quality of relative immobile assets and supporting the adoption and absorption of technology based assets' (p. 304). This contention, which is well argued by the authors, leads them to take a more pessimistic view of the likelihood of a closer relationship between government and the private sector than that urged by the present author (Dunning 1993). Instead, they believe that 'the opposite trend prevails' (p. 303), and that efforts focused on capturing the largest possible returns on indigenously mobile created assets, rather than on the upgrading of the complementary location-bound assets, is, in the long run, bound to be counter-productive.

Chapters 10 and 11 describe how two of the most economically powerful continental European countries have coped with globalization. At first sight, the differences are more marked than the similarities. Charles Albert Michalet traces the nationalistic and mercantilistic philosophy of France back to the time of Colbert; and argues that, although the policies of French administrations of the 1980s towards inward and outward investment underwent a complete volte-face, these were only embraced reluctantly in the light of the imperatives of globalization and regional integration. It, then, comes as no surprise that some of the most vociferous critics of globalization[29] are French politicians or bureaucrats—as documented by Michalet at the end of his chapter.

By contrast, Martin Welge and Dirk Holtbrügge portray Germany as one of the most outward-oriented industrialized economies. Certainly, as the authors observe, no other advanced country has gone through such dynamic and fundamental structural changes in the last decade as has Germany. While, in recent years, Germany has been preoccupied with the consequences of unification, and its economic interdependence with other countries in the EU is deeper than that with the rest of the world, it has always taken a relaxed attitude towards both inward and outward FDI.

At the same time, as Welge and Holtbrügge point out, the German government (like its Japanese counterpart) has done little to remove institutional and other impediments to inbound FDI via the acquisition route; and, to this extent, its reaction to globalization has been less than wholehearted.

However, the authors reserve their harshest criticism for the German government's handling of industrial policy, which they claim has been more directed to supporting ailing and mature sectors than encouraging dynamic new ones; and also for its failure to reduce the inflexibility of labour markets or help allay the fears of the German trade unions about the downsides of globalization. Welge and Holtbrügge also contend (and this will come as a surprise to many people) that German educational policies have been only partially successful in adjusting to the needs of the modern world. Indeed, the chapter gives the overall impression that, as in the French case, German macro-organizational policy is geared more to exploiting the benefits of European integration than those of globalization.

Turning next to a smaller, less central European economy, Magnus Blomström and Ari Kokko in Chapter 12 argue that, historically, most of the macro-organizational strategy of the Swedish government has been influenced by its FDI policies; and that these policies have been fashioned by an economy in which 'big business thrives' (p. 369) and in which foreign firms have always played a major role. This particular characteristic explains several historical differences between the Swedish experience and that of its European neighbours to the south. Until the 1990s, the authors argue, most constituents of the Swedish economy, including labour unions, were generally quite positive about the perceived benefits of outward investment, but were less comfortable with those of inward investment. Consequently, for most of the latter post-war period, one sees very few government regulations on outbound MNE activity, but a close scrutiny being made of most kinds of inbound FDI—and particularly of that targeted to resource and sensitive sectors. One also sees macro-organizational policy directed to supporting the competitiveness of large Swedish firms, particularly those in technology-advanced sectors. Blomstrom and Kokko suggest that one reason that Swedish trade unions initially accepted a liberal policy towards outward FDI was the successful pursuance of full employment policies by the Swedish government. However, their approach towards inward investment has been less welcoming, mainly because they perceive that foreign ownership might weaken their bargaining position or participation in strategic decision-taking.

The authors next proceed to suggest that the prospects of Sweden joining the

EU and globalization are causing a reappraisal of Swedish FDI policy—and, with it, industrial policy as well. Partly, they assert, this is because the performance of the Swedish economy has not lived up to expectations—even though some major Swedish MNEs have improved their global competitive positions. Partly, too, the increased unemployment levels of the early 1990s have increased the attractions of inbound FDI and reduced those of outbound FDI. And finally, as a result of its integration with the rest of Europe, Sweden has had to harmonize most of its laws and regulations towards inward investment. One interesting conclusion which Blomström and Kokko draw from their analysis is that globalization is forcing a convergence of the macro-organizational policies of nation states at similar stages of development, and that, in this new environment, the Swedish approach to FDI 'will probably look more like those in other small open economies' (p. 374).

Travelling now eastwards from Europe, Terutomo Ozawa, in Chapter 13, takes a dynamic view of the interface between the Japanese government and the market. He emphasizes Japan's particular political ideology that national governance should help harness and steer market forces in a way which promotes national economic goals and the comparative dynamic advantage of indigenous resources and capabilities. At the same time, as the Japanese industrial structure has moved from being national-asset based to knowledge based, the government's macro-organizational role—and particularly that of the Ministry of Industry and Trade (MITI)—has changed from being that of a 'national industrial architect' to a 'trade-conflict negotiator'—and 'a vision-builder'. Ozawa also observes that the outcome of the managed market has not always been as intended. In fact, it has created two differently structured sectors. The first is an outward-focused super-efficient sector which drives Japan's Schumpeterian-type exports and foreign investments. The second is an inner-dependent sheltered and over-regulated sector which has been trapped in a vicious circle of declining competition. While the pragmatic and adaptive style of Japanese governance has done much to foster the former sectors, it has also done little to discourage large uncompetitive sectors of industry which can survive only by investing abroad in low-cost environments.

Chapters 14 and 15 pay especial attention to the consequences of technological change and globalization for the organization of economic activity in two developing regions of the world—Asia and Latin America. As Sanjaya Lall points out in his chapter, most of East Asia—partly for cultural and sociological reasons—has followed the Japanese style of market-based capitalism.[30] In both Korea and Taiwan—the subject matter of Chapter 15—strong governments, with the close cooperation of private enterprise, have patterned the course of economic development—although, as that development has proceeded, the operational intervention of the state has been greatly reduced. However, while acknowledging the similarities in intent and philosophy, Lall also emphasizes the differences in the interface between the public and private sector in Korea and Taiwan. For example, he explains that, whereas in the Chinese tradition, the role of the small entrepreneurial firm has been of critical importance, in Korea—as in Japan—industrial development has been more concentrated within the hands of the large trading companies—that is, the Chaebol. Lall also evaluates the success and failures of the two systems and the lessons to be drawn from them.

While for the last two decades East Asian economies have generally followed a pattern of export-led development, and government policy has been primarily directed to promoting an orderly upgrading of that development,[31] most Latin American countries have given priority to building up strong indigenous industries. In this respect, they have followed the lead of much of continental Europe and the USA a century or more earlier; except that, in Latin America, governments were often controlled by military regimes, rather than being democratically elected.

After outlining his concept of the developmental state, and comparing it with the minimalist state, Claudio Frischtak pays especial attention to the interface between markets and governments in the case of Argentina and Brazil. He argues that, in response to recent technological advances and globalization, both countries have introduced a series of economic measures which represent a major volte-face in policy. These have consisted of three main strands. First, a social investment policy aimed (in Frischtak's words) at 'crowding in' private investment by providing physical and other supportive infrastructure, and by targeting sectors that offer large externalities to the rest of the economy. Secondly, there was the wholesale removal of a plethora of laws and regulations which exacerbated market inefficiencies; these included a substantial reduction of tariffs, and, in Argentina's case, the removal of most impediments to in-bound foreign investment and the technology transfers. Competition policy was also tightened. Thirdly, both countries pursued privatization programmes.

Frischtak asserts that, in general, these macro-organizational reforms—very much on the lines of those earlier adopted in East Asia—are having beneficial effects. What appears to be much more difficult to achieve is the fiscal and monetary discipline necessary to ensure macro-economic adjustment and stability. Frischtak makes this observation despite the relative success of some Latin American countries (e.g. Argentina, Chile, Columbia, and earlier Mexico) in reducing their inflation rates and pursuing sensible exchange-rate policies.

Drawing upon the contents of the previous chapters, Part Three of the volume considers how far it is possible to generalize about the appropriate responses of nation states to globalization. In Chapter 16 John Stopford points to both similarities and differences in the reactions of governments. On the one hand, there has been a largely universal movement towards the deregulation and liberalization of markets for all kinds of assets, goods, and services, which, itself, has aided the cross-border mobility of some firm-specific assets—notably of technology and organizational capabilities. Most countries have also introduced a series of macroeconomic reforms more attuned to the needs of the international market place.

However, the actions of governments to reconfigure their macro-organizational policies better to harness and upgrade the resources and capabilities within their jurisdiction have been much more piecemeal and disparate. Some—at least until very recently—have confined their attention to ensuring that the main vehicles of globalization—namely, trade and FDI, helped to promote, rather than inhibited, their national economic goals. Others, in acknowledging a need to restructure their micro-management policies, have concentrated on improving the competitive advantages of their firms—for example by initiating appropriate national innovation policies and encouraging entrepreneurship and inter-firm rivalry. But relatively few appear to have given much attention to how best nations might create or restructure institutions or improve the quality of general-purpose inputs—a point particularly stressed by myself in Chapter 3 and by Ham and Mowery in Chapter 9. And—of the countries studied[32]—only in the case of Japan can one reasonably conclude that a systemic or holistic response of government to globalization has been practised.

In his chapter, Stopford also takes up some of the issues raised in the introductory chapter and explored in more detail in the country case studies. He is particularly interested in the alternative policies of governments to reconfigure dynamic comparative advantage and in the different reactions to globalization of leading and catch-up nations. He elaborates on a number of paradoxes of contemporary global markets—and especially the impact of modern technology on the size of firms and industries and on the emergence of regional clusters in the light of increased mobility of firm-specific assets. He also gives some attention to the consequences of globalization for the organization of firms and states, and the extent to which cross-border alliances between these entities is likely to promote a more heterarchical organizational structure of each.

More generally, Stopford believes that globalization is leading to a range of conflicting trends, acting simultaneously at global, regional, national, and subnational levels. He suggests that the dynamism of these trends, and the new sources of competition arising from them, pose enormous challenges both to scholarly thinking and to policy-makers. His prognosis for meeting these challenges is not an optimistic one. In his own words, he believes that 'the needs for consistency and for broad consensus within the national policy fly in the face of established concepts and institutions' (p. 478); and that the dilemmas remain unresolved problems at least in terms of accepted logic.

In the final chapter of this volume—Chapter 17—Monty Graham touches on the development of various supra-national governmental regimes since the early post-war period. He suggests that the justification for such regimes has been to ensure that the actions of both firms—and governments—to capture the economic rent from their respective activities do not operate to the detriment of global economic welfare. While, in the 1970s, most of the efforts of nation states, and particularly those from developing countries, were geared towards establishing a supra-national regime to prevent MNEs from engaging in unacceptable business practices;[33] more recently attention has been directed to ensuring that the market-distorting policies of national administrations should be minimized.

However, in general, Graham is critical of the ways in which supra-national regimes have responded to the deepening structural integration between countries. Obvious exceptions include explicit bilateral agreements, more formal regional arrangements, notably the EU, and the more specialized international agencies, or clubs, which deal with such issues as intellectual property rights and technical standards.

But, looking at the history of GATT, one can observe only a very modest recognition of the implications of the increasing mobility of cross-border investment capital, or, indeed, of services—even though, as Graham points out, these issues were on the agenda at Havana in 1944. As a consequence, there are, in the mid-1990s, no established rules of the game for national governments to follow in their extra-market actions to attract economic activity to their boundaries. At the same time, it is the foreign production of MNEs, not trade in goods, which is the main modality of international commerce; and, in deciding where to locate their activities, MNEs would appear to be influenced less by trade-related incentives or disincentives, and more by the policies of governments towards corporate investment in general, and FDI in particular. As several chapters in this volume show, the former policies include a whole gamut of macro-organizational instruments, each of which may affect the costs of doing business in a particular country relative to others in which the MNE might consider locating its value-adding activities.

While many of these policies may be justifiable on non-economic grounds, and some may be market-facilitating—in the short or long run—others are most certainly akin to the beggar-my-neighbour trade wars of the inter-war years, which, in the end, benefited none of the participants. Yet, competition policy, investment incentives, rights of establishment, labour laws, environmental regulations, and fiscal policy can all be used to distort the operation of market forces as they affect the geographic allocation of resources; and in doing so, not only reduce world economic welfare, but endanger the very *raison d'être* of globalization.

In the final pages of his analysis of how the leading supra-national regimes are likely to evolve, Graham acknowledges the huge difficulties of arriving at an accord on those issues—and even on the appropriate institution(s) to be responsible for them. Most certainly—again, if the GATT's experience is anything to go by—this is likely to be a slow and incremental process, as so many very different interests are involved. Yet, time is not an ally to the negotiators. Events, and their repercussions, move at a much more rapid pace than they did half a century ago. There is a very real danger that, unless determined efforts are made by national governments both better to coordinate their regulatory responses to globalization and to build up an ethos of trust, cooperation and transparency, the retrenchment of the world economy in the 1930s, brought about by beggar-my-neighbour and trade policies, could be repeated in the next two decades by non-trade protectionist policies.[34] However, such a backtracking on all that has been accomplished over the past half century would be much more serious, not just to the growth and stability of the world economy, but to the very foundation of the modern global community.

NOTES

1. Among the monographs most relevant to our own interests we might mention Olson (1982), Evans, Rueschemeyer, and Stocpol (1985), Gamble (1987), Wolf (1988), Audretsch (1989), Heertji (1989), Helm (1989), Stiglitz (1989), Ostry (1990), Wade (1990), Colclough and Manor (1991), Kuttner (1991), Stopford and Strange (1991), Osborne and Gaebler (1992), Putterman and Rueschemeyer (1992), Amsden, Kochanowicz, and Taylor (1994), Chang (1994*b*), Chang and Rowthorn (1995), Ohmae (1995), Sally (1995), and Dunning and Narula (1996).
2. Scholars differ in their interpretation of both the meaning of globalization and the extent to which it has occurred. Most authors in this volume, however, see it as a continuing process, which is by no means completed.
3. Notably those associated with increased unemployment and job insecurity, a more uneven distribution of income, social unrest, an erosion of national sovereignty, and a loss of tribal identity. One author (Barber 1995) has gone as far as to claim that the same technological advances which have prompted globalization and rising world gross national product (GNP) are being used by those, who are opposed to economic interdependence, to better to achieve their ends.
4. As, indeed, was found to be the case with the German 'miracle' a decade or more earlier.
5. Most authors in the volume use the expression national governments, rather than the nation state. It is, however, assumed that the latter refers to the spatial area of jurisdiction of the former. But see, in particular, Susan Strange's views on this issue in Ch. 4.
6. Cf. internationalization. For more details, see Ch. 5 of this volume.
7. This volume will be mainly concerned with the consequences globalization is having on the structure of economic activity, rather than on the level of such activity. In this respect, we find it useful to distinguish between *macro-economic* policies of governments, e.g. interest rate, monetary, fiscal, and exchange-rate policies; and *macro-organizational* policies, e.g. competition, technology, industrial, trade, environment, and educational policies.
8. And often, of equal importance, to stop it from flowing to another country.
9. For a succinct and recent review of these changes, see especially Ruigrok and Val Tulder (1995). See also Chapters 1 and 2 of this volume.
10. Previously the European Community (EC), and prior to that the European Economic Community (EEC).
11. Including those to do with economic change and resolving conflicts between its constituents. For a more detailed analysis of the ways in which globalization may affect the domestic economic policy of national governments in a variety of spheres, see Dunning (1992).

12. A key issue which has surrounded, and continues to surround, the benefits of economic integration, both in North America and in Europe.
13. As, for example, articulated in Dunning (1997: ch. 14).
14. As described, most recently, by Kozul-Wright (1995).
15. Some commentators would, in fact, argue that apparently market distorting measures, in the short run, might be necessary to facilitate socially efficient markets in the longer run. For a recent exposition of this view, see Amsden (1992).
16. Such as an efficient educational system, transportation and communication network, and technological infrastructure.
17. At the same time, these economies were also growing faster than other economies, and it is always easier to adjust to economic change in a growth than in a no growth situation.
18. A phrase coined by Ann Markusen (1994).
19. See, particularly, various reports issued by the UN Centre on Transnational Corporations (UNCTC), now the Division of Transnational Corporations and Investment of UNCTAD.
20. Such as the Guidelines to MNEs issued by the OECD in 1976 and the abortive UN Code of Conduct for Transnational Corporations (TNCs), as described in Dunning (1993: ch. 20).
21. The year 1925 saw the end of the gold standard, which had been a major constraint on the independent economic actions of national governments over the previous century.
22. Export-processing and efficiency-seeking as compared with resource-based and strategic asset-seeking.
23. Some authors, for example, largely concentrate their attention specifically on how globalization is affecting the foreign direct investment policies of governments; and on how they are adapting specific macro-organizational strategies (e.g. technology and education policies) to increasing intergovernment competition for mobile created assets.
24. For an interesting analysis of how governments may and do respond to cross-border economic integration, see Panic (1995).
25. In describing some of these changes, Lipsey also sets them within the context of globalization.
26. Notably Porter (1990) and the talk he gave at the workshop sponsored by the Carnegie Bosch Institute on Governments, Globalization and International Business, at Georgetown University, Washington DC, in June 1995.
27. In Hirschman's (1970) terminology, to adopt a 'voice' rather than an 'exit' strategy.
28. A point also argued at some length by Kuttner (1991).
29. Most of this volume was completed before the backlash to globalization was making itself felt. However, increasingly in a variety of papers and monographs, the possible disbenefits—particularly some of the geo-economic and social costs of globalization—are being emphasized. See, e.g. Luttvach (1993), Barber (1995), Krugman and Venables (1995), Langhorne (1996), and Dunning (1997: ch. 14).
30. The city states of Singapore and Hong Kong have pursued their own distinct (but rather different) brands of capitalism. For an examination of these, see Wade (1989).
31. There is every sign that the late industrializing economies of Malaysia, Thailand, Indonesia, and the Philippines are following broadly similar paths.
32. It could be argued that the governments of other countries not covered in our volume, e.g. Singapore, have also adopted this kind of strategy.

33. By means mainly of establishing guidelines of behaviour or codes of conduct for MNEs.
34. The need for inter-government cooperation on national regulatory policies in a global economy is stressed by several authors in OECD (1994).

REFERENCES

Amsden, A. H. (1992), 'A Theory of Government Intervention in Late Industrialization', in L. Putterman and D. Rueschemeyer (eds.), *State and Market in Development: Synergy or Rivalry* (Boulder, Colo.: Lynne Rienner).

—— Kochanowicz, J., and Taylor, L. (1994), *The Market Meets its Match: Restructuring the Economies of Eastern Europe* (Cambridge, Mass.: Harvard University Press).

Audretsch, D. B. (1989), *The Market and the State* (New York: Harvester Wheatsheaf).

Barber, B. R. (1995), *Jihad vs. McWorld* (New York: Times Books).

Bardham, P. (1990), 'Symposium on the State in Economic Development', *Journal of Economic Perspectives*, 4/3: 3–7.

Chang, H. J. (1994*a*), 'State Institutions and Structural Change', *Structural Change and Economic Dynamics*, 5/2: 293–313.

—— (1994*b*), *The Political Economy of Industrial Policy* (London: Macmillan).

—— and Rowthorn, R. (1995) (eds.), *The Role of the State in Economic Change* (Oxford: Oxford University Press).

Colclough, C., and Manor, J. (1991) (eds.), *States or Markets* (Oxford: Oxford University Press).

Datta-Chaudhuni, M. (1990), 'Market Failure and Governance Failure', *Journal of Economic Perspectives*, 4/3: 25–39.

Dunning, J. H. (1992), 'The Global Economy, Domestic Governance Strategies and Transnational Corporations: Interactions and Policy Implications', *Transnational Corporations*, 1/3: 7–46.

—— (1993), *Multinational Enterprises and the Global Economy* (Wokingham: Addison Wesley).

—— (1994), *Globalization: The Challenge for National Economic Regimes* (The Geary Lecture for 1993; Dublin: Economic and Social Research Institute).

—— (1997), *Alliance Capitalism and Global Business* (London: Routledge).

—— and Narula, R. (1996) (eds.), *Foreign Direct Investment and Governments* (London: Routledge).

Evans, P., Rueschemeyer, D., and Stocpol, T. (1985) (eds.), *Bringing the State Back In* (Cambridge: Cambridge University Press).

Gamble, A. (1987), *The Free Market and the Strong State* (London: Macmillan).

Grestchmann, K. (1991), 'Analysing the Public Sector: The Received View in Economics and its Shortcomings', in F.-X. Kaufman (ed.), *The Public Sector: Challenge for Coordination and Learning* (Berlin: Walter de Gruyter).

Hämäläinen, T. J. (1994), 'The Evolving Role of Government in Economic Organization' (mimeo; Newark: Rutgers University).

Heertji, A. (1989), *The Economic Role of the State* (Oxford: Basil Blackwell).

Helm, D. (1989) (ed.), *The Economic Borders of the State* (Oxford: Oxford University Press).

Hirschman, A. (1970), *Exit Voice and Loyalty* (Cambridge, Mass.: Harvard University Press).

Kindleberger, C. (1974), 'Size of Firm and Size of Nation State', in J. H. Dunning (ed.), *Economic Analysis and the Multinational Enterprise* (London: Allen and Unwin).

Kobrin, S. (1995), 'Regional Integration Globally in a Networked Economy', *Transnational Corporations*, 4/2: 15–33.

Kozul-Wright, R. (1995), 'The Myth of Anglo-Saxon Capitalism: Reconstructing the History of the American State', in H. J. Chang and R. Rowthorn (eds.), *The Role of the State in Economic Change* (Oxford: Oxford University Press).

Krueger, A. O. (1990), 'Government Failures in Development', *Journal of Economic Perspectives*, 4 (Summer), 9–23.

Krugman, P., and Venables, A. J. (1995), 'Globalization and the Inequalities of Nations', *Quarterly Journal of Economics*, 100/4: 858–79.

Kuttner, R. (1991), *The End of Laissez Faire* (New York: A. J. Knopf).

Langhorne, R. (1996), 'The Causes and Consequences of Globalization' (mimeo; Newark: Rutgers University Center on Global Change and Government).

Luttvach, E. N. (1993), 'The Coming Global War for Economic Power', *The International Economy* (September/October), 18–22.

Markusen, A. (1994), *Sticky Places in Slippery Spaces: The Political Economy of Post-War Fast Growth Regions* (Rutgers University Working Paper No. 79; New Brunswick Center for Urban Policy Research).

Naisbitt, J. (1994), *Global Paradox* (New York: William Morrow & Company).

North, D. (1993), 'Institutions, Transaction Costs and Productivity in the Long Run', paper presented to Eighth World Productivity Congress, Stockholm (May).

OECD (1994): Organization for Economic Cooperation and Development, *Regulatory Cooperation for an Interdependent World* (Paris: OECD).

Ohmae, K. (1995), *The End of the Nation State: The Rise of Regional Economies* (London: HarperCollins).

Olson, M. (1982), *The Rise and Decline of Nations: Economic Growth, Stagflation, and Social Rigidities* (New Haven: Yale University Press).

Osborne, D., and Gaebler, T. (1992), *Reinventing Government: How the Entrepreneurial Spirit is Transforming the Public Sector* (Reading, Mass.: Addison Wesley).

Ostry, S. (1990), *Governments and Corporations in a Shrinking World: Trade and Innovation Policies in the United States, Europe and Japan* (New York: Council on Foreign Relations).

Panic, M. (1988), *National Management of the International Economy* (London: Macmillan).

—— (1995), 'International Economic Integration and the Changing Role of National Governments', in H. J. Chang and R. Rowthorn (eds.), *The Role of the State in Economic Change* (Oxford: Oxford University Press).

Porter, M. E. (1990), *The Competitive Advantage of Nations* (New York: Free Press).

Putterman, L., and Rueschemeyer, L. (1992), *State and Market on Development Synergy or Rivalry* (Boulder, Colo.: Lynne Rienner).

Ruigrok, W., and Val Tulder, R. (1995), *The Logic of International Restructuring* (London: Routledge).

Sally, R. (1995), *States and Firms* (London: Routledge).

Stiglitz, J. (1989), *The Economic Role of the State* (Oxford: Basil Blackwell).

Storper, M., and Scott, A. J. (1995), 'The Wealth of Regions', *Futures*, 27/5: 505–26.

Stopford, J., and Strange, S. (1991), *Rival States, Rival Firms: Competition for World Market Shares* (Cambridge: Cambridge University Press).

Wade, R. (1989), 'The Role of Government in Overcoming Market Failure: Taiwan, Republic of Korea and Japan', in H. Hughes (ed.), *Achieving Industrialization in East Asia* (Sydney: Cambridge University Press).

—— (1990), *Governing the Market: Economic Theory and the Role of Government in East Asian Industrialization* (Princeton: Princeton University Press).

Wallis, J. J., and North, D. C. (1986), 'Measuring the Transaction Sector in the American Economy 1870–1970', in S. L. Engerman and R. E. Gallman (eds.), *Long Term Factors in American Economic Growth* (Chicago: University of Chicago Press).

Wolf, M. (1988), *Markets or Governments* (Cambridge, Mass.: MIT Press).

World Bank (1991), *World Development Report* (Oxford: Oxford University Press).

PART ONE

THE ANALYTICAL FRAMEWORK

1

Governments and the Macro-Organization of Economic Activity: *A Historical and Spatial Perspective*

John H. Dunning

1. Introduction

The optimal role of governments[1] in the organization of economic activity has long been a subject of intense—and sometimes passionate—controversy. Yet a study of the writings of the leading scholars of the past two centuries reveals that these have reflected not only their personal ideologies, and the economic and institutional milieu of the time in which they lived, but the particular issues addressed by them. Indeed, while not wishing to underestimate the real differences of opinions among social scientists about the rationale for, and the appropriate content of, government involvement in the creation and management of resources within that jurisdiction, it is, nevertheless, possible to identify a distinct evolutionary pattern of scholarly thinking, and the reasons for it.

This first chapter has two main tasks. The first is to trace the lineage of academic writings since the time of Adam Smith, on the respective roles of markets, hierarchies, inter-firm alliances, and governments as modes of organizing economic activity in a capitalist economy; and also to analyse why, and in what ways, economists, political scientists, and organizational theorists have differed in their interpretation of the optimal role of governments. The second is to examine the implications of the internationalization, and more recently the globalization, of economic activity for the governance of resource creation and deployment, and the extent to which national administrations and supra-national regimes need to modify their agendas and policy prescriptions in the light of the growing mobility of many tangible and intangible assets. The chapter will further argue that changing patterns of demand and technological advances—especially as they have impacted on the coordinating and transaction costs of value-added activity, and on the institutions and cultural infrastructure underpinning such activity—have critically affected the merits of alternative modes of economic organization; and that, over the years, the optimal combination of these modes has undergone a marked change.

The chapter proceeds in the following way. Section 2 examines the main historical thrust of thinking about the economic legitimacy of democratically elected governments over the past 200 years. The following section deals with some of the main justifications for government intervention set out in the literature; and Section 4 goes on to present an evaluation of these justifications. The chapter then proceeds to analyse the implications of the spatial widening of value-added activity; and suggests that such widening, and, in particular, the emergence of the globalizing economy, is significantly affecting 'best-practice' organizational arrangements for both the creation and the deployment of organizing domestic resources.

2. An Evolutionary Approach to Economic Organization

In taking a bird's-eye view of the economic organization of democratic societies over the past two centuries, it is useful to distinguish between two quite different functions which governments may perform. The first is as an initiator and overseer of the economic system[2], which sets the legal and institutional framework within which the resources and capabilities in its jurisdiction are created and deployed; and as an arbitrator as and when disputes arise between economic agents.[3] The second is as an owner of assets, and as a *participator* in, or *influencer* of, the way these assets are utilized. The former functions are the special and unique responsibility of governments;[4] the latter can frequently be undertaken by either public or private institutions. Much of the changing attitudes of scholars towards government intervention over the past two centuries reflects their perceptions of the appropriate balance between these two roles and their interface with other institutions in achieving societal goals.

We begin by offering a schema—set out in Table 1.1—which identifies three stages in the evolution of market-based capitalism, which we have called respectively *entrepreneurial*, *hierarchical*, and *alliance* capitalism. While the nomenclature and the timing of the stages may be open to question, there can be little doubt that the macro-economic and organizational[5] environment for the management of physical and human resources has dramatically changed over the past 200 years. In particular, the increasing complexity and specialization of economic activity, the growing interdependence of many intermediate product markets, the accelerating movement towards an information- and innovation-driven economy, the widening territorial boundaries of firms, the increasing significance of created assets (e.g. human skills and technological capacity) in the value-adding process, the evolvement of new institutions and organizational forms, and a re-evaluation of cultures and behavioural norms have all impacted on the costs and benefits of alternative resource allocative systems, and, in particular, the relative advantages of markets, firms, and governments as modes of governance.

At the time of Adam Smith, and the emergence of *entrepreneurial* capitalism, production was mainly undertaken by relatively small, single-activity family firms; and most transactions were conducted at arms'-length prices between independent buyers and sellers. For the most part, the division of labour was elemental,

TABLE 1.1. Some features of the three ages of capitalism

	Phase 1 ENTREPRENEURIAL CAPITALISM (1770–1875)	Phase 2 HIERARCHICAL CAPITALISM (1875–1980)	Phase 3 ALLIANCE OR FLEXIBLE CAPITALISM (1980–?)
Markets	Small and fragmentary, local and national: mainly competitive	National or international: increasingly oligopolistic	Regional and global: dynamic and more competitive
Specialization	Simple and modest, based mainly on distribution of natural assets	Becoming more complex: both national and international	Extensive and interdependent: the paradox of an increasing global division of labour based on location of created assets, together with the sub-national specialized clusters of economic activity
Key resources	Natural assets, e.g. fruits of the land and relatively unskilled labour	Physical and some knowledge capital	Tangible assets, e.g. infrastructure and technological capacity Intangible assets, e.g. human competence and knowledge, information, organizational and learning capability
Mobility of assets	Little except for finance capital, and some emigration	Gradually increasing via MNE operations	Substantial mobility of *firm specific* created assets. But less mobility of some *location specific* created assets
Organization	Factory, small firms	Large integrated corporate hierarchies	More inter-firm alliances, single firm heterarchies, corporate networks
Production system	D form, batch	M form, mass or scale	Innovation driven: flexible
Government role	Limited involvement: active	Growing intervention: growth	More systemic and market enabling:

TABLE 1.1. Cont'd

	Phase 1 ENTREPRENEURIAL CAPITALISM (1770–1875)	Phase 2 HIERARCHICAL CAPITALISM (1875–1980)	Phase 3 ALLIANCE OR FLEXIBLE CAPITALISM (1989–?)
	role confined to provision of public utilities, fiscal policy and social welfare	in welfare providing services. In inter-war years considerable protectionism	less regulation of individual markets
Government structure	Local/national legislation	National legislation, limited supra-national institutions	Greater plurality of governmental forms, especially at sub-national and supra-national levels
International activities	Classical trade, very little foreign production	Market and natural resource seeking FDI: growth of intra-industry trade	Substantial efficiency and strategic asset-seeking FDI: more cross hauling of FDI and growth of cross-border strategic alliances
Cross-border integration	Of product and finance markets	Fluctuating: cf. inter-war years with early post-Second-World-War period	Increasing, through corporate and regional integration
Hegemonic power	UK	USA	No single country

and markets were independent of one another and spatially limited. Firms made relatively little use of created assets in the production process. The institution of political democracy was still in its infancy.

In such conditions it was not surprising that the market was the favoured signal for, and modality of, resource allocation, as the transaction and coordinating costs associated with it were insignificant, particularly when compared with those of hierarchies[6]; while, public administrations had neither the experience nor the motivation to organize economic activity efficiently. It was not surprising, either, that the dominant scholastic paradigm which emerged at that time was that of *laissez-faire*; and this was so, not because markets were thought to be perfect, but because the disbenefits of non-market intervention were perceived to be so much greater than the benefits.[7]

The century which followed, which we have called *hierarchical* capitalism, saw the emergence of the multi-activity firm and the gradual internalization by corporations of a range of intermediate product markets. While, frequently, such internalization—or, in the case of inter-firm cooperative agreements, quasi-internalization—helped circumvent endemic failure and enabled the economies of common governance of inter-related activities to be better exploited, it also led to sub-optimal market structures and to unacceptable business practices; hence, the justification for government intervention to counteract structural distortions.

Economists also began to justify an interventionist role by national governments on other grounds. Already, following on the writings of Alexander Hamilton (1751–1804) and Frederick List (1798–1846),[8] a new school of political economists was asserting that nations seeking to 'catch up' in the development process needed some temporary protection against their established competitors if they were properly to exploit their dynamic comparative advantages.[9] Faced, too, with some of the downsides of nineteenth-century capitalism, scholars were arguing for governments to shelter the less fortunate members of society by taking a more active role in promoting social welfare—for example, by such means as the Factory Acts (1819–1901) and Poor Laws (1782–1834) in the UK. As economic activity became more complex, and an increasing number of products took on the form of public goods, governments saw fit to engage in some activities which, at the time, the private sector was not prepared to undertake—and yet which were market-facilitating and welfare-enhancing. Examples include the construction of a wide range of infrastructural facilities—including canals, roads, and railroads—all of which involved a high ratio of fixed to variable costs of production and had extremely long pay-back periods.

In the present century, additional aspects of the macro-organizational role of governments have been recognized in the literature. The concept of externalities and the distinction between social and private costs and benefits were especially highlighted by Alfred Marshall (1920) and A. C. Pigou (1932), while the severe unemployment in industrial economies for much of the inter-war years led other economists, notably J. M. Keynes (1936), to urge for more positive interventionism by national governments, which, they believed, was critical if the benefits of the market system were to be fully realized.

At the same time, a different group of scholars was pointing to the increasing costs of coordinating economic activity (Commons 1924, 1934), and to those associated with technological advances and other structural changes (Schumpeter 1934, 1942; Beveridge 1944). While some economists of this era[10] distinguished between systemic and structural market failures, there was no real attempt to evaluate the alternative ways of coping with the former. This was because, until the writings of Ronald Coase, the role of transaction costs in determining the organization of economic activity had not been incorporated into mainstream economic theory.[11]

Moreover, there was little scholarly discussion of the role of governments as overseers of the organization of economic activity, and of how the economic system, for which they were responsible, might require adaptation because of the changing circumstances. Because of this, the debate between the interventionists and the champions of the 'free' market system became polarized; and it was, indeed, the failures of increasing socio-economic government intervention—which, perhaps, reached its peak in the third quarter of the twentieth century—that led to a renaissance of market-based economics, so vigorously propounded by Friedrich Hayek, Milton Friedman, James Buchanan, and Robert Lucas. Indeed, given the contemporary economic environment, one may be tempted to conclude that, not since the time of Adam Smith (1723–90), has liberal economics so dominated political actions.[12]

Yet, it may be that not all is as it seems. It is one thing to argue that, within a modern capitalist economy, market forces should play a more decisive role as a mechanism for resource allocation. It is, however, quite another to argue that, by themselves, such forces are sufficient to ensure the efficient organization of the economic system of which they are part—particularly in the knowledge-based and globalizing economy of the 1990s. It is quite clear that, along with the liberalization of individual markets, and the regulation of many value-added activities, new (or revitalized) organizational forms are emerging. Within the framework of an innovation-driven market economy, too, there is room for a plurality of organizational arrangements. Indeed, in such an economy, cooperation—for example, between firms and their suppliers, between the research and development (R&D) and manufacturing departments of a firm, between labour and management, and between the private and public sector—is often a critical ingredient of economic success. Hence, the term alliance capitalism[13] has been coined to reflect the kind of socio-institutional structure now emerging in market-based economies.

The two distinctive features of alliance capitalism are its emphasis, first, on the partnership between the various organizational modes of resource allocation, and, second, on the role assigned to government as the overseer of the economic system and the ultimate arbitrator of the functions undertaken by both private and public institutions. Of course, it is recognized that governments, on behalf of their constituents, may have other objectives; and, indeed, as a society becomes more prosperous, the trade-offs between further economic growth and other goals may change.[14] But, having said this, the economic and social milieu of the 1990s is such that, even if the role of government as a direct participator in national economies is declining, its function as (i) a creator and sustainer of the institutional, legal, and commercial infrastructure, (ii) a fashioner of value systems and ideologies, and (iii) a provider of a focal point or consensus around which resource allocative decisions can be coordinated is becoming more, rather than less, critical (Chang 1994). Indeed, it is our contention that not only are the costs of supervising a systemic market-based economy rising all the time, but the role of government in affecting decisions taken by the main organizing entities in individual market transactions continues to be a decisive one. The following sections will elaborate on this thesis in some detail.

One other aspect of alliance capitalism, which will be discussed more fully in Section 5 of this chapter, is the growing structural integration of the world economy. *Inter alia*, this is leading to a network of cross-border collaborative agreements, not only between firms of different nationality, but between firms and foreign governments, between national governments, and between interest groups and participants in the value-added process located in different countries. Such alliances may be both market-facilitating and market-distorting. However, one of the consequences of the globalizing economy is the renewed attention now being given to intergovernmental cooperation and supra-national regimes, as a means of reducing or circumventing undesirable market distorting practices of both firms and national governments. Moreover, this is occurring not only in the field of cross-border commerce, but in several other areas of macro-organizational policy which affect the disposition of resources and capabilities between and within nation states.

3. A Typology of Approaches to Economic Organization

Any attempt to classify the writings of past and contemporary scholars on the organization of economic activity is bound to be subjective, and to reflect the purposes for which it is being made. In this chapter I shall identify *six* different perceptions of the role of government (and for the most part national government) in a market-oriented economy. I would also observe that the great majority of scholars have confined their attention to the organization of economic activity within the context of either a closed economy or one in which cross-border trade is mainly conducted at arm's-length prices between independent parties.[15] Only since the 1970s, for example, have the implications of the activities of multinational hierarchies been explicitly analysed and Section 5 will consider some of these.

I now turn to discuss the lineage of academic scholarship associated with these six approaches, each of which, apart from the first, may be viewed as departures from a perfectly competitive market situation, as perceived by classical and neoclassical economists. For the most part, too, the approaches presume that the extent and form of government involvement are dependent on the extent and character of market imperfections—although, until recently, rarely has any attempt been made to assess whether or not the intervention by government is more cost effective than the market it replaces.[16] For the most part, too, academic research has concentrated on the role of government as controller, regulator, participator or influencer of *particular kinds* of resource disposition, rather than as an initiator and supervisor of the system by which all resources are created and deployed.

Although it is possible to identify a trajectory of scholarly research about the merit of alternative organizational modes, most of the philosophies, theories, and policy prescriptions articulated cannot be divorced from the particular circumstances of their time. For example, although Adam Smith is usually portrayed as an ardent supporter of free markets, his analysis of the situations in which government intervention is justified—if modified to embrace the institutional, technological, and social environment of the late twentieth century—suggests that he was fully aware of the role of governments as overseers of an economic system in which market forces might flourish. Indeed, a close reading of Smith's analysis of the functions of government is quite consistent with the tenets of modern institutional economics; and the fact that their systemic activities were less in evidence than they are today largely reflects the relative simplicity of eighteenth-century economic life, as compared with its contemporary equivalent. Similarly, while, in the context of the US economy of the 1990s, the views of Frederick List might be considered highly protectionist, in the context of that of the German economy of the 1830s, they are entirely in accord with that part of contemporary transaction-cost theory which argues for the need of extra-market action to facilitate the restructuring of an economy in line with its comparative dynamic advantage.

Let us now discuss the lineage of the six approaches to the role of government.

3.1. The Philosophical/Ideological View on how Economic Activity should be Organized

This view essentially reflects that of the nature of society and the 'right' (rather than the most efficient) way to organize economic activity. Scholars who prescribed such views rarely sought to offer a rigorous economic defence for them. The Mercantilists of the sixteenth and seventeenth centuries, for example, believed that the political and economic interests of the state should be the primary justification for economic activity; and, not surprisingly, accorded the rulers of the state direct responsibility for advancing this goal. The two centuries which followed saw a reaction to the Mercantilist philosophy, which was spearheaded by Quesnay (1694–1774) and the French Physiocrats, who believed in the natural law or the 'natural' order of things. Their economic principles were encapsulated in the classic maxim '*laissez faire et laissez passer, le monde va de lui-même*' or 'let do and let alone and the world goes by itself'. To the Physiocrats the role of the state was to regulate affairs to follow the natural order 'ordained by God and susceptible to the discovery of man'. They maintained that 'governments should never extend their influence in economic affairs beyond the minimum absolutely essential to the protection of life and property and the maintenance of freedom of contracts' (Ferguson 1938: 50).

Although philosophical and ideological elements were also contained in the writings of some of the English classical and neoclassical scholars—for example, David Hume (1711–76), Adam Smith, Jeremy Bentham, and Ludwig Von Mises (1881–1973)[17]—the growing sophistication of societies over the last 200 years, which *inter alia* has reflected the increasing dependence on the upgrading of human skills and physical capacity—has tended to lessen the appeal of this kind of approach. However, as a direct result of the less desirable social consequences of the industrial revolution, a new school of thought—which might be dubbed the social welfare school of economics—emerged. The founder of this school was a French historian, Jean Charles Simonde de Sismondi (1773–1843).[18] To begin with, Sismondi was an admirer of Adam Smith, but, in his later writings, he vigorously attacked wealth accumulation both as an end in itself and for its detrimental effect on the poor.

After Sismondi, the course of social economics took two distinct paths. The first was that of *socialist* economics, which urged the collective ownership of property and an active, participatory role of the state in all aspects of economic affairs. Such an approach to economic organization was initially explored by French and English social reformers such as Claude Saint Simon (1760–1825), Jean Louis Blanc (1811–82), and Robert Owen (1771–1858), and by the German state socialists such as Johann Rodbertus (1805–75) and Ferdinand Lassalle (1825–64), but most extensively, and fervently, by Karl Marx (1818–83).

The second path was that of *welfare* economics, which, while firmly rooted in classical and neoclassical theoretical analysis, was built around the concept of the social welfare of the community (rather than the economic self-interest of individual,) and the distribution (in addition to the size) of the national dividend. Hints of scholarly dissatisfaction with the hedonism of Jeremy Bentham, and a realization that the theory of competitive markets did not allow for the less welcome extra-market diseconomies of consumption and production, were first explicitly mentioned in the writings of Henry Sidgwick (1838–90).[19] However, it was Vilfredo Pareto (1848–1923) and A. C. Pigou who provided the intellectual apparatus for identifying the situations in which the social costs and benefits of economic activity might diverge from those resulting from free-market transactions; and of how governments might intervene to optimize—or come near to optimizing—the marginal social net product.

The writings of both Pareto and Pigou—and indeed that of Marx before them —cannot solely be classified to the philosophical–ideological approach to economic organization. Indeed, with the growing complexity of most Western societies and the development of more rigorous economic and social analysis, most scholars came to adopt a less polemical course of reasoning. For example, notwithstanding his contempt for the self-interest promoted by the free enterprise system, and his belief that class warfare would eventually lead to its destruction, several of the writings of Karl Marx foreshadowed not only the kind of state-guided capitalism currently favoured by many East Asian countries, but the critical role played by institutions in determining the success or failure of free markets.

In more recent years, there has been some resurgence in the ideological aspects of economic organization—mainly as a result of the practical failures of dogmatic socialism. The 'high priests' of the unfettered market in the second half of the present century have been Friedreich Von Hayek and Milton Friedman. Indeed, given the post-1945 economic and political milieu, it may be reasonably argued that Hayek—in advancing his philosophy of contractarianism[20]—was even more ideologically attuned to personal liberty and against state interventionism than Adam Smith himself. Having experienced the ultimate consequences of fascist-style governments in the inter-war years, Hayek was apprehensive, lest, in the aftermath of the Second World War, socialism would engulf large parts of Europe and pose a serious challenge to capitalism and to civil liberty.

While acknowledging the concerns of Hayek, other economists of his generation did not share his confidence in either the efficiency or the social justice of the market economy. In particular, in the 1960s and 1970s, the theoretical and ideological insights of Nicholas Kaldor, Albert Hirschman, and Raoul Prebisch were used by policy-makers in both developed and developing countries to justify a whole series of market-interventionist policies. However, as it turned out, far from advancing social welfare, such policies frequently inhibited the economic restructuring and growth on which such welfare depended.

3.2. **The Cost-Benefit View of Alternative Organizational forms**

There are several variants of this view. Most begin with the presumption that, in a situation of perfect competition, markets are the best instrument for allocating scarce resources, and the only justification for external intervention is that, in one way or other, markets fail to perform in a Pareto-optimal fashion. Again, I would observe that those presumptions make no explicit reference to the costs of setting up and sustaining the efficient working of either particular markets or the market system as a whole.

Yet, as I shall argue later in this chapter, it is the systemic costs and benefits of coordinating economic activity that have become such an important component of the total resource allocative process in recent years; and that, quite frequently, the process can best be achieved by a partnership between alternative organizational entities. A review of scholarly research over the past two centuries suggests that five kinds of market imperfections stand out above all others; and it is the presence of these imperfections which has usually led to a discussion of the appropriate role of government in counteracting their adverse affects. I shall briefly discuss each of these in turn; they are taken up in more detail by Richard Lipsey in Chapter 2.

3.2.1. Structural Market Distortions

Perhaps the most widely accepted interventionist role of government is to restrict or counteract any actions on the part of the participants in a market to inhibit the efficient operation of competitive forces. The most obvious case is that of monopolistic or monopsonistic pricing behaviour, but there are many other instances when, through restricting entry into goods or factor markets, or by engaging in excessive product differentiation or anti-competitive practices, sellers (or buyers) might behave in a socially unacceptable fashion.

Such a need for government action has been well recognized by economists since Adam Smith first maintained that the state had a duty to protect the general public from 'extortionate practices',[21] and from the innate selfishness of competing businessmen. At the same time, Smith was quick to denounce any market-distorting behaviour on the part of the state itself. While there remains little disagreement among economists about the need to minimize both private and public structural market imperfections, there is less consensus on the merits and demerits of the alternative organizational arrangements for promoting dynamic allocative efficiency, or those which might best accommodate plant or firm specific economies of scale. Other areas for dispute over the ideal market structure include the trade-off between the benefits of the risk diversification and common governance of related activities, and the opportunities that a domestic multi-activity or multinational enterprise (MNE) may have for engaging in cross-subsidization, transfer price manipulation, and other business practices not available to the single-activity enterprise.

The recent explosive growth in strategic alliances—particularly cross-border alliances—is creating an additional dilemma for competition policy. On the one hand, the alliances may enable the participating firms to be more competitive in global markets; on the other, they may better enable the collaborating firms to crowd out smaller competitors, and/or reduce the contestability of markets. Such trade-offs as these are becoming more, rather than less, prolific in the contemporary globalizing economy—and, as several economists have observed[22]—are requiring national governments, regional authorities, and supra-national regimes to reconsider their anti-trust and competition policies, which were originally formulated in a very different economic environment.

3.2.2. Externalities and Social Welfare

Most contemporary studies of economic organization tend to address the causes of endemic, rather than those of structural, market failure. Endemic market failure refers to the inability of markets to perform in a Pareto-optimal way because of intrinsic market impurities, rather than because of any distorting behaviour of the participants of the market. The rest of this section will consider some of these from a historical perspective.

The idea that a particular market transaction may affect individuals or institutions, other than those engaging in the transaction—that is, that give rise to externalities and a divergence between private and social costs and benefits—dates back to the time of David Hume, Adam Smith, and Jeremy Bentham. According to Rostow (1990: 49), Hume and Smith were 'acutely conscious of external economies that governments should assure were exploited and external diseconomies that government should prevent'. Bentham held that, if it could be shown that government action enhances the happiness of the community more than it diminishes it, then such action would be justified (Ekelund and Hebert 1975: 111). In spite of his defence of an individualist utilitarian creed, John Stuart Mill

(1806–73) took a similar view. He argued that, on humanitarian grounds, it was the state's responsibility to redress the increasing divergence between social and (private) economic welfare, which he believed had been brought about by the industrial revolution.

The implications of wider and deeper levels of economic specialization for extra-market activities, and the possible divergence between the private and social benefits of masket forces were well recognized by Alfred Marshall. Here a quote from his classic work (Marshall 1920: 241) is worth repeating:

> The development of the organism whether social or physical involves an increasing subdivision of functions between its separate parts on the one hand, and on the other a more intimate connection between them. Each part gets to be less and less self-sufficient, to depend for its well being more and more on other parts, so that any disorder in any part of the highly developed organism will affect other parts also.

Although Marshall is also credited as being the father of welfare economics,[23] it was his one-time student and successor to his Chair of Economics at Cambridge University—A. C. Pigou (1877–1959)—who formalized the conditions in which extra-market intervention might be necessary to ensure that competitive market transactions were to advance the wider social good. However, although, in principle, wherever there are externalities to a particular economic activity, there may be a case for increasing or reducing that activity or redistributing some of its costs and/or benefits, this does not necessarily mean that action by public authorities is the best way for this to be achieved. Indeed, over the past century, perhaps the main mode of overcoming the failure of markets to capture the externalities of transactions has been for business enterprises to internalize these markets.

Clearly, however, there are instances—particularly in the provision of public goods—where governments may well be the most suitable organizational mode. This has been acknowledge by almost all scholars from the time of Smith, J. S. Mill, and John McCullogh (1789–1864) onwards. McCullogh, for example, was particularly critical of the principle of *laissez-faire* when it came to the social functions of government, and referred to it as savouring 'more the policy of a parrot than of a statesman or philosopher' (McCulloch 1848: 156).

It is, however, worth observing that, in the absence of serious economic analysis, it is not possible to evaluate the optimal role of government either in reconciling social and private costs and benefits or in the provision of public goods. Some services which in the nineteenth century were best supplied by governments are now at least as well provided by private enterprise;[24] while others, which have become too costly for even groups of firms to produce and which generate enormous externalities, may now be best supplied by public authorities—or public authorities jointly with private corporations. One can, however, point to the need for governments in their overseeing role to take more account of the increasing interdependency of economic activities. One may also observe that, as certain social issues (e.g. those to do with the environment) have risen on the political agenda, the efficacy of traditional resource-allocative mechanisms has been further questioned.

3.2.3. The Issue of Structural Unemployment

Economists have always recognized that it is the unique and critical task of governments to engage in responsible and efficient macro-economic management, even though—at least since the abolition of the gold standard in 1925—there has been much controversy over how this task can be best done. Although this chapter—indeed this volume—is primarily concerned with macro-organizational issues, the question of the role of the appropriate macro-economic arrangements for dealing with unemployment is worthy of some attention—especially since (so we would argue!), in modern times, an increasing proportion of unemployment is due to dynamic structural forces rather than to any overall deficiency in the demand for goods or services.[25]

For most of the nineteenth- and early twentieth-century economists were almost exclusively concerned with structural unemployment. Adam Smith, Jeremy Bentham, and Saint-Simon each advocated the use of public works to reduce the jobless population; while John McCulloch was one of the first economists to argue for the provision of unemployment assistance. By the mid-nineteenth century there was also some acknowledgement that governments can play a role in the upgrading of a country's human and physical resources. John Stuart Mill, for example, strongly believed that government had a duty to provide general education to reduce economic and social inequities, and to prepare men and women for their duties as 'intelligent consumers and trained producers' (Ferguson 1938). This theme was later echoed in the writings of Robert Owen, Karl Marx, Alfred Marshall, and Henry Sidgwick.

The seminal contribution of J. M. Keynes to macro-economic theory and policy-making is germane to our interests in so far as he believed that, unaided, market forces could not always ensure the full and efficient employment of resources, and that government intervention might be necessary to achieve this goal. At the same time, Keynes did not challenge the market system *per se*. He argued, as did the Austrian economists before him, that any inability of the market properly to perform its functions was not a reflection of the system itself—that is, of endemic market failure—but rather the result of the failure of governments properly to execute their own responsibilities. In particular, Keynes argued that, in the inter-war years, neither the UK nor the US government was efficiently managing its fiscal and monetary affairs; and that, were they to do so, then markets would operate in textbook fashion.

In short, although in one sense Keynes was a traditional neoclassicist, in another he posed a great challenge to *laissez-faire* orthodoxy. Moreover, to the extent that he argued that governments may sometimes be justified in extending their macro-economic boundaries to embrace issues of competition, education and science, and industry, they were eagerly (although often incorrectly) seized on by the policy-makers of the day—and particularly by Franklin D. Roosevelt—as an excuse for more widespread state involvement in economic affairs. Indeed, throughout the 1930s, and in the early post-war period, the Keynsian paradigm formed the basis for macro-economic policy in most Western countries.

Keynes was mainly concerned with unemployment caused by lack of effective demand.[26] Only peripherally did he concern himself with structural unemployment, although he clearly recognized that rigidities in the factor and product markets could impede the successful implementation of his policy prescriptions. The significance of these rigidities was first explored in depth by William Beveridge—a scholar and social reformer who was the architect of the modern welfare state in Britain. In his view, the central weakness of the unplanned market economy was its incapacity not only to generate sufficient and steady demand for its products, but to cope with a 'local misdirection of demand' and 'the disorganization of the labour market' (Beveridge 1994: 28). However, unlike Keynes, Beveridge believed that demand-side fiscal and monetary policies were not enough to cure unemployment, and particularly that caused by technological change. Such unemployment, according to Beveridge, was a reflection of the failure of markets efficiently to adjust to changes in supply-and-demand conditions. While in some cases this was due to structural impediments—for example, on the part of firms or organized labour—in others it was not. In these latter instances, Beveridge recommended government intervention—for example, introducing worker-retraining schemes, encouraging the occupational and geographical mobility of labour, providing additional risk capital, and fostering the relocation of industry.

While Beveridge's policy prescriptions were most certainly more interventionist than those of Keynes, many of them, like those of the Cambridge economists, were intended to facilitate the efficient workings of markets, rather than to replace them. However, the distinction between these two rationales for intervention were obscured by both policy-makers and academic scholars. Partly, this was because the dynamic and static functions of market forces had been insufficiently distinguished. This, itself, reflected the fact that economists at the time gave little real attention to technological change as an endogenous variable affecting economic welfare, and one which, by definition, is incompatible with a situation of perfect competition.

And, of course, more than anything else, it has been technological change which has challenged the full employment policies of governments in the post-war period, and particularly since 1970; and it has been the inability or unwillingness of individuals and firms to bear the social costs of technological change that has led economists to urge governments (on behalf of the communities they represent) to help absorb such costs. This responsibility has been embraced more fully by some governments than by others. This reflects partly the differing ability of governments to shoulder the costs of such change, and partly their political or ideological differences on the need for such intervention.

The interaction between technological change and the structure of economic activity was first seriously articulated by Karl Marx, although several classical economists (e.g. J. S. Mill and McCullogh) had anticipated it. According to Marx, the historical development of economies proceeds in a stepwise progression from feudalism to capitalism, and then to socialism, and is fashioned by the interplay between institutional and technological forms. In particular, he argued that history was a series of class struggles, and that each class put its own interests above the national interests (Olson 1965). This, he concluded, was bound to lead to the self-destruction of capitalism. Governments might attempt to compensate for the deficiencies of the market system; but, in the end, 'it was socially impossible for a government to set things right' (Heilbroner 1965: 140). To Marx, the only answer was a Communist state.

Marx had only a rudimentary understanding about the economics of technical change in a capitalist society. It was left to Joseph Schumpeter (1883–1950) to explain the ways in which innovations impacted on economic organization. He coined the expression 'creative destruction' to describe a situation in which innovations led to the obsolescence of existing products and ways of doing things, and hence structural shifts in demand-and-supply conditions. More than any other economist, Schumpeter explicitly distinguished between the static and dynamic components of market failure. While he rejected Marx's diagnosis of capitalistic ills, he did believe that increasingly rapid technological change would necessitate a bigger and more influential role for national governments, if the benefits of such change were to be exploited at minimum social costs. In Schumpeter's writings, too, we also see the distinction between the social and private consequences of innovatory activities, and the notion that firms may under-invest in R&D as they cannot fully appropriate the gains of their innovations. As economic organization has become increasingly innovation-driven, the need for a sympathetic institutional environment to minimize structural adjustment costs has become more urgent. The contributions of Nat Rosenberg, Christopher Freeman, Keith Pavitt, Richard Nelson, and Stanley Winter in the 1970s and 1980s in adding to our knowledge on these issues is particularly noteworthy.[27] In this respect, and as later chapters in this volume will demonstrate in more detail, it is also clear that the actions taken by governments both to encourage their own firms to innovate new products and to minimize the costs of structural adjustment have been one of the main ingredients of their post-war success. But, like Keynes, by and large, the economists justifying such government intervention have done so on the basis that it is necessary to *facilitate* the market system rather than to *replace* it.

3.2.4. Institutions, Transactions, and Coordination Costs

Perhaps the most thought-provoking—and certainly the least understood—contribution to our understanding of the economics of organization has been that which focuses on the *transaction* and *coordination* costs of economic activity, rather than on the *production* or *transformation* costs. Here, the thesis is a deceptively simple one. In conditions of perfect competition, the transaction and coordinating costs of using the market as a mode of allocating scarce resources are zero. This is because the information necessary to engage in economic activity is assumed to be complete; there is no uncertainty attached to contracts, and there is no interaction between buyers and sellers, except at the point of contract completion. It is further presumed that there are no externalities to market transactions and, in consequence, there is no incentive for firms to capture the economies of common governance. This scenario of perfect knowledge and no uncertainty reduces the role of organizations, other than markets, to that of a black box. In perfect market conditions, *homo economicus* reigns supreme.

The practical unreality of these assumptions provided the initial challenge to English classical economics by a group of French and German scholars.[28] Strongly influenced by Hegelian philosophy, they questioned the idea of economic determinism, the universality of classical doctrines and the strategy of individualistic self-interest. Essentially, they argued that any study of economic phenomena had to be set within a particular historical, institutional, and spatial context which might vary over time and space; and, that, because of this, an inductive method of scientific approach was at least as relevant as its deductive counterpart.

The belief that the efficiency of economic organization cannot be separated from the institutional framework of which it is part spawned a new branch of economic thought in the nineteenth century, which has had a chequered influence. Two distinct strands may be identified. The first—to which we give only passing attention[29]—is what might be called a *socio-organizational* variant, the modern inheritors of which are scholars interested in the sociology of organization and institutions, and of the way individuals and interest groups may influence the decisions taken by public agencies. The lineage of this group of scholars dates back to Karl Marx; and among its most vociferous contemporary exponents is Mancur Olson (1965, 1979, 1982).

The other stream of thought is more evolutionary, and focuses the impact of institutions on the costs and benefits of coordinating economic activity. The premiss is that, as economic development proceeds, the costs of organizing production and exchange increases. The question of interest is not why markets fail, but under what conditions alternative forms of governance may be more cost-effective. In their analysis, however, most institutionalists make no presumption that the visible hand of hierarchies and governments is necessarily preferable to the *invisible* hand of markets.

While Smith and Ricardo fully recognized that the specialization of value-added activities might lead to productivity gains in the deployment of resources, neither paid any attention to its effects on the volume and complexity of transactions. In particular, they made no attempt to explore such concepts as asset specificity, bounded rationality, opportunistic behaviour, information asymmetry, and the economies (and diseconomies) of the common governance of related activities. While Smith recognized that the classical duties of government became more extended as the society 'advanced in civilization', it was a French sociologist,

Émile Durkheim (1893), who first provided the analytical underpinnings to the German historical school.

Durkheim's thesis was that the hallmark of 'elevated' societies was the increased specialization of production and exchange. In particular, he argued that this required a reappraisal of the 'existing processes of government involvement' both in the provision of legal and social institutions and in the minimization of the costs of market transactions. Durkheim identified several such pervasive market failures. These included the presence of externalities and spillovers,[30] the difficulty of coordinating an increasingly sophisticated infrastructure of public goods, the need for a tighter protection of property rights, a reduced coincidence of ideologies and values brought about by a separation of tasks, and an increasing differentiation between managerial information and cognitive frames.

Durkheim's views had relatively little impact on orthodox economic thinking in the years before the First World War, which tended to be dominated by the Austrian School of economists.[31] It did, however, strike a sympathetic chord with a group of US scholars who were questioning some of the socio-cultural foundations of neoclassical economics, and particularly its failure to recognize the need for institutional adaptation to the technological and organizational changes. Although Thorsten Veblen (1857–1929)[32] is commonly regarded as the leader of this school, the later writings of Wesley Mitchell (1874–1948) and John Commons (1862–1945) were more influential. Commons, in particular, developed a theory of collective action by the state (and other non-market institutions) which he saw as essential to an understanding of the realities of economic life. Commons focused on the *transaction* as the vehicle for organizing resource usage, and for the building of institutions. In his analysis, he took an interdisciplinary and a dynamic perspective. He foresaw that, as economic activity became more complex and highly specialized, and as human beings and institutions gained in experience and learning, then so did both the costs and benefits of transactions.

Although Commons failed to make inroads into traditional mainstream economic theory before the First World War,[33] he did provide the intellectual backing for some of the welfare reforms initiated by the US federal government in the 1930s. It was, however, left to a British economist—Ronald Coase—to provide the theoretical underpinning of the contemporary revival of institutional economics. Coase, himself, was not an institutionalist, nor, indeed, did he have much to say about the role of government in economic affairs. But, in his seminal essay on the theory of the firm, Coase (1937) not only explained why competitive markets may not always be the most cost-effective way of translating goods and services; he also identified the situations in which market failure could best be overcome by firms, replacing (i.e. internalizing) the market by administrative fiat.[34]

Over the last half century, the theory of market failure has been extended and refined by several economists following in the tradition of Coase, and by behaviourists such as Herbert Simon (1947, 1959) and organizational scholars such as Oliver Williamson (1975, 1985). In principle, there is no reason why the methodologies devised to evaluate the choice between markets and hierarchies as modes of resource creation and deployment should not be extended to that between governments and markets, or between governments and hierarchies. But, until recently, however, economists have been reluctant to do so. One exception has been Coase himself (1960), who analysed the various ways in which negative externalities of market transactions may be overcome by private or public administrative fiat. More specifically,

> The problem is one of choosing the appropriate social arrangement for dealing with the harmful affects. All solutions have costs and there is no reason to suppose that government regulation is called for simply because the problem is not well handled by the market or the firm. Satisfactory views on policy can only come from a patient study of how, in practice, the market, firms and governments handle the problem of harmful effects. (Coase 1960: 18)

In the last twenty years or so, economists and organizational scholars have given more attention to evaluating the costs and benefits of alternative organizational forms. Mancur Olson, for example (1965, 1979), has proposed a theory of economic organization based on the concept of fiscal equivalence.[35] Like Coase and J. M. Clark (1923) before him, Olson concentrates his attention on the problem of negative environmental externalities. Another group of scholars—for example, Charles Wolf (1988), Robert Wade (1988), Joseph Stiglitz (1989), and Ann Krueger (1990)—have attempted to formalize the conditions under which governments might successfully intervene either to replace or to facilitate other organizational arrangements; and also to analyse the costs of non-market failure. Among the limitations of direct government intervention identified by these scholars, are—to quote my own words:

> The rent seeking activities of powerful pressure groups; the magnification of market failures (e.g. with respect to the supply of environmental or social products) by the news media or other politically motivated interests; the inability of governments to attract the best talents (due *inter alia* to ineffective incentive systems); the lack of commercial expertise and bounded rationality of public decision takers; the pursuance of non-economic (especially ideological) goals by politicians; the inadequacy of market related performance indicators which may lead to the establishment of sub-optimal standards (e.g. with respect to budgets, investment and control of information flows); the high-time discount (or short-termism) of political decision takers; the lack of market pressures to minimize X inefficiency, especially in the case of public monopolies; uncertainties and ambiguities inherent in the provision of goods and services, which are in the domain of governments, e.g. defense equipment, educational and health services; and the lack of a coordinated system of governance (cf. with that in case of private hierarchies); and the difficulty of adjusting policies and institutional structures to quickly meet the needs of technological and economic change. (Dunning 1994: 30)

In a recent analysis of the political economy of industrial policy, Ha-Joon Chang (1994) treats all costs of state intervention as transaction costs. Such costs, he argues, are justifiable as long as they yield net benefits exceeding those offered by the market or by market-based hierarchies. In addition to the rationale for government intervention to advance the efficiency of particular markets, Chang—like the present author (Dunning 1994)—suggests that governments can help lower the transaction and coordination costs of the economic *system* by ensuring that the activities of private and public institutions are suited to the needs of the day. This they may do by fostering an ethos and value system among contracting agents which reduce the gains from opportunism; and, by encouraging an ambience of inter-firm cooperation wherever such cooperation is likely to lead to a more socially acceptable allocation of resources and capabilities.

Perhaps the most interesting facet of Chang's work is his recognition that an 'exit' approach to the failure of markets, or of governments, efficiently to coordinate economic activity is not always the first best strategy.[36] The fact that markets fail does not necessarily warrant their replacement by hierarchies or governments. The fact that there are political constraints on governments to perform efficiently does not mean that they should take no corrective action. Sometimes, indeed, 'exiting' from a problem may create more problems that it alleviates. On those occasions, a 'voice' strategy to reduce the costs (or to increase the benefits) of political failure may be the preferable response. But, this, according to Chang, almost certainly requires a reconfiguration of the institutional design of government.

A good example of institutional redesign is the reaction of Japanese firms to market failure. Rather than internalize the markets (an 'exit' response), they have tended to pursue a strategy of reducing the coordinating costs of markets by way of inter-firm cooperative alliances, and by the Japanese government providing market-facilitating facilities.[37]

Research into the ways in which governments, in their capacity of overseers of the wealth-creating activities within their jurisdiction, can help advance these by reducing the structural costs of readjustment and the *X* inefficiency of non-market organizational modes is still in its infancy. But, in the tradition of Marx and Commons, scholars such as Douglass North are encouraging scholars to refocus their attention on the role of institutions in affecting the efficiency of market-based economic systems.

The focus of North's work (e.g. North 1981, 1990, 1993) is on the increasing transaction costs of twentieth-century society.[38] These, he asserts, are the direct result of technological and organizational advances, and their impact on institutional arrangements. But North goes beyond Durkheim (1964) in identifying the coordination costs which result from the increasing complexity of economic activity. He suggests that, as national economies have become richer, goods and services with high transaction costs have become increasingly important. Although he accepts that some product and process innovations (e.g. the computer and satellite communications) have helped reduce transaction costs and macro-level market failures, he believes that most have caused them to increase. While he observes that, in the private sector, the response to such failures has been the development of more efficient hierarchies and/or inter-corporate alliances,[39] he suggests that extra-market organizational modes (e.g. public institutions) have, in general, been much less successful in adapting to the demands made on them.

North is ambivalent about the impact of national government involvement on institutional design.[40] While arguing that the shift in the locus of decision-making of economic organization from economic to political has adversely affected a country's productivity and competitiveness (North 1993), he also contends that governments can play a positive role in encouraging the institutions within their ambiance of responsibility to react to (and, in some cases, actively to facilitate) structural change in a way which is consistent with the societal good. In his writings North takes an incremental approach to economic development. He believes that the trajectory of change is set by the character of established institutions and their ability to adjust to change in the most cost-effective way. To use his own words:

> Well specified and enforced property rights, decentralized political and economic decision taking and effective competition have been the underlying institutional structure for the organizational changes allowing modern economies to reap the productivity gains of the technology. (North 1993: 14, 18)[41]

However, in echoing Durkheim's views a century earlier, North then goes on to argue that many technological and organizational advances are undermining traditional institutions built upon informal restraints—and especially the family, personal relationships, and repetitive individual exchanges. In their place, new institutions have emerged, which have given rise to new transaction costs. North believes that those societies whose governments have fostered the institutional environment by which economic agents are able to take advantage of the new technological advances (e.g. by reducing uncertainty, encouraging flexible economic organizations, releasing creative entrepreneurial talent, and minimizing environmental volatility) are those which are best equipped to succeed in the contemporary world economy.

3.2.5. Technology and Organizational Change

Although Section 3.2.3 has given some attention to the dynamics of structural change, we shall complete our historical survey by briefly considering the role of non-market institutions as facilitators or inhibitors of that change. In general, the consensus of scholarly opinion is more sympathetic to a participatory role of government in assisting or reducing the adjustment costs of change than in affecting the static allocation of resources. Thus, it is not surprising that one of the first scholarly pleas for government intervention was made by a German economist, Frederick List;[42] and that this was because he viewed the existing system of free trade between nations to be market-distorting and argued from the perspective of the long-term economic advantages of the German economy. In his belief that countries passed through various stages of development, he justified some degree of import protection by latecomer nations. This was not because of any static misallocation of resources in the German economy, but because German firms needed some temporary alleviation from established foreign manufacturers if they were to restructure their value-added activities in line with their potential or dynamic comparative advantages.[43]

It was not, however, until well after the second generation of major technological advances had occurred in the third quarter of the nineteenth century that the issue of dynamic market imperfections gained the attention of mainstream economists. Basically, the argument was that not only were the costs of structural adjustment sometimes too great for unaided markets to bear;[44] but that the social benefits of such adjustments were often greater than the private benefits. Although the germs of a dynamic theory of organizational structure had earlier been voiced by such scholars as Ricardo, J. S. Mill, Saint-Simon, and the socio-economic theorizing of Marx, it was not until Schumpeter explicitly identified innovation, or, as he put it, 'new combinations of productive means', as the main driver of economic change, that the properties of dynamic markets were properly identified.[45] Like Marx, Schumpeter believed that technological progress would lead to instabilities in production and exchange, demand new organizational structures, and encourage more influential governments. However, unlike Marx, he did not regard innovations as a catalyst for the demise of market-based capitalism. Rather, he perceived them as vehicles for a reconfiguration of the established institutional norms, embedded value systems, and the traditional exchange patterns between the main organizational entities.[46]

Schumpeter, then, was essentially concerned with the structural forces underlying and influencing economic development, and with the ways in which institutions might adjust to these forces. In particular, he doubted that, unaided, free markets could offer the necessary inducements for firms, consumers, and workers to undertake the changes needed; and that governments might need to intervene to ensure that the social net benefits of restructuring were optimized. In contemporary economic parlance, Schumpeter's analysis can be expressed in terms of the transaction and coordination costs of innovation-led development, which, he observed, do not occur in any predictable pattern.

Later scholars have built upon Schumpeter's ideas and related organizational change to a series of long-term technological trajectories. Carlota Perez (1983), for example, has identified a series of time-related clusters of radical innovations which, she claims, have been watersheds in the economic evolution of countries. However, unlike Schumpeter, she believes that the long waves between these watersheds—as, for example, identified by Nikolai Kondratiev (1926)—are not primarily the result of economic forces, but rather the manifestation of the 'harmonious or disharmonious behaviour of the total socio-economic and institutional system'. In her view, quantum leaps in the best-practice frontier of value-added activity (Perez 1983: 358) require shifts not only in the techno-economic organization of economic activity, but in the socio-institutional fabric of society. In a later contribution with Christopher Freeman, Perez explores the institutional changes forced by the first industrial revolution (*circa* the late 1700s) and those of the second (*circa* the late 1800s) and goes on to argue that the global economy is currently undergoing a third industrial revolution as a result of a constellation of radical innovations in computers, electronics and telecommunications (Freeman and Perez 1988).

The analysis of Perez and the Sussex economists[47] not only fits in very nicely with the ideas of Douglass North. It is also complementary to the writings of such economists as Nelson and Winter (1982),[48] which are primarily directed to examining the behavioural responses of institutions to innovatory change. Issues such as the appropriate incentives or penalties to encourage organizational adjustments, and the implications of new technological trajectories for organizational learning, routines, search processes, path dependencies, the distribution of information and capabilities, and inter-firm transaction costs, are at the core of contemporary debate. These and related issues are being increasingly explored in the literature, and are discussed in more detail in the following chapters. They are mentioned here, partly because, they are among the most germane to our understanding of the micro- and macro-organization of resource allocation; and, also to emphasize that scholarly analysis is currently being conducted in a very different socio-institutional environment to that in which earlier economists framed their ideas.

4. Conclusions of the Historical Review

The general conclusion of our historical review is that past scholars have had a considerable amount to say about the way in which market-based capitalist economies are, and should be, organized. I do not wish to minimize the differences between their opinions or their policy prescriptions, but it is, none the less, the case that their writings often address very different aspects of the role of governments.

A number of specific conclusions can be drawn. Let me highlight six of these. *First, wherever economic activity involves transaction and coordination costs, it is not possible to formulate an optimum mix of alternative organizational modes which are universally applicable.* Much depends on the circumstances facing particular countries at the time. As Chang (1994: 135) has sagaciously observed:

> neither the market, nor the state, nor any other economic institution is perfect as a coordination mechanism. Each institution has its costs and benefits, and is therefore better than others under certain conditions and worse under other conditions. This means that different countries facing different conditions can, and should have different mixes of the market, the state and other institutions. And in fact . . . even economies that are usually lumped together as 'capitalist' or 'market' economies have been based on substantially different institutional mixes.

A similar view is expressed by Aronson and Ott (1991: 525), who write:

Some (countries) will assign more functions to government than others will, and some will have a stronger taste for public services than others will. Moreover, the allocation of responsibilities between different levels of government will also vary, with some countries relying more on the central government than others. The differences exist because groups have different political systems, because the demographic forces at work differ, because countries differ in income and wealth and because people differ in their preferences for publicly supplied goods and services.

Secondly, in retrospect, it is clear that the main thrust of historical research has been to evaluate alternative organizational arrangements in terms of their impact on market failure. Only in the last half century has attention been given to the *endemic* benefits and disbenefits of alternative modes of governance, as are primarily reflected in the costs of such governance and of the synergistic interaction between North-type institutions.

Thirdly, and allied to the second conclusion, differences among scholars have strongly reflected the time-frame of their analyses. For example, most of the ideas and prescriptions of the classical economists about the role of governments tended to assume that the wealth of a nation rested in its *natural* resources, which, apart from population, were perceived to be largely fixed.[49] Later, the historical, institutional, and Schumpeterian schools all viewed the evolution of economies in terms of their ability to *create* new assets and capabilities, notably technology, capital, human skills, and managerial expertise. It was in the production and dissemination of these assets, and in their ability to adjust to changing factor and product markets, that economists now saw the ingredients of growth. Thus if, for example, one takes a longitudinal view to market-based capitalism (Stiglitz 1989), it can be demonstrated that, in the early stages of development, governments play a critical function in setting up a market system and providing assets of a public-goods character (e.g. social infrastructure) to enable the efficient production of privately financed goods and services. Assuming the absence of major innovations, the role of governments may then be expected to decline—particularly where there is little uncertainty, and few economies of scale or externalities of production or consumption. But, then, as economic growth becomes more dependent on technological and organizational innovations, and as these involve increasingly large expenditures on human resource development and supportive physical infrastructure, the systemic functions of government again become important; even though, in some areas, its role as a producer and regulator might decrease.[50] The next section of this chapter will suggest that the emergence of a globally, or regionally, integrated world economy is also requiring a re-examination of the role of national governments in domestic resource allocation.

Fourth, although the debate on the optimal structure of organizational arrangements still remains heavily overloaded with value judgements, over the last fifty years it has taken on a more objective or technical character. Although most obviously demonstrated in the management of macro-economic affairs, the need for a more coherent and holistic governance of the macro-organization of economic activity is becoming increasingly recognized.[51] But there is a long way to go. While there are a plethora of writings on the organizational structures of corporations, and on how these may need to be modified in the light of technological advances and globalization,[52] the study of the governance of government remains in its infancy. The transaction-costs paradigm, as applied to the management of hierarchies and inter-firm alliances, has yet to be applied to that of government-related institutions; and there remain major differences in the structures of authority in the private and public sectors (Shultz 1979).[53]

Fifth, until quite recently, scholars have generally opined that, governments, in their intervention in organization of economic activity, have been more likely to adversely affect economic welfare than to advance it, although the scope and depth of the adversity has varied according to particular circumstances of the time. Very gradually, however, as society has become more complex, the role of government has been more positively acknowledged. Today, in many—especially East Asian—societies, governments and markets work in close association with each other; and, in its 1992 annual report, the World Bank emphasized the complementarity between the two forms of organizational arrangements. Again, the exact nature of the partnership between the public and private sectors partly depends on the nature of the production or transaction functions being undertaken,[54] but perhaps the most notable feature of the successful market-oriented economies of recent years has been the ways in which governments and markets systemically interact with each other, rather than on the extent to which one or the other produces or exchanges (or influences the production or exchange of) particular goods and services.

According, for example, to Amsden, Kochanowicz, and Taylor (1994), the primary reason for the failure of Eastern European countries to develop a market-based economy in the last five years is that they have chosen to adopt an Anglo-Saxon type of capitalism which, while suited to the needs of nineteenth-century England and the UK, has 'resulted in high social costs and low rates of return when applied to the project of restructuring Eastern Europe under the competitive conditions of technologically advanced twentieth century capitalism' (Amsden *et al.* 1994: 2). This, the authors suggest, is in marked contrast to the East Asian (including Chinese) model of economic development which has long recognized the need to adapt the structure of its market-based capitalism to the unique characteristics of its own institutions.

Sixth, the views of scholars about the efficacy of alternative organizational forms—and particularly of the role of government—strongly reflects the particular issues being addressed; and these have varied greatly over time and space. Take, for example, the economic justification of government intervention. In the mid-nineteenth century it was largely directed to protecting the emerging industries of the (then) newly industrializing nations against the abuses of the factory system from foreign competition. In the late nineteenth century, with the growing power and concentration of big business (especially) in the USA, attention shifted to anti-trust policy. In the inter-war years the rationale of government intervention was directed to reducing unemployment, while, in the 1940s, attention switched to the need for social reform. Growing environmental concerns in the 1970s further intensified the plea for government involvement, while in the 1980s and 1990s the role of government in fostering competitiveness by a range of market-facilitating and strategically related policies became the 'flavour of the month'!

5. Spatial Dimension of the Organization of Economic Activity

In the historical analysis, I have largely ignored the spatial dimension of economic activity. This was not deliberate, but rather a reflection of the fact that, for the most part, scholars—including some of the most recent contributors to the debate—have given little attention to the ways in which the geography of value-added activity and markets may affect the optimal governance of resource allocation. The one exception to this statement is the consideration given by economists to the consequences of trade in goods and services on the role of governments, but even here, until very recently, it had been assumed that such inter-country transactions are conducted between independent parties at arm's-length prices (Dunning 1995).

How exactly—if at all—does the widening of the territorial boundaries of economic activity affect the way societies organize the disposition of their natural and created assets? If division of labour is limited by the extent of the market, does it matter if that market is a foreign, rather than a domestic, one? Is it of any consequence if resources and capabilities are mobile across national borders? Should one be interested in where firms undertake their R&D activities? If, as Douglass North and others have asserted, institutions critically affect the costs of structural adjustment, does it make any difference if these institutions are foreign-owned? And, what if the externalities of market transactions primarily affect individuals and organizations in foreign rather than in home countries?

It is questions such as these which some of the chapters in this volume will be addressing. Here we will present some general thoughts. We shall do so by considering the determinants of economic organization first in a *closed* economy, which we define as one completely isolated from the rest of the world; secondly, in a *partially open* economy, which is one in which there are cross-border transactions, but which primarily take the form of arm's-length trade in goods and services; and, thirdly, in a *fully open* economy, which we shall identify as an economy which is structurally integrated with the rest of the world, and one in which there is a plurality of economic transactions, including FDI by MNEs and a range of collaborative ventures (UNCTAD 1993; Dunning 1994).

5.1. A Closed Economy

The main feature of a closed economy is the equivalence between political and economic space. This reflects the fact that the resources and capabilities originate or are created, and are deployed within the domain of particular nation states. Both product and factor markets are exclusively domestic, and there is no cross-border trade, investment, or migration. Economic agents—including national governments—are assumed to be completely unaffected by the behaviour of their counterparts in other nation states.

In such circumstances, the costs and benefits of alternative organizational arrangements and the optimal structure of such arrangements are entirely determined by the structure of domestic resources and capabilities, and by consumer tastes. More particularly, the rationale and consequences of government intervention are influenced by the configuration of the transaction and coordination costs of alternative modes of governance, and of how these may be affected by indigenous supply or demand-induced changes.

5.2. A Partially Open Economy

Assume, now, some transactions take place between economic agents located in different countries. What impact is this likely to have on the costs and benefits of alternative domestic organizational forms—and in particular the role of government? Since external transactions are presumed to be entirely governed by market forces, it is the degree to which markets are imperfect, or are perceived to lead to less than optimal domestic resource allocation, that will determine the extent to which extra-market activities are undertaken.

In such circumstances, governments might step in and, by a variety of policy instruments (e.g. tariffs, quotas, subsidies, etc.), affect the quality, composition, and terms of trade. Such intervention might be either market-facilitating or market-distorting. It may seek both to counteract anti-competitive behaviour by foreign buyers or sellers, and/or by international cartels, and to promote import-substituting policies in the belief these may protect or advance its domestic industries.

Much, of course, will depend on the kinds of coordinating and transaction costs which are specific to cross-border trade. Protectionism, for example, is a response to foreign competition, which has been historically justified by the inability of the country's domestic markets efficiently to adjust to structural change. By contrast, as firms seek to sell to, or buy from, less familiar territories, the costs of market search, uncertainties about future supply conditions, and imperfect knowledge about the tastes of foreign consumers are all likely to increase their transaction costs. Sometimes, other kinds of markets (e.g. insurance and futures markets) may help modify these risks; in others, particularly where political risk is involved, governments may choose to initiate or subsidize insurance or investment-guarantee schemes. In still other cases, the social benefits of cross-border information-gathering and dissemination may justify the role of public authorities as information brokers.[55] National administrations may also act to ensure that their environmental or cultural objectives are not impeded by the trade in certain goods or services, while exposure to foreign competition, particularly in sectors of burgeoning comparative advantage, may require a more focused attention by governments on reducing the costs of structural adjustment. Clearly, too, macroeconomic policies may need to be modified or extended to embrace the issues relating to balance of payments and the external value of the currency, but consideration of these is outside the brief of this volume.[56]

In short, the opening-up of an economy to international trade is likely to pose new problems for the organization of domestic resources. It may help reduce structural market imperfections and better enable an economy to promote its comparative advantage and benefit from scale economies. It may also lead to more endemic market failure by adding to the transaction and coordination costs of domestic economic activity.

A review of both the historical and contemporary literature on international trade reveals that relatively little attention has been given to the interaction between different forms of economic organization and international trade regimes. This is primarily because most trade theorists have adopted (and still adopt) a neoclassical perspective to evaluating the costs and benefits of trade, and regard institutional issues of secondary importance. Strategic trade theory (see e.g. Krugman 1986, 1991) has introduced an industrial-organizational and behavioural perspective into trade theory, but its main emphasis has been on structural market distortions. Although the consequences of endemic market failure[57] and the role of institutions in affecting the optimum level and pattern of trade have been explored by such scholars as Lipsey and Dobson (1987) and the present author (Dunning 1995), there is much work still be done.

5.3. **A Fully Open Economy**

It is, however, the macro-organizational consequences of being part of a fully open and structurally integrated economy that is the main focus of interest of this volume. Because of space limitations, this chapter will confine its attention to FDI—and particularly integrated FDI—as the main vehicle by which economies are linked to each other.[58] According to the UN (UNCTAD 1995), there are more than 38,500 corporations which engage in FDI; these now account for one-third of the non-agricultural world output; and about the same proportion of this amount is produced outside their home countries.

Much has been written about the features of the emerging global economy,[59] but we would emphasize four in particular. These are:

1. the increasing mobility of firm-specific resources and capabilities—especially knowledge-related assets—across national boundaries;
2. the growing significance of cross-border transactions which are either intra-firm, or between firms with ongoing cooperative agreements;
3. the dramatic reduction in long-distance transportation and communication costs and of the psychic and cultural barriers between countries;
4. the growing importance of location-bound assets, notably an educated labour force and a sophisticated physical infrastructure, in influencing the siting of the value-added activities by MNEs.

Closely associated with globalization—and sometimes fashioning its rationale and its shape—have been a series of far-reaching technological and organizational advances. Three particular characteristics of such advances may be identified.

1. Apart from the experiences of a few developing countries rich in natural resources, economic progress is being increasingly conditioned by the abilities of private institutions—sometimes in conjunction with public institutions —to innovate new assets, and to upgrade the efficiency at which these may be utilized with their existing resources and capabilities.
2. Not only do a rising proportion of created assets contain a strong 'public-goods' element, but the market for them is highly imperfect; in addition, they frequently have multiple uses—i.e. are not sector specific. Such assets include an educated labour force, technological capability, and a sophisticated legal and commercial infrastructure.
3. Since there is some suggestion that globalization is encouraging some convergence in the economic structure, at least among high- and medium-income countries (Williamson 1995), it follows that the way in which a nation's physical and human assets are organized becomes a critically important determinant of a nation's economic performance. Moreover, in so far as governments, as overseers and participants in the resource creative and allocative process, play any role at all, their actions in affecting the competitiveness of firms located within their domain are likely to affect that performance.

To what extent is the globalization of economic activity likely to affect the ways in which national economies organize their resource creation and deployment? How far does it require a reappraisal of established institutional modes? What are the likely costs and benefits of markets, hierarchies, inter-firm alliances, and governments as organizing arrangements on a fully open economy? What are likely to be the consequences of globalization for inter-government relations?

It is the purpose of this volume to explore these propositions in some depth. The basic issue relates to the impact of the extension of economic space[60] on the costs and benefits of the interaction between economic agents—be they interactions in the production or exchange process. In so far as transformation, coordination, and transaction costs of alternative modes are affected, then so will be the appropriate structure of organizational arrangements and most likely, too, the configuration of the socio-institutional system.

In the historical section of this chapter, we used the concept of market failure to examine the costs and benefits of alternative modes of governance. We concluded that no one mode was intrinsically preferable to another as a vehicle for coordinating economic activity; and that the optimum combination of modes was likely to vary across both time and space.

It is possible to adopt a similar approach in examining the impact of the increasing porosity of national boundaries. Here our review of received literature can be brief as it has only been in the last thirty-five years that scholars have given serious consideration to the interaction between FDI and the domestic macro-organizational strategies of governments. One is, however, permitted some glimpses of the views of past scholars. The Mercantilists, for example, favoured government support for outbound investment[61] as long as it helped provide raw materials for, or increase employment in, the home country. Adam Smith was less enthusiastic about the benefits of capital exports, although he recognized that, when they promoted the agricultural development of the recipient countries, they could also be to the advantage of sending countries. Ricardo was generally opposed to foreign investment, fearing that it would be at the expense of its domestic counterpart.[62] J. S. Mill did not agree. Writing in 1848, he argued that capital exports could help arrest the declining profitability of domestic capital, and provide the home country with cheaper food and raw materials, as well as access to new markets.

In their writings, all the classical economists took it for granted that there was only limited mobility of capital across national boundaries—although Mill recognized that, as capital became more cosmopolitan, customers and institutions would converge and suspicion of foreigners would diminish. For the most part, they also assumed that the allocation of international economic activity was largely based on the distribution of *natural* resources—although both Smith and Ricardo, both of whom acknowledged the possible role of innovation in promoting economic growth. Later in the nineteenth century, economists such as Bagehot and Marshall accepted the increasing significance of portfolio capital exports. However, they strongly believed that these were best organized through the brokerage of the international capital market.

At the same time, economists were beginning to explore the consequences of tariffs and other trade barriers, not only for the location, but also for the organization of value-added activity. In Germany, for example, there was a lively debate on the relative merits of FDI and international cartels[63] as cross-border organizational arrangements; while Marx was not slow to speculate on how his theory of the internalization of labour markets might be applied to the transnationalization of capital. By contrast, in the USA, the institutionalists confined their analysis to domestic issues, although the origins of hierarchical capitalism—as later recounted by Alfred Chandler (1962, 1977)—were no less relevant in explaining the initial territorial expansion by US firms.

During the inter-war years, Bertil Ohlin (1933) made a seminal contribution by extending location theory into the international arena; while J. H. Williams (1929: 203) not only recognized the growth of FDI as a modality of international commerce, but was prepared explicitly to state that enterprises undertaking such investment provided 'an organic interconnection of international trade, movement of productive factors, transport and market organization'. However, neither economists nor the location theorists of the time—for example, Weber (1929) and Hotelling (1929)—embraced the costs and benefits of alternative organizational modes in their analyses. Of the few scholars who did this, special mention may be made of Alfred Plummer (1934), whose work on international trusts paved the way for a discussion of cross-border market failure, which is now a cornerstone of the theory of the MNE.

In the light of the severe unemployment in the inter-war years, it is surprising that more attention was not given to the social costs and benefits of outbound or inbound FDI. Keynes, although generally sceptical of the advantages of portfolio capital exports (Keynes 1924), had little to say about the territorial expansion of firms;[64] and, while the protectionist policies of governments in the 1930s most certainly took account of the likely consequences for capital inflows, academic scholars made few pronouncements on the subject.[65] There were also some murmurings—particularly in countries becoming heavily reliant on FDI (e.g. Canada and Australia)—about the impact of inbound MNE activity on economic sovereignty.

During the Second World War and for the first part of the post-1945 period, governments of most developed countries intervened in the workings of the free market both to limit outward direct investment and to encourage inward direct investment. Initially, this action was justified on balance-of-payments grounds, but subsequent theorizing by McDougall (1960) and Jasay (1960), and some empirical research on the profitability of home and foreign investment (Dunning 1970), upheld the contention that the marginal social product of FDI was frequently less than that of its domestic equivalent—i.e. there were external costs to FDI. However, later research by Reddaway, Potter, and Taylor (1968) and Bergsten, Horst, and Moran (1978) questioned these findings. Not only did they argue that FDI might bring a whole range of benefits to the investing companies and home countries beyond any profits earned[66] (e.g. a feedback of technical knowledge, additional exports, and so on), but, in the absence of such investment, the overall competitive position of the investing firms might be disadvantaged. The Brookings study, in particular, asserted that, if foreign (and more particularly US) direct investment was not advancing the welfare of the home country as much as it should, this was probably due to market-distorting economic policies on the part of home or host governments, or to the anti-competitive behaviour of the investing firms. The authors were the first not only to examine the ways in which outbound FDI might require some modification to domestic macro-organizational policies, but also to suggest new instruments (e.g. investment guarantee schemes), which might reduce cross-border guarantee imperfections in product and factor markets.

In retrospect, the analysis of Bergsten, Horst, and Moran and its policy prescriptions were highly prophetic of much of the contemporary debate about the impact of globalization on domestic institutions and macro-organizational structures. In particular, their plea for a more systemic evaluation of the effects of MNE activity, and for a strengthening of international rules to head off conflicts among nations, was both original and highly pertinent. At the same time, the study lacked the analytical foundation for analysing the suitability of the respective organizational modes in coping with the effects of the internationalization of production. Moreover, at the time, few MNEs were operating an integrated strategy towards their foreign operations; in consequence two of the key benefits of cross-border hierarchies—namely, the specialization and common governance of interrelated activities and the spreading of environmental risk and volatility (Kogut 1985)—were given only passing attention.

It was left to a following generation of scholars interested in explaining the increasingly rapid growth of FDI and MNE activity to provide the theoretical insights on these issues. Essentially, they did so by internationalizing the market-failure paradigm. The writings of scholars such as Stephen Hymer, J. C. McManus, Mark Casson, Peter Buckley, Alan Rugman, Jean-François Hennart and many others are not the subject of this chapter.[67] But, their methodology of approach—which has since been extended to explain the growth of cross-border non-equity alliances—is highly relevant to our understanding of how a fully open economy may affect the optimal organization of domestic activities. There are, for example, specific market failures associated with cross-border value-added activities; and almost all of these reflect the additional transaction and coordination costs and/or benefits of producing in different political, institutional, and cultural environments. Thus, on the one hand, the opening-up of national boundaries to FDI might reduce structural imperfections in domestic markets. Similarly, corporate and regional integration may lessen the need for national government regulation of domestic activities. On the other hand, the global competitiveness of enterprises is increasingly dependent on the efficient provision of complementary assets which governments are frequently best suited to supply—or, at least, to oversee.

I have already observed in the historical analysis that scholars have increasingly come to stress not only the importance of the transaction and coordination costs of economic activity, but also the need for flexible institutions and organizational modes. This is changing the role of government—making it sometimes more important, sometimes less important,[68] and sometimes changing its character completely. Frequently, too, the impact of change has been industry and/or issue specific. Thus, while, for example, US government intervention in agriculture has been long accepted,[69] it has been viewed with a great deal of suspicion in the service and manufacturing sectors, where most of the activities of the world's most globalized firms are concentrated (Kozul-Wright 1995).

Similarly, it might be argued that the widening territorial boundaries of economic activity bring their own particular transaction or coordinating costs. These costs largely arise because of the very diverse institutions involved in transactions. More specifically, they reflect the additional complexities of human interaction arising from different educational backgrounds, languages, cultures, ideologies, and social objectives. Likewise, even within market-based economies, the institutional framework and the perceptions of the role of governments, hierarchies, and markets themselves differ—together with a reaction to failure of organizational failure.[70] Finally, the structures of the organizational modalities may vary. In consequence, so will the degree to which such modalities complement or compete with each other.[71]

In the past two decades, a substantial amount of literature has been concerned with the response of governments to the growing significance of the cross-border activities of firms, and the acknowledgement that the key assets to wealth creation—namely, technology, entrepreneurship, and organizational skills—are often highly mobile across national boundaries. But, while the quicksilver nature of these assets have widened the arena of market-based organizational modalities, including private hierarchies, the domain of national governments has remained mainly unchanged. It is this growing dichotomy between the boundaries of economic and political jurisdiction which is necessitating a reappraisal of the institutional framework of national economic systems. Sometimes, this means a reorientation of the overseeing roles of governments; and sometimes, of their role as conflict managers and as stabilizers of last resort (Panic 1995); and sometimes of their regulatory, participatory or advisory roles. But, sometimes, it also suggests that governments—like firms—should engage in cross-border alliances to exchange information and ideas and, where appropriate, to coordinate policies.

The advent of globalization is, then, not only demanding that governments reconsider their functions, *vis-à-vis* those of other organizational modes, but on how they interact with each other. Yet, because the interests of the constituents of government are primarily nationalistic, such interaction tends to be adversarial, rather than cooperative. Although some progress had been made towards the coordination of inter-governmental macro-economic policies, this is not the case with most macro-organization policies. And, this is primarily because—using Douglass North's language—the transaction costs of the necessary institutional changes are currently perceived to outweigh the perceived benefits; or, to put it more bluntly—governments prefer to compete rather than to cooperate with each other. As globalization proceeds, the trade-offs between the benefits of inter-government competition and cooperation, and indeed of the role and organization of supranational economic regimes, may well be expected to change.[72]

6. A Final Footnote

In evaluating the views of social scientists about the macro-economic organizational framework of market-oriented economies, scholarly thought may well be entering a new phase. This is partly the outcome of a new generation of technological advances and the increasing structural integration of markets, hierarchies, and government policies across geographical space; and, partly because, since the mid-1970s, there has been a wave of new thinking among economists, organizational theorists, and business analysts on the role of institutions and organizational modes in strategic decision-taking. Although it is my personal opinion that a dynamic interpretation of the transactions–institutions paradigm probably offers the most fruitful avenue for further research, there can surely be little question that the topic of macro-economic organization is, itself, worthy of more study than it has so far had.

The challenges to interpret the implications of the institutional framework of the late twentieth century are at least as daunting as those facing past scholars in their search to understand the macro-organizational implications of the introduction of the factory-based system at the end of the eighteenth century, and the advent of hierarchical capitalism at the end of the nineteenth century. Yet, alongside the evolvement of market-based capitalism have been advances in the intellectual content of scholarly research. Perhaps the main contribution of the classical and neoclassical economists was to further our understanding about the nature of markets as an economic phenomena; while that of the institutionalists was (and is) to emphasize the significance of institutions as both economic and social phenomena. But, apart from the writings of socialists, there have been only fragmentary attempts systematically to explore the role of government in an industrial society; and even fewer rigorously to analyse the interaction between different economic agents. With the advent of an arsenal of new theoretical tools, and a growing appreciation of the need to adopt a holistic and interdisciplinary approach to the study of organizational arrangements and structures, these lacunae in scholarly thinking are gradually being closed.

NOTES

I wish to express my appreciation to Alison McKaig-Berliner of Rutgers University, for her valuable research assistance in the preparation of this chapter. I am also indebted for the exchange of ideas I have had with another of my Ph.D. students, Timo Hämäläinen.

1. I use the term governments to embrace all forms of polity—be it at a local, regional, national, or supra-national level.
2. On behalf of the constituents which it represents.
3. Or, in Milton Friedman's words 'to do something the market cannot do for itself ready to determine, arbitrate and monitor the rules of the game' (Friedman 1962: 27).
4. According to Ekelund and Hebert (1975: 476), these unique functions include the making of laws that embrace contracts and property rights and the power to coin money. As an umpire, the state provides the functions associated with the police, courts, and monetary authorities.
5. By macro-organizational policies I mean policies of governments designed to affect the structure rather than the level of economic activity which is undertaken within their jurisdictional domain.
6. The concept of limited liability had yet to be introduced.
7. For example, classical economists believed that *laissez-faire* was not so much about allowing efficient markets to work as it was about not allowing powerful governments to take control (Steiner 1953).
8. In the case of each of the nineteenth-century scholars named, rather than our citing their writings, the reader is invited to consult Sills (1968) for a brief biography and compilation of their major works.
9. It is pertinent to note there are traces of these thoughts in Smith's writings. Indeed,

he argued for the granting of monopolies to infant industries and to those businesses attempting to establish international trade linkages (Smith 1776: bk iv, ch. 11).

10. i.e. the first and second quarters of the twentieth century.
11. Indeed, the real influence of Coase on micro-economic thought was not apparent until the 1970s.
12. Or, at least, did so until the early 1990s.
13. Also called 'relational', 'collective', and 'cooperative' capitalism (see Lazonick 1992; Dunning 1994).
14. However, in some cases, social and economic goals may be complementary to each other. Examples include some environmental protection schemes and expenditures on health care.
15. What I shall refer to later as a partially open economy.
16. But see, e.g., Wade (1988), Wolf (1988), and Chang (1994).
17. Noticeably the concept of utilitarianism, which viewed laws as being man-made, and, as such, were to be evaluated by their degree of social utility (Robbins 1953).
18. For a review of Sismondi's writings, see Gide and Rist (1915).
19. Although before that, David Hume, Adam Smith, Jeremy Bentham, and John Stuart Mill were well aware of the concept of externalities.
20. In the words of Ha Joon Chang (1994: 14), contractarianism is 'a position that no other person or authority can impose his/her or its own ethical judgement on the individual, since the individual knows best what his situation is and what his best option in that situation is'. Any interference with the making of individual decisions is seen as violating the innate right to freedom of the individual. According to this view, individuals (or firms) should be left free to make their own contracts and should not be coerced into any transaction however beneficial it may appear to an outsider.
21. e.g. with respect to state monopolies, bounties, embargoes, and high tariffs (Smith 1776; Ferguson 1938). Both J. S. Mill and Henry Sidgwick also advocated government action to curb monopolistic abuses.
22. See particularly Graham and Richardson (1996), Graham (1996) and Graham, Chapter 17 in this volume.
23. According to Blaug and Sturgess (1983: 252), Marshall's decision to take up economics originated in a moral purpose, and one general conclusion of his early writings was that a redistribution of income from rich to poor would increase overall satisfaction. In his subsequent writings, the great neoclassicist fully recognized that state interference in free markets might be necessary in order to promote the maximum satisfaction of society (Ekelund and Hebert 1975).
24. McKenzie and Lee (1991) give various examples. They include the postal service, several public utilities, and some highways.
25. More correctly, perhaps, one should say that the natural rate of unemployment has been increasing and that this is due to the inability of economies speedily to absorb or restructure those unemployed as a result of structural change.
26. According to Stein (1988: 46–8), Keynes believed that what he was prescribing did not confer additional powers to the state, but rather 'new rules for exercising the traditional and inescapable powers of government'. The state simply had to get its monetary and fiscal policy right. Therefore, the structural reforms called for by Communism and Fascism as radical alternatives to the free-market mechanism at the time were not needed to cure its systemic ills.

27. For a review of contemporary theories of technical change, see Dosi *et al.* (1988) and Freeman and Soete (1990); for a review of the interaction between technical change and international trade, see Dosi *et al.* (1990); and for a review of some of the organizational implications of technical change, see Dosi *et al.* (1992).
28. Led by Wilhelm Roscher (1817–94).
29. Not because we consider it unimportant, but because it takes us far outside the domain of economics or even political economy.
30. In his own words (which can be compared with those of Marshall on p. 54): 'When society is made up of segments, whatever is produced in one of the segments has little chance of re-echoing in the others as the segmental organization is strong. The cellular system naturally lends itself to the localization of social events and their consequences. This is no longer true when society is made up of a system of organs. According to their mutual dependence, what strikes one strikes the others and thus every change even slightly significant takes a general intent' (Durkheim 1964: 223).
31. Notably Friedrich Von Mises (1851–1926), Eugen Von Bohm-Bowerk (1851–1914) and Karl Menger (1840–1921). The Austrian economists attributed most market failures to government intervention and to the existence of government created impediments to the coordinating process of the market system. In their opinion, disturbances did not arise from some intrinsic attribute of the exchange process itself, but rather from factors exogenous to the process—and more especially from government intervention (Barry 1991: 81). One exception to this view was that of Adolph Wagner (1835–1917), who, like Durkheim, saw an increasing role for the state in education, public health, transport and communications, and public utilities.
32. Better known for his analysis of conspicuous consumption.
33. This was possibly because his focus of interest was primarily directed to legal and social, rather than economic, issues.
34. In particular, Coase emphasized such transaction costs of using markets as 'discovering what the relevant prices are' and 'negotiating and concluding a separate contract for each exchange transaction'.
35. To quote directly from Olson (1979: 184): 'What is the necessary condition for a jurisdiction to deal optimally with an environmental problem? The necessary condition is that the domain of the environmental problem must match the boundaries of the political jurisdiction. There must be what I like to call "fiscal equivalence". The taxing or regulating area must match the benefit area. If the argument I have made here is correct, we should see in the world about us various developments that would suggest a tendency, however faint, in the direction of fiscal equivalence.'
36. The concept of 'entry' and 'voice' responses to economic problems was first introduced by Albert Hirschman (1970) to explain the reactions of nation states to threats to their sovereignty. Borrowing from Hirschman's terminology, we can identify two reactions to the presence of market or government failure. The first is to 'exit' when action is directed to finding some alternative organizational route (e.g. by internalizing market or eliminating government intervention. The second is a 'voice' strategy where efforts are made to improve the efficiency of the existing organizational arrangements (e.g. by reducing information asymmetries and opportunism between buyers and sellers, or by streamlining the governance of government).
37. Although we do not imply that the role of Japanese government was (or is) always market supporting!
38. As demonstrated, e.g., by Wallis and North (1986). Becker and Murphy (1992) argue

that the degree of division of labour in a modern economy is ultimately limited by the costs of coordinating specialized workers who perform complementary, but increasingly complex, tasks.

39. Although it should be emphasized that, as long as there is effective competition between hierarchies, this organizational form is entirely consistent with free-market principles.
40. North (1993: 3) defines institutions as 'humanly devised constraints imposed on human interaction. They consist of formal values, informal constraints (norms of behavior, conventions and self-imposed conduct) and the enforcement characteristics of both. In short, they are the structure that humans impose on their dealings with each other.'
41. North (ibid) quotes from a study by Christainsen and Haverman (1981) which suggests that US federal regulations may have been responsible. However, he also argues that the indirect impact of regulations in terms of increasing uncertainty and foregone production might be even greater—particularly in the Third World.
42. Earlier Alexander Hamilton had made much the same plea for protectionism against European imports into the USA.
43. For a contemporary view of the interventionist policies pursued by the US government, particularly in the first half of the nineteenth century, see Kuttner (1991) and Kozul-Wright (1995).
44. *Inter alia*, this reflected the growing fixed costs of production, the longer time for returns on these outlays to be generated, the rising externalities of markets, and the growing transaction and coordination costs of economic activity.
45. In the first part of the 1900s, serious attention began to be given to the inabilities of the capitalist system. These were two main streams of thought. The first was essentially concerned with cyclical fluctuations in economic activity and the possible imbalances of aggregate supply and demand. The second was concern with the long-run effects on technological change on economic and social structure.
46. Hence, the expression 'creative' destruction. It will also be observed that Schumpeter's reaction to technological process was more 'voice'-oriented than that of Marx.
47. Notably, Christopher Freeman, Keith Pavitt, and Luc Soete.
48. See, too, some pertinent contributions by Chesnais (1982, 1988), and various authors in Dosi *et al.* (1988) and OECD (1992).
49. See especially the work of Thomas Malthus (1776–1836). However, both Smith and Ricardo were interested in explaining its determinants of economic progress.
50. For some alternative views of economists and organizational scholars on the reasons for this and why relationships between the public and private sectors have been more adversarial in the USA and the UK than in continental Europe and Japan, see Chandler (1990), Steiner (1953), Galbraith (1994), and Shultz (1979).
51. See e.g. Chapters 8 and 13 in this volume.
52. See, e.g., Bartlett and Ghoshal (1989) and Hedlund (1993).
53. It also varies according to the rationale for and form of government intervention. Compare, for example, the effects of anti-trust legislation, environmental legislation, corporation taxation, and R&D subsidies as an import protection on domestic firms and markets (McConnell 1980).
54. As has already been suggested, in different countries and at different time periods, the costs and benefits of the different organizational arrangements will change.
55. The Japanese government, for example, puts a major effort into understanding the competition, institutions, technologies, and consumer preferences in foreign markets.

It has established a worldwide market-intelligence system that produces and disseminates vast amounts of information for private and public policy-makers.

56. But see some remarks by Susan Strange in Chapter 4.
57. Particularly, those to do with externalities, structural adjustment, counteracting trade-distorting practices of other countries, information asymmetries, uncertainties, and learning by doing.
58. Data reveal that the value of foreign sales of MNEs in 1992 exceeded that of non-agricultural exports; and, over the past fifteen years, FDI has increased at twice the rate of exports (UNCTAD 1995).
59. See, e.g., Chapter 5 by Stephen Kobrin and Chapter 16 by John Stopford in this volume, the literature surveyed in Dunning (1994), and Nunnenkamp *et al.* (1994).
60. Political space may effectively be enlarged or reduced by the splitting-up or merging of countries.
61. Particularly when undertaken by the chartered trading companies.
62. At the same time, Ricardo was reluctant to recommend government action, as he believed that there were natural institutional checks on capital exports. In particular, he maintained that capital owners (in the first part of the nineteenth century) would be 'loath to take the risk of allowing the capital to go out of their immediate control'; or, if they accompanied their capital, to forsake their homeland and submit themselves to strange regimes and unfamiliar laws, even with the prospects of more favourable returns (Ricardo 1911: 83). The antecedents of the contemporary theory of FDI and international production are traced in Dunning *et al.* (1986).
63. See, e.g., the writings of Levy (1911) and Hilferding (1910).
64. Although, in various of his writings, he acknowledged that the free movement of capital and goods could undermine the power of national fiscal policy and, more generally, erode national sovereignty.
65. An exception was the Canadian economist Jacob Viner.
66. *Inter alia*, this was because, while the taxation on profits earned by the foreign subsidiaries would accrue to the host country, that of domestic investment would accrue to the home country.
67. These are described in some detail in Dunning (1993) and Caves (1996).
68. All too frequently, importance is measured by the percentage of government expenditure to GNP. But, this is an extremely poor measure of the effectiveness of government as an organizational instrument. The Japanese experience demonstrates that effective government intervention does not have to be expensive. Even excluding defence expenditure, Japan has one of the lowest ratios of government expenditure to GDP, yet the Japanese government has probably had a more critical influence on market forces than any of its foreign counterparts.
69. i.e. in the form of price-support schemes, subsidies to farming, R&D, and guaranteed returns on investment.
70. In Japan, for example, the 'voice' strategy of dealing with both market and political failure is more widely practised than the 'exit' strategy.
71. Cf., e.g., the adversarial business–government mentality in the USA and the UK over the last century with that of the more conciliatory and high-trust business–government relationships in Germany and Japan.
72. For a recent examination of the impact of international integration on the role of national governments, see Panic (1995). In his contribution, Panic identifies four possible responses of national governments to the emergence of globalization of the

world economy, namely (i) try to reverse the process of globalization by insulating their economies from those of the rest of the world, (ii) cooperate in a way that the consequences of their policies are similar to those which might have been achieved by a supra-national authority, (iii) engage in political integration with nation states transpiring some of their authority to a regional or supra-national regime, and (iv) let the market mechanism reconcile any conflicts which might arise among national governments or between themselves and supra-national regimes. Panic thinks that an amalgam of these responses is the most likely scenario to emerge in the next decade or so; and, as a result, the framing and implementation of distinctive national economic policies will become more, rather than less, difficult (Panic 1995: esp. 67–74).

REFERENCES

Amsden, A., Kochanowicz, J., and Taylor, L. (1994), *The Market Meets its Match: Restructuring the Economies of Eastern Europe* (Cambridge Mass.: Harvard University Press).

Aronson, J. R., and Ott, A. F. (1991), 'The Growth of the Public Sector', in D. Greenaway, M. Bleaney, and I. M. T. Stewart (eds.), *Companion to Contemporary Economic Thought* (London: Routledge), 523–46.

Barry, N. P. (1991), 'Austrian Economics: A Dissent from Orthodoxy', in D. Greenaway, M. Bleaney, and I. M. T. Stewart (eds.), *Companion to Contemporary Economic Thought* (London: Routledge), 68–87.

Bartlett, C. G., and Ghoshal, S. (1989), *Managing across Borders: The Transnational Solution* (Boston: Harvard Business School Press).

Becker, G. S., and Murphy, K. M. (1992), 'The Division of Labour: Coordinating Costs and Knowledge', *Quarterly Journal of Economics*, 107/4: 1138–59.

Bergsten, C. F., Horst, T., and Moran, T. (1978), *American Multinationals and American Interests* (Washington: Brookings Institution).

Beveridge, W. H. (1944), *Full Employment in a Free Society* (London: Allen & Unwin).

Blaug, M., and Sturgess, P. (1983) (eds.), *Who's Who in Economics: A Biographical Dictionary of Major Economists 1700–1981* (Cambridge, Mass.: MIT Press).

Caves, R. (1996), *Multinational Firms and Economic Analysis* (rev. edn.; Cambridge: Cambridge University Press).

Chandler, A. D., Jr. (1962), *Strategy and Structure: The History of American Industrial Enterprise* (Cambridge, Mass.: MIT Press).

—— (1977), *The Invisible Hand: The Managerial Revolution in American Business* (Cambridge, Mass.: Harvard University Press).

—— (1990), *Scale and Scope: The Dynamics of Industrial Capitalism* (Cambridge, Mass.: Harvard University Press).

Chang, H. J. (1994), *The Political Economy of Industrial Policy* (New York: St Martin's Press).

Chesnais, F. (1982), 'Schumpeterian Recovery and the Schumpeterian Perspective—Some Unsettled Issues and an Alternative Interpretation', in H. Giersch (ed.), *Emerging Technologies: Consequences for Economic Growth, Structural Change and Employment* (Tübingen: J. C. B. Mohr).

—— (1988), 'Multinational Enterprises and the International Diffusion of Technology', in G. Dosi, C. Freeman, R. Nelson, G. Silverberg, and L. Soete (eds.), *Technical Change and Economic Theory* (London: Pinter Publishers).

Christainsen, G., and Haverman, R. H. (1981), 'Public Regulations and the Slowdown in Productivity Growth', *American Economic Review*, 80 (May), 355–61.

Clark, J. M. (1923), *Studies in the Economics of Overhead Costs* (Chicago: University of Chicago Press).

Coase, R. H. (1937), 'The Nature of the Firm', *Economica*, NS 4 (November), 386–405.

—— (1960), 'The Problem of Social Cost', *Journal of Law and Economics*, 3: 1–10.

Commons, J. R. (1924), *The Legal Foundations of Capitalism* (Madison: University of Wisconsin Press; repr. 1957).

—— (1934), *Institutional Economics* (Madison: University of Wisconsin Press; repr. 1959).

Dosi, G., Freeman, C., Nelson, R., Silverberg, G., and Soete, L. (1988) (eds.), *Technical Change and Economic Theory* (London: Pinter Publishers).

—— Pavitt, K., and Soete, L. (1990), *Technical Change and International Trade* (New York: Harvester Wheatsheaf).

—— Giannetti, R., and Toninelli, P. A. (1992) (eds.), *Technology and Enterprise in a Historical Perspective* (Oxford: Oxford University Press), 119–63.

Dunning, J. H. (1970), *Studies in International Investment* (London: Allen & Unwin).

—— (1993), *Multinational Enterprises and the Global Economy* (Wokingham: Addison Wesley).

—— (1994), *Globalization, Economic Restructuring and Development* (The 6th Prebisch Lecture; Geneva: UNCTAD).

—— (1995), 'What's Wrong—and Right—with Trade Theory?', *International Trade Journal*, 9/2: 153–202.

—— (1996), *Alliance Capitalism and Global Business* (London and New York: Routledge).

—— Cantwell, J., and Corley, T. A. B. (1986), 'The Theory of the Multinational Enterprise: Some Historical Antecedents', in P. Hertner and G. Jones (eds.), *Multinationals: Theory and History* (Farnborough: Gower Press), 19–41.

Durkheim, E. (1964), *The Division of Labor in Society* (New York: The Free Press) (originally published in German in 1893).

Ekelund, R. B., Jr., and Hebert, R. F. (1975), *A History of Economic Theory and Method* (New York: McGraw-Hill Book Company).

Ferguson, J. M. (1938), *Landmarks of Economic Thought* (New York: American Business Fundamentals).

Freeman, C., and Perez, C. (1988), 'Structural Crises of Adjustment: Business Cycles, and Investment Behavior', in G. Dosi, C. Freeman, R. Nelson, G. Silverberg, and L. Soete (eds.), *Technical Change and Economic Theory* (London: Pinter Publishers).

—— and Soete, L. (1990) (ed.), *New Explorations in the Economics of Technical Change* (London: Pinter Publishers).

Friedman, M. (1962), *Capitalism and Freedom* (Chicago: University of Chicago Press).

Galbraith, J. K. (1994), *A Journey Through Economic Time: A Firsthand View* (Boston: Houghton Mifflin Co.).

Gide, C., and Rist, C. (1915), *A History of Economic Doctrines* (London: George G. Harrap).

Graham, E. M. (1996), *Global Corporations and National Governments* (Washington: Institute for International Economics).

Graham, E. M., and Richardson, J. D. (1996), *Global Competition Policy* (Washington: Institute for International Economics).

Grestchmann, K. (1991), 'Analysing the Public Sector: The Received View in Economics and its Shortcomings', in F.-X. Kaufman (ed.), *The Public Sector: Challenge for Coordination and Learning* (Berlin: Walter de Gruyter).

Hämäläinen, T. J. (1994), 'The Evolving Role of Government in Economic Organization' (mimeo; Newark: Rutgers University).

Hedlund, G. (1993) (ed.), *TNCs and Organizational Issues: UN Library on Transnational Corporations* (London: Routledge).

Heilbroner, R. L. (1965), *The Worldly Philosophers: The Lives, Times and Ideas of the Great Economic Thinkers* (New York: Simon & Schuster).

Hilferding, R. (1910), *Finance Capital: A Study of Latest Phase of Capitalist Development* (Eng. trans.; London: 1981).

Hotelling, H. (1929), 'Stability in Competition', *Economic Journal*, 29: 41–57.

Jasay, A. E. (1960), 'The Social Choice between Home and Foreign Investment', *Economic Record*, 38: 105–13.

Keynes, J. M. (1924), 'Foreign Investment and the National Advantage', *The Nation and The Athenaeum*, 35 (August), 584–7.

—— (1936), *The General Theory of Employment Interest and Money* (London: Macmillan).

Kogut, B. (1985), 'Designing Global Strategies: Profiting from Operational Flexibility', *Sloan Management Review*, 26 (Fall), 27–38.

Kondratiev, N. (1926), 'The Long Waves in Economic Life', *Review of Economics and Statistics*, 17.

Kozul-Wright, R. (1995), 'The Myth of Anglo-Saxon Capitalism: Reconstructing the History of the American State', in H.-J. Chang and R. Rowthorn (eds.), *The Role of the State in Economic Change* (Oxford: Oxford University Press).

Krugman, P. (1986) (ed.), *Strategic Trade Policy and the New International Economies* (Cambridge, Mass.: MIT Press).

—— (1991), *Rethinking International Trade* (Cambridge, Mass.: MIT Press).

Krueger, A. O. (1990), 'Economists' Changing Perceptions of Government', *Weltwirtschaftliches Archiv*, 126: 417–31.

Kuttner, R. (1991), *The End of Laissez Faire* (New York: Alfred A Knopf).

Lazonick, W. (1992), 'Business Organizational and Competitive Advantage: Capitalist Transformations in the Twentieth Century', in G. Dosi, R. Gianetti, and P. A. Toninelli (eds.), *Technology and Enterprise in Historical Perspective* (Oxford: Oxford University Press).

Levy, H. (1911), *Monopoly and Competition: A Study in English Industrial Organization* (Eng. trans.) (London: Macmillan).

Lipsey, R. G., and Dobson, W. (1987), *Shaping Comparative Advantage* (Ontario: Prentice Hall for C. D. Howe Institute).

McConnell, J. W. (1980), *Ideas of the Great Economists* (2nd edn., New York: Barnes & Noble Books).

McCulloch, J. (1848), *Treatise on the Succession to Property Vacant by Death* (London: Rongmar, Brown, Green & Lagmans).

McDougall, G. D. A. (1960), 'The Benefits and Costs of Private Investment from Abroad', *Economic Record*, 36: 13–35.

McKenzie, R. B., and Lee, D. R. (1991), *Quicksilver Capital* (New York: The Free Press).

Markusen, A. (1996), 'Sticky Places in Slippery Spaces: The Political Economy of Post-War Fast Growth Regions', *Economic Geography*, 72/3, 293–313.

Marshall, A. (1920), *Principles of Economics* (8th edn., London Macmillan).

Mill, J. S. (1848), *Principles of Political Economy* (London: J. W. Parker); ed. with introduction by Jonathan Riley (Oxford: Oxford University Press, 1994).

Nelson, R. R., and Winter, S. G. (1982), *An Evolutionary Theory of Economic Change* (Cambridge, Mass.: Belknap Press of Harvard University Press).

North, D. (1981), *Structure and Change in Economic History* (New York: Norton).

—— (1990), Institutions, International Change and Economic Performance (Cambridge: Cambridge University Press).

—— (1993), 'Institutions, Transaction Costs and Productivity in the Long Run' (paper presented to Eighth World Productivity Congress, Stockholm, May).

Nunnenkamp, P., Gundlach, E., and Agarwal, J. (1994), *Globalization of Production and Markets* (Tübingen: J. C. B. Mohr).

OECD (1992): Organization for Economic Cooperation and Development, *Technology and the Economy* (Paris: OECD).

Ohlin, B. (1933), *Inter-Regional and International Trade* (Cambridge, Mass.: Harvard University Press; rev. edn., 1967).

Olson, M. (1965), *The Logic of Collective Action: Public Goods and the Theory of Groups* (Cambridge, Mass.: Harvard University Press).

—— (1969), 'Fiscal equivalence', *American Economic Review* (May), 479–87.

—— (1979), 'On Regional Pollution and Fiscal Equivalence', in H. Siebert, I. Walter, and K. Zimmermann (eds.), *Regional Environmental Policy: The Economic Issues* (New York: New York University Press), 181–6.

—— (1982), *The Rise and Decline of Nations: Economic Growth, Stagflation, and Social Rigidities* (New Haven: Yale University Press).

Panic, M. (1995), 'International Economic Integration and the Changing Role of National Governments', in H.-J. Chang and R. Rowthorn (eds.), *The Role of the State in Economic Change* (Oxford: Oxford University Press).

Perez, C. (1983), 'Structural Change and Assimilation of New Technologies in the Economic and Social Systems', *Futures*, 15 (October), 357–75.

Pigou, A. C. (1932), *The Economics of Welfare* (4th edn., London: Macmillan).

Plummer, A. (1934), *International Combines in Modern History* (London: Pitman).

Reddaway, N. B., Potter, S. T., and Taylor, C. T. (1968), *The Effects of UK Direct Investment Overseas* (Cambridge: Cambridge University Press).

Ricardo, D. (1911), *The Principles of Political Economy and Taxation* (first pub. 1817; republished with introduction by Donald Winch, London: J. M. Dent, 1992).

Robbins, L. (1953), *The Theory of Economic Policy* (London: Macmillan).

Rostow, W. W. (1990), *Theories of Economic Growth from David Hume to the Present: With a Perspective on the Next Century* (New York: Oxford University Press).

Schumpeter, J. A. (1934), *The Theory of Economics Development* (New York: Harper & Row).

—— (1942), *Capitalism, Socialism and Democracy* (New York: Harper & Row).

Shultz, G. P. (1979), 'The Abrasive Interface', *Harvard Business Review* (November–December), 93–7.

Sills, D. L. (1968) (ed.), *International Encyclopaedia of the Social Sciences*, 18 vols. (London: Macmillan).

Simon, H. A. (1947), *Administrative Behavior* (New York: Macmillan).

—— (1959), 'Theories of Decision Taking in Economics and Behavioral Science', *American Economic Review*, 49: 255–83.

Smith, A. (1776), *The Wealth of Nations* (repr. 1910, London: Everyman's Library).

Stein, H. (1988), *Presidential Economics: The Making of Economic Policy from Roosevelt to Reagan and Beyond* (2nd edn., Washington: American Enterprise Institute for Public Policy Research).

Steiner, G. A. (1953), *Government's Role in Economic Life* (New York: McGraw-Hill Book Co. Inc.).

Stiglitz, J. (1989), *The Economic Role of the State* (Oxford: Basil Blackwell).

UNCTAD (1993): United Nations Conference on Trade and Development, *World Investment Report: Transnational Corporations and Integrated International Production* (New York: United Nations).

—— (1994), *World Investment Report 1994: Transnational Corporations, Employment and the Workplace* (New York: United Nations).

—— (1995), *World Investment Report: Transnational Corporations and Competitiveness* (New York: United Nations).

Wade, R. (1988), 'The Role of Government in Overcoming Market Failure in Taiwan, Republic of Korea and Japan', in H. Hughes (ed.), *Achieving Industrialization in East Asia* (Cambridge: Cambridge University Press).

Wallis, J. J., and North, D. C. (1986), 'Measuring the Transaction Sector in the American Economy, 1870–1970', in S. L. Engerman and R. E. Gallman (eds.), *Long-Term Factors in American Economic Growth* (Chicago: University of Chicago Press).

Weber, A. (1929), *Über den Standort der Industrien*, trans. as *The Theory of Location of Industries* (Chicago: University of Chicago Press).

Williams, J. H. (1929), 'The Theory of International Trade Reconsidered', *Economic Journal*, 39: 195–209.

Williamson, J. G. (1995), Globalization, Convergence and History (NBER Working Paper No. 5259; Cambridge, Mass.: NBER).

Williamson, O. E. (1975), *Markets and Hierarchies, Analysis and Antitrust Implications* (New York: The Free Press).

—— (1985), *The Economic Institutions of Capitalism* (New York: The Free Press).

Wolf, C. J. (1988), *Markets or Governments* (Cambridge, Mass: MIT Press).

World Bank (1991), *World Development Report* (Oxford: Oxford University Press).

2

Globalization and National Government Policies: *An Economist's View*

Richard G. Lipsey

1. **Introduction**

The previous chapter provided a historical analysis of the views of economists on the place of government in the economy and also discussed the complications introduced when governments operate in highly open economies rather than closed or partially open ones. In this chapter we look at the first of these issues as it is usually developed in standard economics texts, and then go on to suggest ways in which the place of government needs to be reassessed in the light of recent massive changes in economic structure, one of the most important of which is globalization.

Although the primary theme of this volume is the impact of globalization on the policy of national governments, the view taken in this chapter is that globalization is but a subset of the immense number of structural adjustments that the world is undergoing as a result of the evolution of a related group of new technologies usually referred to as information and communications technologies (ICT). Since the ICT revolution is causing many structural adjustments, including globalization, and since the rethinking of the role of governments is to a great extent driven by all of these structural changes, it is often hard to know what is due to globalization and what is due to other aspects of the adjustments wrought by the ICT revolution. So the scope of this chapter is the nature of the ICT revolution, the deep structural adjustments that it is inducing, including globalization, and the rethinking of the place of government in the economy, one major driving force of which is globalization.

The next section of this chapter begins with technological and structural change in general and ends with globalization in particular. Section 3 deals with what economists have traditionally regarded as the functions of the nation state. Section 4 develops the chapter's main theme, which is how technological change and globalization are altering views about the place of government in the economy and, in the process, leading to a new clash of ideologies. This theme is being played out against the background of technological change as an ongoing process that requires continual adjustment of the economic structure, one element of which is government economic policy.

2. Technological Change, Structural Adjustments, and Globalization

It is generally agreed that material living standards have risen over most of the last two centuries. The source of this gain is not an increasing volume of the products consumed 100, let alone 200, years ago, and made by the methods then in use. The source is the host of new products that are produced in new ways. We do have ten times as much market value of consumption as our Victorian ancestors had (measured in constant dollars), but we consume it largely in terms of new commodities produced with new techniques.

2.1. Technological Change

The above point is important.[1] Technological advances transform our lives by inventing new, undreamed of products and producing them in new, undreamed of ways.

> Victorians could not have imagined modern dental and medical equipment, penicillin, pain killers, bypass operations, catscans, surgery at a distance, safe births and abortions, personal computers, compact disks, TVs, opportunities for cheap, fast, world-wide travel, safe food of great variety, central heating, elimination of endless kitchen drudgery by either wives or masses of servants through the use of detergents, washing machines, vacuum cleaners, and a host of other new household products that their great grandchildren take for granted. (Lipsey 1993: 4)

As Rosenberg and Birdzell say in *How the West Grew Rich*, the success of the industrial Western economies over the past two centuries has been based not on inventing a particular technology, but in creating a society in which innovation occurred continuously.

> the West's path to wealth involved and required a society willing to tolerate and accept social and political change far more drastic than any previous revolution. . . . The West has grown rich, by comparison to other economies, by allowing its economic sector the autonomy to experiment in the development of new and diverse products, methods of manufacture, modes of enterprise organisation, market relations, methods of transportation and communication and relations between capital and labour. (Rosenberg and Birdzell 1986: 332–3)

2.1.1. A Structuralist Theory of Growth

Mokyr (1990) distinguishes three sources of economic growth: 'Solovian', capital accumulation, 'Smithian', expansion of markets, and 'Schumpeterian', technological change.[2] Virtually all students of technology agree that, in the long term, Schumpeterian growth is the dominant force. The version of the structuralist theory presented by Lipsey and Bekar (1995) distinguishes three key aspects: *technology*, the *facilitating structure*, and *economic performance*.

'Technology' refers to the specifications of the products (both goods and services) that are made, and the processes by which they are made. Some technology is codifiable—for example, in the form of formulae or blueprints—while much of it is held in terms of tacit knowledge that is acquired by operating existing equipment.

Technologies work within a 'facilitating structure' which includes: the nature and physical location of capital goods; the nature and allocation of labour and human capital; the financial and institutional organization of production units; market structures (running from perfect competition to monopoly); the infrastructure; private-sector financial institutions; markets and other means of effecting economic transactions; public-sector institutions such as private property (laws and protection); local and national government activity designed to facilitate or control economic activity, and similar activity at the supra-national level.

The existing technology interacts with the existing facilitating structure to produce 'economic results', such as specific outputs at the micro-level and the size and distribution of the GDP, and employment and unemployment at the macro-level.

Modern aggregate growth theories, whether they treat technology as exogenous or endogenous, do not model the structure. Structuralists who follow Freeman and Perez (1988) handle technology, structure, and results all together in one overarching concept called a techno-economic paradigm (TEP). We separate these three concepts in order to make contact with what we see in economic history and in the micro-economic literature on technological change. For example, radical new technologies are, of necessity, initially inserted into structures adapted to old technologies, and do not realize their full potential until the structures are changed to fit them. This was vividly illustrated at the turn of the last century when the electrification of factories did not dramatically raise productivity until the structure of factories had been changed from what was suitable for steam power to what was suitable for electric power (David 1991).

More generally, as the technology changes, the facilitating structure adapts to it, but with a lag. Thus, when rapid technological developments occur in widely used technologies, the current structure becomes ill adapted to the new technology. The required rapid changes in the structure will then tend to occur in a 'conflict-ridden process'[3] as many of the old industrial locations, institutions, behaviour patterns, and public policies, which worked well under the old technologies, become less effective or even dysfunctional under the new.

The causal linkages between changes in technology and changes in the facilitating structure do not all flow from technology to structure. Changes in the latter can cause changes in the former. For example, as Douglass North has emphasized, changes in defined property rights can cause changes in innovative activity leading to new technologies. (See, for example, North 1990 and his comment in Stiglitz 1989.)

2.1.2. Technological Change in History

Social and economic evolution has been linked with technology at least since the Neolithic agricultural revolution.[4] Technological change has been going on more or less continually in Western societies since that time, sometimes at a fast pace and sometimes slowly. These changes range from numerous small improvements in existing technologies through to occasional major changes in 'enabling technologies', which are technologies that are widely used in various forms throughout the whole economy.[5] Changes in these require major adjustments in the 'facilitating structure' (changes which Lipsey and Bekar call 'deep structural adjustments', or DSAs).

Without claiming that their classification is exhaustive, Lipsey and Bekar (1995) identify four categories of enabling technologies, changes in which have caused DSAs in past history. These are *information and communications technologies* (e.g. writing, printing, and current computer-related technologies), *materials technologies* (e.g. bronze, iron, and modern, purpose-made materials), *power delivery systems* (e.g. water, wind, steam, electricity), and *transportation technologies* (e.g. the wheel, the horse, efficient three-masted sailing vessels, canals, railroads, steamships, automobiles, aircraft).

Currently, the world is undergoing DSAs in response to ICT revolution, assisted by major reductions in transport costs brought about by a host of innovations such as containerization and massive increases in the size of ships. The ICT revolution is based on a host of related electronic technologies, such as automatic telephones employing fibre optic lines, interactive and high definition television, faxes, and satellite communications. At the core, and driving the DSAs, is the computer. As a result of the ICT revolution, our ability to collect, analyse, and transmit data, and to coordinate activities worldwide, has increased massively, while the costs of doing so have fallen dramatically.

2.2. **Changing Structure and Performance**

The ICT revolution is causing massive changes in the facilitating structure and in economic performance.

2.2.1. Structure

From mass production to lean production. Fordism or mass production is giving way to lean production, flexible manufacturing, or Toyotaism, as it is variously called. On the shop floor, the system of dedicated machines tended by unskilled labour engaged in repetitive tasks and producing masses of identical products is being replaced by relatively skilled workers operating in flexible teams doing many tasks on a whole section of the assembly line. Production is typically of short runs of differentiated versions of some generic product, often tailored to meet a specific customer's needs. At the administrative level, the numerous middle managers who passed information up and down the chain of command have been replaced by computers and a more flexible management form of semi-independent groups who are linked laterally rather than vertically. Increasingly, the ability of a firm to be flexible over time has become more important than traditional cost minimization at a point in time. As a result, traditional distinctions between managers and the managed are being eroded whenever they hamper flexibility and learning capabilities.

Deindustrialization and servicization. These shifts have accentuated a trend observable throughout this century: the growing importance of the service sector that was partly masked initially by the larger movement from rural to urban occupations. Manufacturing employment typically reached a peak of somewhere between 25 and 35 per cent of the labour force in most industrialized societies earlier in this century. Since then, the proportion has been steadily declining and shows no signs of stabilizing yet. At the same time, the proportion of the labour force employed in services has been growing steadily until it is now the largest single sector by employment in all industrialized economies. Note, however, that, as with agriculture, total output of manufactured goods has continued to rise, but productivity has risen even faster, so that manufacturing employment has fallen.

The 'servicization' of the economy has a number of different sources. First, the decline in employment in manufacturing is partly a measure of its vast success in raising manufacturing productivity so that more can be produced with less inputs especially labour. Secondly, the shift to services is partly driven by consumers' tastes. As real incomes rise, people spend a lower proportion of their incomes on durable consumers' goods and a rising proportion on such services as medical care, world travel, and restaurant eating. Thirdly, much of the apparent shift is due to redefinitions of an unchanged activity from manufacturing to services. A range of service activities that used to be conducted in-house by manufacturing firms, and so recorded as manufacturing activities, is now contracted out to firms specializing in a wide range of activities such as product design, marketing, accounting, cleaning, and maintenance, and so recorded as service activities. Fourthly, some of the shift is due to a real increase in the importance of the service side of manufacturing, such as design and marketing. So not only are these activities more likely to be recorded as service activities; more real resources are being devoted to them relative to on-line production. Finally, by making them more efficient, the ICT revolution has encouraged many service activities. Travel agents now have real time access to travel and vacation possibilities; financial advisers monitor the performance of worldwide investment opportunities by the minute; courier services deliver packages worldwide, tracking them at every stage of their journey. The Internet is providing entirely new channels for the communication of information that is diminishing the importance of some older service activities such as brokerage and various information services and increasing the importance of many new service activities.

Economies of scope and scale. In manufacturing, the introduction of computers and other information technologies has slashed the minimum efficient scale of production for many product lines. Fixed costs are now covered by small runs of many product lines, so that scope has replaced scale as the dominant determinant of production economies in many consumers' goods industries. Further, the applications of both advanced materials and computers have eliminated economies of scale in such traditional industries as steel manufacturing, as shown, for example, by the rise of the mini-mills.

The organization of service production has also changed rapidly. On the one hand, firms operating on a global scale in law, accounting, and other traditional services are replacing many of the old individual operators. On the other, many service activities are being developed by independent contractors often working out of their homes.

As it was with the introduction of electricity, so it is with the ICT revolution: in some areas, scale economies are increasing the size of the firm; in others, it has become efficient to be small. There is no certainty, therefore, that the average level of industrial concentration will rise over the whole economy—although it is certainly doing so in some industries.

Labour markets. Human capital is becoming an increasingly important factor. Skill requirements for previously low-skilled jobs have risen as design, production, and marketing increasingly involve creating and processing information. The power and the role of unions have been altered both by the need to adopt flexible production techniques which are incompatible with rigid job demarkation rules, and by the development of a global market in low-skilled labour.

Social organizations. If the first industrial revolution took work out of the home and into the factory, the current ICT revolution is putting much of it back. This is permitting flexible work relations and flexible hours. As the suburb becomes occupied during the working day, social relations and tacit social control mechanisms are altering.

The new ICT technologies have redefined our notions of time and distance. For example, the Internet makes it easy for like-minded individuals located throughout the world to link up into a single group. The changes in human interaction and information transfer resulting from myriad such developments are among the largest ever to occur in history—comparable to those wrought by the printing press.

2.2.2. Performance

Major changes in economic performance are accompanying the current technological revolutions and the DSAs that follow in their wake.

The overall rate of growth of the world economy has slowed down over the last two decades. This is typical of a period of DSA in which the gradual introduction of major new technologies entails large adjustment costs and the technologies cannot produce at their full potential until the economy's facilitating structure has been adapted to suit the new technological regime.

In the industrialized countries, rapid technological changes are causing the patterns of the geographical, occupational, sectoral, and skill requirements in the demands for labour to shift faster than labour supplies can adjust. The result in countries with fairly flexible labour markets is rising inequalities in the distribution of pre-tax, pre-transfer income (but relatively low long-term unemployment). This is particularly evident in Canada and the USA. The result in countries with relatively inflexible labour markets, such as some of the countries of the EU, is increased structural (long-term) unemployment (but relatively small increases in income inequalities). (See e.g. Freeman and Soete 1994.)

To some extent at least, these are transitional phenomena, which will last for a decade or two until the labour supply adjusts to the new patterns of demand. Full adjustment, however, must await the departure from the labour force of those with obsolete skills who cannot, or will not, retrain, and the entrance of a new generation trained in the newly required skills. Today there is a major debate as to how much of the increase in income inequalities and unemployment will be transitional, such as is expected with any major DSA, and how much will be more persistent, due to long-term, technologically driven changes in the structure of the demand for labour relative to the structure of supply, once all supply-side adjustments have taken place.

2.3. Globalization

2.3.1. Causes

Many of the structural changes discussed above can be grouped under the general heading that is of most concern to this volume: an increased globalization of the world's economies. This is an acceleration of a process that is largely driven by technological change and that has been going on for hundreds of years—but with the recent addition of the cross-border integration of production of many manufactured goods and services within the common ownership of MNEs.

Although technological change is probably the most important cause of globalization, two important contributory causes are the dramatic revival of the market economy in erstwhile communist regions, and the changes in the development strategies on the part of most of the developing nations from being inward-looking, import-substituting, foreign-investment-hostile to being outward-looking, export-promoting, foreign-investment-welcoming. Part of this switch, which is discussed more fully later in this chapter, was due to a failure in practice of the heavily interventionist model of economic development and its replacement by a more market-oriented model. Part was also due to globalization itself, which made it increasingly costly to operate an inward-looking policy.

2.3.2. Scope

International trade has been important ever since the Bronze Age began in the third millennium BC. It expanded with the development of three-masted sailing vessels in the early modern period, and saw a major expansion with the industrial revolution's growing demand for raw materials and the development of the iron steam ship. With some shorter-term variations, it has been growing ever since. Today's globalization, however, is much more than just an expansion in trade.

Markets for many goods are globalizing, driven by the development of universal tastes for some globally advertised goods such as designer jeans and high-quality footwear.

Financial markets are almost fully globalized and, as Chapter 5 shows, are largely operated by electronic devices. The combination of cheap, easy communications and massive stocks of short-term capital has made these markets international and volatile, responding to every expectation of future movements in interest and exchange rates. No longer is the exchange rate dominated in the short term by current-account transactions. Although these transactions do still strongly influence the trend of actual exchange rates over 5–10-year periods, capital flows can take actual rates far from purchasing power rates and hold them there for quite long periods of time.

Many service industries are globalizing. Accounting and legal firms were early movers in this development. Since then, the ability to communicate instantly around the world has allowed many service activities to relocate. It is now routine to keep accounts of such things as credit-card transactions and frequent flyer points in countries with educated but cheap labour, such as India, Ireland, and the West Indies. The ICT revolution has made it possible for many service firms in developed nations to provide services to other countries in a wide range of activities including architecture, factory and product design, land conservation, and management consultancies. Education is now a major export of several developed nations, not only through bringing students to a country's educational institutions, but through the growing effectiveness of the techniques of distant learning. Dramatically, the use of mechanical hands for surgical operations, combined with new communications systems, is giving rise to distant surgery which may allow advanced nations to export surgical skills around the world—a valuable export for the advanced nations and a boon to those who would otherwise be denied access to such skills. Services are already close to a third of total exports in several industrialized countries, and rising (and are probably under-reported relative to goods exports).

Many corporations are *regionalizing*, developing presences across Europe, or North America, or the Asia Pacific, with some presence outside their own areas. More and more corporations are *globalizing* and are increasingly coordinating their production and trading activities within a network of cross-border, internal and external relationships which serve their global strategic interests. As a result, FDI, which grew in the nineteenth century to exploit overseas resources, has exploded in the last quarter of the twentieth century. Investment in manufacturing facilities and trade in manufactured goods are now complements to, rather than substitutes for, each other. In the last decade or so, the big development in FDI has been growth of the service sector. For the half dozen or so major home countries for international service industries, service-FDI now dominates manufacturing-FDI in both flows and accumulated stocks (UNCTAD 1994).

The ICT and transport revolutions have allowed production units to be delinked from design units, and allowed parts that are manufactured throughout the world to be delivered to assembly plants when and where they are needed. Depending on the need to achieve low-cost production or to tap a pool of human capital, firms are relocating production units all over the world. This requires a degree of coordination that was impossible just a few decades ago, when parts all needed to be made reasonably close to the final assembly point. Although these developments have not made firms indifferent to their location, they have greatly widened their choices to include most of the world. By reducing the importance of transport and coordination costs, the ICT revolution has increased the importance of other variables such as international relative wages, the skills of the labour force, and the 'friendliness' of government policy.

> what follows is the creation of national comparative advantages based on human capital and technological infrastructure. Thus, while multinationals are still engaged in direct investment, they are . . . increasingly assuming the role of an orchestrator of production and transactions with a system of cross-border internal and external relationships, which may, or may not, involve equity investment, but which are intended to serve its global interests. (Dunning 1993: 602)

This last point raises one of the major contrasts between trade in the last forty years and all previous trading regimes. Until recently, manufactured goods were mainly produced in the high-income, industrialized countries and traded for primary products and semi-manufactured goods coming from the less developed countries (now officially called 'developing countries'). Today, the newly industrialized and the developing nations export a wide range of manufactured goods (both final consumers' goods and parts) to the older industrialized nations of Europe and North America.[6]

3. Traditional Views of the Role of National Governments

Of course, government policies change under the impact of many influences other than technological change; but our brief in this chapter is to consider the influence on policy of globalization which is a manifestation of current technological changes. The DSAs associated with the changes in enabling technologies include major induced changes in government policies.

Most macro-growth theories model technological change as a continuous series of small shocks. If this were the whole story, the facilitating structure, including those parts of it which are created or controlled by government policy, would be adjusting slowly and continuously to these technological changes. Our reading of technological history suggests, as we have already pointed out, that the continuous changes in technology are punctuated by occasional major shocks caused by revolutions in an enabling technology and necessitating DSAs. When this happens, the facilitating structure is put under great stress and must change rapidly. Attempts to control pornography and other undesirable material on the Internet provide one small example of the conflict-ridden process involved in adjusting the structure of government policy to the new technologies. In all previous historical experience, once major shifts have been accomplished, periods of secular boom have often followed as newly established technologies are further developed within a relatively stable facilitating structure. The years 1945–75 were the last such period.

This then is the background for the current rethinking of government policy: a period, 1945–75, in which the facilitating structure was relatively stable has been followed by a period of rapid structural change through which we are now living. Before we discuss these issues more fully in Section 3 we need to outline the reasons for government economic policy traditionally held by economists, and whose evolution was described in the previous chapter. The background is the belief that the market is a relatively efficient method of coordinating decentralized decision-making. To argue this case, economists have used two different types of analysis.

3.1. Two Defences of the Market Economy

The first defence of the market economy is informal in the sense that it is not laid out in equations leading to some formal mathematical result.[7] But it does follow from some hard reasoning, and it has been subjected to some searching intellectual probing. It is based on three propositions. First, the market system coordinates decentralized economic decisions better than any known alternative. It does this by generating price signals that reflect relative national scarcities without anyone ever having to calculate them or even to know what they are. Producers and consumers react to these prices, and, in seeking to maximize their well-being, they generate a relatively efficient allocation of resources that satisfies human wants better than any other form of organization could do *within the confines of existing technology*. Secondly, markets tend to decentralize power more and to involve less coercion and opportunities for corruption than does any alternative type of organizing mechanism. Thirdly, the rewards and the flexibility of the market system are conducive to growth by encouraging the exploration of opportunities for innovation by decentralized, profit-seeking decision-takers competing against each other and employing privately owned capital. (On this last point, see Rosenberg and Birdzell 1986.)

The *formal defence*, which dates back at least as far as Pigou (1920), arose because economists wanted to be more precise about just what the market economy did so well. To do this, they developed the proof that an idealization of the market economy called perfect competition would lead, in equilibrium, to an *optimum* allocation of resources. In this idealization, not only is the market economy a better way of organizing economic decisions than known alternatives; it is the best way: it achieves optimality; there can be nothing better. Although optimality can be shown not only statically, but also at every point along a dynamic adjustment path, the proof requires constant technology and tastes. It has nothing to say, therefore, about the performance of an economy that is growing under the impact of endogenous, path-dependant, technological change.

3.2. Major Reasons for Government Intervention

The rest of this part of the chapter puts on the record material that is well known to economists, and takes up many of the issues dealt with by John Dunning in the previous chapter. Given the formal defence, that the performance of a successfully functioning (perfectly competitive) market cannot be improved on, economists derive one of the major classes of reasons for government intervention from what are called 'market failures'.

3.2.1. Market Failures

Common property resources. Economic theory, and a host of empirical evidence, show that, in market economies, common property resources such as fisheries, public grazing land, and forests will be over-exploited, often to the point of destruction.[8] A major area of government activity is to regulate the use of common property resources. This can be done, for example, by creating property rights in the form of tradeable quotas to exploit the resources. The total quota is set at the optimal level of exploitation and the individual quota units go to the highest bidders (and thus, by implication, the most efficient of the potential users). With common property resources, the biggest problems facing governments lie not in figuring out what needs to be done but in having the courage to proclaim the solution and the ability to enforce it.

Public goods. Another class of market failure comes from goods that, once produced, can be consumed by everyone (called non-rivalrous) and the consumption of which cannot be controlled (called non-excludable). If everyone can use a publicly broadcast television signal, it is non-rivalrous. If its consumption cannot be prevented, it is non-appropriable. There is then no way for a private firm to produce the product for profit because the firm cannot make its use conditional on a payment. The state is the obvious producer of such public goods as police protection and national defence. It should be noted that, if consumption can be prevented, as with a fenced park, or if social conscience can be relied on, as with public television, a non-rivalrous good or service can be produced by private organizations. Also, since non-excludability is a technical matter, it changes as technology changes. Pay TV provides a good example of how a once non-excludable, non-rivalrous product can be made excludable by technological developments.

Externalities. An externality, or third-party effect, is an effect of an activity that is felt by some who are not directly parties in that activity. For example, a negative externality is caused when production of some good creates pollution which affects parties other than the firm and its customers. Similarly, if private production creates amenities for which the firm cannot charge, a positive externality is conferred on the beneficiaries. Economic theory shows that goods with negative externalities will tend to be overproduced because the costs conferred on outsiders are not taken into account by either the producer or the consumer. In contrast, goods with positive externalities will tend to be underproduced because the producer cannot collect for the external benefits that are produced. In each case, there is a reason for the government to intervene to alter the outcome that would be produced by the free market. This can be done with rules and regulations, taxes and subsidies, or, as is usually favoured by economists in the case of negative externalities, transferable rights to create that externality. The state must create these property rights, then monitor and enforce their use.

Information asymmetries. Markets work best when the same information is available to buyers and to sellers, so that they each have similar knowledge of what to expect from any bargain that they reach. Information asymmetries can lead to various market failures, of which 'adverse selection' is but one example. Typically, individuals buying insurance know more about their exposure to risk than do the companies selling it. As a consequence, when the companies charge a rate that allows them to cover all their costs over all the policies they write, those buyers who are most exposed to risk will find the insurance a bargain, while those who are least exposed to risk will find the rate expensive. This alters people's behaviour over what would happen if the company could write a policy for each individual that adequately reflected that individual's own risk exposure.

It is not obvious that the government can improve on the market's performance when asymmetric information is the problem. Stiglitz (1986) has shown, however, that governments can improve matters in most such cases by judicious intervention into market transactions.

The concept of workable competition. Using the result that perfect competition leads to an optimum allocation of resources, many economists have argued that all deviations from perfect competition should be regarded as market failures. However, perfect competition requires, among other things, the absence of both differentiated products and significant scale economies. A differentiated product means that each product line is different from every other product line of the same generic product, both within and across firms. Significant scale economies occur whenever the minimum efficient size (MES) of the firm is large in relation to the total market demand at a price that fully covers costs. Since one or both of these conditions is present in the great majority of manufactured goods and services, it is not very satisfactory to regard everything but perfect competition as a 'market failure'. After all, if the market leads to the formation of large firms because they are more efficient than small firms, it seems odd to call this a 'market failure'.

In practice, governments and many applied economists have used a concept called 'workable competition': the maximum amount of rivalry among firms that is consistent with efficient exploitation of current product and process technologies. Competition policy, which goes by various names in various countries, typically seeks to prevent firms from merging to obtain significant power over their markets (except where this confers a cost advantage due to scale economies), or colluding while remaining separate entities, to keep prices high by restricting inter-firm competition. Across all developed countries there can be seen an unresolved conflict between declaring anti-social all market power *per se* or only that which reduces workable competition.

A special case of this problem arises with so-called natural monopolies, which occur when there is room in some market for only one firm operating profitably at the minimum efficient scale. In this case, it is usually agreed that state intervention is desirable. The two major solutions used in the past have been either for the state to operate the monopoly as a nationalized industry or to leave it in private hands while regulating its behaviour.

3.2.2. Other Reasons for Intervention

There are two important reasons for government intervention other than market failures. Both of these relate to social rather than economic considerations.

Paternalism and the imposition of social values. Paternalism occurs when the behaviour of individuals is regulated on the grounds that some public official knows better than the individual what is in the individual's own best interests. Social values are imposed when an individual's behaviour is regulated to make it conform to what is called for by assumed social values which the individual may or may not share.

Paternalistic measures have most justification when they concern minors, who are in any case subject to others taking decisions for them, and in 'one-off' events where the individual has no chance to learn from experience and often does not know what expert knowledge has to say. Seat belts are an example.

Laws creating 'no-victim crimes' are usually either paternalistic of the we-know-better-than-you sort, or attempts to impose behaviour conforming to assumed community values on individuals who do not share them. Methodological individualists usually oppose all such interventions, while others who believe there is a place for the state other than satisfying individual values, or who believe that tastes can and should be influenced, often support such measures.

Altering the distribution of income and wealth. The second reason, which is much more important than the first, is to alter the distribution of income on grounds of equity. This can be done by government expenditures and transfer payments that go to groups identified as needy, or by taxes that fall disproportionately on groups identified as more than averagely better off.

Some types of activity, such as state provision of primary education, fall into several types of justification. Two of the most important in the case of education involve social justice, that every child should be assured a minimum education independent of its parents' ability to pay, and externalities, that all citizens benefit from an improvement in the average educational level.

Assessment of the legitimate redistributive function of the state is made difficult by the undoubted fact that, throughout history, rulers have used this function to appropriate wealth from the economically successful to finance foreign adventures or domestic consumption by themselves and their allies. The modern version of this behaviour occurs in a democracy when the majority uses the tax-expenditure system to appropriate income and wealth from the minority for reasons not supported by any commonly accepted standards of justice.

3.3. **Restraints on Government Intervention**

In recent times, economists have been at pains to emphasize that the above list of potential benefits does not provide sufficient conditions for government intervention. Successful intervention requires that the benefits of such intervention exceed the costs. These costs are associated both with unavoidable intervention costs and with avoidable ones, which are usually associated with what are called 'government failures'.

3.3.1. Unavoidable Costs of Intervention

There are three major types of unavoidable costs of intervention. *Internal costs* arise because everything that government does uses resources. *Direct external costs* are costs that government activity imposes directly on other identifiable agents in such forms as increased production costs, compliance costs, and losses in productivity. Quite apart from actual expenditures, government intervention may reduce the incentive for experimentation, innovation, and the introduction of new products. *Indirect external costs* are costs that spread beyond those immediately affected by the intervention. For example, government regulations designed to ensure the safety of new drugs delay the introduction of all drugs, including those that are safe. The benefits of such regulations are the unsafe drugs that are detected before they reach the market and the costs are the delays in introducing the safe ones. Tax-shifting causes other indirect external costs when the burden of taxes ends up on agents not intended to bear the burden. High marginal rates of income tax provide a disincentive to save, while deduction of interest from taxable income provides an incentive to accumulate debt. Steeply progressive rates of income tax strongly penalize any activity that produces an irregular income stream (typical of risky activities) over other activities that produce a regular stream of the same total pre-tax value of lifetime income.

3.3.2. Government Failure

Governments can fail either because they do not do the things that could produce social benefit, or because they do do things that produce social loss. Although the errors of omission may be serious, particularly in these times of government retrenchment, there is little more to say about them, so we shall concentrate on the errors of commission, mentioning two broad classes.

Rigidities. Although both technology and market conditions change continually, government behaviour is hard to change. For example, today's natural monopolies can be quickly turned into highly competitive industries by technological changes such as have recently occurred in telecommunications. If the old natural monopoly was highly regulated or, worse still, nationalized, alterations in government policy to suit the new conditions are often long in coming. The delay can hurt the competitive advantage of a country's industries if other countries adjust faster. The same is true of almost any set of government laws, rules, and regulations. Conditions change, and the required policy alterations can be long delayed—particularly if there is a vocal interest group that will be hurt by the needed adjustments. This is one reason why economists prefer market-based rather than command-based methods of intervention where some intervention is required: they adjust automatically to changing market conditions.

Public choice. Governments have goals of their own, not the least of which, in a democracy, is getting re-elected. Public-choice theory, the branch of economics that investigates government failures that result from this type of motivation, has identified many sources. A typical one is the tendency to do things that benefit a small, identifiable group at a cost to a large, diffuse group. The net benefit may be negative, but the gain to each member of the small benefiting group may be large and visible, while the loss to each individual in the large losing group may be small enough to be ignored. If many such choices are made, the whole society, including those that benefit from one such choice, may be losers.

3.3.3. When Do Governments Fail?

Can we identify circumstances that make government failure more or less likely? One of the most common situations is when the policy is captured by one of the interest groups which it affects. Classic examples occur when regulatory bodies are captured by the industry they are meant to regulate and when nationalized industries are run in the interests of their employees rather than their customers. The ability to protect a policy from such capture varies with the political institutions and political practices of each country.

Another source of failure is where a country lacks the administrative capability to operate a policy successfully. What one political jurisdiction can do successfully may become a dismal failure under another jurisdiction. In our current research, we have examples of policies that worked well under a Canadian provincial government and failed when transferred to the federal government for what would seem to be small differences in the methods of administration. If administrative competencies differ in material ways between provincial and federal governments in one country, they will differ much more across countries.

Social attitudes that are inappropriate to particular policies are another source of failure. Many of the policies that work well in Japan and the newly industrialized countries (NICs) would fail dismally if transferred to the USA or Canada, because their success depends on cooperation between the private and public sectors based on a trust that is largely lacking in these countries.

Given the right social attitudes, government policies will work best when there is a self-interest in cooperation among private-sector firms which the government can build on but which cannot emerge from non-cooperative self-interested decisions. Such a situation seems to exist with pre-competitive research, as described in a later section.

This issue of government success and failure is taken up again in a more general context at the end of this chapter.

4. Rethinking the Place of Government

During the 1990s a major reassessment of the place of the state in the modern economy has been taking place in most countries. The twentieth century has seen an evolution towards ever larger and the ever more intrusive governments. That trend is now being rethought and reversed to a significant extent. The trend towards diminished government activity is associated with a number of items such as a fuller understanding of the limits of state power to alter economic and social behaviour in ways that are generally thought to be desirable, and the accepted failure of older interventionist models of the government's place in the economy.

At the same time, new possibilities for the government's place in the economy are being suggested. One of the most important factors in this change is an increasing concern with economic growth and international competitiveness, along with an understanding that growth and technological change are largely endogenous and hence capable of being influenced by public policy, certainly for the worse, and possibly for the better.

4.1. Rethinking Economic Growth

4.1.1. Endogenous Technological Change

Endogenous technological change is the current hot topic in growth-theorizing. Its impact seems quite different, however, depending on which of the two main paradigmatic approaches to modelling growth is used.

One approach uses highly aggregated models. A macro-production function relates GDP to two or three aggregate inputs, usually taken to be labour, human capital, and physical capital. Technology alters the production function as a result of a series of more or less small, continuous shocks which are assumed to be either exogenous and random, or endogenous but still continuous in nature. Growth in GDP results from changes in any of the three inputs and from changes in technology. This approach is in the tradition of the growth models pioneered by Robert Solow in the late 1950s, but, in some of its later manifestations, aggregate technology is made into an endogenous variable.

The second approach is the structuralist, micro-approach that was introduced at the beginning of this chapter. It is in the tradition of Joseph Schumpeter and those who argue that growth is inextricably bound up with history and can be adequately understood only as part of a path-dependent, largely irreversible, historical process. It also holds that an assessment of innovation policies requires a detailed modelling of the process of technological change and the structure through which it operates.[9]

While macro-economists still debate the value of allowing for endogenous technological change in their models, students of technology have long agreed that both the R and the D of R&D expenditure respond to some significant extent, but not exclusively, to economic incentives. After all, development is a costly activity engaged in by firms in pursuit of profit and it would be surprising if it did not respond to economic incentives. In his path-breaking book, *Inside the Black Box*, Nate Rosenberg (1982) argues, on the basis of rich micro-evidence, that basic scientific research is also responsive to economic incentives, partly because much of it is now conducted in industrial research labs and partly because of the operation of some subtle incentive mechanisms which operate even when pure research is conducted in non-profit organizations.

4.1.2. Policy Implications of Endogenous Technological Change

If endogenous technological change lies at the heart of economic growth, governments cannot avoid influencing growth, since almost every government policy, including those related to education, competition, and redistribution, will have some influence on the amount, location, and direction of technological change. Some economists argue, however, that endogenous technological change should not be inserted into macro-growth models because this will encourage governments to engage in misguided technology-enhancing interventions. Romer (1995) reports on this argument while not condoning it. It would seem a little late, however, to lock the barn door against the policy implications of endogenous technological change. Writing in 1834, John Rae, one of the first economists to perceive the implications of endogenous technological change, made the following points: 'instead of pursuing a policy of non-intervention, the "legislator" should stimulate foreign trade and technical progress, encourage the transfer of knowledge, tax luxuries, and use tariffs to protect infant industries' (Hennings 1987: 40).

Schumpeter and other theorists of endogenous technical change have typically followed the policy lines pointed out by Rae. Thus, the substantive policy issue today is not 'Is technological change endogenous?' but 'Given that it is, what is the best government policy response?'

Policy with respect to technological change is made more complex by the massive externalities associated with changes in fundamental technologies, particularly those that Lipsey and Bekar (1995) call enabling technologies. A new enabling technology, such as the steam engine, electricity, the computer, or (if it comes) practical superconductivity, has effects that reverberate throughout the entire economy, and only a few of the resulting benefits can be appropriated by the initial inventors and innovators. Furthermore, innovations often occur in clusters whose total impact greatly exceeds the sum of the separate impacts that would have occurred if each had been established on its own without the others being in place. In the early nineteenth century, the combination of steam power with the new textile technologies had a vastly greater effect than either had had separately in the eighteenth century. Later in the nineteenth century, the railroad, the steam-powered iron ship, the telegraph, and refrigeration constituted such a mutually re-enforcing cluster of innovations (Rosenberg 1982: ch. 3).

If we stick to the concepts of neoclassical economics, we would say that innovations confer massive externalities which have the potential to create market failures on a large scale. This, in turn, provides scope for government policies to have major efficiency-increasing effects, at least in principle.

If we use the concepts of the group of non-orthodox economists who follow the lead given by Schumpeter (and John Rae before him), we will argue that the whole concept of an optimum allocation of resources, and the 'market failures' that result when that optimum is not achieved by free markets, is meaningless in a world of endogenous technological change with its accompanying uncertainties. While maximization concepts can be applied to risk, there is no way to determine a maximizing set of decisions when the outcomes are subject to significant uncertainties. Given the uncertainties associated with major technological advances, there is no way of knowing, even in a probabilistic sense, if a particular avenue of investigation will turn out to be blind or have a pot of gold at its end. Only after time and money have been spent investigating that alley, does one know its potential. It follows that there is no unique, best choice among alternative courses of action each entailing significant uncertainties, nor is there an optimal amount of resources that a society should devote to research and development of new technologies whose value might be massive if successful and zero if not.[10] Because most things governments do affect technological change and economic growth, they must make judgements about that influence and adjust their policies accordingly. They cannot avoid having such policies, but they cannot pretend to make optimal decisions on them. Good and bad policies can be assessed in terms of meeting stated objectives of influencing the amount and direction of R&D devoted to technological change, but an optimal set of policies does not exist.

Whether one takes this unorthodox 'structuralist' position or the more orthodox neoclassical position, the existence of endogenous technological change gives the government a responsibility for assessing the growth impact of a wide array of polices—a responsibility that it would not have if technological change were exogenous.

One of the major advantages of private over state ownership of industry is that the former encourages many experimental approaches to problems involving uncertainty, while the latter tends to emphasize a focused commitment to the particular approach backed by the state monopoly. It is precisely where there are major problems of uncertainty, rather than mere risk, that competition among privately owned firms has its greatest advantage over state-owned monopolies.

4.2. Rethinking the Defences of the Market System

Experience of the demise of Communism, and the emphasis on dynamic growth performance that resulted from studying the reasons for that demise, have led to a reassessment of the advantages of the price system.

4.2.1. The Price System vs. Central Planning

On economic matters, the great doctrinal debate of the twentieth century was between the free market and central planning as alternative means of organizing and coordinating economic affairs. The rise of the Asian Tigers, often called newly industrialized countries (NICs), South Korea, Taiwan, Singapore, and Hong Kong, was one of the first strong signs that the advantage in the doctrinal battle was shifting towards the market economies. Then came the dramatic fall of Communism in Eastern Europe, combined with the even more dramatic growth in those parts of Communist China which were left free to market forces.[11] The twentieth-century battle of ideologies is now over, with the market system the conclusive winner over the centrally planned system of economic organization. Rarely in human history has a great social issue been resolved so conclusively.

Out of these experiences has come a measure of agreement that 'policies that ignore or work against market forces are usually counterproductive' (UN 1992: 20). As explained in detail below, this consensus has been followed by the outbreak of a new battle of ideologies. No serious protagonist in this new debate advocates returning to central planning, but many do argue that 'there is room for proactive policies as long as they work through market forces and take them as their criterion of success' (UN 1992: 20). Those on the other side of the debate are sceptical that governments have any place to play in wealth creation beyond setting the background conditions.

(b) The formal defence

The formal defence of the price system outlined in Section 3 is based on a model in which tastes and technology are constant.[12] It concentrates on resource allocation and says nothing about economic growth that is driven by technological change. The static model deals with inter-temporal issues by having dated inputs and outputs as well as futures markets, but it does not have endogenous, path dependant, technological change.

Although central planning has displayed some important static inefficiencies, its major failure was its inability to create the degree of technological dynamism generated by capitalist societies. Nor did it prove adept at copying and adapting other people's technologies—as did Japan and the NICs in modern times, and the Europeans in earlier times when many technological advances originating in China and the Islamic countries were adopted and improved by Europeans.

So, on the issues that concern us today—growth and international competitiveness in a globalizing world—the formal defence of the price system is silent. However, the informal defence is eloquent on these matters and much hard thinking and appeals to evidence have gone into the study of why economies based on decentralized price systems will be more conducive to growth than ones where decisions on inventions, and innovation are highly centralized. (See e.g. Rosenberg and Birdzell 1986.)

4.3. Rethinking the Scope of Governments

The deep structural adjustments required by major changes in enabling technologies often include expansions and contractions of overall political power as well as reallocations of such power among various levels of government.

4.3.1. Alterations of Power

The globalization brought about by the ICT revolution has reduced government power in some traditional areas. Sophisticated communications, and vast amounts of short-term capital in the hands of TNCs, make it impossible for governments to control international capital movements in the ways that they routinely did in the era of fixed exchange rates from 1945 to 1970. Indeed, the globalization of capital markets had a lot to do with the breakdown of Bretton Woods system of fixed exchange rates.

The assets that confer today's national competitive advantages tend to be both created and highly mobile. This severely restricts any individual government's ability of follow policies that affect these assets and that differ markedly from policies followed by other governments. Although this takes little space to say, its effects in limiting policy independence are profound.

The increasing difficulty that governments face in dictating what their citizens will see and hear curtail the efficacy of information-restriction policies exercised in the interest of many varied purposes, from supporting a repressive dictatorship at one extreme to encouraging local cultural industries at the other. Access to the Internet, for example, provides a massive hole in the information-restricting barriers which governments of many countries such as Singapore and China have tried to erect.

A commonly heard extreme view, that the national government has lost all of its power over economic matters, does not seem to stand up to investigation.[13] To some extent, governments have discovered limitations to their power with respect to macro-economic policies that were probably always there but were not appreciated until revealed by decades of experience. Furthermore, markets have always punished unsustainable policies, such as seriously overvalued exchange rates or persistent, large budget deficits, but in today's globalized financial markets the moment of reckoning often comes much faster than it once did.

In other areas, governments have gained power. For example, computers have made possible the collection and cross referencing of masses of data about individual citizens and firms. The technology exists today to locate any inconsistent statements given to two different government authorities and, unless it is controlled by political means, this possibility may soon be realized. Developments in genetics may also increase government power in many areas. For example, genetic screening to discover predispositions of various groups to various afflictions may assist government health services. Analogous developments promise breakthroughs in crime prevention and detection. As a final example, traffic control will see massive changes in the next decade as it becomes possible to track cars through urban streets and to monitor speed with technologies vastly more advanced than following speeders with police cruisers.

This discussion suggests that those who emphasize the loss of national power tend to concentrate on the broad macro-economic issues such as tariffs, exchange rates, and fiscal stabilization policies. However, when one looks at micro-areas —or, as John Dunning calls it, macro-organizational policy—where a vast amount of both national and local government activity occurs, modern technologies are giving governments a wide range of increasing powers. Since the big macro-issues tend to be related to globalization, while the micro-issues tend not to be, different answers are likely to be given to the questions, 'What is globalization doing to government power?' and 'What are current technological changes doing to government power?'

4.3.2. Reallocations of Power

Reallocations are tending to transfer some of the powers of national governments upwards to supranational bodies and others downwards to more local levels of government. On the one hand, globalization is requiring supervision at the international level of many issues involving trade and investment. The importance to most countries of a relatively free flow of international trade has led them to transfer power over trade restrictions to supra-national bodies such as the World Trade Organization (WTO), which is GATT's successor, the EU, NAFTA, and a host of other trade liberalizing arrangements. The interrelation of trade and investment brought about by the ICT revolution has caused modern trade liberalizing agreements to be expanded to include measures to ensure the free flow and 'national treatment' of foreign investment.

Systems frictions provide another powerful reason for the reallocation of power to supranational authorities. These arise when, owing to globalization of trade and investment, policies with respect to such matters as labour practices, industrial competition, R&D support, subsidies, and intellectual property protection, which were formerly thought to be of purely domestic interest, arouse international concern because they affect international flows of trade, FDI, and factors of production (Ostry 1990). Trade liberalizing arrangements are now working towards 'deep integration' in which the sources of systems frictions are subject to agreed international control which implies major transfers of power from national to supra-national levels of government. Some of these issues are taken up further by Monty Graham in Chapter 17 of this volume.

More generally, supra-national organizations are needed to prohibit certain activities and to regulate others. Prohibition is needed in two types of situation. The first is where the policy game played by individual governments is of the prisoner's-dilemma variety (non-cooperative behaviour starts by helping individuals but ends up hurting everyone), as with tariffs. Here, international organizations are already well developed. The WTO and various regional free trading agreements, such as the EU, NAFTA, and MERCOSUR, allow countries to tie their hands in advance, preventing them from taking individual actions in prisoner's-dilemma situations. The second is where the policy game is zero-sum (one person's gain is another's loss), as when countries compete to attract some given set of footloose industries. The new policies for 'deep integration' allow governments to tie their hands against using 'domestic' policies for international purposes and thus to avoid playing such zero-sum games. Regulation, rather than prohibition, is called for where the policy game is positive sum so that everyone gains, as with the creation and transfer of new technologies. In these cases, good policies are needed, not to stop the game from being played, but to help in playing it better.

Pulling in the other direction, consciousness of regional identities and the decline of broad identification with the nation state, which are also related to the globalization caused by the ICT revolution, are causing pressures for the devolution of some powers to lower levels of authority. Provided that acceptable allocations are achieved, there is no need to find these two pressures contradictory. If common markets (or at least modern free trade areas) are maintained among the local authorities, there is little reason to oppose the devolution of considerable power with respect to cultural and community matters to local authorities, although doing so is often a conflict-ridden process.

Determining an appropriate allocation of functions between local, national, and international levels of government, and willingness to pass some power upwards to supra-national authorities and some downwards to state and local authorities, is one of the most important tasks facing modern national governments. This is not something that can be done once and for all. A future set of DSAs, in response to some future revolutions in enabling technologies, may require some different shifts, such as a transfer of major powers back to the national level.

4.4. Rethinking Redistributive Policies

Major reassessments are occurring with redistributive social policies. My brief for this chapter allows insufficient space to do more than mention these issues, although, of course, they are an important part of rethinking government policy.

It is now accepted that many existing welfare measures are counter-productive, hurting the very groups they were intended to help, at least in the long run. This is an argument not to stop trying to assist those in need but rather to do so in a more realistic way than was attempted in the past.

It is now understood that measures designed to influence equity or static efficiency (efficiency at a moment of time) can also affect the dynamic growth behaviour of the economy in both desirable and undesirable ways. This was the sensible grain of truth buried amidst some of the excesses of 'supply-side economics'. In the popular discussion, this concern often comes out as concern over 'competitiveness' which recognizes that these issues have increased force in a globalized world with high mobility of wealth-creating assets owned by individuals and firms.[14]

4.5. Rethinking Market Power Issues

4.5.1. Regulation

Perfect competition not the standard. The realization that the economy is constantly changing under the impact of endogenous technological change has been behind much of the rethinking of market power issues. Hopefully, there is a growing understanding of the validity of Schumpeter's argument against making perfect competition the desirable market structure and regarding departures from it as failures of the market in any real sense. As Schumpeter long ago observed, technological change does more to raise living standards over the decades than removing market imperfections could ever do, and it is the search for market-power-based profits that drives technological advance. Here, the formal defence of the price system is not just irrelevant; it is downright misleading.

Changing natural monopolies. Yesterday's natural monopoly is today's fiercely competitive industry.[15] Transfers of written and oral communications—natural monopolies of the post office and the telephone system earlier in the century—are now possible through a variety of electronic means. However, major constraints on further competition occur when governments protect their monopoly of the post office and publicly owned telephones systems against entry and are slow to change regulations that were designed to protect consumers against the exercise of private-sector monopoly power in telecommunications that has long since evaporated.

Globalization, driven by technological change, has also greatly increased the amount of international competition. A high degree of domestic concentration, even a single firm in one country, is not a serious threat if domestic firms are competing internationally. A host of modern forms of cooperation for the development and diffusion of technologies, such as alliances, licensing agreements, and cooperative ventures, are no longer sufficient to prove intent to monopolize. Often they are ways of responding to internationally competitive situations. Domestic competition policies need to be deeply and quickly adjusted to keep abreast of the technologically driven changes in the conditions of international competition.

Encouraging creative destruction. There is a Schumpeterian case for abandoning all regulation of natural monopolies (and oligopolies). It is that there are no natural monopolies in the very long run when technological change is endogenous. The larger the profits that are earned by an existing natural monopoly, the greater the incentive for technological advance to destroy that monopoly. In this view, regulation slows technological advance because it removes the incentive for creative destruction by holding present profits closer to normal levels.

The opposing argument is that the natural monopoly will continue long enough that profits should be controlled in the interest of social justice, even if that retards the process of creative destruction. If this position is accepted, governments need to stand ready to relax the relevant controls once it becomes clear that new technologies are destroying the 'naturalness' of some current monopoly. All too often, governments get into the absurd position of using their full legal power to preserve a monopoly that they originally controlled in order to protect consumers from 'monopolistic exploitation'.

4.5.2. Public Ownership

The acceptance of the case for the market puts the onus of proof on those who believe that the government should own some firm or industry. Once again, experience of technological change has altered views from what they were fifty or a hundred years ago.

Karl Marx wrote at a time when the introduction of steam-powered factories had greatly increased the typical size of the efficient firm and he bequeathed to his followers the belief that, in production, larger was always better. Ironically, just as he was writing, the electricity revolution was leading to massive changes in scale economies. The unit drive, each machine having its own power supply in the form of an appropriately sized electric motor, made small-sized parts manufacturers efficient, giving rise to the industrial structure we still have today in which large plants assemble components made in many small and medium-sized parts-manufacturing firms. Marx's legacy to twentieth-century Communist and social democratic governments of an obsessive concern with scale economies is an excellent illustration of the general lesson: because constant changes in technology require constant adaptation in the facilitating structure, to assume that one structure (such as heavy industrial concentration) is the universal route to economic prosperity is to misunderstand the dynamics of technical change.

The short and long runs. Evidence differs on how efficiently nationalized industries run their affairs from day to day. What often happens when politicians get involved directly in operating decisions is, first, that the industry gets captured by its workers, who earn incomes well above free market rates (which also happened in regulated industries in the USA), and then losses occur because governments are unwilling to raise prices enough to cover the high wages. When independent boards are set up, but the government remains responsible for providing capital funds, capital tends to be under-provided. The experience of nationalized industries in most countries was of rationing by queues—for example, in the UK telephones took months to obtain and in many areas ordinary citizens could obtain only shared party lines until privatization in the 1980s. When the industry is cut loose from political control in respect of both its current operating and capital investment decisions, there is often not too much difference between private and public ownership (and thus not much reason to have public ownership) in the short and long runs.

The very long run. Emphasis on technological change puts stress on the long-term adaptability of publicly owned industries. We have already observed that the failure of central planning was rooted in its failure to produce and manage technological change. Many nationalized industries were created monopolies in the sense that the private market could sustain more than one competing firm. This was the case, for example, with virtually all of the industries nationalized by the British Labour government in 1945–50. Much evidence suggests, however, that the technological dynamism of one monopoly will fall short of that of two or three competing firms, each of which can operate at its efficient scale. The reason why competition among several firms is more conducive to technological change than is production by a single profit-maximizing monopoly, unstressed in the literature of economic theory, is that the most intense oligopolistic competition is in innovation. Firms can get prices and capacity wrong and recover, but if they fall behind in the innovative race, they will quickly go under. This was a lesson that was driven home when globalization brought firms in Europe and North America into intense competition with Japanese and other Asian firms with very different R&D policies.[16]

4.6. **Rethinking Policies for Growth in Developing Countries**

Globalization caused by the ICT revolution, combined with changes in transport costs, has dramatically altered possibilities for trade. Among other things, components made anywhere in the world can now be delivered precisely when and where they are wanted, thus opening up niches for parts to be manufactured in the developing nations and sold to the advanced nations.

4.6.1. The New Development Model

For developing countries, as both Chapters 14 and 15 in this volume show, the reassessment of the price system and the implications of globalization have involved a major alteration of the older development model that was inward-looking, import-substituting, state-monopoly centred, and heavily interventionist in subsidization, price-setting, and resource allocation. The revised model calls for a more outward-looking, trade-oriented, market-facilitating-based route to development. It has not, however, been *laissez-faire* in economic policy. As shown in detail by writers such as Pack and Westphal (1986), Wade (1990), Lipsey and Carlaw (1996), and Lipsey and Wills (1996), most of the developing nations have used a battery of science and technology (S&T) and industrial policies to encourage both the transfer from abroad, and the local development of, technologies suitable to their conditions. Theirs is more typically managed capitalism rather than *laissez-faire* capitalism. Reviewing the recent shift to a more market-driven approach to economic development, Stanley Fischer (in Williamson 1990: 28) distinguished two possible approaches:

> One, the Chilean or Thatcher approach, requires the government to set the right policies and incentives, to behave consistently and credibly, and then to step out of the way in the expectation that, eventually, growth will return. This approach seems to work, eventually, at least in those countries that have the institutional capacity to support it.
>
> The alternative, East Asian approach is one in which the government takes a more active and ongoing role, in some interpretations operating an industrial policy. The East Asian experience proves that small government, consistent policies, an undervalued currency, export promotion and explicitly time-limited import protection through tariffs, and an educated and disciplined labour force, combined with entrepreneurial skills, create economic growth.[17]

4.6.2. The New Infant Industry Model

Few countries have developed a modern industrial structure without a protective tariff at the early stages of their development. Economists have sought to rationalize the infant-industry argument by appeal to static economies of scale (thereby begging the question of why private finance could not be raised to allow firms to attain a size sufficient to exploit the scale economies implicit in existing technologies). The real significance of the infant-industry argument is in the dynamic path that industries must follow as they develop through the creation and acquisition of technologies and the supporting structure, including human capital.

In Schumpeter's model, and in the classic article by Kenneth Arrow (1962), any new technological advance becomes freely available once it is developed. Research on diffusion shows otherwise. Diffusion is a slow and costly matter. It is slow because firms keep technologies secret for competitive reasons, because technologies can only be adopted when the necessary facilitating structure is in place (the required structure is simple in some cases but complex in others), and because much knowledge is *tacit* in that it cannot be written down and learned from books, but instead must be learned by doing and by using. Diffusion is costly because technologies seldom exist in one generic form that is of equal use to everyone.

This has immediate implications for policy in countries at all stages of development: diffusion of technologies is an important economic variable which can be helped or hindered by market structures, institutions, and government policy. Within one national industry there is often a wide divergence of technologies in use. Some of this divergence is due to the long lifetime of much of the equipment which embodies technology, and some is due to the slow rate of diffusion of tacit knowledge.

It follows that developing countries, whether they be Germany and France trying to catch up with Britain in the nineteenth century, or the countries of South-East Asia trying to industrialize in the late twentieth century, cannot assume that relevant new technologies will flow easily to them across international borders. Nor can they assume that, even if technologies are installed locally by multinationals, the knowledge will diffuse easily to local users. Technology transfer policies, between nations and within one nation, may be important parts of a development strategy—something that would never have been suggested by the formal defence of the price system. Many neoclassical economists, however, contest this view, arguing that production functions are the same the world over. (See e.g. Mankeiv 1995.)

Singapore and South Korea, for example, have elaborate policies to identify and encourage the next generation of technology and to ensure the transfer to locals of technological knowledge used by transnational corporations operating within their borders. (See Lipsey and Wills 1996.) As another example, Canada has a successful policy, called the Industrial Research Assistance Program (IRAP), in which agents assist firms to identify better technologies than the ones now in use and help management to adapt these technologies so that they can adopt them.

Currently, the issues discussed in this section are the subject of intense debate among economists. Many neoclassical economists disagree with what has been said above and argue that the NICs' successes are fully accounted for by the accumulation of human and physical capital, while technology policies brought marginal benefit at best and retarded growth at worst.

4.7. **Rethinking Policies for Growth in Developed Countries**

4.7.1. General Policies

Concern about growth and international competitiveness in a rapidly globalizing world lies behind many current controversies concerning the government's place in the economy. The background to these controversies is the realization of the failure of centrally planned economies to produce sustained growth combined with the new understanding that governments have played different roles in the growth process in different countries.

Studies by historians of technological change have identified many active roles played by governments. For example, in their final chapter, Rosenberg and Birdzell (1986) note several key roles that governments have played in the past (and they make many more points throughout their book). Governments have established law and order. They have established and enforced property rights. They have encouraged trade with a wide variety of measures such as issuing sound money, standardizing products, maintaining harbours, lighthouses, and other navigational aids. They have helped in factor creation by establishing elementary schools, trade schools, and institutions of higher education. In the late nineteenth century, Germany established its system of trade schools whereby every male student who does not go on to higher education learns a trade. This massive factor-creation policy has been the basis of German comparative advantage in producing mainline consumer's goods with state-of-the-art technologies over the whole of the twentieth century. Both German and American universities have been quick to establish departments in the various applied sciences as these disciplines emerged. (See Nelson 1993.)

4.7.2. The Increasingly Important Role of Created Assets

Many of the new technologies are knowledge-based in the sense that human capital is the most important resource required. As a result, comparative advantage in much manufacturing and service production depends today more on acquired advantages in the form of human capital and favourable business climates created by public policy than on natural resources and geographic location. Indeed, a significant amount of education is required to qualify as 'unskilled' labour in modern industrial production. Adrian Wood (1994) in his study of the new industrial trade finds it necessary to distinguish three classes of workers: non-skilled, those without the minimum skills needed for modern industrial production, which includes many in less developed countries which have not emphasized education; low-skilled, those who have the minimum education needed for employment in modern goods and services industries; and skilled, those who hold down the high-quality jobs. Governments have a responsibility to create human capital and the favourable conditions that give physical capital the best working environment. The NICs, and the second generation of Asian industrializing countries, have all been particularly good at education policy, which requires identifying the skills that will be needed in the future by this generation of students and setting out to provide them. Unlike India, they have put their bets on universal literacy and a secondary education for all.

Functional illiteracy and innumeracy among the bottom third of the skill level in many advanced industrial countries is a matter of growing concern. In today's knowledge-intensive world, if educational attainment levels do not keep pace, the lower third of the population may be condemned to (i) Third World pay scales or (ii) subsidized employment or (iii) a life on unemployment and social security.

4.7.3. Policies Concerning FDI

As several of the country studies in this book emphasize, many governments have been hostile to FDI in the past. In today's globalizing world, it is impossible to erect major walls around a country and ensure development within the domestic economy alone. To stay on a sustained growth path, a country needs to be a part of the global economy, and to do this, most countries need substantial presences of TNCs within their borders.[18] As result, most countries, developed and developing, are in competition to attract high-quality FDI.

In the past, outward-bound FDI has often been viewed as a loss of national job-creating capacity. Today, with the understanding that in many areas firms need to be international in scope, outward-bound FDI is seen as an important step in turning successful domestic industries into truly global competitors.

A key part of government policy is the treatment of foreign-owned relative to home-owned firms. One group, that includes Robert Reich (1991), argues that policy should encourage the domestic location of firms that produce high incomes and good jobs and that it matters little who owns them. Another group, which includes Michael Porter (1990) and Lester Thurow (1992), argues that policy should encourage domestic ownership.

As discussed in Chapter 9, the technology-support initiatives of many countries, such as the US SEMATECH, are currently open only to home-owned firms. As a result, many firms that are major creators of domestic jobs are denied support, while many firms that do most of their production in foreign countries are included. Many economists argue that countries would benefit from treating all firms based in their jurisdictions equally (as, for example, the three NAFTA countries must do to firms owned in any NAFTA country). Be that as it may, this is an important function of government on which a policy is needed, the default policy being to treat all firms the same.

4.7.4. S&T and Innovation Policies

The consensus on the superiority of the price system as a general coordinating mechanism for economic decisions has been followed not by 'the end of history' but, just as one should have expected, by a new battle of ideologies—a battle that is being waged in both the developed and the developing countries. Both of the two ideologies that are now competing accept the importance of having market-oriented economies, as argued by the informal defence of the price system. One, however, advocates a basically *laissez-faire* approach to economic (but not necessarily social) policy, such as is espoused, but not always followed, in the USA and the UK, while the second advocates what Wade (1990) calls 'managed market economies'. While the market is the final test of success or failure in this latter approach, substantial, coordinated government assistance is to be given to encourage technological change in a way that is systematically oriented towards innovation and growth. Managed market policies are found in some European countries, in Japan, and in many of the NICs.

As Ham and Mowery point out in Chapter 9, many economists, particularly in the USA, strongly believe that the government has no constructive place to play in the process of technological change, other than getting the background right. Others, more commonly found in Europe, Japan, and the rapidly developing nations, feel with equal strength that there is a case for a significant government presence in the R&D activities that are related to many new technologies. (See especially the chapters on France and Japan in this volume.) Both groups were represented at the conference that led to this book and both expressed their views strongly.

My own view is that case studies, such as are found in Lipsey and Carlaw (1996), show that neither of the extreme views—that government policies designed to encourage innovation succeed easily or always fail—is tenable. Instead, the real issue seems to be to identify the types of policies that are likely to succeed and the political conditions that encourage success rather than failure.[19] The policy debate has many aspects and we can touch on only a few for purposes of illustrating the major issues.

Empirical generalizations about invention and innovation. To start with, one needs to know quite a bit about the innovative process. Here are a few relevant generalizations drawn from Lipsey and Carlaw (1996).

- *Embryonic technologies.* Major innovations never bring new technologies into the world in fully developed form. Instead, these technologies first appear in a crude embryonic state with only a few specific uses. Improvements and diffusion then occur simultaneously as the technology is made more efficient and adapted for use over an increasingly wide range of applications. The more fundamental is the innovation, running up to major innovations in enabling technologies, the more marked is this process of long and slow evolution from crude prototypes with narrow use, to highly efficient products and processes with a vast range of applications.
- *Innovation involves uncertainty.* Because innovation means doing something not done before, there is an element of uncertainty (in Frank Knight's sense of the term) in all innovation. It is often impossible even to enumerate in advance the *possible outcomes* of a particular line of research. Time and money is often spent investigating specific avenues of research to discover if they are blind alleys or full of immensely rich pots of gold. As a result, massive sums are sometimes spent with no positive results, while trivial expenditures sometimes produce results of great value. Furthermore, the search for one objective often produces results of value for quite different objectives. All this implies that agents will not be able to assign probabilities to

different occurrences in order to conduct risk analysis as conventionally defined.

- *Uncertainty about applications.* Uncertainty is involved not only in making some initial technological breakthrough but also with respect to the range of applications that some new technology may have. The steam engine, electricity, the telephone, radio, the laser, the computer, the video-cassette recorder (VCR), and fibre optics are examples of technologies that were thought during the first decade of their life to have very limited potential—and they did have very limited actual applications at first. (See Rosenberg 1994.)
- *Innovation requires flexibility.* Because firms grope in an uncertain world towards better lines of innovative activity as experience accumulates, successful innovators learn from their experience and constantly alter their courses of action.
- *Success requires commercialization.* A successful technological advance is not sufficient for economic gain. Many countries have developed new technologies only to find that they are uneconomical or that some other country succeeds in commercializing them. As shown by Teece (1992), there is many a potential slip between the development of some new technology and depositing large profits in the bank. Furthermore, major commercial success can come from minor technological advances if they are buttressed by an effective set of complementary assets (as were IBM's first PCs).

Assisting pre-competitive research. Research can be roughly divided into pre-competitive, the results of which cannot be legally appropriated, and competitive, the results of which are appropriable. Pre-competitive research is an area in which market failures of various sorts can be significant. Firms doing such research often keep the results as closely guarded secrets, hoping to be able to develop commercially viable applications in advance of competitors. As a result, competing firms may all be doing similar pre-competitive research leading to wasteful duplication and a wastefully large total volume. In contrast, if firms feel they cannot guard the results, they will be motivated to do much less than is socially desirable, and much less than they would do if they were all cooperating as one decision-making unit.

Government coordination that allows firms to commit themselves to cooperation at the pre-competitive level and then to compete in later development can in principle avoid the underproduction where secrecy is not possible and the overproduction and duplication where secrecy is possible. This, as we shall see in more detail in the next section, is an area in which the Japanese have been particularly successful. In the USA, SEMATECH started to support such research but then moved on, with much less success, to supporting particular firms. In the UK's ALVEY programme, an attempt was made to support pre-competitive and competitive research with a single tool and this mixture of conflicting objectives brought failure. The evidence suggests that government assistance in coordinating and assisting pre-competitive research can be effective, but making it so is no easy task.

Picking winners by bureaucrats. Older industrial policies took the form of subsidizing favoured firms, often in declining industries or ones that were being asked to locate in regions chosen by policy-makers. Such subsidization is now out of favour, although it persists in many isolated cases.

More modern polices are directed at encouraging potential 'winners'. How to do so is subject to much current debate. Some economists argue that the market should be left to itself to select winners and losers. Others argue that many governments pick and back potential winners and those that do not will find their industries falling behind in the globalized competitive game in which innovation is so important.

Four arguments are commonly heard against the crude picking of winners by government bureaucrats. First, given the conditions summarized in the bullet points above, picking the next generation of winning technologies is no easy task and more mistakes than successes will be typical, even among the best private-sector entrepreneurs. Bureaucrats, risking other people's money, are unlikely, even with the best of intentions, to do as well at picking winners than private-sector entrepreneurs risking money of their own (or of their shareholders', to whom they are directly responsible). Secondly, political considerations are likely to have too much influence on any government's decisions on which technologies and firms are potential winners. Thirdly, in a process as fraught with uncertainty as is the development of new technologies, the pluralism of the market is preferable to the unified decisions of governments, who often put all their eggs in one basket. Fourthly, bureaucrats and politicians are notoriously unwilling to cut off an activity when evidence suggests failure—a necessary procedure when dealing successfully with uncertainty.

In support of the above arguments, the evidence shows that programmes for which government bureaucrats have mainly determined the target technologies have produced many costly failures. Examples are the French programme for developing the micro-electronics industry, the British ALVEY software development programme, the Anglo-French Concord, and the British AGR and the Canadian CANDU nuclear reactors (Lipsey and Carlaw 1996).

Assisting the private sector to select and promote winners. In contrast to what we have seen above, those programmes that have succeeded have often been based on cooperation between the private and public sectors rather than on bureaucratic choice of potential winners. This may be described as a policy of public–private sector cooperation to select and back potential successes rather than bureaucratic picking of specific winners.

The potential for this type of policy is illustrated by what is probably the world's most successful innovation-assisting public institution, Japan's Ministry of Industry and Trade (MITI).[20] Before targeting a new potential winner, MITI spends up to two years consulting private-sector firms and, with rare exceptions, commits itself only to projects that firms are willing to back with their own money. Relying on user feedback from industry and academia, MITI then selects its potential new winning technologies, and firms and government cooperate to produce fundamental, pre-commercial research. This allows all firms to enter the stage of competitive research on a more or less equal footing.

In general, MITI's policy recognizes that fundamental innovations require changes in the facilitating structure, and the more prepared and flexible is that structure, the more readily will new technologies, whether home developed or imported, be turned into successful innovations. MITI's policy structure amounts to a blueprint for designing and operating efficient interfaces between fundamental innovations and the facilitating structure, plus the tacit knowledge derived from doing this repeatedly.

Japan also provides some subsidization and some protection of the home market to give a secure base for product development, but only where MITI and private industry both identify potential winners and the private sector is risking substantial sums of its own. It is also understood that success in the export market is required if the support is to continue, and, even then, the object of the policy is to get the technology sufficiently developed so that firms can continue without MITI's assistance.

This innovation-producing framework positions Japan to produce the set of supporting innovations in production-level structure that are necessary to exploit commercially a fundamental invention when it emerges—*no matter in what country it is originally produced.* This is almost the exact opposite to policies of many other countries which have produced technological breakthroughs that they could not exploit commercially because they lacked the necessary facilitating structure. MITI's policy also allows commercial results to emerge even when projects targeting fundamental breakthroughs fail, as with the very large-scale integrated circuits (VLSI).

Of course, MITI has failures as well as successes, which is what is expected with anything as uncertain as the development and commercialization of new technologies. For example, MITI's concentration on commercial viability has sometimes led to excessive caution, as when it tried to prevent Tokyo Tsushin Kogyo (TTK) from buying Western Electric's as-yet commercially unproven transistor technology in 1953. Fortunately for the Japanese, MITI was unsuccessful and, on the basis of this technology, TTK went on to become Sony![21]

The procedures for 'picking and pushing winners' vary among each of the NICs that has run active industrial policies, South Korea, Singapore, and Taiwan (Wade 1990). For example, the Taiwanese government has even gone so far as to establish start-up companies in some new targeted sector, transferring them to the private sector after they have become established. Singapore spent upwards of $US1,000,000 in identifying the software industry as a future source of industrial strength years before it became so and did this at a time when programs were usually embedded in computers and given away free to purchasers of hardware (Lipsey and Wills 1996).

These policies seem to be suitable to the cultures of Asian countries, many of whose governments are mainly concerned with encouraging growth rather than brokering conflicting special and regional interests as in the USA and Canada. Also, the export orientation gives the policies a cut-off point that substitutes for the bottom line in the private sector and prevents failed initiatives from persisting indefinitely as they have elsewhere. We cannot, however, be sure how well such policies would work in other nations that have different cultures, different political systems, different facilitating structures, and different amounts and types of institutional competencies.

US successes. In spite of the above evidence, many observers, particularly in the USA and both inside and outside the economics profession, argue that governments have little potential to influence the process of technological change in a useful way. The reality is that US policies have sometimes been successful in encouraging technological change and the industries that depend on it, particularly at the early stages of the development of new technologies. Current examples are found in the chapter by Ham and Mowrey in this volume. One of the several examples of successful government assistance in earlier times will have to suffice here. In its early stages, the US commercial aircraft industry received substantial assistance from the National Advisory Committee on Aeronautics (NACA) which supported invention and innovation in the aircraft industry through its government-operated experimental facilities. Among other things, NACA pioneered the development of large wind tunnels; it provided essential test data that led to the development of such innovations as the 'NACA cowl'; it demonstrated the superiority of airframes designed with a retractable landing gear.

Conclusion. A host of S&T and innovation policies have been used in various countries. The great success of some and the massive failure of others suggest several lessons. First, there is scope for major government activity in the area of encouraging technological change. Secondly, there is also enormous scope for wasteful failure. Thirdly, the expectations are poor for big technology pushes that require massive changes in the existing facilitating structure or even the development of wholly new structures; the successes have tended to be those that accept the path dependency of technological change, going for significant advances that build on existing strengths and not trying for the great leaps in the technological dark that unfortunately seem to attract politicians. Fourthly, although no assistance is clearly better than bad assistance, good assistance is often better than none—at least in some circumstances in some countries. How individual countries should exploit that scope, if they should do so at all, is likely to continue to be one of the great debates of the next few decades.

4.8. What Kind of Future Government?

In his Geary lecture, John Dunning issues a powerful call for reinventing the role of government. In concluding he writes (1994: 29):

> To some extent, too, the problem is one of re-forming opinions and attitudes towards the role of governments. I believe we need a new vocabulary to promote the image of government as a public good rather than as a necessary evil. We need a 'perestroika' of government. We need to recognise that, just as 'Fordism' is an out-dated method of organising work, so the kind of government interventionism appropriate to a 'Fordist' environment is outdated. And, just like the emerging managerial structure of 21st century firms, we need governments to be lean, flexible and anticipatory of change. The new paradigm of government should eschew such negative or emotive sounding words such as 'command', 'intervention', 'regulation', and replace them by words such as 'empower', 'steer', 'co-operative', 'co-ordination' and 'systemic'. Moreover, not only must governments recognise the need for a much more integrated and holistic system of organising their responsibilities, which demands a 'spider's web' rather than a 'hub and spoke' relationship between the various decision taking departments and the core of government, viz the cabinet of the Prime Minister or President; but, for all those affected by governments, and particularly the ordinary tax payers, to take a more positive view of the benefits which only the former can produce. (Dunning, 1994)

It is clear that many of the old beliefs of the abilities of government are no longer held—particularly those based on the view that governments could do better than markets in areas where there was no obvious market failure, and that governments could fine tune the economy to remain in a state of full employment without significant inflation.

The type of new relations between the government and the private sector that Dunning envisages is closer to what one currently finds in the NICs and Japan than in North America and Europe. We may see them adopted more generally. In contrast, however, it is possible to argue that the ways in which governments will change, as change they will, will differ dramatically across nations. All are impacted by globalization and the other DSAs associated with the ICT revolution. But how they respond in terms of altering their current policies and making changes in the structure of government itself may depend on many country-specific factors.

The adjustments may vary with the objectives of government policy. What is needed from a government in an economy that is basically catching up technologically is rather different from what is needed when the country's industries are on the cutting edge of new technologies. Some of the close relationships between government and the private sector in the NICs were more appropriate to, and possibly easier to manage, in catch-up rather than leading-edge situations.

The adjustment may vary with governmental capacity. What a government is capable of depends on a number of things. One important influence is the basic constitution. The US government was successfully designed to be ineffective. Parliamentary systems that operate in the multi-party situations that result, for example, from proportional representation have their characteristic problems. Parliamentary systems with two or three dominant parties, such as typically result from the first-past-the-post electoral system, have different characteristics. The central governments of large and diverse federations with strong regional governments must broker regional interests in ways that are not required in smaller more homogenous countries. Governments operating under each of these constitutional arrangements will have different strengths, weaknesses, and core competencies.

What governments are able to do effectively also depends on their civil services. Some, such as the UK, have the tradition of hiring intelligent amateurs; others, such as France, of going for technocrats. Some, such as the UK, are able to tap the best talent in the country because of salary and social prestige afforded to the job; others, who shall go unmentioned, have to put up mainly with the second rate or worse. Some, such as Germany, hire mainly by merit with only occasional top jobs being decided on political grounds; in others, such as the USA, political appointees extend well down the scale. Some, such as the Indian, are recruited straight out of school or university and some, such as the Korean, typically have private-sector experience.

What governments are able to do also depends on how easy it is for special-interest groups to capture specific policies and turn them to their own uses. For example, a few tentative US attempts at the kind of labour market policies that are on Dunning's agenda appear to have been captured by organized labour and are unlikely, therefore, to accomplish their original goals.

In summary, various public-sector institutions have different institutional capabilities, based partly on constitutional differences, partly on the power relations between various special-interest groups, partly on the nature of their civil services, and partly on the accumulated 'learning by doing' in operating their country's typical set of policy instruments over the past. At one extreme, variants of the kind of private–public sector relations that Dunning envisages probably already exist in Japan, South Korea, Taiwan, and Singapore. At the other extreme, developing them in the USA would be a very tall order, as virtually all of the characteristics discussed above go against the effective development of that sort of working relation. Various European countries lie between these two extremes. As Ham and Mowery put it in Chapter 9 of this volume:

> Above all, there is little evidence that the closer relationships between government and private sector that are advocated by Dunning (1993), and that do appear to have had positive results in other postwar economies, are being forged [in the USA] in response to globalization. Instead, the opposite trend currently appears to be dominant.

The same can be said for Canada, and I suspect for the UK, and possibly also for some other countries of the EU.

This discussion of institutional capabilities is important for at least three reasons. First, it shows that it is not enough to have policies that are well designed in the abstract. Policies must work through an institutional structure and their success depends to a great extent on the institutional competencies of those administering them. Secondly, as long as they are understood to be talking about the institutional capabilities of their own public sectors, US economists may be right in asserting that minimal government is preferable to activist government, while Asian economists are also right in asserting the opposite. Thirdly, it is not obvious that all, or even most, governments throughout the world will evolve in the way that Dunning suggests. Some have; others may; for the rest, the Dunning manifesto will be an unattainable height to be admired or feared as they evolve along other lines of public-sector development.

It is possible that, by early in the twenty-first century, we will see big national differences in the directions of evolution of national governmental institutions and public–private sector relations. Some countries may follow the Dunning track while others may work towards a more minimalist role for government. If so, dynamic comparative advantage will no doubt be affected with countries on the 'Dunning track' succeeding in areas where governments can play an important part in technological developments, and countries that follow the more minimalist role for government succeeding in areas where private-sector imitative is most effective when it operates without public-sector 'assistance', which, given inappropriate institutions, can all too easily turn into hindrance.

Only time will tell. In the meantime we can surely say that we live in an era of massive technological change, major restructuring, increasing globalization, and heavy pressure to rework government policy from top to bottom.

NOTES

For financial support I am indebted to the Canadian Institute for Advanced Research and the Social Science and Humanities Research Council of Canada, and for their many comments and criticisms I thank Ken Carlaw, John Dunning, Richard Harris, David Mowery, Craig Riddell, Nathan Rosenberg, and Ed Safarian.

1. This section is based on Lipsey (1993).
2. This section is based on Lipsey and Bekar (1995).
3. This phrase is due to Freeman and Perez (1988).
4. The close link between technology and social and economic behaviour does not imply technological determinism. The evidence is that identical technologies introduced into different societies with different facilitating structures have very different impacts—which would not be so if technology determined everything.
5. These and other empirical generalizations about the nature of technological change stated in this chapter are drawn from Lipsey (1993 and 1994), Lipsey and Bekar (1995), and Lipsey and Carlaw (1996).
6. As an additional aspect of globalization, the drug trade has passed into the hands of illegal multinational organizations which are amassing great pools of wealth and whose international coordination problems are made easier by the ICT revolution. The serious social and economic repercussions of this massive trade are largely self-inflicted wounds which would disappear, as did the similar problems associated with the 1920s US liquor trade, if drugs were legalized and then sensibly controlled.
7. This section is based on Lipsey (1994).

8. The qualification 'in market economies' is important because, as das Gupta (1995) has recently argued, custom and social taboos have often worked well in traditional societies to prevent over-exploitation of the commons—at least until overpopulation put unbearable stresses on such systems. This point is not, however, uncontroversial, as there is substantial evidence that the expansion of *Homo sapiens* and their forebears into new areas was accompanied by massive extinctions of numerous animal species.
9. These two views are not mutually exclusive; both have strengths and weaknesses and there is no reason why we cannot learn from both. None the less, the approaches represent different routes to understanding the nature of the growth process and different research programmes.
10. This is argued in detail in e.g. Nelson and Winter (1982) and Lipsey and Carlaw (1995).
11. China may develop dreadful problems, but that will not be because market determination has replaced central planning, but because its government is unable to deliver the necessary background institutions and infrastructure, including environmental protection, and measures to alleviate growing income inequalities.
12. Sadly, in this section I am being more prescriptive than descriptive. Students are still exposed almost exclusively to the formal defence and many still go into the world thinking that the optimality of perfect competition is the main reason why we prefer the price system to its alternatives.
13. See the detailed discussion in *The Economist* (1995).
14. I cannot accept Krugman's (1994) position that everything that matters about competitiveness can be measured by productivity. For one obvious counter-example, policies that sustain an increasingly overvalued exchange rate will harm a country's competitiveness in spite of a good productivity record. Given path dependency of technological change, it may be of little consolation to observe that, sooner or later, the overvaluation will prove unsustainable. In the context of an earlier debate between Lawrence (1984) and Thurow (1985) on the same issue, Lipsey (1987) showed how the view that *only productivity matters* depends on the use of a perfectly competitive model. See also John Dunning's critique of Krugman (Dunning 1995) and Krugman's reply in the same issue. After reading the latter, I reread Krugman (1994) and found no evidence of criticism without knowledge of content nor of unprofessional behaviour, at least on Dunning's part. Of course, we can agree with Krugman in criticizing those who argue that trade and industrial development are zero-sum games. But Krugman goes much further, condemning work on competitiveness by writers such as Porter who are too sophisticated to fall into the zero-sum fallacy.
15. 'Competitive industries' refers not to the fiction of perfectly competitive manufacturing and service industries but to industries in which the firms engage in rivalrous behaviour with respect to identified competitors.
16. See Porter (1990) for evidence on the power of competition to encourage innovations, and Dertouzos *et al.* (1989) for evidence on the importance of competition in innovations.
17. Some readers of earlier versions of this chapter have asked if the differences between Fischer's two sets of policies are more apparent than real. The common thread is that, for any policy to be successfully operated, the country in question must have the requisite institutional capability. But the battery of S&T and related policies operated by Singapore and South Korea puts their approach into a different camp

from those countries, such as Chile and the USA, where the public sector's role is mainly to provide the right background conditions—plus relatively minimal interventions in terms of S&T and industrial policies. The current and growing debate in the academic literature between those who give substantial credit to the activist policies of the NICs and those who emphasize only those policies condoned by fairly narrowly understood neoclassical economics is certainly about differences that the protagonists perceive to be real.

18. Japan manages, as in so many things, to be an exception, having very little foreign presence in its economy.
19. A preliminary attempt to do just this is to be found in Lipsey and Carlaw (1996). We are currently expanding this work into a monograph due for completion in late 1997.
20. The best single reference on MITI is still Johnson (1982).
21. Lipsey and Carlaw (1996) study some of MITI's failures and argue that many occurred because MITI violated its own procedures that created its many successes.

REFERENCES

Arrow, K. (1962), 'Economic Welfare and the Allocation of Resources for Invention', in *The Rate and Direction of Economic Activity: Economic and Social Factors* (Princeton: National Bureau of Economic Research).

Cohen, S. C., and Zysman, J. (1987), *Manufacturing Matters* (New York: Basic Books).

Das Gupta, P. (1995), *An Inquiry into Well-Being and Destitution* (Oxford: Oxford University Press).

David, P. (1991), 'Computer and Dynamo: The Modern Productivity Paradox in a Not-Too-Distant-Mirror', in *Technology and Productivity* (Paris: OECD), 315–47.

Dertouzos, L., and Solow, R. (1989), *Made in America* (Cambridge, Mass.: MIT Press).

Dudley, L. (1991), *The Word and The Sword: How Techniques of Information and Violence have Shaped our World* (Cambridge: Cambridge University Press).

Dunning, J. H. (1993), *Multinational Enterprises and the Global Economy* (Reading, Mass.: Addison-Wesley).

—— (1994), *Globalization: The Challenge for National Economic Regimes* (The Geary Lecture for 1993; Dublin: Economic and Social Research Institute).

—— (1995), 'Think Again Professor Krugman, Competitiveness Does Matter', *International Executive*, 37: 315–24.

The Economist (1995), 'The Myth of the Powerless State' (7 October), 15–16.

Freeman, C., and Soete, L. (1994), *Work for All or Mass Unemployment* (London: Pinter).

—— and Perez, C. (1988), 'Structural Crises of Adjustment: Business Cycles and Investment Behaviour', in G. Dosi, C. Freeman, R. Nelson, G. Silverberg, and L. Soete (eds.), *Technical Change and Economic Theory* (London: Pinter Publishers).

Greenwald, B., and Stiglitz, J. (1986), 'Externalities in Economies with Imperfect Information and Incomplete Markets', *Quarterly Journal of Economics*, 101/2 (May), 229–64.

Hennings, K. (1987), 'John Rae', in *The New Palgrave: A Dictionary of Economics* (London: Macmillan), 39–40.

Johnson, C. (1982), *MITI and the Japanese Miracle: The Growth of Industrial Policy, 1925–1975* (Stanford, Calif.: Stanford University Press).

Krugman, P. (1994), *Peddling Prosperity: Economic Sense and Nonsense in the Age of Diminished Expectations* (New York: W. W. Norton & Company).

Lawrence, R. (1984), *Can America Compete?* (Washington: Brookings Institution).

Lipsey, R. G. (1987), 'Models Matter When Discussing Competitiveness', in *Shaping Comparative Advantage* (Toronto: C. D. Howe Institute).

—— (1993), 'Globalization, Technological Change and Economic Growth' (Annual Sir Charles Carter Lecture; Belfast: Northern Ireland Economic Development Office).

—— (1994), 'Markets, Technological Change and Economic Growth', Quaid-I-Azam Invited Lecture, in *The Pakistan Development Review*, 33/4: 327–52.

—— and Bekar, C. (1995), 'A Structuralist View of Technical Change and Economic Growth', in T. J. Courchene (ed.), *Technology, Information and Public Policy* (Kingston, Ont.: John Deutsch Institute).

—— and Carlaw, K. (1996), 'A Structuralist View of Innovation Policy', in P. Howitt (ed.), *The Implications of Knowledge Based Growth* (Calgary: University of Calgary Press).

—— and Wills, R. (1996), 'Science and Technology Policies in Asia Pacific Countries: Challenges and Opportunities for Canada', in R. Harris (ed.), *Growing Importance of the Asia-Pacific Region in the World Economy: Implications for Canada* (Calgary: University of Calgary Press).

Mankeiv, G. (1995), 'The Growth of Nations', *Brookings Papers on Economic Activity*, i.

Mokyr, J. (1990), *The Lever of Riches* (New York: Oxford University Press).

Nelson, R. (1993) (ed.), *National Innovation Systems: A Comparative Analysis* (Oxford: Oxford University Press).

—— and Winter, S. (1982), *An Evolutionary Theory of Economic Change* (Cambridge, Mass.: Harvard University Press).

—— (1994), 'American Universities and Technical Advance in Industry', *Research Policy* (Spring).

North, D. C. (1990), *Institutions, Institutional Change and Economic Performance* (Cambridge: Cambridge University Press).

Ostry, S. (1990), *Governments and Corporations in a Shrinking World: Trade and Innovation Policies in the United States and Japan* (New York: Council on Foreign Relations Press).

Pack, H., and Westphal, L. E. (1986), 'Industrial Strategy and Technological Change: Theory or Reality', *Journal of Development Economics*, 22: 87–128.

Pigou, A. C. (1920), *The Economics of Welfare* (London: Macmillan; 4th edn., 1960).

Porter, M. (1990), *The Competitive Advantage of Nations* (New York: The Free Press).

Rae, J. (1905), *The Sociological Theory of Capital* (New York: Macmillan) (first published in 1834 as *Statement of Some New Principles on the Subject of Political Economy Exposing the Fallacies of the System of Free Trade and of Some Other Doctrines Maintained in the Wealth of Nations*).

Reich, R. (1991), *The Work of Nations* (New York: Ranff).

Romer, P. (1995), 'Comment on Mankiev', *Brookings Papers on Economic Activity*, i.

Rosenberg, N. (1982), *Inside the Black Box: Technology and Economics* (Cambridge: Cambridge University Press).

—— (1994), 'Uncertainty and Technological Change' (mimeo; Stanford, Calif.: Centre for Economic Policy Research).

—— and Birdzell, L. E. (1986), *How the West Grew Rich* (New York: Basic Books).

Stiglitz, J. E. (1986), *Economics of the Public Sector* (New York: Norton).

—— *et al.* (1989), *The Economic Role of the State* (Oxford: Basil Blackwell).

Teece, D. J. (1992), 'Strategies for Capturing the Financial Benefits from Technological Innovation', in *Technology and the Wealth of Nations* (Stanford, Calif.: Stanford University Press).

Thurow, L. (1985), *The Zero-Sum Solution* (New York: Simon & Schuster).

—— (1992), *Head to Head: The Coming Economic Battle among Japan, Europe and America* (New York: William Morrow).

UNCTAD (1994): United Nations Conference on Trade and Development, *World Investment Report 1994: Transnational Corporations, Employment and the Workplace* (New York: United Nations).

UN (1992): United Nations, *Globalization and Developing Countries: Investment, Trade and Technology Linkages in the 1990s* (United Nations Symposium in the Hague, March).

Wade, R. (1990), *Governing the Market: Economic Theory and the Role of Government in East Asian Industrialization* (Princeton: Princeton University Press).

Williamson, J. (1990) (ed.), *Latin American Adjustment* (Washington: Institute for International Economics).

Wood, A. (1994), *North–South Trade, Employment and Inequality* (Oxford: Oxford University Press).

3

A Business Analytic Approach to Governments and Globalization

John H. Dunning

1. **Introduction**

National governments can and do play a decisive role in affecting the competitiveness of the economic activities located within their borders. They do so both by providing the appropriate incentives for domestic firms to upgrade the quality of their ownership-specific assets; and by ensuring that the location-bound general purpose inputs (including educational facilities and communications infrastructure), necessary for these assets to be fully and efficiently utilized, are available. The advent of globalization does not materially alter this fact. But, in a variety of ways, globalization may require a reappraisal both by firms of their strategies to create and sustain core competencies, and by governments as they seek to make the best use of these competencies within their area of jurisdiction. This is the subject matter of this chapter.

2. **Globalization and the Strategy of Firms**

From the viewpoint of firms, one of the main consequences of globalization—or more correctly the forces leading to it—is that it is requiring them to reconsider not only the locational configuration of the home bases for their strategically distinct businesses, but how this configuration affects the rest of their foreign and domestic operations. The underlying idea is that, as world economic events and technological advances are deepening the structural interdependence between nations—and particularly that between advanced industrial nations—the diamonds of competitive advantages of those nations become linked in such a way that enterprises—and especially large MNEs—find it advantageous to disperse at least some of their home bases from their country of ownership to other countries. In the 1990s we see an increasing number of companies such as ABB, Philips of Eindhoven, IBM, 3M, and Nestlé establishing multiple home bases in countries other than that where their headquarters are situated.

What, then, determines the location of the home base of a particular business? Sometimes it is historical accident; yet, once embedded in a particular location, that business may take on a life of its own and attract 'virtuous' clusters of related activities. Sometimes it is (or was) determined by the availability of a particular natural resource or group of resources; and sometimes it is (or was) drawn by the presence of related firms, customers, or a pool of skilled labour. But, in today's innovation-led economy it is being increasingly influenced by the availability and quality of location-specific 'created' assets; and, most noticeably, the kind of infrastructure which fosters entrepreneurship and knowledge accumulation, and that helps to lower distance-related transaction costs. Often, too, by the policies they adopt to regional or urban development, sub-national governments may influence the locational competitiveness of different home bases.

The siting of the home bases of firms is, then, partly influenced by the presence of *national* agglomeration economies (e.g. an efficient telecommunications network), and partly by that of *micro-regional* clusters of economic activity. Although the advantages of regional clusters arise independently of the extent to which participating firms engage in international activities, they may well affect their ability to compete in the global market place. Fig. 3.1 illustrates a selection of regional clusters in the USA. Most of these also house the 'domestic' home bases of the leading enterprises—including MNEs—in the sectors; and sometimes, too, the 'foreign' home bases of foreign-owned firms. Some reflect the presence of natural resources, or a favourable access to national or international transport networks; but many are based on a mixture of opportunism and the availability of immobile created assets and a supportive infrastructure. These latter advantages embrace both Marshallian-type agglomeration economies and the actions taken by local governments to foster cluster building.

While this figure is illustrative of the geography of concentration of economic activity, it tells us nothing about either the organizational structure or the economic viability of such clusters. But, as Anna Lee Saxenian (1994) has demonstrated in her comparison of the Silicon Valley and Route 128 (in Massachusetts) clusters of urban development, state governments may play a critical role in affecting the form, efficiency, and growth of these clusters.

Quite independently, then, of the role of national governments, the effect of globalization on the spatial distribution of the value-added activity is twofold. On the one hand, as a result of improved transport and communications facilities and lower artificial barriers to trade, it helps facilitate the movement of created assets, and with it the specialization of economic activity—including that normally associated with the home base of a particular business. On the other hand, it upgrades the capability of micro-regional spatial units to provide the complementary or support services necessary for these mobile assets to be properly assimilated and exploited; and it does so precisely as a means of minimizing the spatial transaction costs associated with the deployment of these location-bound assets.

The combined result of these forces is that the global strategy of firms is changed in two ways. First, it is no longer necessary for them to locate their home base for each of their distinct businesses in their country of origin. Though this may usually be the case—particularly for MNEs from the larger and more prosperous countries—in circumstances where the foreign diamonds of competitive advantage

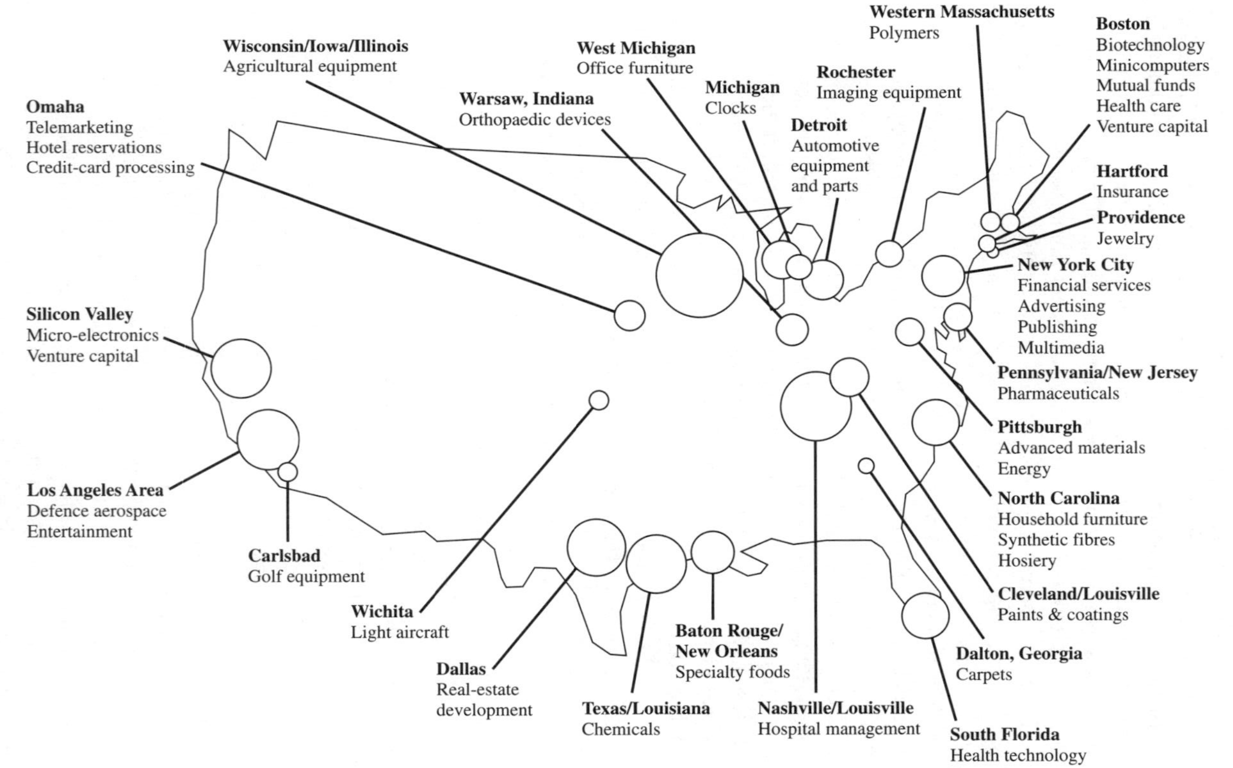

FIG 3.1. Selected regional clusters in the USA of competitive industries

offer better resources and capabilities, such home bases are likely to be dispersed. In a globalizing economy, then, the need to locate the corporate headquarters of an MNE—and particularly one producing a wide range of products requiring different factor inputs or serving different markets in its home country—is likely to become less imperative than once it was. As a general principal, firms should locate new product-line bases in the country which offers the most favourable location-bound endowments for their innovation; and regional subsidiaries of MNEs should specialize in those activities in which they have a competitive advantage, and supply the output of these activities to regional or global markets.

As regards value-added activities other than those of the home base, globalization is likely to lead to a geographical dispersion of these—primarily via FDI and cross-border strategic alliances—whenever it is more efficient (i) to source basic factors (capital, raw materials, and generalized labour) from a foreign outlet, (ii) to secure or improve market access, and/or (iii) selectively to tap into particular skills, technologies, or learning experiences. While the location of the resource-based and market-seeking operations of MNEs is fairly self-evident, that of the third kind is primarily determined by the availability of the complementary created assets which the investing firms perceive they need if they are to make the best use of their own core competences. Sometimes these assets are, themselves, core competencies of related firms (e.g. suppliers); and sometimes they are part of the technological, educational, and legal infrastructure which provides the general (but no less essential) inputs to firms.

In a survey recently conducted by the author, Dunning (1996), it was found that the contribution of the foreign affiliates to the global competitiveness of 144 of the largest industrial MNEs[1] was perceived (by the senior executives participating in the survey) to be both substantial and growing. As might be expected, this contribution was closely related to the degree of multinationality of the investing firms. Thus, on a scale of 1 to 7—1 indicating that, in the opinion of the responding firm, all its competitive advantages were derived from its domestic operations, and 7 that all its advantages were derived as a result of foreign operations—MNEs whose foreign affiliates accounted for less than 15 per cent of their global assets or employment ranked the value of access to foreign-located natural resources and unskilled labour as 3.04, access to foreign-created assets as 2.30, and access to linkages with foreign-related firms (e.g. agglomeration economies) as 3.06. The corresponding values given by MNEs with 60 per cent or more of their assets or employment being accounted for by their foreign affiliates were 4.56, 3.73, and 4.87.

While the survey did not specifically concern itself with the location of multiple home bases, it was quite clear from the responses of firms that the foreign countries from which they were most likely to augment their competitive advantages comprised the triad of the USA, the EU, and Japan. Indeed, one or other of these was mentioned as the most important source of the base for exploiting or obtaining new technologies by 83 per cent of firms; and for exploiting or obtaining new technologies by 73 per cent of respondents (Dunning 1996).

Sourcing Factors

- Assembly in numerous countries to tap lower labour costs

Securing Market Access

- Manufacturing facilities in the USA to hedge against OMA and protectionism
- Joint venture with Rover in the UK, oriented towards the European market, including product development, marketing, and production

Selective Tapping into Foreign Diamonds

- Design studios in California and Germany
- Development of station wagon and all-terrain vehicle in the USA

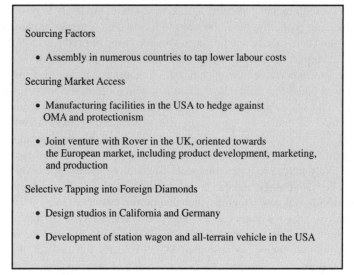

FIG 3.2. The dispersed activities of the Honda Motor Company

As might be expected, the estimated significance of the foreign operations of MNEs was industry, country, and firm-specific. Further illustrations of the ways in which two companies—the Novo Nordisk Group, a Danish firm, and the Honda Motor Company—geographically disperse their value-added activities and, in so doing, tap into foreign diamonds are set out in Figs. 3.2 and 3.3.

3. The Changing Roles of Government

3.1. Some General Remarks

In other writings, both Michael Porter and the present author have argued that the unique and critical role of modern democratic governments is to create and sustain an efficient economic system (Porter 1990; Dunning 1994[2]). What exactly does this mean? From the viewpoint of upgrading the competitiveness of the resources and capabilities within their jurisdictions, we believe it means five things. First, governments must create and effectively communicate to their constituents a distinctive and challenging economic vision. This they will normally do after consulting with a broad range of these constituents. Secondly, they must ensure that the institutions responsible for translating that vision into reality are both willing and able to adjust to the changes required of them by a learning and innovation-driven economy.

Thirdly, it is the responsibility of national administrations to ensure that the availability, quality, and cost effectiveness of general purpose inputs match up

Sourcing Factors

- Capital sourced worldwide
- Pancreases sourced from 20+ countries

Securing Market Access

- Created marketing joint ventures to reach local doctors and hospitals
- Established insulin-making and packaging facilities in France, South America, Japan, and the USA

  Located major enzyme production facilities in the USA to serve sophisticated customers, e.g. detergents and high fructose corn syrup

Selective Tapping into Foreign Diamonds

- Acquired Zymotech in Seattle, Washington, for expertise in genetically engineered insulin
- Rapid approval in Japan relative to Denmark led to the establishment of a genetic engineering R&D facility in Japan

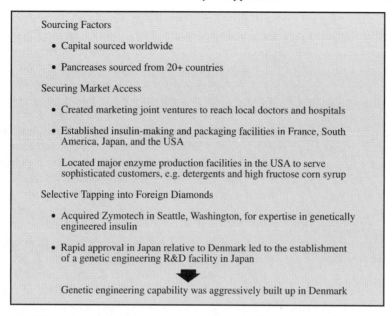

Genetic engineering capability was aggressively built up in Denmark

FIG 3.3. The dispersed activities of the Novo Nordisk Group

to the standards of their global competitors. By such inputs we mean location-bound societal assets which firms need to use jointly with their core advantages to produce goods and services. At one time, these assets mainly consisted of transport facilities and public utilities. Today they embrace all forms of educational and telecommunications infrastructure necessary to foster an efficient and modern innovation-led economy.

Fourthly, governments need to create and sustain an institutional framework and ethos that facilitates a continuous upgrading of the resources and capabilities within its jurisdiction. This not only means ensuring that markets for wealth-creating assets function efficiently, but that entrepreneurship is adequately motivated, consumers are persuaded to be more demanding of technical standards and product quality, and that there is a sufficient quality of inter-firm rivalry to promote learning and a continual improvement of asset usage. This last task of government serves to remind us that it is not only the kind of industries a nation or region competes in that matters, but how firms compete in these sectors. Finally, it encompasses the regular monitoring of various laws, regulations, and regimes (e.g. with respect to anti-trust, labour unions, and intellectual property rights) which help to lower the transaction and coordination costs of dynamic business activity.

Fifthly, governments should do everything to encourage, and nothing to impede the formation of micro-regional clusters development, as it is becoming increasingly apparent that the competitiveness of a country's industries is dependent not only on the efforts of the constituent firms, but also on ways in which they interact with their suppliers, customers, and competitors.[3] Partly, as we have already noted, this kind of inter-firm cooperation is independent of spatial considerations; but partly, at least, it can be strengthened if the activities are in close proximity to each other. This is particularly the case where the transaction costs of doing business rise as the physical or psychic distance between the firms engaging in these activities question increases. Such costs are likely to be more pronounced in the case of firms using pooled factor services, interdependent technologies, and idiosyncratic intermediate products; and where tacit knowledge, trust, and commitment are important intangible assets. The City of London is a classic example of a clustering of business services whose efficiency is dependent on their close physical proximity with other services which need to be jointly used with them.[4] A more recent example is the congregation of multi-media service providers in lower Manhattan, New York.

Because it is only recently that economists and business scholars have begun to give attention to the spatial 'stickiness' of some kinds of economic activity which exist, in spite of advantages of globalization earlier described, we will give a little more attention to this aspect of government involvement. How, if at all, is the role of government affected by the fact that some value activities are becoming location bound, while others are becoming more footloose?

3.2. Governments and Micro-Regional Clusters

In many respects, we believe that it is by avoiding inappropriate policies, rather than taking positive action, that governments can best promote an efficient intra-national distribution of economic activity. Such inappropriate policies arise through the understandable, but not necessarily judicious, intervention by governments to promote a locational strategy which aims at reducing the disparities in incomes and growth in the micro-regions within their jurisdictions. We set out some of these impediments in Fig. 3.4. Of these, perhaps the first two are the ones most widely practised by governments and by regional authorities such as the European Commission.

Here, however, it is important to distinguish between two motives for government intervention. The first is to reduce the external *diseconomies* of industrial concentration,[5] and/or assist the spatial dispersal of both mobile and immobile resources in a way that encourages new clusters. Such measures are essentially designed to reduce endemic market failure and to assist the efficient disposition of resources. The second motive is directed to helping micro-regions to offset their declining competitive advantages, in the same way as national governments have subsidized declining or inefficient firms or industries in the past. Policies of this kind, ostensibly aimed at promoting a 'balanced' development, are more likely to distort, rather than improve, the spatial distribution of economic activity.

National and regional governments are also prone to subsidizing economic activities in backward or distressed regions and, again, this is politically under-

- 'Balanced-development' policies across states and regions
- Incentives or requirements to locate in backward/distressed areas
- Poor transportation and communications infrastructure
- Uniformity in vocational training and university curricula
- University research priorities set independently of local company needs
- Policies that encourage vertical integration (e.g. licensing requirements, reservation of sectors for small firms)
- Tolerance of monopolies/cartels

FIG 3.4. Government impediments to cluster formation

standable, and, in some cases, economically justifiable. These cases include a conjunction of three sets of circumstances: (i) there is a substantial social investment at stake, (ii) the micro-region could be made economically viable again in a cost effective way, and (iii) it costs the community more to relocate people outside the region than to relocate jobs inside the region. But, excepting these instances, if there is a rationale for government intervention, it has to be argued on non-economic grounds!

What, then, might be the positive role of national governments in cluster-upgrading or the creation of new clusters, using the framework of the diamond of competitive advantage? Fig. 3.5 highlights some of these. Essentially, it can be seen that these are an extension of their more general functions identified earlier, although in this figure we have tried to be a little more specific. It will be observed that, although the gains from cluster formation are usually attributable to the presence of related and supporting industries, governments may affect access to the agglomeration economies of micro-regions through the other facets of the diamond. Those items identified in bold print arise specifically as a result of globalization, which we will deal with in the next section of this chapter.

Some of the suggested initiatives in Fig. 3.5 are primarily the responsibility of national governments; others are the responsibility of sub-national authorities (e.g. of states, micro-regions, or cities). Most are fairly self-evident; almost all are intended to lower the transaction or coordinating costs associated with cluster formation or deepening by, for example, assisting data-gathering, reducing information asymmetries, facilitating intra-regional communications, aiding the

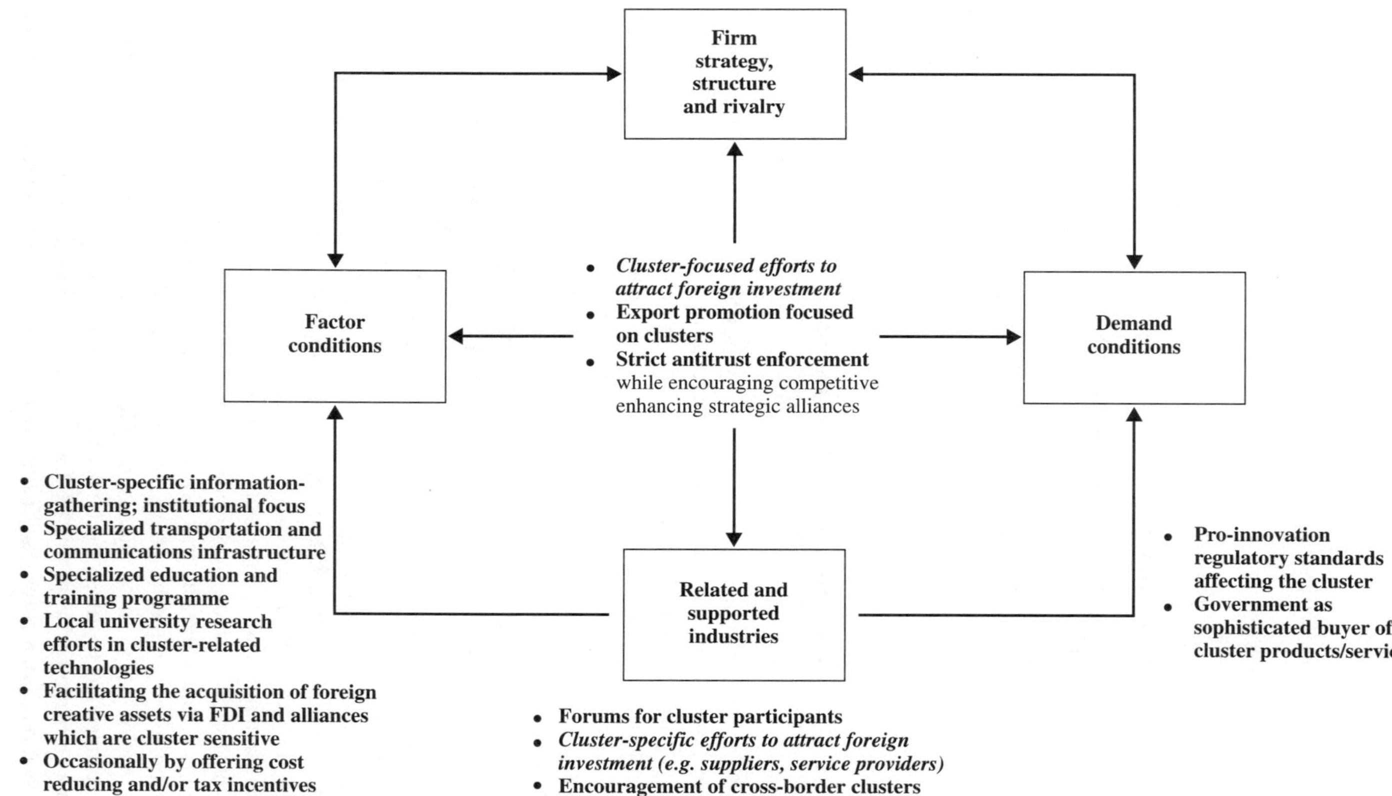
Firm strategy, structure and rivalry
Factor conditions
Demand conditions
Related and supported industries
• Cluster-focused efforts to attract foreign investment
• Export promotion focused on clusters
• Strict antitrust enforcement while encouraging competitive enhancing strategic alliances
• Cluster-specific information-gathering; institutional focus
• Specialized transportation and communications infrastructure
• Specialized education and training programme
• Local university research efforts in cluster-related technologies
• Facilitating the acquisition of foreign creative assets via FDI and alliances which are cluster sensitive
• Occasionally by offering cost reducing and/or tax incentives
• Forums for cluster participants
• Cluster-specific efforts to attract foreign investment (e.g. suppliers, service providers)
• Encouragement of cross-border clusters
• Pro-innovation regulatory standards affecting the cluster
• Government as sophisticated buyer of cluster products/services

Fig 3.5. Role of government in cluster-upgrading

absorptive capacity of spatially linked immobile assets, and capturing the economic and social externalities of interrelated activities. Some, however, are strictly conditional on particular circumstances. Thus, while economists would not generally support the subsidization of either natural or created assets to foster cluster formation, it may be appropriate, particularly in the case of countries seeking to catch up with their established foreign competitors, for some temporary cost-reducing or tax incentives to be offered to firms, conditional, for example, on their locating their activities in certain regions,[6] or on their achieving a certain level of performance, to be provided to these firms.

We would also observe that the appropriate role of government in cluster-upgrading is also likely to vary according to the structure of cluster activity. Ann Markusen (1996), for example, has distinguished between four ways of organizing micro-regional business activity, each of which is likely to make a different contribution to the prosperity of the 'sticky' place of which it is a part.[7] These are (i) the *flexible specialization* rubric, as typified by the Italian textile industry in Prato, North Italy, the watch industry of Switzerland, and the cork industry of Portugal, (ii) *hub-and-spoke* industrial districts where the pattern of economic activity is centred on a number of 'flagship' corporations or strategic centres (e.g. Toyota City in Japan and the Seattle industrial district), (iii) the *satellite industrial platform*, which is mainly made up of the affiliates of extra-regional firms (e.g. as export-processing and free trade zones in developing countries), and (iv) the *non-market-centred district*, where the local economy revolves around either a group of top-ranking educational institutions or a number of major government-owned administrative or research installations, as along Route 128 in the USA and the M4 corridor in the UK. Clearly, government action to promote type (iii) clusters, which tend to result in only a shallow integration of higher value activity, and type (i) or (ii) clusters, which could lead to more structural embeddedness, will be very different. Moreover, while most clusters of related activities tend to be somewhat vulnerable to economic fluctuations, types (i) and (ii) because they are reliant on a few large firms, or on specialized export markets, are likely to be especially so.

We would make one final point at this stage. Later chapters in this volume will identify some country-specific similarities and differences in the role of national governments and the emerging global economy; in Chapter 16 John Stopford will draw some general conclusions about these. But even the most casual reading of the literature suggests that the influences of different governments on the four facets of the diamond of competitive advantage differ enormously. This is not to aver that there is one particular model of government intervention which is superior to all others; in any event, at least some of the assets of 'good' government are largely location-bound—that is, they cannot be transplanted to other countries. At the same time, it would be unusual if successful policies pursued by governments in one country (e.g. towards education and training, entrepreneurship and savings, raising environmental standards of quality, anti-trust legislation, and collecting and disseminating public information

—to give just a few examples) did not contain at least some lessons for other governments. The ability to identify and judiciously adapt 'best-practice' techniques of governments from other countries[8] to one's own particular economic, institutional and cultural situation is, indeed, becoming a core competency in its own right![9]

3.3. Governments and Globalization

Using, once again, the idea of linked diamonds as our unit of analysis, there are two ways in which national (or sub-national) governments may be affected by globalization. The first is directly by the changes it occasions in the interface between governments—and, in particular, those brought about by intergovernment rivalry. The second is by the way in which the four main facets of the diamond are affected by cross-border structural integration—and especially by FDI and the activities of MNEs; and on how this, in turn, may require modifications to the governance of governments, and to their systemic and operational roles.[10]

3.3.1. Interface between Governments

Since most of this volume is concerned with this issue, we will touch upon it only briefly in this chapter. While globalization is only one of the factors making for 'competing' governments,[11] it is as a direct result of the increased mobility of many firm specific assets, notably technology and organizational capacities, and some kinds of previously immobile assets (e.g. managerial and professional labour), that governments are required to consider the actions of other national administrations, who compete for these assets, when designing and implementing their own policies. For most of recent industrial history, nation states have been primarily linked by their trade and macro-economic policies, the latter in as much as interest rates may affect cross-border capital flows, and the exchange rates the real costs of production. But it is the growing mobility of created assets which is tending to bring about the deep integration between national government policies. While it is too early to identify a clear convergence or harmonization among such policies, there is little doubt that, in some areas—including, for example, those most affecting the cross-border location of activity such as FDI and competition policy—there is considerable pressure to do so. On the other hand, as long as there remain differences between countries—not only in their economic and market structures, but in their institutions, cultural mores, social priorities, and political ideologies—government policies are likely to remain differentiated from each other, just as the strategies of successful MNEs—even within the same sector—are distinct from one another.

3.3.2. Globalization and the Diamond

There have been various attempts by scholars to explain the cross-border linkages between the diamond of one country and that of another. Alan Rugman, for example (Rugman and D'Cruz 1991; Rugman 1992, 1993), favours the concept of the double or multiple diamond. Elsewhere (Dunning 1992, 1993) the present author has introduced international business activity as an exogenous variable (like government) into the Porter model, and has sought to consider its influence on each of the four facets of the domestic diamond. Also, earlier in this chapter we acknowledged that, to advance their global strategies, diversified MNEs might wish to establish multiple home bases for at least some of their strategic distinct business.

While each of these various approaches attempts to identify and evaluate some of the effects of the geographical integration of economic activity, from either a sectoral or a country perspective, none gives much attention to the ways in which governments may influence the response of individuals, firms, and industries to their exposures to foreign diamonds. Yet the manner in which governments operationalize their various functions and responsibilities[12] could critically determine both the speed and the ultimate success of the adjustment process. Let us explain what we mean by examining briefly each of the four facets of the diamond.

Factor endowments. Through inward and outward FDI, cross-border alliances and trade in intermediate products, the competitiveness of a country's location-specific endowments is exposed to the actions of foreign economic agents. Where the value activities of an industry are confined to its national borders, this competitiveness (or lack of it) is revealed in its trade and payments balances with other countries. Where, however, its firms are free to produce in other countries, then it is the ability of that country—or, more specifically, the institutions of that country—to provide the location-based resources necessary to retain these footloose assets and attract those of foreign firms that is a better measure of its competitiveness.

What, then, should the government's reaction to globalization be? To some extent, this will depend on the type of factor endowments being considered. For natural assets, for example, it may be comparatively little, except to ensure that the social infrastructure necessary for their efficient production and distribution is available. Yet even here, as is shown with many agricultural products their value in global markets is not only derived from the physical properties of the products *per se*, but from the way they are processed and marketed.[13] However, in the case of created assets, governments may exercise a more decisive role. Some examples include helping to improve the quality of general inputs (e.g. via education and training policies), easing the flexibility of the labour market, ensuring that the capital market operates efficiently, implementing appropriate tax policies, supporting pre-competitive research, easing the access or acquisition of foreign skills and technologies, and facilitating the upgrading of domestic factor endowments by foreign firms. While we accept that most of these roles of government apply no less in a closed economy, globalization does impose a new urgency of action; and, perhaps, emphasizes the need for a closer complementarity of interests between the private and public sectors than existed previously.

Market structure and inter-firm rivalry. Both technological advances and globalization have added several new dimensions to the competition between firms. Like many other aspects of structural integration, they have been ambivalent in their effects. On the one hand, in some instances, they have helped reduce the concentration of production within a country and intensified inter-firm rivalry—as, for example, in the automotive, pharmaceutical, and banking industries. On the other hand, they have led to a wave of cross-border M&As and strategic alliances which has made for a more pronounced oligopolistic competition.

While changes in market structure have not gone unnoticed by governments, by and large, they have taken little action to influence them. This is principally, one feels, because they believe that, on balance, globalization is leading to more, rather than less, competition; and that technological forces are compelling firms to engage in more M&As, and strategic alliances, in order to take full advantage of firm-level scale economies and speed up the process of innovation, *vis-à-vis* their foreign competitors. Whether or not this view is correct remains to be seen; but, sooner or later, governments will have to articulate their competition policies better than they are currently doing, and, as Monty Graham points out in Chapter 17, these issues are also now on the agenda of international agencies, notably the WTO and the OECD.

Globalization is also compelling governments to take a more active stance in promoting an ethos, or mindset, of competitiveness. Margaret Thatcher's Conservative government of the 1980s is a classic example of the kind of influence a government can have on the attitude to wealth creation of both individuals and institutions; and also on entrepreneurship. Though many of the changes instituted during the Thatcher years were an attempt to resolve internal economic problems, there is little doubt that the threat to UK prosperity, brought about by relocation of UK investment and the possible loss of in-bound investment to other parts of the EU, was a major factor in promoting policies which not only deregulated and liberalized UK markets—including labour markets—but initiated a whole range of fiscal and other incentives to motivate people and firms to upgrade their resources and capabilities and to become more aggressively competitive.[14]

Upgrading consumer expectations. Though it is not always necessary for superior-quality or low-price products to be produced where they are sold, there can be little doubt that the pressure of Japanese affiliates in the US and European automotive and consumer electronics industries has heightened the awareness of US consumers to the standards which are commonplace in Japan. At the same time, in their efforts to penetrate the Japanese market, foreign firms have had to take serious account of the particular demands of Japanese customers.

Deep structural integration is then leading to a convergence of consumer expectations and needs—at least as far as tradable goods and services are concerned. In the main, because firms are increasingly seeking new markets through continuous product improvement and innovations, this is resulting in a harmonization of consumer standards—at least among internationally traded branded goods—

to the highest level—although sometimes the improvements may be cosmetic rather than substantive.

What, if anything, does this imply for national governments? First, it means that more attention is likely to be focused on the cross-border harmonization of technical and quality standards (ISO 9000 is an attempt to do just this[15]). Secondly, it means that governments need to study, and where appropriate adapt and implement, the 'first best' practices of other governments in respect of consumer protection, health and safety, and the environment.[16] While, in some cases, such intervention may add to the costs of production, in others, especially in the area of environmental regulations, there are suggestions that firms which pursue the most rigorous standards are, in fact, the most competitive (Lundan 1996). And, thirdly, it again emphasizes the role of government as a setter of an ethos, which encourages the consumers of both intermediate and final goods and services, to be more rigorous and sophisticated in their demands of producers.[17]

Related and supporting industries. A previous section of this chapter has already analysed in some detail the ways in which national and sub-national governments may aid or inhibit the development of regional clusters. Referring back to Fig. 3.5, we suggest that the response of governments may affect cluster formation in four main ways. First, in their cluster-focused efforts, they may wish to take into account the particular and special locational, and other, needs of foreign firms—as, indeed, they have done in the siting of free trade and export-processing zones. Secondly, they can, and do, reduce the social transaction costs, and particularly those to do with information inadequacies or asymmetries, as they affect both potential foreign investors and local firms seeking to establish partnerships with foreign firms. Most of the US states, for example, have offices in Europe and Japan, specifically designed to promote the advantages of their own resources and capabilities; and most national commerce or trade departments help provide information—particularly to small and medium-sized firms—about the opportunities for licensing or other forms of cross-border licensing.

Thirdly, and more generally, in better recognizing the contribution of the affiliates of foreign firms to cluster development, sub-national governments may need not only to upgrade the locational attractiveness of the micro-regions for which they are responsible, but to do so in a way which maximizes its spillover benefits (e.g. to suppliers, service providers, and so on).[18] This may require some reprioritization of the spatial distribution of the social capital of national governments; and also of the taxation and expenditure plans of sub-national governments.

Fourthly, as indicated earlier, technological forces and the liberalization of cross-border markets have changed not only the international and intra-national structure of economic activity, but the competitive advantages of firms of different ownership. This creates certain tensions and dilemmas for national and regional governments. On the one hand, they wish to maximize the economic welfare of the constituents of the country or region they represent. On the other, they wish to avoid any marked spatial disparities of income and wealth; and any undue reliance on foreign ownership. We do not pretend to have a solution to these dilemmas, but we do believe that globalization is likely to sharpen the distinction between the options open to governments.

4. Conclusions

One of the features of globalization is that it is refocusing scholarly attention on the respective roles of firms and governments in advancing the competitiveness of a country or region within a country. In so doing, we are reminded of the distinction between locationally mobile and locationally bound created assets. In an innovation-driven economy, the competitiveness of firms increasingly depends on their ability to create and efficiently to organize the use of distinctive core competences in one or other lines of their business. Although, once produced, these assets, or their rights, are often transferable across national boundaries, their initial creation requires a strong home base. However, while the possession of these assets is a necessary condition for their success, it is not a sufficient condition. To be used effectively, the core competences of firms need to be combined with other assets which are sourced from *other* firms or from non-market institutions. Frequently, these complementary assets are location bound; and frequently, too—as in the case of an educated labour force and an efficient transportation and communications network—their availability and quality are strongly influenced by the actions (or inactions) of national or sub-national governments. Indeed, since many mobile assets are becoming easier to access, it is the uniqueness and quality of location-bound assets, and the way firms are able to coordinate these with their own core advantages, that are, perhaps, the most important components of a country's competitive advantage.

This suggests that governments and firms are best considered as partners in the wealth-creating process. Although, in a market economy, it is the competitiveness of private corporations which determines a nation's prosperity, this competitiveness rests, too, on the five tasks of government described earlier being effectively implemented. If this is not done, then two things are likely to happen. First, where they are able, firms will 'vote with their feet' and relocate their value-added activities in countries which offer them more hospitable location-bound resources. Secondly, the capacity of the domestic economy—and particularly that of clusters of related firms—to absorb the benefits of inward direct investment and advance the home-base competences of MNEs will be reduced.

We have illustrated in this chapter the geographical widening of the home bases of MNEs. Where this is a result of market forces and consistent with the comparative dynamic advantages of both exporting and recipient countries, it is to be welcomed. Where it is a result of structurally distorting policies on the part of either the private or the public sector, it is to be deplored. Where it reflects the failure of governments to compete effectively, because of their inability to ensure the general purpose infrastructure necessary to create and absorb new wealth-creating assets, it is to be regretted.

We have also discussed the growing spatial interdependence between firms in innovation-led economies and the importance of cluster development. While acknowledging that there may be agglomeration diseconomies, current technological developments and the liberalization of many cross-border markets is increasing locational specificity or 'stickiness' as an asset in its own right. In our opinion, unless there are strong non-economic reasons for such intervention, governments should do nothing to hinder market-led concentrations of economic activity; indeed, where they perceive that the social net benefits of clusters exceed the net benefits to the participants in the cluster, they should encourage them. The nature and form of that action will depend on the types of clusters formed; but its aim should be to advance both the static and the dynamic comparative advantage both of the infrastructure of the region, and of the producing firms within it.

A final section of this chapter considered the ways in which the growing structural integration of the world economy links the diamonds of competitive advantage of countries' regions within economies. It again emphasized the interface between the export or import of mobile created assets by firms and the location-specific created assets of countries, and the role of governments in providing the institutional and enabling background for both sets of assets to respond efficiently to the challenges of economic change. It finally confirmed that, alongside the renaissance of market forces, there is the need for strong and wise government to ensure that these forces operate both to advance economic and social welfare, and to do so with the least amount of structural or endemic imperfections.

NOTES

Based upon a presentation by Michael Porter at the Carnegie Bosch Conference in Washington. I am indebted to Professor Porter for permitting me to make full use of the material contained in his presentation. All the diagrams and exhibits have been produced by Professor Porter, although Table 3.4 has been slightly modified by the author.

1. These firms accounted for about 40% of the global FDI stock of industrial MNEs in 1993.
2. See also Chapter 1 of this volume.
3. As set out, e.g., in Porter (1990) and in Alan Rugman and Joseph D'Cruz's five partners network model (Rugman and D'Cruz 1995). For analysis of the concept of alliance capitalism and its implications for the competitive advantages of firms, see Dunning (1995).
4. As documented in some detail by Dunning and Morgan (1971) over twenty years ago.
5. As, for example, occurred in the early post-war period, when the UK government tried to steer economic activity away from a congested London and towards the provinces.
6. As in the case of export-processing zones (McIntyre *et al.* forthcoming). For a review of the role of cost-reducing and fiscal incentives in attracting FDI, see UNCTAD (1995); for the actions taken by state governments in the USA to attract inward investment (be it from foreign or domestic firms), see Coughlin *et al.* (1991) and

Donaghue (1997). The danger is, of course, that such locational tournaments may spark off 'beggar-my-neighbour' competitive bidding between states or regions, which is more cluster-distorting than cluster-facilitating. See also an interesting paper, Mytelka (1996).

7. For an alternative classification of the structure of regions, see Storper and Harrison (1991) and Miles and Snow (1992).
8. Again, the comparative advantage of governments varies according to the functions performed. For example, the policies of the Japanese government on education, savings, and corporate investment are worth close scrutiny, while their anti-trust policies and support of agriculture and some less competitive sectors leave much to be desired.
9. As, indeed, is the ability to adapt and utilize best-practice techniques from throughout the world an important competitive advantage of firms.
10. As identified in the Introduction to this volume.
11. For example, no less important is the trend towards the convergence of economic structures among advanced nations and the growing significance of created assets, the quality and availability of which tend to be more influenced by governments than that of natural resources.
12. As identified and discussed by various contributors to this volume.
13. Ohmae (1990: 175) gives an illustration of the price of Blue Mountain coffee, which sells in Japan for four times the price of Brazilian coffee. 'Is it four times better?' he asks. 'Probably not,' he replies. 'Blind taste tests show little difference. What is different, however, is the clever and determined branding of the coffee. In other words, a managed effort to add value.' In his book, Ohmae goes on to cite other examples of branding creating large margins of value, including Kobe beef and Koshikari rice, both of which are produced in Japan.
14. The issue of governments influencing the ethos of competition is dealt with in Dunning (1991).
15. For a description of the provisions of ISO 9000, which is becoming an increasingly accepted standard for quality management, see, e.g., Peach (1994).
16. In some cases, these may be received as public goods; in others as affecting the design, contents, quality and usage of private goods.
17. Although we accept that there is nothing like inter-firm competition to ensure this!
18. The importance of related industries is particularly well seen in the case of the Portuguese cork industry, which is focused in two regions: Sante Maria de Feira and Sotubal. The efficiency of several hundred cork producers is aided by the presence of specialized cork processing machinery manufacturers, strong local wine and port producers, several large bottling companies, and a number of cork-related training and research institutes. I am indebted to Michael Porter for providing me with this example.

REFERENCES

Coughlin, C. C., Terza, J. V., and Arromdee, V. (1991), 'State Characteristics and the Location of Foreign Direct Investment within the US', *Review of Economics and Statistics*, 73: 675–83.

Donahue, J. D. (1997), *Disunited States* (New York: Basic Books).

Dunning, J. H. (1991), 'Governments, Economic Organization and International Competitiveness', in L. G. Mattson and B. Stymne (eds.), *Corporate and Industry Strategies for Europe* (Rotterdam: Elsevier Science Publishers), 41–74.

—— (1992), 'The Competitive Advantage of Nations and TNC Activities', *Transnational Corporations*, 1 (February), 135–68.

—— (1993), 'Internationalizing Porter's Diamond', *Management International Review*, 33/2 (special issue), 7–15.

—— (1994), *Globalization: The Challenge for National Economic Regimes* (The Geary Lecture for 1993; Dublin: Economic and Social Research Institute).

—— (1995), 'Reappraising the Eclectic Paradigm in the Age of Alliance Capitalism', *Journal of International Business Studies*, 26/3: 461–91.

—— (1996), 'The Geographical Sources of the Competitiveness of Firms: Some Results of a New Survey', *Transnational Corporations*, 5/3.

—— and Morgan, E. V. (1971), *An Economic Study of the City of London* (London: Allen and Unwin).

Lundun, S. (1996), 'Internationalization and Environmental Strategy in the Pulp and Paper Industry' (Ph.D. dissertation, Newark: Rutgers University).

McIntyre, J., Narula, R., and Trevino, L. J. (forthcoming), 'The Role of Export Processing Zones for Host Countries and Multinationals: A Mutually Beneficial Relationship', *International Trade Journal*, 10/4: 435–66.

Markusen, A. (1996), 'Sticky Places in Slippery Spaces: The Political Economy of Post-War Fast Growth Regions', *Economic Geography*, 72/3: 293–313.

Miles, R. E., and Snow, C. C. (1992), 'Causes of Failure in Network Organization', *California Management Review*, 34: 53–72.

Mytelka, L. K. (1996), 'Locational Tournaments, Strategic Partnerships and the State' (mimeo; Ottawa: Carletion University).

Ohmae, K. (1990), *The Borderless World* (New York: Harper Business).

Peach, R. (1994) (ed.), *The ISO 9000 Handbook* (Fairfax, Va.: CEEM Information Services).

Porter, M. E. (1990), *The Competitive Advantage of Nations* (New York: The Free Press).

Rugman, A. M. (1992), 'Porter Takes the Wrong Turn', *Business Quarterly*, 56/3 (Winter), 59–64.

—— (1993) (ed.), *Management International Review*, 33/2 (special edition on Michael Porter's *Diamond of Competitive Advantage*).

—— and D'Cruz, J. R. (1991), *Fast Forward: Improving Canada's International Competitiveness* (Toronto: Kodah Canada).

—— —— (1995), 'The Five Partners Business Network Model' (mimeo; Toronto: University of Toronto).

Saxenian, A. L. (1994), *Regional Advantage: Culture and Competition in Silicon Valley and Route 128* (Cambridge, Mass.: Harvard University Press).

Storper, M., and Harrison, B. (1991), 'Flexibility, Hierarchy and Regional Development: The Changing Structure of Industrial Production Systems and their Forms of Governance in the 1990s', *Research Policy*, 20: 207–422.

UNCTAD (1995): United Nations Conference on Trade and Development, *Incentives and Foreign Direct Investment* (TD/B/ITNC/Misc 1; Geneva: United Nations).

4

An International Political Economy Perspective

Susan Strange

1. Introduction

Many economists and a good few political scientists have only a dim idea of what is meant by international political economy. The term is equally obscure to most general readers. To understand what to expect therefore from 'an international political economy perspective' on the topic of this book calls first for a clear definition that differentiates my perspective from that of an economist or a political scientist. That it is indeed different will be clear from what follows.

Having once clarified where we are starting from, it will then—and only then—be possible to consider in greater detail what effects globalization may have on economic activity, on the wealth and on the stability of the economic system, and on the range of options open to governments, firms, and individual employees and consumers. Are any of these likely to be freer, better off, more secure than they were fifty or a hundred years ago? Are their life chances—their 'entitlements' in Amartya Sen's phrasing—more or less equal when compared to those of others than they were fifty or a hundred years ago?

At this point, economists may already object that such questions are not strictly their concern. But they would be wrong. Wealth can easily translate into power, and power into privilege. The central idea that many economists have been brought up to believe in is that 'economics is the study of wealth-creation and distribution'. As such, they were led to believe, it could be divorced from the study of the social and political causes and consequences of any economic change, or of any system of production or of finance. To my mind (and to that of many sociologists, historians, and lawyers), such an unnatural divorce is a quite preposterous idea. As John Dunning writes in Chapter 1, it is one that was never accepted for a moment by Adam Smith, John Stuart Mill, Karl Marx, or John Maynard Keynes. There is not—and never has been—a clear dividing line in the real world between what is economic and what is political, between the policies chosen for 'economic' reasons whether by governments or by firms, and policies chosen for security, to ensure the survival of the state or of the enterprise.

Since this book is being put together in the year that the London School of Economics and Political Science celebrated its first centenary—and since the story of how and why one of the leading international centres of economic research was set up is germane to my argument—the reasons for its establishment are worth recalling. Its founders were Beatrice and Sidney Webb and George Bernard Shaw, supported by a group of social reformers in Britain known as the Fabians. Its name, linking economics and political science, reveals an underlying conviction that social reform—the purpose of the Fabian Society—required a better understanding of the workings of the economy. Today, only the most rabid and bigoted of neoclassical ideologues among economists can possibly contemplate the arbitrary divorce of economy from society, or from politics. One has only to contemplate the political nature of the post-soviet economy to recognize that separating politics from economics in the name of 'science' is to pass from the real world into one of fantasy and illusion.

Having explained the basis of the approach of this chapter, and thus the foundations for my subsequent observations on globalization, we must next pay some brief attention to the matter of definitions. Two very simple points have to be made. The first is that international political economy (IPE) is more than the politics of international economic relations (PIER), even though many books and their authors that claim to belong in IPE are actually no more than PIER. IPE therefore, cannot possibly be limited to those issues that governments—and particularly major governments, like that of the USA—consider to be on the agenda for discussion with the governments of other states. It has to be concerned with wider issues, such as those concerned with environmental protection, where the conflict of interests, and of policies, is not so much between states as between generations of human beings. The welfare of the world's children, too, is an issue to which some governments pay lip-service but where the real conflict is more between parents, and especially mothers, and non-parents than it is between governments.

The second point is even more relevant to several of the chapters in this book. It is that IPE properly concerns the broadly defined welfare of the world economy as a whole, not just the welfare of any one national economy within it. It is the study of how the total system works, its political and its economic aspects, and of the social consequences of its functioning for generations, for genders, for regions and cities, for sectors of business and occupations. It is not, therefore, the same as *comparative* political economy. Several of the chapters included here consider the ways in which different national economies and their governments have responded to globalization or have failed to do so. That is interesting enough in its way. But it is not international political economy as understood by the present writer. The question, 'What should governments do?', or (even more narrowly) the question 'What should *my* government do?' has often characterized much academic work in the USA. Such a question assumes that the welfare of the USA (and the short-term welfare at that) not only is, but should be, the paramount concern of US intellectuals. The narrow-minded implication is that what happens to the rest of the world is not worth serious consideration. Such an introverted, short-sighted, ungenerous, illiberal, and small-minded notion of the purpose of scholarship and research in the world of the 1990s is quite unworthy of the US academic community.

2. Where does Authority Lie?

There are two more theoretical points to be made before proceeding to discuss the consequences for government, for business, and for society of the globalization of the economy. They come from a concern that has preoccupied this writer for the past four years. It has been with the question, where does authority actually lie in the international political economy? Who, or what, is really in charge? The capacity of governments of states, those political authorities defined by territorial frontiers, to manage the destinies of the societies for whom they are responsible seems to me to be much less than it was fifty years ago.

The sensation of lost power, naturally enough, has been most acutely felt in those countries which were most accustomed to exercising power. The Americans, much more than the Finns, say, or the Mexicans or Canadians, were inclined in the 1970s and 1980s to assume that the sense of increased impotence and heightened vulnerability they felt was peculiar to them. It was not, although many Americans chose to think so.

There emerged what came to be known as the declinist school of thought among US academics that eagerly latched onto hegemonic stability theory as the obvious explanation of any disorder, financial or commercial, that could be perceived as afflicting the world economy. The theory originated with Charles Kindleberger's explanation of the length and depth of the world economic depression of the 1930s. Contrary to much liberal theory, which blamed it on commercial protection, Kindleberger's explanation was essentially financial. The global market economy, he argued, required hegemonic financial management to maintain economic stability. In the 1930s Britain, which had filled the role in the nineteenth century, was too weak to do so any more, and the USA was unwilling and unaware of what was required.

It is only fair to Kindleberger to insist that his explanation of economic history has been grossly distorted by some of the exponents of hegemonic stability theory. Intentionally or not, they shifted Kindleberger's emphasis on the system's need for strong financial management to stressing its need for freer international trade. Entranced by the simplicity of the hegemonic stability hypothesis, moreover, these neo-liberal writers failed to give serious consideration to two alternative explanations of disorder in the world economy of the 1970s and after: first, that structural change was making the whole system much more difficult to manage than it had been for the British in the nineteenth century; or, secondly, that disorder resulted when US governments started to abuse their hegemonic position for unilateralist, short-term national advantage. No, they insisted, if the world economy was in disorder, it must be because of the decline of US power.

But to back up their explanation, they used some very inappropriate and irrelevant indicators of declining power. Much was made of the fact that the US share of world GNP, and its share of world production, and world exports of manufactured goods was much less in the 1970s than these shares had been in the 1950s. All had grown in absolute terms, but not so fast as European or Japanese industrial trade and production. It did not follow that US structural power—its influence over political and economic outcomes—had also declined. In matters of international security, the military capabilities, and especially the nuclear weaponry, of the USA was still unmatched. In international finance, the international use of its currency, the dollar, meant that the decisions of the USA still prevailed in the management of exchange rates and the evolution of expanding financial markets. And in international trade, the greater size and openness of the US domestic economy made its regulatory and monetary policies more important to the managers of transnational corporations than the policies of any other government in the world (Strange 1982). Yet it was nearly a decade before the first of my American friends in international relations came round to questioning the conventional view that US power had declined. (Nau 1990; Nye 1990).

To insist that the USA was still dominant in structural terms was not inconsistent, of course, with agreeing that there was growing disorder in the world economy; merely that there might be other explanations for the disorder. The fallacy of the declinist school, in short, was to assume that, if a state lost power *relative to the market*, that power must have passed to another state—to the Germans or the Japanese. The truth was that, by the 1970s and 1980s, the government of the USA, in common with those of other nation states, no longer had the authority over market forces and either its national or the global economy that it had enjoyed in the early years after the Second World War.

Although by now this is much more widely recognized, it does imply two much more fundamental and important propositions about the nature of politics and economics that need to be made explicit if the international political economy view of globalization is to make any sort of sense.

3. The Limits of Politics

The first proposition concerns the limits of what we understand by 'politics'. Should we continue to think of politics as limited to what politicians do? Is the study of government—as departments of political science are sometimes called in British universities—confined to the activities and constitutions, written or unwritten, of governments of territorial states? Hardly so. In everyday language, we academics talk—quite a lot—about academic politics—which departments and which colleagues are gaining control over resources, financial and human, which factions are guiding the university in which direction, privileging some activities and constraining others. In doing so, we acknowledge that politics is a game that people play in all sorts of contexts—within families, inside the firm, among members of golf and other sports clubs, in church groups, within pressure groups and business associations, in parent–teacher associations, in labour unions—in fact in almost any social group of human beings it is possible to think of. Politics, in short, may be defined as the activities by which an individual or a group of individuals seeks to win the support of other wills for some objective that they wish to achieve. It can be to get a car pool or a baby-sitting rota organized. Or it may be to effect the takeover of another enterprise, replacing its present management with another. The means may be by persuasion or by coercion, or by an astute combination of the two. It is not essentially different from the activities in which politicians engage when they are building coalitions or marshalling votes behind a bill.

Once that hypothesis—that politics is not limited to the conduct of politicians and governments—is accepted, we can start to think of *firms as arenas of politics* and their executives as players—actors in the language of international relations—in the IPE. That was an important conclusion reached in collaboration with John Stopford in our joint study of the 'new diplomacy' of bargaining between foreign firms and host governments (Stopford and Strange 1991: 22). Using the perspective of international political economy, we found great interdependence between firms and governments, so that it was not only governments which create problems for business, but also firms which create problems for governments.

4. **Who has Power?**

The second fundamental hypothesis, related to the first but conceptually distinct from it, concerns the nature of power. Now power is something that economists find hard to handle. It cannot be measured. Different kinds of power are fungible. Power may be used for a variety of purposes, not always rational ones. It is also something that scholars in international relations have often treated in a superficial and unsatisfactory fashion. Thinking of relations between states, they have sought to reduce power to resources, the sum of capabilities derived from territory, population, natural resources, industrial production, military might. The results of such calculations were always pathetic. When it came to contests of power, the small and weak sometimes defeated the large and strong. Speed, surprise, technical superiority, and flexibility won battles, as good generals and military historians always knew, and as effective chief executive officers also well understand.

It is preferable, therefore, to think of power in terms of outcomes. And outcomes may be determined by two kinds of power—relational power, in which one actor gets another to do what he (she, or they) wants, and structural power, in which one actor determines how the game is played, under what rules and conventions, or—even more effective—persuades others that his (her, or their) beliefs, ideologies, and value preferences are right and desirable and therefore should be adopted by all right-minded people. Those who have structural power are recognizable because they are able to affect the range of options within which others can choose what to do. It may seem that the others choose freely, but the risks and penalties of going outside that range of options are so punitive that they are not seriously considered.

Those two theoretical premisses seem to me to be necessary in order to give coherent answers to the question 'How does globalization affect the business of government, and the management of business?'

5. Globalization—Problems for Governments

By globalization the political economist means the coincidental effects of three major changes: the accelerated internationalization of production; the sharply increased mobility of capital; and the greater mobility of knowledge or information, from communication of messages to the transfer of technology. The internationalization of production can be gauged by the rising proportion of production (and of sales) of goods and services that is under the direction and control of enterprises outside the frontiers of the state.[1] The increased mobility of capital can be (roughly) gauged by the daily or annual turnover of foreign exchange transactions, and of credit instruments such as shares or bonds, in international financial markets. It has been a necessary condition for the striking increase in foreign investment flows between countries. And the mobility of information is reflected, though only partially, by the increased flow of communications—telephone traffic, chiefly—although there is no measure of messages passed by computers to other computers, nor of technologies developed in one place and applied in another.

Six major problems for governments result. They can be briefly described and explained.[2]

5.1. Counter-Cyclical Economic Management

Fifty years ago, most economists were convinced that governments had it in their power to correct the tendency of market economies to oscillate between boom and slump. By countervailing power, as J. K. Galbraith called it, and following Keynesian analysis and doctrine, demand in the economy could be checked when the economy became overheated, and stimulated when investment and consumption showed signs of flagging. Now, the government of the USA still has some means to counteract a slowdown in economic growth. Ronald Reagan did it in the early 1980s by a series of judicious tax cuts. In 1995 US export industries were boosted by the Administration's decision to allow a free fall for the dollar in the foreign exchange markets. But other governments, in Europe especially, have lost the power to manage the national economy. Mitterrand tried it in the early 1980s but had to abandon the attempt in face of capital flight and the loss of confidence in the franc in financial markets.

Naturally enough, few politicians, in office or out of it, are honest enough to admit their impotence, compared to past decades, to cut unemployment rates and to raise national rates of economic growth. Globalization and the integration of national economies in one world market economy means that Keynesian counter-cyclical intervention has to be global and systemic, collectively agreed, coordinated, and financed. But governments answerable to national electorates find that degree of cooperation beyond their power, as the record of the European Bank for Reconstruction and Development (EBRD) clearly shows.

5.2. **Financial Stability**

Globalization, or more particularly the mobility of capital, has made it harder for most governments to manage the national currency so as to provide firms with stable money. Money, that is, which keeps its value in terms of goods and services within the national economy, and which keeps its value in terms of exchange rates with other currencies. The Germans would doubtless protest that they have managed to keep the Deutschmark stable. But economists would note that the task has been made easier by the virtuous circle by which a strong mark means lower costs of imports, counterbalancing other inflationary forces and convincing the markets that capital is safer in Germany than elsewhere, so allowing the mark to strengthen once again. For France, the price of shadowing the mark by keeping the franc within the limits set by the exchange-rate mechanism (ERM) has been high and rising unemployment. And it is possible that, as the bill for German unification has to be paid, even the Bundesbank may find stable money hard to maintain.

5.3. **Financing State Budgets**

It is a fact that by the 1990s the governments of most rich countries were resorting to debt to supplement taxes as a means of financing their spending. From an international political economy perspective, it can be argued that they were tempted to do so by the readiness of financial markets, domestic and foreign, to accommodate them; and that they were obliged to do so by the immunity from tax conferred by globalization on many large enterprises. If corporate taxes could not be raised for fear of losing national competitiveness as a host country, and personal taxes, direct and indirect, were felt to be already up against a political ceiling of electoral resistance, borrowing was an easier option for most states than cutting spending. (Even for states who were spending much less than the USA on defence, the costs of maintaining the kind of welfare system expected by the voters were rising rather than falling.) The multinationals protest that they do not evade paying taxes, but their protests are often less than convincing. Not only are holding companies often located in tax havens where tax demands are minimal, but, when it comes to calculating tax liability to the various governments where their main productive operations take place, there is no such thing as a clear international tax regime. Negotiations between each corporate treasury and the two or more tax authorities concerned take place in private. The two hosts share an interest in exacting as much tax as possible, but at the same time are rivals, inhibited by rivalry from making demands so heavy that the company is frightened away (Picciotto 1992).

5.4. Industrial and Competition Policy

For governments, globalization has meant that what John Dunning calls macro-organizational policy has become more crucial to the welfare of most developed states than foreign or defence policy. In his terms, this includes first of all industrial policy—the way governments treat firms, domestic or foreign, that operate within their legal jurisdiction. An important aspect of industrial policy is making sure that there is enough competition within the national economy to keep the enterprises established there competitive in world markets. But in the world market economy it has proved impossible to reach agreement among governments on an international regime or set of rules preventing any form of discrimination against foreign firms, or ensuring there are no administrative barriers to entry for newcomers.

While the move to liberalization and privatization of protected state-owned monopolies shows that there are strong incentives for governments to favour competition, there are also strong incentives for private interests to resist. Economic history from the beginnings of capitalist development is full of examples of vested interests colluding amongst themselves to gain oligopolistic rents at the expense of consumers and of would-be competitors. One of the consequences of globalization is that such cartelizing behaviour is much more difficult for governments—and for political economists—to monitor or control. Either the cartel is tolerated because the consequences for trade of an unmanaged market are considered too costly, as in the case of shipping or diamonds or steel. Or the cartel has prudently relocated itself where the authorities, as in Switzerland, do not concern themselves with what goes on among the members. In yet other sectors—European airlines or Japanese banks and securities houses are two example—while one government (in both these cases, the US government) wants more competition, the others resist.

Closely related to this aspect of competition policy are issues of environmental protection, of state promotion of scientific and technical research and of public provision of an infrastructure congenial to trade and production of goods and services. Business looks not only for an adequate supply of water and electric power but for efficient, cheap, and fast transport and communication systems and a safe and clean environment. Not least, firms look for an educated and reliable labour force; illiterate, unskilled, unreliable workers can prove a false economy, however low the wages.

Two further aspects of macro-organizational policy affected by globalization of business are so important that they deserve separate consideration. One is the management of labour relations. The other is the prevention of crime and the maintenance of law and civil order.

5.5. Managing Labour Relations

Wherever political change over the past century has introduced some element of democratic control over government, the result has been that the state has intervened in the labour market to protect the interests of labour from the demands of management. First unions were made legal. Then the right to strike was secured in law. And in some countries—post-war Germany is the obvious example—the law guaranteed the representation of employees in corporate policy-making processes. In others, neo-corporatist mechanisms gave unions equal representation with management in collective responsibility for national economic decisions. All that has been changed—or is being changed—by globalization. The political responsibility for maintaining good labour relations and avoiding industrial strife has largely shifted out of the hands of government into corporate boardrooms. It is the managers who now have the delicate diplomatic task of reconciling the essentially opposed interests of their high-wage workers at home with their low-wage workers in developing or ex-socialist countries. This is a classic illustration of the point made at the beginning that politics is no longer to be seen as a domain exclusive to the politicians.

5.6. Crime Prevention

Maintaining law and order within the state and defending its territory and people from external attack have always been the chief justifications for the existence of the state. For most rich developed countries, the fear of invasion by their neighbours is dwindling, even if it is too early to be quite sure that major war between them really is obsolete. Maintaining law and order within the territorial state is another matter. It is not only legitimate productive enterprise that has shifted from its original national market economy to a world market economy. Organized crime has also gone global, exploiting the potential for great profit from an unregulated world market for drugs, and also increasingly for weapons, and even for illegal immigrants. In 1994 representatives of major governments met for the first time in Naples—appropriately enough—to discuss the common problems of controlling the mafias. The Italians and others were aware that the criminal organizations in Colombia, the USA, the former USSR, Japan, and China were combining to defeat the efforts of police to stop their criminal activities and to prevent the laundering of their profits. It was clear that the existing cooperative arrangements such as Interpol and Europol between national police forces lacked the transnational powers necessary to combat this new transnational threat to established law and order. This aspect of globalization has been discussed by academics and officials in recent sessions of the International Studies Association. It is an aspect of political and economic change that deserves more attention than it has so far been given in the business schools of the USA, Europe, and Japan.

6. Globalization—Problems for Business

Globalization for business means two kinds of problems. There are problems arising from increased competition in a larger market. And there are problems arising from the inadequacies or shortcomings of governments. The first kind will be seen by some as a problem, by others as an opportunity. Globalization in the communications business, for instance, opens up enormous opportunities for expansion and high profits for the major telecommunications firms. Globalization in financial services has already given unprecedented new opportunities to a broker like Merrill Lynch, which employs 44,000 people and operates in thirty-one countries. Since the mid-1970s its assets, profits, and revenues have shot up, and one-fifth of the latter now comes from outside the USA (*The Economist* 1995: 15). Of course, opportunity seldom comes without cost or without risk and American securities firms who dominate international financial markets have done so by taking on a good deal of their customers' risks.

Advising managers how to cope with the challenges of increased competition is the job of professors of international business. Political economists are more concerned with the other kind of problems such as those arising from the inadequacies of government. This is the other side of the coin of the six major policy areas listed above; here the authority and the effective power of states has been substantially weakened as a result of globalization.

Rather than go through them all, one by one, let us take the function of government which can most adversely affect business—money and finance. For this, we have to distinguish between the lack of stability in the international monetary system—specifically, exchange-rate volatility—and the lack of stability in the international financial system—the demand–supply relationship in markets for various forms of credit (loans, shares, bonds, certificates of deposit (CDs), securitized assets options, and hedges).

On the first, there is a wealth of literature concerning the necessary and sufficient conditions—they are significantly lacking—for a fixed-rate system, or even for the slightly flexible fixed rate 'Bretton Woods' system that worked briefly from 1958 to about 1968. Some of it wishfully but incorrectly idealizes that period—and that of the almost equally short-lived pre-1914 gold standard—as a paradise lost of monetary stability. This literature has surely contributed to the marked nostalgia in business circles for fixed exchange rates. This is shown by the almost universal support from European business leaders for a common European currency which would, it is often supposed, eliminate the ups and downs of currency values inside the European Union.[3]

What seems to be lacking in the economics literature, and which should perhaps be of greater concern in schools of business and management, is serious research based on actual corporate experience of the effects on company profits of instability in exchange rates. There is evidence, for instance, that British firms were handicapped in competition with German firms by the overvaluation of sterling at the beginning and end of the 1980s (Jenkins 1995).[4] It is not yet clear how seriously German firms, or Japanese firms, have been similarly handicapped by the overvaluation—in terms of purchasing power parity—of their currencies in 1995/6. Nor, so far as I know, is there much recent research to show in more detail how exchange-rate changes differentially affect, for example, the firm with a relatively large profit base in its local currency as compared with one more dependent on a variety of foreign markets. What is probable is that large, old, diversified MNEs such as ICI or Dupont are better able to manage this instability than small, new ones without corresponding financial reserves to fall back on.

Some of the same questions arise in connection with the instabilities in stock and bond markets and the international financial system generally. Is a firm like Morgan Stanley better or worse off in terms of economic risk exposure when 40 per cent of its revenues come from outside the USA instead of 25 per cent as in 1990 (*The Economist* 1995: 27)? More broadly, is the German model of capitalism, inhibiting mergers and acquisitions and having bank capital more firmly linked to corporate customers, inherently kinder to firms in a high-risk financial environment than what Albert (1991) calls the 'Anglo-Saxon' model of capitalism?

Problems for business of another kind result from the multiplication of political uncertainties that follows globalization of markets. Instead of uncertainty about what the home government is planning in policy areas relevant to business, corporate managers have to cope with similar uncertainties about the intentions of government in all the countries in which they operate. The trade in arms is a good example. National policies vary from the openly supportive, through the discriminatory ('Our potential enemies must not have them; our potential allies are welcome to have them'), to the prohibitive. What with anti-dumping measures, countervailing duties, and bilaterally negotiated voluntary export restrictions (VERs), international trade generally has become much more of a snakes-and-ladders game for business than it used to be in the 1960s. That seems a much more likely explanation than an ideological devotion to principles of free trade for the practically unanimous anxiety reflected by business associations when it looked as though the Uruguay Round of multilateral trade negotiations might end in disagreement. Such a hypothesis would be supported if business in all the developed countries were to decide that its interests would be served if it was to lobby hard in favour of the tougher rules on trade dispute settlement contained in the WTO agreement.

7. Globalization—Problems for People

From a political-economy perspective, the bottom line, the who-gets-what questions, should be asked not only about governments and business but also about people. How are individual men and women, families and children, affected by globalization? The social philosopher, Emma Rothschild has reminded us that the liberal ideas in politics and economics that emerged in eighteenth-century Europe and America were all about freedom and security for the individual man and woman, not freedom and security for the state. That perversion of the liberal idea came in only after the Napoleonic Wars, with the Congress of Vienna and the emergence of strong centralized states. She has argued that the 'new politics of the 1990s' is rediscovering a concern for the freedom of the individual and his or her security from the state and from the market (Rothschild 1995). That idea, certainly, is in accord with trends in IPE.

If, as this chapter began by suggesting, politics is a game that corporate executives as well as politicians play, there are many political and social issues affecting the life and death of people that globalization raises for which firms, no less than governments and other non-state sources of social authority, share responsibility. Many are fundamentally questions of ethics and morality, going far beyond the conventional boundaries of politics and economics. Such questions often result from technological innovations, As such, they are coming to be more readily recognized in business schools than they are in most departments of economics.

Of course, concern with ethical issues does not always lead to finding the answers. Too often, it reveals only that there are no easy general answers, either for governments or for firms. Both need to decide whether there are any absolute rules or principles of moral conduct that must be observed at all times, whether or not they are politically convenient or economically profitable. That is—and always has been—a difficult question. Both also have to decide where their loyalties lie. To whom do they have a prior moral responsibility? For the firms, there are often conflicts of interest between the shareholders and other creditors, and between both and the suppliers, distributors, and employees. Which has the better claim to corporate protection against the forces of globalization?

These forces, moreover, are creating new moral and social dilemmas for management. To raise just one specific issue, what about the wives and children of jetsetting salesmen and managers? Globalization of the business means that managers—predominantly men—have to spend more time away from home. Families—wives especially—have to cope without their support for much longer than just the working day, or week. Though I am not greatly in sympathy with some of the rhetoric of the sort of gender studies currently fashionable among militant feminists, especially in the USA, its protagonists do have a point that capitalist development has been predominantly male-dominated, and that the interests of women have often taken second place. But times are changing. The retail businesses that have traditionally employed women may have things to teach manufacturing firms, not only about equal opportunity but about more flexible systems of working. And the example of universities may be worth looking at too. Here there is already a more truly global labour market, and young academics tend, more perhaps than young managers, to marry fellow graduate students. Increasingly, employers are being asked to make two-person job offers. But if this is considered impractical, what other solutions can firms suggest?

Of the many other social and essentially moral issues raised for ordinary people by globalization, I would mention only two that seem to me deserving of further discussion. One is consumer protection. The transnational firm is often caught between two contending ideas. The governments of developed states under political pressures hold that the state must protect the consumer with product safety rules, applied in law and if necessary by the courts. This necessarily imposes costs on firms—costs which are passed on to consumers. Meanwhile the governments of developing countries have the interests of poorer people to consider. They want cheaper goods, more than safer ones. Take medicines as an example. Standard rules on pharmaceuticals mean higher prices. In a world market where the poor customers certainly outnumber the rich ones, whose side should the firms be on?

The other issue for firms and for governments concerns pensions and provision for old age. At present, the expectation in the developed countries is that retirement should not mean a drop in living standards. Whether provided by the state or by the company, the insurance costs necessary to provide such pensions are heavy. In countries like Japan, where the transition from a population profile typical of early industrialization to one of mature industrialization has been exceptionally rapid, the burden of paying for such pensions on working-age groups is likely to be very heavy; a falling birth rate plus a falling death rate adds to the demographic disproportion between the generations. How do firms cope? Do they have two pension policies for their employees, one in the old, and another in the young industrialized countries? Do they let the employees choose? Or do they give way to pressure on the firm to provide subsidized pension plans for all, or just for senior managers? This is just one among many examples of the new complexities facing managers as well as politicians under the pressures of globalization.

Politicians, however, do not have to be told that there are no simple rule-of-thumb principles to guide them, or that the best is often the enemy of the good and compromise is therefore unavoidable for those with the responsibility of being in authority. For managers, such home truths may be less easy to accept. The pseudo-rationalism inseparable from neoclassical economics has dominated much teaching of management in business schools. The time has perhaps come to recognize the contribution of political economy to an understanding of globalization and its consequences, and to acknowledge that there is no general theory to guide corporate strategy at every turn of the market, in every culture, and in every kind of business. There are no infallible, universal panaceas to ensure the success or even the survival of the enterprise. And the latest fad will be no certain remedy for bad or complacent leadership in business—any more than it is in government.

NOTES

1. FDI, often used as a measure of international production, actually underestimates the role of the MNE. The statistics do not reflect joint ventures in which the foreign partner, armed with advanced technology and established access to foreign markets, makes only a small financial investment. Nor do they do justice to the growing importance in the globalization process of licensing arrangements, franchising, or contracting in

which the foreign licensor, franchisor, or contractor may make no financial transfer at all but still maintains control of the resources and the enterprise.

2. It would not be difficult to find more than six problems for governments. But for reasons of space it seems more useful to identify just those that are most important for governments and for the societies to whom, sooner or later, governments are accountable.
3. Paradoxically, there is almost as much general support for European monetary union from European labour unions, even though it is by no means clear that this would help workers to get and keep jobs or to maintain their incomes (Verdun 1995).
4. An earlier study of the British North American Council (BNAC) by Blin and others had argued that large firms, at least, were able to manage exchange-rate instability. Jenkins argues that, on the contrary, even large firms lack both the information and the organizational structure to cope with these risks. Trading in futures and derivatives is of only limited, short-term value.

REFERENCES

Albert, M. (1991), *Capitalisme contre Capitalisme* (Paris: Le Seuil).

The Economist (1995), 'Wall Street Survey' (15 April).

Jenkins, R. (1995), 'Corporate Management of Exchange Rate Misalignment: The Experience of UK Firms 1979–1982 and 1987–1992' (unpublished doctoral thesis, University of London).

Murphy, C., and Tooze, R. (1991) (eds.), *The New International Political Economy* (Boulder, Colo.: Lynne Riener).

Nau, H. (1990), *The Myth of America's Decline* (New York: Oxford University Press).

Nye, J. (1990), *Bound to Lead: The Changing Nature of American Power* (New York: Basic Books).

Picciotto, S. (1992), *International Business Taxation* (London: Quorum Books).

Rothschild, E. (1995), 'What is Security?' in *The Quest for World Order*, special issue of *Daedalus*, journal of the American Academy of Arts and Sciences, 124/3: 53–98.

Stopford, J. M., and Strange, S. (1991), *Rival States, Rival Firms: Competitions for World Market Shares* (Cambridge: Cambridge University Press).

Strange, S. (1982), 'Still an Extraordinary Power: America's Role in a Global Monetary System', in R. Lombra and W. Witte (eds.), *Political Economy of International and Domestic Monetary Relations* (Ames, Ia.: Iowa University Press).

—— (1995), 'The Defective State', in *What Future for the State?*, special issue of *Daedalus*, journal of the American Academy of Arts and Sciences, 124/2: 55–74.

—— (1996), *The Retreat of the State: Power Diffused in the World Economy* (Cambridge: Cambridge University Press).

Verdun, A. (1995), 'Europe's Struggle with the Global Political Economy: A Study of how EMU is Perceived' (Ph.D. thesis, Florence: European University Institute).

5

The Architecture of Globalization: *State Sovereignty in a Networked Global Economy*

Stephen J. Kobrin

1. **Introduction**

> Geographical space as a source of explanation affects all historical realities, all spatially defined phenomena; states, societies, cultures and economies.
>
> (Braudel 1986: 20)

In 1904 H. J. Mackinder—delivering what was to become a very well-known paper—told the Royal Geographic Society that the Columbian epoch was drawing to a close and the political system would henceforth be worldwide in scope. Mackinder spoke as the first global economy (Krugman 1992) was approaching its zenith—the period from 1870 to 1914 which has been called 'the high water mark' of an open, integrated international economy and the 'golden age' of international economic integration (UNCTAD 1993).[1]

Pre-1914 levels of international trade and investment—both relatively and absolutely—were striking; world trade grew by almost 50 per cent per decade from the mid-nineteenth to early twentieth century and international capital investments by 64 per cent per decade during the forty years before the First World War. By most measures, the degree of internationalization of the first global economy compares favourably with that of the current or second. To cite one relative comparison, at their late twentieth-century peak Japan's capital exports (relative to GDP) were only about half of Great Britain's at the turn of the century (Wolf 1995: 22).[2]

As the twentieth century draws to a close, there is general agreement that major changes in the scope and organization of international economic activities are taking place, but there is considerable disagreement over their interpretation (Dicken 1994). Some argue that the interrelated economic and technological developments which are emerging as critical components of *globalization* will result in deep structural adjustments, perhaps leading to one of the major periods of change of this millennium (Lipsey and Bekar 1995). The French author and politician Jean-Marie Guehenno (1995), for example, links emerging global networks with the death of nation states and the state structure.

Others claim that all that has ended is what Eric Hobsbawm (1994) calls the 'age of extremes', the economic dislocations and mass destruction—real or threatened—which have characterized the 'short' twentieth century from 1914 to the end of the Cold War in 1991. Martin Wolf (1995) believes that what has died is not the state, but the delusion of its omnipotence which existed from the 1950s through the 1990s. One implication of this line of argument is that with the end of the 'age of extremes' we are now able to return to the open, international world economy of the early twentieth century; that what appears to be dramatic change is actually a return to normalcy.

Thus, Milton Freedman (1989) claims that the world is less internationalized today than it was in 1913 or 1929 and the Vice-Chairman of the Federal Reserve has observed that 'a great deal of what we have been witnessing since 1950 is simply getting the world back to the level of integration that had been achieved in 1914' (Bradsher 1995). The underlying issue, however, is not whether the level or rate of growth of trade and investment or interdependence are greater in 1995 than they were in 1895. It is whether a qualitative structural change is taking place and that cannot be demonstrated by quantitative arguments involving cross-temporal comparisons of economic data (Michalet 1994).

There is no question that the late-twentieth-century world economy differs significantly from that of a century ago in many respects. First, it is *broader* in terms of the number of national markets encompassed (albeit to varying degrees) as constituent units. Secondly, it is *deeper* in terms of the density and velocity of interaction, of flows of trade and investment, than it was prior to 1914.

Thirdly, and perhaps most important, the dominant mode of organization of international economic transactions has changed significantly since Mackinder's time: from the market (trade and portfolio investment) to hierarchy or the internationalization of production through the MNE.[3] By the early 1990s, 37,000 transnational corporations with worldwide sales of about $US5.5 trillion controlled about one-third of the world's private-sector productive assets and the UN Programme on Transnationals could conclude that 'international production has become a central structural characteristic of the world economy' (UNCTAD 1993: 101).[4]

The critical question is whether *globalization* defines a change in degree or in kind—an extension of the modern international world economy into somewhat unfamiliar territory or a systemic transformation which entails both changes in quantity (breadth and depth) and quality, defining new structures and new modes of functioning.

Put differently, is a *global* world economy merely 'more' international or does the word imply a deep change in political-economic structure? If the distinction is to have meaning, it is important to be precise about definitions. *International* is a relatively new word dating from the late eighteenth century,[5] a modern concept which was not relevant before the emergence of territorially defined nation states and national markets. An international economy *links* discrete, mutually exclusive, geographic national markets through cross-border flows of trade and investment.

'The world-wide international economy is one in which the principal entities are nation states, and involves the process of the growing interconnection between national economies . . . [it] is an aggregate of nationally-located functions' (Hirst and Thompson 1992: 358–60). An international economy is unambiguously *modern*; it involves relations between sovereign units of the post-Westphalian state system and hierarchically structured, often vertically integrated, discrete economic actors. It is profoundly *geographic* in that borders of states and markets are of the essence. The internationalization of production discussed above is not necessarily inconsistent with this framework: MNEs are seen by many observers as national firms with a clear centre or home country which engage in international operations.

In this chapter I shall argue that *globalization* does have substantive meaning, that we are in the midst of a qualitative transformation of the international world economy. My argument is based on three related propositions. First, dramatic increases in the scale of technology in many industries—in its cost, risk, and complexity—have rendered even the largest national markets too small to be meaningful economic units; they are no longer the 'principal entities' of the world economy. National markets are *fused* transnationally rather than linked across borders.

Secondly, the recent explosion of transnational strategic alliances is a manifestation of a fundamental change in the mode of organization of international economic transactions from markets and/or hierarchies (i.e. trade and MNEs) to *postmodern* global networks. Last, and related to the second point, the emerging global economy is integrated through information systems and information technology rather than hierarchical organizational structures.

My primary interest in this chapter is the impact of globalization of the world economy—defined in terms of scale, mode of organization, and means of integration—on states and the states system. I assert that globalization compromises the basic symmetry of political and economic organization, of nation states and national markets, characteristic of the present century.

A asymmetry of geographic scope is emerging as economic units (markets) expand in space well beyond the limits of political units (national territories). More important is the emerging asymmetry in mode of organization as politics remains geographically grounded in the modern territorially based sovereign state system while major sectors of the world economy are organized in terms of postmodern electronic networks. Geographic space is losing meaning as a basis for the organization of markets.

The next section of this chapter deals with the three components of globalization in some considerable detail: the scale of technology; networks as a mode of economic organization; and information technology as a means of international integration (the last two are difficult to separate analytically). I then turn to a summary of the emerging networked global economy and explore its implications for states and the state system. The chapter concludes with some thoughts about likely futures.

2. Globalization

2.1. Scale of Technology

An international world economy is constructed through the mutual interconnection or cross-border integration of national economic spaces. It is one step in an evolutionary process of the expansion of integrated markets in geographic space: from local to national to regional to international (UNCTAD 1994). That raises a pertinent but little considered question: why should markets spread geographically beyond a local area or region?

The simplest explanation, and the oldest, is that the supply of some goods is found in one locale and their demand in another: for example, precious metals, spices, and petroleum. The geographic expansion of markets also allows for a more productive division of labour: gains from specialization, exploitation of differences in resource endowments, and the adaptation of skills.[6] Last, spreading fixed capital costs over a larger market area can reduce unit costs and produce gains from scale.[7] With the exception of resource-seeking industries such as petroleum, the spatial expansion of markets has been efficiency driven, exploiting gains from specialization, factor cost differences, and scale.

This chapter is concerned with transnationally integrated industries where internationalization is driven by scale rather than specialization; where a process Kenichi Ohmae (1990) characterizes as a dramatic shift from a variable to a fixed-cost environment has occurred. He notes that, in a number of critical industries, the scale of production and/or technology has increased to the point where fixed costs must be amortized over a larger market base than is available in even the largest national markets. The result is 'globalization'.

In the mid-1990s, it is the cost and risk of technology rather than the need for larger production runs that are the primary motivation for the transnational integration of markets. In many strategic industries international markets are required fully to amortize the enormous R&D expenses associated with rapidly evolving process and product technology. There are only a few sectors (e.g. the automotive industry and construction equipment) in which the fixed costs of manufacture are the motivation for international market integration, and even there developments such as computer-aided design/manufacture and flexible production are reducing rapidly the number of units needed fully to exploit scale economies.

While the point is difficult to 'prove', F. M. Scherer (1974) has concluded that in only a very small minority of industries is concentration approaching oligopoly at the *national level* justified by production-scale economies in the US market.[8] In a previous study (Kobrin 1991), I found that technological intensity was the primary determinant of the transnational integration of US firms and that proxies for manufacturing scale were not significant.[9]

On the other hand, there is no question that the cost, risk, and pace of technological development have increased significantly since the 1950s.[10] For example, *constant dollar* research and development expenditures for US industry increased almost five and one-half fold between 1953 and 1990; they increased 150 per cent between 1980 and 1990 alone. R&D spending as a percentage of sales for US industry doubled in the sixteen years between 1976 and 1992: from 1.9 to 3.8 per cent (Jankowski 1992; *Business Week* 1994*a*).

As the extent of a company's R&D effort is mandated by the nature of its technology and competition rather than its size, this rapid growth of spending requires a corresponding expansion of sales—and ultimately, internationalization—if profitability is to be maintained.[11] At this point it appears that even the global integration of markets by a single firm may no longer be sufficient to offset the huge costs and risks of technological development in a number of *strategic* industries. The last decade has seen an exponential increase in the number of technology-driven collaborative agreements or strategic alliances among leading multinationals from the major industrial countries.

2.2. Strategic Alliances

Strategic alliances are central to my argument for two reasons. First, in many instances they are an indicator that the *scale* of technology—the cost, risk, and complexity of R&D—has grown to the point where it is beyond the reach of even the largest and most global firms. Secondly, alliances are a manifestation of the substitution of a cooperative global network for trade and investment by a single firm; they represent a change in the *mode* of organization of international economic transactions.

Although comprehensive data on alliances do not exist, virtually every attempt at data-gathering reveals their dramatic growth over the last decade; one study estimated a 31 per cent compound annual growth rate for the number of high-technology alliances over the 1980s.[12] The vast majority of alliances are triad-based; most studies find that over 90 per cent of all agreements are between firms from North America, Europe, and Japan (US Congress 1994). Alliances also tend to be concentrated in a limited number of industries: typically automobiles and high-technology sectors such as pharmaceuticals, biotechnology, aerospace, information technology, and new materials (US Congress 1994).

The motivations for strategic alliances are complex and varied (Mytelka 1991). One is clearly market access: the need to compete in all major markets, or at least in all the legs of the triad, simultaneously. A second reflects the continued importance of national boundaries: government preferences for 'local' firms in industries such as aerospace where an alliance with a national or regional firm may be a necessary requisite of sales to either the military or a national airline. Thirdly, one can never dismiss an interest in making competition less onerous as a motive for collaboration.[13]

The most important motivation for alliance formation, however, is the increasing cost, risk, and complexity of technology.[14] Even the world's largest and most international firms can no longer 'bet the company' on the next generation of semiconductors or jumbo jets; in many industries the cost of a competitive R&D budget has risen to the point where it is no longer possible to 'go it alone'. An example is provided by the alliance between IBM, Siemens, and Toshiba to develop a 256 megabyte chip motivated by the need to share an estimated $US1 billion in development costs and the large associated risks (UNCTAD 1993).

Perhaps more important, technologies have become so complex and rapidly changing that even industry leaders cannot master them internally. An analysis of over 4,000 strategic alliances where innovation or an exchange of technology represented at least part of the agreement concluded that 'cooperation has to be understood in the light of attempts made by companies to cope with the complexity and the interrelatedness of different fields of technology and their efforts to gain time and reduce uncertainty in joint undertakings during a period of technological uncertainty. Other motives appear to play a very limited role' (Hagedoorn 1993: 378).

In summary, the evidence strongly suggests that the minimum size of markets needed to support technological development in industries such as aerospace, semiconductors, and pharmaceuticals is now larger than the largest national markets. In the emerging global economy international integration is a requisite of a competitive R&D budget; national markets are *fused* transnationally rather than linked through cross-border transactions.

Furthermore, in some industries single firm globalization no longer appears sufficient as even the largest multinationals must cooperate to deal with the cost, risk, and complexity of technology.[15] The motive for transnational collaboration is a combination of scale (in terms of cost and risk) *and* inter-firm specialization. Alliances represent a transformation of the mode of organization of international economic transactions from hierarchically structured MNEs to networks. It is to that subject that I now turn.

2.3. Network Forms of Organization

The fundamental issue addressed by institutional economics is the governance of economic transactions. Strategic alliances represent a networked mode of organization of international economic transactions which can be distinguished from both trade (markets) and multinational firms (hierarchies). One central question, which is pertinent here, is whether 'markets, hierarchies and networks are discrete organizational alternatives employing distinctive control mechanisms or plural forms on a continuum employing, price, authority and trust simultaneously' (Jones and Hesterly 1993: 3).[16]

Oliver Williamson (1991: 280) includes hybrids or *networks*—'various forms of long-term contracting, reciprocal trading, regulation, franchising and the like' —with *markets* and *hierarchies* as generic forms of economic organization. He locates hybrids on a continuum between markets and hierarchies, the polar modes of economic organization. Similarly, Wayne Baker (1990) argues that most real organizational forms fall between market and hierarchy and suggests that they are an intermediate or hybrid form of interface.

In a very influential article, however, Walter Powell (1990) argues against portraying economic exchange as a continuum with markets and hierarchies at the poles and hybrids in between. Network forms of organization—typified by reciprocal patterns of communication and exchange—represent a *distinctive* mode of coordinating economic activity and economic organization.[17]

Similarly, an OECD (1992: 78) report concludes that networks are a distinctive form of economic organization and the 'notion of the continuum fails to capture the complex realities of know-how trading and knowledge exchange in innovation. Networks . . . represent a type of arrangement with its own specific distinctive features which henceforth must be considered in *its own right*' (emphasis in original).

If networks are significantly different from both markets and hierarchies, trade, multinational firms, and alliances represent distinct modes of organization of international economic transactions. Trade involves production by national firms in national markets linked by 'arm's-length' spot exchanges, typically of raw materials, commodities, and finished goods. MNEs internalize production: the firm's administrative hierarchy becomes the primary mode of organization of the international economy. In the integrated international firm, the exchange of intermediate goods through intra-industry and intra-firm trade becomes increasingly important.

International strategic alliances signal the replacement of integrated transnational hierarchies by global networks, by a cooperative and reciprocal organization of economic transactions. The basic unit and venue of production become ambiguous; indeed there is a real question about the appropriateness of these terms. As will be discussed more extensively below, the most important flows across transnational networks are intangible: knowledge and information.

Although the periods overlap and are approximate, trade was the primary mode of integration of the international economy from the late nineteenth century through the first two post-Second World War decades and the internationalization of production through MNEs from the mid-1960s until the mid-1980s. Alliances or networked integration emerged in the late 1980s as a significant mode of integration. Two caveats are important. First, I am not proposing a 'stage theory' of international integration, but rather am concerned with changes in the dominant mode over time. Secondly, reality is complex and messy and there are large sectors of every economy where production has remained entirely national and 'networks' are confined to television and job-seekers.

2.4. The Means of Integration

Firms internalize or coordinate economic activity administratively because it is more efficient than relying on markets, given transaction costs and/or market imperfections. Thomas Malone and John Rockart (1993) argue that the electronics and information revolution has resulted in a turnabout, making extra-firm coordination cheaper and more efficient once again. Electronic information technology facilitates the integration of geographically dispersed operations and allows networked coordination to replace ownership and hierarchy as a primary mode of control (Dicken 1994). One result is the emergence of flexible networks replacing production by a single large firm. Hierarchical, vertically integrated transnational firms have 'fragmented' into 'diverse' networks reintegrated through information technology (Parker 1992: 9).

There is widespread agreement that electronic information systems are critical to alliances. Albert Bressand, Catherine Distler, and Kalypso Nicolaidis (1989), for example, argue that electronic networks play a central role in wealth creation as production and transactions merge into complex, information-intensive processes; networks are a manifestation of the blurring of the boundary between the factory and the market place. Clarence Brown (1988) makes a similar point: as intra-firm integration increasingly depends on electronic information technologies, modern manufacturing enterprises are coming to have a great deal in common with information service firms. He notes that this applies to inter-firm links—to subcontractors and customers—and that these linkages are rapidly becoming global in scope.

It is directly relevant that in 1995 *Fortune* combined the Industrial and Service 500, arguing that the new economy has virtually obliterated the distinction between industrial and service business. They note the digital revolution has 'dematerialized' manufacturing, citing one source claiming that three-quarters of the value added in manufacturing is now information (Stewart 1995). All firms, regardless of sector, are becoming information processors.

Networks, and especially transnational networks, are creatures of the information age: postmodern organizations held together by information technology (Clegg 1990). Computers, facsimile machines, high-resolution monitors, and modems have been called the 'threads' of the global web (Reich 1991), of the emerging electronically networked world economy.

2.5. A Networked World Economy

In this chapter I argue that a global economy differs in kind from the international economy which preceded it in two critical and inter-related respects. First, in many industries the scale of technology has driven the limits of markets well beyond those of national borders. Secondly, in many of these same industries electronically integrated networks are replacing hierarchies as the most important mode of organization of international economic transactions.

In the nineteenth century, all production took place in discrete national markets which were linked through cross-border trade and portfolio investment. Although levels of interdependence were high and policy autonomy constrained, there is no question that the national market was the basic unit in the international system.

As noted above, the very use of the term *international* implies the existence of discrete and meaningful national economic (and political) units.

In contrast, in the late twentieth century national markets are losing meaning as discrete units of the world economy: the scale of technology is *fusing* them into a larger whole. Thus Dicken (1994: 106 n.1) contrasts the international or cross-boundary economy with globalization which implies 'a degree of purpositive functional integration among geographically dispersed activities'. Hirst and Thompson (1992) depict national economies being subsumed and rearticulated into the global system, and argue that the international economy is becoming autonimized.

National borders are not irrelevant. Nation states have differing interests and objectives and attempt to enforce their will on firms and other governments; national boundaries still 'create significant differentials on the global economic surface' (Dicken 1992: 149). The critical point, however, is that globalization implies that the national economy is no longer the unit of economic accounting or the frame of reference for economic strategies (Castells 1993).[18]

In a sense, the fusion of national markets represents a return to an earlier stage in the evolution of the capitalist world economy. Hobsbawm (1979: 135) argues that, in contrast to the past 300 years when production was local and the world economy was based on territorially defined national economies, the current phase of development is marked by the re-emergence of transnational elements. 'The national economy is no longer the building block of the world economy, but has a rival in the immediately global market which can be supplied directly by firms capable of organizing their production and distribution in principle without reference to state boundaries.'

Increasingly, network metaphors are used to describe the emerging world economy: a shift from standardized mass production to flexible production, from vertically integrated, large-scale organizations to disaggregation of the value chain and horizontally networked economic units (Michalet 1991; Castells 1993; *The Economist* 1993; UNCTAD 1993). In Dunning's (1994) terms, hierarchical enterprises are being replaced by alliance capitalism.[19]

The emergence of networks as a basic mode of organization of international economic transactions may be of more profound importance than increases in the scale of technology. It is important to conceive of a networked world economy in terms of a complex web of transactions rather than a series of dyadic or triadic cooperative arrangements between firms. A large multinational firm may well be involved in tens if not hundreds of alliances linking various parts of its organization with others. Dicken (1994) characterizes these webs as multilateral rather than bilateral and polygamous rather than monogamous.

The modern international economic system of cross-border linkages between discrete national markets is being replaced by a global, postmodern, networked mode of organization where the very concept of geographically based economic activity may not even be relevant. It is to the impact of globalization on states and the inter-state system that we now turn.

3. The Impact on States and the State System

Robert Keohane (1993) observes that sovereignty is typically discussed rather than defined. Formal sovereignty is a legal concept implying supremacy within a territory and independence of outside authorities in the exercise of state authority. In contrast, autonomy and effectiveness are political constructs; the former implies that a state can and does make its own decisions with regard to internal and external issues and the latter is a measure of the extent to which its purposes are achieved.

Internal sovereignty entails legitimization of the state *vis-à-vis* competing domestic claimants. It conceptualizes the state in the Weberian sense as having an effective monopoly of force over a territory and population, the 'undisputed right to determine the framework of rules, regulations and policies within a given territory and to govern accordingly' (Held and McGrew 1993: 265).

External sovereignty involves the basic principles on which the modern interstate order is based—the division of the political order into fixed, territitorially defined, and mutually exclusive enclaves (Ruggie 1993) and mutual recognition that each state represents a specific society within an exclusive domain (Barkin and Cronin 1994).[20] In fact, Hendrik Spruyt (1994) argues that a primary explanation for the spread of sovereign territorial institutions was that respective jurisdictions, and thus limits to authority, could be specified precisely through agreement on fixed borders.

In examining the impact of globalization on states and the state system one must separate analytically constraints imposed on autonomy or effectiveness, from affects on formal sovereignty. Two sets of questions need to be asked. First, are the constraints that globalization imposes on state autonomy qualitatively different from those resulting from the interdependence associated with an international or cross-border world economy? If so, at what point do constraints on state autonomy compromise formal internal sovereignty? Secondly, will the emergence of an electronically networked global economy compromise external sovereignty—the idea of territoriality itself as a mode of economic, and possibly political organization? I believe the second question to be, by far, the more important.

3.1. Globalization and Autonomy

State autonomy has never been absolute and decision-making power has always been constrained by international economic transactions; the trade-off between the efficiency gains from cross-border economic activity and lost autonomy is far from new. The problem facing governments is 'how to benefit from international exchange while maintaining as much autonomy as possible' (Keohane and Nye 1989: 248).

What is new this time around? Even if one grants that flows of trade and investment are greater in both absolute and relative terms in 1995 than in 1895 and there is 'more' interdependence (however measured), that is still only a quantitative difference. Why should globalization have a qualitatively different impact on state autonomy?

One answer is the nature of interdependence in a global world economy. First, the scale of technology in many strategic industries presents states with a discrete decision rather than a marginal trade-off: participate in the world economy or forgo technological development. In strategic industries where markets are fused transnationally, autonomy or independence is severely constrained. Secondly, the spread of networks as a mode of organization of economic transactions renders borders problematic as economic constructs.

Participation in an international economy presents states with a trade-off between efficiency and a loss of autonomy, and in many instances governments have chosen to preserve the latter. Without judging their economic merit, in opting for import substitution policies such as forcing local production of automobiles, policy-makers were willing to trade off higher local costs for automobiles (reduced efficiency) for the promise of a more developed industrial capability and increased future autonomy.

That option is not available in industries such as telecommunications, pharmaceuticals, semiconductors, and aerospace, where even the largest national markets are too small to support the R&D efforts needed to remain competitive. If transnational markets are an absolute requisite of continued technological innovation, governments face a discrete zero-one decision rather than a continuous, marginal trade-off. Accepting higher costs (e.g. lower efficiency) for some degree of autonomy is not a realistic possibility; mutual dependence is inevitable and breaking its bonds implies a degree of withdrawal that few states could tolerate. The choice is to compete transnationally or forgo the next generation of microprocessors, pharmaceuticals, or telecommunications technology entirely.

At a minimum, states must allow their firms to participate in global markets. While in theory governments could participate in the global economy while closing their borders to participation by others, that option is not viable in practice. At least in these strategic industries, independence or autonomy is a very limited option.

At this point in many high-technology industries, participating in the global economy implies participating through alliances and cooperative efforts. As Zacher (1992: 60) notes, '[states] are becoming increasingly *enmeshed* in a network of interdependencies and regulatory and/or collaborative arrangements from which exit is generally not a feasible option' (emphasis in original).

In an electronically networked global economy the borders of national markets, and thus the distinction between the domestic and international economy (or domestic and international policy), become problematic. In *Being Digital*, Nicholas Negroponte (1995) makes a nice distinction between trade in *atoms* and trade in *bits*. Atoms take the form of tangible material which must cross borders physically and can be controlled by political authorities. Bits, on the other hand, are transmitted electronically, typically by satellite, which renders the borders of national markets virtually meaningless.

If software is imported in the form of disks and manuals, it is subject to border controls, tariffs, and the like. However, if it is transmitted digitally—downloaded from the Internet, for example—any sort of control becomes problematic and autonomy is directly constrained.

State autonomy or independent decision-making power is clearly compromised by the fusion of markets and the emergence of an electronically networked global economy. Indeed, in the strategic industries of concern here national markets have lost meaning as economic constructs. They are too small to support competitive technological development efforts and territorial borders are no longer clear lines of separation between the domestic and international economies.

The question remains, however, at what point do constraints on state autonomy affect formal sovereignty? Geoffrey Goodwin (1974: 101) asks 'whether the capacity of states to order their own internal affairs and to conduct their own external policies has been so undermined or eroded as to make the concept of state sovereignty increasingly irrelevant in practice despite its persistence in legal and diplomatic convention'. Although this question is not immediately answerable, it is, none the less, critically important.

4.2. **External Sovereignty**

Although all forms of political organization *occupy* geographic space, all are not *territorial*: systems of rule 'predicated on and defined by fixed territorial parameters' (Spruyt 1994: 35). The distinguishing characteristic of the modern state is that it is territorial, and that of the modern state system is that it organizes geographic space. As James Anderson (1986: 117) notes: 'Modern states . . . are all territorial in that they explicitly claim, and are based on, particular geographic territories, as distinct from merely occupying geographic space which is true of all social organizations . . . territory is typically continuous and totally enclosed by a clearly demarcated and defended boundary.'[21]

What makes the modern state system historically unique is this 'differentiation' into 'territorially defined, fixed and mutually exclusive enclaves of legitimate dominion' (Ruggie 1993: 151). Joseph Camilleri and Jim Falk (1992: 238) argue that the first function of the sovereign state was the organization of space and that the spatial qualities of the state are 'integral to the notion of sovereignty and international relations theory.'[22]

The modern construction of economics is also inherently territorial; the idea of both a market and the international economy are geographic constructs. In his *Principles* Alfred Marshall (1961: 270) quotes Cournot to define a market spatially as 'not any particular market place in which things are bought and sold, but the whole of any region in which buyers and sellers are in such free intercourse with one another that the prices of the same goods tend to equality easily and quickly'. Economic integration is the extension of markets in geographic space (Cooper 1986).

National markets were created by political authorities to *territorialize* economic activity.[23] In general, regional markets—the EU is the best example—are motivated by the need to expand the geographic bounds of national markets to increase efficiency in terms of specialization and/or scale. An international economy, then, is comprised of national or regional economic spaces linked through economic transactions. In part, globalization involves 'deepening' or closer integration across national, regional, and global geographic spaces (UNCTAD 1994: 118).

An argument has been made that, regardless of how international the world economy becomes, at the end of the day all economic activity takes place within national boundaries (UNCTAD 1994: 119). The implication is that even the most integrated MNE does not alter the basic geographic structure of the world economy; any given step in the production process or any given economic transaction can be located precisely in geographic space and thus assigned unambiguously to a specific national territorial jurisdiction and national market. While that argument may hold for a modern international economy, it is not necessarily valid in a postmodern, electronically networked global economy.

The geographic definition of markets is created rather than inherent; to some extent it is a result of the path of development of the modern political-economic system. There is nothing in the nature of markets that demands that they be defined spatially. Many of the emerging global networks construct markets in electronic rather than geographic space. The international financial system provides both the best current example and a metaphor for the future.

The world financial market is not comprised of linked national markets; in fact, it is not comprised of geographic locations at all. It is a network integrated through electronic information systems—hundreds of thousands of electronic monitors in trading rooms all over the world linked together through satellites (Wriston 1992). It is a system which is no longer nationally centred, 'in which national markets, physically separate, function as if they were all in the same place'. Global financial integration has been described as 'the end of geography' (Stopford and Strange 1991: 40; O'Brien 1992).

If a trader in New York presses a key on her computer and buys German Marks in London, where did the transaction take place? Chase Manhattan Corporation has built a centre to process transactions worth trillions of dollars each year in Bournemouth England linked by satellite to its offices in New York, Hong Kong, Luxembourg, and Tokyo. Would anyone argue that all of these 'transactions' can be located in the UK (*Business Week* 1994*b*: 52, 53)?

Another example of a postmodern global network is provided by the Indian software industry which has evolved from sending Indian programmers abroad to work at a client's site (known as 'body-shopping') to satellite linkages through which programmers physically situated in India work directly on the client's host computer, wherever in the world it is located (Pandit 1995). If an Indian programmer located in Bangalore edits a program on a computer in New York, there is no question that economic value has been created. Did the transaction take place in India or the USA? Which jurisdiction gets to tax it or control it?

Do the concepts of geographic space apply to cyberspace? What do jurisdictions and boundaries mean when markets take the form of information systems? One can question whether all economic activity takes place within national boundaries or even whether economic activity can occur in more than one place at the same time. At the end of the day, the real question is whether the spatial concepts of borders, territory, and jurisdiction apply to electronically organized global networks.

The information revolution—the linking of telecommunications and computers—makes the very idea of a market as a geographic construct obsolete; they have become global networks rather than places (Nye 1990). Ruggie (1993: 172) suggests that a non-territorial region is emerging in the world economy, 'a decentered yet integrated space-of-flows . . . which exists along side the spaces-of-places that we call national economies'. He goes on to note that in this non-territorial region the distinctions between internal and external become problematic.[24]

In summary, the very idea of a national market as an economic (or political) construct appears to have lost meaning in the postmodern world economy. Given the emergence of electronic global networks, neither territoriality nor mutually exclusive geographic organization retains relevance. The result has been to strip markets of both geographic and political meaning; to raise questions about the meaning of sovereignty in its external sense of a system ordered in terms of mutually exclusive territoriality.

Sovereignty and modernity cannot be separated. Both entail the unambiguous and mutually exclusive ordering of space; both are profoundly geographic. Camilleri and Falk (1992: 11) go so far as to claim that 'Sovereignty, both as an idea and an institution, lies at the heart of the modern and therefore Western experience of space and time'.[25]

Both Gianfranco Poggi (1990) and Friedrich Kratochwil (1986) note a crisis of territoriality. The latter observes that the fact that political systems are territorial and boundary-maintaining and economic systems are not affects the very core of the state as a political entity. It is to that asymmetry that we now turn.

5. The Changing Domains of Political and Economic Geography

During most of the twentieth century there has been a rough symmetry between politics and economics: both nation states and national markets have been bounded by the same set of unambiguous borders and organized geographically. Nation states and national markets, however, are but one of a number of historical modes of organizing political and economic authority and, in historical terms, relatively short-lived ones at that (Kennedy 1993; Ruggie 1993). It is not unreasonable to argue that the symmetry between states and markets in both geographic scope and mode of organization—which we tend to take as the natural order of things—is characteristic only of a very brief window of time: perhaps the 100 years spanning the late nineteenth to late twentieth centuries.

Martin Parker (1992) makes a nice distinction between 'post-modern' as a historical period and 'postmodern' as a theoretical perspective (he uses the hyphen to distinguish between the two). Thus, one can meaningfully talk about a modern or post-Westphalian political-economic system structured in terms of unambiguous territorial jurisdiction or the transition from modern to 'post-modern' organizations in terms of the disintegration of vertically integrated hierarchical firms, without assuming a 'postmodern' epistemology.

In the late twentieth century, a post-modern global economy is situated in a modern political system. As noted above, in many of the industries now regarded as strategic, the minimal market size needed to support a competitive R&D effort is larger than even the largest national markets. Perhaps of more fundamental importance, politics is still organized in terms of geography—territory and borders—while economic activity is increasingly organized in terms of electronic networks. The result is a developing asymmetry of scope and mode of organization between a modern, territorially based, and geographically organized international political system comprised of nation states and an emerging postmodern world economy where national markets, and indeed the very concepts of territoriality and geography, are becoming less relevant.

That being said, one caveat is necessary. Neither the international nor the global world economy is all encompassing. Many sectors of economic activity are still domestic and little affected by cross-border transactions; many others remain grounded in a cross-border or international economy. While the focus of this chapter is on 'post-modern' as a historical period rather than 'postmodern' as an epistemology, the simultaneous existence of domestic, international, and global economies would not be inconsistent with the latter.

6. **Back to the Future?**

Geoffrey de Joinville, a thirteenth-century French medieval lord, acquired a considerable portion of Ireland through a 'strategic alliance'. His half-sister's husband—the uncle of the queen of England—arranged a marriage with Matilda, granddaughter of Walter de Lacy, Lord of Meath, who brought substantial Irish lands with her (Bartlett 1993). After his marriage, de Joinville owed simultaneous allegiance to the kings of England and France.

Neither de Joinville's fiefdoms nor the international financial market are modern, geographically based forms of political or economic organization. Political control in one case and economic transactions in the other are organized without regard to mutually exclusive geography or meaningful and discrete borders. To a large extent both pre- and postmodern forms of organization are aterritorial.

Almost twenty years ago Hedley Bull (1977) argued that the emergence of a modern and secular counterpart of Western Christendom, with its characteristic overlapping authority and multiple loyalties, was within the realm of possibility. The post-modern future may well resemble the medieval past more closely—at least metaphorically—than the more immediate, geographically organized world of national markets and nation states.

Although medieval 'states' occupied geographic space, politics was not organized in terms of unambiguous geography. Political authority took the form of hierarchical personal relationships, of often overlapping and intertwined mutual obligations and rights, as de Joinville well illustrates. Borders were diffuse, representing a projection of power rather than a limit of sovereignty.

While the medieval analogy has very obvious limits, the past may well contain applicable lessons for the future. A neat, unambiguous ordering of economic and political authority along geographic lines may no longer be the norm. Borders are diffuse and permeable, compromised by transnational integration and global telecommunications. Relationships are increasingly networked rather than hierarchical, with both individuals and organizations enmeshed in complex, polygamous worldwide webs. Multiple and competing loyalties result.

James Rosenau foresees the emergence of a dual system of sovereignty-bound and sovereignty free-actors—or state-centric and multicentric worlds—coexisting together. 'The result is a paradigm that neither circumvents nor negates the state-centric model but posits sovereignty-bound and sovereignty-free actors as inhabitants of separate worlds that interact in such a way as to make their coexistence possible' (Rosenau 1990: 247).

One of the primary characteristics of modernity is a lack of ambiguity. The international political system is structured in terms of discrete and mutually exclusive geography: disputed border areas aside, every point in geographic space belongs unambiguously to a single nation state and market. With very few exceptions, every individual under the law, including corporations, is a citizen of a single state. Similarly, the essence of the modern integrated economic organization is a clear hierarchy and a single chain of command: one boss, one company. Every individual, and every transaction, can be located in organizational space.

We may well be at a point of transition comparable to what Ruggie (1983: 273) describes as the 'most important contextual change in international politics in this millennium: the shift from the medieval to the modern international system'. The emergence of an electronically networked global economy may herald an analogous transition to a post-modern political-economic system.

There is, however, a danger in trying to project modern assumptions into a post-modern era. Linearity or unrepeatable time is basic to modernity (Camilleri and Falk 1992). We assume that time's arrow is unidirectional and that progress is irreversible; that there is a historic progression from classical to medieval to modern to—perhaps—post-modern. That assumption may be wrong.

7. Whither the State?

This chapter has argued that globalization will markedly constrain the autonomy and effectiveness of states and, at a minimum, raise serious questions about the meaning of internal and external sovereignty. One point should be clear: I am not claiming that the state will wither away or even be rendered impotent. Rather, that globalization will affect the structure and functioning of both states and the inter-state system.

At a minimum states remain responsible for any number of critical functions: for the welfare of their citizens, for basic social and physical infrastructure, and for ensuring economic viability, albeit in a very different context. Furthermore, while globalization will transform relatively large numbers of critical, strategic sectors, it certainly does not affect all sectors, firms, and individuals equally. There will still be firms that function as domestic actors and those that function in a more traditional international or cross-border economy.

I believe, however, that there is no question that the meaning of sovereignty will evolve and that the state's role relative to supra- and sub-national actors will change. The medieval *analogy* is useful. It should be clear at this point that I agree with Hirst and Thompson (1995: 422) that the political order is becoming more polycentric, with states seen as 'one level' in a very complex system of often overlapping and competing agencies of governance.

There is certainly some recognition of the need for some sort of control at the center. The WTO (for example) has been given greater adjudication powers than its predecessor (the GATT) and is now attempting to reach agreement on a set of rules governing FDI. Furthermore, regional agreements such as the EU, NAFTA, and the Association of South-East Asian Nations (ASEAN) appear to be proliferating. While the future of the EU is far from clear at this point, the fact that a common currency is even on the table has major implications for state sovereignty.

At the same time, there appears to be increasing pressure for devolution of powers downwards to sub-national entities, whether they are individual states in federal systems such as the USA or regions within Europe. The situation is complicated further by the rise of non-governmental organizations (NGOs) as important actors in international politics; one thinks immediately of Greenpeace in environmental politics or Amnesty International in human rights.

The modern system of political and economic organization may well have been an exception. There is no reason to assume that a lack of geographic ambiguity, or even territoriality itself, is inherent in the human condition.[26] The post-modern era may well resemble the medieval in terms of ambiguity, multiple loyalties, multiple levels of authority, and the coexistence of multiple types of political and economic actors. It is certainly consistent with a postmodern world-view to reject the 'modernist narrative of progress' and 'embrace many simultaneously different and even contradictory accounts of reality' (Camilleri and Falk 1992: 52).

A medieval lord dealt with allegiances to multiple sovereigns, perhaps an emperor, and the coexistence of secular and sacred authority as the norm. Is there any reason a postmodern could not deal with sub-national, national, regional, international, and supra-national authorities simultaneously? Or with multiple and ill-defined allegiances? Or with a system ordered on some basis other than geography?

This chapter has argued that globalization entails the technologically driven expansion of the scope of markets well beyond the limits of even the largest national territories, and the replacement of markets and hierarchies by relational networks as the mode of organization of international economic transactions. I believe that both signify the emergence of a post-modern world economy that is not consistent with a modern, territorially defined, international political system. While the emerging asymmetry could be resolved by some sort of 'world order', I do not think that is likely in the foreseeable future. Modern economic and political actors will have to learn to deal with the ambiguity and uncertainty of the post-modern future.

NOTES

I would like to thank Mark Casson, John Dunning, Vicki Golich, Ben Gomes-Cassares, John Ikenberry, Robert Keohane, Bruce Kogut, Robert Kudrle, Richard Lipsey, Richard Locke, Tom Malnight, Simon Reich, John Ruggie, Karl Sauvant, John Stopford and Raymond Vernon for comments on previous drafts. The Reginald Jones Center at the Wharton School provided partial support for this research.

1. Krugman (1992: 10–13) argues that by nineteenth-century standards present levels of economic integration are not exceptional. Dunning (1993: 476) concludes that, although complete economic interdependence has never existed in practice, 'it came near to it in the second and third quarters of the nineteenth century'. See also Streeten (1992: 125–6).
2. Krugman (1992: 12–13) argues that the ratio of trade to output achieved by the industrial countries in 1913 was not achieved again until the early 1970s. Rates of growth of trade and investment are certainly comparable, at the least in terms of orders of magnitude, for the forty years prior to the First and following the Second World Wars. From the 1820s through 1913 world trade grew at 46% per decade; from 1874 to 1913 capital invested abroad grew at a striking rate of 64% per decade. Between 1860 and 1913 Great Britain, for example, invested between 25 and 40% of its gross domestic savings overseas, Sodersten (1980). Rosecrance et al. (1977) argue that, prior to the First World War, international trade was a higher proportion of national income and direct and indirect investment a larger fraction of GNP than at present (the mid-1970s).
3. See also Dunning's description of globalization in his Prebish lecture (Dunning 1994). A significant proportion of what appears to be trade is actually cross-border intra-firm transfers, and sales of subsidiaries of MNEs located outside the home country now substantially exceed the value of goods 'traded' internationally. At this point, UNCTAD (1995) estimates that intra-firm trade accounts for about 35% of all international transactions and for the US sales of affiliates exceeds cross-border sales of goods and services by a factor of 2.5 to 1.

4. For a dissenting view on the tendency towards the internationalization of production, see Gordon (1988: 24–65).
5. The *Oxford English Dictionary* attributes its first use to Bentham in 1780 in a discussion of international jurisprudence in which he explicitly states that the word is a new one.
6. *Smithian* growth results from 'the creation of commerce and voluntary exchange between two previously disjoint units—be they individuals, villages, regions, countries or continents' (Parker 1984: 1). See also Mokyr (1990: 4–6).
7. Historically, fixed capital was confined to buildings and vehicles such as warehouses, harbours, docks, and ships (Hicks 1969; Parker 1984). As North and Thomas (1973) note, transaction costs—search, negotiation, and enforcement—are subject to scale economies, and an expanding market can increase income in the absence of technological change.
8. Scale economies and notions such as minimally efficient plant size are notoriously difficult to measure in practice, especially across a range of industries. Similarly, Bain concluded that in the USA only two industries—automobiles and typewriters—had 'very important' scale economies—where the minimal optimal plant scale exceeded 10% of the national market. (Five industries—cement, farm machinery, tractors, rayon, and steel—had 'moderately important' plant scale economies.) A study of the smaller UK market reported similar results. In only eleven industries did minimum efficient plant scale exceed 10% of the national market. Reported in Dicken and Lloyd (1990). Furthermore, while minimum efficient plant size does appear to have increased over the past few decades, recent developments may well reverse that trend. The introduction of computer-aided manufacturing and the general application of electronic technology to production allows for efficient manufacture at lower volumes; in the automotive industry, for example, minimum efficient plant size may have declined significantly.
9. Using US Department of Commerce data, the ratio of intra-firm international sales to all international sales was used as an index of integration (on an industry basis). R&D intensity as well as a number of control variables were significant determinants of the index. Although a proxy for manufacturing scale economies was not, the considerable conceptual and measurement problems associated with this concept limit generalization.
10. Industrial R&D laboratories were first established in the mid- to late-nineteenth century for tasks such as testing and grading of materials, quality control, and writing specifications. General Electric established a laboratory for materials-testing in the early 1870s, the Pennsylvania Railroad established a chemical laboratory in 1874, Kodak's experimental and testing facility was founded in 1890, and Du Pont's in 1900 (*Research Management* 1986: 6–8, and Mowery and Rosenberg 1989). Nelson (1992) notes that, during the first industrial revolution, invention was largely a result of individuals working alone. R&D laboratories tied to particular business firms first appeared at the end of the nineteenth century, first in chemical firms and later in those producing electrical products. After the First World War industrial research turned to product and process development and the fixed costs associated with technology grew rapidly. For example, the number of research laboratories in the US manufacturing sector grew twenty-fold from 1899 to 1945; correspondingly, the number of scientific personnel employed grew tenfold from 1921 to 1940 (Mowery and Rosenberg 1989: tables 4.1, 4.2, 4.3, 4.4, and 4.5).

11. The point can be illustrated anecdotally. For example, in 1993, Merck spent 11.2% of its sales on R&D and 43.7% of its sales were outside the USA. If it were forced to support the costs of technological development, which are exogenously determined, on its US volume alone (64.3% of the total), it would have had to spend 21% of its sales of R&D, a proportion not tenable over any but the shortest time period. Corresponding figures for some other firms, that is R&D spending as a proportion of US sales only, are: Intel, 22%; Pfizer, 24%; Motorola, 17%; Lilly, 24% (data obtained from *Business Week* 1994; *Forbes* 1994).
12. See Osborn and Baughn (1990); Mytelka (1991); Gomes-Casseres (1993); and Terpstra and Simonin (1993) among many others. The LARA/CEREM database, for example, of 1,086 agreements involving at least one European partner, shows an average of 67 a year in 1980–2, 133 in 1983–5, and 243 in 1986–7 (Mytelka 1991: 10–11.) In a study of alliances in the computer industry alone, Gomes-Casseres reports a more than sixfold increase from under 4 a year in 1975–80 to 26 per year in 1985–9. The compound growth rate was contained in a Predicast study (cited by Lewis E. Platt, President and CEO of Hewlett Packard at the Wharton School on 12 Sept. 1993) which estimated a 31% compound annual growth rate of high-technology strategic alliances over the 1980s.
13. Raymond Vernon argues that this is the primary motivation for the current wave of strategic alliances (letter to the author, Nov. 1993).
14. Again, while generalization is difficult, existing data do appear to support technology as the dominant driver of inter-firm cooperative agreements. An OECD (1992) report, for example, sums evidence from 'one of the best data banks' to conclude that R&D cooperation represents the single most important objective of inter-firm agreements. Technologically intensive industries appear to dominate. For example, Terpstra and Simonin (1993) found that 60% of the agreements they studied were in industries that are technology intensive (an additional 16% were in the automotive sector). Similarly, in reviewing a number of empirical studies Mytelka (1991: 9) concludes that knowledge production and sharing is an increasingly important component of strategic partnerships. Similarly, in her study of the commercial aircraft industry, Golick (1992) found reducing R&D costs, scale economies, and increased market size to be important motivations for cross-border collaboration. A recent US government report concluded that developments encouraging the formation of alliances include: technological levelling, convergence in product markets, slow growth, excess capacity, shorter life cycles, escalating R&D costs, and increasingly complex product and process technologies (Office of Technology Assessment 1993).
15. A caveat is necessary. Although the growth of alliances has been dramatic over the last decade, their presence is not universal. While the data are still fragmentary, alliances appear to concentrate in industries characterized by technological or capital intensity. It should be noted, however, that these industries (e.g. aerospace, semiconductors, telecommunications, and automobiles) are the most important strategically in terms of national economic competitiveness and security.
16. The literature on networks is large and growing. For an introduction and references, see Miles and Snow (1986); Wellman and Berkowitz (1988); Ghoshal and Bartlett (1990); Nohria and Eccles (1992).
17. Powell (1990: 299) characterizes the continuum view as quiescent and mechanical and argues that by 'sticking to the twin pillars of markets and hierarchies, our attention is deflected from a diversity of organizational designs that are neither fish nor

fowl, nor some mongrel hybrid, but a distinctly different form'. See also Thorelli (1986) and Jarillo (1988).

18. As markets become fused and truly integrated, it is becoming increasingly difficult to distinguish one nation's products, technologies, and firms from another's (Blumental 1988; Lee and Reed 1991; Reich 1991).
19. See also Harvey (1990) for references to the large and growing literature on this topic.
20. External sovereignty includes the concept of 'juristical statehood', that states are organizations recognized by established states as sovereign (Keohane 1993: 96).
21. The mode of organization of the modern state is territoriality; it exerts control over its population and over economic actors (and the economy) through its exclusive control over territory (Sack 1981). Sovereignty is an inherently territorial concept: 'The condition of sovereignty for a state is control of its own real-estate' (Lucas 1993: 263). See also Bull (1977), James (1986), and Poggi (1990) among a large number of other authors discussing this subject.
22. Similarly, Krasner (1993: 259) argues that the 'central characteristic' of the sovereignty regime is exclusive control over a given territory.
23. As Braudel notes, their development was far from spontaneous: 'The national market was a form of coherence imposed by both political ambitions . . . and by the capitalist tensions created by trade . . . a political space transformed by the state into a coherent and unified economic space . . . a large scale economy, territorialized so to speak, and sufficiently coherent for governments to be able to shape and manœuvre it to some extent . . .' (Braudel 1977: 99; 1986: 277, 294).
24. Also see Castells and Henderson (1987: 1–17).
25. Similarly, Ruggie (1993: 159) argues that the concept of sovereignty is no more than the 'doctrinal counterpart of the application of single-point perspectival forms to the spatial organization of politics'.
26. Ruggie (1993: 49) notes at least three ways in which systems of rule have differed from the modern territorial state. First, they need not be territorial at all; secondly, they need not be territorially fixed; and, thirdly, they may not entail mutual exclusion.

REFERENCES

Anderson, J. (1986), 'The Modernity of States', in James Anderson (ed.), *The Rise of the Modern State* (Atlantic Highlands, NJ: Humanities Press International, Inc.).

Baker, W. E. (1990), 'Market Networks and Corporate Behavior', *American Journal of Sociology*, 96: 589–625.

Barkin, J. S., and Cronin, B. (1994), 'The State and the Nation—Changing Norms and the Rules of Sovereignty in International Relations', *International Organization*, 48: 107–30.

Bartlett, R. (1993), *The Making of Europe* (Princeton: Princeton University Press).

Blumental, W. M. (1988), 'The World Economy and Technological Change', *Foreign Affairs*, 66: 529–550.

Bradsher, K. (1995), 'Back to the Thrilling Trades of Yesteryear', *New York Times* (12 March), p. E5.

Braudel, F. (1977), *Afterthoughts on Material Civilization and Capitalism* (Baltimore: Johns Hopkins University Press).

—— (1986), *The Perspective of the World Civilization and Capitalism: 15th–18th Century*, iii (New York: Perennial Library, Harper and Row).

Bressand, A., Distler, C., and Nicolaidis, K. (1989), 'Networks at the Heart of the Service Economy', in A. Bressand and K. Nicolaidis (eds.), *Strategic Trends in Services* (New York: Ballinger).

Brown, C. J. (1988), 'New Concepts for a Changing International Economy', *Washington Quarterly*, 11: 86–94.

Bull, H. (1977), *The Anarchical Society: A Study of Order in World Politics* (New York: Columbia University Press).

Business Week (1994*a*), 'R&D Scoreboard' (27 June), 78–103.

—— (1994*b*), 'Technobanking Takes Off' (18 November), 52–3.

Camilleri, J., and Falk, J. (1992), *The End of Sovereignty?* (Aldershot, Hants.: Edward Elgar).

Castells, M. (1993), 'The Informational Economy and the New International Division of Labor', in M. Carnoy, M. Castells, S. S. Cohen, and F. H. Cardoso (eds.), *The New Global Economy in the Information Age* (University Park, Pa.: The Pennsylvania State University Press).

—— and Henderson, J. (1987), 'Techno-Economic Restructuring, Socio-Political Processes and Spatial Transformation: A Global Perspective', in J. Henderson and M. Castells (eds.), *Global Restructuring and Territorial Development* (Beverly Hills: Sage Publishers).

Clegg, S. R. (1990), *Modern Organizations* (London: Sage).

Cooper, R. N. (1986), *Economic Policy in an Interdependent World* (Cambridge, Mass.: The MIT Press).

Dell, E. (1986), *The Politics of Economic Interdependence* (New York: St Martin's Press).

Dicken, P. (1992), *Global Shift* (2nd edn., New York: Guilford Press).

—— (1994), 'The Roepke Lecture in Economic Geography: Global–Local Tensions: Firms and States in the Global Space-Economy', *Economic Geography*, 70: 101–2.

—— and Lloyd, P. E. (1990), *Location in Space: Theoretical Perspectives in the Economic Geography* (New York: HarperCollins).

Dunning, J. (1993), *Multinational Enterprises and the Global Economy* (Reading, Mass.: Addison-Wesley).

—— (1994), *Globalization, Economic Restructuring and Development* (The 6th Prebisch Lecture; Geneva: UNCTAD).

The Economist (1993), 'The Global Firm: RIP' (6 February), 69.

Forbes (1994), 'The International 500' (18 June).

Freedman. M. (1989), 'Internationalization of the US Economy', *Fraser Forum,* quoted in J. G. Ruggie, *At Home Abroad, Abroad at Home: International Liberalization and Domestic Stability in the New World Economy* (Jean Monnet Chair Papers, Robert Schuman Centre, European University, 1995).

Ghoshal, S., and Bartlett, C. A. (1990), 'The Multinational Corporation as a Strategic Network', *Academy of Management Review*, 15: 603–25.

Golick, V. (1992), 'From Competition to Collaboration: The Challenge of Commercial-Class Aircraft Manufacturing', *International Organization*, 46: 899–934.

Gomes-Casseres, B. (1993), 'Computers: Alliances and Industry Evolution', in D. B. Yoffee (ed.), *Beyond Free Trade: Firms, Governments and Global Competition* (Boston: Harvard Business School Press).

Goodwin, G. L. (1974), 'The Erosion of External Sovereignty?', in Ghita Ionescu (ed.), *Between Sovereignty and Integration* (New York: John Wiley & Sons).

Gordon, D. M. (1988), 'The Global Economy: New Edifice or Crumbling Foundations?', *New Left Review* (March–April), 24–65.

Guehenno, J.-M. (1995), *The End of the Nation State* (Minneapolis: University of Minnesota Press).

Hagedoorn, J. (1993), 'Understanding the Role of Strategic Technology Partnering: Interorganizational Modes of Cooperation and Sectoral Differences', *Strategic Management Journal*, 14: 371–85.

Harvey, D. (1990), *The Condition of Postmodernity* (Cambridge, Mass.: Blackwell Publishers).

Held, D., and McGrew, A. (1993), 'Globalization and the Liberal Democratic State', *Government and Opposition*, 28: 265.

Hicks, J. (1969), *A Theory of Economic History* (Oxford: Oxford University Press).

Hirst, P., and Thompson. G. (1992), 'The Problem of Globalization: International Economic Relations, National Economic Management and the Formation of Trading Blocs', *Economy and Society*, 21: 358–60.

—— (1995), 'Globalization and the Future of the Nation State', *Economy and Society*, 24: 408–42.

Hobsbawm, E. J. (1979), 'The Development of the World Economy', *Cambridge Journal of Economics*, 3: 305–18.

—— (1994), *The Age of Extremes: A History of the World 1914–1991* (New York: Pantheon Books).

James, A. (1986), *Sovereign Statehood: The Basis of International Society* (London: Allen & Unwin).

Jankowski, J. E., Jr. (1992), *National Patterns of R&D Resources* (NSF 92–330; Washington: National Science Foundation).

Jarillo, J. C. (1988), 'On Strategic Networks', *Strategic Management Journal*, 9: 31–41.

Jones, C., and Hesterly, W. S. (1993), 'A Network Organization: Alternative Governance Form or a Glorified Market?' (paper presented at the Academy of Management Meeting, Atlanta, August).

Kennedy, P. (1993), *Preparing for the Twenty-First Century* (New York: Random House).

Keohane, R. O. (1993), 'Sovereignty, Interdependence, and International Institutions', in L. B. Miller and M. J. Smith (eds.), *Ideas and Ideals: Essays on Politics in Honor of Stanley Hoffman* (Boulder, Colo.: Westview Press).

—— and Nye, J. S. (1989), *Power and Interdependence* (Glenview, Ill.: Scott Foresman & Company).

Kobrin, Stephen J. (1991), 'An Empirical Analysis of the Determinants of Global Integration', *Strategic Management Journal*, 121: 17–32.

Krasner, S. D. (1993), 'Westphalia and All That', in J. Goldstein and R. O. Keohane (eds.), *Ideas and Foreign Policy* (Ithaca, NY: Cornell University Press).

Kratochwil, F. (1986), 'Of Systems, Boundaries, and Territoriality: An Inquiry into the Formation of the State System', *World Politics*, 39: 27–52.

Krugman, P. R. (1992), 'A Global Economy is Not the Wave of the Future', *Financial Executive* (March–April), 10–13.

Lee, T. H., and Reed, P. P. (1991) (eds.), *National Interests in an Age of Global Technology* (Washington: National Academy Press).

Levine, R. A. (1994), 'France and the World', *Foreign Policy*, 95: 184–97.

Lipsey, R. G., and Bekar, C. (1995), 'A Structuralist View of Technical Change and Economic Growth', in T. J. Courchene (ed.), *Technology, Information and Public Policy* (Kingston, Ont.: John Deutsch Institute).

Lucas, J. (1993), *The End of the Twentieth Century and the End of the Modern Age* (New York: Ticknor & Fields).

Mackinder, H. J. (1904), 'The Geographical Pivot of History', *Geographical Journal*, 23: 421–44.

Malone, T. W., and Rockart, J. F. (1993), 'How Will Information Technology Reshape Organizations? Computers as Coordination Technology', in S. Bradley, J. A. Hausman, and R. L. Nolan (eds.), *Globalization, Technology, and Competition: The Fusion of Technology and Computers in the 1990s* (Boston: Harvard Business School Press).

Marshall, A. (1961), *Principles of Economics* (8th edn.; London: Macmillan).

Michalet, C.-A. (1991), 'Strategic Partnerships and the Changing Internationalization Process', in L. K. Mytelka (ed.), *Strategic Partnerships and the World Economy* (Rutherford, NJ: Fairleigh Dickinson University Press).

—— (1994), 'Transnational Corporations and the Changing International Economic System', *Transnational Corporations*, 3: 6–22.

Miles, R., and Snow, C. C. (1986), 'Organizations: New Concepts for New Norms', *California Management Review*, 27: 62–73.

Mokyr, J. (1990), *The Lever of Riches: Technological Creativity and Economic Progress* (New York: Oxford University Press).

Mowery, D. C., and Rosenberg, N. (1989), *Technology and the Pursuit of Economic Growth* (Cambridge: Cambridge University Press).

Mytelka, L. K. (1991), *Strategic Partnerships: States, Firms and International Competition* (Rutherford, NJ: Fairleigh Dickinson University Press).

Negroponte, N. (1995), *Being Digital* (1st edn., New York: Knopf).

Nelson, R. (1992), 'The Role of Firms in Technical Advance: A Perspective from Evolutionary Theory', in G. D. R. Giannetti and P. A. Toninelli (eds.), *Technology and Enterprise in Historical Perspective* (Oxford: Oxford University Press).

Nohria, N., and Eccles, R. C. (1992), *Networks and Organizations: Structure Form and Action* (Boston: Harvard Business School Press).

North, D. C., and Thomas, R. P. (1973), *The Rise of the Western World: A New Economic History*. (Cambridge: Cambridge University Press).

Nye, J. S., Jr. (1990), *Bound to Lead: The Changing Nature of American Power* (New York: Basic Books).

O'Brien, R. (1992), *Global Financial Integration: The End of Geography* (London: Pinter Publishers).

OECD (1992): Organization for Economic Cooperation and Development, *Technology and the Economy: The Key Relationship* (Paris: OECD).

Ohmae, K. (1990), *The Borderless World* (New York: Harper Business).

Osborn, R. N., and Baughn, C. C. (1990), 'Forms of Interorganizational Governance for Multinational Alliances', *Academy of Management Journal*, 33: 503–19.

Pandit, S. K. (1995), 'Wired to the Rest of the World', *Financial Times* (10 January), 12.

Parker, M. (1992), 'Post-Modern Organizations or Postmodern Theory?', *Organization Studies*, 13: 1–17.

Parker, W. N. (1984), *Europe, America and the Wider World: Essays on the Economic History of Western Capitalism* (Cambridge: Cambridge University Press).

Poggi, G. (1990), *The State: Its Nature, Development and Prospects* (Stanford, Calif.: Stanford University Press).

Powell, W. W. (1990), 'Neither Market nor Hierarchy: Network Forms of Organization', *Research in Organization Behavior*, 12: 295–316.

Reich, R. B. (1991), *The Work of Nations* (New York: Alfred A. Knopf).

Research Management (1986), 'What our Organization can Learn from the Historians', 29: 6–8.

Rosecrance, R., Alexandroff, A., Koehler, W., Kroll, J., Laquer, S., and Stocker, J. (1977), 'Whither Interdependence', *International Organization*, 31: 385–424.

Rosenau, J. (1990), *Turbulence in World Politics* (Princeton: Princeton University Press).

Ruggie, J. G. (1983), 'Continuity and Transformation in the World Polity: Toward a Neorealist Syntheses', *World Politics*, 271–85.

—— (1993), 'Territoriality and Beyond: Problematizing Modernity in International Relations', *International Organization*, 47: 139–74.

Sack, R. D. (1981), 'Territorial Bases of Power', in A. D. Burnett and P. J. Taylor (eds.), *Political Studies from Spatial Perspectives* (London: John Wiley).

Scherer, F. M. (1974), 'Economies of Scale and Industrial Concentration', in H. Goldschmitt, H. M. Mann, and J. F. Weston (eds.), *Industrial Concentration: The New Learning* (Boston: Little Brown & Company).

Sodersten, B. (1980), *International Economics*, (2nd edn., New York: St Martin's Press).

Spruyt, H. (1994), *The Sovereign State and its Competitors* (Princeton: Princeton University Press).

Stewart, T. A. (1995), 'A New 500 for the New Economy', *Fortune* (15 May), 168–78.

Stopford, J. M., and Strange, S. (1991), *Rival States, Rival Firms: Competition for World Market Shares* (Cambridge: Cambridge University Press).

Streeten, P. (1992), 'Interdependence and Integration of the World Economy: The Role of States and Firms', *Transnational Corporations*, 1: 125–36.

Terpstra, V., and Simonin, B. L. (1993), 'Strategic Alliances in the Triad: An Exploratory Study', *Journal of International Marketing*, 1: 4–25.

Thorelli, H. B. (1986), 'Networks: Between Markets and Hierarchies', *Strategic Management Journal*, 7: 37–51.

US Congress, Office of Technology Assessment (1993), *Multinationals and the National Interest: Playing by Different Rules* (OTA-ITE-569; Washington: US Government Printing Office).

—— (1994), *Multinationals and the US Technology Base* (OTA-ITE-612; Washington: US Government Printing Office).

UNCTAD (1993): United Nations Conference on Trade and Development, *World Investment Report 1993: Transnational Corporations and Integrated International Production* (ST/CTC/156; New York: United Nations).

—— (1994), *World Investment Report 1994: Transnational Corporations, Employment and the Workplace* (DTCI/10; Geneva: United Nations).

—— (1995), *Trends in Foreign Direct Investment* (TD/B/ITNC/2; Geneva: United Nations).

United Nations Economic and Social Council (1993), *Transnational Corporations in World Development: A Re-examination* (New York: United Nations).

Wellman, B., and Berkowitz, S. D. (1988), *Social Structures: A Network Approach* (Cambridge: Cambridge University Press).

Williamson, O. E. (1991), 'Comparative Economic Organization: The Analysis of Discrete Structural Alternatives', *Administrative Science Quarterly*, 36: 280–96.

Wolf, M. (1995), 'Globalization and the State', *Financial Times* (18 September), 22.

Wriston, W. B. (1992), *The Twilight of Sovereignty* (New York: Charles Scribners' & Sons).

Zacher, M. (1992), 'The Decaying Pillars of the Westphalian Temple: Implications for International Order and Governance', in J. N. Rosenau and E.-O. Czempiel (eds.), *Governance without Government: Order and Change in World Politics* (Cambridge: Cambridge University Press).

PART TWO

COUNTRY CASE STUDIES

6

Canada

Alan M. Rugman

1. Introduction

There are three themes pursued in this chapter. They are all consistent with the mainstream literature on international business and globalization, as summarized and integrated in a comprehensive manner in Dunning (1993*a*). They all stem from the fact that Canada (while a member of the G7) is still a relatively small, open, trading economy rather than a triad power. It does nearly 80 per cent of its trade and has two-thirds of its stocks of inward and outward FDI with its triad neighbour, the USA. These data are provided in Rugman (1990) and Eden (1994*b*). As Canada is one-tenth the economic size of the USA, there are asymmetries in the trade, investment, and corporate strategic relationships between the USA and Canada. The Canada–US Free Trade Agreement (FTA) of 1989 and the North American Free Trade Agreement (NAFTA) of 1994 provide an institutional framework which reflects the high degree of economic interdependence and the strong corporate linkages between the two economies. For analysis of the investment provisions of NAFTA and its linkages to the FTA in terms of corporate strategic management and adjustment policies, the reader is invited to read Rugman (1994*b*).

The first theme pursued is that globalization, from a Canadian perspective, means regionalization. By virtue of the FTA and NAFTA, Canadian-based firms have secure and reasonably predictable access to the world's largest market. The rules-based regime of the FTA and NAFTA is preferable to the former US dominated power-based system, but many subtle political and managerial challenges remain, since market access is not perfectly secure. For example, the USA retains its right to use trade remedy laws in the form of countervailing duty (CVD) and anti-dumping (AD) actions, and these can be used in an abusive manner to harass Canadian traders (Rugman and Anderson 1987; Hart 1994; Anderson 1995). The FTA and NAFTA set up a unique system of binational panels to review CVD and AD duties, and several major US rulings have been reversed, including those on pork and softwood lumber (Hart 1994; Anderson 1995). So the first nuance of Canadian management is how to achieve better and more secure access to the US triad market, working within the parameters of the FTA and NAFTA. There is unfinished business here (Warner and Rugman 1994).

The second characteristic of Canadian strategic management is related to the first and is the need to develop skills in 'national responsiveness', due to the asymmetries in size of the US and Canadian economies. Bartlett and Ghoshal (1989) have developed the notion of national responsiveness in a managerial context. Even when Canadian managers pursue the three generic strategies of cost, differentiation, and focus (Porter 1980), there is an additional requirement to have national responsiveness (Rugman 1994*c*). With Canada being one-tenth the size of the US market, a global strategy for a Canadian manager often means operating in the large US triad market. For example, lumber exporters cannot rely on cost advantage alone in the face of a CVD case, brought by rival US lumber producers. Instead, they need to develop US-based coalitions (such as with the US furniture industry and US housing industry) in order to offset contingent protection. This is a clear case of the need for managerial skills in national responsiveness. In a related manner, Canadian forestry, chemical, and other export sectors need to develop national responsiveness skills to deal with the US environmentalist movement, since sub-national levels of US government can pass laws affecting Canadian business and deny Canadians market access. For example, the California newspaper recycling law could require that Canadian forestry firms access paper from the 'urban forest' (by building de-inking plants in California) rather than exporting newsprint using the forests of British Columbia. Some of these issues of environmental regulations and the forced switch of market access modality by the MNE are discussed in Rugman (1995). The dominant role of national responsiveness for Canadian managers has been articulated by Rugman (1994*c*) within the 'double-diamond' framework of Rugman and D'Cruz (1991, 1993), which is a simple, although controversial, extension to Canada of the single home-diamond model of Porter (1990), Porter (1991). For a criticism of this model, see Porter and Armstrong (1992) and a reply to these criticisms in Rugman and Verbeke (1993).

The third theme affecting Canadian competitiveness and analysis of globalization is the large amount of foreign ownership. This somewhat complicates the nature of business–government relations in Canada, since more than one-third of the manufacturing sector is foreign owned, with over two-thirds of this being US FDI in Canada. In recent years, both Canadian-owned and foreign-owned firms have shared a common concern about efficiency and competitiveness. For example, both sets of firms were strong advocates of the FTA and NAFTA (Rugman 1988*a*: 1993, 1994*b*). A new theoretical framework can be useful in analysing the contribution of both foreign-owned and Canadian-owned firms to Canadian competitiveness. This is the D'Cruz and Rugman (1992, 1993) flagship model of a business network. It will be the basis for the analysis in this chapter of the first two issues. However, in the next section the foreign-ownership issue is explored in detail, with regionalization and the flagship analytical framework to follow.

2. Foreign Ownership and Strategic Management

A major complexity in the analysis of Canadian strategic management and the reaction of the Canadian government to regional and global economic issues comes from the large amount of foreign ownership of the manufacturing sector. There was as much as 60 per cent foreign control in the late 1960s (with 75 per cent of this being US FDI in Canada.) This led to the economic nationalist Watkins Report (Watkins *et al.* 1968) and the subsequent introduction of the Foreign Investment Review Agency (FIRA) to screen foreign investment in 1974. The objective of FIRA was to review every foreign investment and assess its net economic benefits on the basis of performance requirements such as employment, regional development, Canadian participation, taxes paid, and so on. Although FIRA acted as a major deterrent to foreign investment in 1980–2, when nationalist Herb Gray was Minister of Industry, Trade and Commerce, for most of the period from 1974 until its demise in 1985, it was a 'paper tiger' (Rugman 1980; Rugman and Waverman 1991; Safarian 1993).

One of the first acts of the new Conservative government of Brian Mulroney was to abolish FIRA and replace it with Investment Canada, an agency designed to attract FDI, rather than scare it away. In an empirical analysis of the cases reviewed by FIRA between 1974 and 1985, and then by Investment Canada over the 1985–90 period, no significant difference was found, in terms of discrimination between triad-based inward FDI into Canada even across major industry sectors (Rugman and Waverman 1991). By 1990 the issue of foreign control was fading away, despite polemics, such as by Mel Hurtig (1991), and analysis by Jenkins (1992), both of which still advocated regulation of US FDI in Canada. In 1987 foreign affiliates controlled 53 per cent of the Canadian manufacturing sector, although in 1986 it was 47 per cent. In 1993, foreign control of Canada's non-financial industries was only 25 per cent, down from 36 per cent in 1970 (Statistics Canada 1995).

Despite the decrease in the percentage of foreign control of the manufacturing industry, the Canadian economy still has a legacy of foreign ownership. For example, many of the senior managers in Canadian firms (foreign owned as well as Canadian owned) learned their roles over the last thirty years in a political atmosphere fraught with tension over the issue of foreign control and its alleged threat to Canadian sovereignty. The debate over the FTA in the 1986–8 period, and the 1988 federal election campaign, was the catharsis which finally changed the Canadian managerial—not to mention government—mindset from a protected, subservient one towards the outward looking, globalization-driven one of today.

One of the major turning-points on the path to globalization in Canada was the 1983 submission by the Canadian Manufacturers' Association (CMA) to the Macdonald Commission (1985). As reported in Rugman (1988*a*, 1990) the CMA brief supported an FTA with the USA, instead of its century-old reliance on protection. Subsequently, the Canadian private sector strongly supported both the negotiation of the FTA (Hart 1994) and helped to 'sell' it in the 1988 election (Rugman 1988*a*, 1988*b*; Doern and Tomlin 1991). So one of the biggest changes in recent Canadian history, in both government policy and management practice, is the change from a foreign-ownership attitude of dependence towards one of 'complex interdependence' and innovation (Keohane and Nye 1977; Eden 1994*b*).

TABLE 6.1. FDI between Canada and the USA, 1985–1994

Year	Canadian FDI in the USA ($Can.m.) (1)	US FDI in Canada ($Can.m.) (2)	Net position ($Can.m.) (1)–(2)	(1)/(2) (%)
1985	39,586	67,874	–28,288	58.3
1986	42,027	69,241	–27,214	60.7
1987	46,091	74,194	–28,103	62.1
1988	48,809	76,345	–27,536	63.9
1989	52,615	80,877	–28,262	65.1
1990	55,475	84,353	–28,878	65.8
1991	58,256	86,813	–28,557	67.1
1992	61,806	89,013	–27,207	69.4
1993	61,645	90,589	–28,944	68.0
1994	67,739	96,032	–28,293	70.5
Average rate of Increase	6.2%	3.9%		

Note: Ratios for the last column in previous years are: 1975: 18.7; 1979: 28.4; 1984: 48.0 (Rugman 1985).

Source: Statistics Canada (1995).

One of the first studies to demonstrate both the decline in foreign ownership but also the growth of outward Canadian FDI, with its associated maturing of Canadian-based MNEs, was the C. D. Howe-sponsored study on Canadian FDI in the USA (Rugman 1985). Although Canada's economy is under one-tenth the size of the US economy, it was shown that the ratio of Canadian FDI in the USA over US FDI in Canada had increased from under 20 per cent in 1975 to 58 per cent by 1985. Table 6.1 updates this study and reveals that the ratio has subsequently increased to 70 per cent by 1994.

The main point of these statistics on bilateral FDI is that Canadian-owned MNEs are doing a major part of their business in one of the world's largest triad markets, the USA. The largest Canadian MNEs, such as Seagram, Alcan, Moore, Northern Telecom, Noranda, Bombardier, Horsham, and Magna have an average of 60 per cent of their sales in the USA—one of the highest ratios in the world (Rugman and McIlveen 1985). In contrast, the largest US-owned MNEs have only a 25 per cent ratio of foreign to total (F/T) sales, because of their large domestic market (Rugman 1990; Rugman and McIlveen 1985). Tables 6.2 and 6.3 contrast the Canadian-owned firms (with an F/T of 46 per cent) with US firms in Canada (with an F/T of 17 per cent). Subsequent work by other Canadian researchers has confirmed the recent growth of Canadian FDI in the USA and the focus of Canadian-owned MNEs on the US market—see, for example, Eden (1994*a*: chs. 1, 7, 8, 13) and all the contributions in Globerman (1994). In a related study, Crookell (1990) examined the impact of globalization on the strategic management practices of both foreign-owned and Canadian-owned firms after the FTA.

TABLE 6.2. The largest Canadian-owned companies, by size

Firm	Industry (1990)	Sales (1993) ($Can.m.)	F/T[a] (1990) (%)
1. BCE	Telecom.	19,827	31
2. George Weston	Food & stores	11,931	21
3. Alcan Aluminium	Metal	9,329	87
4. Ontario Hydro	Electric utility	8,363	n.a.
5. Thomson	Publishing & travel	7,545	89
6. Hydro-Quebec	Electric utility	7,036	52
7. Seagram	Beverage	6,761	97
8. Canadian Pacific	Diversified	6,579	26
9. Univa	Merchandise	6,207	n.a.
10. Power Corp. of Canada	Management	6,087	n.a.
11. Oshawa Group	Food store	5,728	n.a.
12. Hudson's Bay	Retail	5,441	0
13. Noranda	Integrated forest	5,255	68
14. Brascan	Diversified	5,130	n.a.
15. Petro-Canada	Oil & gas	4,507	0
16. Bombardier[b]	Transportation equip.	4,448	90
17. TransCanada Pipelines	Pipelines	4,242	28
18. Canadian National Railway	Transportation	4,200	11
19. Onex	Diversified	4,025	39
20. Canada Post	Postal service	3,909	n.a.
Average		6,828	46
TOTAL		136,550	

Note: n.a. = not available.

[a] F/T is the ratio of foreign (F) to total (T) sales.

[b] 1992 data.

Sources: Industry and F/T: *Canadian Business* (June 1991); Sales: *Financial Post 500* (Summer 1994).

3. **Regional Strategic Management for Canadian Firms**

Against this background of deep integration of the Canadian and US economic systems and the interdependence of corporate performance, it will be useful in the remainder of the chapter to develop a case study of the competitiveness and strategic management issues facing a Canadian industry. Because it has large elements of foreign ownership and also because of its core relevance for Canada's manufacturing industry, an appropriate sector to examine is the Canadian chemical industry. This is an industry with both large MNEs, small and medium-sized enterprises (SMEs), foreign-owned enterprises, Canadian-owned enterprises, and a strong interaction between business and government. The chemical industry will be analysed using an appropriate framework, the flagship model of a business network, developed recently by D'Cruz and Rugman (1992, 1993), as discussed below. This model is consistent with Dunning's attempt to incorporate network and alliance relationships into the eclectic paradigm (Dunning 1995).

TABLE 6.3. The largest foreign-owned companies in Canada, by size

Firm	Industry (1990)	Sales (1993) ($Can.m.)	F/T[a] (1990) (%)	Ownership (1993) (%)
1. General Motors Canada	Automobiles	21,777	64	USA (100)
2. Ford Motor of Canada	Automobiles	15,918	n.a.	USA (94)
3. Chrysler Canada Ltd.	Automobiles	13,595	71	USA (100)
4. Imperial Oil Ltd.	Oil	7,809	5	USA (70)
5. IBM Canada	Inform. tech.	6,698	0	USA (100)
6. Shell Canada	Oil	4,701	20	Neth. (78)
7. Canada Safeway	Food store	4,457	0	USA (100)
8. Amoco Canada Petroleum	Oil	4,086	n.a.	USA (100)
9. Sears Canada Inc.	Retail	3,939	n.a.	USA (61)
10. Maple Leaf Foods	Food	3,035	n.a.	Britain (56)
11. Total Petroleum Ltd.	Oil	3,004	n.a.	France (52)
12. Great Atlantic & Pacific	Food store	2,709	n.a.	USA (100)
13. Mitsui & Co. (Canada)	Import/export	2,423	0	Japan (100)
14. Honda Canada Inc.	Automobiles	2,246	n.a.	Japan (100)
15. United Westburne Inc.	Wholesale	2,152	20	France (69)
16. Consumer's Gas	Gas	1,801	5	Britain (85)
17. Cargill	Grains	1,794	0	USA (100)
18. Canadian Ultramar	Petroleum	1,725	2	USA (100)
19. Price Costco Canada	n.a.	1,675	n.a.	USA (100)
20. Medis Health and Pharm.	n.a.	1,669	n.a.	USA (100)
Average		5,361	17	
TOTAL		107,213		

Note: n.a. = not available.

[a] F/T is the ratio of foreign (F) to total (T) sales; the firms must have 50% or greater foreign ownership.

Sources: Industry and F/T: *Canadian Business* (June 1991); Sales and Ownership: *Financial Post 500* (Summer 1994).

The associated reason for choosing the Canadian chemicals sector for analysis is the rapid pace of change in an industry much affected by globalization pressures and also by the institutional changes signalled by the FTA and NAFTA (see Rugman 1993, 1994*a*, 1994*b*). Indeed, chemicals has been affected in a dramatic manner by the 'regionalization' of strategy across the border into a North American context. The nature of the Canadian manager's 'double diamond' framework has been explained elsewhere (Rugman and D'Cruz 1993) and this approach is fully compatible with the flagship model, which is the focus of this chapter.

3.1. Strategic Management and the Canadian Chemical Industry

This section reports on a test of the flagship framework of D'Cruz and Rugman (1992, 1993) in the Canadian chemical industry. The analysis determines what role manufacturers in each of the five Standard Industrial Code (SIC) speciality chemicals groups (paints, soaps and detergents, adhesives, agricultural chemicals, and organic chemicals) play within the flagship framework. More specifically, the analysis determines whether firms in the Canadian industry are flagships, key suppliers, or key customers. The relationships that manufacturers in each sector have with their competitors and with the non-business infrastructure are also examined. This particular field study can be generalized, since we consider the nature and quality of the relationships that firms in these sectors have with their partners in the network, and how addressing weaknesses in these relationships can increase international competitiveness. This study complements another test of the flagship model with respect to the global telecommunications industry (D'Cruz and Rugman 1994*a*, 1994*b*). A more detailed, but unpublished, version of this part of the paper is available in D'Cruz *et al.* (1995). The flagship model is further developed in D'Cruz (1995).

The Canadian chemical industry is composed of two types of firms: MNEs and SMEs. Both types are faced with the same challenge and overarching strategic objective: how to become useful participants in the increasingly internationalized structure of the global chemicals industry. However, for each type of firm, the appropriate strategy to adopt in order successfully to attain this objective is heavily influenced by the structure of the network relationships in which it participates.

Canadian managers of MNEs are confronted with a dual challenge. During the current phase of global restructuring, Canadian managers must find ways to sell the benefits and capabilities of the Canadian operation in various forums at head office, based on the needs of the parent's plans for a rationalized global network. Unless they succeed in this objective, they will not have sufficient resources at their disposal to fulfil the second objective, which is to refocus and concentrate the contribution of the Canadian operation to the MNE's global network. In other words, Canadian managers of MNE subsidiaries need to find a niche within the global operations of the parent companies. This niche will usually consist of establishing key supplier relationships, either directly with the parent (an intra-firm key supplier relationship) or with independent MNE flagships in the form of regional or global supplier arrangements (an inter-firm key supplier relationship). This contrasts with the pre-FTA competitive environment where many Canadian subsidiaries operated as miniature replica flagships within the Canadian domestic market.

For SMEs, healthy key customer relations with relevant MNE flagships are critical for survival in an economy increasingly driven by global benchmarks of competitiveness. SMEs are, in several key respects, better placed to benefit from globalization than some subsidiary operations of MNEs. For example, SMEs can help MNEs to access small markets that require flexibility and quick response. This natural alignment of interests means that SMEs have been and can continue to be a source of dynamism and growth in the Canadian chemicals industry. In the next section, the flagship model is reviewed. Then the model is applied to the five chemical sectors examined.

4. The Flagship Business Network Model

The flagship model uses a business-systems approach, which is becoming increasingly appropriate in industries where internationalization and globalization are advanced. By 'business systems' is meant the vertical chain of companies that interact with each other from the manufacture of basic raw materials to final consumption. Conventional relationships in such systems are characterized by arm's-length competition between firms as they buy and sell. Such relationships, which are well explained in the 'five forces' model of competitive advantage (Porter 1980), are based, to a large extent, on the development and exercise of market power. They tend to foster a short-term orientation among participants, with each participant being concerned primarily with its own profitability. The flagship model, in contrast, is based on the development of collaborative relationships among major players in a business system. Its focus is on strategies that are mutually reinforcing. By their very nature, such relationships tend to foster and depend upon a collective long-term orientation among the parties concerned. Hence, they form an important facilitating mechanism for the development of long-term competitiveness (D'Cruz and Rugman 1992, 1993; Rugman and D'Cruz 1993).

There are two key features of the flagship business network. The first is the presence of a flagship firm itself, that pulls the network together and provides leadership for the strategic management of the network as a whole; and the second is the existence of firms that have established key relationships with that flagship. These relationships are illustrated in Fig. 6.1 by black arrows that cross organizational boundaries, symbolizing the nature of inter-firm collaboration that characterizes them. Conventional arm's-length relationships are shown as grey arrows that stop at organizational boundaries.

I now turn to discuss the competitive-enhancing roles played by the constituents of the flagship network of the Canadian chemical industry, paying particular reference to its role in the regional market of which it is part.

4.1. Flagship Firms

The flagship firm is the heart of the flagship business network. It is usually an MNE that provides the network with strategic and organizational leadership. Flagship firms are critical to competitiveness in so far as they provide direction and leadership beyond the resources that, from an accounting perspective, lie directly under the flagship's management control. In other words, flagship firms extend their influence throughout the network in such a way that the quality of business leadership provided by the flagship will directly affect the competitive position of the other key players in the network—namely, the flagship's key suppliers, key customers, and selected competitors. The relationship between the flagship and the non-business infrastructure can also affect the competitiveness of

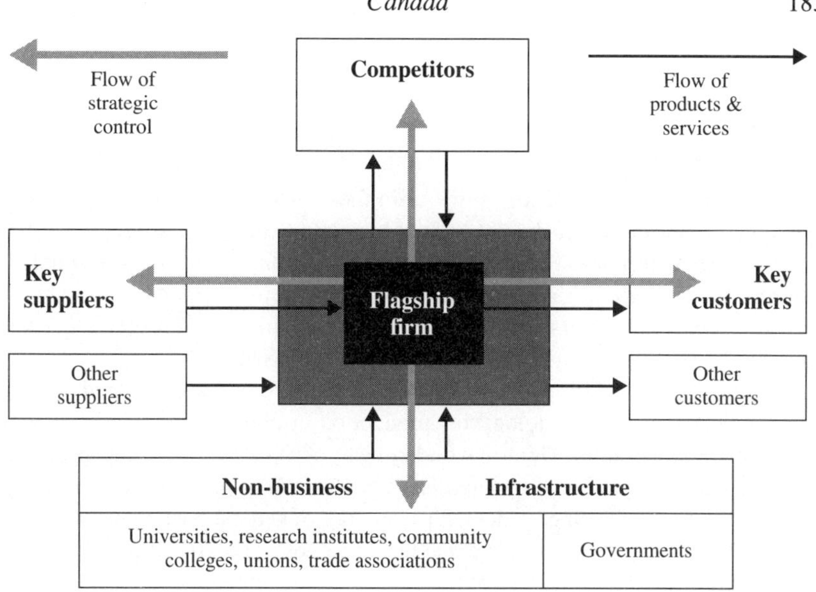

FIG 6.1. Elements of a business network

the overall network. Each of these relationships within the network is described later in this section.

The strongest instance of a flagship firm operating from a home base in Canada was a subsidiary of Sterling Chemicals Inc. known as Sterling Pulp Chemicals Ltd. This company has its Canadian head office in Toronto and operates a chlorine dioxide-based business in two sectors—bleaching systems for the pulp industry and disinfection systems for water treatment. The technology and commercial vision for this business have been developed in Canada by Sterling Pulp and its predecessor companies. In implementing this vision, it has made extensive use of network relationships with its partners in the business system, as shown below.

4.2. **Key Suppliers**

Key suppliers have established long-term relationships with the flagship of the network. In other words, although these firms may be completely independent of the flagship from an ownership perspective, a close convergence of the strategic interests of the two gives rise to a business relationship that is more stable and involved than one based purely upon arm's-length transactions. This type of relationship has become increasingly common in the global economy since the mid-1980s.

The role of the flagship in the key supplier–flagship relationship is to direct key suppliers with respect to:

1. the supplier's role and mandate in the value chain;
2. the quality standards and product specifications to which the key supplier must adhere; and
3. the organizational parameters of the key supplier–flagship relationship.

The flagship will direct the key supplier in these three areas in accordance with the strategic objectives of the network as a whole (Rugman and D'Cruz 1993). For example, with respect to the organizational parameters of the key supplier–flagship relationship, flagships that have recently been concerned with reducing inventory costs have started to require their suppliers to adopt electronic data interchange (EDI) systems to streamline the supply network.

Sterling's relationships with its key Canadian suppliers are instructive. Sterling has designed the technology for production of chlorine dioxide by its customers using generators which have also been designed by Sterling. However, the generators are produced by suppliers who have long-term relationships with Sterling. Similarly, Sterling works with a network of general contractors who have the expertise to install the generators at the customer's site. In contrast, Sterling's relationship with Ontario Hydro has become a major strategic issue that threatens its future competitiveness. Electric power is a major input for Sterling's plants which produce sodium chlorate, the raw material from which its customers produce chlorine dioxide. Ontario Hydro's rates for Sterling's Thunder Bay plant have risen to the level where they make production in Ontario uneconomic. Unless it can obtain power at competitive prices, Sterling may have to consider locating expansion capacity in the USA, where power rates are substantially lower.

With respect to the role of the flagship in establishing the key supplier's mandate in the value chain, recent developments in the relationship between automotive original equipment manufacturers (OEMs) and their key suppliers are also instructive. In the late 1980s the automotive OEMs, in their capacity as flagships, sought to shift greater responsibility for the quality of their output to selected-parts producers by mandating that a small number of these firms would be designated as 'tier-one' parts manufacturers and would be responsible for complete subsystems rather than just individual components in the final product. In this case, the flagships in the network initiated a fundamental reorganization of responsibilities throughout this business system, highlighting the degree to which flagships can exert influence beyond their own corporate 'boundaries' and throughout the network.

4.3. **Key Customers**

The relationship of flagships to their key customers is based on the former developing strategies to support the prosperity and profitability of the latter. The flagship provides broad strategic guidance to the customer and essentially dictates what the customer should be buying and, by implication, producing. The flagship firm-key customer relationship with which the flagship model is most concerned is one in which the key customer is a producer that is using the output of the flagship firm as an intermediate input. Usually, the flagship–key customer relationship revolves around the flagship firm's production of a critical input for the key customer's own production. Key customers are often SMEs and their network relationships need to be carefully explored.

Sterling's relationships with its customers in the pulp industry offer a number of useful lessons. Sterling is working with one of its key customers to find ways to develop closed-loop systems for using chlorine dioxide to bleach pulp. These systems allow pulp mills to meet and exceed government emission regulations regarding free chlorine, a major environmental concern for the pulp industry. By addressing an important strategic issue facing its key customers, Sterling not only helps the Canadian pulp industry maintain its competitiveness but also consolidates its own position in the business system.

4.4. Key Competitors

The flagship firm in a network can interact in various ways with selected competitors, which in turn are often also flagship firms. While the inclusion of competitors is uncommon in traditional business models, they are included in more modern analyses such as the flagship framework to reflect the growing complexities of the international economy and the fact that MNEs are rarely singular in their strategic objectives. In reality, all MNEs pursue several strategic objectives at any given point in time and some of these are often best served by cooperating with firms that have complementary objectives—even though these same firms might be rivals with respect to other strategic objectives. Research at pre-competitive levels of product development is one area where cooperation between 'competitors' has become increasingly common. As discussed below, Dupont Canada has a relationship with the Japanese MNE Kansai in the chemical business. For data on the large increase in strategic alliances and the growth of 'network corporations', which is fully consistent with this aspect of the flagship framework, see, for example, McKern (1994) and some of the essays in Nohria and Eccles (1992).

4.5. Non-Business Infrastructure

The final relationship identified in the network in Fig. 6.1 is that between the flagship and the non-business infrastructure. The non-business infrastructure consists of both government and a group of institutions that are 'network partners'. These include: independent research centres, universities, community colleges, and industry associations. The government non-business infrastructure includes all government-based granting agencies, support services offered through various arms of the government infrastructure, as well as any *ad hoc* programmes and initiatives. The non-business infrastructure–flagship firm relationship is critical to the competitiveness of the network and to the ability of the flagship to lead the network effectively. On the one hand, government has ultimate responsibility for shaping major elements of the economic environment within which the business network must operate (through its control over fiscal policy, monetary policy, and the legal environment in which business must be conducted). On the other hand, the other network partners (especially the flagship firm) can be conducive to collaborative research projects, can supply business with a pool of skilled labour (the education system), and so on.

Again, an example from Sterling's experience is informative. Much of the fundamental technology for using chlorine dioxide in the pulp process was developed by collaboration between Sterling and the Pulp and Paper Centre of the University of Toronto. This collaboration has been in existence for many years and was inspired by the work of Dr Howard Rapson of the University of Toronto, an acknowledged intellectual giant in the field. Over the years, Sterling and the university team have developed improved processes to manufacture chlorine dioxide and are developing the technology for the closed-loop system for use in pulp mills. Without the latter, it might not be possible to meet current and future environmental standards. Both Sterling and the University have had essential roles in this collaboration. Sterling provided the strategic leadership for the commercial aspects of the project and made important financial contributions to the research. On the other hand, the university provided the research environment and talent for the projects.

In summary, then, the relevance of the flagship model to competitiveness lies in the contribution of network relationships and the roles of key suppliers, key customers, and flagships. An understanding of where a particular firm, or, in some instances, an entire industry, lies with respect to the particular network with which it is associated is critical for the formulation of a business strategy which makes sense. Strategies aimed at increasing competitiveness need to be based upon an understanding of the importance of establishing 'key' status with a flagship for firms that are not in a flagship position themselves.

5. Strategy in the Canadian Chemical Industry

In this study, five segments of the Canadian chemical industry are considered; paints and varnish (SIC 3751), soaps and cleaning compounds (SIC 3761), adhesives (SIC 3792), agrochemicals (SIC 372), and the more general inorganic and organic chemical groups (SIC 371 and 3799). These first four segments accounted for approximately 21.7 per cent of the entire chemical industry's (SIC 37) shipments in 1992, which were valued at $Can.21,489.4 million (preliminary data for 1993 value shipments at $Can.22,515 million). Of this share, adhesives accounted for 1.3 per cent of the total ($Can.276.9 million), soap and cleaning compounds 7.7 per cent ($Can.1,651.3 million), paint and varnishes 6.7 per cent ($Can.1,445.7 million), and agrochemicals 6.0 per cent ($Can.1,282.4 million). In addition, the critical role played by producers of industrial inorganic and organic chemicals (SIC groups 371 and 3799) as suppliers to firms in these four groups is also considered in detail. However, because of the eclectic nature of the activities of firms in these two SIC groups, we have not treated them as a separate business system as we did for the other four groups. Organic and inorganic chemicals accounted for 43.9 per cent of shipments in 1992, or $Can.9,437.1 million. The scope of this study therefore covers products which accounted for 65.6 per cent of the chemical industry's shipments in 1992. The only major sub-groups within SIC 37 excluded from the analysis are pharmaceuticals, plastic and synthetic resins, and toilet preparations. Relative to the other nine major SIC groups, chemicals ranked third in terms of value of shipments in 1991, after transport and food.

5.1. **The Paint-Business System**

The Canadian paint-business system comprises two distinct segments: industrial and decorative. With respect to shipments, both segments are approximately equal in size. However, in their organizational and operational characteristics, they are quite different. The paint-business system can also be illustrated by Fig. 6.1. Sources of value added in the industry come from the boxes on the top left representing joint ventures (JVs) for raw materials and JVs for R&D, through the box of key suppliers, to the flagship firms. The value chain extends from the production of basic inputs to the retail or wholesale distribution of the final product, moving from left to right.

The paint industry made shipments worth $Can.1,498.7 million in 1993, reflecting continued growth and recovery from the recession when industry shipments reached a low of $Can.1,370.6 million in 1991. However, pre-1990 shipment levels ($Can.1,659.6 million in 1989) have yet to be reattained. In 1992 there were 131 establishments in this sector, wages and salaries accounted for 28 per cent of variable input costs, and value added for the industry as a whole equalled $Can.829.6 million, or 57 per cent of the value of shipments.

The industrial segment serves primarily the automotive industry in both OEM assembly plants and the refinish aftermarket. The firms in this segment are essentially all large MNEs whose relationships with the automotive OEMs are organized to shadow the North American patterns of OEM operations. Output is concentrated in the hands of just a few large players and a few smaller niche players. The MNEs that account for most of this sector's output include BASF Coatings and Inks Canada Ltd., Dupont Canada Inc., PPG Canada Inc., and Akzo Coatings Ltd.

The key issues for paint manufacturers in the industrial segment revolve around the importance of the automotive OEMs as flagships. Indeed, in some instances, paint manufacturers have developed a strategy of serving only the automotive OEM market. For example, Dupont Canada Inc. produced paint for both the decorative and the broader industrial segments when it entered the business in 1956. However, its focus has progressively narrowed to the point where today it produces paint only for the automotive industry. PPG Canada Inc. is also highly focused in the area of automotive finishes, although the company does still manufacture some industrial coatings in Canada.

The suppliers to the automotive OEMs are responsible for researching colour trends, new product development, and technical support. Each of the major paint manufactures serving the automotive OEMs is capable of covering all of the stages in the paint process. Yet, the automotive OEMs generally distribute different assembly lines among the different paint manufacturers and also distribute responsibility for the different layers in the automotive painting process (i.e. E-coat, topcoats, clearcoats, primers, etc.) to different companies. Generally, each OEM facility has two suppliers. Only four Canadian automotive plants are sole-sourced. One reason for multiple sourcing by the automotive OEMs is that the paint manufacturer may have led in the development of certain products. For example, PPG established an early market position in E-coat. Another reason relates to the efforts by the OEM flagships to keep their suppliers competitive and to avoid becoming too dependent in any one area upon a given supplier.

In addition to dealing directly with the OEMs, paint manufacturers are also key suppliers to the automotive parts suppliers—who in turn supply painted parts to the OEM. In this instance, however, the paint manufacturer interacts with the part manufacturer that has won a contract with an automotive OEM. In this case, the automotive OEM is still clearly acting as the flagship, even though the paint manufacturer is submitting its bid to the automotive parts manufacturer. One important technological development in the parts segment has been the increased use of flexible fascias. The widespread use of these products has required paint manufacturers to develop flexible finishes that have to match the colours of the rest of the body of the car.

Most of the paint manufacturers that have specialized in the automotive OEM segment have also developed relations with the Japanese transplants. In order to enhance their relationship with the Japanese automobile manufacturers, Dupont Canada has established a joint venture with a major Japanese paint supplier—Kansai. In this case, the flagship status of the automobile manufacturer and the key supplier role played by the paint manufacturer are again evident. To become a supplier to the Japanese OEMs, the joint venture needed to adopt a different technology—the technology that the Japanese OEMs were familiar with in their domestic operations in Japan. Furthermore, the joint venture was required to source its basic inputs from the traditional suppliers to Kansai Paint Co. Ltd. Even though Dupont Canada would like to source more inputs from its own supplier network, the strategic force in this relationship has clearly been the Japanese OEMs.

The paint manufacturers that serve the automotive OEMs are organized to conform to the spacial organization of the OEMs themselves. In the case of Dupont Canada, sales contracts with the automotive OEMs (both North American and Japanese) are negotiated in Detroit (indeed, Dupont Canada has a reputation in the industry for having regionalized the structure of its operations most rapidly). Likewise, all of PPG's contracts with the North American-based automotive OEMs are negotiated on a regional basis by the OEM office in Detroit. However, business with the transplants (mainly Japanese firms) is negotiated by the Canadian subsidiary. In the OEM paint segment we also find significant examples of horizontal integration. For example, in addition to being a major paint supplier to the automotive OEMs, PPG also supplies glass and Dupont Canada supplies engineering plastics, fibres, and windshield laminating adhesive film.

In contrast to their role as key supplier to the automotive OEMs, the paint manufacturers act as flagships in the refinishing business. The reason for this is that they control and support the technology used by the body shops to match paints in repair work. Body shops must usually enter into exclusive contracts with their paint suppliers.

The decorative segment of the paint industry is much less technically advanced than the industrial segment and is also dominated by MNEs. Producers in this segment can be distinguished according to the type of distribution channels they use: (i) those that distribute through their own retail outlets (e.g. Sherwin Williams); (ii) those that produce private label products for, or distribute their own products through, mass retail outlets (e.g. Sico Inc.); and (iii) those that distribute their products only through smaller independent retail outlets. With respect to the paint manufacturers that have positioned themselves in the upscale markets (e.g. Para Paints Canada Inc.), the critical business relationship is the key customer relationship they can develop with the large integrated chemical manufacturers. Through these relationships, the paint manufacturers gain access to the output of research programmes that only the larger chemical companies can support. The large companies are willing to share this information with the smaller paint manufacturers because these do not represent a strategic threat to the flagship and because these SMEs are small enough to be able to access markets in which the MNE would otherwise not be able to sell its products (in the case of high-end decorative paint manufacturers, most could be classified as medium-sized enterprises (MEs)).

One of the key issues in this segment concerns the strategic integrity of the distinction between low-cost/low-service producers and the high-quality/high-service producers. With respect to the former category, producers have established key supplier relationships with large retailers (e.g. Sico's relationship with Sears). As key suppliers, these paint manufacturers are mandated to supply the retail flagship with a reasonable product at very competitive prices. The product can be sold either under the original manufacturer's name (as with the Durral line sold through the Price Club/Costco chain) or as a private-label brand (Canadian Tire's Mastercraft line of paints). The question that arises is whether the retail flagships will be content to continue to limit their activities to the high-volume/low-margin segment they have traditionally occupied, or whether they will attempt eventually to increase their share of the higher-quality segment of the decorative market. In several industries (including soaps and detergents), the large, aggressive mass merchandisers such as Wal-Mart are attempting to carve out a flagship role for themselves. It remains to be seen how the current shake-up in the retail sector and the flagship aspirations of several of the larger retailers will affect the decorative paint manufacturers.

In summary, Canadian paint manufacturers pursue their strategic interests by establishing key relationships with flagship firms. In this industrial segment, the predominant flagship relationship of the Canadian paint manufacturers is a key supplier relationship with the automotive OEMs. The strength and focus of this particular flagship relationship have led to considerable stability in this segment of the Canadian chemicals industry, a stability predicated upon the continued health of the Canadian automotive industry.

The decorative segment is more volatile. Depending upon which distribution network they are affiliated with, decorative paint producers have stronger key relationships either with the large integrated chemical companies (mainly from SIC 371 and 3799) that produce the inputs for paint production or with the flagship mass merchandisers. The decorative paint manufacturers that have positioned themselves in the high end of the market must actively market their products—much of the distinctive value of the output from these paint manufacturers originates in the ability of their flagship chemical suppliers to provide them with ingredients that impart to the final product its special qualities (e.g. zero volative organic compounds, durability, washability, resistance to UV rays, and so on). The decorative paint manufacturers that have positioned themselves in the low-cost segment of the market are concerned with volume and have therefore benefited from their relationships as key suppliers to the flagship mass merchandisers.

5.2. The Soap-and-Detergent Business System

The soap-and-detergent business system comprises two broad groups of manufacturers: name-brand producers and private-label producers. Name-brand production accounts for approximately 80 per cent of industry shipments (with 60 per cent going to the consumer market and 20 per cent going to the commercial/institutional market), while private-label production accounts for the remaining 20 per cent (most of which goes to the consumer market). Another way of describing the Canadian market, then, is that 80 per cent of it is consumer and 20 per cent of it is commercial/institutional. In 1991, raw materials accounted for 49 per cent of the cost of inputs, containers 19 per cent, wages 26 per cent, miscellaneous services and inputs 4 per cent, and fuel and electricity 2 per cent. Total shipments in 1991 were worth $Can.1.7 billion. Value added equalled $Can.887 million, or roughly 52 per cent of shipments.

The industry is dominated by foreign MNEs. Procter and Gamble Inc. and Lever Brothers Ltd. are the predominant name-brand producers for the consumer market, with approximately 75 per cent market share. The rest of the consumer market is divided between: (i) smaller, specialized Canadian producers (often regionally based) such as Lavo Ltée (Montreal); (ii) MNEs that service a smaller share of the market through a distribution presence only (or minimal manufacturing) such as Colgate-Palmolive Canada Inc.; and (iii) private-label manufacturers such as Witco Canada Inc. and CCL Industries Inc. The industrial segment is also dominated by MNEs, such as Diversey and Ecolab Ltd., that specialize in producing cleaning and sanitizing products for the hospitality, institutional, and industrial markets.

Two MNEs have acted as flagship firms in the soap and detergent industry: Lever Brothers Ltd. and Procter and Gamble Inc. These companies are characterized by significant levels of both vertical and horizontal integration. Lever Brothers Ltd., for example, has integrated backwards into higher value-added inputs such as isethionate and fatty acids and have sourced other critical inputs from third-party suppliers.

Key suppliers to these flagship firms are the large integrated chemical companies. For example, Rhône-Poulenc has been a key supplier of surfactants to many of the major soap-and-detergent manufacturers in Canada (Procter and Gamble Inc., Colgate-Palmolive Canada Inc., Lever Brothers Ltd., Diversey Corporation, and CCL Industries Inc.). As a key supplier, Rhône-Poulenc interacts with its flagship customers on a North American basis reflecting the nature of flagship strategy in this industry.

In some cases, the soap-and-detergent flagships will closely coordinate the activities of several of their key suppliers. For example, the production of ethoxylate for a major soap-and-detergent manufacturer involved the coordination of three key suppliers: one supplied the ethylene oxide; alcohol was supplied by another; and the third supplier provided the reactors on a service-fee basis. Therefore, in addition to negotiating all of the contracts for the inputs with its key suppliers, the soap and detergent manufacturer also directed its key suppliers to do the blending of a critical input for them.

Although Procter and Gamble and Lever continue to act as flagships, their longstanding flagship positions have been challenged in the mid-1990s, and the networks for which they have served as a hub for so long are on the verge of radical transformation. Competition for flagship status in this industry has emerged in the retail sector, both from traditional retailers, such as Loblaws, and from the new entrants in the Canadian retailing scene, mass merchandisers such as Price Club and Wal-Mart.

The new entrants in the Canadian retail sector have set new standards for efficient distribution networks and heightened price competition. While the soap-and-detergent industry has always been subject to price pressure from retailers (since soaps and detergents are among the 'basic products' that retailers frequently feature as specials), the traditional soap-and-detergent flagships will probably see their leverage with respect to retailers substantially eroded because of both the increased market power of the new retailers that have entered the market recently and the rise of the private-label segment. Furthermore, with advertising costs already accounting for approximately 25 per cent of selling price, it is unlikely that the soap-and-detergent manufacturers will be able to improve their leverage with respect to the retailers by means of increased promotion at the consumer level.

The soap-and-detergent business in Canada continues to be viable. However, the traditional flagship status of the MNEs operating in this sector is under attack from the retail sector. The strategic question faced by managers in the soap-and-detergent industry then is whether to engage the retailers head on in a battle to maintain flagship status or whether to adapt to fundamental changes in the network by developing key-supplier relationships with retailers. In most cases, the confrontational approach will not be successful. Firms in the soap-and-detergent sector need to attempt to increase their leverage with respect to retailers through development of stronger name-brand recognition while simultaneously seeking common ground with them.

5.3. **The Adhesives Business System**

The adhesives-business system in Canada is dominated by MNEs. The industry can be roughly divided according to the quality of output between low- and medium-performance products that are produced for local industrial and consumer markets and high-performance products that are produced for new industrial applications such as in the automotive and aerospace industries. The Canadian market is relatively small, and therefore production in Canada is limited to the low- and medium-performance products. High-performance needs are served through imports. These products account for approximately 35 per cent of the Canadian market, and are associated predominantly with the automotive OEM sector. The industry does not export to any significant degree.

Shipments in 1993 were valued at $Can.300.3 million. The total cost of inputs into the manufacture of these shipments was $Can.200.1 million. Raw materials accounted for $Can.124.8 million (62 per cent of total cost), wages $Can.71.7 million (36 per cent), and fuel and electricity $Can.3.7 million (2 per cent). The cost structure of the industry has been affected considerably by the ratification of the FTA in 1989 and by the continued liberalization of trade in NAFTA. Prior to these agreements, basic inputs accounted for upwards of 76 per cent of manufacturing costs, while wages accounted for only 22 per cent of total cost. Trade liberalization has therefore contributed to a lowering of overall production costs and led to a significant increase in the relative share of wages in the sector's cost structure.

Canadian adhesives manufacturers usually specialize in producing either for the consumer market or for the commercial/industrial market. The principal producers for the industrial market include Nacan Products Ltd., Swift Adhesives Inc., H. B. Fuller Canada Inc., Helmitin Canada Inc., and Halltech Inc. The producers that dominate the retail/consumer market include Roberts Company Canada Ltd., Lepages Ltd., and Canadian Adhesives Ltd. A few firms produce for both segments; these include 3M and Dural. In value terms, the industrial segment accounts for approximately 80 per cent of the total adhesives market.

Adhesive manufacturers in Canada act as key customers to the large integrated chemical producers and as key suppliers to large manufacturers such as the automotive OEMs. In effect, the adhesive and sealant manufacturers play an intermediary role in the value chain that links the flagship producers of the basic inputs into the manufacture of adhesives and sealants and the flagship commercial end users of these products. A stylized characterization of the new product-development processes in this relationship is as follows: (1) the end user (e.g. automotive OEM, packaging facility, and so on) communicates a new need to the adhesive producer (such as a reduced volatile organic compound product); (2) the adhesive manufacturer tries to supply this product if the new specifications are not too technically demanding; (3) if the technical implications of the end-user's needs are more complex, then the adhesive producer will be dependent upon its suppliers of basic inputs to provide the required innovation (e.g. in the form of a new polymer system) to create a product with the qualities demanded by the end user.

The Canadian adhesive manufacturers have established key customer relationships with the large integrated North American chemical producers. In the four main product categories (hot melts, water-based synthetic adhesives, water-based natural adhesives, and solvent-based adhesives) the Canadian manufacturers have heavily integrated backwards for some products and not for others. Further, where they have not integrated, there has been a strong trend towards a greater concentration of suppliers and the development of closer, more long-term relationships with those that remain.

With respect to the production of hot melts (which have been one of the fastest growing segments), the main inputs are often sourced from independent suppliers. The three main inputs are wax, EVACs, and tackifying resins. A fourth input, that is more important from a quality perspective than a cost perspective, is anti-oxidants. The main producer of wax is International Waxes Inc. EVACs are produced by AT Plastics (the only major Canadian-based producer), Dupont Canada, Exxon, and Atochem. Tackifying resins are all imported from the USA. The principal manufacturers of this input are Arizona, Eastman, Exxon, and Hercules. Finally, anti-oxidants are produced by, and mainly sourced from, Ciba-Geigy Canada Ltd. The significance of large integrated chemical MNEs as suppliers is clear. North American producers of hot melts, such as Nacan Products Ltd., have not vertically integrated any of these basic inputs.

With respect to water-based synthetic resins, PVAc and EVA account for approximately 90 per cent of basic inputs by value. PVAc production has been integrated into the value chain of the large adhesive producers such as Dural, Nacan, and Reichold, which together account for more than 80 per cent of PVAc output in Canada. The principal producers of EVA are Nacan (National Starch), Reichold, and Air Products. An input into the production of water-based synthetic resins that has not been internalized by the adhesive producers is plasticizers.

These are produced mainly by large chemical MNEs such as Monsanto and Velsicol.

With respect to water-based natural adhesive production, the two most important inputs are starch (dextrins) and casein. Starch production for adhesive production is almost completely internalized, with only a few firms, including National Starch, accounting for the bulk of production in Canada. Casein, on the other hand, is imported. It is a traded commodity for which key supplier relationships have not been found necessary.

Production of solvent-based adhesives, which have been on the decline for environmental reasons, is characterized by linkages with large MNE chemical producers for all significant inputs: solvents and neoprene. Solvents account for approximately 80 per cent of the input for this product. The most commonly used solvents include xylene, toluene, MEK, and hexane. Imperial Oil and Shell are the main suppliers of these inputs. It should be noted that a very small fraction of Imperial Oil and Shell's output of these products is destined for the adhesives industry. In the case of Neprene, which accounts for the other 20 per cent of the input into solvent-based adhesive production, it is the only supplier of this input in Canada.

With respect to their role as key suppliers, the principal customers of the adhesive producers have been packagers (40 per cent of the industrial market) and the automotive OEMs (35 per cent of the industrial market). As is the case in the industrial-paint segment, the adhesives producers have established key supplier relationships that reflect the growing need for product customization and high-quality service to accompany the product. In some instances, adhesive manufacturers develop such close relationships with customers that the adhesive manufacturer will assume responsibility for managing supply to the customer. For example, as a key supplier to some customers, Nacan will determine the adhesive needs of its customer on site and will initiate a shipment—the customer is not involved in the order process until the invoice stage.

A key issue facing Canadian adhesive manufacturers is the erosion of their Canadian customer base. For example, whereas furniture manufacturers used to be a significant market segment, this industry has been largely rationalized on a North American basis, with very little manufacturing remaining in Ontario. A related problem concerns the Canadian industry's traditional emphasis on production of lower- to medium-performance products and the lack of technical capability as a growing share of the adhesives market moves towards higher-performance products.

Therefore, in their role as key customers of the flagship integrated chemical producers, the adhesive producers should continue to develop these relationships by finding niches where they may be able to market new products based upon new formulations developed by the flagships. With respect to their role as key suppliers to flagship customers, the adhesive producers need to focus upon the needs of their customers both in terms of technical requirements as well as with respect to organizational issues where their customers are in the process of integrating their operations on a North American basis.

5.4. The Agrochemical Business System

The agrochemical industry can be divided between fertilizer production and pesticide production. The two sectors are radically different from each other in terms of the structure of shipments. The fertilizer industry is characterized by low levels of imports (approximately one-fifth of the domestic market) and high export volumes (approximately two-thirds the value of total shipments). In contrast, roughly half of the domestic market for pesticides is served by imports, and exports account for only one-tenth the value of total shipments. With respect to the industry's cost structure, in 1991 63.5 per cent of input costs were accounted for by raw inputs, 15.8 per cent by wages, 9.0 per cent by fuel, 1.6 per cent by containers, and the remaining 10.1 per cent by various other costs. Shipments were valued at $Can.1,282.4 million in 1992 (preliminary data suggest that shipments for 1993 will be valued at $Can.1,452.8 million). We will focus our analysis here upon the flagship relationships and the competitiveness of the pesticides industry.

As with all of the other sectors examined in this chapter, the agricultural chemicals sector is dominated by MNEs. For the most part, the main function of the Canadian subsidiaries of these firms has been distribution and the mixing of active ingredients to create the final product. The principal players in this market are Ciba Geigy, Zeneca, Hoechst, Monsanto, Rhône-Poulenc Canada, Rohm and Haas Canada, Sandoz, and Uniroyal Chemical Ltd. Some firms in this market, such as BASF, Dupont Canada, and ICI, do not manufacture pesticides in Canada but do act as distributors. Almost 90 per cent of the industry's output is for the agricultural market and, of this, approximately 77 per cent is herbicides. Most firms do not conduct R&D in Canada or maintain only small research laboratories (a few significant exceptions will be discussed below).

This sector is characterized by some clear examples of flagship activity. In the 'greenhouse' segment, Plant Products Company Ltd. stands out as having several strong flagship qualities. With respect to suppliers, strong, cooperative long-term relationships have been fostered with an emphasis on quality and trust. In terms of the direction of product development, the company has sought to develop relationships both with key competitors as well as with the non-business infrastructure (namely a research relationship with Laval University) towards maintaining the ability to develop cutting-edge technologies in-house (especially in the area of biological controls). As a result, Plant Products Company Ltd. is responsible for the first biological fungicide registration in Canada. In its relationship with Laval, the university laboratory does the basic research, while Plant Products Company Ltd. takes care of patents, registrations, and market research.

Another example of flagship activity in the agricultural chemicals industry is Uniroyal Chemical Ltd. Uniroyal maintains a sophisticated R&D facility in Guelph which is integrated into Uniroyal's global R&D programme. The high level of technical ability at the Canadian operation has translated into two forms of flagship role. First, with respect to the parent R&D facility in Connecticut, the Canadian R&D facility plays a key leadership role (while at the same time also fitting into Uniroyal Chemical's international organizational structure). For example, the Guelph facility supplies 100 per cent of the in-house compounds for biological screening in Connecticut, where environmental chemistry is conducted. In effect, the high technical capacity of the Canadian operation has made it an important part of Uniroyal Chemical's global R&D organization.

Another area in which Uniroyal Chemical's technical capacity has given it a flagship role is with respect to field-testing and its relationship with customers. Its field-testing programme is among the most sophisticated in Canada and the company works closely with customers to determine and then provide for their needs. In addition, Uniroyal will attempt to develop differentiated products for its customers.

Finally, Uniroyal Chemical's relationship with the non-business infrastructure has been critical to the company's success, both with respect to competitors and with respect to its internal relationship with the rest of the company's global operations. Whereas numerous examples can be found in the Canadian chemical industry of MNEs reducing or completely eliminating the R&D capacity of their Canadian operations (e.g. the closing of Shell's R&D facility in Oakville and the moving of Diversey's R&D facility to Chicago), Uniroyal Chemical Ltd. is an example of a viable R&D operation in Canada and of the benefits of having good R&D conducted in Canada. Part of Uniroyal's success in this regard should be associated with government support of research programmes. For example, from 1962 to 1983, the National Research Council's IRAP programme which supported R&D at the Uniroyal research laboratory was critical to the laboratory's success.

The Canadian agrochemical industry is among the most competitive sub-sectors of the Canadian chemicals industry. This competitiveness derives from a combination of 'natural' factors (proximity to a large market, availability of basic inputs at world-competitive prices) and less 'natural' factors (positive contribution of government programmes to R&D efforts, favourable precedents for joint business–university research efforts, good international reputation developed by Canadian scientific community, and so on). This sector therefore provides other sub-sectors of the chemical industry with examples of viable Canadian operations that are integrated into the global operations of their parents. However, to remain viable the agrochemical producers must continue to nurture their network relationships.

6. **Conclusions**

Three broad conclusions for the competitiveness of Canadian firms and the Canadian economy emerge from this analysis of the Canadian chemical sector: (1) the significance for competitiveness of key supplier relationships for subsidiaries of MNEs in the face of the rapid regionalization of the Canadian industry; (2) the significance for competitiveness of key customer relationships of SMEs with flagship suppliers; and (3) the importance of the non-business infrastructure to the continued dynamism and entrepreneurial contribution of SMEs. These three findings confirm the analytical strength and predictive ability of the flagship business network model. They are also consistent with the theoretical work of Dunning (1995) on ways to incorporate cooperative production and strategic alliances by MNEs into the eclectic paradigm.

6.1. The Key Supplier Relationships of MNEs

This research suggests that the Canadian chemical industry has adapted too slowly to the growing significance of regional economic integration in North America. More specifically, many Canadian chemical companies have not understood clearly enough the need for a transition from their earlier stand-alone organizational structures (that were viable primarily because of high tariff barriers) to the key supplier and key customer roles demanded by internationalization in an industry dominated by MNEs. Even when managers did recognize this (e.g. in firms such as Dupont Canada, Alkaril, Hart), they could not resolve the problem. Whether a firm is a subsidiary of an MNE or an independent and much smaller niche player, establishing strong relationships with flagships is the key to the future survival of Canadian chemical companies.

Many of the larger MNEs in Canada are now doing very well as key suppliers. For example, in the paints industry key suppliers such as PPG and Dupont Canada have profitable businesses as key suppliers to the US and Japanese automobile makers (OEMs) in Canada. The strategic direction for these businesses is partly determined in the USA, but the production mandate to implement these contracts can result in a successful Canadian business, with many jobs, profits for the company, and a net positive contribution to Canada's social and economic well-being. Therefore, managers of MNEs need to continue to adopt a North American strategic vision. Especially important within the context of MNEs will be the ability of Canadian managers to articulate in the appropriate North American regional forums the Canadian subsidiary's potential contribution as a key supplier.

6.2. The Key Customer Relationships of SMEs

Somewhat in contrast to the dramatic retrenchment affecting the larger MNEs, there is a more subtle change affecting SMEs. These are often 'niche' players driven by entrepreneurs who have a sense of the market. The SMEs are close to their customers; they can build and maintain long-term successful businesses through their marketing skills and flexibility.

The SMEs act as intermediaries between the larger MNE suppliers and the wholesale or national distributors. Their flexibility and marketing know-how are vital firm-specific advantages. They can use their laboratories to customize products and/or respond very quickly to customer demands. They can manage these service functions better than larger MNE suppliers. As 'key customers' of the MNEs, they can actually expand the total market for the MNEs, while not acting as a threat to them. In this sense, the SMEs have to manage the key supplier role with skill and foresight. They can develop close working relationships with a variety of MNEs provided they preserve secrecy and develop a reputation for discretion and non-disclosure to rival MNEs.

SMEs therefore promise to be a source of considerable growth and dynamism in the Canadian chemicals industry as MNEs seek to rationalize the productive structure of their global (or regional) operations while at the same time accessing as many markets as they can. SMEs are, in effect, the keys to new markets in so far as (*a*) they are able to penetrate markets that are simply too small for MNEs to cater to, given the scale of operations to which most MNEs are committed; and (*b*) they allow for more rapid roll-out of technological advances by making smaller, more specialized product development economically viable.

6.3. Support from Non-Business Infrastructure

With Canadian-based chemical MNEs consolidating their R&D functions outside Canada, there has been less opportunity for technical training 'on the job' in the Canadian chemical industry. This has occurred especially in the agrochemical sector. Therefore, more of the burden for technical training will shift to the Canadian educational system. However, the skills to be a successful MNE network manager are often missing in today's Canadian chemicals industry.

Managers who started their careers running branch plants for which Canada was the market now often find themselves in a radically different organizational and strategic environment. As long as Canada was a protected market, the reason for the existence of the Canadian operation was obvious and needed no explaining. Now, after the FTA and NAFTA, the contribution of the Canadian operation to the company's global strategy is no longer so obvious (at least not to head office) and Canadian managers are finding that they need to operate on a North American regional basis. Canadian managers therefore need to develop the managerial skills relevant to international network forms of corporate organization, as illustrated by the flagship model discussed here. Therefore, although Canadian universities provide the industry with an ample supply of graduates in engineering and chemistry, the radical change which the industry has experienced and the continued exposure of the industry to the forces of globalization and international benchmarking have given rise to the need for skill sets which the industry is not used to needing and which the non-business infrastructure is not yet equipped to produce.

6.4. Regionalization and Government Policy

A key theme in this volume is the interaction between domestic government policy and competitiveness. In the Canadian context the response of the federal governments of Prime Ministers Brian Mulroney (1984–93) and Jean Chrétien (since 1993) to the pressures of globalization has been to endorse and promote a strategy of regionalization. The Mulroney conservative government negotiated and won the election of 1988 on the substance of the Canada–US FTA, a set of rules aimed to enhance access to the large US triad market for Canadian firms. The Chrétien liberal government approved NAFTA immediately after entering into office in November 1993 and thereby committed itself to the regionalization strategy designed by the previous federal government.

An important conclusion of this chapter is that successive Canadian governments have had little choice other than to adopt a regionalization strategy of market access to the dominant US economy. In the past decade, governments have been influenced by large Canadian-based MNEs who were keen advocates of both the FTA and NAFTA. Indeed, the actual details of the negotiations of the FTA were largely determined by business leaders serving on Canada's International Trade Advisory Committee (ITAC) in the 1986–8 period. Evidence for this assertion is set out in Hart *et al.* (1994) and Rugman (1988*a*), both of whom present 'insider' analyses of the negotiating process—Hart as a member of the Canadian negotiating team led by Simon Reisman, and Rugman as the only academic member of ITAC. While the influence of business groups was somewhat reduced in NAFTA, it is apparent that items such as the rules of origin for automobiles, textiles, and apparel reflect sectoral lobbying conveyed through the participation of industry groups in ITAC and on the sectoral advisory committees on international trade (SAGITs) in Canada, and on the parallel committees in the USA (with the Mexican process being relatively opaque in comparison).

In short, the evidence from the complex institutional fabric of the FTA and NAFTA provides strong support for the regionalization thesis of this chapter and for the related point that the main role of the Canadian federal governments in the last decade has been facilitate market access to the USA for Canadian business. This strategy of regionalization has been called a policy of continentalism by its critics (see, e.g., Hurtig 1991), but it is now the reality of Canada's role in the world economy.

Such a strategy (implemented by both the Canadian federal and provincial governments) has most certainly helped advance the competitiveness of Canadian resources and capabilities. No longer is there any serious support for the alternative nationalist strategy in which Canadian governments would adopt an industrial policy by giving mandatory direction to business in dealing with issues of global competitiveness. Instead, Canadian governments have emerged as a partner of business, with the explicit intention of helping Canadian-based firms to integrate themselves better into the US economy. The result is a series of North American 'regional' business networks or clusters in which Canadian firms operate as if there were no border (Rugman and D'Cruz 1991, 1994).

With the US–Canadian border disappearing, there is a different role for government—no longer one defined by the political nationalism of the border but one defined by the interdependence of business. The power and autonomy of Canadian governments to pursue independent efficiency-based macro-organizational policies have been curtailed since the 1960s. Recently, the integration of the US and Canadian goods and factor markets has matched the previous integration of the North American financial markets. For the last thirty years Canadian interest rates (and Canadian monetary policy) have been determined by the US Federal Reserve System (Rugman 1980). Over this period the value of the Canadian dollar has followed in lock step with changes in the US dollar against the Japanese yen, European, and other non-American currencies.

Canada's macro-organizational policies have become increasingly correlated with US ones (although not completely harmonized in goods and factor markets, since both the FTA and NAFTA provide for national treatment rather than reciprocity). To this extent, Canada represents the maturation of the regionalization concept—a country completely interdependent with its US neighbour due to financial, goods, and factor-market integration. Canada may even be a precursor of events in other countries. As 'alliance capitalism' becomes the norm in the triad, the small open economies (like Canada) will be drawn into the regional networks of the triad leaders. Then the role of the home government's policy will matter much less than that of the relevant triad government. In turn, business strategy in countries like Canada will become much less home-base oriented and much more responsive to the rules and regulations of its dominant triad partners.

NOTE

This paper was presented at the Carnegie Bosch Foundation Conference on 'Governments, Globalization and International Business', 15–16 June 1995, Georgetown University, Washington, DC. Revised: December 1995. Helpful comments have been made by Joseph R. D'Cruz and John Dunning.

REFERENCES

Anderson, A. (1995), *Seeking Common Ground: Canada–U.S. Trade Dispute Settlement Policy in the Nineties* (Boulder, Colo.: Westview Press).

Bartlett, C., and Ghoshal, S. (1989), *Managing across Borders: The Transnational Solution* (Boston: Harvard Business School Press).

Crookell, H. (1990), *Canadian–American Trade and Investment under the Free Trade Agreement* (Westport, Conn.: Quorum Books).

D'Cruz, J. (1995), 'The Theory of the Flagship Firm' (mimeo; Faculty of Management, University of Toronto).

—— and Rugman, A. (1992), *New Compacts for Canadian Competitiveness* (Toronto: Kodak Canada).

—— —— (1993), 'Developing International Competitiveness: The Five Partners Model', *Business Quarterly*, 58/2 (Winter), 101–7.

—— —— (1994*a*), 'The Five Partners Model: France Telecom, Alcatel, and the Global Telecommunications Industry', *European Management Review*, 12/1: 59–66.

—— —— (1994*b*), 'Business Network Theory and the Canadian Telecommunications Industry', *International Business Review*, 3/3: 275–88.

—— Gestrin, M., and Rugman, A. (1995), 'Is the Canadian Manager an Endangered Species?' (mimeo of study prepared for Ontario's Ministerial Advisory Committee on Chemicals; Faculty of Management, University of Toronto).

Doern, G., and Tomlin, B. (1991), *Faith and Fear: The Free Trade Story* (Toronto: Stoddart).

Dunning, J. (1993*a*), *Multinational Enterprises and the Global Economy* (Wokingham: Addison-Wesley).

—— (1993*b*), *The Globalization of Business: The Challenge of the 1990s* (London: Routledge).

—— (1995), 'Reappraising the Eclectic Paradigm in an Age of Alliance Capitalism', *Journal of International Business Studies*, 26: 461–91.

Eden, L. (1994*a*) (ed.), *Multinationals in North America* (Calgary: University of Calgary Press).

—— (1994*b*), *Multinationals as Agents of Change: Setting New Canadian Policy on Foreign Direct Investment* (Ottawa: Industry Canada Discussion Paper No. 1).

Globerman, S. (1994) (ed.), *Canadian-Based Multinationals* (Calgary: University of Calgary Press).

Hart, M., *et al.* (1994), *Decision at Midnight: Inside the Canada–U.S. Free Trade Negotiations* (Vancouver: University of British Columbia Press).

Hurtig, M. (1991), *The Betrayal of Canada* (Toronto: Stoddart).

Jenkins, B. (1992), *The Paradox of Continental Production: National Investment Policies in North America* (Ithaca, NY: Cornell University Press).

Keohane, R., and Nye, J. (1977), *Power and Interdependence* (Boston: Little Brown).

Macdonald, D. (1985), *Report of the Royal Commission on the Economic Union and Development Prospects for Canada* (Ottawa: Supply and Services).

McKern, B. (1994), 'International Network Corporations in a Global Economy' (Pittsburgh: Carnegie Bosch Institute Working Paper No. 94–9).

Nohria, N., and Eccles, R. (1992) (eds.), *Networks and Organizations: Structure, Form and Action* (Boston: Harvard Business School Press).

Porter, M. E. (1980), *Competitive Strategy: Techniques for Analyzing Industries and Competitors* (New York: The Free Press).

—— (1990), *The Competitive Advantage of Nations* (New York: The Free Press).

—— (1991), *Canada at the Crossroads* (Ottawa: Business Council on National Issues).

—— and Armstrong, J. (1992), 'Dialogue on Canada at the Crossroads', *Business Quarterly*, 56/4 (Spring), 6–10.

Rugman, A. (1980), *Multinationals in Canada: Theory, Performance and Economic Impact* (Boston: Martinus Nijhoff/Kluwer.)

—— (1985), *Outward Bound: Canadian Direct Investment in the United States* (Toronto: C. D. Howe Institute.)

Rugman, A. (1988*a*), 'Why Business Supports Free Trade', in J. Crispo (ed.), *Free Trade: The Real Story* (Toronto: Gage).

—— (1988*b*), 'Multinationals and the Free Trade Agreement', in M. Gold and D. Leyton Brown (eds.), *Trade-Off on Free Trade* (Toronto: Carswell).

—— (1990), *Multinationals and Canada–United States Free Trade* (Columbia, SC: University of South Carolina Press.)

—— (1993), 'Drawing the Border for a Multinational Enterprise and a Nation-State', in L. Eden and E. Potter (eds.), *Multinationals in the Global Political Economy* (New York: St Martin's Press).

—— (1994*a*), 'A Canadian Perspective on NAFTA', *The International Executive*, 36/1 (January–February), 33–54.

—— (1994*b*) (ed.), *Foreign Investment and NAFTA* (Columbia, SC: University of South Carolina Press).

—— (1994*c*), 'Strategic Management and Canadian Multinational Enterprises', in S. Globerman (ed.), *Canadian-Based Multinationals* (Calgary: University of Calgary Press).

—— (1995), 'Environmental Regulations and International Competitiveness', *The International Executive*, 37/5 (September–October 1995), 451–65.

—— and Anderson, A. (1987), *Administered Protection in America* (London: Routledge).

—— and D'Cruz, J. (1991), *Fast Forward: Improving Canada's International Competitiveness* (Toronto: Kodak Canada Inc.).

—— —— (1993), 'The "Double Diamond" Model of International Competitiveness', *Management International Review*, 33/2: 17–40.

—— —— (1994), 'A Theory of Business Networks', in L. Eden (ed.), *Multinationals in North America* (Calgary: University of Calgary Press).

—— and McIlveen, J. (1985), *Megafirms: Strategies for Canada's Multinationals* (Toronto: Methuen).

—— and Verbeke, A. (1993), 'Foreign Subsidiaries and Multinational Strategic Management: An Extension and Correction of Porter's Single Diamond Framework', *Management International Review*, 33 (Special Issue 2), 71–84.

—— and Waverman, L. (1991) 'Foreign Ownership and Corporate Strategy', in L. Waverman (ed.), *Corporate Globalization through Mergers and Acquisitions* (Calgary: University of Calgary Press).

—— D'Cruz, J., and Verbeke, A. (1995), 'Internalization and De-Internalization: Will Business Networks Replace Multinationals?', in G. Boyd (ed.), *Competitive and Co-operative Macromanagement* (Aldershot: Edward Elgar).

Safarian, A. (1993), *Multinational Enterprise and Public Policy: A Study of the Industrial Countries* (Aldershot: Edward Elgar).

Statistics Canada (1995), *Canada's International Investment Position 1994* (Cat. No. 67–202, Table 27, Ottawa: Statistics Canada, March).

Warner, M., and Rugman, A. (1994), 'Competitiveness: An Emerging Strategy of Discrimination in U.S. Antitrust and R&D Policy?', *Law and Policy in International Business*, 25 (Spring), 945–82.

Watkins, M., *et al.* (1968), *Foreign Ownership and the Structure of Canadian Industry* (Ottawa: The Queen's Printer).

7

Australia

Hal Hill and Bruce McKern

1. **Introduction**

Australia is well suited to a comparative study of globalization and international business for a number of reasons. First, its economic structure is unusual, 'mid-way' according to one popular view (Arndt 1965), exhibiting characteristics of both developing and developed countries. Among the former are its heavy, though declining, reliance on commodity exports, its large external debt, and its net imports of both capital and technology. The latter characteristics include high living standards and social indicators, which place it in the middle ranks of the OECD group.

Secondly, the country embarked on a set of major economic policy reforms during the 1980s, which transformed it from one of the most inward-looking and protectionist of countries, to one in which the liberal policy agenda is in the ascendancy (with a few notable exceptions, discussed below). Consequently, it provides an excellent 'laboratory' for an assessment of the impact of liberalization and globalization on an economy, albeit one in which the reform agenda remains incomplete and the micro, firm-level impacts are still being played out.

A third reason for interest is that Australia is on the periphery of, and increasingly enmeshed with, the dynamic East Asian region. Probably in no other OECD economy are national fortunes more closely linked to developments in this region. Consequently, Australia's involvement in the seemingly inexorable rise of East Asia provides a valuable case study of one of the most important dimensions of globalization in the late twentieth century.

Furthermore, Australia has for most of its history been open to FDI, apart from restrictions in a few sectors, with the result that foreign corporations are major actors in the economy, especially in mining and manufacturing industry.

The theme of this book is the reciprocal relationship between national governments, influencing the business context in a country, and international corporations, executing strategies of global expansion. The interest in this two-way interaction is relatively new, although governments have long been concerned with the impact of FDI investment on their economies. Earlier work on the rationale for FDI (see, e.g., Hymer, Caves, and others) emphasized growth beyond domestic markets and the exploitation of intangible assets of technical and managerial know-how, usually associated with oligopolistic industry structures.

In this framework, firm-specific ownership advantages are the primary enabling factor for FDI. Other studies focused on country-specific variables (Kravis and Lipsey 1982, for example), including government policies, as attractors of FDI. Dunning's eclectic paradigm (Dunning 1977, 1979) combined firm-specific factors (ownership advantages) with country-specific factors (location advantages, including government) to explain the foreign location decisions of investors. Dunning also explains the adoption of a hierarchical form for the exploitation of the firm's intangible assets in foreign countries in terms of ownership advantages, resulting in internalization or cross-border corporate ownership, which results in lower transaction costs than contracting in imperfect markets for such assets.

Porter focused attention on the home country of the international corporation, and specifically on a complex of four variables he described as the 'diamond of competitive advantage' which collectively determine the competitive posture and competences of a country's domestic firms, thus fitting them for success or failure in international markets. Porter's work is supported by detailed analyses of a number of countries, identifying revealed comparative advantage for each country, but using a richer definition of the term which includes foreign penetration through direct investment as well as export trade performance. Government is not central to the model and Porter does not support intervention except where it enhances infrastructure or competitive conditions. His model pays little attention to national culture as an explanatory variable.

Globalization describes the growing integration of the world economy, primarily through the cross-border activities of international corporations (ICs). The growth of globalization is due to both demand-side and supply-side influences. On the demand side, a convergence of living standards in the rich triad, coupled with widely distributed international media, has led to a higher share of demand for products and services that are globally more homogeneous. On the supply side, rapid transport and cheaper communications technology, coupled with deregulation, privatization, and lower trade and investment barriers, make it more possible for firms to exploit economies of scale and scope by adopting a globally integrated strategy for their businesses.

The paramount role of the international corporation in the deepening integration of the world economy through trade and investment is well established. The sales of international corporations were equivalent to one-quarter of the world's GDP in 1992 (UNCTAD 1994) and a higher proportion of private-sector output. The total foreign sales of international corporations in 1992 were estimated at $US4.8 trillion. Total world exports of goods and services were $US4.5 trillion, so ICs' sales in host countries are already more important than arm's-length international trade. A considerable portion of export trade is conducted between the affiliates of ICs—approximately one-third. In fact, in manufactured products, arm's-length trade now has the minority role; transactions internal to ICs (i.e. between affiliates) account for 75 per cent of world trade in such goods.

The importance of trade to the major economies is underlined in Table 7.1. A more complete measure of the activity of foreign firms in a country is the effective foreign-penetration ratio, which measures imports plus local sales by foreign corporations in a country, less exports by those companies, as a percentage of total national demand. For manufacturing industry, these ratios range from 9.1 per cent (Japan) to 24.5 per cent (the USA) and 47.3 per cent (France). Data for Australia are not available on this basis, but we note that the foreign share of turnover in manufacturing was about 30 per cent and the share of imports in total demand 25 per cent in 1990 (OECD 1994*a*). So for Australian manufacturing the effective foreign penetration ratio was in excess of 30 per cent and perhaps as high as 50 per cent. Foreign participation was also high in the mining sector, which is mainly export-oriented.

TABLE 7.1. Exports, selected countries, 1993

Country	1993 (% of GDP)	1970–93 (% increase)
Australia	19	36
Canada	30	30
USA	10	67
Netherlands	68	n.a.
Sweden	33	38
UK	25	9
Japan	9	−18
Korea[a]	29	107
New Zealand	31	35
Singapore	169	66

Notes: Data refer to exports of goods and non-factor services.
n.a. = not available.

[a] Korean data refer to 1992.

Source: World Bank (1995).

As is well known, the majority of global FDI flows have originated from, and flowed into, the highly developed countries of the triad (UNCTAD 1994). Foreign ownership, measured as share of employment, ranged from as little as 1 per cent in Japan (in 1989) to 37.8 per cent in Canada (in 1980). Australia was at 26.3 per cent in 1980. Japan is the low outlier in measures of import and investment penetration, and Germany is also low on indicators of inward foreign investment. A further indicator of the importance of FDI is the ratio of inward FDI stock to GDP (Table 7.2). For Australia, this ratio is 27 per cent, second highest among the comparison group after Singapore (91 per cent). Australia's outward investment also shows complementarity to its inward investment with respect to the USA and the UK (see Table 7.11). However, like other countries, Australia's investment in Japan is low; conversely, its investments in New Zealand are disproportionally high, due to proximity and long-standing political and cultural ties.

Given the importance of country conditions to the competitive strengths of home country firms, and the substantial and deepening presence of international corporations in the economies of most countries, it is to be expected that country competitiveness is modified by the presence of ICs. As Rugman argues, the competitiveness of a country like Canada, host to a high level of FDI, is determined, not solely by Canadian environmental factors, but also by the 'diamond' of its major trade and investment partner, the USA (Rugman 1991). The proximity of the USA, under the open trade environment of recent years, crowned by NAFTA, has a big influence on the demand pattern facing Canadian firms. Also, US-based ICs operating in Canada have an impact on Canadian managerial and technical competences and the competitive conditions of its industry.

Australia, like Canada a host to much FDI, might be expected to be influenced in a similar way, although without the benefit of proximity to the vast US market. It is not clear how far spatially the idea of a 'double diamond' can be extended while remaining meaningful. In Australia's case, it is spatially very diverse, as its trade ranges from the EU to the USA and Asia, while the FDI influences are due to ICs based in the USA, the UK, and Japan, with smaller representation from a number of other countries. Australia's managerial and technical strengths are undoubtedly influenced by the strengths of international firms based in these triad countries, which transfer technologies and managerial practices developed in their home markets. These skills have an impact in two ways: the foreign-based firms' strengths are deployed in Australian markets, and this affects exports and outward investments; and, by competing with indigenous firms, they help to diffuse best practice amongst Australian firms, inducing them to be stronger. The process is indirect and its importance difficult to assess. Certainly, by comparison with Canada, whose companies face the opportunities and the threats of a now virtually integrated North American market, the influence on Australia of the foreign diamonds must be much attenuated. We return to this question in Section 5 of the chapter.

Another influence of foreign 'diamonds' is the exposure of a country's ICs to the competitive conditions of other host countries in which they operate. Foreign firms may gain some of the advantages of firms originating in a particular country, thus eroding the special advantages of local firms. The attraction of the USA for foreign ICs establishing R&D centres is an obvious example. How extensive this equalizing process may be is not yet clear, as it depends on the ease of transfer of the competences associated with the special conditions of the country. Those that are deeply embedded in cultural values are more resistant to transfer. Also, resistance to IC penetration, whether by government action or for other reasons, can delay diffusion. The difficulty of foreign access to the Japanese market enabled Japanese firms to maintain the advantages of their manufacturing system, with its special features, for many years. Foreign firms had little opportunity to be exposed to the demonstration effect of these innovations. They also found the techniques difficult to transmit to home countries, where industry clusters had to be re-educated and workforces retrained.

An important component of the country-specific conditions is government. Government affects the micro-economic context of business as well as the macro-economic settings, and both influence the actions of ICs. Likewise, ICs are powerful organizations, and their actions are often important to a country's economy and, ultimately, to the conditions for its international success. In Chapter 1 of this volume Dunning makes the case for paying greater attention to this interaction. Australia, with a high level of foreign ownership and a recent programme of micro-economic reform, provides an interesting case for considering these issues. In this chapter we show the importance of the institutional setting to Australia's international economic performance, arguing that evolution of the institutional arrangements was a necessary precondition to the adaptation of the economy under globalization.

The chapter is organized as follows. Section 2 provides a general overview of Australia's international integration from a comparative perspective. Sections 3–5 place Australia's growing internationalization in context. The policy reforms of the 1980s are described and assessed (Section 3), relating them to a range of macro-economic performance indicators (Section 4). These sections provide essential background information, since the reforms were crucial in shifting Australia towards a much more international orientation. Similarly, the macro-economic setting (in particular the country's low saving rate) is important, for it has the potential to nullify many of the significant reform achievements. The liberalization achieved thus far could well be disrupted by serious macro-economic imbalances.

Section 5 develops the internationalization theme further by examining trends in equity capital flows and technology effort. Section 6 provides another of the building blocks in our argument by analysing the development of ever stronger ties with East Asia. Section 7 takes a more micro-economic perspective by examining the impact of the major changes discussed earlier on business enterprises, and Section 8 presents our conclusions.

2. **International Comparisons**

It is useful first to provide a few international comparisons of the nature, trends, and extent of Australia's international commercial engagement. These comparisons provide the backdrop for the more detailed analysis to follow. The broad picture to emerge from these comparisons is one of a prosperous economy. Indeed, if recent World Bank estimates are to be believed, Australia's *per capita* wealth, incorporating a measure for natural resources, is the highest in the world. This estimate places Australia, at about $US835,000, comfortably ahead of second-placed Canada at $704,000, and well ahead of the USA at $421,000 (*Asian Wall Street Journal*, 18 Sept. 1995). On per capita GDP comparisons, however, Australia appears much lower in the world league. Historically, it has been an isolated, rather inward-looking economy, but over the past decade it has undertaken a significant shift towards a stronger international orientation. There are a number of dimensions of this reorientation, to be discussed shortly. The two most important have been a concerted attempt to halt and reverse the long drift towards dirigisme, and developments in transport and communication which have lowered the costs of isolation or, in Australian parlance, the 'tyranny of distance'.[1]

Australia is not an especially significant international trader, nor does trade assume a major role in its economy. As a percentage of GDP, trade is less important than that of its usual group of comparators, middle-sized OECD economies such as Canada and The Netherlands (see Table 7.1). The share is also a good deal lower than that of middle-sized Western Pacific economies. However, although Australia's international trade has been growing more slowly than that of the Asian tigers, it has been increasing faster (from a lower base) than in most OECD economies, reaching 20 per cent of GDP in 1995. The increasing importance of trade since 1970 in fact reverses a long-term decline for most of this century. This trend, as Anderson (1987: table 7.6) pointed out, resulted in Australia's being an 'outlier' for most of this century, as one of the few OECD economies to retreat from the international economy. Comparisons of this kind need to make allowances for country size, factor endowments, location, membership of preferential commercial arrangements, and so on. But two of the major themes of this chapter—starting from behind most countries and yet quickly becoming more internationally oriented—are partially illustrated by the data in Table 7.1. Trends in intra-industry trade indices provide additional support for these propositions: the indices rose significantly during the 1980s, in the case of all commodities, at a rate at least comparable to other countries. Nevertheless, the ratios are generally below those of North America and the newly industrializing economies (NIEs).

FDI data reveal a broadly similar picture, especially with regard to outward flows (see Table 7.2). Unlike most other OECD economies, Australia has long been a consistent net importer of capital and technology. These two factors, combined with a reasonably open posture towards equity capital inflows, have resulted in high levels of foreign ownership in most sectors of the economy. Among the comparisons in Table 7.2, only Singapore—the world's largest recipient of FDI (relative to the size of its economy)—has a higher inward FDI stock ratio. Moreover, the Australian ratio has risen much faster than that of any country in the comparison.

The data on outward flows are equally revealing. Australia was traditionally a minor international investor, for the reasons mentioned above, with in addition a policy of actively discouraging such investments through controls on capital outflows. As is discussed in more detail below, the removal of these controls in late 1983 ushered in a major transformation. Although Australian FDI abroad is still comparatively modest, since 1980 the ratio of these stocks to GDP has increased much faster than that of any 'northern' OECD country. Only the Korean and New Zealand ratios have risen faster, in both cases following major policy liberalizations on the capital account. By these indicators, Australian business clearly exhibits a strong global interdependence, and one that is increasing significantly over time.[2]

TABLE 7.2. Foreign investment stocks, selected countries, 1992

Country	Inward		Outward	
	1992 (% of GDP)	1980–92 (% increase)	1992 (% of GDP)	1980–92 (% increase)
Australia	27.0	203	9.9	560
Canada	24.6	21	17.7	99
USA	7.1	125	8.3	–2
Netherlands	26.1	129	41.1	64
Sweden	6.4	137	22.9	398
UK	19.2	59	24.5	59
Japan	1.1	−63	6.8	325
Korea	2.4	20	1.5	650
New Zealand	13.9	38	10.5	855
Singapore	91.4	54	14.3	131

Sources: UNCTAD (1994); World Bank (1982, 1994).

A third, indirect illustration of comparative global interdependence is given by R&D intensities. As the literature on technology and trade emphasizes (see, e.g., studies as diverse as Nelson (1993) and Grossman and Helpman (1991)), investments in R&D are one of the key determinants of a firm's competitive advantage, and hence its propensity for global integration. Among advanced economies, FDI flows are underpinned increasingly by such R&D investments.

Here also, Australia is something of an outlier (see Table 7.3). Its R&D expenditures, relative to GDP, are among the lowest in the OECD, exceeding only those of Italy, Iceland, and Ireland among the Europeans, although broadly similar to Canada. Significantly, the ratio is now also less than that of most of the Asian tigers. Furthermore, Australia's share of R&D performed by business ranks lower still, at merely one-quarter that of the USA, Japan, and Sweden. The reasons for these pronounced differences will be explored below. It is sufficient to note here that economic structure and a long history of dependence on private capital inflows are key explanations. Australia's modest R&D base, and its concentration on a few highly specialized niches, have major implications for the country's future path of global interdependence.

3. **Major Policy Reforms**

Australia entered the 1980s with its membership of the 'Antarctic Club' fully intact.[3] Although its record of macro-economic management remained reasonably sound, and its productivity growth not too far below international standards in the 1960s and 1970s (OECD 1994*b*: 56), its economic performance had been inferior to most other OECD economies during the long post-war economic

TABLE 7.3. Comparative R&D indicators, selected countries, late 1980s (%)

Country	R&D/GDP	Business[a] R&D/GDP	Share of total R&D	
			Private[b]	Business[a]
Australia	1.4	0.5	61	37
Canada	1.5	0.8	42	55
USA	2.9	1.9	48	73
Italy	1.2	0.8	42	57
Sweden	3.0	2.0	61	67
UK	2.3	1.5	49	67
Korea	1.0	n.a.	81	n.a.
Japan	2.9	2.1	78	66

Note: n.a. = not available.

[a] 'Business' refers to incorporated enterprises, both public and private. Business R&D data refer to 1990/1.

[b] 'Private' refers to all non-government enterprises.

Sources: Nelson (1993: 26, 264, 356), Business R&D: ABS, *1990–91 Research and Experimental Development, Australia* (Cat. 8112.0) (1993).

boom.[4] Barriers to international trade were among the highest in the OECD, and showing no sign of decline. Capital controls restricted outward investment, and there had been periods of chauvinism towards inward FDI from the 1960s through the 1970s (focused on natural resources) to the 1980s (when the focus was on real estate). The labour market was one of the most rigid in the world and financial markets were tightly regulated. The tax structure was inefficient and stifling. Inter-state commerce was restricted and 'orderly-marketing' schemes proliferated. These institutional features were sustainable only as long as a large and internationally efficient commodity sector was able to finance the inefficiencies inherent in such a highly regulated system. The consequence was decline in the comparative ranking of Australia in terms of per capita GDP.

The importance of the institutional setting is demonstrated by the impact of a major shift in the government's view of its role. During the decade, significant policy reforms were introduced, at a pace which surprised many people. Some of the factors which precipitated change[5] include: a gradual realization that Australia's international economic ranking was slipping; a secular decline in the real price of most major commodity exports; a growing appreciation among élite political and administrative circles of the costs of high levels of protection and regulation; and the advent of a reform-oriented Labor government in early 1983.

Central to the policy reforms, and to the development of a more international economy, has been trade liberalization. During the 1970s, with the exception of New Zealand, Australia's effective protection rates were the highest in the OECD. Moreover, there was extensive resort to non-tariff barriers, and rates were highly dispersed. Industries which were of particular interest to then emerging Asian

TABLE 7.4. Assistance for manufacturing, 1978/9–1992/3 (%)

	1978/9	1983/4	1989/90	1992/3
Average nominal rate of assistance	15	13	9	7
Standard deviation	15	16	11	8
Average effective rate of assistance	24	22	15	12
Standard deviation	30	43	22	16

Source: Fane (1995: 10), citing Industry Commission data.

exporters—textile, clothing, footwear (TCF)—were among the most heavily protected. Through to the early 1980s, there were minor reductions, but the most heavily protected sectors continued to receive very high assistance, resulting in still wider dispersion of effective rates (see Table 7.4). Thereafter, under the impetus of the Labor administration, rates began to fall quickly. A decade into the reforms, average effective rates were about half the previous levels, while the dispersion of these rates was cut still further. Non-tariff barriers have been largely abolished. The government has given a commitment to setting tariff rates at a maximum 5 per cent by the end of the decade, except for the sensitive areas of TCF and the automotive industry, where the reforms will proceed more slowly.[6]

Financial market and exchange-rate liberalizations were also introduced early in the reform period. After a long history of heavy management, the Australian dollar was floated in late 1983. As a necessary corollary, restrictions on the international movement of capital were removed. Australia had traditionally adopted a liberal posture towards capital inflows, including equity capital. But outflows had been controlled, resulting in very small levels of direct investment abroad. Over the same period, the tightly regulated financial market was opened up to new competitors, and most interest-rate and sectoral restrictions were removed. The previous administration had been moving in this direction, following an influential inquiry on the subject.

So much for the positive side of the reform ledger. Progress has been slower in other areas.[7] Government business enterprises have been subject to major reforms, and many have been partially or fully privatized. Most state-based utility companies have been corporatized and now operate in at least a 'contestable' environment. The highly regulated transport and communications industry has been subject to partial reform. In 1990, for example, the government abolished the long-established two-airline policy, which not only prohibited new entrants, but also effectively precluded any competition among the two existing firms. By contrast, entry to the telecommunications industry has been only partly opened up. The uneven pace of progress, and the potential for further reform, are underscored by a series of 'international bench marking reports' by a government research agency, the Bureau of Industry Economics (BIE various). For example, with regard to international ports, Australia's 'crane rates' (container moves per hour per crane) are reportedly low by international best-practice standards, and improving only slowly; the country's waterfront charges for non-containerized cargo are also comparatively high. By contrast, costs at Australia's specialized coal ports are among the lowest in the world.

Also, the tax system has been overhauled, the tax base broadened, and top marginal income-tax rates reduced. However, while attracting much business and academic support, a value-added tax has not been introduced, nor is one in prospect. In consequence, there is high reliance on income tax, with the top marginal rate on individuals cutting in at little more than the level of average weekly earnings.

The two major shortcomings in the area of micro-economic reform have been the labour market and federal fiscal relations. Australian unemployment rates remain at European levels, reflecting, in addition to macro-economic mismanagement, continuing rigidities in the labour market, extensive government intervention, and a strong (though diminishing) union presence. There have been some reforms over the past decade: real wage growth has been curbed by an 'accord' between the government, unions, and employers; union amalgamations have proceeded, thus reducing inter-union territorial disputes; more emphasis has been placed on work-site negotiations; and Australia's once notorious record for industrial disputation has improved greatly.

But the reforms still leave the country with one of the most tightly regulated labour markets in the OECD, and much more so than the dynamic 'full employment' economies of East Asia.[8] Although, in common with most OECD countries, labour unrest has declined, a recent survey shows Australia seventh in the OECD countries in working days lost over the period 1990–4 (*The Economist*, 20 Apr. 1996). Labour productivity has grown rather slowly since the late 1970s, including the reform-oriented 1980s (OECD 1994*b*; Lowe 1995). It is difficult to demonstrate conclusively a link between the pace of reform and the rate of growth in labour productivity, especially as there is considerable inter-industry variation in these rates. One hopeful sign is a marked acceleration in the 1990s, although it is possible that this reflects in part the effects of strong economic growth during the recovery following the early 1990s recession.

Australia's federal structure has also frustrated the reform programme. While the federal government maintains responsibility for macro-economic management, the division of fiscal responsibilities has never been satisfactorily resolved, and there is much overlap in the areas of social policy such as education and health. In the crucial area of micro-economic reform, the acquiescence of the eight state and territory governments is essential. Unfortunately, the sometimes acrimonious relationships between the two tiers of government on fiscal issues has resulted in an uncooperative spirit towards these reforms. Nevertheless, the states, to varying degrees, have instituted reforms in their own areas of responsibility. The State of New South Wales led the way under a reformist market-oriented Liberal government from the mid-1980s, and has corporatized or privatized many of its business operations, introduced private-sector contracting and privately owned

TABLE 7.5. Rankings in world competitiveness, 1994

Factor	Australian ranking	Number one rank
Domestic strength	20	USA
Internationalization	24	USA
Government	9	Singapore
Finance	15	USA
Infrastructure	5	Norway
Management	18	Japan
S&T	16	Japan
People	12	Singapore
OVERALL	15	USA

Source: World Economic Forum/International Institute for Management Development (June 1994).

and financed infrastructure development, as well as extensive reform of public departments. Victoria has also made substantial progress in reform. More remains to be done, however.

Thus, in sum there has been significant progress in the past decade. Major reforms have been introduced with far-reaching implications for Australia's place in the global economy. It is important to note, too, that the reforms have been interactive and 'positive sum', in the sense that changes in one area have facilitated initiatives elsewhere. A good example is trade-policy liberalization, where the exposure of more sectors of the economy to international competition has increased the pressure for reform in other sectors. The now 'unprotected' industries have plausibly made the case that tariff reductions are sustainable only if the process of micro-economic reform proceeds in a comprehensive fashion.

But, notwithstanding the progress to date, much remains to be done, both at the micro-level, as adumbrated above, and at the macro-level, to which we now turn. Australia's real per capita GDP is some 20 per cent below that of Canada, and the productivity of industry may be as much as 27 per cent below that of the USA (Forsyth 1994). Australia's rankings in the annual World Competitiveness Report provide at least some indication of the magnitude of this unfinished reform agenda (see Table 7.5). Australia was ranked below most OECD economies, and the Asian tigers, in the most recent assessment. Only in infrastructure and government was it in the top ten countries. Significantly, it performed worst on the 'internationalization' variable. The 1994 ranking is broadly similar to that of previous years.

4. **The Macro-Economic Context**

The macro-economic environment supporting these micro-economic reforms has been satisfactory is some respects, but notably deficient in other areas. It is important to examine these developments briefly, since, if the major problem

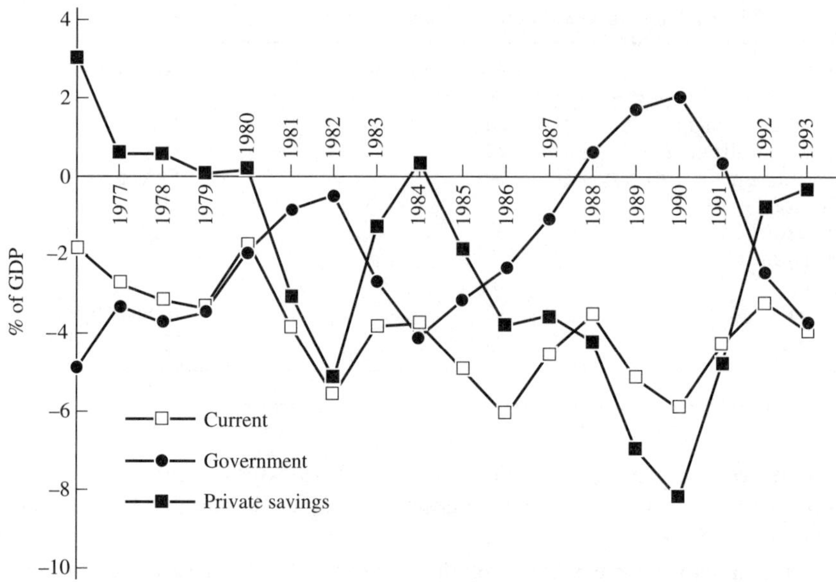

Note: Years refer to financial years (1993 to 1992/3, etc.) *Source*: Reserve Bank of Australia, *Bulletin*, various issues.

FIG 7.1. Macro-economic balances

areas are not resolved, they have the potential to disrupt the genuinely significant achievements and frustrate the path towards an internationally oriented and efficient economy. The purpose of this section is to examine briefly the salient features of the macro-environment. We also allude to some of the effects of the reforms. We do not attempt to provide a comprehensive assessment, which would be beyond the scope of this chapter, and arguably premature.

Throughout most of the reform period, fiscal policy was reasonably conservative. The Labor administration inherited a large fiscal deficit in 1982/3, in consequence partly of a severe recession (see Fig. 7.1). The government proceeded to reduce this deficit progressively through the decade. By 1987/8 a modest surplus had been achieved, and was maintained for the next three years, before another serious recession forced a change in policy. For a short period, also, the administration reversed the post-war trend towards an ever-larger government presence in the economy. Economic growth remained quite buoyant during this period, although inflation continued to exceed that of major trading partners, while remaining below 10 per cent after 1983 (see Fig. 7.2). The recession of the early 1990s was the major mistake in macro-economic management over this period. Extremely tight monetary policy resulted in a 'hard landing', with reductions in per capita income for two years and unemployment rates in excess of 10 per cent. Inflation did, however, fall sharply. After several years of low inflation, there is now some prospect that inflationary expectations have been eradicated and that low inflation may be a durable policy achievement.

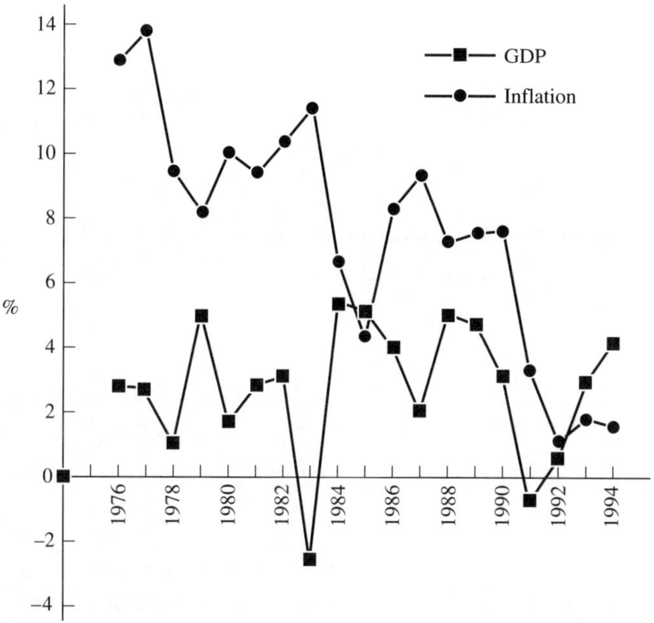

Note: Years refer to financial years (1994 to 1993 /4, etc.)

Source: Reserve Bank of Australia, *Bulletin*, various issues.

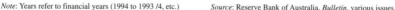

FIG 7.2. Growth and inflation

In the newly liberal commercial environment the government has, however, been far less successful in promoting domestic savings, managing external debt and the exchange rate, and responding to exogenous trade shocks. One key element of the process of globalization, the opening of the international capital account, altered the commercial and economic management rules of the game rapidly, and for both governments and financial institutions the new environment has posed great challenges. Firms' commercial horizons broadened immeasurably, as we shall see shortly, and there was a flurry of aggressive highly leveraged international expansion. But financial institutions were rather slow to adjust to the changes. Less than a decade after the liberalization, many of the country's most prominent business conglomerates had collapsed, and several major banks were in great financial difficulty.[9]

In some respects, macro-economic management was also one of the casualties of the liberalization. A case in point is the exchange rate. The floating of the Australian dollar initially had the desired effect of delivering a competitive exchange rate. When commodity prices fell sharply in the mid-1980s, and with it Australia's terms of trade, the nominal exchange rate also declined. Even though inflation continued to exceed that of major trading partners, the decline was substantial enough for the real effective rate also to fall significantly (see Fig. 7.3). The economy recovered strongly from the terms of trade decline (see Fig. 7.2), but again began to experience unsustainably large current-account deficits. To

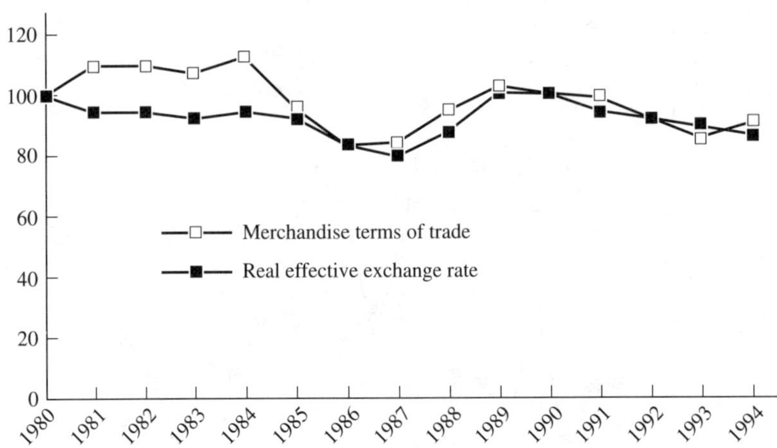

FIG 7.3. The terms of trade and the exchange rate

cool an overheated economy, the government adopted a moderately conservative fiscal policy, as noted (see Fig. 7.1). But the fiscal restraint proved insufficient, and so the government resorted to ever-tighter monetary policy. By the end of the 1980s interest rates were at record levels, in excess of 10 per cent in real terms. The consequent mismatch between fiscal and monetary policy proved disastrous. Capital inflow led to a substantial appreciation of the Australian dollar, eroding the competitive benefits achieved a few years earlier. Ultimately the current-account deficit was brought under control through the extremely crude and costly mechanism of the country's worst recession since the 1930s—two years of negative per capita growth and unemployment peaking in excess of 11 per cent of the workforce.

The high and rising current-account deficit of course reflects a shortage of domestic savings. No economic issue has attracted more attention in Australia over the past decade than the level of savings and external debt.[10] Current-account deficits *per se* need not be a cause for concern, provided the marginal rate of return on borrowed funds exceeds the interest rate and, by extension, domestic savings remain buoyant. As shown in Fig. 7.4, however, Australia's high current-account deficits have been accompanied by a secular deterioration in the savings rate. It has not been uncommon for up to one-quarter of the country's investment to be financed by foreign savings. Unfortunately, there is no evidence that this trend is about to be reversed.

The origins of this poor saving rate are complex, and beyond the scope of this chapter. But two general observations are pertinent on each of the major components, public and private savings. First, the government's apparent achievement of moderately conservative fiscal policy, as illustrated in Figure 7.1, is somewhat illusory. As a major national report on the subject demonstrated (Fitzgerald 1993), the usual practice of reporting financial statements significantly

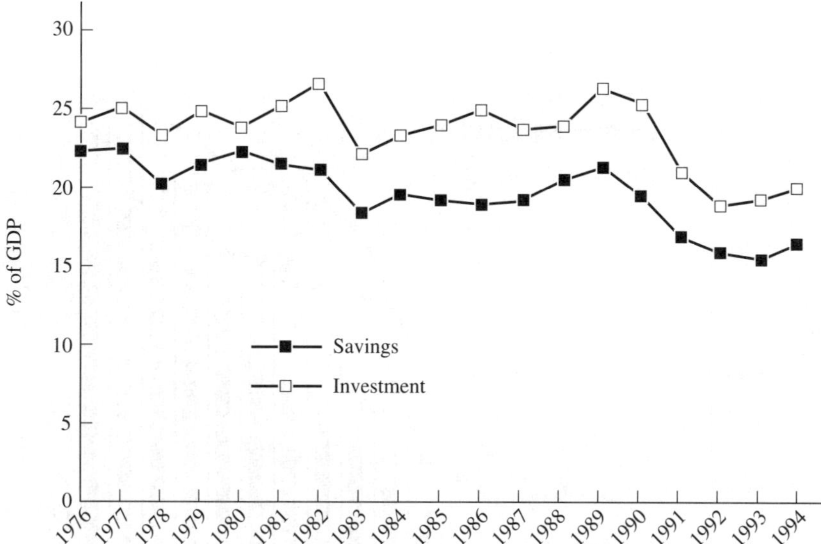

FIG 7.4. Savings and investment

understates public debt, mainly because it excludes a variety of formal obligations by Australian governments to its employees such as unfunded superannuation entitlements. A revised set of estimates prepared by Fitzgerald (1993) suggests that net public-sector debt is some $A300 billion, about double the official estimate, and almost double the nation's net external indebtedness. There was a good deal of discussion in Australia during the late 1980s of the fact that the country recorded ever larger current-account deficits despite having a fiscal surplus. That is, its experience seemed to be at odds with the popular 'twin-deficits' explanation for the 1980s US current-account deficits. Of course, the national accounts identity can explain why a deficit on one account and a surplus on another may coexist. But, in addition, the Fitzgerald report drew attention to the frequently neglected point that, depending on how they are measured, fiscal 'surpluses' may be illusory, because, in Australia's case, of a failure to report properly all financial obligations.

Secondly, while it is more difficult to explain the apparently poor rate of private-sector saving, the tax system is likely to be a significant variable. For example, a recent comparison of real effective tax rates for individual investors on average marginal personal tax rates found that Australia had one of the highest rates. At over 50 per cent, it exceeded the OECD average of 40 per cent, and was far higher than in the high saving East Asian economies, five of which had a rate of less than 10 per cent (Pender and Ross 1995).

The savings shortfall has resulted in extremely rapid external debt accumulation. Australia now has one of the largest external debts, relative to the size of its economy, within the OECD bloc. Exceeding $A200 billion, gross external

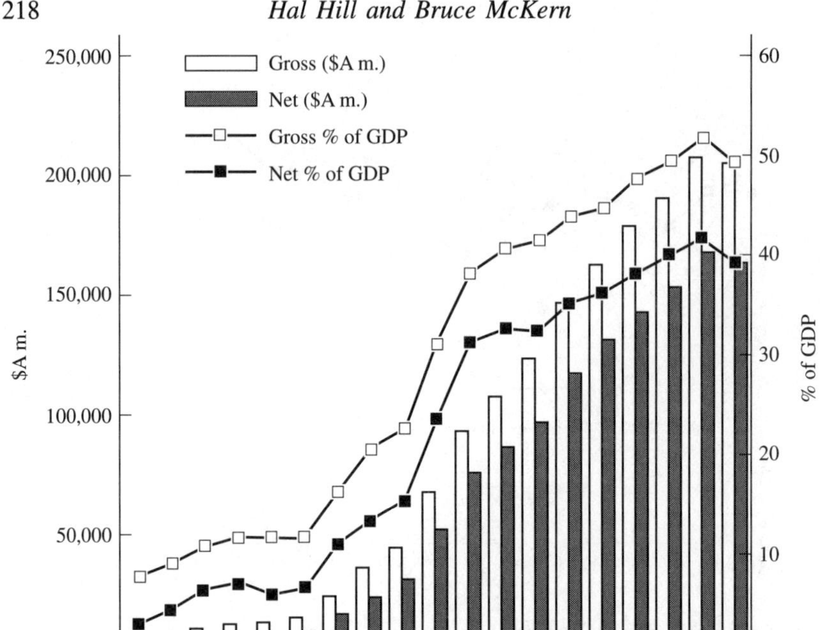

Note: Data as at 30 June each year.

Source: ABS, *Balance of Payments*, Australia (Cat. 5303) and *Australian National Accounts* (Cat. 5204), various issues.

FIG 7.5. External debt

debt is now equivalent to over half of GDP; the present ratio is seven times that of the mid-1970s (see Fig. 7.5). Net external debt has risen more slowly, owing to the increase in foreign assets following the capital market liberalization of 1983. The increase in the debt to GDP ratio is partly explained by measurement effects resulting from the depreciation of the Australian dollar. Nevertheless there can be little doubt that the debt is increasing at an unsustainable rate (a point highlighted by some recent international financial press reporting[11] that the Australian economy is more exposed internationally than any other OECD economy apart from Mexico). A reversal of the trend requires, at the broadest level, higher public- and private-sector savings, while at the micro-level a continuation of the reforms commenced in the mid-1980s as a high priority.

This analysis highlights the critical importance of macro-economic management in a reform programme designed to make the Australian economy more internationally oriented. Macro-management, of itself, is not the key ingredient in the process; rather, the essential building blocks have been trade liberalization, the opening of the capital account, the floating of the dollar, and the attempts at broad-ranging micro-economic reform, as yet incomplete. But the macro-element is essential, in that poor management can jeopardize the micro-reforms. Growth could be retarded, as occurred in the early 1990s. A low savings rate could

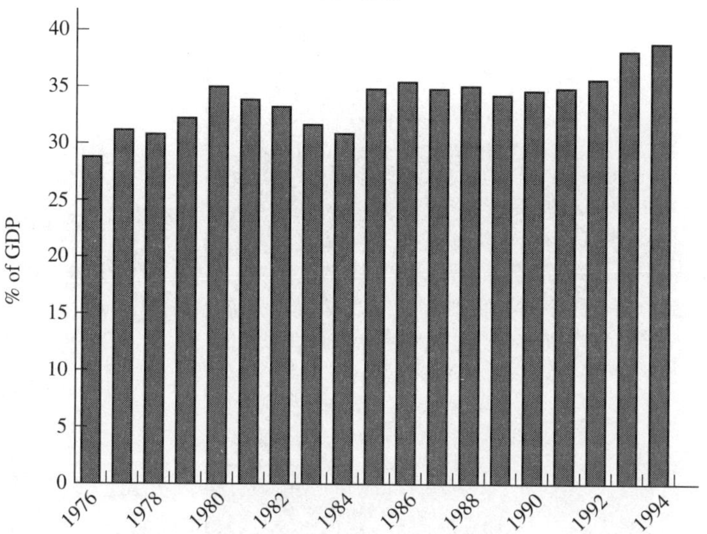

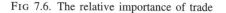

Notes: Exports and imports of goods and services as a percentage of GDP. Years refer to financial years (1993 to 1992/3, etc.)

Source: ABS, *Balance of Payments, Australia* (Cat. 5303), various issues.

FIG 7.6. The relative importance of trade

frustrate the necessary retooling which is required for rapid structural change. More generally, macro-economic mismanagement renders more difficult the prospect of achieving durable reforms. Reform is an inherently destabilizing process which inevitably produces both winners and losers. The conservative social-welfare function, in Australia as elsewhere, generally weights these losses more highly than the gains. If in addition economic mismanagement and cyclical factors generate a downturn in economic activity, the political consensus in favour of reform tends to evaporate. This has been the Australian experience of the early 1990s. While there has been no significant backtracking on reform, the forward momentum has slowed appreciably, most notably in the area of micro-economic reform of non-tradeable activities (see BIE, various).

To complete this review of broad trends, we turn to trade patterns and in particular the composition of exports over the reform period. The picture here is moderately encouraging in at least two respects. First, the Australian economy has become unambiguously more international in the sense that the trade share in the economy has risen, from about 31–3 per cent in the early 1980s to 35–8 per cent a decade later (see Fig. 7.6). Secondly, the composition of exports has moved in the desired direction. Minerals still dominate exports, accounting consistently for almost 40 per cent of exports over the last decade. But the reliance on unprocessed rural products has fallen significantly, and in their place more income-elastic manufactures and services have assumed a greater role (see Fig. 7.7). In the case of the so-called 'elaborately transformed manufactures' (ETMs), annual export growth in real terms over the period 1985–93 was 14.5

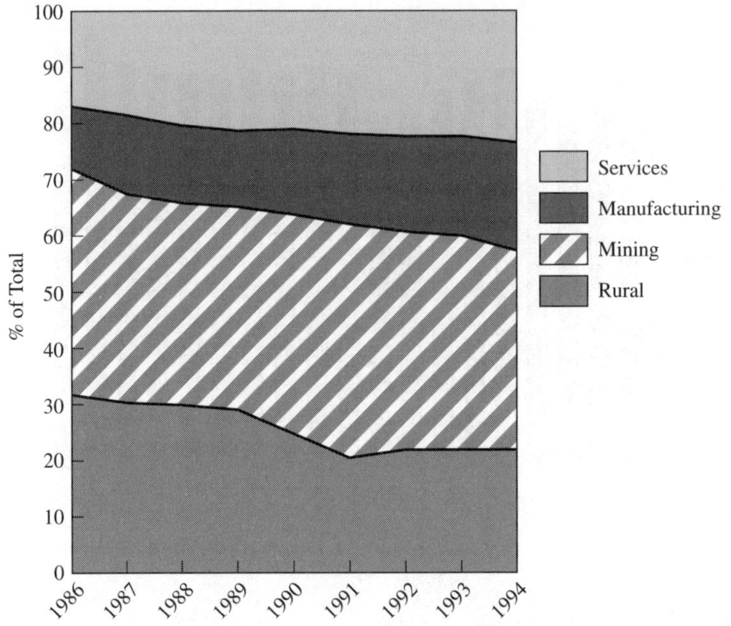

Note: Years refer to financial years (1993 to 1992/3, etc.). *Source*: ABS, *Balance of Payments*, Australia (Cat. 5303), various issues.

FIG 7.7. Composition of exports

per cent, as compared with just 1.8 per cent for the period 1979–85. By contrast, import growth of these items over the whole period was in the range of 5–6 per cent, with little sub-period variation (Sheehan 1994: 6). This is presumptive evidence of efficient, export-oriented industrial growth during the reform period.

Australian service exports grew over the period 1985–91 at an annual average rate (in $US terms) of 17 per cent, exceeding both the average international and Asian rates, of 13.6 and 14.6 per cent respectively, over the same period (AUSTRADE 1994: 37). The services sector is also expected to generate most of the employment growth over the 1990s (BIE various).

We will return to the growth of these 'non-traditional' exports below, but it is worth noting here that high value-added industries such as resource-based processing, international education, and tourism have been prominent in the new export growth industries. These conclusions are necessarily tentative: the time period is too short to draw definitive conclusions; economic cycles and commodity-price fluctuations obscure the picture; and the mechanics of the link between reform and supply response have not been adequately investigated. Nevertheless, is seems that exposure of Australian industry to the winds of international competition, coupled with liberalization of economic management and diminution in the role of state enterprises, has shifted the economy substantially towards international integration.

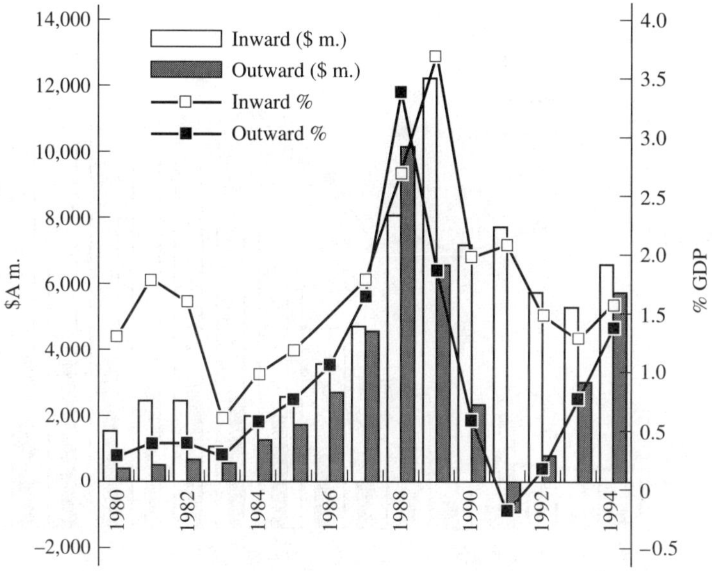

Note: Data refer to financial years (1993 to 1992/3, etc), and include direct investment only.
Source: ABS, *International Investment Position*, Australia (Cat. 5305), various issues.

FIG 7.8. Foreign Investment, flows

5. Foreign Investment, Technology, and the Basis of Competitive Advantage

5.1. Foreign Direct Investment

As foreshadowed above (see Table 7.2), rising international investment flows are the clearest indication of the growing globalization of Australian business. Here, the impact of policy reform has been quite unambiguous. Australia has always been a significant recipient of equity capital, and it could be expected that capital flows would have increased in the 1980s in line with worldwide trends. But both inflows and outflows rose rapidly in the 1980s (see Fig. 7.8). Outflows increased substantially following the removal of capital controls in late 1983. In the peak year of 1988 outflows actually exceeded inflows, the first occasion in recorded Australian history. The outflows rose from about 0.3 per cent of GDP annually before the lifting of controls to five or more times this ratio for several years. Inward flows as a percentage of GDP also rose substantially, though not as sharply. In both cases the recession led to sharp declines, although by 1992–3 a strong recovery was evident.[12] As a result of these changes, in the decade after capital-account liberalization, the stock of inward investment as a share of GDP was some 60 per cent higher, while the outward stock was three times as large (see Fig. 7.9).

Since capital controls were lifted, Australia has essentially had no policy

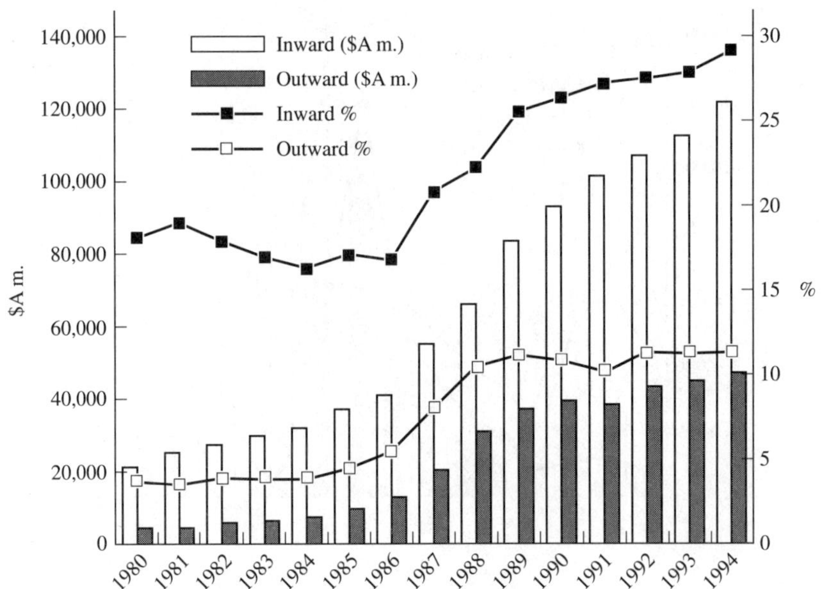

Note: As at 30 June each year. Data refer to direct investment only.
Source: ABS, *International Investment Position, Australia* (Cat. 5305), various issues.

FIG 7.9. Foreign Investment, stocks

towards international investment flows. A 'screening' mechanism for major inward flows has been maintained in the form of the Foreign Investment Review Board within the Department of the Treasury. The board has been maintained principally as a monitoring mechanism, and as an exercise in political window dressing to placate political opposition to increased foreign ownership. Only in the case of real-estate investments has it ever exerted any authority, and even here its impact has been very minor. 'Strategic' sectors such as the media are also subject to government regulation. But otherwise the regime is largely neutral as between foreign and domestic investors.

Inward FDI in Australian manufacturing is well explained by the eclectic paradigm. Inward foreign ownership has focused on sectors which are highly R&D- or marketing-intensive, human capital-intensive, concentrated, with high levels of protection, and where multi-plant operations are common (Ratnayake 1993). Tariffs were a major factor in supporting inward investment during much of the post-war period, as Brash (1966) much earlier noted, leading to an inefficient domestically oriented manufacturing sector. The rich resources of the mining sector attracted foreign firms that possessed ownership advantages arising from access to markets and experience in the industry. Vertical integration was not a major motive (McKern 1976). The major sources of inward FDI (see Table 7.11) were the USA (stock in 1993 31.5 per cent of the total), the UK (23.1 per cent) and Japan (15.6 per cent), and the main destinations of outward flows were the UK (29.4 per cent) and the USA (24.5 per cent). The principal puzzle in relation to investment flows is why their regional composition has differed considerably from that of the trade flows. We address this issue in Section 7.[13]

5.2. **Technology**

As noted above (see Table 7.3), Australian investment in R&D is low by OECD standards, both in total and especially in the business sector. It might be expected that the process of internationalization would increase the R&D effort to the extent that there is a reallocation of resources towards 'comparative advantage' in R&D-intensive activities. The data show no clear trend, other than some increase in business R&D (see Table 7.6). Given the very short period under observation, it is premature to reach any conclusion concerning trends.

Close to 45 per cent of Australian business expenditure on R&D is undertaken by affiliates of ICs (which collectively account for some 30 per cent of sales in manufacturing) (OECD 1994*a*). ICs' affiliates in Australia are thus more research-intensive than Australian domestic firms, as might be expected given the sectors in which they predominate. But business spending on R&D in Australia, at 0.5 per cent of GDP, is low by comparison with other developed countries (see Table 7.3) and about one-quarter, relative to GDP, of the level of spending in the USA or Japan. Australia is thus, unlike most OECD economies, dependent on inflows of technology. A crude indicator in support of this point is given in Table 7.8, which shows that in 1990–1 payments abroad for technical know-how exceeded receipts from abroad by a large margin. Further evidence is the ratio of the net balance of technology payments to business R&D spending, which averaged 20% between 1980 and 1990 (OECD 1994*a*). For the USA and Japan, this ratio is negative or close to zero. Imported technology substitutes, in some degree, for local development efforts in Australia.

A number of factors explain Australia's low R&D effort. One is economic structure, and in particular the importance of low R&D-intensive resource sectors (mining and rural industry). (The Canadian figure is low for similar reasons.) Another is the preponderance of small-scale commercial enterprises. To the extent that private R&D is associated with scale, this factor also explains Australia's low ratio. Thirdly, Australia's past heavy reliance on FDI inflows may have meant that the country has been bypassed by ICs as a research centre.

The R&D done by foreign firms in Australia is predominantly undertaken by the affiliates of US, UK, and Japanese ICs, which account for 40, 28, and 5.5 per cent of business spending respectively. When these proportions are compared with the relative ownership of inward FDI stock by country (see Table 7.11), it appears that US and British ICs undertake more R&D in Australia, and Japanese ICs less, than the proportions of their FDI stock would imply. In sharp contrast to Canada and the UK, practically all the spending on R&D by foreign firms in Australia is financed by the local affiliates rather than by the parent. These pieces of evidence, and other work (Stubbs 1968; McKern 1981), support the

TABLE 7.6. Trends in Australian R&D expenditure (% of GDP)

Year	Total expenditure	Business expenditure
1984/5	1.1	0.3
1985/6	1.2	0.4
1986/7	1.3	0.5
1987/8	1.2	0.5
1988/9	1.3	0.5
1989/90	n.a.	0.5
1990/1	1.3	0.5
1991/2	1.4	0.5
1992/3	1.6	0.7

Source: ABS, *Research and Experimental Development, Australia* (Cat. 8112.0), various issues.

view that the affiliates of foreign firms rely to a large extent on parent technology, and that a major part of their local technology expenditure is on development and adaptation of products to the Australian market. Given the economies of scale in R&D, ICs tend to centralize research as well as a good part of their development effort, unless a particular country offers special features such as a large and demanding market, inexpensive research personnel of high quality, or idiosyncrasies of the local environment which could lead to valuable breakthroughs. So it is not surprising that ICs have little interest in locating major research centres in the small Australian market, although they could take advantage of able scientific personnel at reasonable cost. (An exception is the minerals industry, where production is at world scale and sufficient to support local R&D efforts.)

Future patterns of R&D investment are likely to be determined by government expenditure priorities more than any other factor, for at least two reasons. First, over half of the R&D expenditures in 1990–1 were in the government and (predominantly state-funded) higher education sectors (see Table 7.6). Secondly, a good deal of private R&D expenditure is in fact government funded or at least subsidized. And, as noted above, Australia is and will continue to be for some time a net importer of technology.

Although Australian scientific and engineering education resources are comparatively strong, this technological dependence and low R&D investment will not be altered quickly. Indeed, one of the major policy issues for government is the avoidance of costly and ineffective R&D promotional programmes. The restructuring now occurring in Australian industry has prompted the government, under pressure from public opinion, to be seen to be accelerating the shift towards a 'high-technology' economy. In the process, several programmes designed in effect to subsidize private-sector R&D activities have been introduced. A tax concession of 150 per cent of R&D spending, introduced in 1985, was extended in 1992. The government has funded a number of key research centres operating jointly between universities and industry. And the mandate of the government-

TABLE 7.7. Composition of Australian R&D expenditure, 1992/3 (% of total)

Sector undertaking R&D	%
Business enterprises	44.2
private	(40.3)
public	(3.9)
General government	27.6
Higher education	26.9
Private non-profit	1.3
TOTAL	100.00
TOTAL ($Am.)	6,308.8

Source: ABS, *1992–93 Research and Experimental Development, Australia* (Cat. 8112.0) (1995), and previous issues.

TABLE 7.8. Payments for technical know-how, 1992/3 ($Am.)

	Location of recipient or payer	
	Australia	Abroad
Payments	35.2	445.4
Receipts	137.2	144.9
Net Receipts	102	–300.5

Source: ABS, *1992–93 Research and Experimental Development, Australia* (Cat. 8112.0) (1995).

funded Commonwealth Scientific and Industrial Research Organization has been redirected towards commercial applications. This is an example of government taking steps to reduce transaction costs and uncertainties for firms in an area vital for competitiveness, and likely to generate positive externalities. It is too early to evaluate the effectiveness of these changes, although some preliminary assessments are favourable.[14]

5.3. Other Factors Determining Competitive Advantage

As the most recent OECD report on the Australian economy concludes, Australia's rate of total factor productivity growth (TFPG) lagged behind the OECD average from 1987 to 1992, after exceeding the average during the period 1980–6 (OECD 1994*b*). During the 1987–92 period, Australian TFPG was about 60 per cent of the OECD average, suggesting that the reforms discussed above have not yet had a positive effect, or that other factors are inhibiting improvement. In the conclusion to this section, we survey some of these factors.

Enrolments in university and other tertiary education in Australia equal or exceed those of major EU countries and Japan, but are considerably lower than in the USA or Canada. Although education expenditure as a percentage of GDP (5.5 per cent) was not far below the OECD average of 6.5 per cent, expenditure per student relative to GDP was well below the average (OECD 1994*b*). Comparisons of the outputs are difficult to make, as Australia has not participated in international tests of achievement (because of opposition by teachers' unions) since 1983, when it ranked in the lower half of a comparison group in mathematics and science abilities. It is likely that its position has slipped further since then. Many parents, dissatisfied with the public-schooling system, have turned to private schooling for their children. Interestingly, the ratio of private-education expenditure to public expenditure is still considerably lower in Australia than the OECD average. For Australia, the ratio is 17 per cent, compared with the USA (27 per cent), Japan (35 per cent), and Germany (37.5 per cent) (OECD 1994*b*).

Given the success of privatization in many fields of government activity, the lack of alternatives to public education in Australia may be a negative factor. At present, there are only very limited opportunities for private university education, most institutions being funded mainly by the federal government. Funding is administratively determined, with the result that there is no clear nexus between resource allocation and educational performance. There appears to be a case of government failure here, for which the solution should incorporate market mechanisms. As the governments (state and federal) have the responsibility for education, this would seem to be an area in which fresh thinking and a market orientation could bring benefits.

Training undertaken by business firms is encouraged by a taxation incentive, the Training Guarantee, which levies a tax on firms that spend less than a threshold amount on employee training. The scheme is an attempt to address the free-rider problem of private expenditure on training. The scheme has been in force for too short a period to evaluate its effectiveness, but it does not apply to small firms, where training is usually less likely to be done.

As Table 7.5 shows, Australia is ranked eighteenth in the 1994 World Competitiveness Report rankings on quality of management. An OECD Survey (OECD 1994*b*) claims that the educational attainments of Australian managers have not in the past been much higher than those of the rest of the workforce. This is probably an exaggeration, but, as the survey suggests, the protected nature of industry in the past and the emphasis on mining and rural industry have probably inhibited the development of internationally oriented capable managers. Although business schools and programmes for executives have existed for many years, there has been much more interest in the development of good managers in the last decade. A recent proliferation of these schools, of which a few have adopted an international orientation, is evidence of this greater awareness. The most serious weakness is in research relevant to Australian management.

The exposure of Australian firms to international trade through tariff reduction has been a key source of external competitive pressure. Within the country, efforts are also under way to eliminate barriers to inter-state commerce. Although the

Constitution guarantees free commerce between the states, its purpose has been frustrated by differing regulations and standards within state jurisdictions. Recent legislation of all seven governments has been enacted to create uniformity of regulations and mutual recognition of professional and occupational qualifications. Although anti-competitive behaviour is prohibited under the Trade Practices Act, 1974, government business activities, certain professions, agricultural producers, and statutory marketing authorities are exempt. A recent Committee of Inquiry (Hilmer *et al.* 1993) proposed sweeping reforms in competition policy, to end these exemptions, to force government businesses to comply with principles of competitive neutrality, and to open contestable areas of government responsibility to free competition.

One of the obstacles to industrial reform has been the interdependence of capital and labour in Australia's highly centralized industrial-relations structure. The centralized system persists, despite erosion of the unions' membership base, and government action has been employed to bring about a joint response to global pressures. To effect major reductions in protection, the federal government intervened strongly in several sectors where agreement between companies and unions was necessary. A collaborative plan for the steel industry was developed that provided for workforce reductions coupled with new investment in more efficient plant. This scheme has been a success, if measured by improvements in the productivity and international competitive position of the major steel producer, BHP. A government plan for the automotive industry has been effective in encouraging consolidations, new investment, and workforce reductions, with tariff reductions phased in over an extended period.

6. The Reorientation towards East Asia

Intimately related to the growing internationalization of the Australian economy has been its dramatic reorientation towards, and deeper engagement with, the dynamic East Asian region.[15] This process pre-dates the liberalization thrust, but the two have become powerfully intertwined over the past decade. It is important to understand this major realignment in Australia's commercial relationships. Not only have these countries been a central element of the process of internationalization, but they have also shaped and hastened the process. The latter has occurred through a variety of channels: the spectacular growth in Asia has awakened Australian firms to new commercial opportunities beyond national shores; the extraordinary growth of highly international economies has contributed to the dawning consensus in Australia of the merits of liberalization; and a desire to negotiate access to the markets of these booming economies has hastened the reduction of import barriers at home.

The speed with which this East Asian orientation has occurred is underlined by the fact that, in the immediate post-war period, Australia was in many respects a distant, though prosperous, British outpost, trading mainly with the UK and the

TABLE 7.9. Destination of Australian trade, 1950–1992 (% of total)

Destination	Early 1950s[a]	1970[b]	1992[b]
Total trade			
USA	10	19.2	16.5
EU12	62	29.2	17.6
Japan	5	20.3	21.5
Other NE Asia	7	4.2	14.2
SE Asia	–[c]	4.3	9.3
SW Pacific	5	5.4	5.4
Other	11	17.4	15.5
TOTAL	100	100	100
Exports			
USA	7	12.8	9.2
EU12	63	22.4	13.5
Japan	8	27.7	25.8
Other NE Asia	6	5.6	17.0
SE Asia	–[c]	6.0	10.6
SW Pacific	7	7.9	6.3
Other	8	17.6	17.4
TOTAL	100	100	100

[a] Data refer to 1951/2–1954/5.
[b] Data based on UN trade data tapes.
[c] Incl. in Other NE Asia.

Sources: Early 1950s: Anderson and Garnaut (1987: 19); 1970 and 1992: International Economic Data Bank (IEDB), Research School of Pacific and Asian Studies, Australian National University.

rest of Europe, receiving most of its foreign investment from the UK, and peopled almost exclusively from Britain. Less than four decades later East Asia has come to dominate the country's trade and to supply a rapidly rising share of its capital imports, migrants, and tourists.

The most pronounced reorientation has been in trade. In the early 1950s over 60 per cent of Australia's merchandise trade was with Western Europe, some two-thirds of which was with the UK (Table 7.9). Over the next forty years an amazingly rapid shift in trade shares occurred. Europe shrank to less than one-quarter of the early post-war figure. Australia's trade with the USA assumed rising importance in the 1950s and 1960s (though its share has declined since 1970). In the rising East Asian share, Japan was initially the key factor, and it continues to be Australia's largest trading partner in the region. Japan's rapid growth laid the foundations for this trade expansion, but two other factors were of special importance. The first has been intense complementarity between the two countries, one a resource-poor, densely populated, rapidly industrializing nation, the other resource rich, and (of significance as tourism began to grow very quickly) abundantly endowed with natural amenities, but with a small work-force. The second factor has been creative and far-sighted diplomacy on the part of the two countries, which has enabled both peoples to overcome the historical legacy of mistrust and hostility.[16]

During the 1970s and 1980s Japan's share of trade peaked at a little under one-quarter of the total, and its role as Australia's most rapidly growing trade partner shifted to the dynamic developing economies of East Asia. By the early 1990s these economies in aggregate were more important trading partners than Japan; as export markets they were larger than the combined total of the USA and the EU. The expansion was particularly important in the case of developing North-East Asia (Garnaut 1989), with the share of Australia's trade with the four major economies in this group rising by over 300 per cent in just a little over two decades. Here, also, high rates of economic and trade expansion, combined with strong complementarity in resource trade, underpinned much of the growth. From the late 1970s accelerating growth in China provided a major additional stimulus.

This Northern group tended to overshadow the smaller economies of South-East Asia. Nevertheless, the latter's share of Australia's trade also more than doubled over this period (EAAU 1992). High growth in ASEAN, combined with proximity and moderate complementarity, explain much of this growth. The ASEAN economies are small actors on the international stage, the size of their combined economies being little greater than that of Australia (at official exchange rates). Yet by the early 1990s they were more important export markets for Australia than either the USA or the EU.

Table 7.10 enables these trends to be viewed in broader context by presenting trade-intensity measures for trade within Asia-Pacific, together with the EU for the purposes of comparison.[17] There are intense trading relationships within and across the Pacific, as illustrated by these indices. For example, Australia's trade with Japan is about four times larger than what would be expected on the basis of the two countries' shares of world trade, while its trade with ASEAN and the Developing North-East Asia (DNEA) region is about double expected shares.

The East Asian trade matrix is similarly intense, with indices in excess of unity in all cases. The figures are particularly high for trade within the two East Asian sub-groups, ASEAN and the DNEA economies, in both cases driven by proximity and complementarily, in addition to the institutional arrangements within ASEAN. The trans-Pacific intensities are somewhat lower, although those for the USA are at least unity, and almost double this for Australia and Japan. The broad stability of these indices over time, in most instances, indicates that most of the increased trade among these countries and regions is the result of their enlarged importance in world trade, rather than the rising intensity of the trading relationships.

Proximity, familiarity, institutional arrangements, and other residual factors are the key to this strong Asia–Pacific trade relationship. Estimates of complementarity and country bias (not reproduced here)[18] show that with Japan there is strong complementarity, defined here as a matching of the commodity composition of a country's exports (or imports) and its partner's imports (or exports).

TABLE 7.10. Trade intensities, 1970 and 1991

Country	Australia	ASEAN	DNEA	Japan	Canada	USA	EU12
1970							
Australia		2.4	1.8	4.7	0.6	1.0	0.6
ASEAN	1.6	8.9	2.5	3.8	0.2	1.3	0.4
DNEA[a]	1.3	3.1	4.3	2.0	0.6	2.2	0.4
Japan	2.1	3.4	5.2		0.7	2.3	0.3
Canada	0.8	0.2	0.5	0.8		5.1	0.4
USA	1.6	1.1	1.4	1.7	4.9		0.7
EU12	0.8	0.4	0.4	0.2	0.3	0.6	0.7
1991							
Australia		2.1	1.9	4.1	0.5	0.7	0.3
ASEAN	1.8	3.9	1.6	2.8	0.3	1.3	0.4
DNEA[a]	1.3	1.6	2.9	2.0	0.6	1.7	0.4
Japan	1.9	2.4	2.4		0.7	2.0	0.5
Canada	0.5	0.2	0.4	0.8		5.2	0.2
USA	1.9	1.0	1.2	1.8	6.0		0.6
EU12	0.5	0.3	0.3	0.3	0.3	0.5	1.5

Note: Data refer to three-year averages, and include intra-bloc trade (in the case of ASEAN, DNEA, and EU).

[a] DNEA includes Hong Kong, China, South Korea, and Taiwan.

Source: IEDB.

But in virtually all other cases the complementarity indices are close to unity. There are significant country biases in Western Pacific trade, with the country-bias indices well above unity, and in about half the cases exceeding two. These country biases also lay the foundations for durable instances of regional cooperation, ranging from the broadest of initiatives such as the Asia Pacific Economic Cooperation (APEC) to the highly developed, institutionalized arrangements such as the EU, NAFTA, ASEAN, and CER (Closer Economic Relations—between Australia and New Zealand).

Most other dimensions of the relationship also portray a picture of closer engagement. The movement of people is further reinforcing Australia's economic, political, and cultural reorientation towards Asia and the Pacific. Australia has long maintained an immigration programme which, relative to its population base, is one of the largest in the world. Until the 1950s this migration was almost exclusively from the UK. During the 1950s the programme was extended to the rest of Europe. Profound changes occurred in migration policy during the 1970s, when the racial basis for selection of migrants was replaced by criteria relating to skills and family connections.

This change in policy regime, combined with growing European prosperity, had a dramatic impact on migration patterns. In the mid-1960s, for example, the UK (and Ireland) were by far the most important source of immigration, constituting over half of the total. In contrast, by the early 1990s the UK share, while still the largest, had shrunk to just one-fifth of its 1960s share. Moreover, it was the only country outside the Asia-Pacific in the top ten. Asia has quickly replaced Europe as the major source region. Whereas only one Asian nation was in the top ten in 1966–7, by 1991–2 eight of the top ten were in Asia (see Shu and Khoo 1993 for more details).

Despite the usual measurement and conceptual problems, it is clear that services trade is following the same regional pattern. Indeed, the connections may be even more intense, since, as is well known, proximity is usually a more important determinant of the regional composition of services trade as compared to merchandise trade. Two components of services trade in particular deserve mention: education and tourism. The Western Pacific now dominates Australia's tourism flows, providing 65 per cent of the inflows and absorbing 58 per cent of the outflows. In 1993 North-East Asia was easily the largest source of tourism, comparable in size to the combined European–American total, and trebling in share since the late 1970s. The numbers from South-East Asia are much smaller, but they too have been growing rapidly.

Education provides another example of increasingly intense services trade in which proximity and comparative advantage play an important role. Following major policy changes in the mid-1980s, the hitherto intensely regulated education sector began to display flexibility and a capacity to innovate in response to market demand. By the early 1990s about 60,000–70,000 students were arriving annually for the purpose of study, about 80 per cent of whom were from Asia. In 1991–2, the major source countries were Hong Kong (9,200), Malaysia (8,700), Indonesia (6,600), and Japan (5,300). In most of these markets, Australia is among the top three overseas suppliers of education services (Shu and Khoo 1993: 46).

Investment patterns are the only case where there has not yet been such a pronounced reorientation, as is illustrated in Table 7.11. Indeed, there is a surprising lack of symmetry between the regional composition of exports and outward investments. These differences are sufficiently important to require some explanation.

Historically the UK was the dominant investor, and, even though its position has waned, it still accounted for almost one-quarter of the stock of inward investment in mid-1992. Together with the rest of Europe, Japan, and North America, the 'OECD North' accounts for over 85 per cent of the stock of inward investment. In this respect, the pattern of inward FDI in Australia has mirrored the pattern of FDI in the developed triad. During the 1980s the share of Japan rose sharply, while in the early 1990s investments from other North-East Asian economies have also increased.

It is not surprising that the OECD North dominates inward-investment flows. But the converse, concerning outward flows, is more puzzling. Over 70 per cent of the stock of Australian outward investment in 1992 was located in these countries,[19] almost five times the total East Asian share and about eight times the 9 per cent share of Developing East Asia.

TABLE 7.11. Regional composition of foreign investment stocks, 1980 and 1993 (% of total)

Source Region	Inward	
	1980	1993
USA	38.4	31.5
UK	30.4	23.1
Other EU	9.3	8.0
Japan	6.4	15.6
Other OECD	—[a]	6.4
ASEAN	1.4	1.5
Other countries[b]	14.1	13.9
Destination Region	**Outward**	
	1980	1993
USA	15.9	24.5
UK	14.2	29.4
New Zealand	15.3	15.8
Other OECD	—[b]	8.5
ASEAN	10.1	7.8
Papua New Guinea	19.5	4.6
Other countries[b]	25.0	9.4

Note: Data as at 30 June each year.

[a] Included in other countries.

[b] Includes unallocated investment.

Source: ABS, *International Investment Position, Australia* (Cat. 5305), various issues.

This figure is puzzling for three reasons. First, it is contrary to the postulates of the foreign-investment literature, according to which investors from small nations tend to locate primarily in geographically proximate regions. Such a pattern is dictated by transactions costs and information flows for these firms, which lack the 'global-scanning' capacity of the really large multinationals.

Secondly, these shares represent a reversal of the trend which was evident up to the early 1980s, and which did conform to the standard foreign-investment theory concerning the impact of proximity in the case of small investors. In some years prior to the early 1980s, for example, the adjacent economies of ASEAN, Papua New Guinea, and New Zealand absorbed well over half the outward total.

The third reason why the figures are puzzling is that the investment trend is quite the opposite to that of trade, which, as noted above, reveals ever deeper engagement with East Asia.[20]

Several factors contributed to this pattern. First, the relaxation of capital controls clearly had a major impact on investment flows, as noted above. The outward pattern before 1983 generally had been one of very small flows, in a tightly regulated policy environment. Small investments naturally had a strong orientation to adjacent economies. The lifting of capital controls enabled firms to undertake investments on a much larger scale, unrestricted by capital constraints.

A number of large Australian-owned companies, seeking growth beyond the domestic market, had initially been either sceptical of Asia's future or deterred by its unfamiliarity, and looked for opportunities in the developed world. CSR, Boral, and James Hardie, all active in the building-materials industry, invested in the USA and Europe. Their particular competence was efficiency in a large domestic industry, and their strategy involved partial rationalization of the same industry abroad. Through acquisitions, Boral became the largest brick producer in the USA. Other venturers abroad included Bond Corp. in the brewing industry, TNT in the express freight business, and News Corp. in electronic and print media. None of these sectors is technologically very sophisticated. The source of the firms' advantage appeared to be managerial and organizational competences, honed through experience in a competitive Australian industry. These large firms looked to invest in the developed triad markets, for much the same reasons as did multinationals based in the USA, Europe, and Japan.

Examples of firms with a particular technological competence are more rare, but their numbers are growing. They include Telectronics, in cardiac pacemakers, where regulatory requirements and the large market of the USA encouraged foreign expansion, and Memtec, in the liquid-separation business, based on innovative membrane technology. The larger minerals companies developed skills in managing and financing large projects and finding markets for the output that were comparable with the best in the world, and this gave them an edge for investment in other countries.

Secondly, the international commercial environment changed markedly over this decade. In the early 1980s a number of ASEAN countries introduced more restrictive investment regimes, followed shortly afterwards by the region's first recession in more than two decades. A number of well-publicized disputes between Australian firms and their ASEAN joint venture partners over this period also contributed to a souring of perceptions. This occurred precisely at the same time that the OECD economies began to grow strongly, in the context also of far more liberal investment regimes than were on offer in ASEAN (Singapore excepted). In a number of instances, most obviously the UK, the benefits of 'cultural proximity' outweighed those of geographic proximity.

Thirdly, and related to the second point, there was the special case of the USA, which over the decade became the world's largest capital importer. The USA sucked in capital from all over the world; Australia was no exception, with the US share of its outward investment stock doubling, from 16 per cent in 1980 to 25 per cent in 1992. Finally, Australia's major export market, Japan, has always been a minor recipient of direct investment (see Table 7.2), and so Australian investors have been forced to look elsewhere.

Data from the 1990s, recently unpublished, suggest that a reversal of the regional composition of Australian outward investment may be under way (Access

Economics 1994; see also the recent BIE survey of forty-five Australian ICs). There are always lags in business perceptions and investment decisions. The recent profitability of investments in Asia has been comparable to the best anywhere. The senior management of Australian firms which had an unsatisfactory South-East Asian experience in the 1970s to 1980s has largely moved on. As a case in point, new management at Boral Ltd. has recently been placing more emphasis on Asia. It is also possible that small-scale investments to the region are understated, particularly now that the absence of international capital controls renders much more difficult the task of collecting accurate outward-flows data.[21] The much higher levels of intra-industry trade observed in Australia's trade with its immediate neighbours, ASEAN and New Zealand (see Table 7.2), are also presumptive evidence of significant trade-investment relationships. Nevertheless, the overall conclusion must be that Australia's growing internationalization, as measured by rising trade shares and increased focus on East Asia, has not been fundamentally investment-led. Rather, it seems that trade has been leading investment in Australia's growing engagement with the region.

7. Responses at the Level of Firm and Industry

It is clear that the reforms of the past decade have resulted in a more internationally oriented and efficient economy. Some dimensions of this process of internationalization have obviously been beneficial, such as the exposure of Australian companies to more intense international competition, and the removal of restrictions on international investment activities. The link between the reforms and firm-level responses is, however, under-researched. Which elements of the reform package were the most important? How much of the presumed efficiency gains is due to scaling up and reduced market and product fragmentation, and how much due to broader innovatory behaviour? How important have international benchmarking comparisons been, especially between affiliates?

The reform process has also sparked a vigorous debate concerning the most effective means of hastening the internationalization of the Australia economy. As noted above, the old debate concerning the merits of protection versus free trade disappeared surprisingly quickly during the reform process. The focus has now shifted to a debate between two schools who essentially agree on ends. The first group, comprising mostly academic economists, the Treasury, and the Industry Commission, favours a *laissez-faire* approach, emphasizing the importance of getting the macro-economic fundamentals (including the exchange rate) 'right', and pressing on with the unfinished micro-economic reform agenda. Most members of this group would also support some commercial initiatives of the government, but limited mainly to the fields of information and commercial promotion activities (trade fairs, and so on).

The second group, comprising business economists, the trade unions, and some business groups, agrees with such an approach, but argues that it is insufficient.

It needs to be supplemented, it is maintained, by a 'managed', 'strategic' export policy, in which the government and business associations identify promising activities, and marshal resources to overcome information gaps and other alleged market failures. No one group is in the policy ascendancy, and so it is not possible to verify empirically which of these approaches has been the most effective.

It is worth emphasizing in the context of this debate that there may indeed be a case for government intervention to overcome information bottlenecks (especially for small-to-medium firms with little international commercial experience), and to promote R&D activities. But the Australian record of micro-level intervention, at both federal and state levels of administration, reveals a political economy structure which is vulnerable to capture by vested interests. It is this consideration, as much as any economic rationale, which motivates the first group, and will probably ensure that neither of the two major political parties would seriously consider a more interventionist approach.[22] As Dunning implies in Chapter 1, the solution may lie between the two positions: government intervention where transaction costs or lack of information make private organization of the particular resources unattractive; predominantly free-market approaches in other cases. It is not obvious that Australian conditions should favour one mechanism or the other as uniquely appropriate.

In the remainder of this section, we refer briefly to the limited amount of empirical research undertaken on the firm- and industry-level impacts of reforms. Stewardson (1995) provides an account of changes within BHP, Australia's largest corporation, the only one to rank (No. 88) within the UNCTAD top 100 ICs, and the fourth largest mining corporation in the world. The company's internationalization since 1980 has been very rapid. Its workforce is now 25 per cent foreign, compared to 1 per cent in 1980. In the mid-1980s, Australian domestic sales accounted for 53 per cent of the company's total sales, followed by exports from Australia of 35 per cent and overseas-sourced sales of 12 per cent. By 1993–4 the shares of all three sources were approximately the same. Sales to the economies of East Asia constitute BHP's largest single market outside Australia, and these countries are likely to overtake Australia shortly. The company has investments in virtually every major country, as well as many minor ones, and in 1995 consolidated its position as a global copper company with a major US acquisition, Magma.

A number of factors have propelled this outward expansion: the company has 'outgrown' the Australian market, other countries' mining and energy regimes have become more attractive, and international acquisitions have had a snowballing effect in sales and commercial orientation. Policy reforms have also had some impact on BHP's outward expansion, particularly the removal of capital controls. As Demura (1995) points out, productivity increased significantly during the reform process, a result of economies of scale, the introduction of new technologies, and the shift to higher value exports. The reforms, which were introduced in the context of a government-business industry restructuring package, facilitated much of these improvements.

Other industry case studies also point to major and positive effects from the reforms. As noted above, the state-based electricity companies have been corporatized, and in some instances privatized, and new competitive structures have been introduced. A recent study (Pierce *et al.* 1995) of the industry in the largest state, New South Wales, shows that, following these policy changes, the real price of electricity has fallen (faster than international benchmark prices) and service quality has improved.

A similar conclusion is reached by Oster and Antioch (1995) in their study of the banking industry after the major reforms of 1983, although they are careful to stress the difficulties associated with measuring the value and quality of output. Both the electricity and banking industries have remained essentially domestic industries, with limited forays abroad. By contrast, the education and health industries have internationalized quickly and, along with tourism, have generated major service exports. Both industries enjoy cost advantages over US and European suppliers, enhanced by a proximity advantage in the rapidly expanding South-East Asian market. The major government contribution here has simply been unshackling the industries and allowing them to compete internationally, supplemented at the margin by some promotional support in opening up new markets and establishing a presence in them.

Ergas and Wright (1994) present preliminary results from the most detailed recent survey of firms—962 in total—conducted by the Australian Manufacturing Council in 1993–4. The findings provide further evidence of the link between policy reform and performance. As expected, the more international a firm, the more it is likely to monitor a rival's performance, to be attentive to customer satisfaction and product quality, to extend its learning process, and to focus on industrial-relations issues. Reduced protection has had a number of important effects, among which lower levels of product fragmentation rank highly.

Ergas and Wright (1994: 91–2) also probe for the determinants of firm-level performance, concluding: 'Competitive conditions . . . do play a significant role in determining product quality and in reducing intra-industry dispersion in performance. However, by far the strongest relationships . . . link superior performance to export orientation—not to competition *per se*.'

The study of service exporters referred to earlier (AUSTRADE 1994) concluded that increased competition in Australia was a major factor in inducing firms to go abroad, a result consistent with that of Ergas and Wright (1994). Services exports have increased by 10 per cent per annum in the last decade, much of it Asia-oriented. A recent variant of services exports has been a programme which has succeeded in attracting eighty regional headquarters or major offices of international corporations to establish in Australia.

Also notable are the results of Sheehan *et al.* (1994) who, although not undertaking firm-level research, probed at the industry level for determinants of the dramatic improvement in Australian ETM export performance referred to above. They concluded (1994: 21 ff.) that rising competitiveness in the first half of the

1980s, resulting primarily from exchange-rate movements and wage controls, was the major stimulant to growth, alongside a supportive international environment, especially in East Asia.

However, they assert that, while cost advantages were the trigger for the initial increase, they alone could not sustain the growth. (We note that this cost advantage was substantially eroded for a period around 1990—see Fig. 7.3.) Instead they argue that a change in 'business culture' was under way. The success of a few firms generated positive externalities in the sense that the 'leaders' acted as a powerful demonstration effect for the 'followers'. More controversially, they argue that 'policy ETMs' (sectors where the government played an active role in promoting restructuring and inducing firms to look outward) in industries such as pharmaceuticals, computing equipment, transport, and telecommunications equipment, appear to have exhibited superior performance to the 'non-policy' group. The counterfactual proposition, however, is a powerful one, and it is not immediately obvious that policy was the main arbiter of success, nor of course that the social cost-benefit analysis of the schemes was always positive. Moreover, the data are not robust enough and the time period too short to reach firm conclusions, while the ETMs include some low value-added products along with more technology-intensive items. This is clearly an area where further research is required.

ETMs exports constituted some 23 per cent of total merchandise exports in 1995, reaching into many corners of the world. For example, Australian-built ferries ply the English Channel; Hong Kong's new airport will have an Australian weather radar system; an Australian company provided the signalling systems for a large new Indonesian railway project; and an Australian firm is handling the master planning for the $A2 billion Yokuska Islands development in Tokyo Bay (Department of Foreign Affairs and Trade 1996).

Amongst the larger companies, there are a few with substantial international activity. BTR Nylex, Elders, and Pacific Dunlop have foreign assets approaching their domestic investment, and BHP, CSR, Boral, and Pioneer hold foreign assets equal to some 50 per cent of their domestic assets. Other work suggests that there are some 2,500 small to medium-sized Australian firms that export about 10 per cent of their sales, and a further 500 that export 10–40 per cent of sales, with another 400 exporting over 40 per cent (EPAC 1995). These exports total around $A6 billion per year. These smaller firms operate mainly in niche segments of markets in Asia and the Pacific. It is argued that their primary reason for internationalizing was lack of opportunity in the domestic market.

8. Conclusion

This survey of Australia's experience of a major experiment in micro-economic reform has a positive conclusion. Australia embarked on a clear change of direction in the early 1980s towards integration with the emerging global economy.

Declining relative standards of living and comparisons of other indicators with the rest of the developed world made the need for change obvious. At the same time, there was growing acceptance of the need to reform both the non-market and business sectors of government at the federal and state levels.

We believe the experience to date is positive in many respects. Australia has made significant progress towards the vision of an open, competitive economy. It has moved firmly to establish itself in the Asian region as a complementary trading partner for the fast-growing nations to the north. Foreign investment by Australian firms has expanded rapidly, albeit skewed towards the developed world, and appears to be shifting recently to follow trade towards East Asia.

The role of government policy has been crucial to these developments, in our view. In Australia, unlike the USA, government has always had an important role, particularly since 1940. The wage-fixing system, the system of protection, and regulation in many sectors are all symptoms of the acceptance of a strong role for government. For these reasons, reform in Australian had to be initiated by government, even as it was being forced upon the country by growing globalization. Government has adopted a new role towards business and in the process is reforming itself. Australian firms and the local affiliates of international corporations face stronger competition in the domestic market than in the past, and their offshore subsidiaries are exposed to the competitive conditions of other countries. Growing integration with the rest of world economy is forcing these firms to develop sharply focused strategies, to recognize and enhance their key competences, and to capitalize on those strengths. It is also requiring them to learn how to manage the greater complexity of international operations.

Although we consider the scorecard positive, it is still to early to reach strong conclusions. Macro-economic management, although not directly part of the reform agenda, has the potential if mishandled to undo many of the major reform achievements. If, on the other hand, the present direction of change continues without the dislocation of a currency crisis, Australia may have set itself on a path of global integration that will greatly enhance its influence and prosperity. As a country undertaking a fundamental transformation of its position in the world, the successes and failures of government policy should be of considerable interest to other countries. Likewise, the strategies and operational policies employed by Australian-based firms in the process of internationalization are undergoing change. As outlined earlier, the reasons for and direction of outward investment have changed over time. The nature of these changes is not yet well understood, yet they should be of interest to other international corporations.

We end by making a call for further work. In a number of areas the lack of systematic analysis makes it difficult to draw sound conclusions. In particular, there is a great need in Australia for more detailed firm-level research to understand the forces at work during this period of internationalization, such as the 'transmission mechanism' linking micro-reforms and firm strategies. More needs to be known about the process of internationalization of Australian firms, their strategies and organizational forms, and the sources of success and failure. This work would provide guidance to improve the effectiveness of government policies and assist business to accommodate more easily to change.

NOTES

1. The phrase 'tyranny of distance' was developed originally by a leading Australian historian in reference to the barriers imposed by huge internal distances. But it has come into more common usage to refer also to *international* distances. Its diminished importance as an obstacle to Australian economic development is the result not only of declining real transport and communication costs, but a major shift in the locus of economic activity.
2. Notwithstanding the very rapid increase in outward FDI, the ratio in Table 7.2 underlines the modest absolute size in comparison to that of other middle-sized OECD economies with a longer history of international investment. As further illustration, there is just one Australia-based company, BHP, ranked 88, in the top 100 MNCs as listed in UNCTAD (1994). By contrast, Canada and The Netherlands have three companies, Sweden four, and Switzerland six.
3. We owe this term to Ross Garnaut, and his observation that the five commodity-dependent economies closest to Antarctica—Argentina, Australia, Chile, New Zealand, and South Africa—all turned inward in the post-war period. By the mid-1990s all had made major U-turns in policy, with the possible exception of South Africa.
4. According to estimates prepared by Maddison (1989: 19), Australia had the highest *per capita* GDP among sixteen OECD countries in 1900 and was some 50% above the OECD average. By 1987 it had slipped to a below-average ninth position.
5. Garnaut (1994*b*) provides a detailed analysis of the political economy of these reforms, written partly from an 'insider's' perspective. Kelly (1992) is an account of the decade's change written by one of the nation's most authoritative political journalists.
6. For further analysis, and reference to the extensive literature on the subject, see Albon and Falvey (1992).
7. These issues are examined comprehensively by the contributors to Forsyth (1992).
8. See Fane (1995) for a strong statement of the case for labour-market reform. A detailed study of the case for industrial-relations reform, including more emphasis on enterprise-level negotiations, is contained in Hilmer *et al.* (1993).
9. For an illuminating account of the spectacular rise and fall of these enterprises by one the country's leading financial journalists, see Sykes (1994).
10. For a representative sample of perspectives, see, e.g., Arndt (1989), Pitchford (1990) Nguyen (1992), Collins (1994).
11. See, e.g., the suggestion in *The Economist* (Nov. 1995): 'A Mexican wave could mean adios amigo.'
12. Recent, as yet unpublished, research by the BIE suggests that the trend towards rising outward investment will accelerate. For example, in their survey of 45 major

Australian ICs (35 in manufacturing, 10 in services), it was found that 63% of their projected net new investment over the period 1995–9 will be abroad, as compared to 43% over the period 1987–94.

13. See Howe (1994) for a detailed examination of international investment trends, and Bora (1995) for a discussion of policy issues.
14. For a discussion of this and other related issues, see BIE (1993) and Gregory (1993).
15. This section draws on Hill (1994).
16. For a detailed analysis of Australia–Japan economic relations over the period of rapid growth 1945–65, see Drysdale (1967).
17. For an explanation of these trade intensity concepts, see Drysdale and Garnaut (1982).
18. Based on International Economic Data Bank, Research School of Pacific Studies, Australian National University.
19. Assuming, plausibly, that most of the 'other' category falls into this grouping.
20. The recent BIE survey of outward investment by 45 major Australian companies confirmed such a regional shift. The distribution of their investments in 1980 and 1994 respectively was UK (11.8% in 1980, 39.3% in 1994), USA (13.1%, 21.8%), New Zealand (8.1%, 14.7%), Papua New Guinea (5.8%, 4.5%), ASEAN (28.3%, 5.9%), Hong Kong (17.6%, 2.8%), other (15.4%, 11.0%).
21. It is possible also, as suggested by the EAAU (1994) report, that Australia's high dependence on imported capital has restricted outward-investment flows to the region, a factor which results from the Australian subsidiaries' subservience to the headquarter's global investment decisions. Documentation of such a phenomenon is, of course, extremely difficult.
22. The debate on recent industrial policy is well summed up by Smith (1995). Key references from a variety of perspectives include Garnaut (1989), Marsh (1994), and Sheehan, Pappas, and Cheng (1994).

REFERENCES

Access Economics (1994), *Australia in Asia* (Canberra: Access Economics).

Albon, R., and Falvey, R. (1992), 'Trade Policy and Microeconomic Reform in Australian Manufacturing', in Forsyth (1992), 145–63.

AMC (1994): Australian Manufacturing Council, *Leading the Way: A Study of Best Manufacturing in Australia and New Zealand* (Canberra: AMC).

Anderson, K. (1987), 'Tariffs and the Manufacturing Sector', in Maddock and McLean (1987), 165–94.

—— and Garnaut, R. (1987), *Australian Protectionism: Extent, Causes and Effects* (Sydney: Allen and Unwin).

Andersen, P., Dwyer, J., and Gruen, D. (1995) (eds.), *Productivity and Growth* (Sydney: Reserve Bank of Australia).

Arndt, H. W. (1965), 'Australia: Developed, Developing or Midway?', *Economic Record*, 41/95: 318–40.

—— (1989), 'Australia's Current Account and Debt Problem: A Skeptical View of the Pitchford Thesis' (Centre for Economic Policy Research, Discussion Paper No. 219; Australian National University, Canberra).

AUSTRADE (1994), *Intelligent Exports and the Silent Revolution in Services* (Canberra: Australian Government Publishing Service).

BIE (various): Bureau of Industry Economics, *News* (Canberra: BIE).

—— (1993), *R&D, Innovation and Competitiveness: An Evaluation of the Research and Development Tax Concession* (Research Report 50, Canberra: Australian Government Publishing Service).

Bora, B. (1995), 'The Implications of Globalisation for Australian Foreign Investment Policy', in EPAC (1995), 89–111.

Brash, D. J. (1966), *American Investment in Australian Industry* (Canberra: Australian National University Press).

Caves, R. E. (1971), 'International Corporations: The Industrial Economics of Foreign Investment', *Economica*, 38: 1–27.

Collins, S. (1994), 'Experiences with Current Account Deficits among East Asian Economies: Lessons for Australia?', in Lowe and Dwyer (1994), 274–303.

Demura, P. (1995), 'Productivity Change in the Australian Steel Industry: BHP Steel 1982–95', in Andersen *et al.* (1995), 172–84.

Department of Foreign Affairs and Trade (1996), *Insight*, 5/2 (26 February).

Drysdale, P. D. (1967), 'Japanese–Australian Trade' (unpublished doctoral dissertation, Canberra: Australian National University).

—— and Garnaut, R. (1982), 'Trade Intensities and the Analysis of Bilateral Trade Flows in a Many-Country World: A Survey', *Hitotsubashi Journal of Economics*, 22/2: 62–84.

—— —— (1993), 'The Pacific: An Application of a General Theory of Economic Integration', in C. F. Bergsten and M. Noland (eds.), *Pacific Dynamism and the International Economic System* (Washington: Institute for International Economics), 183–223.

Dunning, J. H. (1977), 'Trade, Location of Economic Activity and the Multinational Enterprise: A Search for an Eclectic Approach', in O. B. Hesselborn and P. M. Wikman (eds.), *The International Allocation of Economic Activity* (London: Macmillan).

—— (1979), 'Explaining the Changing Pattern of International Production: In Defence of Eclectic Theory', *Oxford Bulletin of Economics and Statistics*, 41: 269–96.

(EAAU) (1992): East Asian Analytical Unit, *Australia's Business Challenge: South-East Asia in the 1990s* (Canberra: Department of Foreign Affairs and Trade, Australian Government Publishing Service).

—— (1994), *Changing Tack: Australian Investment in South-East Asia* (Canberra: Department of Foreign Affairs and Trade, Australian Government Publishing Service).

EPAC (1995): Economic Planning Advisory Commission, *Globalisation: Issues for Australia* (Commission Paper No. 5; Canberra: Australian Government Publishing Service).

Ergas, H., and Wright, M. (1994), 'Internationalisation, Firm Conduct and Productivity', in P. Lowe and J. Dwyer (1994), 51–105.

Fane, G. (1995), 'Economic Reform and Deregulation in Australia' (Discussion Paper No. 310; Centre for Economic Policy Research, Australian National University, Canberra).

Fitzgerald, V. W. (1993), *National Saving: A Report to the Treasurer* (Canberra: Australian Government Publishing Service).

Forsyth, P. (1992) (ed.), *Microeconomic Reform in Australia* (Sydney: Allen & Unwin).

—— (1994), 'Microeconomic Reform: Where to from Here?', *Policy* (Winter), 1994.

Garnaut, R. (1989), *Australia and the Northeast Asian Ascendancy* (Canberra: Australian Government Publishing Service).

Garnaut, R. (1994*a*), 'The Floating Dollar and the Australian Structural Transition: Some Asia Pacific Context', *Economic Record*, 70/208: 80–96.

—— (1994*b*), 'Australia', in J. Williamson (ed.), *The Political Economy of Policy Reform* (Washington: Institute for International Economics), 51–72.

Gregory, R. G. (1993), 'The Australian Innovation System', in Nelson (1993), 324–52.

Grossman, G. M., and Helpman, E. (1991), *Innovation and Growth in the Global Economy* (Cambridge, Mass.: MIT Press).

Hill, H. (1994), 'Australia's Asia-Pacific Connections' (Economics Division Working Papers (East Asia) 94/2; Research School of Pacific and Asian Studies, Australian National University, Canberra).

Hilmer, F. G., *et al.* (1993), *Working Relations: A Fresh Start for Australian Enterprises* (Melbourne: Business Council of Australia).

Howe, J. (1994), 'Internationalisation, Trade and Foreign Direct Investment', in Lowe and Dwyer (1994), 111–55.

Hymer, S. H. (1976), *The International Operations of National Firms: A Study of Foreign Direct Investment* (Cambridge, Mass.: MIT Press).

INDECS (1992), *State of Play 7: The Australian Economic Policy Debate* (Sydney: Allen & Unwin).

Kelly, P. (1992), *The End of Certainty: The Story of the 1980s* (Sydney: Allen & Unwin).

Kravis, R., and Lipsey, R. E. (1982), 'The Location of Overseas Production for Export by US Multinational Firms, *Journal of International Economics*, 12: 201–23.

Lloyd, P. J. (1995), 'The Nature of Globalisation', in EPAC (1995), 11–31.

Lowe, P. (1995), 'Labour-Productivity Growth and Relative Wages: 1978–94', in Andersen *et al.* (1995), 93–134.

—— and Dwyer, J. (1994) (eds.), *International Integration of the Australian Economy* (Sydney: Reserve Bank of Australia).

Maddison, A. (1989), *The World Economy in the 20th Century* (Development Centre Studies; Paris: OECD).

Maddock, R., and McLean, I. W. (1987) (eds.), *The Australian Economy in the Long Run* (Cambridge: Cambridge University Press).

Marsh, I. (1994) (ed.), *Australian Business in the Asia Pacific Region: The Case for Strategic Policy* (Melbourne: Longman Cheshire).

McKern, R. B. (1976), *Multinational Enterprise and Natural Resources* (Sydney: McGraw Hill).

—— (1981), 'Technology Transfer in Australian Firms', in *The Economic Implications of Patents in Australia* (Canberra: Australian Patents Office), 189–98.

Nelson, R. R. (1993) (ed.), *National Innovation Systems: A Comparative Analysis* (New York: Oxford University Press).

Nguyen, D. T. (1992), 'The Role of Policy Reform in Managing Australia's External Debt', in A. J. MacIntyre and K. Jayasuriya (eds.), *The Dynamics of Economic Policy Reform in South-East Asia and the South-West Pacific* (Singapore: Oxford University Press), 178–97.

OECD (1994*a*): Organization for Economic Cooperation and Development, *The Performance of Foreign Affiliates in OECD Countries* (Paris: OECD).

—— (1994*b*), *OECD Economic Surveys: Australia* (Paris: OECD).

Oster, A., and Antioch, L. (1995), 'Measuring Productivity in the Australian Banking Sector', in Andersen *et al.* (1995), 201–12.

Pender, H., and Ross, S. (1995), *Business Taxation in Australia and Asia* (Commission

Paper No. 4; Canberra: Economic Planning Advisory Commission, Australian Government Publishing Service).

Pierce, J., *et al.* (1995), 'The Performance of the NSW Electricity Supply Industry', in Andersen *et al.* (1995), 185–200.

Pitchford, J. D. (1990), *Australia's Foreign Debt—Myths and Realities* (Sydney: Allen & Unwin).

Ratnayake, R. (1993), 'Factors Affecting Inter-Industry Variation of Foreign Ownership of Manufacturing Industry', *Applied Economics*, 25: 653–9.

Rugman, A. (1991), 'Diamond in the Rough', *Insight* (University of Western Ontario).

Sheehan, P., Pappas, N., and Cheng, E. (1994), *The Rebirth of Australian Industry* (Melbourne: Centre for Strategic Economic Studies, Victoria University).

Shu, J., and Khoo, S. E. (1993), *Australia's Population Trends and Prospects 1992* (Canberra: Bureau of Immigration Research, Australian Government Publishing Service).

Smith, H. (1995), 'Recent Writings on Australia's Industry Policy', *Agenda*, 2/4: 479–88.

Stewardson, B. R. (1995), 'The Globalization of BHP', in EPAC (1995), 51–9.

Stubbs, P. (1968), *Innovation and Research* (Cheshire: Sydney).

Sykes, T. (1994), *The Bold Riders: Behind Australia's Corporate Collapses* (Sydney: Allen & Unwin).

UNCTAD (1994): United Nations Conference on Trade and Development, *World Investment Report 1994: Transnational Corporations, Employment and the Workplace* (New York: United Nations).

World Bank (1982), *World Development Report 1982* (Washington: World Bank).

—— (1994), *World Development Report 1994* (Washington: World Bank).

—— (1995), *World Development Report 1995* (Washington: World Bank).

8

The United Kingdom

Neil Hood and Stephen Young

1. Introduction

This chapter concerns the evaluation of selected aspects of the development of macro-organizational policy in the UK, principally covering the period since the late 1970s. It does so against the background of the conceptual frameworks considered by Dunning and Lipsey within this volume (Chapters 1 and 2), and in the light of Dunning's earlier work on this subject (Dunning 1992).

In view of the open nature of the economy, its tradition of liberal policies on both trade and FDI, and its strong vested interest in both, the UK is an economy in which it would be expected that the impact of the forces of global economic change would be particularly evident. That this is the case is confirmed within this chapter. At the same time, and supporting views expressed by Dunning (1992), it is difficult to imply any direct correlation between developments in the global economy and the radical changes in UK economic policy in general or in macro-organizational strategy over this particular period.

While what has occurred falls short of a systemic approach to counteract market-distorting behaviour or to build up created assets, there is little doubt that there have been consistent themes pursued since the Conservative government came to power in 1979. Deregulation, privatization, the restructuring of the handling of labour disputes, and so on have been driven by a clear philosophy concerning the role of the market and the negative economic and social effects of certain types of market distortions. Therefore it could be argued that, while the motivation was a political paradigm, it took the form of pursuing policies designed to achieve an adjustment in the relative competitive position of the UK among its economic peer group of nations. In that particular sense, whether expressed formally as a reform of macro-organizational strategies, much change was achieved which had the effect of better positioning the UK of the late 1990s to be able to live with the consequences of globalization. As will be evident in Section 3, the specific language of policies designed to enhance competitiveness did not emerge in the UK until the late 1980s and early 1990s, but many of the previous policy components were pointing in that direction.

In order to confine the topic of this chapter to manageable proportions, we propose to view the question of the evolution of macro-organizational policies in the UK from the perspective of its approach to FDI policy, and to cover related issues with that in mind. Clearly FDI is a particularly relevant driver of globalization and an arena within which government and business interaction can be readily studied in the UK. The chapter is in five main sections, starting with a review of the background to inward and outward FDI and reviewing its contribution. The second section provides an overview of the radical directional policy changes which were implemented in the UK between the late 1970s and the early 1990s in order to enhance competitiveness. This includes a more detailed and critical review of five ingredients of policy: namely, macro-economic management; FDI; technology and R&D; employment, training, and the labour market; and those directed towards regional economic development. The third section briefly reviews three sectoral cases which amply illustrate some of the policy challenges which have emerged for UK governments over this period as a consequence of the growing globalization of economic activity. These are the electronics industry in Scotland; the automotive industry; and the financial-services sector represented by the City of London. Section four explores the degree to which EU policies have aided or retarded FDI and competitiveness in the UK; while the final section sets out some conclusions and propositions regarding UK competitiveness and the policies which have been adopted to enhance it.

2. FDI, International Business, and UK Competitiveness

2.1. The Statistical Position

The UK has played a leading role in the history of global FDI since its earliest days. It was the location for the first US FDIs in the 1850s, including particularly Singer, and was the pioneer manufacturing investor in the USA, in the form of J. & P. Coats (Wilkins 1970, 1989). The network of UK FDI abroad expanded throughout the Empire, and it was not until the 1970s and 1980s that a belated reorientation to developed countries, and particularly back to the USA, occurred. The recent history of inward FDI again shows the UK as a major location first for the post-Second World War growth of US investment and more recently for Japanese investment capital.

The contemporary situation is summarized in Tables 8.1 and 8.2 and Figs. 8.1 and 8.2. During the 1980s UK outflows and inflows were the highest as a proportion of GDP of any G7 country (see Fig. 8.3); in stock terms, the UK in 1992 (see Fig. 8.4) was second to the USA as a recipient of inward investment, and third behind the USA and (marginally) Japan as an outward investor. Fig. 8.5 records the pre-eminent position of the UK within the EU: this position was sustained on an annual-flow basis until the end of the 1980s, when substantial declines occurred on both outward and inward sides. UNCTAD (1994) explains this in terms of the waning wave of cross-border mergers and acquisitions and the UK recession, which was deeper and longer than in most other countries—although it would be premature to speak of fundamental changes in the UK's attractiveness to inward FDI or commitment to outward FDI.[1] Sectorally some 35 per cent

TABLE 8.1. Measures of performance of overseas-owned and all enterprises in manufacturing in the UK, 1991

	Overseas-owned	All enterprises	
			Overseas-owned as per cent of all enterprises
Number of enterprises	1,470	127,907	1.1
Employment (000)	774.8	4,506.8	17.2
Net output (£m.)	30,475	135,208	22.5
Gross value added (£m.)	22,818	105,095	21.7
Net capital expenditure (£m.)	4,373	13,056	33.5
Gross wages and salaries (£m.)	12,396	60,389	20.5
			Ratio of overseas owned to all enterprises
Employment per enterprise (no.)	527	35	15.1
Net output per employee (£)	39,334	30,003	1.31
Gross value added per employee (£)	29,451	23,321	1.26
Gross wages and salaries per employee (£)	15,999	13,401	1.19

Source: Central Statistical Office (1991).

TABLE 8.2. Industrial structure of overseas-owned and all manufacturing enterprises in the UK, 1991

Industry	Share of total employment		Net output per employee	
	Overseas-owned (%)	All enterprises (%)	Overseas-owned (£)	All enterprises (£)
Chemical industry	11.9	6.2	n.a.	53,097
Mechanical engineering	13.2	12.1	33,371	28,201
Office machinery & data-processing equipment	4.3	1.4	54,925	46,384
Electrical & electronic engineering	13.1	10.3	29,619	25,830
Automobiles & parts	13.5	5.4	26,547	26,636
Food, drink, & tobacco	10.2	12.7	37,160	34,906
Paper, printing, & publishing	8.7	9.7	49,310	35,856
All other industries	25.1	42.2	n.a.	n.a.
All manufacturing	100.0	100.0	—	—
Number	774.8	4,506.4	39,334	29,936

Source: Central Statistical Office (1991).

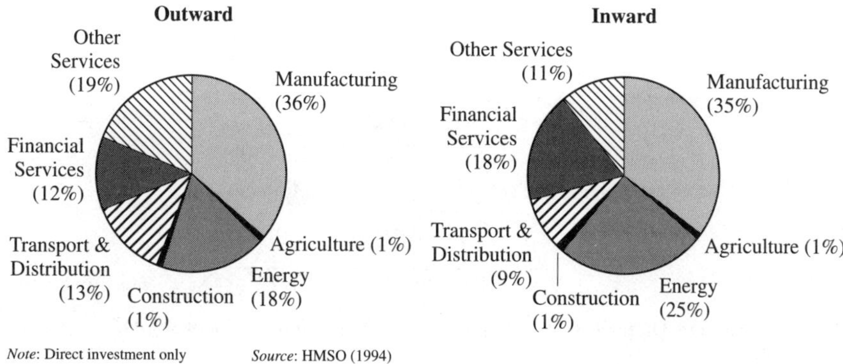

FIG 8.1. Book value of stock of UK investment by sector, 1992

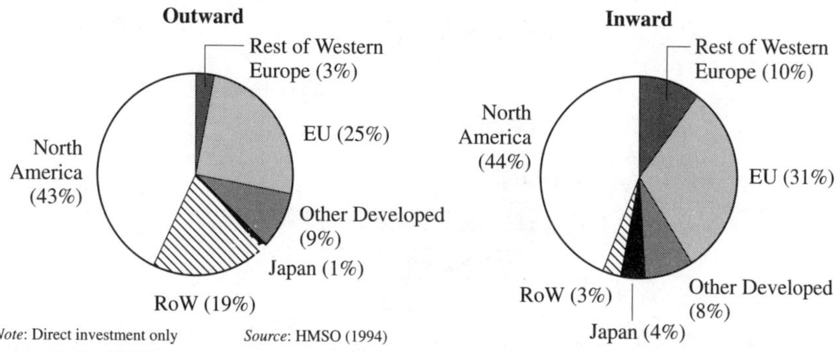

FIG 8.2. Book value of stock of UK investment by area, 1992

of both outward and inward investment is in manufacturing, and North America represents around 44 per cent of outward and inward FDI (see Figs. 8.1 and 8.2).

There have been numerous survey studies of the factors influencing FDI into manufacturing industry in the UK (see the review in Hood and Young 1995). Proximity to markets and labour considerations (costs, availability, and quality) are consistently shown to be of major significance, especially in the country-choice decision, followed at the second level by transport costs and availability and incentives. As for the choice of regional location within the UK, while market proximity, labour, and transport variables are again of critical importance, issues of incentives and sites or premises are also important determinants. Hourly labour costs in manufacturing in the UK are below those of the other G7 countries and all the northern European countries, with low non-wage costs being a particular issue in the comparison with the latter. There are important EU policy controversies here. Low labour costs are primarily a consequence of the UK's poor economic performance, but currently UK labour-cost competitiveness is also linked to the country's withdrawal from the EU's ERM and, some would argue, to its refusal to sign up for the Social Charter in the Maastricht Treaty.

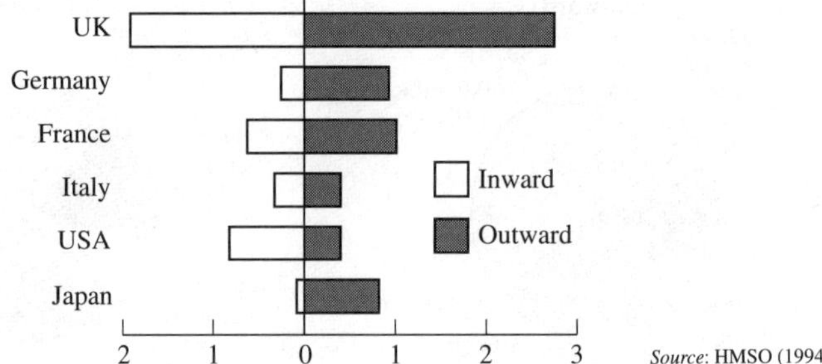

Source: HMSO (1994)

FIG 8.3. Foreign Direct Investment Flows as a Proportion of Country GDP 1981–1991

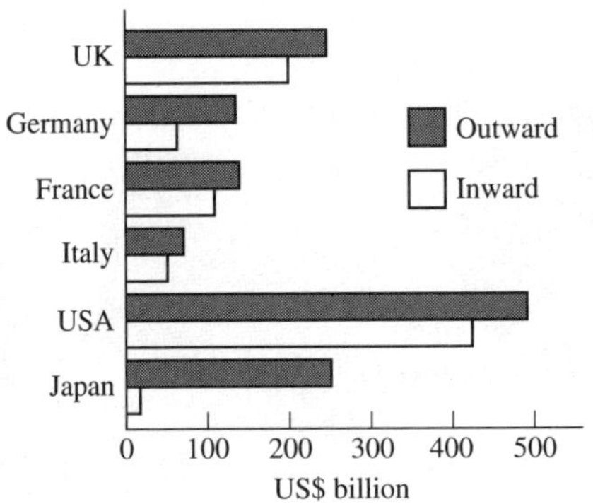

Source: HMSO (1995)

FIG 8.4. Comparison of Stock of Direct Investment in 1992

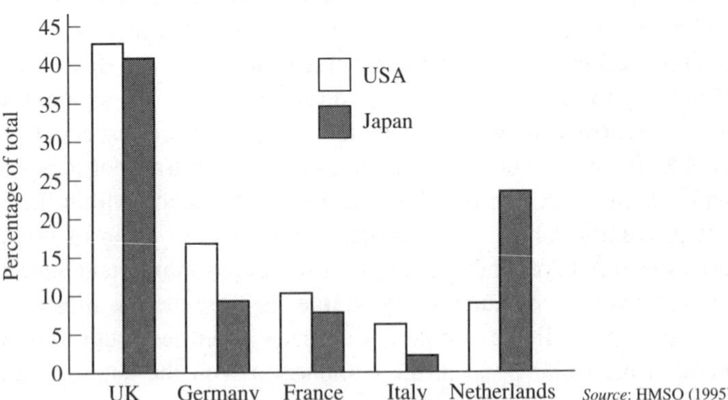

Source: HMSO (1995)

FIG 8.5. Main Recipients of US and Japanese Investments in the EU

Incentives in the UK, when expressed as a percentage of value added or ecu per employee, are, however, the lowest in the EU (Peters 1995).

Table 8.1 shows the performance of inward investors in manufacturing, and provides a number of comparisons between the overseas-owned sector and all enterprises in the UK, highlighting the well-known facts regarding the larger size of foreign affiliates, and their higher productivity, investment, and levels of wages and salaries. During the years 1981–91, moreover, foreign manufacturing firms improved their relative performance on all these measures as compared with UK enterprises as a whole, a considerable achievement given the revival of domestic industry (Central Statistical Office 1981, 1991). To complete this introductory picture, Table 8.2 summarizes the sectoral pattern within manufacturing, revealing a more concentrated structure and one more strongly oriented towards high-technology industries than for UK industry as a whole. A note of caution emerges, however, from consideration of R&D spending the share of overseas-owned enterprises declined at the end of the 1980s, with electronics and vehicles showing significant falls in share.

Performance data for UK outward direct investment are more difficult to obtain. Considering the structural pattern of outward FDI in manufacturing, this is rather more growth-sector oriented than the structure of UK industry as a whole; but it still reveals a lower share in high-technology sectors than is the case for the structure of inward FDI. One basis for comparison is the comparative performance of US affiliates of UK MNEs versus other overseas-owned enterprises: Graham and Krugman (1991: table 3.5) show that, on the measures of value added, compensation, R&D, and imports and exports per employee, UK figures were below those of all other major countries (with the single exception of The Netherlands for value added per workers); and, in the first three of these measures, UK firms performed less well than the average US manufacturing firm.[2]

Analysing the structural pattern of inward and outward FDI, Dunning (1985) concluded that the ownership-specific advantages of MNEs have assisted the UK to adjust to sectors in which it is most competitive and to improve the efficiency of existing sectors; and that MNEs have adjusted to the changing locational advantages of the UK to a greater extent than have uni-national enterprises.

2.2. The Contribution of Inward and Outward Direct Investment

Beginning with Dunning's (1958) pioneering research on US manufacturing in the UK, there have been a variety of studies of inward FDI. The most comprehensive research on economic and political issues was that undertaken by Steuer *et al.* (1973). Its conclusions were hedged but found that: 'On economic grounds and grounds of national autonomy we express few arguments against inward investment' (p. 15); and that: 'concerns over the multinational firm and inward investment on the grounds of monopoly power, technology and the balance of payments are not well founded. At the same time, some drawbacks have been indicated . . .' (p. 12). Reviewing later evidence and including results of their own research, the present authors (Young *et al.* 1988) confirmed the conclusion that net impact of inbound FDI was probably beneficial but were more qualified in their conclusions. Positive contributions confirmed relate to the role of international investment as a complement to cross-border trade, to the competitive stimuli induced by MNE activity, and to the transfer of managerial skills and knowledge. The qualifications included the cyclical variability and relative decline in competitiveness of inward foreign affiliates (particularly those of US origin); the lack of strong linkages to domestically owned firms in many sectors (which has at least as much to do with UK competitiveness as with multinationals), and the limited decision-making capacity of most MNE affiliates.

The early work on UK outward FDI was primarily concerned with macroeconomic and balance-of-payments considerations, with the results revolving around the assumed counterfactual situation. Reddaway (1968) assumed that, if UK firms had not invested abroad, alternative investment in the UK was not a possibility: in consequence the balance of payments and employment effects were positive. This conclusion was supported by subsequent research (Houston and Dunning 1976; Shepherd *et al.* 1985; Stopford and Turner 1985), albeit, perhaps, with more caution. Some concerns were expressed about the politically motivated nature of some UK FDI into the USA during the 1970s, but the economic environment within the UK was adverse. There are further anxieties over the characteristics and performance of UK outward FDI into the USA, as noted above; and at 'the loss of some structural autonomy on the part of the UK' (Dunning 1985: 47) (derived, of course, from inward as well as outward investment). Generally, however, the substantial UK outflows are regarded as a necessary response to globalization, with important learning effects deriving, in particular, from overseas FDI in developed countries.

2.3. **Interpreting UK FDI Patterns and Contributions**

There is no question that the most interesting and revealing work on inward FDI (not yet matched by equivalent study of outward FDI) concerns the microeconomic behaviour and performance of foreign-based MNEs in the UK, and their role in generating dynamic comparative advantages. The international business-management literature contains a number of contributions relating to the possibility of the emergence of 'developmental' MNE affiliates, essentially world product mandate (WPM) operations, and to the required conditions for their establishment or evolution. The present authors (Young *et al.* 1994*a*) have argued that one or a small number of sectorally or technologically diverse WPM subsidiaries could not themselves set in motion a positive process of cumulative causation. Drawing on the work of Dunning (1988), Cantwell (1989), Porter (1990), and others, however, it is possible to identify two routes to the generation of clusters, a necessary prerequisite for self-sustaining growth. The two routes proposed are via local sourcing or technological innovation, and are shown in Table 8.3, with

TABLE 8.3. Two possible routes to cluster formation involving inward investment and MNE subsidiaries

	Local-sourcing route	Technological-innovation route
Conditions		
• Company	WPM subsidiary/product specialist/ strategic leader[a] (local design and development capabilities, autonomy in purchasing, marketing responsibilities)	WPM subsidiary/product specialist/strategic leader[a] (R&D capabilities to support subsidiary; access to basic research of parent)
• Country	• Local supplier capabilities (technological and volume capabilities; quality, delivery, price)	• Local scientific, educational, technological tradition
	• Local content requirements	• Availability of research professionals and other labour requirements
Host government requirements	• Macro-economic framework • Infrastructure, education, R&D support, and other public goods • Policies to facilitate efficient resource allocation • Environmental conditions: research parks, innovation centres, public venture funds (inc. support for university–industry research linkages) Government procedure	
	• Availability of assistance to indigenous suppliers	• Assistance to upgrade Miniature Replica-type subsidiaries; creative aftercare policies
	Targeted attraction policies including appropriate regional policy incentives	
	• Competitor/complementary companies	• R&D intensive companies using related technologies
	• Supply companies (to fill gaps)	• Internationally mobile R&D investments using related technologies
Outcomes	• Generation of complete value-adding chains in particular sectors • Agglomerative economies • Self-sustaining industrial growth	• Generation of technological clusters • Technological agglomeration • Enhancement of indigenous technological capabilities

[a] The illustrations relate to WPM-type subsidiary rather than subsidiary centres of excellence. However, for example, a manufacturing centre of excellence would be linked to the local-sourcing route to cluster formation, and an R&D centre would be linked to the technological-innovation route.

Source: Young *et al.* (1994*a*).

a critical role for government in terms of each of the constituents of Porter's diamond of comparative advantage.

Applying this framework to inward investment into the UK, it is apparent that the WPM subsidiary is an elusive phenomenon. This is certainly true of FDI outside the core regions of the UK, and of German FDI more widely (Hood *et al.* 1995*b*). Papanastassiou and Pearce (1996) do, however, identify some evolution in the innovatory roles of MNE subsidiaries in Europe, with those in the UK occupying a more strategic position than their counterparts in Belgium, Greece, or Portugal. The authors suggest that UK subsidiaries are not simply low-cost-based operations specializing in the production of inputs as part of an EU-wide network: rather they may play a leading creative position in an MNE's European activities (that is, regional product mandate, if not WPM status). However (and relevant to the discussion following), the UK subsidiaries did not seem to have a deep relationship with local factors, either subcontractors or research institutions and universities.

Using the technological accumulation paradigm, Cantwell and Dunning (1991) have distinguished between the roles of MNEs as promoters of virtuous cycles of increasing technological capability or vicious cycles of declining technological capability. Applying this paradigm to the UK, the authors compare the pharmaceutical and automotive industries. In the latter instance, the declining locational attractiveness of the UK contributed to a vicious cycle with reduced inward investment and MNE activity less directed to high-value activities; in turn this reduced the industry's ability to compete—that is, until the mid-1980s and the wave of Japanese FDI, which has helped convert a vicious cycle into a virtuous one. In the pharmaceutical industry, by comparison, from the early 1950s foreign producers acted as a competitive challenge to an already strong indigenous industry. Between them they generated a critical mass of innovatory capacity, both human and physical, producing substantial agglomerative economies and further reinforcing the attractiveness of the industry in the UK. The case of financial services in the City of London reveals similar positive economies of agglomeration, although these are perhaps under threat in the light of recent events.

Young *et al.* (1994*a*) make a distinction between this technological innovation route to dynamic comparative advantage, and the local sourcing route where emphasis is placed upon supplier and subcontractor linkages. Thus vertical disintegration of production is linked to collaborative partnerships between MNEs and suppliers, encouraging geographical clustering to minimize transaction and transportation costs and to maximize networking benefits. There have been numerous survey studies of OEM–supplier relationships in respect of both particular regions of the UK and particular nationalities of investor (see, e.g., Morris 1989; Connor 1990; Peck 1990; Thoburn and Takashima 1993). The results are difficult to interpret in any general way, but there are a number of points worth noting. First, given that MNEs in the UK are generally conceived and operated as pan-European enterprises, customer–supplier links may also be pan-European, and the likelihood of clustering at a regional or even UK level is rather limited. Secondly, studies in sectors such as electronics have shown that locally sourced items were mainly relatively bulky, low value, simple technology components, characterized by subcontracting for cost-cutting and risk reduction for MNEs. Thirdly, national-government and EU policies towards Japanese investors (e.g. the formerly operated policy of imposing AD duties on 'screwdriver' plants, and 'voluntary' local content agreements) seem to have been effective in both requiring and encouraging commitment to the development of long-term supplier relationships. Fourthly, as with the technological accumulation model, the critical issue in development or dependency, virtuous or vicious cycles, is the competitiveness of the domestic supplier base.

The conclusion of the Young *et al.* (1994*a*) research was that setting in motion a positive process of cumulative causation and utilizing the capabilities of inward-investing MNEs required an integrated policy approach, beginning with a stable macro-economic environment through effective macro-organizational policies to active and efficient micro-organizational policies. It is to an evaluation of such policies in a UK context that this chapter now turns.

3. **Government Policies, International Business, and UK Competitiveness**

3.1. **Context**

Coinciding with the beginnings of Dunning's era of alliance capitalism, UK policy took a sharp change in direction following the return of a Conservative government under Margaret Thatcher in 1979. Against an external tradition of openness to inward investment and support of international free trade, the UK government proceeded systematically to address many of the internal rigidities within the economy in labour and capital markets as well as its fundamental structure. In consequence, for example, the removal of exchange controls helped to boost UK outward direct investment flows; while confrontational policies were directed to the abuse of trade-union power in industrial disputes and to the reform of wage-bargaining. The privatization programme gathered momentum from the early 1980s as the cornerstone of opening up markets to competition and encouraging wider share ownership as part of the promotion of the 'enterprise culture'.

Many of these changes were painful, but are widely recognized as being necessary. There is not scope within this chapter fully to evaluate their longer-term impact on the UK economy, but several indicators are worthy of comment. For example, since 1975 there has been a fall of 35 per cent in manufacturing employment in the UK, as against 20 per cent in Europe as a whole and a relatively constant figure in the USA. This trend was accelerated in the UK in the 1981–3 recession when a policy of sustaining a high value of the pound highlighted the low relative levels of UK productivity and lack of competitiveness in many parts of the manufacturing sector. One direct outcome of this was a rapid rise in manufacturing productivity in the UK in the 1980s. This created further opportunities for inward FDI, but employment continued to decline in spite of the high levels of inward investment in manufacturing recorded in the previous section. At least partly in consequence of the government policies pursued, productivity (output per hour worked) rose rapidly in the UK over the 1979–92 period—namely, by 4.6 per cent per annum compared to 2.9 per cent in France, 1.8 per cent in Germany, 3.6 per cent in Japan, and 2.4 per cent in the USA. However, by other criteria, such as unit labour costs measured in a common currency and in terms of levels of productivity, the UK relative improvement within the G5 (though improving) has been less impressive (McKinsey Global Institute 1993). Thus, although the UK has many world-beating companies, average productivity levels in manufacturing, in terms of value added per hour worked, has still not risen to that of major competitors such as France, Germany, the USA, and Japan, although the productivity shortfall in services is rather less—as is evidenced, for example, in the section on the City of London.

3.2. **UK competitiveness policy**

There is little doubt that the objective of a sustained improvement in competitiveness has been a continuing theme of UK governments since 1979, although the first comprehensive government audit of the country's competitive position was not made until 1994. At that time, it was recognized that what was required was 'further underlying improvement in long term productivity, control of costs, and a performance in many aspects of national life that compares favourably with others' (HMSO 1994: 9). The core presumption in this policy approach is that the UK is in vigorous competition with other nations in a global economy. There was also a strongly held government belief that the primary responsibility for improving the UK's competitiveness lay with firms and that its own role was to create the right kind of enabling environment. The latter has included the desire to provide a stable macro-economic framework which enabled business to plan ahead with confidence; policies to make markets work more efficiently as well as broadening the influence of market disciplines on resource attraction throughout the economy; the pursuit of tax policies designed to encourage enterprise which do not act as hindrances to economic efficiency; and, finally, the aim to improve value for money in the services which are provided by the public sector.

One of the most obvious and influential examples of the outworking of this philosophy is evidenced in the privatization programme. Between 1979 and 1994 almost two-thirds of the industries under state control and around one million public-sector jobs were transferred into the private sector. This expansion of the market economy has involved almost fifty major businesses in sectors as diverse as automobiles, steel, airlines, and utilities. Several of the companies involved are both substantial exporters and outward investors. Meanwhile the market liberalization associated with privatization in areas such as telecommunications and electricity generation, distribution and supply, has acted as a stimulant for related inward investment, not least because this has created the opportunity to use the UK as a base for subsequent penetration of other EU markets as their own privatization policies have subsequently emerged (Hood and McArthur 1994).

The radical and diverse nature of the post-1979 policy environment in the UK has been such that, within the confines of this chapter, it is possible to give only selective coverage of some of its various elements within this section. For example, the 1994 white paper (HMSO 1994) in fact identified ten main factors influencing competitiveness and reviewed the UK policy approach to each of them. The bias in those selected is towards the component elements of macro-organizational policy, including those involving the enhancement of created assets.

3.3. **Macro Economic Policy**

Although involving a planned reduction in corporate and personal taxation levels and a progressive switch from direct to indirect taxation over the period since 1979, the dominant thrust of UK macro-policy has been on the monetary side. For example, there is little doubt that the UK's inflation rate in the 1970s was much too high and well above that of its competitors. Progress in remedying this during the 1980s was mixed, not least because of the rigidities in several parts of the economy. It was, therefore, not until late 1992 that the cumulative effect of policies to control inflation could claim to have been effective. By then it was credible to set a target annual range of 1–4 per cent for underlying inflation at a time when earnings growth in the country was at its lowest level for twenty-five years. It is not unreasonable to assume that the UK commitment to low inflation, combined with a resistance to the social overhead cost escalation as required in the social contract of the Maastricht Treaty (from which the UK has opted out), has helped the country to gain substantial inward investment flows following from the completion of the Single Market—or, more accurately, those which came to Europe following the announcement of its completion.

Exchange-rate policy has been another important policy arena for the UK over this period, but one in which fortunes have been mixed. For example, the policy of maintaining a high relative value of sterling during the 1981–3 recession had the effect of overpricing UK exports, accelerating manufacturing restructuring, and raising unemployment. At the same time, it also placed considerable pressure on UK firms to upgrade their manufacturing productivity. Viewed in retrospect, the resulting gain in competitiveness has probably been worth the price, but the full impact of the resulting loss of capacity has taken time to work through the economy and into inflation and balance-of-trade effects. In the opposite direction, and while aiming for exchange-rate stability, the UK has experienced two distinctive sterling events over the past decade which have had substantial competitive consequences. The first was in 1984/5, when sterling was very weak against the US dollar, and the second was in September 1992, when the UK left the ERM after a period of considerable currency turbulence. These events were the outcome of a combination of earlier UK policy decisions and of events external to the UK economy. In the latter context, in particular, the effective devaluation which followed further enhanced the ability of UK-based business to gain from the expansion of exports into the Single Market and further induced expansion projects within the foreign-owned sector (Hood *et al.* 1995*a*).

3.4. **FDI Policy**

UK policies on both outward and inward FDI have been relatively liberal for most of the post-Second World War period, and became progressively more so in the period since 1979 (Hood and Young 1981; Safarian 1993). On the outward side, the UK government has continued to be active in the promotion of the interests of its investors as would be expected from a major home country. Over the period under consideration, such activity has included opposition to unitary tax measures in the USA and certain EU proposals such as the draft Vredeling Directive regarding employee consultation, the requirement for two-tier boards, and so on. Arguably, however, the major enabling contributions came in other directions, in that the abolition of exchange controls, the gains in relative productivity, and the adoption of Single Market measures all contributed to the reorientation of UK-outward FDI away from historically protected and formerly colonial markets, towards the EU and the USA. Thus the mid-1990s witnessed not only a substantial growth in overseas assets, but a strategic reorientation within the asset stock and one which reflected the trading relationships of the end of the twentieth century rather than at its beginning.

As regards inward FDI, UK policy has remained liberal over this period. In another context the present authors have characterized the UK policy in the 1980s as one of 'bounded prejudice', combining liberalization with occasional interventionism (Young *et al.* 1988: 197). For example, takeovers may be investigated on competition grounds and the Industry Act 1975 gives powers (not used hitherto) to prohibit acquisitions against the national interest. There are also a limited number of specific sectoral measures, as evidenced, for example, in the limitation of foreign ownership in British Aerospace plc and Rolls Royce plc to 29.5 per cent of the voting equity in view of their defence and technology interests. However, although there are still constraints in a number of UK sectors, the erosion of sectoral boundaries, together with privatization and market liberalization in the UK, have opened up some new areas for inward FDI. For example, the review of the duopoly in telecommunications in 1988 has led to the unique awarding of combined telephony and cable licences in the UK, which in turn has led to a wave of foreign investment in a sector which borders on broadcasting

(Hood *et al.* 1993*b*). Meanwhile, and atypical of the general thrust of UK policy, the government has continued to defend UK interests in the oil-exploration and development industry, especially in terms of local-content requirements; and in banking, where the 1987 legislation gave the Bank of England the power to block the purchase of over 15 per cent of the shares of a UK bank from any source.

In the light of the comments made in the opening section of this chapter regarding the contribution of in-bound FDI to the UK economy, one of the notable features of the period since 1979 has been the growth in the number of institutions whose mission is to attract FDI. As a result, intra-UK competition for FDI has grown, as regions compete in order to gain economic benefit at the regional level. While the strategy for these activities is set at national level by the Invest in Britain Bureau (IBB) and incentive levels managed by its parent department (Trade and Industry) according to UK and EU rules, the net effect has been to make the UK an even more welcoming environment for FDI at the local level. Among the consequences of this has been the progressive defining of FDI-targeting policies (Young *et al.* 1994*b*) and the development of after-care programmes to enable the UK to gain from higher value-added developments within subsidiaries (Young and Hood 1994). However, as will be evident later in this section, some of the policy instruments to ensure the latter are not present in the UK. As a general conclusion, the UK policy on inward investment has remained firmly on the macro side, consistently supporting FDI attraction but paying less attention than some of its EU or global competitors to the adoption of macro-organizational policies for its long-run value-added development.

3.5. **Technology and R&D Policy**

The relationships between MNEs, technology, and innovatory capacity have been well explored (*inter alia*) in Dunning (1993). As regards the location of technological capacity, there has been some dispersion since 1970, with the rise of Japan being particularly notable. The UK remains one of the five leading innovating countries in the world and in some areas, such as tobacco-processing, pharmaceuticals, and aircraft, it has registered an above average number of patents (Cantwell and Hodson 1991), even though its share of the patents registered in the top five countries had dropped to under 4 per cent by the late 1980s. However, in its own diagnosis of the UK relative position (HMSO 1994), the government has acknowledged that UK industrial R&D expenditure as a proportion of GDP has lagged behind that of some other leading economies, as had the UK share of US patents, and that there was evidence of lags in the introduction of automation and flexible manufacturing systems in some sectors. Indeed, the UK was the only industrialized country to have a smaller proportion of GDP devoted to R&D in 1991 than it did in 1981.

A full explanation of cause and effect in this large topic is outside the scope of this chapter. Numbers, quality, and recognition of technological qualifications;

the historic split between defence-related R&D and commercial innovation; the scale and scope of venture and development capital; long- and short-term investment horizons, and so on are among the many variables cited in the literature to explain the UK's position. Much of the UK government approach over the study period is captured in its own attempted evaluation of the government contribution to competitiveness through science, engineering, and technology (HMSO 1993). The thrust of this approach has remained enabling, but of a specific type, with an emphasis placed on partnership between government, business, and science communities and the focusing of public resources towards the achievement of economic goals. By contrast, there has been little attempt to provide fiscal incentives for innovation, but rather to place the onus on companies to take advantage of the plethora of initiatives established by governments. These range most recently from the strategic (through Technology Foresight Groups and the expansion of higher education in relevant disciplines) to the financial (through Research Council programmes and the accessing of EU schemes) to those offering assistance with the process of innovation itself. The uptake of these schemes consistently shows that they regularly feature in the plans of inward investors, and that they act as an important element of the generally supportive UK environment.

Beyond that, however, there is little that is truly distinctive about the UK government's general approach to innovation. What is evident, however, is that the southern part of the UK (the south-east region and its environs) already has attributes which place it within the EU core cluster of innovatory centres, and that this has attracted international research interests of many types. Some of the comments in the previous section suggested that there was merit in attempting to extend and deepen the technology infrastructure to support efficient macro-organizational policies, but there is little sign of a willingness to do that in the UK. Thus a paradox is beginning to emerge in the EU between countries such as the UK which consistently view FDI attraction and development as a general policy to sustain economic growth in a quantitative sense and those (such as The Netherlands, France, and Italy) where the focus tends to be directed to the selective targeting of specific qualitative inputs from these sources—as in biotechnology in The Netherlands and electronic R&D in Italy.

3.6. Employment, Training, and Labour-Market Policy

In this area, an enduring UK policy issue has been the association between flexible labour markets and competitiveness. In the 1960s and 1970s wage rises in the UK failed to reflect performance, affordability, and retention needs, and, as a result, firms' labour costs rose faster than those in major competitor nations when expressed in national currencies. Inherent in the inflationary environment of that era was an expectation that exchange-rate depreciation would maintain corporate competitiveness. Associated with this sequence of events were poor industrial relations, high levels of industrial disruption, and increasing unemployment.

The complexity of the environment of that time required a wide-ranging strategy post-1979 by the newly elected Conservative government to improve the working of the labour market. The main objectives were seen as encouraging good employment practices based on a dialogue between employers and employees, local wage determination, financial participation by employees at their place of employment, and so on. In order to improve industrial relations, closed-shop practices were made illegal, as were calls for secondary industrial action. One consequence of this strategy has been continued tensions between the UK and the EU as regards the balance between individual employment rights and the minimization of costs to employers. Equally controversial at the time were some of the actions taken to reform wage-bargaining arrangements, especially when these involved the abolition of mechanisms such as Wages Councils for setting and enforcing statutory minimum-wage rages. These measures, together with others related to work incentives, the discouragement of discrimination in the labour market, and a reduction of the obstacles to labour mobility, have had a profound effect both on the UK labour market and on the perception of the country as a place in which to invest. One of the most conspicuous outcomes lies in a radical change in the industrial-relations climate, the UK strike rate falling well below the EU and OECD averages, as well as that of the USA in the past decade. Employee involvement and participation have also increased very substantially, national multi-employer collective agreements have fallen sharply, and there has been a rapid growth in flexible working patterns, short-term, and contract employment.

A balanced judgement would conclude that the UK has had a good record in deregulating its labour market since the early 1980s, but that its achievements in education and training have been less impressive. As the outcome of these reforms, and the resultant wide differentials between the UK and some of its EU partners in terms of labour flexibility, there are continued allegations of 'social dumping' in the UK and of creating excessively favourable conditions within which the UK can compete to attract inward investment.

Turning more directly to education and training and its relation to international business, there are two important issues for the UK. The first is to have sufficient suitably qualified workers to fill vacancies and encourage flexibility in the wage-bargaining process to allow companies to respond to changing technologies and international competition. Progress in the former area has been mixed. At one end of the spectrum there has been the rapid expansion of higher education in the past decade. At the other there has been a heavy weighting of government schemes towards training for the young and longer-term unemployed as distinct from reskilling those in employment. Equally the UK still shares the general European dilemma which probably requires a fall in the real wages of the unskilled before it is possible to speed up employment creation, yet such policies are a threat to social cohesion.

The policy thrust in the UK has recognized the critical role of skills in competitiveness, and there have been many reforms since 1979 designed to boost the outputs from the education and training system. These have included measures to require employers to take more responsibility for the training and development of their workforce through a series of local enterprise councils; the establishment of new national standards and targets; and initiatives to expand the higher education sector. In the latter case, one in eight entered full-time education post school in 1979, whereas the figure was one in three by 1994. However, even taking all these measures into account, there is still a question as to whether the UK infrastructure is fully adequate to meet the skill needs of international business over the next two decades, and whether the educational and training flexibility has yet caught up with the new labour-market flexibility in the UK.

3.7. **Regional Policy**

Regional policy has been an important instrument in the promotion of inward investment in the UK since its most active period in the mid-1960s. Although its objectives during the 1980s have shifted from attempting to relocate activity from one part of the country to another, towards the development of indigenous potential, the strong connection between regional policy expenditure and inward FDI has remained. Thus an analysis of the ability of particular regions to attract inward investment shows that the major assisted areas of Scotland, northern England, and Wales attract shares of new foreign manufacturing investment well in excess of their relative size (Hill and Munday 1994). In terms of subsidy and incentives, the 1980s witnessed the gradual change towards Regional Selective Assistance (RSA) as the main policy instrument.

While not all inward investment is subject to the effects of regional policy, there is ample evidence that measures such as RSA play an important role in its distribution. For example, in 1993/4, 43 per cent of the inward investment successes recorded by IBB had RSA (or equivalent) support. As has been argued throughout this chapter, supply-side factors play the greater role in determining the attractiveness of the UK and its regions as business locations. At the same time, if the government were to adopt a more active policy towards maximizing the economic benefit from inward investment, there would be a need to make RSA (or its equivalent) more capable of enhancing the innovative and technological base of foreign subsidiaries. For example, because the establishment of R&D capability within such an entity often involves a relatively small capital expenditure and creates few additional jobs, it is not readily assisted by existing RSA rules, which are weighted towards job creation. Pursuing this line of argument would advocate that the UK should take a more integrated approach to regional development in which technology policy rather than inward investment is the major driver.

There is no sign in the mid-1990s of policy development in the UK addressing these issues. Rather, the most recent regional policy review (HMSO 1995) indicates that the question of economic benefit is to be pursued along the lines of developing UK supply chains in the industries relevant to inward investors, disseminating efficient working practices, better targeting of investments which are of greater value to the UK, and ensuring reinvestment by existing investors. All these are essential ingredients of FDI development strategy, but in our opinion they do not address the real challenges for the late 1990s.

4. Sectoral Cases

The impact of globalization on government is likely to be industry specific. Here we illustrate the differential consequences by considering three UK sectors—namely, the electronics industry in Scotland, the automotive industry, and the financial-services sector as represented by the City of London.

4.1. The Electronics Industry in Scotland

This case illustrates the challenges of attempting to create a globally competitive, robust, sustainable high value-added sector *ab initio*, while deficiencies exist in critical aspects of infrastructure, in the environmental conditions for nurturing new start-ups and entrepreneurial behaviour, and in supplier industries.

The small indigenous electronics industry in Scotland which existed in 1945 largely revolved around government purchasing for the UK defence sector; whereas growth in the 1950s and 1960s was chiefly built on inward direct investment from such US companies as IBM, NCR, Burroughs, and Honeywell (Firn and Roberts 1984). The ability of the electronics industry to attract in-bound FDI has been a major success story, so much so that the 25,385 jobs in overseas-owned companies in 1990 accounted for 30 per cent of all foreign-owned manufacturing employment in Scotland (Young *et al.* 1993). The foreign-owned sector was responsible for two-thirds of net output in the electronics industry in Scotland in 1989, and net output per employee averaged £51,100 in MNE affiliates compared with £21,200 in UK-owned firms (Peters *et al.* 1992). Factors influencing the attractiveness of Scotland differ little from those discussed earlier in this chapter. These include market proximity, but also low labour costs and high quality labour, good logistics and communications, and financial incentives. The government role in terms of the provision of effective regional policy incentives was particularly important in the early post-war years, and more recently the Scottish Development Agency's (later Scottish Enterprise) Electronics Division helped provide a significant supportive role. Peters (1995: 265) summarizes Scotland's strategic role as that of providing 'a least cost manufacturing and logistics hub for volume assemblers seeking to exploit . . . European and . . . wider market opportunities'.

Against the benchmarks set out above, fundamental weaknesses exist in the industry. According to Peters (1995) these include:

- The concentration of activity in areas of hardware such as computers and components (especially integrated circuits). Although Scotland accounts for

35 per cent and 20 per cent respectively of European output, higher value-added functions such as design, development, marketing, and monitoring of product and technology markets are under-represented, and this limits the possibilities for exploiting the fastest growing software and services sub-sectors. There are probably only two foreign-owned companies which fall into the category of strategic leaders with global product mandates.
- University–company linkages are weak in research. Supplier linkages are similarly poor (Turok 1993), and there are few illustrations of new companies being formed as spin-offs from inward investment.
- Reliance on high-volume assembly of standard products exposes the economy to adverse cyclical and structural conditions. Between 1980 and 1990 virtually no net additional jobs were created in the sector, and significant volatility was reflected in fourteen closures and ten contractions of US MNEs (Young *et al.* 1993).
- The advantages of Scotland as a manufacturing location are under growing threat from the attractions now offered by the Asia-Pacific region and in Eastern Europe. Similarly there is a widening capability gap between Scotland, and not only Japan and the USA, but also Taiwan and Singapore. These latter locations in particular possess the created assets capable of adding higher value to the operation of electronics companies.

Based on a recent analysis of the industry, a number of key strategic directions have been set out by Scottish Enterprise, the lead Scottish economic development agency, for building a more viable and competitive industry (and indeed ensuring its very survival):

- building world-class advanced factors in critical aspects of infrastructure (logistics, supply, and communications) and skills;
- building world-class commercialization capabilities, to bridge the gap between the industry's assembly capabilities and the economy's research base in advanced technologies such as artificial intelligence and opto-electronics;
- strengthening and developing micro-regional sub-clusters to facilitate agglomeration economies;
- building advanced technology platforms in new areas of technology in which Scotland has world-class capabilities;
- developing Scotland as a centre for the growing electronics sub-sector concerned with multimedia applications.

Implicit in these recommendations is strong government involvement in all aspects of the industry from monitoring emerging technologies to building agglomeration economies and investing in infrastructure, with implications also for regional incentive policies and trade policies. The start which has been made in establishing the Scottish Electronics Forum in 1993, as an industry-led initiative bringing together the leading electronics companies in Scotland, represents a small tip of a very large iceberg.

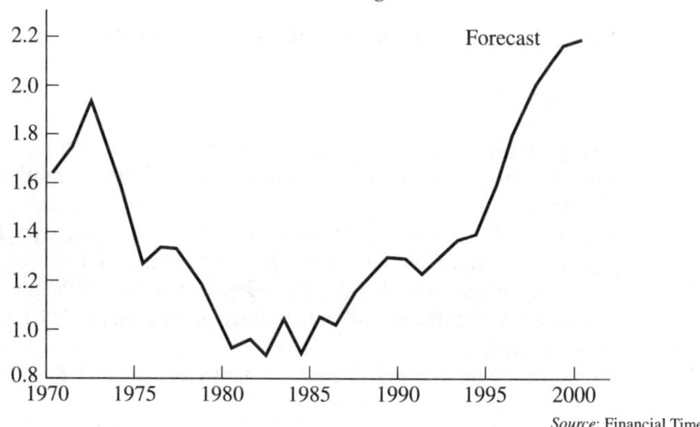

FIG 8.6. Automobile production in the UK

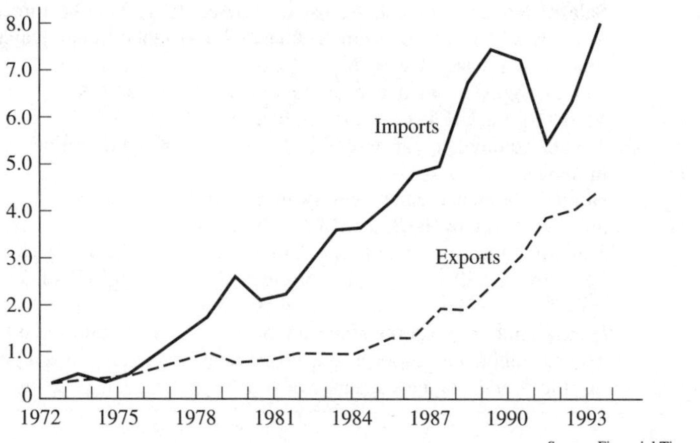

FIG 8.7. Exports and imports of automobiles

4.2. The Automotive Industry

This case charts the massive decline and more recent turnaround of an industry which, except for some small niche producers, is now wholly foreign-owned. It represents a classic example of the halting of a vicious cycle and the development of a virtuous cycle by a new wave of FDI. In the two decades covered by the case, overseas-owned MNEs have played a critical role in both slump and revival. Future prospects for assembly business are optimistic, but long-term recovery is dependent upon a competitive components sector.

Figs. 8.6 and 8.7 record the changing fortunes of the automotive industry, with output falling from a peak of 1.92 million units in 1972 to a nadir of 0.88 million units in 1982; largely as a consequence of Japanese FDI, production had recovered to 1.47 million units in 1994 and is forecast to rise to about 2.2 million

TABLE 8.4. Chronology of major events in the automotive industry in the UK

1975	Nationalization of bankrupt British Leyland and substantial cash injection.
1975–6	UK government financial rescue of Chrysler's UK affiliate.
1978	Sale of Chrysler's European operations to PSA Peugeot–Citroen (France).
1979	Launch of De Lorean car project in Northern Ireland, with £80m. government aid. Company went into liquidation in 1981.
1979	Rover (formerly British Leyland)–Honda technical strategic alliance. Followed by licensing and subcontract production in 1981 and a variety of joint projects.
1970–1980s	Numerous rumours and threats of plant closures in UK by Ford and GM.
1981	Closure of Scottish factory of PSA Peugeot–Citroen (Talbot).
1986	Nissan commence car assembly from kits in Washington (UK). European content reached 80% in 1990.
1988	Sale of Rover to British Aerospace (BAe). In 1993 BAe forced by EU to repay £57m. of government financial assistance made available at time of purchase of Rover.
1989	Honda engine plant began production in Swindon (UK).
1989	Ford acquire UK luxury car-maker Jaguar for £1.6bn.
1992	Toyota commence car assembly in Derby (UK) and engine manufacture in Wales.
1992	Honda commence car assembly in Swindon.
1994	Sale of Rover by BAe to BMW (Germany).
1995	Ford announce investment in UK to produce 25,000 cars a year for Mazda. Ford invest £500m. in a new product range for Jaguar (subject to EU approval of £70m.–£80m. UK aid package). Honda announce £200m. investment to expand Swindon plant. Toyota announce second stage investment of £200m. to double car assembly and engine capacity.

in 2000 (*Financial Times* 1995). The problems of the industry had a major adverse effect on the balance of payments, and in the 1980s it was accounting for more than one-third of the total trade deficit in manufactured goods; it is estimated that in 1997 and 1998 the UK will have a trade surplus in cars for the first time since the early 1970s (Lorenz 1994).

The causes of industry decline are well known: the Central Policy Review Staff study of *The Future of the British Car Industry* (1975: p. v) noted that: 'There are too many manufacturers with too many models, too many plants and too much capacity. Other severe weaknesses are poor quality, bad labour relations, unsatisfactory delivery record, low productivity and too much manpower'. Table 8.4 identifies some of the major consequences at corporate level, with Chrysler selling its loss-making European operations to PSA Peugeot-Citroen after an earlier bail-out by the UK government (Hood and Young 1982), and the nationalization of the effectively bankrupt British Leyland (then Rover Group, now BMW) (Wilks 1984). While Ford and GM retained their UK operations during this period, their activities were substantially run down by switching components' sourcing to continental European plants, increasing tied imports, and halting exports: the UK content of Ford cars fell from 88 per cent to 46 per cent between 1973 and 1984; for GM the fall was from 89 per cent to 22 per cent (Jones 1985). Apart from problems at the firm level which were ubiquitous across the industry, the macro-economic environment was adverse during much of the 1970s and the strength of sterling in the early 1980s was a further factor in the much discussed 'deindustrialization'.

The turnaround in the automotive industry can be very largely credited to Japanese involvement, which initially and rather surprisingly took place through a technical strategic alliance between Rover and Honda starting in 1979. Thereafter Nissan commenced assembly in the UK in 1986, with Honda and Toyota following in 1992, and with the latter two companies also adding engine facilities. The roots of the decision to invest in Europe (as in the USA) undoubtedly lay in the strength of the Yen following the Plaza Accord in 1985 and in non-tariff barriers against car exports from Japan: these operate on a national basis within the EU (e.g. 11 per cent of the domestic market in the UK), to be phased out at the end of a transitional period on 31 December 1999. While there are no EU local-content rules, Japanese producers have informal voluntary agreements with national governments such as the UK to achieve levels of local (European) content of 80 per cent or greater (Hamill and McDermott 1994). The improving competitiveness of the UK through the 1980s, and both pro-business attitudes generally and welcoming attitudes to inward investment specifically, were further positive factors in the industry's turnaround.

UK government financial support for the industry has been substantial throughout the period, from the now discredited interventionism of the 1970s in Chrysler and British Leyland, to the débâcle of the De Lorean car project in Northern Ireland, and latterly to regional investment incentives. More than in any other sector perhaps, the multinational automotive firms have been able to use their bargaining power to the full. In mid-1995 the UK state-aid package for Ford's planned investment in Jaguar (reported at between £70 million and £80 million on an investment of £500 million) was under scrutiny by the European Commission; for its three phases of investment between 1984 and 1988, Nissan received £125 million in capital grants, with further assistance in the form of training grants and infrastructure spending.

Much has been made of the positive demonstration effects throughout UK industry associated with Japanese lean manufacturing techniques and just-in-time deliveries. Productivity levels have improved dramatically throughout the automotive industry, and, allied with low labour costs and the competitive stimulus (or threat) from the Japanese, substantial new investments have been made or are planned by Ford (in Jaguar), GM, and Rover (under BMW ownership since 1994). The uncertainties rest with the automotive supply industry, although major recent investments from Siemens and Bosch are likely to boost the supply infrastructure. Inward investment has increased substantially (although less in Europe

TABLE 8.5. The UK's share of selected world financial markets, 1989–1994 (%)

	1989	1990	1991	1992	1993	1994
Foreign exchange turnover[a]	25	n.a.	n.a.	27	n.a.	n.a.
External bank lending[b]	17	17	16	16	16	17*
Foreign equities turnover[c]	n.a.	n.a.	65	64	58	59
International bond issues	75	60	65	60	60	60
International bonds secondary trading[d]	80	75	70	70	75	75
Financial derivatives trading	8	10	11	14	16	17
Insurance[e]						
Marine insurance	31	31	31	29	n.a.	n.a.
Aviation insurance	37	37	42	45	n.a.	n.a.

Note: Compiled by British Invisibles.
n.a. = not available.
* End September.

Sources: HMSO (1995).
[a] Bank for International Settlements.
[b] London Stock Exchange.
[c] Bank of England estimates.
[d] Futures Industry Association.
[e] Lloyd's of London (net of reinsurance ceded).

than in the USA), but the UK-owned industry has shrunk commensurately and a recent study by Andersen Consulting (1995) concluded that typical UK plants would need to double productivity to achieve world-class levels. In terms of the automotive industry's technological base, the loss of R&D capability by the US MNEs through the 1970s and 1980s is problematic, the future of Rover's R&D under German ownership is uncertain, while Nissan has only a small development centre. With these weaknesses the maturing green shoots still have relatively shallow roots.

4.3. **The City of London**

For most developed countries, finance, insurance, real estate (FIRE), and business services account for over 20 per cent of GDP, which in the case of the UK results in this sector's output being broadly comparable with that of manufacturing. In the past decade, the growth in output of these services in the UK has accounted for half of the total growth in GDP. The City of London accounts for around a third of this output, and about 30 per cent of those employed in finance and related services in the UK are employed therein. By 1992 this employment had exceeded 0.6 million, about one-third higher than in the previous decade. Table 8.5 provides an overview of the competitiveness of the City in selected financial markets.

London's role as a *financial* centre has always stemmed from its position as a domestic and international *commercial* centre, which brought with it a need for markets in insurance, shipping, commodity, foreign currencies, and loans. In contrast to both New York and Tokyo, a high proportion of London's business is international, and among other distinctive features it remains the world's largest centre for foreign-exchange trading, international bond underwriting, cross-border fund management, and metals future trading. This has had important consequences for both inward and outward foreign investment in as much as the international focus in the City has required the adaptation of the UK tax and regulatory rules to facilitate this trade.

There is little doubt that the City of London provides a good illustration of the cumulative effects of historic and current policies designed to create and sustain an asset base which acts to reduce transaction costs. It has been suggested (Corporation of London 1995) that four types of distinctive capability have been the foundation of London's competitive advantage. First, there is the existence of strategic assets. While these include a benign regulatory, tax, and legal environment, the competition between financial centres can reduce their weight as a source of long-term advantage. Thus a more enduring asset might be in the scale and depth of the financial labour pool, and the agglomeration economies which flow from the clustering of supporting services and the existence of liquidity. Secondly, there is the structure of relationships which exists between and within firms. In this context, an important element of a central location is the need to maintain personal contacts and networking with customers and competitors. Thirdly, there is the question of reputation at both a personal and a corporate level, which, though difficult to evaluate, supports agglomeration by a trading and locational association with other major players. The final component is innovation within a setting where patenting is not possible but where the existence of close trading links enables the innovator to gain an appropriate rent for the costs and risks involved. In spite of other innovations in areas such as communications, and the strong pressures for financial services to concentrate, the externalities which create financial centres also give incumbent centres like London considerable advantages over emerging rivals such as Paris and Frankfurt or smaller centres. However, this advantage cannot be taken as given, hence the policy questions which follow.

4.3.1. Policy Challenges

There are four diverse policy areas in which the interaction between investors and government policy is particularly central to the maintenance of the City as a competitive force. The first concerns physical infrastructure within the concentrated area of the centre of London and relates, for example, to the need for the long-term investment planning of public transport or the introduction of road pricing in order to offset agglomeration costs (Daniels 1987). The second lies in the regulatory and tax infrastructure which on the whole has been benign and beneficial to the development of the City. London has profited not only from an open market at home which attracts foreign business to the City, but also from the deterrent effects of restrictive practices elsewhere. The implementation of the GATT agreement with respect to financial services will play an important role in the development of London, depending on the way in which the reciprocal rights of market entry are applied. However, perhaps the most immediate challenge to the UK is in the shift in decision-making on regulations and tax away from the UK government and towards the EU. This could well diminish some aspects of London's competitive advantages if it removes system flexibility and sets up a vicious circle of bureaucracy. International harmonization could well make regulations more remote from practitioner expertise, delay agreements, and politicize the regulatory process. A cognate matter is the rising costs of regulation and compliance, especially in the light of financial scandals over recent years. Estimates by the Corporation of London (1995) suggest that these are broadly comparable as between the USA, the UK, and France at about 3–4 per cent of net operating expenses.

The third policy area surrounds the uncertainties associated with Economic and Monetary Union (EMU)—namely, when it will be achieved, whether the UK will be a member, and how the European System of Central Banks will operate. The UK impact will largely depend on its membership. For example, while, under a single currency, intra-European foreign-exchange dealing and associated currency swaps would disappear, London could gain if there were to be a concentration in the City of transactions between the ecu and other currencies. However, a late, or non-UK, entry could readily see a liquid ecu money market developing in Paris or Frankfurt, leaving London behind the field.

The final policy question surrounds the nature of ownership of the institutions within the City of London. There is no ready correlation between the maintenance of the UK as a leading financial centre and ownership and control. It could be argued that this is simply a consequence of globalization and the relative price of a UK asset base. At the same time, there is an issue as to whether the coherence and integrated nature of the City is enhanced or threatened by increasing levels of foreign ownership in banks, merchant banks, investment management houses, and other institutions. Some of these changes might work against the agglomeration of decision-making; others may enhance it.

4.3.2. Conclusions

The City of London exists because of a long-term build-up of created assets which, in turn, continue to yield good invisible earnings for the UK economy and aid its overall competitiveness. These particular assets also act as facilitators for international trade, and reduce transaction costs on a global basis. These assets are located in the UK but are worldwide in their origin and highly diverse. In aggregate, they are the outcome of a series of reinforcing decisions in a virtuous circle which have built London into a distinctive centre. However, as is evident, there are several sets of forces which could work against its remaining in a pole position. The most uncertain of these seem to relate to the integration of the EU and the UK participation in EMU. It is evident that the UK authorities such as the Treasury and the Bank of England are very alert to these dangers as well as to the expectation that deregulation in other centres and the international harmonization of regulatory practices is already causing London to lose some of its competitive advantages.

4. **The European Dimension**

The questions to be tackled in the penultimate section of the chapter are whether or not policies of the EU have aided or retarded FDI and competitiveness in the UK, and the UK's ability to adapt to the globalization of economic activity. The argument to be presented is that the integration which has taken place in Europe to date has increased the attractiveness of the UK as an inward-investment location. A significant rethink in attitudes is necessary, however, if the UK is to benefit equally from the next stage of development of the Union, which should see greater emphasis on its own efforts to improve the global competitiveness of its resources and firms.

Despite the importance of FDI into, within, and out of the EU, historically FDI and MNE activity have not been seen as issues in their own right by the European Commission, independent of the potential anti-trust problems associated with large firms and the need to encourage cross-border activity among European enterprises (Young and Hood 1993).

Nevertheless, policies, for example, on the liberalization of capital movements have affected MNEs directly. The UK lifted all its exchange controls in 1979, and other countries took significant steps in the same direction after 1985, with Greece being the last country to liberalize on 16 May 1995 (Brewer and Young 1995). Member states still have a variety of controls, principally on inward investment and relating mainly to takeovers from outside the country or the EU and sectoral measures (OECD 1992). Irrespective of the formal position, however, takeovers from abroad are more easily executed in the UK than elsewhere. This is largely due to structural factors, such as the greater proportion of quoted companies, and to regulatory factors, especially those at the level of company law, articles of association and management/board (Booz-Allen Acquisition Services 1989). The upshot is that over 40 per cent of the total value of all cross-border acquisitions in Europe in the recent past have been represented by takeovers of UK companies (Hamill and Castledine 1994), constituting strategic asset-seeking investment. The UK approach is consistent with its liberal attitudes towards inward and outward FDI, and these have probably reinforced its attractiveness as a business location. However, the lack of a level playing field within the EU remains a problem.

While there is still no formal FDI policy in the EU, the most recent European Commission document on competitiveness (CEC 1994: 13) comments that: 'Steps must be taken to ensure that the European Union remains an attractive site for production and investment, including investment from outside the Union', but that in order to generate jobs a more labour-intensive development model should be employed. Considerable attention is also paid to the need to support industrial cooperation, within and outside the Union, which has mainly taken the form of strategic alliances. The absence of an FDI policy has meant, however, that trade and general macro-organizational policies have not been either developed or implemented with foreign-investment consequences in mind. This lack of a coherent policy is leading to overlaps, contradictions, and gaps in policy coverage (Brewer and Young 1995).

4.1. Macro-Economic Policy

Macro-economic strategy within the EU has until recently taken a back seat, although the European Monetary System which introduced the ecu and initiated an ERM dates from 1979. The UK joined the ERM much later and then withdrew one year before the effective collapse of the mechanism in August 1993. The experience in allowing exchange rates to determine domestic policy is now widely seen in the UK to have been a major error, and accounts for attitudes ranging from caution to scepticism about plans for EMU. There have been few academic studies on the effects of membership or non-membership of the ERM on investment and trade. Business surveys consistently show support for exchange-rate stability as a means of reducing transaction costs, but work by the present authors on MNEs in the UK indicates that exchange-rate variability has not been a major factor in long-run investment decision-making (Hood *et al.* 1993*a*). The UK is likely to remain aloof from EMU, at least for a period: however, the damage caused by this is probably greater in terms of exacerbating beggar-thy-neighbour policies (see below) than in adversely affecting FDI flows. It is possible that the beneficial position which the UK enjoys in intra-EU FDI, both inward and outward, could be adversely affected in the longer term if the country remained outside the EMU. But there are other many favourable supply-side factors which would have to be offset by this particular risk before it could be concluded that the UK would necessarily lose out by such a policy stance.

4.2. Macro-Organizational Policies

The macro-organizational policies of the EU have, by contrast, had a major impact on FDI especially through the promotion of European integration, while in turn integration has been reinforced by the policies of the MNEs themselves (Robson 1993; UNCTAD 1993). Moreover, Clegg (1996) has argued that successive enlargements of the Union have enabled inward FDI in manufacturing to grow at least as fast, if not faster, than indigenous European investment. During Mark I integration from 1957 to the mid-1980s market size and tariff discrimination were important determinants of US FDI in the EU, and in the case of Mark II integration (associated with the Single Market) market size and growth and non-tariff barriers have been significant for Japanese and other East Asian investors. In the ten years to June 1993 the EU initiated 252 AD cases (admittedly many fewer than the 483 instituted in the USA during the same period (*Financial Times* 1993; CEC 1993*a*)); these undoubtedly influenced FDI, even if their motives were different. Given the importance of the market size and growth variable in inward FDI into the UK, EU trade policies have clearly been instrumental in supporting new flows of market-seeking investment.

The Single Market programme is an ongoing and long-term one, and many obstacles still remain to the free movement of goods, services, people, and capital. Notwithstanding its slow progress, most MNEs have assumed a single market in their strategic plans leading to substantial cross-border restructuring and rationalized (efficiency-seeking) investment. There is little evidence on the country-specific effects of this process within the EU. The main benefits reported to date by firms from the Single Market programme relate to reductions in transaction costs resulting from the abolition of border controls, lower costs of transport, insurance, intra-EU banking transactions, and so on (Economic and Social Committee 1994). However, a range of substantive barriers remain. These include:

- a failure to implement the principle of mutual recognition of standards;
- problems in accessing public procurement contracts unless the company is established locally;
- restrictions on the free movement of people, e.g. lack of mutual recognition of diplomas and certificates;
- difficulties posed *inter alia* by monopolies, restrictive national legislation, variations in state aid, etc., on the performance and geographical distribution of financial services, airlines, energy, and telecommunications.

It is in respect of public enterprises and services that single-market policies interface with other EU macro-organizational policies, especially those to do with competition and fiscal incentives. The slow pace of deregulation in many continental EU countries and the commitment to support domestic producers has arguably delayed the necessary responses to globalization forces in some sectors. With the faster pace of privatization and deregulation in the UK, it is arguable that UK MNEs should be in a position to benefit from future liberalization elsewhere in the EU (hence UK demands for the opening-up of markets in services); but in the meantime the absence of a level playing field may again work to the disadvantage of the UK.

Considering EU competition policy as a whole, its remit relates to acquisitions, mergers, and alliances with a 'Community dimension'. Its objectives are to prevent harmful cooperation and concentration, while supporting all forms of cooperation (pooled research and development, strategic alliances, and so on) and concentrations which enable enterprises to enhance their competitiveness at EU and global levels (Young and Hood 1993). In general, EU competition policy has appeared to be fairly liberal and its impact rather limited, and more active and aggressive policies are probably required (see also Thomsen and Woolcock

1993). This is in spite of the positive role that FDI has played in some sectors in stimulating competition, by breaking down oligopolistic structures and reducing the dominance of national champions. The UK would probably be a beneficiary of a less reactive approach, but might resist an extension of EU powers on grounds of subsidiarity (see below). It is interesting, nevertheless, that there have been calls by the UK recently (*Financial Times* 1995) for tighter controls on state aid on competition policy and other grounds. This reflects concerns over a number of recent cases of state aid to national producers where the Commission has appeared to back down in the face of national-government pressure.[3]

Apart from the above macro-organizational strategies which are directed to both structural and endemic market distortions, another group of EU policies is aimed at the upgrading of the created assets of indigenous firms. Within the latter category are policies aimed at fostering innovation, research, and technological capabilities, the development of human capital including the adaptation of workers to industrial changes, and improvements in transportation and communications' infrastructures. But EU funding is small in relation to that of national governments. For example, Union R&D represents only 4.5 per cent of spending by member states' governments on civil R&D, rising to 11 per cent for research targeted at industrial technology (Buiges and Sapir 1993). This is not to underestimate the role of such funding in this and other areas, such as the use of Structural Funds for regional regeneration and transEuropean networks. Although, at first, the UK was slow to participate in cross-border projects, at present it is an active participant in and beneficiary of programmes designed to enhance created assets.

4.3. Policy Coordination, Competition, and Conflict

It was noted in the introduction to this section that many EU policies lack coordination and fail to consider their consequences for inward FDI. In reality the problems are much wider than this, with contradictions, competition, and conflicts between the EU and multilateral organizations, between the EU and its member states, and among member states themselves (Brewer and Young 1995). Within the framework of EU regional policy, for example, investment incentives (including FDI incentives) are permitted, with aid ceilings linked to levels of unemployment and living standards. These incentives are influential in FDI decisions at a regional level (Hood and Young 1995). Hence they have encouraged competitive bidding, despite the European Commission's efforts over time to improve the transparency of aid schemes and reduce both the automaticity of aid schemes and the regions qualifying for assistance (Young and Hood 1993). Monitoring and enforcement arrangements vary between countries, and the true level of aid is disguised by the topping-up of capital grant schemes with labour-related subsidies and infrastructure improvements. Irrespective of aid ceilings, therefore, poorer countries may be unable to offer aid at the maximum permissible level, and richer countries can improve their bidding position by investment in created assets on the 'prisoner's-dilemma' principle. Although the Commission and academics are highly critical of existing investment incentives, neither the UK nor other member states have made significant efforts at EU-level reform. (A recent review of regional policy in the UK which virtually ignores EU dimensions, except as sources of funding, is contained in Trade and Industry Committee 1995; see also n. 3.)

The debate over regional policy is allied to a concern over the future of regional development within the EU and the centrifugal or centripetal effects of economic integration. This is discussed at length elsewhere (Young and Hood 1993). It is perhaps worth pointing out, however, that the EU core (the so-called 'blue banana' stretching from the south of England to the north of Italy) contains the key clusters of economic activity. For example, Hilpert (1992) has shown that eight islands of innovation and agglomeration[4] account for 80 per cent of all public R&D expenditures.

Competition between member states extends much more widely to include so-called monetary, fiscal, and social dumping, with the UK being condemned for attempting to undermine the consensus of most of the other EU countries. From a UK perspective, there is undoubtedly an issue of self-interest and economic nationalism, but this is also allied to fundamental philosophical differences between the UK and, most commonly, France and southern European countries.

Linked to this debate is that on 'subsidiarity', the concept which was introduced into EU law by the Treaty on European Union (Maastricht Treaty) of 1992.[5] Detailed discussion of this issue is contained in Centre for Economic Policy Research (1993) and Woolcock (1994). There is a genuine controversy over the economic advantages and disadvantages of policy centralization versus decentralization (with or without coordination). The balance of argument differs according to policy area: the Centre for Economic Policy Research (1993), for example, argues that merger policy is a good illustration of a case where the gains from centralization are high, whereas, in regard to regional policy, centralization is rejected, since this would assume that the EU systematically knows better than member states what the best regional projects are. On the other hand, Brewer and Young (1995) have contended that administrative economies, level playing fields, and relative bargaining power all point to the need for a centralized EU FDI policy. Unfortunately, the subsidiarity principle is principally regarded by the UK government as a means of curbing the powers of the European Commission—that is, limiting EU competence in existing areas of activity and preventing an extension of EU competence into new areas. Julius (1990) has contended that market integration will create a powerful internal dynamic for policy convergence across countries and therefore limit the need for central involvement. Analysing the single-market situation and the application of the 'mutual-recognition' principle, however, Woolcock (1994) concludes that the scope for competition among rules is fairly limited; and, in the context of FDI, the fear must be that the bargaining power of MNEs will encourage a 'race to the bottom' and a bidding-up of incentive offers (of all types). The interpretation of subsidiarity by the UK government can only reinforce this tendency.

4.4. An Industrial Competitiveness Policy for the EU

The problems of the global competitiveness of the EU are now well recognized (CEC 1994). The EU is less specialized in high-technology products and has less of a presence in high-growth markets than either the USA or Japan, and, since 1986, has had a trade deficit in high-technology products. The explanations are complex but one factor is the EU's emphasis on the liberalization of intra- rather than extra-EU markets; the Single Market programme is taking place when globalization is already a reality and when the Asian region is the fastest growing in the world. These phenomena are providing both threats and opportunities for EU enterprises. Although UK MNEs are more externally oriented than their continental counterparts, they share a common weakness in terms of relative inactivity in the fast-growing Asian markets.

In identifying these and other problem areas (e.g. rapid increases in hourly wage rates, higher tax burdens, deficiencies in the promotion of physical and intangible investments by companies), the Commission (CEC 1994) has called for a competitiveness policy for the EU with four basic priorities:[6]

- *the promotion of intangible investment*, particularly training and learning, the promotion of quality, and R&D;
- *the development of industrial cooperation*, both internally and externally;
- *the assurance of fair competition inside the Union and at international level*—internally this means reducing overall public aid and controlling state aids; externally, this means supporting the work of the WTO and developing international rules on competition;
- *the modernization of the role of the public authorities* by continuing deregulation processes in telecommunications and energy, redefining public-service objectives, and simplifying legislation and administrative procedures.

Although inadequate attention is still paid to inward and outward FDI (and especially, in the latter regard, FDI in developed countries and high-growth markets) (for a fuller review, see Burton, Yamin, and Young 1996), other features of the industrial competitiveness policy fully recognize the Commission's role in the macro-organization of economic activity in an era of alliance capitalism. Whether the political support will be forthcoming from the UK or from other member states is, regrettably, much less certain.

4.5. Concluding Remarks

The conclusion of the previous paragraphs is that the UK has benefited significantly from the development of EU to date, especially in terms of its attractiveness as a location for market-seeking inward FDI. However, free-market policies and other factors have also facilitated strategic asset-seeking inward acquisitions, the beneficial impact of which is less certain. The general policy thrust has thus been supportive of the UK government's aim of maximizing the quantity of inward FDI attracted to the country. The nature of decision-making in the EU and the lack of a policy consensus has also enabled the UK to promote and implement a more pro-business philosophy than that in some of its competitors, while ambivalent/negative attitudes towards the ERM do not seem to have been harmful.

For the future, the ability to pursue a similar 'UK-first' strategy will be constrained by changes in decision-making structures. The arguments presented on Economic and Monetary Union in both the UK and continental Europe are as much political as they are economic, and there seem to be major dangers for a number of countries in locking-in exchange rates prematurely. On the other hand, there are economic opportunities for the UK and all member states (subject to concern about centrifugal versus centripetal tendencies) is supporting the Commission's industrial competitiveness initiative, as part of a rational approach towards holistic macro-organizational strategies for the EU.

5. Conclusions and Propositions

Reviewing the content of this chapter in the light of the question as to whether or not the globalizing market place requires a fundamental shift in the role of national governments in the macro-organizational area of policy, an important overall conclusion can be drawn from the UK case. The role of the UK government has changed in that it is much less directly involved in the production of marketable goods and services, and it has redefined its involvement in terms of facilitating the operation of efficient markets. There has also been some attempt to exert a greater influence on the production and efficient usage of created assets, but this effort has been less whole-hearted and focused than those driven by the desire to let markets work. In that regard, this chapter has argued that the UK policy mix towards global economic realities is more optimal than it was in the late 1970s, but remains sub-optimal in some other aspects. In summary, recent UK governments have been clearer on what not to do, than on the types of challenge of 'neo-interventionism' which calls for different types of initiative, especially with regard to created assets. However, it is reasonable to conclude that the UK economy is now in a much better position to handle the challenges of globalization as a result of the policy directions set since the early 1980s. And there has been a growing focus on developing a more holistic intra-government approach to competitiveness which might provide the framework within which the missing macro-organizational ingredients can be added.

Since the core of this chapter has concentrated on FDI, these general conclusions are best amplified within that context. Although research on the subject of FDI (especially inward FDI) and the UK economy has been extensive, very little of this has related its determinants or effects to the substance of either macroeconomic or macro-organizational government policies. Given the preliminary nature of the findings in this chapter and the need for further research, therefore, it is perhaps desirable to express the concluding remarks in this section in the form of a number of propositions and ideas. We shall identify some of these.

1. The historically open UK economy has meant a policy environment supportive of free markets for both inward and (since 1979) outward FDI.
2. The policy philosophy of the UK government over the last fifteen years or so has been that the responsibility for improving competitiveness must lie with the private sector, and that the role of government is one of providing an enabling and pro-business environment aimed at reducing transaction costs.
3. In consequence, UK policy towards inward FDI has focused upon maximizing investment flows not investment quality. This was implicit until fairly recently, but government statements and the rejection of various EU policies suggest it is now explicit. It is supported at the macro-organizational level by active inward-investment promotion policies.
4. Since the attraction policies have not been supported by investment in complementary assets, the contribution of inward FDI is chiefly linked to the existing competitiveness of the sectors to which it is directed. Thus in sectors like pharmaceuticals and financial services, FDI has reinforced competitive advantage. In electronics, positive impacts have been largely static; while in automobiles it is still too early to be totally optimistic about the long-term, dynamic gains from (especially) Japanese and (more recently) German inward FDI. Many of the benefits of inward FDI have thus been restricted to structural upgrading.
5. The effects of liberal policies towards inward acquisitions are uncertain. There may be some beneficial effects in reducing short-termism, where the example of Rover under BMW ownership might be cited as an illustration.
6. Further research is needed on the effects of liberal policies towards outward FDI. On the one hand they have meant (as with inward FDI) exposure to new ideas and technologies and the opportunity to tap wider markets, and so on. On the other hand, the limited evidence from UK FDI in the USA is suggestive of low-technology investments and relatively poor performance.
7. The UK may be regarded as a classic case of a free-market-oriented nation state in a globalizing world. If so, the lessons are that much more commitment is needed to investment in created assets to ensure dynamic gains from FDI and long-term competitiveness.
8. UK government policy-makers have not yet fully understood the importance of infrastructure investment to build complementary assets, develop agglomeration economies, and so on. As such there are long-term concerns about the contribution of FDI, and indeed about sustaining the level of inward flows.
9. EU approaches, conversely, are moving in the direction of competitiveness policy with a recognition of the importance of upgrading infrastructure and

human capital. It is desirable that negotiations in the WTO progress relatively quickly so as to facilitate market opening globally, and hence offset continuing protectionist pressures within some countries of that EU. It is also desirable that EMU is pursued for economic as opposed to political ends.

Finally, however regarded, the UK is a very interesting case of national repositioning under a set of policy imperatives which have, implicitly or explicitly, contributed to its addressing some of the effects of global economic changes. History may enable a clearer line to be drawn between the systematic and the opportunistic components of these changes. The net effect is clearly that by the mid-1990s the UK government in matters of inward FDI does regard itself as actively competing for economic advantage but not yet designing or adopting 'next-step' policies which would maximize the advantages which flow from these. In effect, the policy platform has changed and a new foundation laid. The next decade will demonstrate whether or not this is built upon to advance the long-term comparative advantage of UK resources and capabilities.

NOTES

1. This is an important trend to be monitored, but certainly on the inward side in terms of new investments from the USA and Japan there was little evidence of declining attractiveness of the UK. UK percentage shares of US and Japanese FDI in the EU in 1991–3 were as follows:

	1991	1992	1993
USA	26.3	42.4	60.0
Japan	40.9	44.4	35.5

Sources: JETRO (unpublished); US Dept. of Commerce (1992, 1993, 1994).

2. Data from the US Dept. of Commerce (1992: table 18.2, July) relate to all US affiliates (and not simply those in manufacturing) and a more limited range of performance measures. Here the comparative data are more mixed, although the tendencies indicated by Graham and Krugman are supported.
3. The *Financial Times* (2 May 1995) reported that the UK Trade and Industry Secretary had submitted a confidential memorandum to the EU containing the following proposals:

   - a requirement, where appropriate, that governments commit to privatizing, or finding state partners for, state-owned companies which receive aid;
   - limiting approval of state aid to a fixed period or monitoring approved schemes to determine whether they should continue;

- joint examination, with EU governments, of state aids which threaten to cause job losses in other member states;
- improved procedures for consulting those potentially affected by proposed state aids;
- more use of independent consultants to assess the impact of state aid on competition;
- more rigorous appraisal of aid to 'sensitive' industrial sectors;
- systematic reviews of state aid rules and establishment of guidelines in areas such as state guarantees, indirect investment support, and land, buildings, training, and employment aid;

The latter is very relevant to the comments on p. 260 concerning investment incentives.

4. The ten major European 'islands' of science-based innovation are: Greater London, Rotterdam/Amsterdam, Île de France, the Ruhr area, Frankfurt, Stuttgart, Munich, Lyon/Grenoble, Turin, and Milan.
5. The principle of subsidiarity was introduced into EU law by article 3b of the Maastricht Treaty, specifying that: 'In areas which do not fall within its exclusive competence, the Community shall take action only if and in so far as the objectives of the proposed action cannot be sufficiently achieved by Member States and can therefore, by reason of the scale or effects of the proposed action, be better achieved by the Community.'
6. This is a follow-on from earlier policy papers, particularly CEC (1993*b*).

REFERENCES

Andersen Consulting (1995), *World Manufacturing Competitiveness Study* (London).

Booz-Allen Acquisition Services (1989), *Study on Obstacles to Takeover Bids in the European Community* (Paris: Commission of the European Communities).

Brewer, T., and Young, S., 'European Union Policies and the Problems of Multinational Enterprises', *Journal of World Trade* (1995), 29/1: 33–52.

Buiges, P., and Sapir, A. (1993), 'Community Industrial Policies', in P. Nicolaides (ed.), *Industrial Policy in the European Community: A Necessary Response to European Integration?* (Netherlands: Martinus Nijhoff).

Burton, F., Yamin, M., and Young, S. (1996), 'Introduction—International Business and Europe in Transition', in F. Burton, M. Yamin, and S. Young (eds.), *International Business and Europe in Transition* (London: Macmillan).

Cantwell, J. A. (1989), *Technological Innovation and Multinational Corporations* (Oxford: Blackwell).

—— and Dunning, J. H. (1991), 'MNEs, Technology and the Competitiveness of European Industries', *Aussenwirtschaft*, 46: 45–65.

—— and Hodson, C. (1991), 'Global R&D and British Competitiveness', in M. C. Casson (ed.), *Global Research Strategy and International Competitiveness* (Oxford: Blackwell).

CEC (1993*a*): Commission of the European Communities, *The Commission's Anti-Dumping and Anti-Subsidy Activities* (eleventh annual report from the Commission to the European Parliament, COM (93) 516 final; Brussels: CEC).

—— (1993*b*), *Growth, Competitiveness, Employment* (White Paper, COM (93) 700 final; Brussels: CEC).

—— (1994), *An Industrial Competitiveness Policy for the European Union* (COM (94) 319 final; Brussels CEC).

Central Policy Review Staff (1975), *The Future of the British Car Industry* (London: HMSO).

Central Statistical Office (1981, 1991), *Business Monitor*, PAI002 (London: HMSO).

CEPR (1993): Centre for Economic Policy Research, *Making Sense of Subsidiarity: How Much Centralization for Europe?* (London: CEPR).

Clegg, J. (1996), 'United States Investment in the European Community: The Effects of Market Integration in Perspective', in F. Burton, M. Yamin, and S. Young (eds.), *International Business and Europe in Transition* (London: Macmillan).

Connor, P. (1990), *Japanese Companies and Suppliers in Gwent, South Wales: Locational Influences, Trading Relationships, Imperative for UK Action* (Japanese Management Research Unit Working Paper No. 11; Cardiff Business School, October).

Corporation of London (1995), *The Competitive Position of London's Financial Services*, Final Report by London Business School, March).

Daniels, P. W. (1987), 'Foreign Banks and Metropolitan Development: A Comparison of London and New York', *Tijdschrift voor Economische en Sociale Geografie*, 78: 269–87.

Dunning, J. H. (1958), *American Investment in British Manufacturing Industry* (London: Allen & Unwin).

—— (1985) (ed.), *Multinational Enterprises, Economic Structure and International Competitiveness* (Chichester: John Wiley).

—— (1988), *Multinationals, Technology and Competitiveness* (London: Unwin and Hyman).

—— (1992), 'The Global Economy, Domestic Governance Strategies and Transnational Corporations: Interactions and Policy Implications', *Transnational Corporations*, 1/3: 7–45.

—— (1993), *Multinational Enterprises and the Global Economy* (Wokingham: Addison Wesley).

Economic and Social Committee of the European Communities (1994), *Opinion on the Annual Report on the Functioning of the Internal Market* (COM (94) 55 final; Brussels; 14–15 September).

Financial Times (1993), 'Negotiations Down in the Dumps Over US Draft' (25 November).

—— (1995), 'Quantity, But Not Enough Quality' (16 March).

Firn, J. R., and Roberts, D. (1984), 'High-Technology Industries', in N. Hood and S. Young (eds.), *Industry, Policy and the Scottish Economy* (Edinburgh: Edinburgh University Press).

Graham, E. M., and Krugman, P. R. (1991), *Foreign Direct Investment in the United States* (Washington: Institute for International Economics).

Hamill, J., and Castledine, P. (1994), *Foreign Acquisitions in the UK: Impact and Policy* (Strathclyde International Business Unit Working Paper 94/2; University of Strathclyde, Glasgow, January).

—— and McDermott, M. (1994), *Nissan's European Localization Strategy* (Strathclyde International Business Unit Working Paper 94/7; University of Strathclyde, Glasgow, October).

Hill, S., and Munday, M. (1994), *The Regional Distribution of Foreign Manufacturing Investment in the UK* (London: Macmillan).

Hilpert, U. (1992), *Archipelago Europe—Islands of Innovation: Synthesis Report*, FAST Programme; Brussels: Commission of the European Communities).

HMSO (1993): Her Majesty's Stationery Office, *Realizing Our Potential: A Strategy for Science, Engineering and Technology* (Cm. 2250; London, HMSO).

—— (1994), *Competitiveness—Helping Business to Win* (Cm. 2563; London: HMSO).

—— (1995), *Competitiveness—Forging Ahead* (Cm. 2867; London: HMSO).

Hood, N., and McArthur, D. (1994), 'The Evolution of Internationalisation Strategies in the European Electricity Industry', *Management International Review*, 34/1: 25–48.

—— and Young, S. (1981), 'British Policy and Inward Direct Investment', *Journal of World Trade Law*, 15/3: 231–50.

—— —— (1982), *Multinationals in Retreat: The Scottish Experience* (Edinburgh: Edinburgh University Press).

—— —— (1995), *The Locational Decision-Making Process* (Module 3 in Analytical Skills for Case Officers, Locate in Scotland; Glasgow: Scottish Enterprise).

—— —— Hood, C., and Peters, E. (1993*a*), *The Impact of Exchange Rate Fluctuations on the Foreign Owned Sector in Scotland* (report for Research Division, Scottish Enterprise National, July).

—— —— and Lal, D. (1993*b*), *Internationalisation in European Telecommunications Utilities: Trends, Prospects and the UK Case* (Strathclyde International Business Unit Working Paper 93/13; University of Strathclyde, September).

—— —— and Peters, E. (1995*a*), *Exchange Rate Fluctuations and Multinational Subsidiary Responses* (Strathclyde International Business Unit Working Paper 95/5; University of Strathclyde, February).

—— Taggart, J., Barker, L., and Hood, C. (1995*b*), *German Manufacturing Investment in the British Isles: Interview Results* (report for Scottish Enterprise Research Division, Glasgow, April).

Houston, T., and Dunning, J. H. (1976), *UK Industry Abroad* (London: Financial Times Ltd.).

Jones, D. T. (1985), *The Import Threat to the UK Car Industry* (Science Policy Research Unit; Brighton: University of Sussex).

Julius, D. (1990), *Global Companies and Public Policy* (London: Pinter Publications).

Lorenz, A. (1994), 'The British Car is Dead—Long Live the British Car', *Management Today* (August), 36–42.

McKinsey Global Institute (1993), *Manufacturing Productivity* (Washington, October).

Morris, J. (1989), 'Japanese Inward Investment and the "Importation" of Sub-contracting Complexes: Three Case Studies', *Area*, 21 (1989), 269–77.

OECD (1992): Organization for Economic Cooperation and Development, *International Direct Investment Policies and Trends in the 1980s* (Paris: OECD).

Papanastassiou, M., and Pearce, R. (1996), 'The Creation and Application of Technology by MNEs' Subsidiaries in Europe', in F. Burton, M. Yamin, and S. Young (eds.), *International Business and Europe in Transition* (London: Macmillan).

Peck, F. (1990), 'Nissan in the North East: The Multiplier Effects', *Geography*, 75: 354–57.

Peters, E. (1995), 'Restructuring of Scotland's Information Technology Industries', in A. Amin and J. Tomaney (eds.), *Behind the Myth of European Union* (London: Routledge).

—— Hood, N., and Young, S. (1992), *Foreign Owned Manufacturing Industry in Scotland—Statistical Tabulations* (report for Scottish Enterprise National, Glasgow, June).

Porter, M. E. (1990), *The Competitive Advantage of Nations* (New York: The Free Press).

Reddaway, W. B. (1968), *Effects of UK Direct Investment Overseas* (interim and final reports) (Cambridge: Cambridge University Press).

Robson, P. (1993) (ed.), *Transnational Corporations and Regional Economic Integration* (United Nations Library on Transnational Corporations, 9; London: Routledge).

Safarian, A. E. (1993), *Multinational Enterprise and Public Policy* (Aldershot: Edward Elgar).

Shepherd, D., Silberston, A., and Strange, R. (1985), *British Manufacturing Investment Overseas* (London: Methuen).

Steuer, M. D., Abell, P., Gennard, J., Perlman, M., Rees, R., Scott, B., and Wallis, K. (1973), *The Impact of Foreign Direct Investment on the United Kingdom* (London: HMSO).

Stopford, J. M., and Turner, L. (1985), *Britain and the Multinationals* (Chichester: John Wiley).

Thoburn, J. T., and Takashima, M. (1993), 'Improving British Industrial Performance: Lessons from the Japanese', *National Westminster Bank Quarterly Review* (February), 2–11.

Thomsen, S., and Woolcock, S. (1993), *Direct Investment and European Integration* (London: Royal Institute of International Affairs, Pinter Publishers).

Trade and Industry Committee, House of Commons (1995), *Regional Policy* (HC 356-I, London: HMSO, 29 March), 105–9.

Turok, I. (1993), *Loose Connections? Foreign Investment and Local Linkages in 'Silicon Glen'* (Strathclyde Paper on Planning No. 23; University of Strathclyde, January).

UNCTAD (1993): United Nations Conference on Trade and Development, *World Investment Report 1993: Transnational Corporations and Integrated International Production* (New York: United Nations).

—— (1994), *World Investment Report 1994: Transnational Corporations, Employment and the Workplace* (New York: United Nations).

United Nations (1992), *World Investment Report 1992* (New York: United Nations, Transnational Corporations and Management Division).

US Department of Commerce (1992, 1993, 1994), *Survey of Current Business* (Washington: US Government Printing Office).

Wilkins, M. (1970), *The Emergence of Multinational Enterprise: American Business Abroad from the Colonial Era to 1914* (Cambridge, Mass.: Harvard University Press).

—— (1989), *The History of Foreign Investment in the United States* (Cambridge, Mass.: Harvard University Press).

Wilks, S. (1984), *Industrial Policy and the Motor Industry* (Manchester: Manchester University Press).

Woolcock, S. (1994), *The Single European Market: Centralization or Competition Among National Rules?* (London: Royal Institute of International Affairs).

Young, S., and Hood, N. (1993), 'Inward Investment Policy in the European Community in the 1990s', *Transnational Corporations*, 2/2: 35–62.

—— —— (1994), 'Designing Developmental After-Care Programmes for Foreign Direct Investors in the European Union', *Transnational Corporations*, 3/2 (August), 45–72.

Young, S., and Hood, N. and Hamill, J. (1988), *Foreign Multinationals and the British Economy: Impact and Policy* (London: Croom Helm).

—— —— and Peters, E. (1994*a*), 'Multinational Enterprises and Regional Economic Development', *Regional Studies*, 28/7: 657–77.

—— —— and Wilson, A. (1994*b*), 'Targeting Policy as a Competitive Strategy for European Inward Investment Agencies', *European Urban and Regional Studies*, 1/2: 143–59.

—— Peters, E., and Hood, N. (1993), 'Performance and Employment Change in Overseas-Owned Manufacturing Industry in Scotland', *Scottish Economic Bulletin*, 47: 29–38.

9

The United States of America

Rose Marie Ham and David C. Mowery

1. **Introduction**

In his Geary Lecture for 1993 John Dunning (1994) argued that a defining characteristic of global competition among industrial and industrializing nations in the late twentieth century is the importance of created assets, as opposed to natural resources, in trade and international competitiveness. Examples of 'created assets' include technology, a highly skilled labour force, and physical infrastructure (e.g. the US Interstate Highway System or the Internet). According to Dunning, the growing importance of these factors has changed the role of governments in the response to globalization, even as the process of globalization has constrained and complicated their role. Dunning notes that many types of 'created assets', most notably technology, are highly mobile among the industrial economies. The 'strategic technology policies' of many governments are frustrated by the inability of domestic firms to capture all of the benefits associated with these programmes' support for technology creation. Moreover, efforts by some governments to limit the international movement or spillovers of these created assets create powerful incentives for the creation of interfirm cross-border linkages and alliances that support still higher levels of mobility (Mowery 1994).

A closely related point that receives less attention from Dunning concerns the economic importance of *absorbing*, as well as *creating*, these assets. The economic benefits from many of these resources flow from their application, as much as from their creation. As Chapter 14 shows, some of the most successful post-war industrializing economies, notably those of East Asia, have derived great economic benefit from their absorption of the fruits of other economies' created assets (see also Mowery and Oxley 1995). This absorption task is by no means costless; it is often highly knowledge-intensive, and its effectiveness and feasibility rest on many of the investments needed to create the assets of interest to Dunning.

These observations are apposite to any consideration of the response of the US government to economic globalization during the past two decades. Federal government policies have concentrated on supporting the creation, rather than the absorption or adoption, of internationally mobile competitive assets. Indeed, programmes to support the economic adjustment and training of the least internationally mobile production input—namely, labour—have received relatively little attention, even though the economic well-being of many US workers has declined. In order to highlight these points, this chapter explores the US policy response to globalization in two of the most important classes of created assets: namely, technology and human resources. We shall discuss in some detail relevant developments in US technology policy, intellectual property-rights policy, and investments in human-resource improvement and adjustment.

In our view, the US policy response to globalization is not unlike that of the inebriated gentleman who, having lost his keys, chooses to search for them under the lamp-post; his keys are not there but he continues to search in that area because of the availability of light. The USA resembles this individual in ways that go beyond its bibulous fiscal policy since the mid-1970s. In technology policy, for example, the US government has attempted to 'convert' policies originally developed for the Cold War era to a very different purpose, without recognizing the sharp contrasts in environment and context. At the same time, many private firms in the USA are, at best, ambivalent towards collaborating with government in areas relevant to the creation of the assets that are now important to their international competitiveness. If anything, the Republican political victory of November 1994 and its consequences appear to reflect a deepening hostility.

Our assessment of the federal government response to globalization in the USA is complicated by the presence of several simultaneous trends, not all of which are related to globalization. The rapid internationalization of the US economy since 1970 has been a period of relatively slow growth in productivity and incomes, which has had profound consequences for domestic politics and the US policy response to globalization. Among other things, slow growth in incomes has been associated with severe imbalances in US fiscal policy, which, in turn, have constrained growth in government expenditures on programmes other than middle-class entitlements. Not only have incomes grown more slowly; the distribution of domestic earnings has become more unequal. The end of the Cold War also has shaped the US policy response to globalization, because it provided a political justification for large investments in a national R&D infrastructure that spanned the public sector, industry, and US universities. These investments face an uncertain future and lack the political backing that they enjoyed during the Cold War. The policy developments that we discuss below are responses to one more of these concurrent trends, and cannot be accurately portrayed as responses to economic globalization alone.

2. Globalization and Other Developments since 1970

2.1. International Trade, Investment, and Technology Flows

The importance of international flows of trade, investment, and technology to the US economy has dramatically increased during the past two decades from relatively low levels. With the possible exception of Japan, the rate of growth

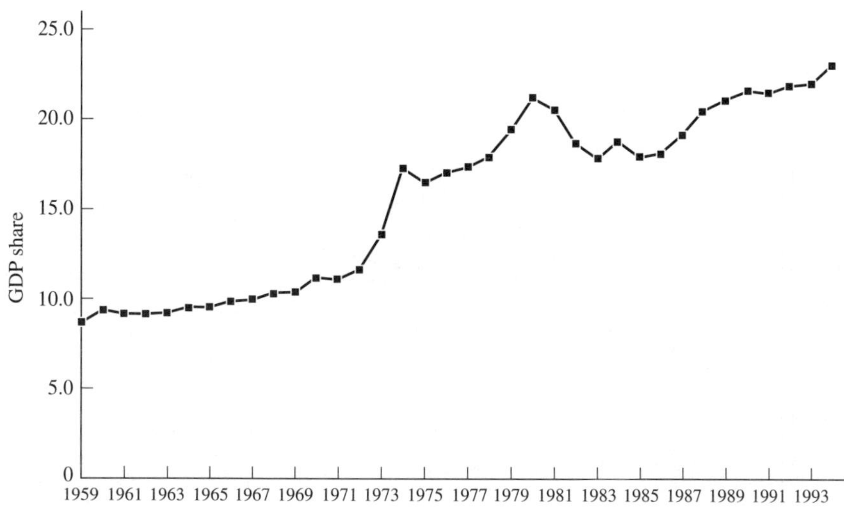

Source: President's Council of Economic Advisers, 1995.

FIG 9.1. International trade share of US GDP, imports and exports, 1959–1994

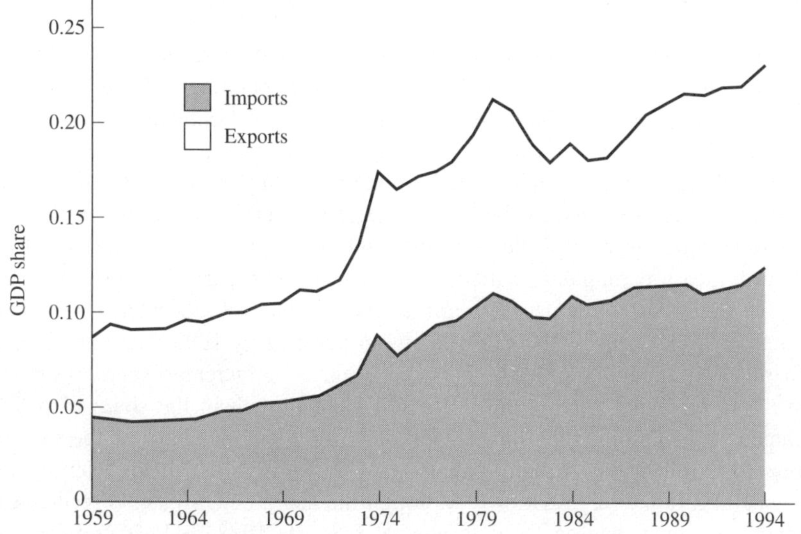

Source: President's Council of Economic Advisers, 1995.

FIG 9.2. Import and export share of US GDP, 1959–1994

in the relevant shares of US economic activity accounted for, or influenced by, foreign transactions has exceeded that of any other G7 economy. The share of GDP accounted for by exports and imports of merchandise and services doubled during 1975–94 from 11 per cent to 22 per cent (see Fig. 9.1), and, during the 1980s, rapid growth in the US merchandise trade deficit (see Fig. 9.2) had

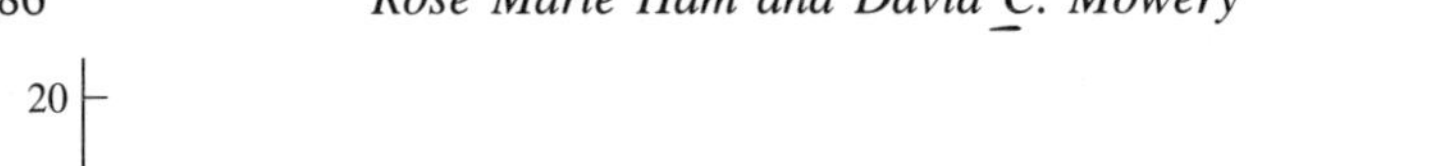

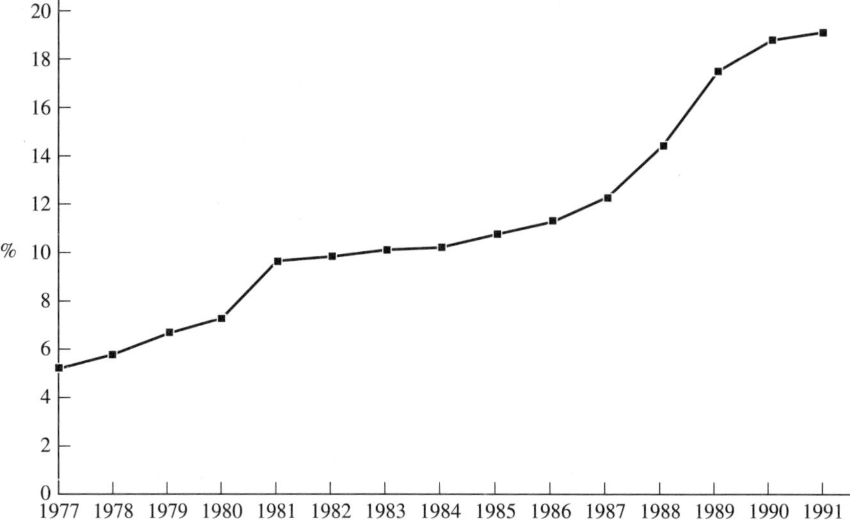

Source: Graham and Krugman, 1995.

FIG 9.3. Foreign affiliates' share of US manufacturing assets, 1977–1991

important consequences for the incomes of skilled and unskilled US workers (see below). Data from Graham and Krugman (1995) spanning a shorter period of time (1977–91) reveal a large increase in the share of US manufacturing assets owned by foreign enterprises, from slightly more than 5 per cent to nearly 20 per cent (see Fig. 9.3). Although the USA remains an important source of FDI outflows, its economy has also become a major host nation for FDI.

International flows of technology into and out of the US economy, which are not well measured in public statistics, also appear to have grown appreciably during the past quarter century. Foreign inventors' share of US patents grew from less than 38 per cent in 1978 to roughly 45 per cent by 1993 (National Science Board 1996, appendix tables 6–7). Interestingly, the increased share of non-US inventors receiving patents did not result from growth in the share of patents granted to inventors from Japan, Germany, or other members of the G7, but appears to reflect the growing patenting by individuals and firms from a more diverse array of foreign nations. Although the share of US patents received by foreign inventors has declined somewhat from its 1988 peak, it remains well above the 1973 level.

Fig. 9.4 shows that, between 1986 and 1993, international flows of technology into and out of the US economy grew markedly.[1] US receipts of royalty and licensing income grew at an average annual rate of 20 per cent during 1986–90, but their growth slowed to 7 per cent per year during 1990–3, and receipts grew by only 2 per cent during 1992–3. The 1992–3 slowdown in nominal growth may reflect the effects of recessions in Western Europe and Japan (receipts from Western Europe actually declined during 1992–3). This overall rise in international technology flows, however, is largely attributable to increased intra-firm

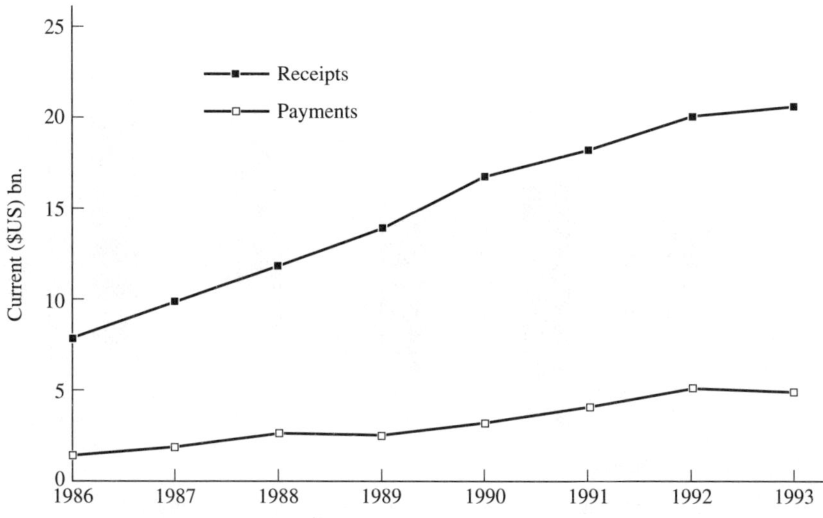

Source: Bureau of Economic Analysis, September, 1994.

FIG 9.4. US royalty and licensing receipts and payments, 1986–1993

flows of technology. In 1992, 80 per cent of US receipts were accounted for by technology exports to foreign affiliates, a modest increase from 75 per cent in 1986, and the average annual growth rate of intra-firm receipts during 1986–92 exceeded that for exports to non-affiliates.

US payments of royalties and licensing fees grew even more rapidly than US receipts between 1986 and 1993, registering an average annual growth rate of 23 per cent between 1986 and 1990, and 16 per cent per year between 1990 and 1993, although these payments declined by 3 per cent in 1992 and 1993. These payments are also dominated by intra-firm transactions, although the share of affiliates is lower. In both 1986 and 1992, intra-firm technology flows accounted for approximately 65 per cent of total US technology imports. The great importance of intra-firm transactions within both technology exports and imports means that the trends depicted in Fig. 9.4 do not permit strong conclusions to be drawn about the technological competitiveness of the US economy.[2]

Other trends also point to higher levels of technological interdependence between the US and foreign economies. During the 1980–9 period, nearly 600 'strategic technology alliances' were formed between US and Japanese firms, and more than 900 between US and European firms (National Science Board 1993). Thus far, very few technology alliances link US firms with firms from such newly industrializing economies as Taiwan or South Korea (Mowery and Oxley 1995), although such links seem likely to increase in the future. In part, the growth in the number of international technology alliances is attributable to the increased importance of foreign sources of technology for US high-technology firms, but it also reflects the economic importance of foreign markets for US firms. For example, foreign markets for commercial aircraft are projected to grow more rapidly than the US domestic market through the year 2010. The rapid growth

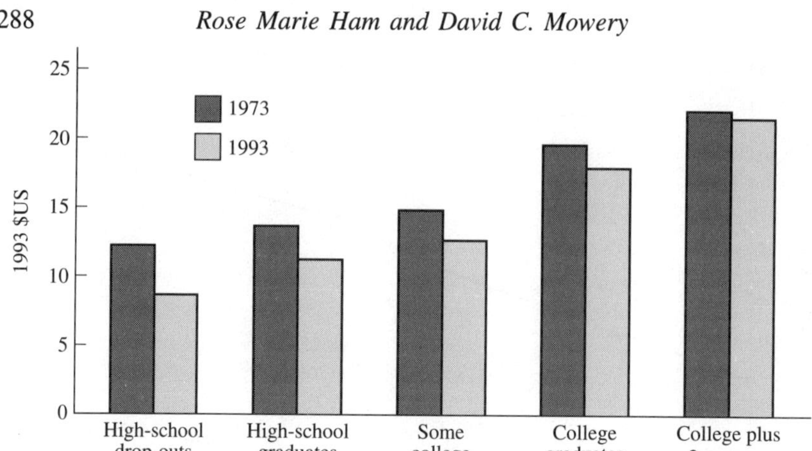

Source: President's Council of Economic Advisers, 1995, based on data from the Economic Policy Institute.

FIG 9.5. Real hourly wages for men by level of education, 1973 and 1993

of foreign markets, combined with the need to recover the costs of new product development, have increased the economic importance to US high-technology firms of penetrating foreign markets (we return to this point below). The growth in alliances in at least some high-technology industries also reflects the response of US and foreign firms to non-tariff barriers to trade and investment, as well as the policies of governments that seek to restrict access to their domestic 'strategic-technology' programmes, such as SEMATECH in the USA and JESSI in Western Europe (Mowery 1994). Paradoxically these and other government efforts to restrict the international mobility of technology-based 'created assets' contribute to the formation of inter-firm alliances that support such mobility.

2.2. Immigration and Incomes

In addition to a more rapid internationalization of the US economy, the period since 1973 has witnessed a significant slowdown in the rate of growth of US domestic household incomes. Real median family incomes grew by less than 1 per cent during the 1973–93 period (President's Council of Economic Advisers 1995: 310), which reflects the lower productivity growth of this period. Although the US economy has exhibited lower unemployment rates than most other industrial economies since the early 1970s, the lowest-paid employed males in this economy have experienced a steady decline in their wages.[3] The distribution of earnings, especially among males, appears to have become more unequal, with a severe decline in real hourly wages among male workers with a high-school education or less (Fig. 9.5) and a somewhat less marked decline in real wages among the lowest decile and quartile of the US labour force.[4] As Freeman and Katz (1994) point out, this growth in wage inequality during the 1980s is virtually unique to the USA among the industrial economies. A portion of the decline in the relative wages of low-skill workers may reflect higher immigration during the 1980s.

An important element of the internationalization of the US economy that until recently has received little attention is the 'internationalization of the US labor market' (Abowd and Freeman 1991: 1), as legal and undocumented immigration expanded the non-native-born share of the US workforce. Although immigrants constituted a significant share of the US labour force in the early decades of this century,[5] they have accounted for a smaller share of US labour-force growth through much of the post-Second World War period. During 1980–8, however, the estimated share of immigrants in the US labour force increased from 6.9 per cent to 9.3 per cent (Borjas *et al.* 1991). Relatively low levels of education among a large share of these immigrants, according to Borjas and colleagues, may have depressed the wages of less-educated workers, since during the 1980s, immigration was a 'major source of the supply of high school dropout workers whereas it was only a much smaller source of the supply of more educated workers' (Borjas *et al.* 1991: 17).[6]

The effects of immigration on low-skill US workers' wages were compounded by the large merchandise trade deficits of the 1980s (see Fig. 9.2). Although Abowd and Freeman (1991) point out that structural change in the US economy during 1960–87 in fact appears to have reduced the share of the US labour force that is directly exposed to import competition, import-competing industries tend to be relatively intensive employers of low-skill US workers, while export-intensive sectors employ higher-skill workers. The large import inflows of the 1980s therefore depressed the wages of low-skilled US workers, reinforcing the effects of immigration:

> In 1985–6, at the height of the trade deficit and after a decade of substantial legal and illegal immigration, the nation's effective supply of high school dropout men was 27 to 32 per cent higher than it would otherwise have been, while the supply of high school dropout women was 28 to 34 per cent higher. By contrast, the nation's effective supply of college graduates was just 8 to 10 per cent higher, exclusively because of immigration. (Borjas *et al.* 1991: 19)

These findings have been disputed by Lawrence and Slaughter (1993), who conclude that changes in the relative demand for skilled and unskilled workers associated with technological change in the US economy have been far more significant than those related to international trade flows.[7] But Lawrence and Slaughter's measures of the skill-intensity of US industries leave much to be desired, and their analysis does not take into account the effects of immigration on the relative supply of low-skilled workers.

The relative contributions of trade, immigration, and technical change to declines in the real wages of low-skilled US workers and increased inequality in the US earnings distribution remain uncertain, but the effects of these three factors have indisputably reinforced one another, and have led to increasing earnings inequality. Since the 1970s the international flows of goods and labour have affected the welfare of less educated US workers in ways consistent with Dunning's arguments, in as much as they increased the returns to investments in such created assets as worker skills. Nevertheless, the USA is unique in the severity of the penalties inflicted on low-wage, male workers during the 1980s, a difference that may reflect institutional factors such as the decline in the economic and political strength of US labour unions.

2.3. **Political Events: Budgetary Policy and the End of the Cold War**

Two other developments since 1970 have influenced the US government's response to globalization: the surge in federal deficit spending and the end of the Cold War. Indeed, as we shall elaborate later in this chapter, these two developments were themselves intertwined—the military tensions of the Cold War contributed to successive increases in federal deficits. Between 1970 and 1995 US federal budget deficits grew from 0.3 per cent of GDP (fiscal 1970) to more than 3 per cent (fiscal 1994).[8] Large federal deficits have increased the merchandise trade deficit, which arguably has affected the distribution of wages within the US labour force. Public-sector deficits have lowered national savings rates, which raised domestic interest rates, reduced domestic investment, and lowered long-term productivity growth. US fiscal policy and politics have thus influenced other trends (the larger trade deficit, slower growth in national incomes, and increasing inequality in the distribution of domestic incomes) that are linked with the internationalization of this economy.

Although much of the long-term rise in the federal budget deficit has been driven by expanded spending on entitlement programmes, notably Social Security and Medicare, the surges in deficit spending are, in fact, related to Cold War defence spending. Moreover, each of these spending surges (Truman's defence build-up at the outset of the Korean War; Johnson's defence build-up for Vietnam; and Reagan's defence build-up of the early 1980s) was associated with a relatively powerful president who exercised strong *de facto* or formal political control over both houses of Congress. Rather than resulting from 'divided government', these deficit surges were associated with unprecedented peacetime presidential influence in defence spending and foreign policy (Hahm *et al.* 1995).[9] The current loss of presidential influence over budgetary policy may thus be an enduring one that flows from changes in the international environment rather than from changes in domestic political power.

The Cold War pattern of defence-led spending surges promoted by politically powerful presidents may be nearing its end, a development that holds some promise for fiscal stabilization. But the politics of federal spending are now linked in a vicious circle with the disappointing performance of US incomes. As taxpayers struggle to maintain or improve living standards with stagnant household incomes, they resist higher taxes or reduced government services, and the costs of current government services are deferred to future generations. The economic results of

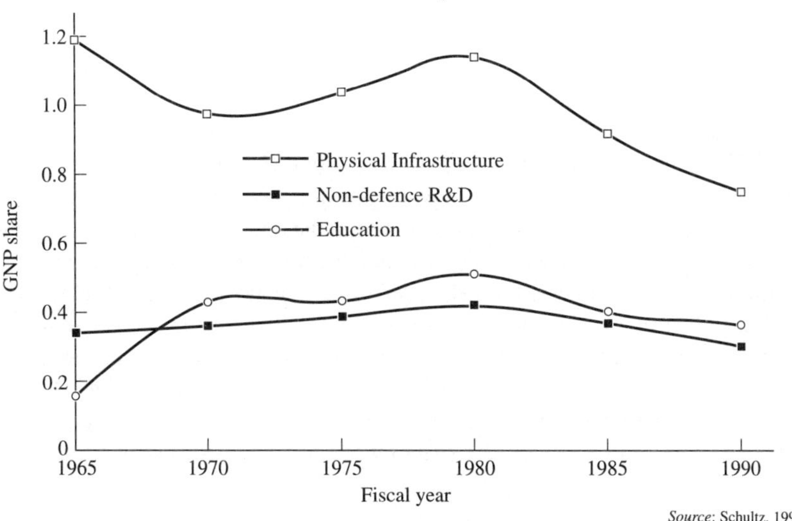

Source: Schultz, 1990.

FIG 9.6. Federal investment spending, 1965–1990

this dynamic reinforce some of the factors (low national savings and investment levels) that tend to depress growth in household incomes.

The evidence from 1993–4 suggests that the political benefits from White House efforts to reduce deficit spending are dwarfed by the costs of such initiatives. At present, it is uncertain whether the Republican Congressional majority will adopt realistic budgetary projections and policies without simultaneously committing to unsustainable tax cuts, maintaining a well-established, bipartisan habit of deferring difficult fiscal decisions. The political costs of restoring fiscal stability are particularly high because any such effort will eventually require a shift in the mix of federal spending away from subsidized consumption by middle-class recipients of entitlements and towards investment in physical and human capital. Deferral of difficult political decisions continues in the current menu of proposed spending reductions, which largely preserve middle-class entitlements at the expense of public-sector investments in physical infrastructure, education, and R&D, and maintain a fifteen-year trend of declining public financial support for investment (see Fig. 9.6).

The Cold War was also largely responsible for much of the structure of post-war US S&T policy. Military and national-security objectives, rather than any comprehensive economic strategy, were the basis for the allocation of the bulk of federal R&D funds, and during the early 1960s defence-related spending accounted for as much as 80 per cent of federal R&D spending. Along with defence-related procurement, this spending assisted the development of such US high-technology industries as semiconductors, computers, and commercial aircraft, and supported the growth of university-based research in such areas as computer science. Post-war US civilian technology policy consisted largely of federal government funding for scientific research, especially basic research in biomedical science, with little or no central coordination or focus on economic objectives; federal funding of development or applied research was confined largely to defence-related areas.

By the early 1980s, however, the situation had changed and new approaches to US technology policy emerged. Military-funded R&D and military procurement contributed less to civilian applications in many technologies; instead, technological developments increasingly flowed in the opposite direction, from civilian to military applications. This change in the direction of technological 'spillovers', combined with declines in the share of total demand accounted for by the US military, has meant that the economic viability of many US defence suppliers of high-technology components and systems now depends on their competitive strength in civilian markets. The economic consequences of these developments are likely to be heightened still further by the prospect of steady reductions in defence R&D and procurement spending during the next decade.[10]

2.4. Conclusion: Globalization, Government, and the US Economy

This section has illuminated the complexity of the various parallel political and economic trends that have affected, and have been affected by, the internationalization of the post-war US economy. The simultaneous operation of these trends means that very few of the putative 'impacts of globalization' can easily be identified as such. Nor can any discrete set of government policies be neatly denoted as 'responses to globalization'; indeed, the set of government policies that can be so characterized is potentially limitless. In the following sections, we shall discuss several policies that deal directly with the created assets of technology and human resources. Specifically, we shall first consider US technology policy and the dilemmas of 'national' technology policy in an open economy; secondly, the closely related efforts of the US government to raise the domestic returns to technology-related assets through efforts to strengthen intellectual property rights; and, thirdly, the absence of significant initiatives in the area of human resources. Because of their extensive treatment elsewhere, we shall not discuss US policies in the international trade and foreign investment areas, or competition policy, all of which will loom large in future multilateral and plurilateral trade negotiations.

Dunning (1993) suggested that the pace and spread of globalization would force governments to develop new relationships with the private sector to support investments in 'created assets' such as infrastructure and technology. Dunning's predictions notwithstanding, the US political climate appears to have become significantly more hostile to such collaborative endeavours. As we shall note below, the (limited) bipartisan support for civilian technology policy initiatives that prevailed within Congress during 1984–94 has been swept away by the upsurge in conservative Republican power in Congress and within state governments.

The current Congressional majority appears to view the best government as one that governs least, and has vowed to 'roll back' federal programmes in all areas save middle-class entitlements and defence. The outlook for a more collaborative relationship between the public and private sectors in the USA is thus mixed at best. This conservative Republican majority gained power with substantial assistance from a large swing in the votes of white males with a high-school education or less (Connelly 1994). In other words, the greatest losers from the economic trends since 1970 supported a political coalition that rhetorically seeks to restore the pre-New Deal order.

3. Technology Policy

For much of the post-war period, US firms have benefited from substantial federal R&D spending through the technological spillovers from defence programmes. At the same time, research results have tended to be diffused relatively slowly across international boundaries, while many foreign firms have been unable quickly to apply these results in commercial markets. None of these conditions now applies; defence technology spillovers are less significant, scientific and technological knowledge moves more quickly within the international economy, while foreign firms have dramatically improved their capabilities to apply advanced scientific and technological knowledge. Since 1960 these latter capabilities have also strengthened significantly relative to those of the USA.[11] In many industries, US firms are now first among equals, rather than dominant firms, in technological capabilities (and in others, well behind the state of the art), and the economic returns from the post-war US R&D system are available to US and foreign firms alike.

3.1. Technology Policy Initiatives Prior to the Clinton Administration

Beginning in the early 1980s, these developments and the competitive pressures noted by Dunning (1994) spawned new initiatives in the technology policies of the Reagan and Bush Administrations, in spite of their rhetorical opposition to policies of direct support for civilian technology development. Federal policy-makers began to experiment with 'strategic' programmes that sought to strengthen civilian technological capabilities by subsidizing joint research, encouraging collaboration between US universities and industry in technology development, and supporting collaboration between US industry and the federal laboratories. In some cases, these programmes sought to emulate the perceived success of collaborative R&D programmes in other nations, such as Japan, without much understanding of the other factors contributing to the success of these foreign programmes. In other respects, these initiatives sought to shift the focus of a portion of existing sources of funding (e.g. the Defence Department) or research

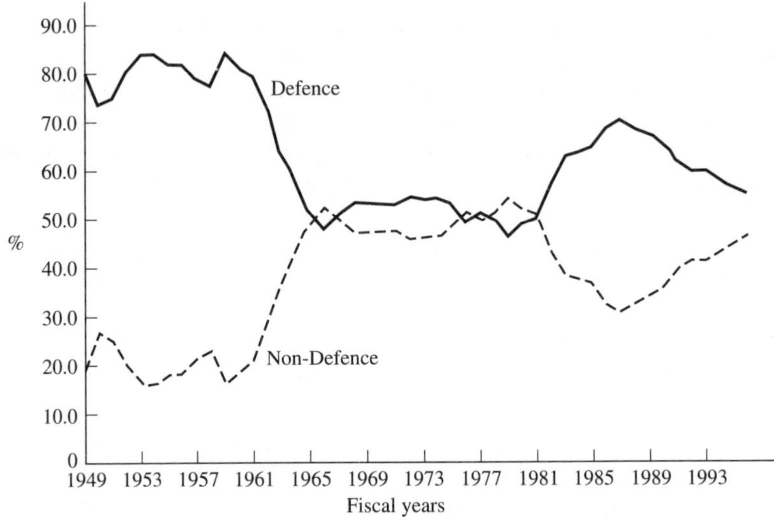

Note: Outlays for fiscal year 1996 are proposed. *Source*: U.S. Office of Management and Budget, 1995.

FIG 9.7. The conduct of federal R&D: Defence and non-defence shares, fiscal years 1949–1996

performers (e.g. universities) to civilian industrial competitiveness, without a more comprehensive restructuring of programmatic or institutional goals and management. As Fig. 9.7 shows, the share of defence outlays in the federal R&D budget rose from approximately 50 per cent to nearly 70 per cent between 1979 and 1987. Before the end of the Reagan Administration, however, this growth trend had been reversed, and the share of defence outlays in the federal R&D budget declined under Bush.

Programmes such as the National Center for Manufacturing Sciences (NCMS), the semiconductor research consortium SEMATECH, the Advanced Technology Program (ATP) of the Department of Commerce, and even the National Science Foundation's Engineering Research Centers all represented new policies that modified the missions of existing programmes or funding agencies. For example, SEMATECH and the NCMS have both relied on expanded funding by the Defence Department for civilian-technology development in 'dual-use' technologies. This approach has been based on the premise that the 'spinoffs' from military to civilian technology applications had become less economically beneficial than in the early post-war years. As the share of total demand accounted for by military markets shrank and military procurement budgets declined, according to this argument, products developed exclusively for military markets have become prohibitively costly and are often unable to incorporate advances from civilian applications rapidly.

These pre-Clinton initiatives expanded the federal role in supporting technology development, especially in high-technology sectors that were believed to be important to both civilian economic competitiveness and national security. A small but growing share of the federal R&D budget began to flow to such 'dual-use' technology development projects, under the approving oversight of Congress. This broad effort to utilize existing programmes for new goals, looking under the figurative lamp-post rather than developing new programmes, has continued under President Clinton.

3.2. The Clinton Technology Policy Agenda

One of the most striking characteristics of the Clinton Administration's 'new direction' in technology policy (Clinton and Gore 1993), especially prior to its collision with the political goals of an ideologically hostile Congress during 1995, is the great continuity between the Republican Administrations of the 1980s and the policies of the current Democratic Administration. Much of the Clinton Administration's 'new direction' in fact consists of expanded funding for initiatives begun at the behest of Congress during the Reagan and Bush Administrations.

3.2.1. Commercial Technology Development and Adoption

The most dramatic reallocation within the civilian federal R&D budget under the Clinton Administration was the large increase in the Commerce Department's R&D budget, which more than doubled after 1992. The Commerce Department became a key agency in the management of jointly funded technology development and adoption programmes with US firms, and this new prominence may have contributed to Republican support for its abolition. Much of the increase in the Commerce Department R&D budget was located in the ATP, which as of December 1995 was in danger of termination by Congress. The ATP provided matching funds for firms and consortia for the development of 'precommercial' technologies.

The Clinton Administration also increased support for federal programmes supporting the adoption of advanced technologies, expanding programmes begun (at the behest of Congress) under the Bush Administration that, nevertheless, remain small by comparison with ATP. The Commerce Department has garnered R&D budget increases for the Manufacturing Extension Partnership programme, administered by the National Institute for Standards and Technology (NIST) of the Commerce Department.

3.2.2. Growth in 'Dual-Use' Technology Programmes in the Clinton Administration

The Clinton Administration also launched several initiatives in the 'dual-use' technology area that extended initiatives that began during the Reagan Administration. Although their growth reflects change in the international political environment as well as change in the technological and economic viability of the US defence industrial base, 'dual-use' R&D programmes provide a political justification for using a portion of the largest single component of the federal R&D budget for civilian purposes, such as national competitiveness.[12]

Among the most widely noted 'dual-use' initiatives of this Administration was the flat-panel display programme, unveiled in 1994 with a projected five-year budget of $US580 million. The programme sought to develop commercially feasible product and process technologies and to establish four US plants to manufacture flat-screen displays for civilian and military applications (Davis and Zachary 1994). The flat-panel display initiative was described at its inception as the first of several technology development programmes in this area that seek to support the development of US technological and manufacturing capabilities for products embodying these technologies for civilian and military markets. (For a critique of the flat-panel displays programme, see Barfield 1994, or Ham and Mowery 1995.)

The 'dual-use R&D' initiative also led to efforts within the Department of Energy's defence-related laboratories (e.g. Los Alamos, Lawrence Livermore, and Sandia National Laboratories) to support 'cooperative research and development agreements' (CRADAs) in dual-use technologies both to assist US industry and to sustain the weapons R&D capabilities of these huge federal laboratories.[13] The number of CRADAs between Department of Energy weapons laboratories and private firms that are supported by the Energy Department's nuclear weapons R&D budget increased from 122 in January 1993 to 326 in July 1994. The Department of Energy has adopted policies at the behest of Congress to limit the mobility of the assets created through these ventures, requiring that any commercial results of these joint R&D projects be manufactured domestically, rather than being transferred to foreign affiliates or foreign firms.

3.3. Enduring Technology Policy Dilemmas

In addition to its consistency with many of the programmatic precedents established by its immediate predecessors, the current Administration's technology policy has faced three major dilemmas that also confronted the Reagan and Bush Administrations: (1) the feasibility and desirability of 'dual-use' technology development programmes; (2) the problems imposed by political requirements to capture the bulk of the economic returns from programmes whose results may benefit foreign firms; and (3) the enduring tension between programmes that support technology development and those supporting technology adoption. All three of these dilemmas have, if anything, been sharpened by the progressive internationalization of the US economy. Moreover, the implications of these dilemmas extend beyond the USA. The size of the US economy, the prominent leadership role of the US government in the post-war liberalization of the global trading system, and the significant presence of the USA in the global S&T system all mean that the domestic policies of this and subsequent administrations to resolve these dilemmas may affect the global trade and R&D systems. Indeed, restrictive US policies could retard or reverse liberalization of these systems.

The Republican Congress elected in November 1994 is strongly opposed to many of the civilian components of the Clinton Administration's technology policy, in spite of the fact that many of these policies originated in the Reagan and Bush Administrations. The severe budget pressures that will typify 1996–2000 provide additional incentives to reduce spending in these and other programmes. Moreover, many private firms that have received funding for projects under the civilian-technology programmes initiated since 1989 have not lobbied aggressively for the preservation of current funding levels for such programmes. Most firms appear to prefer the promise of less regulation and lower taxes to continued funding for programmes for civilian-technology development (Davis and Cooper 1995).

This political environment is, thus, likely to frustrate the Clinton Administration's efforts to reduce the role of defence-related R&D funding in US technology policy. The very existence of the Commerce Department (and many of its programmes) is threatened, and the Department of Energy's ambitious efforts to aid industry are likely to be curtailed. In contrast, the Pentagon budget will remain important for the support of 'dual-use' technology programmes. Given the hostility of many members of the 104th Congress towards civilian-technology programmes, these initiatives may seek political shelter under a national security rationale, and the defence R&D budget will be used to support civilian-technology development, in effect 'remilitarizing' US technology policy. Unfortunately, the feasibility of an ambitious 'dual-use' strategy to meet the civilian-technology policy goals of the current or any other Administration is dubious (Barfield 1994; Ham and Mowery 1995). Moreover, the aggressive pursuit of civilian-technology development subsidies for US firms under the dual-use rubric could undermine efforts to improve multilateral disciplines on such subsidies through the WTO.

Another element of continuity between current and past US technology policies concerns the tension between such policies and international MNEs (many of which are headquartered in the USA), markets, and sources of technology. The political justification for many civilian-technology development programmes (including those supported with Defence Department funds) now rests on the ability of US firms and citizens to capture the economic benefits of these programmes. Unfortunately, the characteristics of the outputs of many of these programmes, the structure of the US firms participating in them, and the structure of the markets for the goods into which the results of these programmes are incorporated, mean that the domestic capture of all or even a majority of the economic benefits from some of these programmes is unfeasible.

Finally, the focus of many Clinton Administration policy-makers, as well as those of previous Administrations, on technology creation and development as the key source of economic benefits overlooks the benefits from technology adoption in a US economy that is now 'first among equals' and is open to international trade and technology flows. Here, too, US policy continues to concentrate public funding and efforts under the lamp-post, relying on older structures and instruments to advance new goals, rather than developing new instruments with a very different focus. Despite its rhetorical support for 'adoption-oriented' policies, the Clinton Administration has concentrated most of its efforts on supporting technology-development programmes and other initiatives that could retard the domestic adoption of important high-technology products. These programmes maintain the long-established focus of US S&T policy on the creation of technological assets, which are highly mobile within the global economy.

4. Intellectual Property Rights

The increased international mobility of technology-based created assets has contributed to a significant shift in US policy towards intellectual property (IP) rights, based on the belief that stronger IP protection could increase the domestic returns to technologies invented by US firms. In addition to strengthening the protection of IP within the USA, the US government has pursued higher levels of international IP protection through bilateral and multilateral negotiations.[14] The 1994 Agreement on Trade-Related Aspects of Intellectual Property Rights of the Uruguay Round has accomplished many of the US negotiating objectives through the establishment of minimum worldwide IP standards, and ushered in important changes to the US domestic IP system. Domestic opposition to some of the provisions of the TRIPS agreement, however, has resulted in the creation of a 'hybrid' US IP system that attempts to incorporate international norms while maintaining aspects of the first-to-invent system that is virtually unique to the USA.

Shifts in US policy towards intellectual property rights began with the 1982 legislation that established the Court of Appeals for the Federal Circuit (CAFC), a specialized tribunal for the adjudication of IP disputes. The CAFC has strengthened the protection granted to patent-holders, since it has upheld patent rights in roughly 80 per cent of the cases before it, a considerable increase over the pre-1982 rate of 30 per cent for the federal bench (Katz and Ordover 1990). Since the formation of the CAFC, the US IP system has continued to favour the creation of IP (by providing and enforcing broad, exclusive rights embodied in patents and other legal forms of protection) over the promotion of its diffusion.

The faith in intellectual property rights as a critical policy tool in improving US competitiveness was exemplified in two other statutes of the 1980s that sought to transform the federal laboratory system into a source of innovations for US firms. First, the Bayh–Dole Patent and Trademark Amendments Act of 1980 permitted federal agencies to grant licences to small businesses and non-profit institutions, including universities, for patents based on research funded by federal agencies at federal and contractor-operated laboratories. Secondly, the Federal Technology Transfer Act of 1986 and amendments passed in 1989 authorized federal laboratories to conduct CRADAs with private firms.[15]

The protection of IP rights also emerged in the 1980s as an important international trade issue for the USA, as US policy-makers became concerned that a growing share of the economic returns to technologies invented in the USA were flowing to foreign firms and economies.[16] A 1988 International Trade Commission (US International Trade Commission 1988) survey estimated that US firms lost over $US23 billion in revenues and sales in 1987 infringements of their IP, and fuelled additional concerns that inadequate worldwide IP protection hindered the competitiveness of US firms.

These concerns led Congress and the Executive branch to initiate a series of policies to strengthen the capabilities of US trade policy-makers to apply pressure (including retaliatory measures) on other governments on a bilateral basis, while also pursuing a complementary multilateral negotiation strategy within the GATT. During the 1980s several domestic policy instruments were instituted at the behest of Congress that sought to improve the protection of IP in selected foreign countries. The Trade and Tariff Act of 1984 extended presidential authority to retaliate against 'unjustifiable' and 'unreasonable' foreign barriers linked to inadequate IP protection (Bayard and Elliot 1994). The 1988 Omnibus Trade and Competitiveness Act promoted an even more aggressive US stance towards strengthening international IP protection. The 'special' 301 provision of the Act directed the US Trade Representative (USTR) to identify the highest-priority instances (based largely, but not solely, on their economic importance) of countries that deny adequate intellectual property protection and to conduct investigations of those practices. Depending on USTR's findings, the legislation may require (with notable exceptions) the President to take retaliatory actions if the accused trading partner does not promptly eliminate the barriers. Bayard and Elliot (1994) reported that since 1985 the USA has brought nine Section 301 IP rights cases, most of which were filed against newly industrializing economies.[17] Seven of these cases are still open, which may reflect the depth of the conflict over this issue between the USA and the target countries.

This arsenal of unilateral weapons was used by US policy-makers to complement multilateral efforts to strengthen the international protection of intellectual property. The Uruguay Round and its TRIPs Agreement established minimum worldwide standards of intellectual property protection, and accomplished many long-sought objectives of the US government.[18] Among other things, the TRIPs agreement extended most-favoured nation status and national treatment to a wide range of IP areas. The agreement also mandated improved or new standards of IP protection and enforcement, and extended such protection to new areas such as trade secrets and integrated circuit designs (see US General Accounting Office 1995 for a more detailed discussion of the GATT/TRIPs agreement). But this agreement may also constrain US retaliation against nations deemed to provide insufficient protection for intellectual property. Conflicts over the IP areas covered by the agreement are now handled through the WTO's dispute-settlement process, which limits the ability of governments to undertake unilateral retaliatory actions in IP disputes with other member countries. Large-economy governments such as the USA or the EU may elect to ignore the rulings of the WTO.

The evolution of US IP policy during 1980–95 represents an attempt by the USA to establish higher levels of international patent protection and a more transparent and coherent system with which to grant and enforce IP rights within other national economies. Since 1994, however, efforts to further this goal by harmonizing the US patent system with those of other economies have encountered vehement domestic opposition. Opposition by small firms and independent inventors in 1994 forced US government authorities to abandon their long-standing effort to align the USA with international standards by adopting a first-to-file system (Cardona 1994). The resulting domestic US system of IP protection is a compromise that illustrates the pivotal role in this aspect of the US response to globalization played by groups concerned primarily with the domestic consequences of changes in the US IP system. Indeed, the political influence of such groups appears to have grown significantly over the course of the IP negotiations. In this area, at least, US multinational firms have not been able to gain all of their goals because of domestic, rather than international, opposition.

Domestic political resistance also influenced the June 1995 implementation of the TRIPs agreement (PL 103–465), which is only a partial step towards harmonization of the US and foreign IP systems. The USA has superimposed features of the internationally accepted first-to-file system upon its existing first-to-invent structure. This 'hybrid' system will continue to grant patents on a first-to-invent basis, but will extend the duration of patent rights to twenty years from the date in which the patent was *filed*.[19] The hybrid US patent system no longer discriminates against inventorship that does not take place within the USA, in conformance with the national treatment and most-favoured-nation provisions of GATT. In a first-to-invent system like that of the USA, however, this modification could increase the costs of designating patent rights, since evidence of inventorship now can be based on activity that took place outside the USA. This would not be an issue in a first-to-file system, in which patent rights are generally allocated to the first inventor to file an application.

In summary, the US response to internationalization in the IP arena is consistent with our earlier description of US policy as characterized by a tendency to use old policies to deal with new realities. In this case, federal policy-makers see stronger IP rights as one means to restrict the mobility of technology-based assets that are inherently mobile across international borders. As in other areas, this US policy response emphasizes technology creation, rather than technology adoption. In IP rights policy, however, the US response to globalization has been surprisingly constrained by domestic constituencies that oppose the positions favoured by US-based multinational firms. The resulting hybrid US system, which is partially but not fully harmonized with international norms, may prove to be an unstable compromise between established institutional structures and new international goals. Although the agreement achieved significant progress towards raising international IP standards, it is a paradoxical outcome to a ten-year campaign by the USA to harmonize standards and norms within the global IP system.

5. Human-Resources Policies

US policies towards investment in the skills of the domestic labour force are relevant to any discussion of this government's response to globalization for a number of reasons. First, the experience of many of the successful post-war economies of Asia and Western Europe suggests that investment in human capital improves the ability of an economy to absorb and apply new technologies developed domestically and abroad (Mowery and Oxley 1995). In other words, a key component of an 'adoption-oriented' national technology policy—namely, one that emphasizes the domestic capture of the economic benefits of technology-based created assets—is investment in the skills of the domestic labour force, an area in which US workers may be deficient.[20] Secondly, the substantial inflows of immigrants since 1970 notwithstanding, the US labour force is an internationally immobile factor of production, relative to capital or technology (see Reich 1990 for a similar argument). The ability of the US economy to capture a large share of the public returns to investments in worker skills exceeds the ability to capture the public returns from its investments in the domestic development of new technologies that are marketed throughout the global economy. Thirdly, the increased inequality in US wages and earnings that has resulted, in part, from internationalization and technological change has been associated with lower wages for the least-skilled portion of the US labour force. Policies to improve the skills of this cohort accordingly might ameliorate trends towards greater inequality. Fourthly, this subject presents an interesting political anomaly—political support for programmes that could benefit those harmed by the economic changes since 1975 has declined in parallel with the economic welfare of these groups. Indeed, the human-resources area illustrates the 'lamp-post' tendency in US policy, revealed in the failure to develop new initiatives and a reliance on outmoded programmes to deal with new requirements for improvement in the skills of the US workforce.

A final reason for focusing on public policies to support investments in worker skills and worker adjustment is the evidence that US workers, particularly relatively low-skill workers, receive little training either before or during entry into the labour market. Fig. 9.8, from Lynch (1994*a*), depicts the share of the labour force of ten industrial nations that receives some firm-provided training. The share of the US labour force receiving such training is among the lowest of these economies. Moreover, when firms do provide training for their workforce, white-collar employees tend to be the primary beneficiaries (Carnevale and Goldstein 1983; Tierney 1983; Cyert and Mowery 1987). Lynch (1994*b*: 10) notes that 'Only 4 per cent of young workers who are not university graduates get formal training at work.' Smaller firms also provide considerably less training *per capita* to their employees than do larger firms; Lusterman (1977) found that firms with 10,000 or more employees spent an average of $US86 per worker on training, while firms with 500–999 employees spent only $US27 per worker.[21] If the anecdotal evidence of corporate downsizing accurately depicts economy-wide trends,

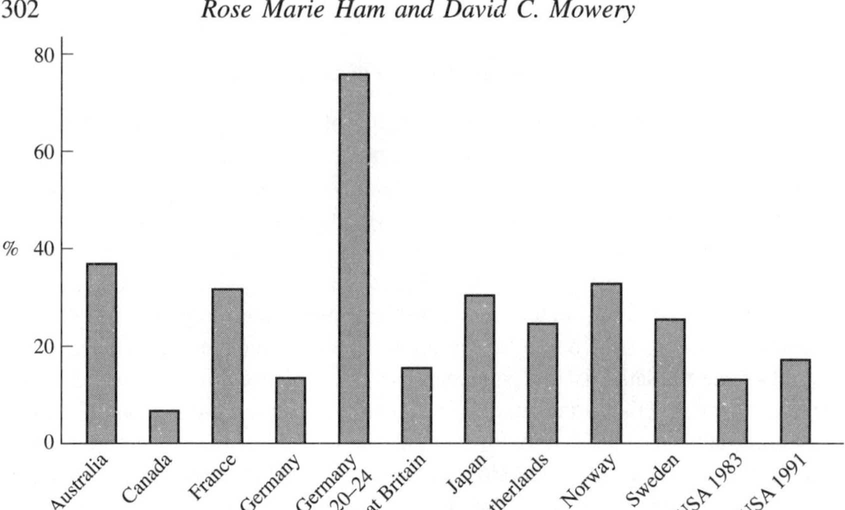

Note: Data refer to the incidence of training in various years in the mid to late 1980s. *Source*: Lynch, 1994a.

FIG 9.8. Incidence of firm-provided training

growth in the share of the US labour force employed in smaller firms could depress still further average levels of employer-provided training.

The tendency of employer-provided training to reinforce, rather than offset, the effects of differences in workers' educational attainment when they enter the workforce is especially problematic for workers with low levels of educational attainment. These workers (high-school drop-outs and even some high-school graduates) often have far less preparation in the basic skills of literacy, numeracy, and problem-solving upon entry into the labour force than is true of labour-force entrants in Japan and many Western European economies (Berg 1994; Hashimoto 1994). Inferior basic skills mean that these US workers may experience longer unemployment spells following displacement by technology or import competition. In addition, low levels of basic skills increase the costs and lower the returns to employers of investments in more specific training, and may also retard the adoption of productivity-enhancing technologies.

The economic reasons for relatively low levels of employer-provided training and the skewed distribution of this training among different skill classes have been extensively discussed (see Lynch 1994*a*). Relatively high levels of domestic inter-firm labour mobility in the US economy, especially among lower-skilled workers, make it difficult for employers to appropriate the returns to their training investments, especially those in basic or generic skills. The disincentive effects of labour-market 'flexibility' are compounded by weaknesses in the USA of institutions that support rigorous apprenticeship programmes that can provide generic, as opposed to highly job-specific training. The necessary level of cooperation among employers, educational institutions, and the federal, state, and local governments to operate such programmes in the USA has been lacking.

(See Berg (1994) for a detailed comparison of training in US and German automotive plants that emphasizes the role of such cooperation; Schneitz (1995) presents a similar analysis for the US and German machine-tool industries).

Although the economic explanation for low levels of investment in US workers' skills appears logical, the lack of political support for more coherent or ambitious efforts in this area, against a backdrop of apparently greater need, is puzzling. Current public policies to support investments of public and private funds in the skills of the employed and unemployed labour force are best described as chaotic. These programmes were identified by the Clinton Administration as a high priority for reform, but federal policies to support adjustment by displaced workers remain a patchwork of categorical programmes, many of which are encumbered with complex eligibility requirements that limit their effectiveness. The US General Accounting Office (1994*a*) found 154 federal employee training programmes with a total budget of $US25 billion in the federal budget for 1993/4, an estimate that includes almost $US9 billion in student-loan programmes. Among the largest programmes designed to assist workers' adjustment to economic change are Trade Adjustment Assistance (TAA), which accounted for $US215 in 1993/4 spending, and the Job Training Partnership Act, which (including its Job Corps component) accounted for $US5.2 billion.

The TAA programme is aimed specifically at the 'losers' from internationalization, workers displaced by import competition. The programme was created in 1962 as part of trade-liberalizing legislation, and expenditures on TAA rose from $US15 million in fiscal 1973 to a peak of roughly $US1.6 billion in 1979/80, a period of significant worker displacement in the US automotive industry. But the Reagan Administration significantly reduced funding for the TAA programme; by 1987, outlays for TAA were roughly $US206 million, and in 1993, TAA received $US211 in funding. Paradoxically, political support for TAA has crumbled during a period of rapid expansion in import penetration of the US economy.

One reason for this programme's limited political support may be its poor track record. TAA's requirements for ascertaining that a worker has been displaced by imports, as opposed to the myriad of other potential causes, severely delays the delivery of income-support payments and virtually precludes retraining for displaced workers. One 1979 study of TAA's operations during the late 1970s found that workers received their first payments an average of fourteen months after layoff (Corson *et al.* 1979). More recent evaluations of TAA (US General Accounting Office 1994*b*) found that programme participants received no training in their first fifteen weeks of unemployment. These problems in this programme illustrate the serious handicaps imposed on 'adjustment-assistance' programmes by strict eligibility requirements that are based on the cause of displacement. However politically appealing such requirements may be, they can impair the success of programmes designed to support worker adjustment.

The other major federal programme for meeting the needs of displaced workers is the Job Training Partnership Act (JTPA), created in 1982 to replace the Comprehensive Employment Training Act. JTPA's primary assistance to displaced workers, however, remains focused on job-search assistance, and the structure of its service delivery system is such that workers with relatively low skills, who are often harder to place in new jobs, tend to be under-served. JTPA also provides relatively little by way of education in basic skills (Cyert and Mowery 1987), which reinforces a tendency for the programme to deal more effectively with relatively better-educated workers within the displaced population.

In summary, the potential economic returns to a stronger set of institutions for the support of investments in the skills of the US labour force appear to be substantial, particularly in an era of rapid internationalization and economic change. But more effective policies require cooperation among institutions (public education, local government, organized labour, and employers) over which the federal government exercises little direct control, and will be difficult to develop in a political atmosphere of considerable mistrust between business and the federal government. Improvements in programmes for displaced workers are also hampered by limited understanding of the factors that are most important to programme success. In the absence of better policies to improve the skills of the low-skilled cohort of the US labour force, current trends towards greater inequality in wages and earnings, and their undesirable political and social correlates, seem likely to continue.

6. Conclusion

The US economy has been transformed since 1975 from one that was relatively insulated from international flows of capital, goods, and technology to a much more internationalized entity. Yet US economic and technology policies have largely failed to recognize, let alone respond effectively to, the implications of such rapid internationalization. Technology policy, IP policies, and human-resources policies all reveal a tendency to look to the past, rather than the realities of the present, for guidance. US policy has concentrated on supporting the creation of technology-based assets, combined with policies to restrict the international mobility of these assets, rather than on the development of a more effective and feasible strategy of strengthening the quality of relatively immobile US assets and supporting the adoption and absorption of technology-based assets.

Although the overall trade and investment policies of the US government have remained liberal, technology policy has seen growing restrictions on foreign access to the US research system; additional restrictions on immigration into the USA are also likely. There is little evidence that the closer relationships between government and the private sector advocated by Dunning (1993), and that do appear to have had positive results in other post-war economies, are being forged in response to globalization. Instead, the opposite trend prevails.

In part, the reactionary style that recently has found favour in US domestic politics reflects the force of other factors, including the end of the Cold War, slow growth in real household incomes, and the widening disparities in the distribution of US incomes. But a surprising recent element in US domestic politics, revealed starkly in the 1994 elections, is a tendency among some of the groups that have suffered the most severe economic penalties to support the rollback of government programmes and regulations that were partly intended to address some of the distributional consequences of economic change.

In many respects, these political developments in the USA reflect a very different vision of the requirements of international competition in the global economy from that described in Dunning (1993). This opposing vision treats governments as inherently incapably of managing investments in infrastructure or other created assets; accordingly, their role is best confined to public goods such as national defence. However unrealistic, this view has gained considerable strength among US business and more surprisingly, among the lower-income voters whose economic interests and declining living standards would lead one to predict the opposite pattern of political behaviour. The political upheaval of November 1994 may itself be reversed in the next several years, but the US domestic political climate has become more conservative and public scepticism about the merits of public intervention in an array of areas has grown in parallel with the internationalization of the US economy.

In addition to the historic lack of support for such a position, another reason for the limited US domestic political support for a 'corporatist' response to globalization may be the tendency of the advocates of a cooperative approach to restrict their search for innovative policies to the area under the lamp-post. To a remarkable degree, even the Clinton Administration's activist approach has responded to globalization by supporting the creation of the technology-based competitive assets that are internationally mobile, while placing less weight on improvements in the ability of US firms and workers to absorb and apply technological advances from external or foreign sources. In addition, this and previous Administrations have all too often simply assigned new objectives to established agencies or programmes, rather than seriously considering the suitability of these goals to the structure or historic goals of these existing programmes. Thus, 'dual-use' programs of defence-related R&D spending are described as a means of improving the competitive and trade performance of US firms, despite abundant evidence that such programmes are of limited effectiveness for civilian-technology development in many areas, and despite the potential of such programmes to undermine multilateral disciplines on R&D subsidies or to result in foreign retaliation.

The response of the current US Administration to globalization reflects another unresolved clash of visions, between advocates of new programmes that are better tailored to the advancement of civilian economic competitiveness and those arguing for a redirection of existing (often, defence-dominated) programmes. Nor are the conflicts between support for technology creation and support for technology adoption resolved in current debates, even among those committed to a new approach to technology policy. The structure of the US central government, with its strict separation of legislative and executive power, makes dramatic policy overhauls difficult. Nevertheless, the failure of the Clinton Administration to develop a more coherent and novel strategy in response to globalization has undermined its political effectiveness in these areas.

This review of the US government's response to globalization suggests that government actions continue to matter a great deal in the modern global economy of mobile capital, goods, and technology. But the mobility of these assets means that the consequences of many government policies will differ from their intended goals. In both the IP and technology-policy areas, for example, the efforts of the US government to develop and implement policies that are intended to capture a larger share of the returns to US-developed technologies have had complicated and sometimes perverse consequences. A more effective US response to globalization must entail a search beyond the lamp-post for policies that are more consistent with the new international economic and political realities, and therefore support the adoption, rather than solely the creation, of the assets and capabilities that underpin international competitiveness.

NOTES

Research for this paper was supported by the Alfred P. Sloan Foundation, the US Air Force Office of Scientific Research, Lawrence Livermore National Laboratory, and the Canadian Institute for Advanced Research.

1. The data in Fig. 9.4 portray trends in US imports and exports of technology, as measured by licensing and royalty income and payments. These data reflect receipts and payments covered by all extant agreements. A more revealing measure, for which the US government does not collect data, concerns the 'balance of trade' on only the contracts and agreements signed during the previous year. Japanese data on new contracts and agreements reveal a dramatic improvement in that nation's importance as an exporter of industrial technology (Mowery and Teece 1993).
2. The apparent increase in the role of foreign affiliates of US multinationals as sources of licensing fees and royalties, for example, could reflect a tendency for these offshore affiliates to receive more advanced technologies from their US parents, as offshore sites have become more attractive locations for advanced production operations than the USA. These trends might also result from stronger international intellectual property rights, which facilitate the arm's-length transfer of technology between parent and affiliate.
3. Freeman and Katz (1994) estimate that the average real wage of the lowest decile of the US labour force declined by 11–17% during 1979–90.
4. Levy and Murnane (1992) note that earnings inequality within age-group and educational cohorts also grew during the 1970s and 1980s. The causes of this trend remain a mystery, although these authors conclude that it may be related to technological change. Increased within-group inequality in earnings is less easily attributed to trade-induced structural change, although this hypothesis cannot be ruled out.
5. Easterlin (1972: 138) estimates that, in 1910, 26% of the US non-farm white labour

force was foreign-born; this proportion was higher in lower-status occupations such as 'craftsmen and operatives' (30%) and 'laborers' (37%).

6. A 1995 report on immigration by the US Census Bureau found 8.7% of the US population in 1994 was foreign-born, the highest share since 1940. Summarizing this unreleased report, Holmes (1995) noted that it found that 20.9% of recent immigrants over the age of 25 had bachelor's degrees, higher than the 14.7% of native-born Americans with four-year college degrees. But 36% of these recent over-25 immigrants had not completed high school, significantly higher than the 17% of native-born Americans who lack high-school degrees. In other words, the distribution of educational attainment within the inflow of immigrant workers is distributed bimodally, with larger shares of this group in the upper and lower tails of the distribution than appears to be true of the native-born US population.
7. Berman *et al.* (1994) also conclude that within-industry shifts in the demand for skilled and unskilled labour account for most of the relative growth in demand for skilled labour in the US economy during the 1980s, and argue that technological change rather than import competition, therefore, is largely responsible for this demand shift.
8. The fiscal 1994 figure nonetheless represented a significant reduction from fiscal 1983's deficit of more than 6% of GDP and fiscal 1992's deficit of nearly 5% of GDP.
9. The contrast with Japan, a parliamentary system with very low levels of defence spending, is particularly interesting. Although the Liberal Democratic Party controlled the Diet for much of the post-war period, its actual control of committees in fact varied with its majority of seats. Strong prime ministers in the Japanese system used their political power to reduce deficits in periods of relative economic prosperity (Hahm *et al.* 1995).
10. During 1960–86 real defence spending on R&D and procurement increased by 2–4% on an annual basis. According to *The Economist* (1994), this trend will probably be replaced by 4% annual reductions in these expenditures through the end of this century. Defence Department spending on research, development, and procurement has already fallen by nearly 50% in real terms since 1986.
11. See Nelson and Wright (1994); much of this foreign challenge to US economic and technological hegemony reflects a remarkable policy success, the post-war reconstruction of foreign economies that was a central goal of post-war US foreign policy.
12. Indeed, the rise of 'dual-use' technology programmes must be placed in the context of the political struggles of the late 1980s and early 1990s between Congress and the White House over federal spending. The budget agreement of 1990, which established separate caps for defence and non-defence spending, created strong incentives for Members of Congress seeking greater funding for technology development programmes to look for these funds within the defence R&D budget by redefining the objectives of these programmes.
13. A CRADA specifies terms under which a private organization provides personnel, equipment, or financing for R&D activities that are consistent with a specific laboratory's broader mission. Most CRADAs include provisions that cover the sharing of IP rights to any technologies resulting from the project.
14. According to Katz and Ordover (1990), at least fourteen Congressional bills passed during the 1980s focused on strengthening domestic and international protection for intellectual property rights.

15. As we noted earlier, the legislation restricted participation in CRADAs to firms that would 'substantially manufacture' the resulting products in the USA.
16. Needless to say, policy-makers' concerns found strong support among such US industries as computer software, entertainment, and pharmaceuticals, few if any of which were experiencing the intensified import competition that emerged during this period in semiconductors and automobiles.
17. Six of the nine cases involve disputes with Brazil, India, China, and Thailand.
18. US negotiating objectives were set forth in the 1988 Omnibus Trade and Competitiveness Act, and included: (1) the enactment and effective enforcement by foreign countries of laws that recognize and adequately protect intellectual property and provide protection against unfair competition; (2) the implementation of adequate and substantive standards and the establishment of effective enforcement procedures to enforce these standards both within member countries and at the border; and (3) the implementation of effective dispute-settlement procedures.
19. This replaces the seventeen-year term measured from grant that has been a part of US law since 1861. This change has conveyed an economic windfall to some US patentholders, since it potentially extends their patent rights for an additional one to two years. US makers of generic drugs have opposed this change in the US patent system because it extends the lives of key pharmaceutical patents (Carey, 1995).
20. Although the evidence remains fragmentary, Lynch (1994*b*: 2) argues that there is 'an emerging consensus that US workers' skills are not on par with those of European and Japanese workers . . .'.
21. Lynch (1994*b*) quotes Bowers and Swaim's (1992) finding that 26% of workers in large establishments received formal company training, significantly higher than the 11% of workers in small establishments.

REFERENCES

Abowd, J. M., and R. B. Freeman (1991), 'Introduction and Summary', in Abowd and Freeman (eds.), *Immigration, Trade, and the Labor Market* (Chicago: University of Chicago for NBER).

AAAS (1994), American Association for the Advancement of Science, Intersociety Working Group, *AAAS Report XIX: Research and Development, FY 1995* (Washington: AAAS).

Barfield, C. (1994), 'Flat Panel Displays: A Second Look', *Issues in Science and Technology* (Winter), 21–5.

Bayard, T. O., and K. A. Elliot (1994), *Reciprocity and Retaliation in US Trade Policy* (Washington: Institute for International Economics).

Berg, P. B. (1994), 'Strategic Adjustments in Training: A Comparative Analysis of the US and German Automobile Industries', in L. M. Lynch (ed.), *Training and the Private Sector: International Comparisons* (Chicago: University of Chicago for the NBER).

Berman, E., Bound, J., and Griliches, Z. (1994), 'Changes in the Demand for Skilled Labor within US Manufacturing: Evidence from the Annual Survey of Manufactures', *Quarterly Journal of Economics*, 367–97.

Borjas, G. J., Freeman, R. B., and Katz, L. F. (1991), 'On the Labor Market Effects of Immigration and Trade' (NBER Working Paper #3761).

Bowers, N., and Swaim, P. (1992), 'Recent Trends in Employment-Related Training and Wages' (unpublished MS, US Congress, Joint Economic Committee).

Bureau of Economic Analysis (1994), *Survey of Current Business* (Washington: US Department of Commerce, Sept.).

Cardona, M. (1994), 'US Says "Not Now" To Resumption of Patent Harmonization Talks', *US Department of Commerce News* (24 January).

Carey, J. (1995), 'A Patent Medicine Called GATT', *Business Week* (15 May), 44.

Carnevale, A. P., and Goldstein, H. (1983), *Employee Training: Its Changing Role and An Analysis of New Data* (Washington: American Society for Training and Development).

Clinton, W. J., and Gore, A., Jr. (1993), *Technology for America's Economic Growth, A New Direction to Build Economic Strength* (Washington: US Government Printing Office).

Connelly, M. (1994), 'Portrait of the Electorate: Who Voted for Whom in the House', *New York Times* (13 November), A15.

Cooper, H. (1994), 'Big Business and Clinton May be Forced to Protect Commerce Department from GOP Ax', *Wall Street Journal* (12 December), A12.

Corson, W. S., Nicholson, W., Richardson, D., and Vayda, A. (1979), *Final Report: Survey of Trade Adjustment Assistance Recipients* (Princeton: Mathematica Policy Research).

Cyert, R. M., and Mowery, D. C. (1987) (eds.), *Technology and Employment: Innovation and Growth in the US Economy* (Washington: National Academy Press).

Davis, B., and Cooper, H. (1995), 'Big Business, Striking It Rich in GOP "Contract", Stands by as Clinton's High-Tech Plans Get Cut', *Wall Street Journal* (7 March), A22.

—— and Zachary, G. P. (1994), 'Electronics Firms Get Push from Clinton to Join Industrial Policy Initiative in Flat-Panel Displays', *Wall Street Journal*, (28 April), A16.

Dunning, J. H. (1994), *Globalization: The Challenge for National Economic Regimes* (The Geary Lecture for 1993; Dublin: Economic and Social Research Institute).

Easterlin, R. A. (1972), 'The American Population', in L. E. Davis, R. A. Easterlin, and W. N. Parker (eds.), *American Economic Growth* (New York: Harper & Row).

The Economist (1994), 'Downdraft: A Survey of Military Aerospace' (3 September).

Freeman, R. B. (1994), 'How Labor Fares in Advanced Economies', in R. B. Freeman (ed.), *Working Under Different Rules* (New York: Russell Sage).

—— and Katz, L. F. (1994), 'Rising Wage Inequality: The United States vs. Other Advanced Countries', in R. B. Freeman (ed.), *Working Under Different Rules* (New York: Russell Sage).

Graham, E. M., and Krugman, P. R. (1995), *Foreign Direct Investment in the United States* (3rd edn., Washington: Institute for International Economics).

Hahm, S. D., Kamlet, M. S., and Mowery, D. C. (1995), 'Institutions Matter: Comparing Deficit Spending in the United States and Japan', *Journal of Public Administration Research and Theory*, 5: 429–50.

Ham, R. M., and Mowery, D. C. (1995), 'Enduring Dilemmas in US Technology Policy', *California Management Review*, 37: 89–107.

Hashimoto, M. (1994), 'Employment-Based Training in Japanese Firms in Japan and in the United States: Experiences of Automobile Manufacturers', in L. M. Lynch (ed.), *Training and the Private Sector: International Comparisons* (Chicago: University of Chicago for the NBER).

Holmes, S. (1995), 'Surprising Rise in Immigration Stirs Up Debate', *New York Times* (30 August), A1.

Institute for Defense Analyses (1991), *DARPA Technical Accomplishments*, ii. *An Historical Review of Selected DARPA Projects* (Alexandria, Va.: Institute for Defense Analyses).

Katz, M., and Ordover, J. (1990), 'R&D Cooperation and Competition', *Brookings Papers on Economic Activity*, 3: 137–204.

Kelley, M. R., and Watkins, T. A. (1995), 'In from the Cold: Prospects for Conversion of the Defense Industrial Base', *Science*, 268 (28 April), 525–32.

Langlois, R., and Mowery, D. C. (1996), 'The Federal Role in the Development of the American Computer Software Industry: An Assessment', D. C. Mowery (ed.), *The International Computer Software Industry: A Comparative Study of Industry Evolution and Structure* (New York: Oxford University Press).

Lawrence, R. Z., and Slaughter, M. J. (1993), 'International Trade and American Wages in the 1980s: Giant Sucking Sound or Small Hiccup?', *Brookings Papers on Economic Activity*, 161–210.

Lepkowski, W. (1994), 'Last Minute Maneuvering Rescues US Technology Policy', *Chemical and Engineering News* (3 January), 13.

Levy, F., and Murnane, R. (1992), 'US Earnings Levels and Earnings Inequality: A Review of Recent Trends and Proposed Explanations', *Journal of Economic Literature*, 30: 1333–81.

Lusterman, S. (1977), *Education and Industry* (New York: The Conference Board).

Lynch, L. M. (1994*a*), 'Payoffs to Alternative Training Strategies at Work', in R. B. Freeman (ed.), *Working Under Different Rules* (New York: Russell Sage).

—— (1994*b*), 'Introduction', in L. M. Lynch (ed.), *Training and the Private Sector: International Comparisons* (Chicago: University of Chicago for the NBER).

Mowery, D. C. (1988) (ed.), *International Collaborative Ventures in US Manufacturing* (Cambridge, Mass.: Ballinger Publishers).

—— (1989), 'Collaborative Ventures Between US and Foreign Manufacturing Firms', *Research Policy*, 18: 19–32.

—— (1994), *Science and Technology Policy in Interdependent Economies* (Dordrecht: Kluwer).

—— (1995), 'The Global Computer Software Industry' (presented at the conference on Coevolution of Industries and National Systems of Innovation, Milan, Italy, 19–21 June).

—— and Rosenberg, N. (1989), *Technology and the Pursuit of Economic Growth* (New York: Cambridge University Press).

—— —— (1993), 'The US National Innovation System', in R. R. Nelson (ed.), *National Innovation Systems: A Comparative Analysis* (New York: Oxford University Press).

—— and Oxley, J. E. (1995), 'Inward Technology Transfer and Competitiveness: The Role of National Innovation Systems', *Cambridge Journal of Economics*, 19: 67–94.

—— and Teece, D. J. (1993), 'Japan's Growing Capabilities in Industrial Technology: Implications for US Managers and Policymakers', *California Management Review*, 9: 9–34.

National Science Board (1993), *Science and Engineering Indicators: 1993* (Washington: National Science Foundation).

—— (1996), *Science and Engineering Indicators: 1996* (Washington: National Science Foundation).

Nelson, R. R. (1984), *High-Technology Policies: A Five-Nation Comparison* (Washington: American Enterprise Institute).

—— and Wright, G. (1994), 'The Erosion of US Technological Leadership as a Factor in Postwar Economic Convergence', in W. J. Baumol, R. R. Nelson, and E. N. Wolff (eds.), *Convergence of Productivity* (New York: Oxford University Press).

President's Council of Economic Advisers (1994), *Economic Report of the President, 1995* (Washington: US Government Printing Office).

Reich, R. B. (1990), 'Who is Us?', *Harvard Business Review* (January–February), 53–674.

Schneitz, K. (1995), 'Industrial Adjustment in the US and German Machine Tool Industries: The Impact of Worker Training' (unpublished MS).

Schultze, C. L. (1990), 'The Federal Budget and the Nation's Economic Health', in H. J. Aaron (ed.), *Setting National Priorities: Policy for the Nineties* (Washington: Brookings Institution).

Semiconductor Equipment Manufacturers' Institute (1993), *Executive Summary Report: Fourth Quarter, 1993* (Mountain View, Calif.: Semiconductor Equipment Manufacturers' Institute).

Singer, P. (1994), 'Flat Panel Displays: An Interesting Test Case for the US', *Semiconductor International* (July), 78–88.

Steinmueller, W. E. (1995), 'The US Software Industry: An Analysis and Interpretive History', in D. C. Mowery (ed.), *The International Computer Software Industry: A Comparative Study of Industry Evolution and Structure* (New York: Oxford University Press).

Tierney, M. L. (1983), 'Employer Provided Education and Training in 1981', in *Training's Benchmarks: A Statistical Sketch of Employer-Provided Training and Education, 1966–1981* (Philadelphia: Higher Education Finance Research Institute, University of Pennsylvania).

US Congress (1995), *Congressional Record*, 9 March (Washington: US Government Printing Office).

US Department of Defense, Flat Panel Display Task Force (1994), *Building US Capabilities in Flat Panel Displays* (Washington: US Department of Defense).

US Department of Defense (1994), *Industrial Capabilities for Defense* (Washington: US Department of Defense).

—— (1995), *Dual Use Technology: A Defense Strategy for Affordable, Leading-Edge Technology* (Washington: US Department of Defense).

US Department of Energy, Task Force on Alternative Futures for the Department of Energy National Laboratories (1995), *Alternative Futures for the Department of Energy National Laboratories* (Washington: US Department of Energy).

US General Accounting Office (1986), *International Trade: Strengthening Trade Law Protection of Intellectual Property Rights* (Washington: US Government Printing Office).

US General Accounting Office (1993), *Technology Transfer: Implementation of CRADAs at NIST, Army, and DOE* (Washington: US Government Printing Office).

US General Accounting Office (1994*a*), *Multiple Employment Training Programs: Conflicting Requirements Hamper Delivery of Services* (Washington: US Government Printing Office).

—— (1994*b*), 'Dislocated Workers: Trade Adjustment Assistance Program Flawed' (statement of Linda G. Morra before the Subcommittee on Employment, Housing and Aviation, Committee on Government Operations, US House of Representatives).

—— (1995), *The General Agreement on Tariffs and Trade: Uruguay Round Final Act Should Produce Overall US Economic Gains*, ii (Washington: US Government Printing Office).

US International Trade Commission (1988), *Foreign Protection of Intellectual Property Rights and the Effect on US Industry and Trade* (Washington: US Government Printing Office).

US Office of Management and Budget, Executive Office of the President (1994), *The Budget of the United States Government for Fiscal 1995* (Washington: US Government Printing Office).

—— (1995), *The Budget of the United States Government for Fiscal 1996* (Washington: US Government Printing Office).

US Office of Science and Technology Policy, Executive Office of the President (1994), *Science in the National Interest* (Washington: Executive Office of the President).

US Office of Technology Assessment, US Congress (1994), *Multinationals and the US Technology Base* (Washington: US Government Printing Office).

10

France

Charles-Albert Michalet

1. **Introduction**

The new rules of the game in globalization are currently calling into question what has sometimes been called 'French singularity', France's own special approach to economic management. The decade of the 1990s marks a watershed in the traditional conception of the role of government in France with respect both to macro-economic policy and to relations with business and the private sector.

Globalization clashes head on with the long history of the French 'Colbertist' model. From the establishment of the great royal manufactories of the seventeenth century for the manufacture of fabrics and porcelain all the way to 'hi-tech Colbertism' (Cohen 1992), with its computer plans, high-speed trains (*train grande vitesse* (*TGV*)) and nuclear and aerospace programmes, it had never truly been questioned.

The Colbertist conception assigns a pre-eminent role to the state in the formulation and implementation of industrial policy. Market forces and corporate strategies play a subordinate role within the framework of a centralized government policy geared to long-term objectives and tailored to the satisfaction of concerns not necessarily coterminous with economic rationality. Industrial policy serves a great design aimed at strengthening the nation's power. Internationally, state control of the national economy must guarantee the accomplishment of a geopolitical design, first safeguarding the nation's independence and next sustaining its influence and its power at the world level. The French model fits quite well with the 'hierarchical-capitalism' type as identified by Dunning in Chapter 1 of this volume.

In short—though this is no doubt to take an excessively schematic view—political considerations have carried the day over economic considerations. In fact, according to the famous quip by the first President of the Fifth Republic, economic and financial matters are the business of the supply corps—the support troops. In an army in the field, these support services are supposed to follow behind the heroic advance of the victorious regiments. We can perhaps pursue the military metaphor to pose the question of which are the generals who conduct economic battles. Behind the state stand the political institutions, the government and parliament. But what makes the French case so special is that in the areas of economics, industry and finance effective power is in the hands of an élite produced by the competitions held by the upper-echelon administration and the engineering schools. 'Technocrats' head the major departments of the ministries, which is what they were recruited for, but they are also in charge of the large enterprises and the major banks. Moreover, they closely advise the ministers, within ministerial cabinets that exert an increasingly strong influence.

The Colbertist model, imbued with the ideas of mercantilism and List-type infant-industry arguments, suffered its first external shock with France's signature of the Treaty of Rome and entry into the Common Market in the late 1950s. However, the opening-up of the economy did not fundamentally impugn the French model. The new great national priority, competitiveness, continued to be compatible with the safeguarding of a national aspiration. With the challenge posed by globalization, however, things could well go otherwise.

The characteristics of globalization—which we need not reiterate here (Dunning 1994*a*; Michalet 1994)—would seem difficult to reconcile with the French 'special approach'. Consequently, the dynamics of globalization could well lead to an open crisis of 'state governance' as well as of 'corporate governance'. Finally, France could find itself confronted with a generalized economic power crisis. Globalization could lead to a revision, more far-reaching than in the case of entry into the Common Market, of a system of values that ever since the revolution of 1789 has made the concept of the nation state the primary principle of coherence of government action. If the French economy comes through this—as it probably will—it will nevertheless emerge radically changed. The logic of globalization will compel the French economy to conform. This means that the programmes of government and of business will have become compatible, in the data-processing sense, with the rules of the game of globalization. In the process, the country risks losing its identity.

Examination of the impact of globalization on state governance and corporate behaviour is crucially important in the case of France. It is, therefore, most appropriate that we turn now to describe the historical nature of the transformation of the French model.

2. The National Aspiration: The French 'Hierarchical-Capitalism' Model (Mid-1960s–Mid-1980s)

During the period from the mid-1960s to the mid-1980s France's national aspiration was expressed through the priority objective—the watchword—of competitiveness. The concept of competitiveness was defined within the framework of an international economy, in which the trade flows of goods and services among nations occupy a predominant place—one that still responds to Ricardian analysis. On the other hand, the first indications of the transformation in nature of the traditional international economy into a global economy characterized by multidimensional integration based not only on export and import flows but also on direct investment flows and financial capital movements were received with apprehension.

2.1. Competitiveness as the Watchword

Affirmation of the primacy of competitiveness, which has constituted the leitmotif since the mid-1960s, was compatible with the French model. Competitiveness was perceived from the outset as an economic war to be waged against foreign competitors on the international market. The battlefield was in fact demarcated mainly by the EU area and, within this, as a confrontation with the German economy, whose industrial power worried French entrepreneurs.

The latter had for decades operated sheltered from international competition. The opening-up of the global economy taught them to know what it was to fear for their survival. It therefore very naturally fell to the state, continuing a long tradition, to take the necessary steps to protect France's industrial potential. The signing of the Treaty of Rome had made recourse to customs duties out of the question, so the only available means of fighting back was the industrial challenge, to borrow the title of a work which, at the time, synthesized the philosophy of the new state interventionism (Stoléru 1969). It is not without significance that the watchword changed from competitiveness to industrial strength. Modernization policy and strengthening of industry had to provide the basis for international competitiveness, the latter being an ability to resist the rising penetration of the domestic market by foreign products. In the final analysis, therefore, the object was less to secure a place for the French economy in the international economy on the basis of comparative advantages than to build a national industrial system that would save France from dependence created by the importation of 'strategic' goods. The latter comprise products with a high-technology content and required intermediate products, which, in the inter-industrial trade-flows matrix, generate downstream or upstream dependence on the outside world. A competitive economy is therefore one with a complex industrial structure such that domestic industry is able to produce the largest possible range of goods, especially goods produced by leading-edge industries and incorporating the most sophisticated knowledge. The existence of leading-edge industries on home soil provides an assurance that the economy will not allow itself to be outgunned by foreign competitors.

The industrial priority reflected the concerns of the technocratic élite, keen to secure independence, and of engineers, keen to secure access to the latest technologies. This conjunction of interests fostered a productivist approach geared to product supply. On the other hand, concern for demand, especially from foreign consumers, took second place to the desire to build a broadly self-reliant economy. Export performance was therefore not the main objective. At best, it was evaluated in terms of its contribution to redressing the trade default, which was worrying because it reflected the weaknesses of the national productive structure, still incapable of fully satisfying domestic needs. Reducing imports, especially of manufactured products, was just as important as raising exports. The opening-up of the economy was perceived as a constraint (the 'external constraint' in technocratic language)—that is, it had a defensive connotation. It was a matter of plugging a gap, not of taking a more active part in international trade flows. The model to be imitated was that of the German economy, whose exports related mainly to 'noble' goods—that is, capital goods. From France's standpoint, the performance of its great neighbour across the Rhine reflected, more than anything else, mastery of the high-technology and productive branches of industry, marketing capability trailed far behind.

Responsibility for achieving the industrial priority objectives was assigned largely to the state. It relied on three major instruments of implementation. The first was the 'burning obligation of the Plan', to use General de Gaulle's phrase. It is a mistake, widespread abroad, to equate the Planning Commissariat of the time to the Soviet Gosplan. Planning did not consist in setting production goals and then imposing them on the production units. The essential purpose of planning was to help create a consensus, around a set of medium-term priorities, among the three social partners—government, employers, and unions—in order to 'reduce uncertainty'. An econometric model of the French economy built by the Projections Department (Direction de la Prévision) of the Ministry of Finance and the National Institute of Statistics and Economic Studies (Institut National de la Statistique et des Études Économiques (INSEE)) furnished a frame of reference by which to identify priorities and needs in light of a given GDP growth target. The process of consultation and agreement was facilitated by the fact that the representatives of both government and employers, products of the same 'great schools', spoke the same language and shared the same economic conceptions. For their part, the union representatives essentially approved this exercise in that it guaranteed the maintenance of strong growth, coupled with a wage-biased distribution of value added, in a situation of full employment. The workers were assured of sharing in the 'fruits of growth', to use the hallowed formula. The Planning Commissariat of the time has several parallels with the Japanese MITI.

The second instrument available to the state to implement its industrial modernization policy was the existence of a large public sector, substantially enlarged by the nationalizations of the immediate post-war period. The public sector encompassed most of the 'national champions' (Michalet 1973). The majority of them had public status or were controlled by the state through a majority interest; they nevertheless belonged to the competitive sector, in contrast to the public enterprises that performed public-service functions by supplying collective goods and services (electricity, gas, railways, postal, and telecommunication services). By their size and their technological capacity the national champions formed the spearhead of French industry in facing up to large foreign enterprises on world markets.

Their competitiveness was strengthened by the third industrial policy instrument: the large industrial projects. These were aimed at strengthening 'lines of production' (*filières*) or sectors regarded as strategic, by reference to the conception mentioned above. They therefore mainly comprised activities with a high-technology content—for example, data-processing, nuclear power, high-speed trains (TGV), aerospace—but also sectors that were inadequately developed or were running out of steam—such as machine tools and shipbuilding. The large projects replaced private initiative and were financed largely out of public funds (subsidies, soft loans, public contracts). It has to be borne in mind that the major banks had been nationalized and it was difficult for them not to support the priorities proclaimed by the government. These types of assistance mainly benefited the large enterprises, the great majority of which belonged to the parapublic sector.

Budget and monetary policy served largely to advance the national aspirations by making it possible to sustain a high rate of growth of production and a steady rise in purchasing power in accordance with the principles of what is generally called the 'Fordist model' (Boyer 1986). In view of the high level of public spending, which helped finance both investment and the 'welfare state', the model was made to work by the acceptance of close to double-digit inflation. The coherence of this Keynesian-inspired macro-economic policy was all the greater for the fact that the 'external constraint' was weak, since the degree of openness of the economy remained limited. This latter condition would prove increasingly difficult to maintain.

2.2. **Controlled Opening-Up of the Economy**

The constant reference to the 'external constraint' in fact reflects the persistence of the trade-balance deficit throughout the period. France had a trade deficit with the OECD countries as a whole. The only surpluses realized were with the less developed countries and, within them, those of the franc zone—the former colonial empire—and the Middle Eastern OPEC members. With this group of countries, exports developed within the framework of 'big contracts', signature of which was closely bound up with the status of diplomatic relations. They depended also on the granting of large loans, financed and guaranteed by public agencies—COFACE and the French Foreign Trade Bank (Banque Française du Commerce Extérieure (BFCE)). Because of the nature of the goods exported (nuclear power stations, railway equipment, iron and steel complexes, armaments, and so on), the great majority of the French exporters' customers were governments and public agencies.

In this setting, the export enterprises—the largest of which took the lion's share—were required more to demonstrate the technical merits of their equipment than to exhibit competitive product-pricing or marketing skill. In view, nevertheless, of the growing importance of foreign trade flows in the economy—exports have accounted for nearly 20 per cent of GDP since the late 1970s—the opening-up of the economy received official blessing with the introduction of the FIFI (physical–financial) model for preparation of the Sixth Plan. The model distinguishes between two economic sectors: the exposed or vulnerable sector, and the protected sector. The exposed sector comprises those enterprises whose activity is geared largely to world markets and which consequently have to contend with the constraint represented by the prices set on those markets. The protected sector comprises those enterprises that operate mainly on the domestic market. This division does not correspond to the distinction between 'tradable and non-tradable goods'; rather it relates to a recognition of the existence of two pricing systems, which in turn reflects the fact that the economy continues to be in large measure administered (through price and exchange control).

Foreign investment—whether French investment abroad or foreign investment in France—was regarded with suspicion.

It is a euphemism to say that French investment abroad was not encouraged by the Administration. The Ministry of Finance looked with a critical eye on capital outflows resulting from decisions by businesses to invest abroad, because such transactions were perceived to threaten the stability of the franc on the foreign exchange market. Moreover, in order to avoid 'crowding-out' of enterprises that pursue purely domestic activities, and also of public financial institutions that borrow heavily on the financial market, large enterprises were required to finance at least 50 per cent of their foreign investments on the international financial market. This constraint would not be lifted until the very last years of the 1970s. The assistance and guarantees obtainable from public financial institutions such as COFACE and the BFCE by enterprises that invested abroad were subject to very strict conditions. To be eligible for such financing, an enterprise had to demonstrate that its foreign activities would generate incremental exports equal in value to at least seven times the amount invested. In sum, foreign investment was not encouraged except to the extent that it helped to alleviate the foreign constraint.

This export priority is mirrored in the enterprises' own strategies. First of all, it is not merely anecdotal to recall that until the end of the 1970s the National Center for French Employers (Centre National du Patronat Français (CNPF)) and the large French enterprises that had investments abroad rejected the appellation 'multinational firm'. The proper definition was 'internationally oriented firm'. This attitude was attributable to the extremely negative image of multinationals that prevailed not only in trade-union circles but also among employers at that time. For the unions, investing abroad meant exporting jobs. For the employers, recognizing the firm's multinational nature meant accepting the risk of being confused with expatriate firms with the bad habit of meddling in countries' internal affairs. For many people, the shock generated by the denunciation of the scheming of International Telegraph and Telephone (ITT) in Chile at the end of the President Allende regime lay in the choice of this ethical position.

The first survey conducted of a sample of French MNEs (Delapierre and Michalet 1976) revealed that the most important motivation for the decision to invest abroad was to circumvent import barriers that other countries had erected (95 per cent of responses). For French enterprises, foreign investment meant pursuing exports by other means. Lowering costs by shifting production was a completely secondary consideration (less than 10 per cent of responses). The target-countries map coincided with the exports map: the EU, North Africa, and sub-Saharan Africa. In the last two areas, the choice of location in many cases harked back to the colonial era. Brazil and Argentina were the only other countries mentioned by a significant number of firms surveyed. Investment abroad was considered to be an extremely risky activity. In the case of the developing countries, many of the responses mentioned the political risk. This concern reflected certain negative experiences associated with decolonization (e.g. Algeria, Indochina). In the case of the USA, there was a strong temptation to locate in the USA because of the size of the market and the need to be close to consumers so as to be able to tailor products to their taste. However, the resounding failures of certain French enterprises (Creusot Loire and above all Renault) gave pause for reflection, despite some positive experiences (Péchiney and the buy-out of Howmett, for example). The choice of a 'multi-domestic' strategy (Porter 1986) was reflected in the enterprises' organizational structure, which was based on a clear-cut separation between domestic activities and international activities, which were the responsibility of a specialized division, often with poor linkages to the firm's other departments (Delapierre and Michalet 1976).

The attitude toward foreign investment in France, too, had a negative connotation, even though rhetoric far outstripped reality. During the mid-1960s the uproar sparked by the closing of the Remington factory in suburban Lyons nearly degenerated into an open diplomatic crisis with the USA. This, together with the shilly-shallying concerning the establishment of Ford at Bordeaux and then at Strasbourg, which led the US company finally to choose a location in Germany, close to the French frontier, illustrated the existence of a prevailing nationalism, amply fuelled by the positions taken by General de Gaulle towards the USA. Subsequently, the government rapidly came to understand that rejecting the presence of foreign businesses on French soil did not prevent those businesses from selling their products on the French market through their subsidiaries located in the EU member countries. Thus, while competition was not avoided, neither was it compensated for by the job creation that would have accompanied their establishment in France. Not long after he succeeded General de Gaulle as President of France, George Pompidou made a reassuring statement before an audience of businessmen during a trip to the USA. He, nevertheless, introduced on that occasion a distinction between 'good' and 'bad' foreign investments which continues to pervade current analyses. 'Good investments' meant those that related to the establishment of a new production unit and created jobs (greenfield investment). The others were those reflected in the buy-out of French enterprises. In practice, this criterion does not seem to have played a very significant role in the direct investment approval decisions taken by the Foreign Investment Commission (Commission des Investissements Étrangers), which was an agency of the Treasury Department of the Ministry of Finance. Cases of rejection of investment applications were extremely rare. This may, however, have been due to prudence on the part of foreign enterprises who submitted approval applications only when they believed their projects did not present any problems, preferring to hold back in the case of projects on which they felt, from prior contacts, that the Administration was not very keen.

The Land Use and Development Agency (Délégation à l'Aménagement du

Territoire (DATAR)), which was set up in the early 1970s, was to play an increasing role in the promotion of foreign investment with the expansion of its network of offices abroad. It should be noted, however, that its mission was limited to attracting foreign businesses to locate in the relatively under-developed port areas (west, south-west) or areas affected by industrial conversion projects (Lorraine, north). This work proved fruitful: in a White Paper published at the end of the 1970s, DATAR was able to announce that foreign investors had responded more positively than French enterprises to land-use and management-policy concerns. For foreign MNEs making their first investment in France, the choice of a depressed region was less expensive than it was for a French enterprise that had to close down facilities in the Paris region before being able to set up in a region regarded as off the beaten track and not very hospitable.

In the last analysis, it seems that, on the eve of the great watershed of the mid-1980s, attracting foreign investment in France was pursued more energetically than promoting French investment abroad. This is not really surprising; it fitted into the logic of an economic policy that gave higher priority to strengthening domestic industry than to securing France's place in the international division of labour. Enlarging on this feature, it can be argued that the pursuit of France's national ambition overshadowed that of its comparative dynamic advantages. What was, in fact, achieved, through decisions not entirely dominated by economic rationality, was the construction of competitive advantages (Porter 1990) and the creation of intangible assets (Dunning 1992). This construction of competitive advantages, in which the state played a decisive role, based on a large public sector and the 'national champions', was accomplished within the framework of an economy amply protected against international competition from outside Europe. The coherence of the French model presupposes that the exposed sectors are closely circumscribed. As soon as the openness of the economy is widened, the 'external constraint' can no longer be reduced to a problem of redressing the trade balance; the very bases of traditional policy are called into question. For that reason, the dynamism of globalization constitutes a major challenge to the French 'special approach'.

3. From a Partially Open Economy to a Fully Open Economy: A Challenge to France's Notion of Uniqueness

The movement from a 'partially open economy' to a 'fully open economy', to use Dunning's (1992) terminology, cast doubt on the French 'special approach' because it was accompanied by weakening of the economic role of the state. This change is evident at two levels: first, in the economic orthodoxy adopted from mid-1982 onwards, which no longer tolerated the state interventionism that had characterized the previous period; and, secondly, in a shift in industrial initiative from the state to business as a consequence of the great upsurge of French investment abroad and the increased presence of foreign enterprises.

The replacement of the Colbertist model by the liberal model, and the reduction in state control of macro-organizational policy consequent on the adoption of global strategies by both domestic and foreign firms, opened up a new and uncertain period which was not yet perceptible at the time when we prepared the first analysis of French competitiveness taking the multinationalization phenomenon into account (Michalet 1985).

3.1. Switch to Economic Orthodoxy

Mid-1982 marks a major turning-point in the traditional conception of economic policy according to J. Attali's *Verbatim* (1993: 375). It marks the beginning of abandonment of the French model in favour of neo-liberal orthodoxy. It is interesting to recall the factors that compelled the government to change course, following the 1981–3 interlude corresponding to the first two years of office of the first socialist President of the Fifth Republic.

The main lines of economic policy over the period 1981–3 represented a rather farcical return to the French model following the more liberal direction imparted to the economy under the seven-year administration of Giscard d'Estaing. Revival of nationalization, revival of the 'national-champions' concept, revival of demand through wage increases, and, finally, revival of macro-organizational policy around the theme of reconquest of the domestic market. The master tactic for reconquering the domestic market (Mistral 1986) was to reduce its penetration by foreign products by strengthening industrial structures around the concept of 'chains of production' (*filières*) or sub-sectors. Schematically, these production lines are meant to describe, for a given product, the activities necessary to its production and distribution. The concept does not differ greatly, at the national economy level, from the 'value-chain' concept introduced by Michael Porter (1985) at the enterprise level. Once again, the machine-tool industry is identified as the main missing link in the industrial sub-sectors structure, the strategic bond that guarantees autonomous functioning of a national economy. The idea of creating a French-style MITI was already in the air, since revival of the Planning Commissariat no longer satisfied the need to manage at a 'meso-economic' level (that of the *filières*) an economy that had been opening up at an ever faster rate during the last few years.

The results of this resurgence of 'Colbertism' were reflected in a sharp rise in inflation, a high trade deficit, and the need to devalue the franc several times. The revival of domestic demand mainly benefited France's trade partners, especially firms building German cars. The failure of this brief resumption of the model of competitiveness based on supply, accompanied by neo-Keynesian economic measures, demonstrated the impossibility of applying a policy of this kind in an open economy. The Socialist government's decision to remain in the then EEC and to comply with the requirements of the European monetary system would be accompanied by somewhat surprising support for neo-liberalism. This new orientation has been followed without respite from then until the time when this chapter is being written (1995), which coincides with the beginning of a new seven-year presidential term.

The new national priority had become that of 'competitive disinflation'. It was accompanied by an anti-inflationary monetary, budget, and social policy. The effort paid off, and for the first time since the post-war period (if we except the short Pinay experience in the early 1950s) inflation was arrested, the annual rise in prices being held constantly below the 3 per cent mark.

The second component of the new economic policy consisted in a reassertion of the role of the market system. The nationalizations programme was halted, and marginal changes were made in the status of the public enterprises, to allow the public enterprises the necessary 'breathing space' which enabled them to set up subsidiaries for some of their activities and conclude joint production agreements with firms (many of them foreign) belonging to the private sector. A series of measures to lighten business taxation and hold wage rates below productivity gains, accompanied by the privatization programmes carried out during the two 'cohabitation' periods (1986–8 and 1993–5), helped redress the division of the value added in favour of profits and restore business profit margins. Businesses would take advantage of these to pay off their debt to the banks and increase their equity funds ratio. At the beginning of the 1990s, business self-financing margins averaged close to 100 per cent (Taddéi and Coriat, 1993: ch. 1).

Yet despite these excellent performances, investment did not take off again, or, more precisely, domestic investment continued to stagnate, whereas direct investment abroad rose sharply from the mid-1980s.

The behaviour of the firms that preferred to invest abroad rather in their country of origin cannot be explained entirely by cyclical factors associated with economic stagnation. It also points, above all, to a significant change in the strategy of the private economic actors, which no longer, as in the past, waited for the state to find the remedy for their difficulties. The 1983 watershed demonstrated that state interventionism did not work in a national economy increasingly integrated into the world economy. Moreover, this integration was no longer limited to goods and services trade flows. France was to discover from the second half of the 1980s that its integration into the world economy was based also on inward as well as outward investment flows and on international capital movements. Unlike the previous period, this new situation of the French economy was no longer the result of deliberate steering by the state but of the dynamics of globalization. The latter thus represented a radical questioning of the French special approach. Globalization could well deal a more radical shock than that caused by the pro-Europe decision of 1983 and the adoption of a neoclassical policy by a socialist government. We, therefore, turn to consider the novel nature of this transformation of the French economy.

3.2. **Towards a Global Integration**

The trend towards a global integration is currently evident at two different levels. First, from the mid-1980s French businesses sharply increased their investments abroad and more and more of them adopted global strategies. Secondly, the presence of foreign enterprises in France strengthened, and the government gave more attention to making the economy attractive in order to try to make up for the outflow of direct investment by French businesses by inflows of foreign capital.

3.2.1. Upsurge of French Investment Abroad

The surge in foreign investment gathered momentum in the mid-1980s. At that time French FDI accounted for only 6 per cent of the world total, and France ranked sixth, far behind the USA and the UK, after Germany and The Netherlands, and on a par with Switzerland, Canada, and Japan. In 1992, the record year, at the fourth rank, French direct investment abroad accounted for 18 per cent of the world total and 32.1 per cent of the EU outflows, to be compared with only 12.2 per cent in 1982–7 (UNCTAD 1994). French enterprises provided employment for 2.3 million people abroad, against 500,000 in 1984. Twelve French enterprises figure on the list of the world's 100 largest concerns in terms of turnover (Hatem and Tordjam 1995). 'France 300', a survey of large to medium-sized enterprises (those with turnover in the FF 1–35 billion range) conducted by the firm of Bain et Cie for the Ministry of Industry, depicts the accelerated multinationalization of French businesses: between 1988 and 1992 the proportion of turnover achieved outside France rose from 48 to 55 per cent, labour force outside France from 21 to 28 per cent, production abroad from 18 to 24 per cent, and R&D carried out abroad from 8 to 13 per cent. The proportion of foreigners among the twenty chief executive officers was 9 per cent in 1982, compared with 5 per cent in 1988.

These performances reflect a significant change in the attitude of enterprise chiefs. According to the above-mentioned survey, 63 per cent of the enterprises surveyed considered the markets on which they operated to be 'global' in nature, compared with only 22 per cent in 1985. There was an increasingly widespread conviction that future growth in foreign-based turnover would stem from expanded location of production facilities abroad, not from incremental exports. Another study, 'France Innovation', conducted by McKinsey, revealed that among heavily export-oriented enterprises (those with average exports in excess of FF 675 million), the rate of growth of production abroad was 80 per cent, against export growth of 62 per cent. Small and medium-sized enterprises (SMEs) were also launching into investment abroad. In 1993 1,400 enterprises with turnover below FF 1 billion set up business abroad (Bricout 1994). At the watershed of the mid-1990s, more and more French enterprises have become convinced that their international competitiveness depends primarily on a dynamic foreign-investment policy and the adoption of a global strategy.

In implementing their global strategies, French enterprises favoured the acquisition or merger entry modality (Pottier 1992). During the period 1988–92 such operations accounted for investments amounting to $US85 billion out of a total of $US115 billion (75 per cent). According to an estimate by KPMG (Hatem and Tordjam 1995: 38), between 1988 and 1992 French enterprises carried out 2,300 acquisition/merger operations, representing 12 per cent of total world transactions of this kind, and ranked third behind US and UK enterprises. The study 'France 300' referred to earlier found that external growth accounted for 75 per cent of the total value of foreign investment by firms in the sample during the period 1988–92, compared with 66 per cent in 1985–8. The decision to pursue external growth on the part of latecomers is not surprising: acquisition of foreign enterprises often offers the fastest way to acquire market share and attain critical size. In the French case this was perceived as being among the five world leaders (in terms of turnover) in a given sector of activity. This latter objective, often mentioned by the heads of many large enterprises, in part represents a resurgence of the 'national-champions' philosophy. It must be added, however, that, in many cases, external growth also catered to the desire to refocus the industrial groups' activities portfolio on products and services they were best placed to supply in international competition.

Europe easily headed the list in terms of geographic targeting of French investment. Between 1985 and 1992, two-thirds of direct investment by French businesses was made in Europe. The USA took second place, with a share of one-quarter. From 1991 to 1993, out of nineteen acquisition operations exceeding $US 1.5 billion, fifteen were carried out in Europe and three in the USA (Hatem and Tordjam 1995: 201). The rest of the world attracted only 10 per cent of investment, with the bulk of it going to Asia. The investment stock data given in Table 10.1 confirm these trends. It is noteworthy, however, that at the beginning of 1992 nearly 93 per cent of the invested capital went to the OECD countries, with the developing countries sharing the remaining 7 per cent. Within the developing countries group, the very low share of investment directed to sub-Saharan Africa and North Africa reflects the increasing withdrawal of French enterprises from regions in which they had traditionally located. While the member countries of the EU continue to occupy first place, since the mid-1980s French businesses have taken a more global approach to their presence abroad, breaking with the trend of the 1960s and 1970s.

French investment abroad is most concentrated in services activities. Table 10.2 shows that in 1992 just over 40 per cent of the stock of French investment abroad was located in mercantile services, headed by banking (17.5 per cent of total investment), insurance, and trade. Investment in manufacturing accounted for only just over one-third of the total; the leading sub-sectors were chemicals and electric and electronic equipment (nearly 10 per cent each), followed by transportation equipment (5 per cent). Over the period 1985–93 two-thirds of French investment was made in services (Hatem and Tordjam 1995: 204). The dynamic international expansion of the banks and insurance companies, reflected also in the sharp rise in portfolio placements abroad (from FF 25 billion in 1980 to FF 220 billion in 1993, is not really a new development. Since the end of the 1960s, the network of foreign windows of French banks had been one of the densest—if not the densest—in the world and their international activities more dynamic

TABLE 10.1. French direct investment abroad, by country, 1992

Country	Employment		Stock of FDI	
	Number (000 wage-earners)	Per cent	Amount (Fbn.)	Per cent
OECD	1,619.0	70.1	624.5	92.9
EU	1,033.0	44.7	420.5	62.5
UK	241.0	10.4	79.5	11.8
Germany	232.0	10.0	124.2	18.5
Spain	211.0	9.1	65.2	9.7
Belgium-Luxembourg	151.0	6.5	64.0	9.5
Italy	121.0	5.2	35.0	5.2
Europe outside EU	103.0	4.5	47.7	7.1
OECD outside Europe	483.0	20.9	156.7	23.3
USA	382.0	16.5	130.9	19.5
Canada	50.0	2.2	15.2	2.3
Japan	16.0	0.7	2.3	0.3
Developing countries	691.0	29.9	48.0	7.1
Maghreb	87.0	3.8	1.6	0.2
Africa	218.0	9.4	10.0	1.5
South America	213.0	9.2	19.6	2.9
Asia, Oceania	140.0	6.1	15.2	2.3
Eastern Europe	33.0	1.4	1.6	0.2
World	2,310.0	100.0	672.5	100.0

[a] Data at 31 Dec. 1991.

Sources: Employment: Direction des Relations Économiques Extérieures (DREE) (1992 data); Stock of FDI: Banque de France; Observatoire de l'Investissement International de la Delegation aux Investissements Étrangers, Ministère de l'Industrie, Paris.

than those of the industrial enterprises (Michalet 1981). The relatively large share of acquisitions and mergers was no doubt due in large part to the operations of the financial establishments.

3.2.2. Increasing Attractiveness of France

The second half of the 1980s was marked by an increasing attraction of foreign investors to France. France's share of total investment inflow rose steadily, from 4.5 per cent in 1984 to 5.6 per cent in 1986 and 6.5 per cent in 1990, to a peak of 14.55 per cent in 1992. At the same date French inward investment was 27.7 per cent of total EU inward investment (UNCTAD 1994). With accumulated FDI valued at FF 100 billion, France ranks fourth in the world among foreign investment host countries, behind the USA, the UK, and Germany.

The relatively strong attraction of the French economy is not really a new

TABLE 10.2. Distribution of French investment abroad, by sector, 1992

Sector	Employment		Stock of FDI[a]	
	Number (000 wage-earners)	Per cent	Amount (Fbn.)	Per cent
Agriculture	n.d.	n.d.	0.5	0.1
Energy	473.0	20.5	61.7	9.2
Agriculture & food industries			33.4	5.0
Manufacturing industry	1,000.0	43.3	228.1	33.9
Metal	n.d.	n.d.	29.8	4.4
Non-metal minerals	n.d.	n.d.	21.8	3.2
Chemical products	n.d.	n.d.	62.9	9.3
Electrical and electronic equipment	n.d.	n.d.	64.2	9.5
Transportation equipment	n.d.	n.d.	34.2	5.1
Rubber and plastics	n.d.	n.d.	15.2	2.3
Others	n.d.	n.d.	n.d.	n.d.
Building, civil engineering	147.8	6.4	10.9	1.6
Services	686.1	29.7	275.2	40.9
Trade	140.9	6.1	41.6	6.2
Credit	n.d.	n.d.	117.7	17.5
Insurance	n.d.	n.d.	55.1	8.2
Others	n.d.	n.d.	n.d.	n.d.
Other industries	n.d.	n.d.	4.0	0.6
TOTAL	2,310.0	100.0	672.9	100.0

Note: n.d. = no data

[a] Outstanding at 31 Dec. 1991

Sources: Employment: DREE (1992 data); Stock of FDI: Banque de France.

development. A survey by the SESSI (Ministry of Industry) found that 1,200 of the 3,000 cases of establishment of subsidiaries of foreign enterprises in France counted in 1991 were set up there as long ago as 1977. Moreover, 300 of these 1,200 subsidiaries engaged only in commercial activities, later converted to production. The acceleration that marked the beginning of the decade is probably explained by the improvement in the country's image as a consequence of economic liberalization.

Paralleling the case of French investment abroad, Europe is the leading source of foreign investment in France. Between 1985 and 1992 three-quarters of investment inflow originated in Europe. Table 10.3 shows that in 1992 nearly 60 per cent of total foreign investment came from other EU countries, with The Netherlands ranking first with 20.4 per cent. At the beginning of the 1990s, the share of investment originating in the USA stood at 19 per cent of the total, down from the two previous decades. In terms of jobs created by foreign subsidiaries, however, the USA ranked first (29.1 per cent), with Germany a distant

TABLE 10.3. Foreign direct investment in France by investing country

Country	Employment		Stock of FDI	
	Number (000 wage-earners)	Per cent	Amount (Fbn.)	Per cent
OECD	715.0[a]	90.9[a]	484.0	95.9
EEC	350.0	44.5	283.5	56.2
Netherlands	37.0	4.7	102.8	20.4
UK	87.0	11.1	61.0	12.1
Germany	132.0	16.8	52.2	10.3
Italy	48.0	6.1	28.6	5.7
Denmark	4.0	0.5	2.2	0.4
BENELUX	40.0	5.1	30.6	6.1
Others	2.0	0.3	5.5	1.1
North America	241.0	30.6	101.4	20.1
USA	229.0	29.1	96.0	19.0
Canada	12.0	1.5	4.8	1.0
Other OECD countries	124.0	15.8	99.1	19.6
Switzerland	78.0	9.9	50.4	10.0
Japan	20.0	2.5	16.1	3.2
Sweden	26.0	3.3	4.4	4.7
Finland	n.d.	n.d.	4.7	0.9
Others	n.d.	n.d.		0.9
Rest of the world	72.0[b]	9.1[b]	20.6	4.1
TOTAL	787.0	100.0	504.6	100.0

Note: n.d. = no data

[a] Excluding Finland.
[b] Including Finland.

Sources: Employment: SESSI (manufacturing industry only); Stock of FDI: Banque de France.

second (16.8 per cent). The enterprises of these two countries are the ones that have been located in France longest.

Foreign investors have carried out acquisitions in order to locate in France. The KGPM reports that 1,500 buy-outs were registered during the period 1988–92. This method is much rarer, however, than in the case of French investment abroad: over the period, such buy-out transactions ($US30 million) accounted for only 5 per cent of the total world value of acquisition or merger transactions and for less than half the value of French acquisitions abroad.

Foreign investors in France are also attracted primarily to services activities. The leading services sub-sectors were finance (banking and insurance), trade, and, far behind, transportation, accounting for 44.7 per cent of total foreign investment in France in 1991 (see Table 10.4). The manufacturing sector accounted for only one-third of total foreign investment in France. This gap has widened in the last decade or so, during which three-quarters of foreign-investment inflow

TABLE 10.4. Foreign establishments in France, by sector, 1991

Sector	Employment		Stock of FDI	
	Number (000 wage-earners)	Per cent	Amount (Fbn.)	Per cent
Agriculture	n.d.	n.d.	0.9	0.2
Energy	n.d.	n.d.	26.5	5.3
Agricultural & food industries	n.d.	n.d.	22.1	4.4
Manufacturing industries	788.0	35.8	177.0	35.1
Metal	19.0	0.9	n.d.	n.d.
Non-metal minerals	37.0	1.7	13.4	2.7
Chemicals	133.0	6.0	43.4	8.6
Founding, metalworking	42.0	1.9	11.2	2.2
Mechanical engineering	93.0	4.2	15.0	3.0
Data processing	56.0	2.5	17.9	3.5
Electrical and electronic equipment	117.0	5.3	16.8	3.3
Transportation equipment	111.0	5.0	22.5	4.5
Textiles, clothing	44.0	2.0	5.4	1.1
Paper, publishing, printing	56.0	2.5	19.0	3.8
Rubber and plastics	53.0	2.4	8.8	1.7
Others	27.0	1.2	3.5	0.7
Building & public works	n.d.	n.d.	1.5	0.3
Services	1,100.0	50.0	225.4	44.7
Trade	n.d.	n.d.	52.5	10.4
Transportation	n.d.	n.d.	4.1	0.8
Credit/insurance	n.d.	n.d.	65.8	13.0
Others	n.d.	n.d.	103.0	20.4
Real Estate, holdings, miscellaneous	n.d.	n.d.	47.4	9.4
TOTAL	2,200.0	100.0	504.3	100.0

Note: n.d. = no data

Sources: Employment SESSI; Stock of FDI: Banque de France.

has gone to services. Within the services sector, alongside locations in the financial sub-sector (13 per cent of the total) and trade (10.4 per cent), good performances were posted in attracting R&D centres. In 1992 there were 417 R&D centres set up by foreign companies, with 25,000 research workers, representing 10 per cent of the industrial research labour force. From 1989 to 1992, thirteen of the twenty-four new research centres set up by multinational enterprises in Europe were located in France (Buck 1994). These results make up for the disappointments recorded in headquarters locating by large non-European companies. Between 1984 and 1993, the number of headquarters establishments of large US and Japanese companies in Europe rose from 815 to 1,000 but only about twenty opted for France (Hatem and Tordjam 1995: 210). The manufacturing activities that attracted the most foreign investors can be divided into two groups. The first group comprises sectors common to foreign investment in France and French investment abroad: chemicals, electrical and electronic equipment, transportation equipment, and non-metal minerals. The second comprises the sectors in which there is little or no cross-investment: data-processing, the paper–publishing–printing group, and mechanical engineering.

3.2.3. The French 'Diamond'

The 'Seven Reasons to Invest in France', as set forth in the booklet of the Foreign Investment Promotion Agency (*Délégation aux Investissements Étrangers*) which was set up in 1992, can be classified by reference to the points of Porter's competitiveness 'diamond' (Porter 1990). But, beyond that approach, the renewed concern to promote foreign investment in France signals the broad lines of what could be the new role of government in globalization.

Let us consider the various points of the 'diamond' for the case of France. First, demand conditions are attractive. The French economy forms part of the EU, the world's largest market. The French market ranks second, behind Germany, with a population of 57.5 million consumers with average *per capita* income of $US23,000 (the average for the EU is $US19,700). Secondly, France offers satisfactory factor-endowment conditions: hourly cost ($US16.2) is lower than in Germany, Belgium, The Netherlands and Sweden, or East Germany. It is lower than or close to that in the USA and Japan. This situation is attributable to the wage moderation that has prevailed since the mid-1980s and the productivity gains achieved, which testify to the high level of training of the labour force. Over the period 1979 to 1992 work productivity rose at an average annual rate of 2.5 per cent, the fastest rate in the EU. Energy cost is the lowest in Europe. Only in the UK are telephone communications cheaper. The road, air, port, and railway infrastructure links the French market to the European and world markets efficiently: the TGV (high-speed train) substantially shortens travel time to the major European cities. R&D is strong: 35,149 patents were registered in 1990 (7.3 per cent of the world total); France ranks second behind Germany in number of research workers and engineers engaged in research (300,000). Concerning the third rating factor, the analyses discussed above show that the large enterprises have been increasingly exposed to international competition, in terms both of trade (France is the world's fourth largest exporter and fourth largest importer) and of foreign investment flows, both inward and outward. Finally, the existence of a large number of efficient SMEs satisfies the requirements of the fourth point of the diamond. They are able to supply the needs of the large enterprises established in France on competitive terms.

To this list of attractiveness factors, which give France a high competitive rating, we can usefully add a series of institutional changes, applying the 'diamond' model as revised by Dunning (1994*b*). These changes should help to alter the still fairly controversial image of the French economy that prevails in the international business community, illustrated by the World Economic Forum's mediocre world competitiveness ranking of France (thirteenth or fourteenth during the early 1990s). First of all, France's foreign-investment control regulations have been substantially relaxed, a development that should change its reputation as a bureaucracy. The decree of 11 February 1992 extended the very liberal regime applied to foreign investments originating in the EU to the vast majority of foreign investments (those amounting to less than FF 50 million and relating to French enterprises with a turnover of less than FF 500 million). Secondly, contrary to widespread opinion abroad, the number of workdays lost through strikes is now one of the lowest in Europe. Finally, business-profits taxation has fallen from 50 per cent in 1985 to 33 per cent in 1993. The rate of return on capital, which was 14.2 per cent in 1993, is 1.5 per cent higher than the average for Europe.

4. Conclusions: An Uncertain Future?

The shape of the 'diamond' ranking the French economy among the high scorers in competitiveness, and putting it near the top of the list of international investors, results both from the policies followed by the dirigiste state and those followed by the liberal state. The first helped to lay the structural bases for competitiveness by fostering the creation of efficient infrastructures, developing leading-edge technologies and a high education level, and by encouraging the creation of large industrial and financial groups. The second made France more attractive by changing the social climate, restoring more room for manœuvre to private initiative and competition and redressing the major macro-economic equilibria.

Economic liberalization has been imposed on the French government both by the Single Market constraints reflected in Brussels 'directives', and by the global strategy followed by an increasing number of firms. The result has been less interventionist government macro-organizational policies, which have effectively phased out the French special approach, with far-reaching transformation of the role of government in the economy. In this setting, stubborn defence of the French language and French audiovisual production strikes one as rather in the nature of a rearguard action. The combined effect of the surge in investment abroad, the increased attractiveness of France as a location for inbound-MNE activity, the conversion to orthodox economics, and the growth in the power of the Commission of the EU is that the state and its administration no longer play the lead role in economic management. The decisions by the large enterprises to locate abroad and the increased emphasis on the presence of foreign subsidiaries in the economy are weakening the state's ability to sustain its traditional control over industrial policy. The initiative no longer lies with the state. It is becoming a mere spectator, at best a facilitator of the growing integration of the national economy into that of the European region and, to a smaller degree, but irreversibly in terms of the world scene, of globalization—an evolution that bears out the analyses of Dunning (1992). In contrast with the 'Glorious Thirty Years' period, the state henceforth expects economic recovery or reduced unemployment to be triggered abroad through the demand of our trade partners and the establishment of new subsidiaries of foreign enterprises. Successive governments, regardless of their ideological orientation, repeat that there is only one possible economic policy. This contrasts sharply with the long period during which the national aspiration was to be served only through France's own strengths deployed according to decisions made in France. This volte-face in the principles of governance has not been deliberate. It has been induced progressively, first through acceptance of the rules of the game of regional integration, which were those of a liberal economy, and then, since the end of the 1980s, through emancipation of the large French concerns which gave priority to the defence or conquest of world market share and capacity to join the club of the world oligopolies.

It is difficult to imagine that the French special approach will be able to withstand the dynamic onslaught of globalization. However, in the mid-1990s the question remains as to whether France will be capable of replacing the old model by a new one. This question stems from the dual crisis of 'state governance' and 'corporate governance'. As early as the end of the 1970s, the large French groups were ready to launch out into globalization. They profited from the opportunity offered by the change in the government's attitude to business from the mid-1980s onwards to expand their presence abroad by stepping up their acquisition/merger transactions. The problem that now arises is that of consolidating the industrial groups created through external growth, many of which need to be rationalized both to make them more competitive and to improve their profitability.

At the same time, the power structure in the large concerns, which traditionally belonged to the top-ranking civil servants, is being called into question. The serious accusations levelled in 1994–5 against the Presidents of Crédit Lyonnais, Alcatel, and Lyonnaise des Eaux point to a deeper malaise which concerns the management structures of large groups. The Cadbury Report (1992) has become bedside reading for heads of enterprises looking for ways to reform what is deemed to be the 'presidentialist' style of operation of the large enterprises. Similarly, the state finds itself limited in its traditional capacity to help public enterprises get back on their feet, in that Brussels looks unfavourably on measures of the kind that benefited Renault, Air France, and, more recently, Crédit Lyonnais. Finally, the fact that foreign pension funds and insurance companies hold at least one-third of the securities quoted on the Paris Stock Exchange poses the threat of a takeover of power by the managers of those financial agencies. Without going so far, we feel that these operators are indeed probably going to exert ever-increasing influence on the management of French businesses. The decision by a growing number of these firms to present their profit-and-loss accounts in accordance with US accounting principles is not a matter of chance or of technical preferences (*Le Monde* 1995).

Globalization is generating a crisis in terms not only of French business leadership but also of definition of the role of the state. Whereas the enterprises—at least the largest ones—favour globalization, the same cannot be said of the state or the administration. Historically, opening up the economy has always been perceived as a constraint—the 'external constraint'. Managing the new rules of the game imposed by globalization is much more difficult than managing the balance of trade—all the more so since the government has to contend with two major domestic difficulties: the quasi stagnation of the economy up to 1993 and, more serious, record high unemployment and the steady increase in the 'excluded' population—the jobless and homeless. A large segment of public opinion feels, more or less consciously, that globalization and the decision to go the way of liberalization are at the root of French society's present ills. A strong current of hostility exists today to the supposed implications of globalization. Expressions of such hostility range from the findings of a Senate committee chaired by M. Arthuis in 1994 denouncing relocations by French enterprises as one of the major causes of unemployment, via demands by the extreme left opposition for France to abandon economic liberalism, return to state interventionism and resume nationalization, to extreme rightist movements that blame everything on immigrant workers and appeal to an exaggerated nationalism in order to demand France's withdrawal from the EU. At the first round of the presidential elections in April 1995 these movements together accounted for 40 per cent of the votes, not counting the opinions of those who supported the traditional parties even though they were not fully convinced of the benefits of a strong franc, competitive disinflation, and commitments to macro-economic convergence as a prelude to transition to a single European currency. It is mainly by taking refuge behind respect for European commitments that successive governments have tried to deal with this movement of refusal to abandon the traditional model. The new economic policy has not so far truly inspired a replacement doctrine.

The only recent official attempt to identify such a doctrine is contained in the report *France in the Year 2000* (*La France de l'an 2000*), prepared by a committee of the Planning Commissariat chaired by Alain Minc and submitted to the Prime Minister in the fall of 1994 (Minc 1994). The title of the first chapter of the report neatly summarizes the diagnosis it presents of the past decade: 'France Successfully Opens Up to the World But at a High Price'. This concept of the social cost of globalization is developed in the rest of the chapter, which concludes with the following judgement: 'France, for its greater good, has played the game of opening up to the world; it has accepted the pressures of international competition. It has held fast. But for failure to make the right internal arbitrages it has permitted the development of an ever growing society of the excluded which has paid the price of this success on behalf of us all' (Minc 1994: 30). Finally, in order to come to terms with a market society open to international competition without widening the social breach created by increasing social inequality and exclusion from mainstream society, France needs a new social compromise to replace that of the high-growth years. The commission recommends 'that it be based on the principle of equity, in contrast to the egalitarian aspiration that has marked the whole of postwar social history' (Minc 1994: 87).

Finally, therefore, the Minc Report urges a change in the historical motto of the French Republic so as to enable France to face up to the 'challenges' of the year 2000. As we suggested at the beginning of this work, it seems indeed unlikely that the French special approach will survive the new principles imposed on the old nation state by the globalizing world economy.

NOTE

The author would like to thank the Foreign Investment Advisory Service (FIAS) for the support it provided in the production of the paper. The opinions expressed are those of the author and do not necessarily represent those of FIAS.

REFERENCES

Attali, J. (1993), *Verbatim (1981–83)* (Paris: Fayard).

Boyer, R. (1986), *Théorie de la régulation* (Paris: La Découverte).

Bricout, J. L. (1994), 'Les P. M. E. aussi', *Économie et Statistiques*, 271–2 (May).

Buck, R. (1994), 'International Investment in Europe, the Role of Science Parks and Technopole', *Communication à l'Observatoire des investissements internationaux* (May).

Cohen, E. (1992), *Colbertisme high tech—Economie des grands projets* (Paris: Hachette).

Delapierre, M., and Michalet, C.-A. (1976), *Les Implantations étrangères en France: Stratégies et structures* (Paris: Calmann Lévy).

Dunning, J. H. (1992), 'The Global Economy, Domestic Governance Strategies and Transnational Corporation', *Transnational Corporations*, 1/3: 7–46.

—— (1994*a*), *Globalization, Economic Restructuring and Development* (The 6th Prebish Lecture; Geneva: UNCTAD).

—— (1994*b*), Re-Evaluating the Benefits of Foreign Direct Investment, *Transnational Corporations*, 3/1: 23–52.

Hatem, F., and Tordjman, J. D. (1995), *La France face à l'investissement international* (Paris: Economica).

Le Monde (1995), 'L'Europe perd la bataille des normes comptables' (31 March).

Michalet, C.-A. (1973), 'The French Case', in R. Vernon (ed.), *Big Business and the State* (Cambridge, Mass.: Harvard University Press).

—— and Delapierre, M. (1975), *Multinationalization of French Firms* (Bloomington, Ind.: Academy of International Business).

—— (1981) (ed.), *Internationalisation des banques et des groupes financiers* (Paris, Edit. CNRS).

—— (1985), 'The Case of France', in J. H. Dunning (ed.), *Multinational Enterprises, Economic Structure and International Competitiveness* (London: J. Wiley & Sons).

—— (1993), 'Globalisation, attractivité et politique industrielle', in B. Coriat and D. Taddéi (eds.), *Entreprise France* (Paris: Le Livre de Poche).

Michalet, C.-A. (1994), 'Transnational Corporations and the Changing International Economic System', *Transnational Corporations*, 3/1.

Minc, A. (1994), *La France de l'an 2000* (Paris: Éditions O. Jacob).

Mistral, J. (1986), 'Régime international et trajectories nationales', in R. Boyer (ed.), *Capitalismes, fin de siècle* (Paris: PUF).

Porter, M. E. (1985), *Competitive Advantage* (New York: The Free Press).

—— (1986) (ed.), *Competition in Global Industries* (Boston: Harvard Business School Press).

—— (1990), *The Competitive Advantage of Nations* (New York: The Free Press).

Pottier, C. (1992), *Stratégies d'acquisition des groupes industriels français* (Paris: Eyrolles).

SESSI (1994), *L'Investissement étranger dans l'industrie française*, 35 (January).

Stoléru, L. (1969), *L'Impératif industriel* (Paris: Seuil).

Taddéi, D., and Coriat, B. (1993), *Made in France* (Paris: Le Livre de Poche).

UNCTAD (1994): United Nations Conference on Trade and Development, *World Investment Report 1994: Transnational Corporations, Employment and the Workplace* (New York: United Nations).

World Economic Forum/IMD (1994), *The World Competitiveness Report 1994* (14th edn., Geneva/Lausanne: World Economic Forum/IMD).

11

Germany

Martin K. Welge and Dirk Holtbrügge

1. Introduction

In the last decade, no other industrialized country has gone through such dynamic and fundamental structural changes as Germany. The fall of the iron curtain in 1989, the unification of East and West Länder in 1990, and the establishment of the Single European Market after 1992 are only the most remarkable milestones which have affected the German economy with new opportunities and threats. At the same time, German companies as an integral part of the global economy are facing and implementing new forms of economic organization like outsourcing, intra-firm trade, cross-border alliances, strategic networks, and other non-equity forms of cooperation (NEC). These challenges not only affect the strategies of both German and foreign firms but also bring about a major rethinking of government attitudes and policies towards FDI and MNEs.

The purpose of this chapter is to analyse the possible impact of globalization on the state governance of FDI and NEC in Germany. To give an overview of the major influential factors on this issue, the economic situation and the international competitiveness of the German economy is described in the following section. In the third section, the role of outward and inward FDI with special reference to the new Länder (*Neue Bundesländer*) is estimated. Attitudes and policies of the German government towards FDI are discussed in the fourth part. Afterwards the features of globalization are outlined and challenges for federal state governance of FDI are deduced. Because of the important role of trade unions in Germany, their position is also briefly discussed. The chapter ends with a short summary and outlook.

2. The German Economy after Unification

2.1. Recent Economic History and Economic Position

Undoubtedly the most outstanding and far-reaching incident in recent German history is the unification of East and West Germany which took place economically on 1 July 1990, and politically three months later on 3 October 1990. The collapse of the former GDR is causing the unified Germany to face the challenge of transforming a socialist economy into a market system. This does not only mean adapting West Germany's laws, regulations, and institutions to the new Länder but also reorganizing and privatizing more than 8,000 former state-owned enterprises and preparing them for international competition. At the same time, there exists a strong political need for economic and social stabilization and for overcoming income and wealth disparities as soon as possible. By 1997, six years after unification, both challenges have been only partially met.

While the German unification was an totally unexpected incident, the European integration was a protracted process of more than forty years. This process reached its peak with the introduction of the Single European Market after 1992. For German firms and firms from other EU countries, the abolishment of border controls and the reduction of government-imposed trade-and-entry barriers provided better market access for exports and hence less pressure for FDI. On the other hand, the EU 1992 programme forced firms to reconfigure their value chain according to locational advantages, reduced transaction costs, and economies of scope. Consequently, the late 1980s were characterized by a massive wave of cross-border alliances, M&As, and the establishment of new foreign subsidiaries.

The unification of 1990 and the introduction of the Single European Market after 1992 not only caused deep structural changes in many companies and in the German economy as a whole but also affected the four main macro-economic goals specified in the Law on Stability and Growth (*Gesetz zur Förderung der Stabilität und des Wachstums der Wirtschaft*). Especially in the first two years after unification, the enormous demand for consumer goods in East Germany caused an increase of GDP with growth rates of nearly 10 per cent in West Germany and more than 20 per cent in East Germany. Because of structural inefficiencies, economic growth slowed down after 1992 and even became negative in 1993. Since demand has decreased more and more, in 1995 the growth rate fell to 1.8 per cent and again reached the low pre-unification level.

Another consequence of unification was a significant rise in *inflation*, with double-digit rates in East Germany in 1991 and 1992. Price increases were less a result of the currency conversion—which was initially considered as overly favourable for East Germans—but rather a reaction to excess demand. Since demand has decreased more and more, in 1995 the inflation rate is expected to reach again the low pre-unification level of less than 3 per cent.

In contrast to inflation, *unemployment* still remains at a rather high level. On 31 June 1995 the unemployment rate reached 8.4 per cent in West Germany and 14.1 per cent in the new Länder. Thus, structural unemployment has become one of the major obstacles to economic and social stabilization.

Finally, *export performance* has also significantly varied in recent years. Traditionally, Germany has had a strong export orientation. Export shares of more than 50 per cent are common in many firms, especially in the chemical, automotive, and mechanical engineering industry. After a steady increase until 1992, however, exports in West Germany declined by 10 per cent in 1993. In the new Länder, exports in 1993 reached only 25 per cent of their 1985 levels. As a consequence, Germany has lost its position as the world's leading exporting nation.

2.2. International Competitiveness

In view of the particular importance of foreign economic relations for the German economy, it seems to be useful to analyse its international competitiveness in more detail. According to the diamond model of Michael Porter (1990),[1] it is affected by six major determinants: factor conditions, demand conditions, related and supporting industries, firm strategy, structure and rivalry, role of government, and the role of chance.

As a country with relatively few natural resources, the economic miracle (*Wirtschaftswunder*) in Germany after the Second World War mainly depended on the ability to create advanced and specialized *factor conditions*. These include highly educated, skilled, and motivated workers as well as a very effective structure for commercial research and development. To some extent competitive advantages of German firms have been powered even by pressure from selective factor disadvantages. As Porter (1990) points out, high labour costs, for example, have been an important stimulus for innovation and automatization, and have prompted German firms to stress quality while moving into more technologically sophisticated industry segments. More and more, however, high labour costs are likely to become one of the most important competitive disadvantages of the German economy. Especially after the fall of the iron curtain, more and more firms have tried to reduce labour costs not by developing innovative and productive technologies, but rather by transferring labour-intensive production to Central and Eastern Europe where money labour costs amount to less than 10 per cent of those in Germany (Holtbrügge 1995).

Demand conditions in Germany are very attractive. Germany is the largest market in the EU and the third largest in the industrialized world, following the USA and Japan. Germany has a population of nearly 82 million customers, with an average *per capita* income of DM 39,990 in 1993. Despite the size of the country, most segments of the domestic market are saturated, particularly in West Germany. As a consequence, even small and medium-sized companies are being forced to sell their products abroad and to adapt themselves to foreign market conditions.

Germany has a close web of *related and supporting industries*. Widespread diversification is the exception and not always very successful. Instead of foreward or backward integration, buyers and suppliers tend to work closely together and often to internationalize themselves sequentially.

Firm strategy and structure are basically characterized by pragmatism, conservatism, and a strong technical as well as scientific orientation. A strong desire for technical perfection and very tough customers have led to a high buyer loyalty to German products and a strong domestic *rivalry*, particularly in those industries where high-product quality is demanded. Because of their technical abilities and conservative customers, German firms are usually successful in those industries with a pronounced experience curve and a strong need for highly qualified and specialized employees. However, they succeed in industries with short product life-cycles or the need for aggressive marketing.

Compared to most other industrialized countries the *involvement of government* in industrial policy is moderate. In contrast to smaller economies, such as Sweden or Switzerland, German macro-organizational policy has focused on antitrust issues rather than productive and scale efficiency. A very important role is played by the Federal Cartel Office (*Bundeskartellamt*) which is independent of the government and provided with powerful instruments to control mergers, cartels, and dominant firms. It has lagged behind many other countries for a long time, but in recent years successful attempts have been made to deregulate, commercialize, and privatize formerly state-owned industries such as telecommunications, power industry, or railways.

Finally, *chance* has played a very favourate role in recent German history. The fall of the iron curtain and the unification of a country which had been divided for more than forty years have offered wide opportunities to develop new markets, to strengthen its international competitiveness, and to sustain economic prosperity. To be able to take advantage of these opportunities, however, the concentration of economic policy on the new Länder—caused by the initial problems of unification—has to be overcome and the global orientation has to be recaptured as soon as possible.

3. The Role of FDI

3.1. General Aspects

As previously pointed out, a distinctive feature of the German economy is its openness and its pronounced international orientation. This does not only mean that German companies face strong competition with foreign firms in the domestic market, but also that they have to develop foreign markets and actively seek investment opportunities abroad. Consequently, the ratios of exports to GDP and of inward and outward FDI stock to GDP are relatively high. Between 1990 and 1993 German FDI accounted for more than 10 per cent of total world investment, ranking third behind the USA and Japan, and on a par with France and the UK (OECD 1994). Comparing the level of FDI with exports, however, it is evident that export orientation is still the dominant feature of internationalization strategies of German firms and that the importance of internationalization via FDI (although notable in absolute terms) is much lower than in other industrialized countries.

After a period of large inward investment in the post-war years, since the early 1970s Germany has been more important as a host country than as a home country for FDI (see Fig. 11.1). While, in 1993, outward FDI amounted to about DM 18,041 million, the respective figure for inward investment was only DM 5,086 million.[2]

One reason for this asymmetry is that labour costs in Germany are among the highest in the world. This motivates German firms to transfer labour-intensive

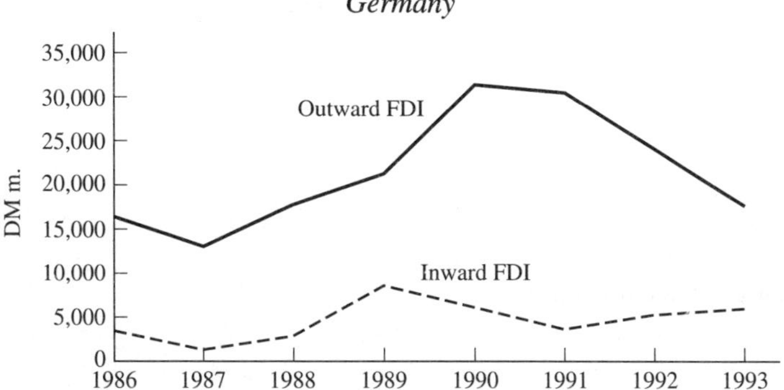

Source: BMW: (1994*b*).

FIG 11.1. Inflows and outflows of German FDI, 1986–1993

production to countries with lower real-wage levels and simultaneously keeps foreign firms from investing in Germany. Since trade restrictions in the EU have been nearly totally removed, many non-EU firms now prefer to establish subsidiaries in Portugal or the UK—that is, in countries with much lower wage levels—and use these transplants as a supply base for the German market.[3]

3.2. **Outward Investment**

Since the end of the First World War, outward direct investment by German firms has increased very rapidly. Its total stock grew by DM 17,950 million in the 1960s, by DM 53,240 million in the 1970s, and by as much as DM 143,296 million in the 1980s. Since 1990, however, German FDI has fallen sharply. In 1993 net transfers amounted for DM 18,041 million and nearly reached the level of 1988. Compared to the peak of 1990, this is a decline of nearly 40 per cent. The main reasons for this recent development cited by BMWi (1994*b*) are as follows.

First, the development of German FDI reflects a general trend of worldwide FDI which declined considerably because of the recession in most industrialized countries in the beginning of the 1990s. Secondly, the significant increase of German FDI in the late 1980s was mainly a response to the proposed creation of a Single European Market after 1992. This process has now largely come to an end, and German firms are now consolidating their overseas assets. Last but not least, since 1989 most German firms have concentrated their activities on the new Länder. As a consequence, the development and penetration of this new market ties up financial and managerial resources that otherwise would have been invested elsewhere.

Table 11.1 shows that the most important target region for German FDI is the rest of Europe. In 1993 nearly 85 per cent of FDI flowed to other European countries with more than 75 per cent of that to members of the EU. A second regional focal point is the USA, with a share of nearly 10 per cent. Compared

TABLE 11.1. Outward FDI from Germany, regional distribution, 1992 and 1993 (DM m.)

Region/country	1992	1993
Europe	20,090	15,199
EU	16,057	11,518
EFTA	2,242	1,758
Central and Eastern Europe	1,593	1,760
Africa	91	−3
America	3,674	1,864
North America	3,320	1,747
USA	2,800	1,737
Central America	124	−4
South America	230	121
Asia	953	901
Japan	300	170
Australia, New Zealand, Oceania	24	179
Industrialized countries	21,919	15,193
Developing countries	1,098	846
TOTAL	24,634	17,978

Source: BMWi (1994*b*).

to other countries, however, it is notable that transfers to the USA declined more than average.

Contrary to the general trend, German FDI in the reforming countries of Central and Eastern Europe is increasing rapidly. With approximately 10 per cent in 1993, it was more than twice as high as German FDI in developing countries and in the emerging markets of South-East Asia. Most attractive among the Central and Eastern European economies are Poland, Hungary, and the Czech and Slovak Republics which, between them, account for nearly 80 per cent of German total investment in this region. In the Commonwealth of Independent States the investment conditions seem more uncertain given the unstable political situation. In addition, there are less advantageous legal and economic conditions for FDI as compared to other parts of this region. Still, in the long term, Russia and, to a lesser extent, the Ukraine offer attractive opportunities for large-scale FDI because of their vast internal markets, their critical need for an efficient expanding consumer goods industry and their enormous natural resources (Welge and Holtbrügge 1993).

For the late 1990s and the beginning of the twenty-first century, the shift of German FDI from the EU and the USA towards Central and Eastern Europe and Asia is expected to continue. For example, a recently published study of the German Chamber of Industry and Commerce (Deutscher Industrie- und Handelstag) revealed that one-third of the interviewed large and medium-sized companies in West Germany indicated that they plan to invest abroad in the next three years. The favoured regions are Central and Eastern Europe followed by Asia, with respective reductions in the EU (DIHT 1993).

Since the late 1980s the major part of German FDI flowed into financial institutions, holding companies, and other property agencies (see Table 11.2). This reflects the overall emerging importance of services and the particular relevance of spatial closeness to local markets in this sector. Among the processing industries, chemical, electrical, and automotive industry and mechanical engineering are of greatest importance. In addition, it is safe to say that FDI is realized especially in those industries in which German firms are particularly competitive in the world market.

According to a survey by the Institute of the German Economy (Institut der deutschen Wirtschaft), the main motive for the decision of German companies to invest abroad is to gain access to foreign markets and to protect their position in markets that are already supplied by exports (Beyfuß and Kitterer 1990). Especially in countries with high trade barriers and governmental control, some firms also expect that the 'goodwill effect' of their investment will cause additional exports to the host country. Thus, FDI and exports are best regarded as being complementary rather than substitutable to each other. In contrast to market-access motives, cost- and procurement-oriented motives are of less importance. However, recent empirical studies, with special reference to Central and Eastern Europe, indicate that, in view of the high wage levels in Germany, the reduction of labour costs is becoming an increasingly important motive for investment abroad by German firms (Holtbrügge 1995).

3.3. **Inward Investment**

Between 1992 and 1993 inward investment in Germany increased moderately from DM 4,614 to DM 5,086 million. As in the case of outward investment, the major countries of origin are neighbouring European countries (see Table 11.3). Until 1992 most prominent among these were member states of the EU, but more recently there has been a shift to EFTA countries. Another notable tendency is the decline of inward investment from Asia. An explanation for this finding might be the weakness of the Japanese economy in the early 1990s and its concentration on South-East Asian countries which has also led to a decline of Japanese FDI in other European countries and in the USA (Tejima 1995).

By far the major portion of inward-investment flows are directed to holding companies and other property agencies (see Table 11.4). In contrast to outward investment, however, since 1990 the share of banks and financial institutions has constantly declined. Inward investment in processing industries has lost importance too. Holding companies, however, often have a strong reference to processing industries, so that their real share might be underestimated in the official figures.

TABLE 11.2. Outward FDI from Germany, sectoral distribution, 1986–1993 (DM m.)

Industry	1986	1987	1988	1989	1990	1991	1992	1993	1986–1993
Service sector									
Holding companies & other property agencies	891	1,274	2,584	3,596	3,132	8,529	5,066	2,408	27,480
Financial institutions	1,814	725	1,524	4,087	4,075	2,106	3,299	3,994	21,624
Insurance companies	740	1,411	2,196	2,124	5,248	1,596	1,125	—	14,440
Real estate and housing	−68	32	32	30	48	55	242	47	418
Manufacturing industries									
Chemical industry	4,288	1,596	2,718	2,367	3,350	2,169	1,816	1,903	20,207
Electrical industry	1,899	528	2,072	2,264	3,819	1,178	1,578	1,431	14,769
Automotive industry	2,199	540	1,021	366	2,991	2,414	3,201	818	13,550
Mechanical engineering	402	565	973	1,062	1,854	1,672	1,568	1,266	9,362
Iron-and-steel-producing industry	213	499	223	298	384	332	514	46	2,509
Oil-and-gas industry	611	447	440	148	124	46	−91	−126	1,599

Source: BMWi (1994*b*).

TABLE 11.3. Inward FDI in Germany, regional distribution, 1992 and 1993 (DM m.)

Region/country	1992	1993
Europe	2,280	2,777
EU	2,898	1,070
EFTA	−779	1,388
Africa	30	41
America	1,093	1,917
North America	1,370	1,662
USA	1,323	1,684
Central America	−273	294
South America	−2	−40
Asia	1,186	358
Australia, New Zealand, Oceania	24	—
TOTAL	4,613	5,093

Source: BMWi (1994*b*).

According to a survey by the Institute of the German Economy, investment by foreign companies in Germany is mainly triggered by market-seeking objectives (Beyfuß 1992). Most important among them are closeness to main customers, access to new markets, protection of positions in markets that are already supplied, and the use of Germany as an export base for the EU market and Central and Eastern Europe. A second group of motives are locational factors such as highly-qualified workers, modern infrastructure, high productivity, and a favourable social climate. Compared to previous studies, however, the survey indicates that the locational disadvantages of Germany as a production location are increasingly exceeding its locational advantages. In particular, high wages and non-wage labour costs, short and inflexible working hours and plant operating times, heavy taxes, strict environmental protection requirements and complicated authorization procedures are becoming major deterrents to new inward investment in Germany (see Table 11.5).

Despite extensive governmental incentives, FDI in East Germany is especially disappointing. In 1992 only 20 per cent, and in 1993 even less than 4 per cent, of total inward investment flowed into the new Länder. In 1991 this figure barely exceeded the respective figure for West Germany. Japanese investment in particular, which was expected to provide a significant stimulus for the restoration of East Germany's economy, remained rather modest. As Waragai (1993) has pointed out, the main reasons for this are unsettled ownership questions, ecological and debt problems, bad infrastructure, and the lack of detailed market and company information. In view of these disappointing figures, however, one has to take into consideration that the investment in the new Länder of those firms which are located in West Germany but owned by foreign companies—like Opel in Eisenach—is not recorded statistically as *foreign* investment. Moreover,

TABLE 11.4. Inward FDI in Germany, sectoral distribution, 1986–1993 (DM m.)

Industry	1986	1987	1988	1989	1990	1991	1992	1993	1986–1993
Service sector									
Holding companies & other property agencies	2,565	739	3,650	5,548	4,976	3,832	4,969	3,207	29,396
Financial institutions	339	576	407	1,350	1,411	1,092	607	–481	5,301
Manufacturing industries									
Electrical industry	48	–414	–52	97	446	–276	–517	652	–19
Non-ferrous metal producing	–39	—	–5	–33	44	–103	151	508	523
Non-ferrous metal working									
Mechanical engineering	–12	–276	–278	–401	24	145	104	221	–476
Food-processing industry	–78	507	–243	–57	19	–334	–155	–87	–428
Automotive industry	243	–643	–83	–3	41	182	–262	–443	–968
Iron-and-steel-producing industry	—	—	4	–39	28	16	–1,083	–73	–1,147
Petrochemistry	300	0	–2,272	–399	126	–378	71	–130	–2,682
Chemical industry	–848	–164	344	–604	–2,113	592	–871	210	–3,454

Source: BMWi (1994*b*).

TABLE 11.5. Germany as a production location compared to other industrialized countries, 1993 (Germany = 100)

Country	Wage costs	Non-wage labour costs	Total labour costs	Productivity	Annual working time	Total tax burden
Germany (West)	100	100	100	100	100	100
USA	83.0	43.6	65.3	86	116.2	74.2
Japan	91.0	83.0	87.4	96	115.2	95.0
France	62.8	71.7	66.8	97	107.6	83.8
UK	66.8	33.8	51.9	60	107.9	53.0
Netherlands	80.5	81.9	81.3	103	105.5	56.2
Portugal	18.4	18.2	18.3	.	115.3	64.5

Source: Institut der deutschen Wirtschaft (1994); own calculations.

some proposed large-scale investments—such as those of Elf Aquitaine and EKO-Stahl—are under preparation and are not yet included in this figures. Nevertheless, investment of foreign firms in the new Länder is much lower than expected.

4. State Governance of FDI

4.1. Protection of Domestic Firms from Foreign Takeovers

The relatively modest inflow of FDI may be somewhat surprising, since the level of state interventionism in foreign economic relations is modest compared with that of most other industrialized countries.[4] There is no foreign trade ministry in Germany, and foreign economic relations are seen principally as the responsibility of firms, not of the government. There are no authorization requirements for FDI, nor for investment by established foreign-controlled enterprises, except for some strategic sectors subject to special conditions. Inward investors simply have to notify the Deutsche Bundesbank if they acquire 20 per cent or more of the shares of a German firm. Indeed, the Law on Foreign Economic Relations (*Außenwirtschaftsgesetz* (*AGW*)) empowers the German government to restrict FDI in order to fulfil its international commitments, to preserve economic stability, and to guarantee national security, but, so far, available measures have been used in only very few exceptional cases. The predominant opinion among German politicians is that openness of the economy was a major factor in post-war success, and still is today. Even under SPD Chancellors Brandt and Schmidt, who put more emphasis on the social aspects of social market economy (*Soziale Marktwirtschaft*), inward investment was perceived to have been beneficial by stimulating competition and importing know-how and new technologies.

Although the legal framework for inward investment, especially for greenfield investment, is, in general, very liberal, there are various informal and indirect mechanisms to protect domestic firms in certain key sectors from foreign takeovers (Berg and Müller 1990; Bailey *et al.* 1994).[5] First of all, the participation of employees in the supervisory board (*Aufsichtsrat*)[6] and the need to consult workers on important decisions regarding investment and employment laid down in the Industrial Relations Act (*Betriebsverfassungsgesetz*) of 1952 and the Codetermination Act (*Mitbestimmungsgesetz*) of 1976 have to be considered. Since foreign firms are generally perceived to be less sensitive to social requirements, the influence of employee representatives is a major impediment to take over a German company.

Secondly, German firms are less reliant on the stock market for raising funds. Rather, they prefer to have close and long-term relationships with banks. Banks, themselves, not only influence the corporate policy of large firms through direct holdings, but, by acting as proxies for private shareholders, they tend to protect them from foreign takeovers. Even if foreign firms are able to acquire a majority of shares in a German company, limited voting rights make it difficult for them to gain full control.

Last but not least, the Cartel Office plays a very important role. All mergers and acquisitions with one firm's sales exceeding DM 2 billion or both firms' sales exceeding DM 1 billion require the approval of the Cartel Office. Furthermore, notice has to be given after the merger has taken place wherever a market share of 20 per cent is reached, or if the newly merged firm employs more than 10,000 employees, or if it has sales over DM 500 million (Berg 1992). As a consequence, hostile foreign takeovers are very difficult, and most tend to be negotiated between the parties.

Informal mechanisms towards inward investment are especially relevant in the case of the new Länder. After German unification in 1990, representative offices of the state property agency Treuhandanstalt[7] were established in New York and Tokyo, and generous tax incentives were (and still are) made available in order to attract foreign investors. The privatization of East German firms, however, has not rested on economic factors solely. Employment guarantees and other political factors have played a very significant role. In many cases firms have been sold not to those making the highest bids, but to those who have submitted the most convincing plans for the revitalization and development of the enterprise concerned. For example, British Petroleum was rejected in its bid for the profitable Minol petrol-filling station group and the Leuna petrochemicals refinery because it was perceived to be concerned with short-term returns only. Instead of BP, the Treuhandanstalt accepted the bid of a consortium comprising Elf Aquitaine, Thyssen, and SB Kauf because it felt that these firms had a strategic interest (Bailey *et al.* 1994). Undoubtedly, this policy of the Treuhandanstalt is one of the main reasons for the disappointing engagement of foreign firms in the new Länder that has already been mentioned elsewhere.

4.2. Promotion of Outward Investment

Because of the enormous growth of outward investment flows during the 1980s, the German government has gradually moved away from the regulation of inward investment to the protection of investment of German firms against restrictive government action abroad (Bailey *et al.* 1994). Not only have agreements with other countries and supra-national organizations been settled, but also special incentives and guarantees to promote outward investment have been made available.[8]

Most important among governmental incentives are bilateral investment guarantee treaties to protect German investors from political risks. Up to 1995, agreements with more than seventy countries in Asia, Africa, Latin-America, and East and Central Europe have been negotiated. Long-term funds are made available by the export promotion programme of the Hermes Kreditversicherungs AG and that of the German Bank for Reconstruction (Kreditanstalt für Wiederaufbau). The German Investment and Development Agency (Deutsche Investitions- und Entwicklungsgesellschaft mbH (*DEG*)) also appropriates equity and equity-like capital for investment in developing countries and countries in transition. A very important function is performed by the National Agency for Foreign Trade Information (Bundesstelle für Außenhandelsinformation (BfAi)) with its world-wide web of trade correspondents in collecting, analysing, and preparing detailed information on foreign markets, industries, and companies. Last but not least, special incentives for FDI in Central and Eastern Europe are also provided.

As in the case of other industrialized countries, it is doubtful whether these incentives have a significant impact on the amount of German FDI. Empirical studies show that—comparing to market- and cost-oriented motives—governmental incentives have only little influence on the investment decision of firms (e.g. Rolfe *et al.* 1993). In the case of Germany, moreover, such incentives are relatively modest and mainly aimed to invigorate firms' own initiatives. Summing up, it may be argued that governmental promotion of outward investment in Germany is likely to support and accelerate the market mechanism rather than to replace it.

5. The Impact of Globalization

5.1. Features of Globalization

Globalization is one of the most frequently discussed concepts in international business today. Of the various definitions of globalization, the one given by McGrew (1992: 23) seems most appropriate to us (see also Dunning 1994):

> Globalization has two distinct phenomena: scope (or stretching) and intensity (or deepening). On the one hand, it defines a set of processes which embrace most of the globe or

which operate world-wide; the concept therefore has a spatial connotation. On the other hand, it also implies an intensification on the levels of interaction, interconnectedness or interdependence between the states and societies which constitute the world community. Accordingly, alongside the stretching goes a deepening of global processes.

The emergence of the globalization phenomenon is regularly attributed to several *environmental factors* that significantly supported this process (Welge 1990; Böttcher 1995).

The most often quoted factor is the convergence of consumer preferences in industrial nations after the Second World War. With increasing levels of disposable income, people, regardless of their cultural or ethnic background, begin to develop similar tastes and lifestyles and demand similar products (Ohmae 1987). Irrespective of whether this tendency results from the universality of human nature, or from the fact that Western countries such as the USA and European nations represent the most advanced industrial economies, it is nevertheless the case that Western lifestyle and patterns of consumption have been widely adopted by all newly industrialized countries, and are now penetrating into the erstwhile Communist regimes of Russia and China. In this respect, it is commonly asserted that the *convergence of consumer preferences* is a function of the increasing trend towards deregulated free market policies which provided the basis for the rapid industrialization of the world economy after the Second World War.

The diffusion process of Western tastes and lifestyle has been supported by significant advances in *transport, telecommunications, and media technology.* These have allowed fashions, trends, ideas, tastes, and so on to be diffused more easily across national borders. In the global era, the power of national borders in separating international operations into neat clusters of distinct areas of competition has faded. Today, large MNEs typically operate all over the world. Because of the increased permeability of country borders, MNEs are able to raise capital, conduct research, buy supplies, and manufacture and market their products wherever they find the best opportunity to do so. Political boundaries are of relevance only if they significantly restrict the scope of options.

The opening of national economies has been mutually facilitated by the *GATT achievements*, which obliged national economies to liberalize product and factor markets. As a consequence, the world economy has recently become highly interdependent, leading to a more rapid spread of goods and services across countries. Technological advances have helped shorten product life cycles. This forces firms to exploit their investments more rapidly in terms of world-market dimensions and volumes.

Based on these developments, patterns of competition and cooperation have rapidly been altered. The three major trade blocs—namely, NAFTA, EU, and Pacific Rim—have fundamentally changed the world economy into a global triad (Ohmae 1989). The triad regions serve as regional hubs for the rest of the world. In industries in which large volumes determine profitability and competitiveness, the ability of firms to survive is increasingly determined by the success in the triad markets.

The question now arises how globalization affects the organization of economic activities. This analysis can conveniently be carried out by using the following dimensions (Böttcher 1996): (i) dispersion of activities, (ii) differentiation of managerial responsibility, (iii) analytical focus, and (iv) management mentality.

Dispersion of activities. Within a global context, investment decisions are seen from a worldwide perspective, incorporating the configuration of existing operations (Kogut 1989; Hedlund 1993). In this respect, it is proposed to configurate single functional elements of the value chain separately (Porter 1986). Thereby, MNEs can gain competitive advantages arising from strategically configuring and integrating segments of the value chain around the world, following a pattern that focuses on the overall advantage for the system as a whole rather than narrowly only on local conditions of either the home or the host country (Porter 1986).

Differentiation of managerial responsibility. Because of their strategically configurated activities around the world, internationally operating subsidiaries are less centred on their parent companies. Since subsidiaries often outweigh home-country operations in terms of the general importance for the business as a whole, it is increasingly considered inappropriate to manage an international business exclusively with a home-country orientation (Bartlett and Ghoshal 1989). This implies that subsidiaries are no longer simply seen as implementors of the strategic concepts of their parent organizations. Rather, they are considered as crucial sources of expertise and know-how. It is believed the MNEs derive sustainable competitive advantage from being able to acquire know-how and strategic information anywhere in the world, and to benefit from the aggregation and exploitation of these resources globally (Nonaka 1988). The diffusion of technological and managerial competence creates the opportunity of scanning for internal or external innovations and new ideas on a global basis (Vernon 1979; Hedlund and Rolander 1990). Competitive advantages arise from synergetic rather than from additive coupling of units (Hedlund 1993).

Analytical focus. The segmentation of MNEs into clusters of dyadic parent–subsidiary relationships is replaced by an *ex ante* neglect of country borders that previously caused an inevitable division of fields of activities along the geographical dimension of nation states in distinct subsidiaries. In the global context, the impact of country borders is considered only when it actually influences MNE activities across borders, and not beforehand by conceptualizing the object of analysis.

The permeability of country borders as well as the strategic configuration of activities result in growing interdependencies between operational activities of subsidiaries. Managing an international business from a global perspective implies, therefore, a significant increase of reciprocal and sequential instead of pooled interdependencies. This also leads to relationships between subsidiaries without direct involvement of headquarters.

Management mentality. In the global context, executives are believed to change their attitudes towards foreign business from an ethnocentric or polycentric to a geocentric mentality. For Perlmutter (1969: 13), a geocentric attitude implies adopting a worldwide approach in headquarters as well as in subsidiaries. 'The firm's subsidiaries are thus neither satellites nor independent city states, but parts of a whole whose focus is on worldwide as well as on local objectives, each part making its unique contribution with its unique competence.' Geocentrism overcomes the dichotomy between global and local in conceiving the performance for each unit as a contribution to the overall success of the business as a whole.

The analysis of the consequences of globalization on the organization of activities of MNEs makes it clear that the international firm is evolving into a very different sort of institution (Dunning 1993*b*: 602): 'It is increasingly assuming the role of an orchestrator of production and transactions within a system of cross-border internal and external relationships, which may, or may not, involve equity investment, but which are intended to serve its global interests.' FDI is not the only means by which the value chain may be fragmented on a worldwide scale. NEC is becoming more prominent, lying in the grey area between arm's-length trade and international FDI (Nunnenkamp *et al.* 1994). The purpose of these cooperative agreements or strategic alliances is to reduce the transaction and production costs of their activities along the value chain, and/or to gain access to complementary resources and capabilities (Welge 1995).

In the following section we shall discuss how governments are required to rethink their domestic economic and macro-organizational strategies in the light of a much greater ease with which resources and capabilities can move within MNEs across national boundaries.

5.2. The Challenges of Globalization for National Governments

As a consequence of the globalization process described above, policy-makers from industrialized countries, especially from the EU and Germany, are facing a major policy dilemma (Nunnenkamp *et al.* 1994: 130). On the one hand, consumers are likely to benefit from intensified trade and investment relations, because increased competition will create positive welfare effects. On the other hand, domestic producers and workers are likely to lose in terms of competitiveness, which will motivate them to resist the increasing international division of labour. Therefore, government might be tempted to intervene in order to ease the adjustment burden for local producers and workers. The effectiveness of such interventions, however, becomes rather questionable. 'The more companies operate on a worldwide scale, the smaller the potential for effective national trade measures is, because evasion becomes easier' (Nunnenkamp *et al.* 1994: 130). Trade barriers can be circumvented by FDI, and restrictions imposed on FDI can be eroded by NEC. Therefore, governments may turn to more innovative protective instruments such as stricter common standards concerning social and ecological production conditions and harmonized competition rules. Some selected options will be discussed in more detail below (Nunnenkamp *et al.* 1994).

5.2.1. Ex ante *Harmonization of Production Standards*

First indications of a more sophisticated protectionism relate to attempts of *ex ante* harmonization of production standards. Common standards, for example, with respect to social and ecological production conditions mean a protectionist device possibly being more restrictive than traditional trade barriers. They would remove an important locational parameter of international competition.

The EU has been among the first to follow the path of *ex ante* harmonization of social production standards. The Maastricht Treaty contains a mandate to issue requirements with respect to the working environment to protect workers' health and safety, working conditions, information and consultation of workers, gender equality, and the integration of workers excluded from the labour market. If these standards were implemented by all EU member nations, locational characteristics would be denied their role of shaping the international division of labour. The implicit assumption of this strategy is that the locational advantages of a rich country like Germany, such as a well-developed infrastructure and a high-skilled workforce, are regarded as fair, whereas locational advantages of poor countries, such as lax environmental regulations and low labour costs, are perceived as unfair. This is the old-fashioned protectionist argument. Therefore, in an integrating world economy, fairness in terms of economic competition should mean a guarantee against discriminination. This can best be realized by strict adherence to the most-favoured-nation treatment clause of the GATT.

In our opinion, however, harmonization is not able to offer a long-term solution to the challenge of globalization for various reasons. First, foreclosing institutional competition implies allocative inefficiency and structural rigidities in the protected economies. Secondly, harmonized standards cannot prevent evasion. Thirdly, it will be difficult to agree on common standards from the very beginning.

5.2.2. Industrial and Technology Policies

In Europe, industrial and technology policies have gained considerable momentum since 1992. The Treaty of Maastricht endows the EU with new and far-reaching competences in this area. Articles 130 and 130i list various policy instruments that aim at industrial targeting and upgrading technological capability. Also comparable measures at the national level are largely exempted from EU provisions against cartelization and mergers.

Past experience, especialiy in Germany, has shown that strategic industrial policy is of limited cost-effectiveness. In Germany, industrial policy has mainly reacted to the adjustment problems of ailing sectors, such as agriculture, mining, iron and steel, shipbuilding, and railways. Most public-support programmes have been prolonged when sectoral adjustment problems have turned out to be persistent. The few examples of industrial targeting in the technologically more advanced industries such as civil aircraft and semiconductors have not been encouraging either (Nunnenkamp *et al.* 1994: 147).

All in all, strategic industrial policy in Germany is not a promising response to the challenges of globalization. Defensive attempts to ease the adjustment burden of mature industries are unlikely to prevent their decline, and will eventually reduce the adjustment flexibility of the whole economy.

5.2.3. Wage Policies

By comparing the US and European reaction patterns to fiercer international competition, it may be concluded that wage discipline is necessary in order to maintain employment of low-skilled workers in industrialized countries. In European countries, wage flexibility and wage differentiation have frequently been resisted, as trade unions have aimed at a greater equality of wages across skills and regions. Recently negotiated agreements in Germany have pointed to an emerging consensus that wage discipline is unavoidable, and that real wage cuts may need to be accepted once job security has become a major concern. It is still questionable, however, whether German trade unions will agree to a more pronounced wage differentiation.

Consequently, the German government is mainly responsible to *overcome incentive problems* and to *improve the conditions* for wage differentiation. In particular, the incentive compatibility of the system of unemployment benefits has to be strengthened in several respects. Strict eligibility criteria should be applied if job offers are declined by beneficiaries. Duration and level of payments should also be linked to the beneficiary's willingness to participate in qualification and retraining programmes (Langhammer and Paqué 1994).

The effectiveness of revising the system of unemployment benefits is likely to remain limited, however, unless trade unions and employers take more responsibility for securing employment. It cannot reasonably be expected that the required change of policies will emerge from government action alone. A concerted action of government, employers' associations, and trade unions (*konzertierte Aktion*) which has been effective in the past could be a workable solution.

5.2.4. Human Capital Formation

Given the permanent change of current and future job requirements in the era of globalization, human capital has to be upgraded in such a way that allows for flexibility and mobility of the workforce. In this respect, as has been echoed in several chapters of this book, human capital formation is of increasing importance under the conditions of globalized production and markets. Consequently school and university curricula have to be revised in cooperation with the business sector. We believe that governments should concentrate on establishing a sound educational basis that allows people to acquire a broad spectrum of specific skills according to changing demands. Being insiders of the German educational system, the authors have some doubts, whether central and regional governments in particular are well prepared to meet these challenges.

As long as German universities are state schools with no clear differentiation in quality and without being allowed to choose their students according to individual admission standards, German university education will lose its competitive edge internationally.

5.2.5. Anti-Trust Legislation for Strategic Alliances

In 1991 a working group at the German Cartel Office dealt with anti-trust implications of strategic alliances (Bundeskartellamt 1991). After reviewing the European Anti-Trust Law as well as the German Anti-Trust Law, three cases—the 'pump case' (KSB/Goulds–Lowara/ITT), IBM/Siemens, and VW/Ford—are examined more closely. Because of space limitations, we will not go into details, but rather concentrate on the conclusions of the working group. First, the working group emphasized that German and European anti-trust laws allow for a wide range of cooperative forms, also between large-scale enterprises. Secondly, their major concern was that, because of the limited sovereignity of all institutions, nobody is able to account for all of the economic and competitive implications and effects of international cooperations among firms. In addressing the issue of globalization, it was felt that the framework of governance has to be made compatible with the dimensions of corporate strategy, in order to prevent the emergence of a legal vacuum. The introduction of the EU-merger control was perceived as a step in the right direction.

Since corporate strategies go beyond European space, securing competition has to be oriented on a worldwide scale. Maintaining free world trade implies that worldwide competition should not be blocked by private-market orders, created by a network of strategic alliances of a few large-scale enterprises.

What is needed, according to their view, is a framework for the world economy and world trade, which has been passed in the Havanna Charter of the UN Conference on Trade and Employment as early as 1948. This charter has never been put into force; however, it contains the necessary framework, especially a code of conduct for trade policy and an international law for cartels and concentration. If these basic ideas of the Havanna Charter could be implemented, the objective of securing the welfare-increasing effects of international division of labour for all nations would not be beyond reach.[9]

5.3. The Role of Trade Unions

Before we describe the position of the German trade unions, it is important to remember the relevant background scenario. As has already been discussed in Section 2.1 of this chapter, the unemployment rate in West Germany amounts to 8.4 per cent, and in the New Länder 14.1 per cent. Many economists believe that this is structural rather than cyclical. Another important issue is the high real costs of labour where Germany ranks number one in the world. Moreover, Germany is of comparative disadvantage with respect to the number of hours worked each year. In France employees work 80 hours more than in Germany, in Italy 280 hours, and in the USA more than 470 hours. As a consequence, production sites are relocated to East European and Southern European countries. The Association of the Chemical Industry (VCI) admits, however, that this has been taken into account by the recent wage negotiations, where rules for more flexible working times have been set up. It is fairly evident that this is a very tough scenario with which the unions have to deal. As an example, we give a brief description of the position of the German Metal Workers Union, the most influential union in Germany.

According to its former president, the union recommends that three major tasks are needed to deal with the challenges of globalization (Steinkühler 1992): first, the German unification should be socially designed; secondly, there should be a common action in the European market in order to improve conditions of work and conditions of life on a European scale; and, thirdly, there has to be an individual response to the Japanese challenge. In this chapter we will deal only with the second and the third tasks.

With respect to the European market, the unions have identified improved exchange of information and experience, definition of common pools and procedures for national union action, and common European bargaining rules negotiated by European institutions that ought to be created as their central fields of concern. Euro-workers' councils are felt to be the adequate instrument for exchange of information and experience (Deppe 1992). There are already examples in Gillette, Bull, VW, and DEC, where European contact levels have been established. Where the second issue is concerned, European cooperation with respect to working time, qualification time, and so on is under way. European wage contracts have not yet been achieved. However, the introduction of a European currency is felt to be a facilitator for the ultimate objective of the principle of 'same wage for the same work'.

The unions believe that they have adequately responded to the Japanese challenge and the implied changes in methods of production by allowing for a more qualified and flexible workforce, by supporting the reorganization of the production process, and by supporting more democratic rather than hierarchical forms of organization of work. They emphasize, however, very strongly, that additional qualification should correspond with additional pay, and that self-determination in team work should not result in self-exploitation. In addition, they also see clearly the danger of massive job losses because of the new principles of organization of work.

Where the attitude of German trade unions to globalization *per se* is concerned, it is very difficult to draw any firm conclusions. In their workshop on the 'Internationalization of the Economy; Challenges for the Trade Unions' held in Düsseldorf in 1993, the issue of globalization was not addressed explicitly. The position put forward in this workshop can be summarized as follows (Zwickel 1994). The unions emphasize future oriented regulation: namely, a modernized wage-negotiation system, strong workers' councils, goal-oriented industry policy, ecological innovation of production structures, and the creation of new jobs in areas such as traffic, communications, energy, and environment. According to their view, this strategy will allow for reduction of mass unemployment and will enhance competitiveness of Germany as a location. How this strategy should be implemented successfully remains totally unclear. All in all, German unions seem to have no workable strategy to deal with the challenges of globalization. Their basic objective is to serve the interests of the workers who have jobs, and not the interests of those who have lost jobs because of relocation of production.

6. Summary and Outlook

The process of globalization is leading to a structural transformation of firms and nations, and is creating new relationships and interdependencies (Dunning 1994: 11). It seems that firms have already responded to this challenge by having changed their strategies, their structures, their management systems, their human resource policy, and so on. Nation states are far behind. The cases of France, Sweden, and also Germany support this judgement very clearly. In an age of 'alliance capitalism', Dunning (1994) suggests that traditional measures of trade and FDI policy are not effective anymore. We predict the role of the state has to change in the same way as the role of the headquarters in global MNEs has done. The state should adopt a role as an administrator and facilitator who sets certain rules of the game. The state will become less powerful and ought to be less interventionist. It should provide favourable locational conditions such as infrastructure, education, entrepreneurial spirit, technological know-how, working conditions, and so on. This context management provides the framework which makes a country competitive and attractive in a global scale.

Taking the case of Germany, we feel that the state has not done its homework well, as the ongoing discussion of Germany as a production location (*Standortdebatte*) clearly indicates. In criticizing the German government, however, one has to take into consideration that there are massive pressures on the administration to take local action. One of these pressures results from high structural unemployment in the country. Another pressure comes from the unions as a very powerful stakeholder, defending wage and working conditions they have been fighting for the last decades. So the government faces a global dilemma. It is very doubtful whether the nation state is the right unit of analysis to solve this dilemma. There are good reasons why supra-national institutions should become major actors in governing FDI and NEC.

NOTES

1. Although frequently criticized (see, e.g., Dunning 1992, 1993a; Rugman and Verbeke 1993), in our opinion the 'diamond' represents the most prominent and useful framework to analyse the international competitiveness of nations.
2. In this chapter, all figures refer to data provided by the German Ministry of Economics (Bundesministerium für Wirtschaft (BMWi)). For our purpose, they are more suitable than those of the Deutsche Bundesbank and the OECD, since they do not include reinvested profits and acquisition of commercial real estate.
3. For example, this strategy is typical for many Japanese automotive firms.
4. For a comparison to other industrialized countries, see OECD (1992) and Bailey *et al.* (1994).
5. In Dunning's terminology (see Chapter 1), these measures may be characterized as macro-organizational policies, since they are designed to affect the structure rather than the level of economic activity.
6. In firms with more than 500 employees one-third, and in firms with more than 2,000 employees half, of supervisory board members must be employees or employee representatives.
7. The activities of the Treuhandanstalt are extensively documented in Treuhandanstalt (1994).
8. For a detailed view of governmental incentives to motivate outward investment, see BMWi (1994a, 1995).
9. This issue is taken up further in Chapter 16.

REFERENCES

Bailey, D., Harte, G. and Sudgen, R. (1994), *Transnationals and Governments* (London: Routledge).

Bartlett, C. A., and Ghoshal, S. (1989), *Managing across Borders: The Transnational Solution* (Boston: Harvard Business School Press).

Berg, H. (1992), 'Wettbewerbspolitik', in D. Bender *et al.* (eds.), *Vahlens Kompendium der Wirtschaftstheorie und Wirtschaftspolitik* (5th edn., Munich: Vahlen), ii. 239–300.

—— and Müller, J. (1990), 'Unfriendly Takeovers: Ursachen, Formen und Wettbewerbswirkungen', *Das Wirtschaftsstudium*, 19/11: 647–52.

Beyfuß, J. (1992), *Ausländische Direktinvestitionen in Deutschland: Bestandsaufnahme und Ergebnisse einer Unternehmensbefragung* (Cologne: Deutscher Instituts-Verlag).

—— and Kitterer, B. H.-J. (1990), *Deutsche Direktinvestitionen im Ausland: Bestandsaufnahme und Ergebnisse einer Unternehmensbefragung* (Cologne: Deutscher Instituts-Verlag).

BMWi (1994*a*): Bundesministerium für Wirtschaft, *Maßnahmen zur Förderung deutscher Direktinvestitionen in den Ländern Mittel- und Osteuropas (MOE) und in den Neuen Unabhängigen Staaten der ehemaligen Sowjetunion (NUS)* (BMWi Dokumentation No. 347; Bonn: BMWi).

—— (1994*b*), *Neuere Entwicklungen und Perspektiven für Direktinvestitionen* (BMWi Dokumentation No. 363; Bonn: BMWi).

—— (1995), *Maßnahmen zur Förderung deutscher Direktinvestitionen im Ausland (ohne Osteuropa)* (BMWi Dokumentation No. 365; Bonn: BMWi).

Böttcher, R. (1996), *Global Network Management* (Wiesbaden: Gabler).

Bundeskartellamt (1991), *Arbeitsunterlage für die Sitzung des Arbeitskreises Kartellrecht am 7. und 8. Oktober 1991.*

Deppe, J. (1992) (ed.), *Euro-Betriebsräte* (Wiesbaden: Gabler).

DIHT (1993): Deutscher Industrie- und Handelstag, *Produktionsverlagerung ins Ausland* (Bonn: DIHT).

Dunning, J. H. (1992), 'The Competitive Advantage of Countries and the Activities of Transnational Corporations', *Transnational Corporations*, 1/1: 135–68.

—— (1993*a*), 'Internationalizing Porters's Diamond', *Management International Review*, 33 (Special Issue), 7–15.

—— (1993*b*), *Multinational Enterprises and the Global Economy* (Wokingham: Addison Wesley).

—— (1994), *Globalization, Economic Restructuring and Development* (The 6th Prebisch Lecture; Geneva: UNCTAD).

Hedlund, G. (1993), 'Assumptions of Hierarchy and Heterarchy, with Applications to the Management of the Multinational Corporation', in S. Ghoshal and D. E. Westney (eds.), *Organization Theory and the Multinational Corporation* (New York: St Martin's Press), 211–36.

—— and Rolander, D. (1990), 'Action in Heterarchies: New Approaches to Managing the MNC', in C. A. Bartlett, Y. Doz, and G. Hedlund (eds.), *Managing the Global Firm* (New York: Routledge), 15–46.

Holtbrügge, D. (1995), *Personalmanagement Multinationaler Unternehmungen in Osteuropa. Bedingungen—Gestaltung—Effizienz* (Wiesbaden: Gabler).

Institut der deutschen Wirtschaft (1994), *Industriestandort Deutschland. Ein graphisches Portrait* (Cologne: Deutscher Instituts-Verlag).

Kogut, B. (1989), 'A Note on Global Strategies', *Strategic Management Journal*, 16: 383–9.

Langhammer, R. J., and Paqué, K.-H. (1994), *Die Folgen des Welthandels: Ein nüchterner Blick in die Zukunft* (Kiel: Institut für Weltwirtschaft).

McGrew, B. G. (1992), 'Conceptualizing Global Politics', in B. G. McGrew and P. G. Lewis (eds.), *Global Politics: Globalization and the Nation State* (Cambridge: Polity Press).

Nonaka, I. (1988), 'Creating Organizational Order out of Chaos: Self-Renewal in Japanese Firms', *California Management Review*, 30 (Spring), 57–73.

Nunnenkamp, P., Gundlach, E., and Agarwal, J. P. (1994), *Globalisation of Products and Markets* (Tübingen: J. C. B. Mohr).

OECD (1992): Organization for Economic Cooperation and Development, *Internationale Direktinvestitionen: Politik und Trends der 80er Jahre* (Paris: OECD).

—— (1994), *Financial Market Trends* (Paris: OECD).

Ohmae, K. (1987), 'The Triad World View', *Journal of Business Strategy*, 7/4: 8–19.

—— (1989), 'Managing in a Borderless World', *Harvard Business Review*, 67/3: 152–61.

Perlmutter, H. V. (1969), 'The Tortuous Evolution of the Multinational Corporation', *Columbia Journal of World Business*, 4: 9–18.

Porter, M. E. (1986), 'Competition in Global Industries: A Conceptual Framework', in M. E. Porter (ed.), *Competition in Global Industries* (Boston: Harvard Business School Press), 15–60.

—— (1990), *The Competitive Advantage of Nations* (New York: The Free Press).

Rolfe, R. J., Ricks, D. A., Pointer, M. M., and McCarthy, M. (1993), 'Determinants of FDI Incentive Preferences of MNEs', *Journal of International Business Studies*, 24/2: 335–55.

Rugman, A. M., and Verbeke, A. (1993), 'Foreign Subsidiaries and Multinational Strategic Management: An Extension and Correction of Porter's Single Diamond Framework', *Management International Review*, 33 (Special Issue), 71–84.

Steinkühler, F. (1992), 'Veränderungen in Europa und ihre Auswirkungen auf die Tarifpolitik', *Personal*, 1: 10–16.

Tejima, S. (1995), 'Future Trends in Japanese Foreign Direct Investment', *Transnational Corporations*, 4/1: 84–96.

Treuhandanstalt (1994), *Dokumentation Treuhandanstalt 1990–1994* (Berlin: Treuhandanstalt).

Vernon, R. (1979), 'International Investment and International Trade in the Product Cycle', *Quarterly Journal of Economics*, 80/2: 190–207.

Waragai, T. (1993), 'Das japanische Engagement in den neuen Bundesländern', *Zeitschrift für Betriebswirtschaft*, 63/11: 1169–79.

Welge, M. K. (1990), 'Globales Management', in M. K. Welge (ed.), *Globales Management: Erfolgreiche Strategien für den Weltmarkt* (Stuttgart: Poeschel), 1–16.

—— (1995), 'Strategische Allianzen', in B. Tietz *et al.* (eds.), *Handwörterbuch des Marketing* (2nd edn.) (Stuttgart: Schäffer-Poeschel), 2397–410.

—— and Holtbrügge, D. (1993), 'Effects of Foreign Direct Investment on Employment in the Former "Centrally Planned Economies" of Central and Eastern Europe', in P. Bailey, A. Parisotto, and G. Renshaw (eds.), *Multinationals and Employment: The Global Economy of the 1990s* (Geneva: International Labour Office), 215–236.

Zwickel, K. (1994), 'Zukunft der Arbeit am Industriestandort Deutschland: Konsequenzen aus der Tarifrunde 1994', *Gewerkschaftliche Monatshefte*, 45/6: 381–9.

12

Sweden

Magnus Blomström and Ari Kokko

1. Introduction

Although Sweden has been ruled by left-wing governments during most of the post-war period, the country has never been able to afford much of inward-orientation, public ownership, and state planning. Instead, productive efficiency and a liberal trade environment have been the cornerstones of Swedish economic policies. In fact, until the early 1990s, the Swedish political climate and the country's economic policies were characterized by consensus and compromise between labour and big business. This unusual macro-organizational setting facilitated the internationalization of Swedish industry in two ways. First, industrial policy supported growth with a strong bias in favour of large firms: given the limited size of the domestic market, the response of large firms was often to grow even larger by expanding foreign operations. Secondly, unlike labour unions in many other parts of the world, the Swedish labour movement did not oppose investment abroad by Swedish multinational enterprises (MNEs). The establishment of foreign affiliates was instead seen as a necessity to keep foreign competitors at stake: even leading Social Democratic politicians argued that 'what is good for Volvo is good for Sweden'. At the same time, the trade unions' attitudes towards inward investment by foreign MNEs were less benign. The country's formal FDI regulations, largely formulated by Social Democratic governments, clearly revealed this asymmetry, with rules concerning inward FDI being significantly more restrictive than those regarding Swedish investment abroad.

By the early 1990s, both these characteristics of the Swedish model had begun to fade. As a result of the increasing globalization of Swedish industry, it is not obvious any more that what is good for large Swedish MNEs, such as Volvo, is also good for Sweden: many MNEs have become so international that they may well decide to exploit innovations and other growth opportunities in their foreign affiliates, rather than at home. In the dim light of the waning Swedish welfare state, where high unemployment has become a serious problem, it is also uncertain whether the labour movement can afford to continue supporting Swedish investment abroad and opposing inward FDI. In addition, the restrictive policies regarding inward FDI began to converge towards those of other European countries during the early 1990s, in preparation for the Swedish accession to the EU.

The purpose of this chapter is to describe the traditional Swedish model of industrial policy and FDI policy, to discuss why the trade unions were so positive towards Swedish investment abroad, and to speculate about the reasons for the changes that have occurred or are under way. In doing this, we shall also illustrate some of the channels through which governments and institutions influence the globalization of private firms.

Anticipating some of the main conclusions, it can be noted that Swedish macro-organizational policy has focused on productive and scale efficiency rather than anti-trust issues, which has facilitated the growth of large firms and oligopolies at the expense of small and medium-sized firms. Competition has been upheld by free trade policies. Once these large firms have exhausted their domestic market opportunities, multinational expansion has been the next step. The focus on large companies and FDI has also been supported by the labour movement. The trade unions' positive views regarding outward FDI seem to have been born from the combination of large centralized labour unions, a welfare state with low unemployment as a major policy objective, and a legal framework guaranteeing union participation in the management of large companies. These factors contributed to reduce the perceived risk of large job losses in Sweden as a result of FDI. The sceptical attitudes towards inward FDI were probably also related to the full employment policies—it was not necessary to try to attract foreign investment for employment reasons—and to the fear that foreign owners would be less willing or able to allow union participation in company decisions. This latter fear arose because not only are the major decisions in foreign-owned firms taken far from Sweden, but the foreign owners may also be less interested in consensus and compromise.

The remainder of the chapter is organized as follows. The next section discusses the role of inward and outward investment for the Swedish economy. Section 3 looks at Swedish industrial policy, and its role for the globalization of Swedish industry. Section 4 focuses on the Swedish labour movement's attitudes towards FDI. Section 5 concludes the chapter by discussing why the Swedish model of FDI policy began to fade away in the late 1980s.

2. The Role of FDI for the Swedish Economy

Both inward and outward FDI have played significant roles for the structure and development of the Swedish economy, although their relative weights have varied over time. Investment abroad has been of great importance for the competitiveness of the leading Swedish companies since the beginning of the twentieth century. Several of today's Swedish MNEs had already established foreign affiliates before the First World War, although the great expansion of foreign operations did not occur until the 1970s and, particularly, the 1980s. Inward investment by foreign companies and individuals was most important before the First World War, but the inflows were also significant during the 1960s, and have grown again during the last decade or so. Yet, in aggregate, it is clear that Sweden has been more important as a home country than as a host country to

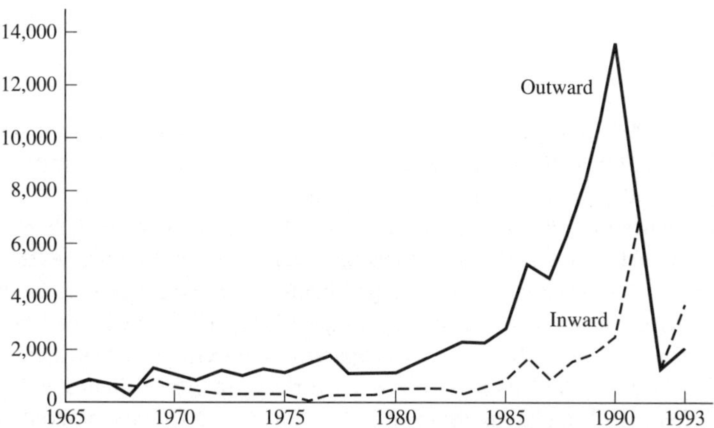

Source: Central Bank of Sweden

FIG 12.1. Inflows and outflows of Swedish FDI, 1965–1993 (Million SEK, fixed 1968 prices)

MNEs. Fig. 12.1, which plots the inward and outward FDI flows during the period 1965–93, shows that the inward investment flows have rarely been comparable to the outward flows.

One reason for the asymmetry, of course, is that Sweden is a small country, and therefore not very attractive as a location for market-seeking FDI. Another reason is that the regulations on inward FDI have been rather restrictive, whereas outward FDI has been promoted by the country's macro-organizational policies, and even by its trade unions. In this section, we outline the growth and structure of outward and inward FDI, and the development of the legal framework for FDI.

2.1. **Outward Investment**

Considering that Sweden is a relatively small country, accounting for less than 1 per cent of the world's GDP, it is home to a remarkable number of large multinationals. An indication of this is that seventeen Swedish MNEs were among the world's 600 largest multinationals in the mid-1980s, which is a high figure even compared to other small, outward-oriented economies such as The Netherlands or Switzerland (UNCTC 1988).[1] In the early 1990s Swedish MNEs accounted for 4 per cent of the world's FDI stock (Olsson 1993). Only three countries—the UK, the Netherlands, and Switzerland—had a higher ratio of outward-FDI stock to GDP at that time (Andersson *et al.* 1996).

Another characteristic feature of Swedish FDI is that the population of large MNEs has remained rather stable over time. Several of today's leading companies, such as Alfa Laval, AGA, SKF, and Ericsson, had grown beyond the national market and become multinational before the First World War. All but one of the twenty largest manufacturing MNEs had already established foreign production affiliates in the 1960s. These top twenty companies account for more than 75 per cent of the foreign employment in Swedish-owned firms, although the total number of Swedish firms with foreign operations is well above 600 (NUTEK 1994). The largest MNEs also hold a strong position in Swedish industry, with more than 50 per cent of the country's total exports and industrial labour force, and 90 per cent of the industrial R&D.

The ownership advantages allowing Swedish firms to extend their international boundaries have almost always been related to technology. A few of the earliest Swedish multinationals emerged thanks to a few major innovations, and have subsequently created a broader range of expertise—SKF (ball bearings), AGA (beacons), and Alfa Laval (the separator) are examples of such companies, and they had all established extensive networks of foreign affiliates within a few years after their foundation.[2] Several of the leading MNEs have based their competitiveness on the long Swedish tradition of metal manufacturing, and gradually moved to more advanced industries, such as sophisticated machinery and transport equipment. A few of the best-known engineering and electronics firms, such as Ericsson (telephones), ASEA (electrical equipment, turbines), Atlas Copco (drilling equipment), and Volvo and SAAB-Scania (transport equipment), belong to this category. A third group comprises MNEs that have drawn directly on abundant local raw materials, such as wood and ferrous metals, and stayed close to their original industry, such as Sandvik (metal products) and Assi-Domän, Stora, and SCA (pulp and paper). The MNEs in the pharmaceutical and medical-equipment sectors (Astra, Gambro, Pharmacia) make up a fourth group, with their strength based on the country's scientific tradition and human-capital resources. This pattern with technology as the main competitive advantage of Swedish MNEs' is still discernible, although some firms now rely heavily on the sales networks created to exploit some initial technological asset (Olsson 1993). Industrial policies supporting the growth and development of large firms that can invest heavily in R&D have enabled many of the old MNEs to stay competitive in spite of changing technologies and market conditions.

Table 12.1 illustrates the industry distribution of Swedish manufacturing FDI, and it can be seen that the electrical and non-electrical machinery categories are quite dominant. Swedish MNEs in the service sector have been less successful, and their foreign employment is only about one-tenth of that in manufacturing MNEs (NUTEK 1994).

The most important reasons for Swedish investment abroad have been to reduce transportation costs, to avoid formal and informal trade barriers, and to get closer to foreign customers (Jordan and Vahlne 1981). Swedish MNEs have rarely invested abroad to secure foreign raw-material supplies, nor has access to cheap foreign labour been an important argument, except in the garment industry after the 1960s (Swedenborg 1979). In other words, market access has been the central motive for FDI. Foreign production has often been considered necessary even where formal trade barriers have been low, to facilitate the development of products that are suited to specific national preferences or product standards,

TABLE 12.1. Sectoral distribution of Swedish manufacturing FDI, producing affiliates, 1970–1990 (%)

	Employment			Total assets		
	1970	1986	1990	1970	1986	1990
Food products	1	1	<1	1	1	<1
Textiles	2	<1	1	1	0	<1
Pulp, paper, and paper products	4	11	18	10	14	23
Chemicals	14	11	10	8	10	15
Metals	10	9	14	13	7	12
Electrical and non-electrical machinery	61	56	48	59	55	39
Transport equipment	2	7	7	4	9	8
Other	6	4	3	6	3	3
TOTAL	100	100	100	100	100	100
Total number of employees	182,087	258,823	316,308			
Total assets, (SEK m.)				15,396	142,854	225,696

Source: Calculated from Andersson *et al.* (1996).

and to avoid discrimination in, for example, public procurement. Sometimes, foreign production has even been an outright requirement, particularly for companies such as ASEA, AGA, and Ericsson (selling e.g. hydro-electric plants, lighthouses, and telephone systems), since their customers are often public authorities that worry about local content and local employment.

The growth of Swedish MNEs has largely coincided with expanding international trade, and the foreign investment has typically targeted the fastest-growing markets. Before the First World War, the main location for Swedish FDI was Europe, and, in particular, Russia. The Russian revolution meant that many of the subsidiaries were nationalized without compensation, but the foreign investments of Swedish firms continued elsewhere during the 1920s. As a result, Sweden became, for the first time, a net exporter of capital. The investments were directed not only to Europe, but increasingly to the USA and Latin America. At the end of the 1920s at least fifty Swedish companies were operating foreign production affiliates (Lundström 1986). The more protectionistic international environment of the 1930s slowed down the foreign expansion. The positive correlation between FDI and trade suggests that the two were probably complements, so that Swedish exports and employment benefited from the foreign operations of the MNEs.

The outflow of FDI did not pick up again until the 1960s (although the introduction of import substitution in Latin America after the Second World War had motivated several companies to establish local production in order to avoid tariffs). At that time, continental Europe became the most important investment location. The main reason appears to have been the formation of the EC and the emerging Common Market: Swedish industry regarded it as necessary to invest within the tariff walls in order to get access to the market (Olsson 1993).

Until the late 1960s outward FDI had not been restricted by government policies: the Central Bank had monitored FDI applications since the 1940s, but mainly in order to ensure that the transaction was a direct investment and not a portfolio investment. In 1969, however, new exchange controls were introduced because of a deteriorating balance-of-payments position. Investment licences were to be granted only if the FDI project could be expected to have a positive impact on the balance of payments, or on the investing company's market position or development potential. In 1974 the exchange regulations were amended, and the opportunities to finance FDI by borrowing in the domestic capital market were severely restricted. Moreover, it was stipulated that licence applications could be denied if the FDI project caused 'exceptional damage' to the national economy—for example, by significantly reducing Swedish employment or by moving strategic company functions abroad (SOU 1980). The trade unions were regularly consulted during the licence administration process, both because their opinions were needed to determine the employment effects of the projects, and to ascertain that they were informed about the foreign-investment plans. Yet, the implementation of the exchange controls was liberal, and it is estimated that only 1 per cent of the licence applications during the second half of the 1970s were denied. These were mainly small projects that would have moved management, financing, and R&D functions abroad (SOU 1980). Hence, the regulations did not stop the growth in outward FDI, and the aggregate outflows doubled during each successive five-year period from 1960 to 1985.

However, the geographical pattern of Swedish FDI flows changed from the early 1970s. In 1972 a free-trade agreement was negotiated between the EC and EFTA (of which Sweden was a member), and this seems to have reduced Swedish industry's need to establish local production in the EC countries. At the same time, the European economies began to suffer from stagflation and *Eurosclerosis*, while the US economy continued growing at a steady pace. Consequently, the USA became the main target for FDI, and the value of the production by Swedish subsidiaries in the USA grew by a factor of eight between 1978 and 1986 (Blomström *et al.* 1989).

Market access also appears to have been a major determinant of the even larger increases in FDI outflows that occurred in the late 1980s. At that time, decisions were taken to deepen the economic integration of the EC countries, and the Single European Market was beginning to emerge. However, there were no signs that Sweden would seek membership in the EC—the membership application was not submitted until several years later, in July 1991. As had been the case in the 1960s, Swedish companies feared that their competitiveness in the Single Market would suffer if they stayed outside. Partly as a response to this

TABLE 12.2. Geographical distribution of Swedish manufacturing FDI, producing affiliates, 1970–1990 (%)

	Employment			Total assets		
	1970	1986	1990	1970	1986	1990
Developed economies	80	83	87	85	91	93
EC12	60	51	56	62	49	63
EC6	45	36	36	47	36	44
EC3	12	11	16	11	10	14
EFTA	10	8	5	10	8	6
North America	7	21	22	12	32	21
USA	5	19	21	7	30	19
Other developed	5	4	3	4	3	3
Developing economies	20	17	13	15	9	7
Latin America	12	12	10	12	8	6
Africa & Asia	8	5	3	3	1	1
TOTAL	100	100	100	100	100	100

Note:
EC6 = Belgium, France, Italy, Luxembourg, Netherlands, Germany.
EC3 = Denmark, Ireland, UK.
EC12 = EC6 + EC3 + Greece, Portugal, Spain.
EFTA = Austria, Finland, Norway, Switzerland.

Source: Calculated from Andersson *et al.* (1996).

threat, the Swedish direct investments in the EC area expanded rapidly, going from a total of SEK 22 billion during the period 1981–6 to SEK 128 billion during the next four years, as shown in Fig. 12.1. Most of this was in the form of acquisitions of British, Dutch, and German companies. Table 12.2 illustrates the changes in the geographical distribution of Swedish FDI. In particular, the table shows the increasing importance of the USA between 1970 and 1986, and the recovery of the EC area after 1986.

It is impossible to determine exactly how much of the FDI boom of the late 1980s was due to the formation of the Single Market, and how much was caused by other factors. The reason is that the period was also characterized by a peak in the Swedish business cycle, with high profits and liquidity in industry, full employment, shortages of skilled labour, high property prices, and a strong Krona, all of which made foreign investment appear easier and more attractive than domestic expansion. Moreover, in 1986, the Swedish controls on international capital movements were liberalized, which in essence meant that there were no more obstacles to outward investment.

2.2. **Inward Investment**

Many foreign firms—mainly from Denmark, Germany, the Netherlands, Norway, and the UK—invested in Sweden during the late nineteenth century, when the country's industrialization was just taking off. Since Sweden was several decades behind these countries in terms of overall industrial development, the foreign investors made important contributions in the fields of technology, management, and marketing and distribution. A significant share of the foreign entrepreneurs also settled permanently in the country, which probably enhanced the positive impact of their investments on Swedish development. Shortly after the turn of the century, it was estimated that there were foreign owners in about a quarter of the industrial firms in Sweden, although only a few companies had foreign majority-owners (Johansson 1968).[3]

However, the increasing foreign ownership of Swedish industry was soon accompanied by fears about diminishing national independence, particularly in connection with foreign acquisitions of Swedish natural resources, such as forest and minerals. For instance, German companies had acquired several mines in the central parts of Sweden during the years before the First World War, and the subsequent shipments of iron ore and other minerals to the German war industry worried the Swedish authorities. Consequently, in order to protect the Swedish natural resources, a law was passed in 1916 to restrict foreign acquisitions of real estate and to prohibit the granting of mining concessions to foreigners. The law was applicable not only to foreign subjects, but also to Swedish companies without so-called 'foreign-ownership restriction clauses'—that is, rules in the company's Articles of Association limiting foreign ownership to 40 per cent of the capital and 20 per cent of the voting power. In addition, the Swedish Companies Act required Swedish citizenship for the executive officers in newly established companies.

The restrictions brought an end to FDI in resource-based activities, but foreign investment in other sectors continued, although the inflows were small until the 1960s. In 1962 foreign companies had significant ownership stakes (i.e. above 10 per cent of the capital) in nearly 500 Swedish firms, employing some 62,000 people (Johansson 1968). About 22,500 people, or 2.5 per cent of the industrial labour force, were employed in majority-owned foreign manufacturing affiliates (SOU 1987). The foreign investments were mainly found in the engineering, chemical, and food-products industries, and in wholesale trade and other services. The USA, the UK, Denmark, and the Netherlands were the leading foreign investors—the German share was low because many German investments had been liquidated, nationalized, or taken over by Swedish companies during and after the Second World War.

The inflows of FDI increased markedly during the 1960s. By 1970 the employment in majority-owned foreign affiliates in Sweden had grown to about 86,000. Slightly less than half of these jobs were in manufacturing, which means that the industrial employment share of foreign firms had nearly doubled in eight years, to 4.5 per cent (Samuelsson 1977).[4] This increase, which was largely the result of foreign acquisitions of Swedish firms, triggered a new debate on the possible negative consequences of foreign ownership of domestic assets, and prompted a revision of the 1916 law on foreign acquisition of Swedish real estate. In 1973 the law was amended to require authorization for all foreign acquisitions of Swedish firms (even those without real-estate holdings) and it was decreed that changes in the foreign-ownership restriction clauses of Swedish companies would also require permission. In addition, exchange controls regulated foreign investment and restricted foreign access to the local capital market: although investment permissions were almost always granted, 50 per cent of the capital had to be sourced abroad.

In spite of these restrictions, inward FDI continued at a moderate level through the 1970s and the first half of the 1980s. By 1985 the aggregate employment in foreign subsidiaries had grown above 140,000, and their employment share in industry was around 9 per cent. The debate on the effects of FDI also continued during this time, both at the legislative level and among other interest groups. For instance, the government commissioned several detailed studies on ownership concentration and international investment flows (SOU 1982, 1983), and the labour movement had already adopted a more restrictive attitude towards foreign investment in the mid-1970s (LO 1976). In addition, the existing regulations on inward investment were reviewed, and the amended 1916 law was replaced by two new laws in 1983.

According to the new Act on foreign acquisitions of Swedish enterprises, prior authorization was required each time a foreigner or a Swedish company without foreign-ownership restriction clauses intended to increase its ownership share of a Swedish enterprise beyond certain levels (10, 20, 40, or 50 per cent of the capital or votes of the enterprise). Authorization was granted on condition that the investment was not 'contrary to the public interest': occasionally, this meant that investment permits were made contingent on specific performance requirements. The Act on foreign acquisitions of real estate contained similar requirements, although it appears to have been more liberal when applied to property used for business purposes. Together with the exchange controls discussed above, and the nationality requirements in the Companies Act, it can be said that these rather restrictive regulations made up the policy concerning inward investment. Concurrently, controls on outward investment were significantly less restrictive, as noted earlier. This asymmetry between attitudes and policies regarding outward and inward FDI—together with the corresponding asymmetry between outward and inward investment flows—is what we refer to when talking about the 'Swedish model' of FDI and FDI policy.

From the late 1980s, several factors contributed to erode the restrictions on inward investment. The exchange regulations were liberalized in two stages, in 1986 and 1990, and the Act on foreign acquisitions of Swedish businesses was abolished in 1992. The nationality requirements in the Companies Act were dropped the same year. The main motive has officially been the wish to adapt to OECD recommendations, but it is likely that the increasing globalization of Swedish industry was also important: the large Swedish investments abroad during the late 1980s made it difficult to defend the restrictive policies at home (Andersson and Fredriksson 1993). Moreover, it is possible that the increasing

TABLE 12.3. Sectoral distribution of inward FDI: Majority-owned foreign affiliates' shares of total employment in Sweden, 1980–1992 (%)

	1980	1985	1990	1992
Mining and manufacturing				
Food products	12	16	19	22
Textiles	8	4	6	11
Wood products	1	2	3	2
Pulp and paper	3	5	8	8
Chemicals	12	16	22	26
Non-metallic minerals	8	13	33	31
Basic metals	5	4	6	16
Engineering	7	10	16	19
Services				
Wholesale trade	19	19	20	22
Retail, hotels, restaurants	1	2	2	2
Communication	3	4	5	5
Banking, insurance, consultancy	2	5	5	5
Other services	3	5	4	10
TOTAL BUSINESS SECTOR	5	7	9	10

Source: NUTEK (1994).

number of cross-border alliances—such as the equity links between ASEA and Brown Boveri, and SAAB and GM—demonstrated the need to reform the Swedish regulations. This type of strategic alliance, which was discouraged by the restrictions on inward FDI, has arguably been essential for the international competitiveness of many Swedish MNEs.

The liberalizations were followed by significant increases in the inflows of FDI. In 1992 there were 2,700 foreign-owned companies in Sweden, employing a total of 224,000 people. More than half of these were found in manufacturing industry, where the foreign-employment share reached 17 per cent. Table 12.3 illustrates the development of the foreign ownership of different sectors of Swedish industry between 1980 and 1992.

The lifting of restrictions was probably not the only explanation for the expansion in foreign ownership: for instance, the Swedish decision to apply for EU membership, announced in 1991, may have made the country more attractive for foreign investors, and the large depreciation of the Swedish Krona in 1992 undoubtedly reduced the foreign-currency prices of Swedish assets. Yet, it is clear that the changing institutional environment has been important, particularly since it has been accompanied by much more positive views regarding the potential benefits of inward FDI (Fredriksson 1994; NUTEK 1994). In fact, the prospect of becoming a more attractive host country for FDI was presented as one of the strongest economic arguments in favour of Swedish EU membership during debates in 1993 and 1994 (Kokko 1994). Another sign of the change in official attitudes was the establishment of an investment promotion agency, Invest in

Sweden, in 1995. Consequently, the foreign acquisitions of Swedish companies have continued at a high level since the early 1990s, and investment inflows surpassed the outflows in both 1993 and 1994. This had not happened since the 1960s.

3. Swedish Macro-Organizational Policy

As noted earlier, Sweden is a small, open economy with a disproportionate number of big successful multinationals. Companies like Volvo, SAAB, Ericsson, ASEA (ABB), and SKF, to mention but a few, are well known worldwide, and Sweden has more companies among the world's leading MNEs than many larger economies such as Italy, Spain, the Netherlands, and Switzerland. Thus, Sweden is a highly concentrated economy where big business thrives, but the flip side of the coin is that it is difficult for new companies to grow large and challenge the incumbents. The reason has largely been the Swedish macro-organizational (and particularly industrial) policies.

By tradition, Swedish industrial policy has stressed the importance of large firms that are able to survive in international competition (Hjalmarsson 1991). In large economies such as the USA or the UK, macro-organizational policy has been influenced by anti-trust ideas that stress competition in domestic factor and product markets. Small countries like Sweden can rarely afford that, because the domestic market can seldom accommodate a large number of efficient firms. Instead, the focus on market structure in the anti-trust tradition has been replaced by a focus on the efficient use of resources within the firm and structural efficiency—that is, the efficiency of an entire industry structure. Achieving economies of scale has been more important than avoiding oligopolies—at the same time, free trade and competition from imports have been promoted to counterbalance the concentrated industry structure. The main policy instruments to achieve these goals have been tax policy, credit market regulations, and R&D policy.

Before the Swedish tax system was reformed in 1991, it was obvious that large established corporations were supported by the tax system, at the expense of younger, smaller, and less capital-intensive enterprises (Mutén 1968). Until about 1990, the formal corporate tax rates were quite high, between 50 and 62 per cent, but there was a large gap between formal and effective rates. The reason was that generous deductions and allowances could be made for investment in machinery, equipment, and inventories, and untaxed profits could be put aside in special investment funds for future use. The main beneficiaries were capital-intensive firms that could make large allowances, and large diversified companies that could cross-subsidize loss-making activities at very low real cost. At the same time, dividends distributed to shareholders were taxed at extremely high marginal rates. This provided another motive for successful companies to grow larger: profits distributed to shareholders would be taxed twice (once as company profit and once as the shareholder's personal income), whereas profits used for investment or to acquire a small competitor would be taxed once or often not at all. Even the shareholders approved, since the increase in the value of their shares was typically larger than the dividend net of taxes (Mutén 1968; Davis and Henrekson 1995).

The regulation of the Swedish credit market has also favoured big business at the expense of small firms. During the whole post-war period, until the end of the 1980s, the Swedish credit market was highly regulated. The development of the welfare state meant that much credit was channelled to the public sector. Housing and construction were also priority sectors, with guaranteed access to funds and subsidized interest rates. However, lending to industry and commerce was often subject to quantitative restrictions, because the priority sectors absorbed much of the available funds and because interest rates were regulated. With this type of restrictions, it was inevitable that commercial banks directed most of their lending to the larger, older, and more successful companies, and to capital-intensive firms that could easily provide collateral (Davis and Henrekson 1995).

Moreover, various measures have been undertaken to encourage Swedish industry to increase its spending on R&D, particularly since 1967, when the Ministry of Industry was created. For example, tax incentives were introduced that allowed companies to make extra deductions for the costs of R&D and various government funds were created to encourage the build-up of competence in enterprises. In 1968 the National Board of Technical Development (STU) was created to support technical research projects, cooperative research, and industrial development. Several areas, such as space technology, energy research, and micro-electronics, have also received special attention during different times. Partly as a result of the public-sector support to industry research, the R&D intensity of Swedish industry is now among the world's highest. It is mainly big business that benefits from these policies, since R&D are activities with very distinct economies of scale. Of the aggregate industrial R&D undertaken in Sweden in the early 1990s, 80 per cent was allocated to four product fields. Three of these fields—transport equipment, electro-technical products, and pharmaceuticals—were dominated by six company groups (NUTEK 1994).

Another channel for Swedish macro-organizational policy has been the direct contacts between the government and leading industrial corporations. In several advanced sectors, such as infrastructure and telecommunications, the government has been the major Swedish customer, and has taken an active role in product and technology development. MNEs such as Ericsson (telecommunications) and ASEA (power plants and high-speed trains) have benefited from this type of interaction, and they have subsequently been able to market the technological innovations abroad, through both direct exports and foreign production.

In summary, it is clear that Swedish macro-organizational policy has supported the development of a highly concentrated industry structure, with large, efficient firms that devote considerable resources to R&D. These industry and firm characteristics are also strong determinants of the high level of internationalization of Swedish industry. Concentrated domestic markets provide important motives to expand operations abroad (Hymer 1976). To become and to remain a successful MNE, the candidate must also possess some firm-specific competitive asset, such as technology, that allows it to survive in tough foreign markets.

4. The Trade Unions' Views

The close connection between macro-organizational policy, large corporations, and FDI has always been supported by the Swedish trade unions. As early as in the 1920s, the central blue-collar union, LO, promoted a productivity-enhancing industrial policy, emphasizing rationalization of firms. In a Trade Union Congress Report from 1930 one can, for instance, read the following: 'Trade unions should promote the planned development of industry, its structural rationalization into larger units, the financial reorganization, and the substitution of old machinery and methods by new plants and innovations' (Fackföreningsrörelsen 1930: 30). While labour organizations in most other countries have opposed outward investment because they have feared job losses and technological erosion, Swedish labour has had a more positive attitude and even encouraged FDI (Hedlund and Otterbeck 1977). Concurrently, Swedish trade unions have been much more sceptical regarding inward FDI, although this could be expected to provide both jobs and technology. The trade unions' perspectives on FDI have been important determinants of the character of the Swedish FDI policies, thanks to their close connections with the ruling Social Democratic Party (Hjalmarsson 1991).

From an academic perspective, the positive view of foreign investment may appear rational, since many studies—both in Sweden and elsewhere—have concluded that the impact of outward FDI on home-country exports and employment is beneficial (see Blomström and Kokko 1994 for a survey of results). The establishment of foreign-production affiliates leads to significant increases in the MNE's foreign market shares, thanks to better contacts with foreign customers. The rising foreign sales boost home-country exports of intermediate products to the affiliates, who require inputs from their parent companies or other firms in the home country. The increases in exports of intermediates are typically large enough to make up for the losses of parent exports to independent customers in the host country. However, it is peculiar that only Swedish labour seems to base its FDI policies on these results.

The reason for the pro-FDI attitudes of the Swedish labour movement is probably to be found in the specific institutional environment of Sweden. Three characteristic features of the Swedish labour market seem to be of central importance. First, Swedish labour is highly organized in a few centralized trade unions. Secondly, the Swedish welfare state has had low unemployment as its main policy objective. Thirdly, the Swedish labour laws have, for a long time, guaranteed worker participation in the management of even the largest MNEs.

The structure of the trade unions, with one strong, centralized organization for all blue-collar workers, has meant that policies have aimed at maximizing the benefits of labour at the national level, rather than at local or company levels.

Hence, the fact that aggregate employment in industry has tended to grow with FDI has had a larger influence on the union's official attitudes than the fact that some jobs in the later stages of the production chain have moved abroad. Moreover, the new jobs created as a result of FDI have typically been 'better' than those lost to foreign affiliates: the labour productivity in the MNEs' home-country operations has been significantly higher than that in the foreign affiliates (Andersson 1993).

The full employment policies that have been pursued by all Swedish governments from the 1930s to the 1990s have also facilitated the unions' objectives to maximize national rather than local welfare. The negative employment effects of FDI at the plant level have usually not been considered as very serious problems by the trade-union leaders, since the workers laid off have seldom had any problems finding new jobs.[5] If suitable jobs were not available in industry, the unemployed workers could almost always find jobs in the expanding public sector. The worker participation in management, finally, has given the trade unions an opportunity to veto or to delay FDI decisions that have threatened to cause serious job losses. In addition, the trade unions were represented in the Central Bank's Currency Board, which was responsible for the administration of exchange controls and FDI licences. Taken together, these institutional arrangements meant that the labour organizations did not perceive very large risks of job losses in connection with Swedish investment abroad. In particular, it was felt that a generally positive attitude to FDI was feasible, since the unions could always respond individually to the least beneficial FDI cases.

Regarding inward FDI, the Swedish trade unions' attitudes have been very cautious, if not outright negative, although the positive employment effects of inward investment should benefit union objectives. However, as a result of the Social Democratic economic policies, unemployment has been extremely low until recently, which may explain why the unions have not appeared eager to attract foreign investment. Another reason for the low priority given to employment creation is that most inward FDI has come in the form of acquisitions of existing companies, rather than as greenfield investments, which makes it difficult to distinguish the net effects on Swedish employment.

The labour movement's suspicious sentiments against foreign investors may also be culturally determined: the foreigners have not always adopted the Swedish traditions of compromise and consensus management, but instead applied more authoritarian management styles. In fact, it appears that the Swedish labour unions are less negatively inclined towards foreign investors from countries with similar labour market traditions, such as the other Nordic countries, than towards American, British, or Dutch investors.

Another reason for disliking inward foreign investment is that the owners of foreign companies are based outside Sweden, which makes it hard for the labour organizations to participate in strategic decisions—the managers of the Swedish subsidiary are seldom the primary decision-makers, but rather representatives with limited power. If the subsidiaries in Sweden make up only a small share of the foreign MNEs' operations, it is also clear that the bargaining position of Swedish labour is relatively weak. Similarly, US trade unions have been opposed to inward FDI, since they have felt that foreign ownership weakens their bargaining position (Bergsten *et al.* 1978).

5. Conclusions: The Erosion of the Swedish Model

The Swedish model of FDI and FDI policy, as it looked at its height during the late 1980s, was characterized by liberal policies towards outward FDI, a more restrictive environment for inward FDI, and a corresponding asymmetry between the magnitudes of inward and outward FDI flows. We have argued in this chapter that the Swedish government's industrial policy and the attitudes of the Swedish trade unions are important explanations for this pattern. A growth-oriented industrial policy, biased towards large firms, has facilitated the emergence of companies with the type of ownership assets that are needed to undertake FDI. The trade unions have supported this industrial policy and the subsequent multinationalization of Swedish firms. Labour's positive attitude towards FDI is explained by some of the central characteristics of the Swedish labour market. Centralized trade unions, operating in a full employment economy, with guaranteed participation in the MNEs' strategic decisions, have little to fear from outward FDI. At the same time, they have little to gain from inward FDI.

Recently, however, it seems as if the Swedish model of FDI and FDI policy has begun to change. Rules and restrictions on inward investment have been liberalized, the attitudes towards inward investment are becoming more positive, and the inflows of FDI have increased markedly. The large-firm bias in industry policies is also being eroded, and the unreservedly positive views on Swedish investment abroad are being questioned. These developments, we suggest, are caused by several fundamental changes in the Swedish economy, and by the increasing globalization of Swedish industry.

First, weak government finances have forced Sweden to give up the objective of a welfare state where the public sector can employ those who lose their jobs in the private sector. As a result, open unemployment presently stands at over 8 per cent, as compared with an average of 2 per cent during the 1980s. The increasing unemployment levels will probably make inward FDI appear increasingly attractive and outward FDI all the more threatening from an employment perspective.

Secondly, the structural effects of FDI may be less beneficial to Swedish labour today than in the past. The Swedish Krona has depreciated heavily against most leading currencies since 1992, and the Swedish real interest rates have been high. This has made Swedish labour relatively cheap (and Swedish capital relatively expensive) and caused worries that the Swedish production stages are becoming more raw-material and labour intensive, while the production in the foreign affiliates of Swedish MNEs is becoming increasingly technology and capital intensive (Andersson 1993). Consequently, Swedish observers have begun to question whether FDI is still good for Swedish labour. Until the mid-1980s, outward FDI entailed a shift in Swedish industry towards activities with higher labour productivity, but it is not obvious that this is still the case. During the late 1980s, the labour productivity in the MNEs' home-country operations fell, while it increased rapidly in most foreign affiliates (Andersson 1993)—this may reflect a relocation of some activities with high value added from plants in Sweden to Swedish foreign affiliates.

The rapid globalization of the Swedish MNEs has also raised serious doubts about the appropriateness and efficiency of the macro-organizational policies that made up the foundation of the Swedish model. Until the late 1980s, economic policies assumed that what is good for large Swedish firms is also good for the Swedish economy. However, the performance of Swedish industry during the past decades has not lived up to expectations. Although industrial policies have supported the large firms, and the R&D intensity in industry has been among the highest in the world, there has been no shift in Swedish exports towards more technology or R&D intensive products (see, e.g., Blomström and Lipsey 1989). Instead, it appears that Swedish MNEs have undertaken the bulk of their R&D at home, but located most of the new production abroad, in their foreign affiliates. In fact, while Sweden as a country has lost world market shares over the past decades, Swedish MNEs—that is, the Swedish parents together with their foreign affiliates—have increased their shares and become more competitive. From the perspective of Swedish taxpayers, this is obviously not an ideal development, since the gains from Swedish R&D subsidies and other public funds are largely exploited outside the country. Consequently, the bias in favour of large firms is eroding, and industrial policies are focusing more and more on supporting small and medium-sized companies that are more likely to keep their production in Sweden.

Thirdly, as a result of its integration with the rest of Europe, Sweden has recently liberalized most laws relating to inward FDI. Together with the depreciating Krona, which has made Swedish assets cheap in an international comparison, this has triggered a rapid increase in the foreign ownership of Swedish industry. It is likely that the increasing investment inflows will make trade unions more used to contacts with foreign owners, and perhaps also less worried about increasing foreign presence in Swedish industry. In this new institutional and international environment, the Swedish policies and approaches to FDI will probably look more like those in other small, open economies.

NOTES

We thank Thomas Andersson, John Dunning, Gösta Karlsson, Leif Mutén, and Martin Welge for helpful comments and the Swedish Council for Research in the Humanities and Social Science for financial support.

1. The Netherlands had eight and Switzerland nine enterprises among the world's 600 largest MNEs in 1985 (see UNCTC 1988).
2. Before the Second World War, Alfa Laval (or Separator, as it was called then) had established eighteen foreign subsidiaries. AGA's international network comprised thirty subsidiaries, while SKF had thirty-three foreign affiliates. See Runblom (1971).
3. About 12 per cent of the aggregate capital of the 1,000 largest industrial companies in Sweden was owned by foreigners in 1905 (see Johansson 1968).
4. Data on employment in minority-owned foreign firms (with foreign ownership stakes between 10 and 50 per cent) are not available after 1962.
5. However, there have been very clear differences between the attitudes of local trade unions and those of the central organizations. Local union leaders have often been very negatively inclined, and have frequently opposed FDI projects. The reason, of course, is that FDI may well lead to job losses and friction at the local level, while the benefits may occur in other companies or other parts of the country, beyond the horizon of local union leaders. See Hedlund and Otterbeck (1977).

REFERENCES

Andersson, T. (1993), 'Utlandsinvesteringar och policy-implikationer' (Working Paper No. 371; Stockholm: Industriens Utredningsinstitut).

—— and Fredriksson, T. (1993), *Sveriges val, EG och direktinvesteringar, Bilaga 7 till EG-konsekvensutredningen* (Stockholm: Norstedts Tryckeri).

—— —— and Svensson, R. (1996), *Multinational Restructuring, Internationalization and Small Economies: The Swedish Case* (London: Routledge).

Bergsten, F., Horst, T., and Moran, T. (1978), *American Multinationals and American Interests* (Washington: Brookings Institution).

Blomström, M., and Kokko, A. (1994), 'Home Country Effects of Foreign Direct Investment', in S. Globerman (ed.), *Canadian-Based Multinationals* (Calgary: University of Calgary Press).

—— and Lipsey, R. E. (1989), 'The Export Performance of US and Swedish Multinationals', *Review of Income and Wealth*, 35: 245–64.

—— —— and Ohlsson, L. (1989), *Economic Relations between the United States and Sweden* (Stockholm: Svenska Handelsbanken).

Davis, S., and M. Henrekson (1995), 'Industrial Policy, Employer Size and Economic Performance in Sweden' (NBER Working Paper No. 5237, August).

Fackföreningsrörelsen (1930), *The International Trade Union Industry Policy Program* (Stockholm: Landsorganisationen).

Fredriksson, T. (1994), 'Utlandsinvesteringarnas betydelse för Sverige', *Aktuellt om Näringspolitik och Ekonomi* (Stockholm: Ministry of Industry and Commerce).

Hedlund, G., and Otterbeck, L. (1977), *The Multinational Corporation, The Nation State and the Trade Unions: An European Perspective* (Ohio: Kent State University Press).

Hjalmarsson, L. (1991), 'The Scandinavian Model of Industrial Policy', in M. Blomström and P. Meller (eds.), *Diverging Paths: Comparing a Century of Scandinavian and Latin American Economic Development* (Baltimore: Johns Hopkins University Press).

Hymer, S. (1976), *The International Operations of National Firms: A Study of Direct Foreign Investment* (Cambridge: MIT Press).

Johansson, H. (1968), *Utländsk företagsetablering i Sverige* (Stockholm: SNS).

Jordan, J. L., and Vahlne, J. E. (1981), 'Domestic Employment Effects of Direct Investment Abroad by Two Swedish Multinationals' (Working Paper No. 13; Multinational Enterprise Programme; Geneva: International Labour Office).

Kokko, A. (1994), 'Sweden: Effects of EU Membership on Investment and Growth', *The World Economy*, 17: 667–77.

LO (1976): Landsorganisationen, *Fackföreningsrörelsen och de multinationella företagen* (Stockholm: LO).

Lundström, R. (1986), 'Swedish Multinational Growth before 1930', in P. Hertner and G. Jones (eds.), *Multinationals: Theory and History* (Aldershot: Gower).

Mutén, L. (1968), *Bolagsbeskattning och kapitalkostnader* (Stockholm: Almqvist och Wiksell).

NUTEK (1994): Swedish National Board for Industrial and Technical Development, *Swedish Industry and Industrial Policy 1994* (Stockholm: Swedish National Board for Industrial and Technical Development).

Olsson, U. (1993), 'Securing the Markets: Swedish Multinationals in a Historical Perspective', in G. Jones and H. G. Schröter (eds.), *The Rise of Multinationals in Continental Europe* (Cheltenham: Edward Elgar).

Runblom, H. (1971), *Svenska företag i Latinamerika: Etableringsmönster och förhandlingstaktik 1900–1940* (Studia historica upsaliensia 35; Stockholm: Läromedelsförlagen).

Samuelsson, H. F. (1977), *Utländska direkta investeringar i Sverige: En ekonometrisk analys av bestämningsfaktorerna* (Stockholm: Industriens Utredningsinstitut).

SOU (1980): Statens Offentliga Utredningar, *Valutareglering och ekonomisk politik: Expertrapport från valutakommittén*, no. 51 (Stockholm: Finansdepartementet).

—— (1982), *Internationella företag i svensk industri: Expertrapport från DIRK*, no. 15 (Stockholm: Industridepartementet).

—— (1983), *Näringspolitiska effekter av internationella investeringar. Betänkande från DIRK*, no. 17 (Stockholm: Industridepartementet).

—— (1987), *Utländska förvärv av svenska företag—en studie av utvecklingen*, no. 37 (Stockholm: Industridepartementet).

Swedenborg, B. (1979), *The Multinational Operations of Swedish Firms* (Stockholm: Industriens Utredningsinstitut).

UNCTC (1988): United Nations Centre on Transnational Corporations, *Transnational Corporations in World Development* (New York: UNCTC).

13

Japan

Terutomo Ozawa

> Nothing seems more likely to establish [industrialization in developing countries] than that mutual communication of knowledge and of all sorts of improvements which an extensive commerce from all countries to all countries naturally, or rather necessarily, carries along with it.
>
> (Adam Smith)

1. **Introduction**

Although the 'flying-geese' (FG) paradigm of economic development has only recently come to be known outside Japan, it best describes the major industrialization-cum-globalization approach long pursued by Japanese policymakers at both government and industry levels, consciously or unconsciously, ever since the start of Japan's modernization in the mid-nineteenth century. It succinctly epitomizes not only Japan's erstwhile—and still-lingering—mentality as a latecomer in global capitalism, but also Japan's current *Zeitgeist* of, and its attitude towards, international economic relations, particularly between the advanced and the developing worlds.

In essence, the paradigm envisions the global economy as a hierarchical system in which a sequential pattern of tandem development among a group of economies occurs through the medium of trade, investment, and knowledge transfers. It is based on a *dynamic evolutionary* perspective of interactive industrial upgrading and growth, a view that the global economy goes through structural renovations because of mutual interactions between 'leader' (lead goose) and 'catching-up' (follower goose) countries.

This analogy of a flight formation of wild geese to this concatenated type of industrial development was originally conceptualized by a Japanese economist, Kaname Akamatsu, in the early 1930s. As he put it, 'It is impossible to study the economic growth of the developing countries in modern times without considering the mutual interactions between these economies and those of the advanced countries' (1962: 1). Indeed, this pursuit of *interactive industrialization* in a global context is a promising avenue any latecomer can exploit for catching-up development, now that the global economy is ever more integrated and the growth stimuli (and, especially, *informational* external economies) are constantly transmitted from the advanced to the developing world, particularly at the hands of MNEs. It behoves any developing country's government, if it intends to modernize its economy, to formulate an appropriate strategy to capitalize on such MNE-facilitated growth opportunities.

The FG paradigm, when reformulated the way it is done in this chapter, provides an ideal framework within which to study the role of the Japanese government, the inter-temporal process of Japan's fostering of industrial growth and competitiveness, and its management of continuous structural upgrading in the context of an ever-globalizing economic environment.[1] It also serves as a framework of analysis for two accompanying pathological problems: one is what may be called the 'Japanese disease', and the other is the 'price-knowledge-flow' syndrome.

The 'Japanese disease' is an advanced case of the 'Dutch disease'. It is caused by the sharp rise in value of the yen, which in turn is aggravated by the rigidified regulatory structure of the Japanese government and its intransigence against deregulation (the government is good at regulating but very poor at deregulating). The 'price-knowledge-flow' syndrome (Ozawa 1996) describes the eventual futility of a neo-mercantilist industrial policy which attempts to build up manufacturing at home under protection and promotion. This is because the very competitiveness fostered at home will inevitably drive up the value of home currency and make home-based production less competitive, forcing domestic firms to transplant production abroad (i.e. a 'hollowing-out' effect). This is akin to David Hume's 'price-specie-flow' theory which describes how mercantilists' efforts to accumulate precious metals via engineering trade surpluses will cause inflation at home, thereby eventually draining out precious metals, again through the external sector. These two problems—which are mutually reinforcing—are the econo-organic pathogeneses that have unfortunately accompanied Japan's managed catching-up growth in the post-Second-World-War period.

In short, Japan's trilogy of government involvement, competitiveness building, and globalization, entailing the two structural pathologies, can be very nicely illustrated within the conceptual framework of the FG paradigm.

2. Akamatsu's 'Fundamental' Pattern of Industrial Growth: A Reformulation

Akamatsu's concept of the FG paradigm is framed in terms of Hegelian dialectics, an approach he called 'synthetic dialectics'. Hence, such a paradigm presupposes incessant (never-ending) inter-temporally connected changes in a country's economic activities, and in its commercial relations with the outside world. His initial studies (1935, 1956) were concerned with the developmental growth path of a particular modern industry in Japan as it was transplanted on to that latecomer economy at the time. Specifically, he found some *common* patterns of industrial growth and trade in cotton yarn, cotton cloth, spinning and weaving machinery, and machines and tools. All these industries exhibited a comparative-advantage–nurturing sequence of 'imports → domestic production → exports', each activity tracing out an inverted V-shaped curve—the reason why he christened this sequential pattern 'a wild-flying-geese formation'. Interestingly, Raymond Vernon's product-cycle theory of trade and investment (1966) is exactly the inverse of this sequence, i.e. 'exports → overseas production → imports', i.e. one experienced by manufacturers in a lead-goose country.

The FG paradigm is then based on an evolutionary vision of how an initially disadvantaged—or non-existent—industry could be developed into a comparatively advantaged industry. This is basically a process of 'import protection as export promotion', if we borrow Paul Krugman's phrase (1984). But there are some major differences between what Krugman conceived as an intervening causal mechanism and what Japanese industry has actually done, as will be seen below.

It is noteworthy that all those manufacturing industries Japan endeavoured to develop at home in its early phases of growth took more than half a century to accomplish—namely, 1870–1940 (Akamatsu 1962). As will be explored below, however, nowadays a modern industry (say, apparel and standardized electric/electronics goods) can be grafted onto the soil of a developing country practically overnight at the hands of MNEs—that is, time-compression takes place along the path of development.

Akamatsu emphasized the fact that, when a non-industrialized country began to import manufactured consumer goods (light-industry goods), its native handicraft industry was usually damaged and destroyed, but that such imports created the domestic markets for potential local substitutes. Thus, a stage was set for the country to capture those newly emerged markets by taking up domestic production under the 'infant-industry' protection scheme. In other words, 'economic nationalism' was inevitably born in the wake of the destruction of the local handicraft industry by imports and the new opportunities to replace such imports with domestic production. 'In this process of recovering the domestic market, there will arise a struggle of economic nationalism in less-advanced countries. This presupposes the accumulation of capital and the technological adaptability of the people in those countries. Further, it calls for the government's protective policy to encourage and promote the consumer goods industries' (Akamatsu 1962: 11). Thus, the opening-up of a traditional society to the market forces of the advanced world gives a strategic role to imports; they serve as a trigger mechanism for industrialization so long as the developing country can meet two conditions: (*a*) the execution of an appropriate developmental policy by the government, and (*b*) the existence of a basic technical and industrial (especially, traditional-craft-production-rooted) foundation to learn modern technology.

In the post-Second World-War period (throughout the 1950s and the early 1960s) Japan continued to pursue the same sequential 'infant-industry' strategy of imports → domestic production → exports as it did in the pre-war years.[2] But such a sequence in the post-war period was accomplished much more rapidly than previously; in other words, as mentioned above, the phenomenon of time

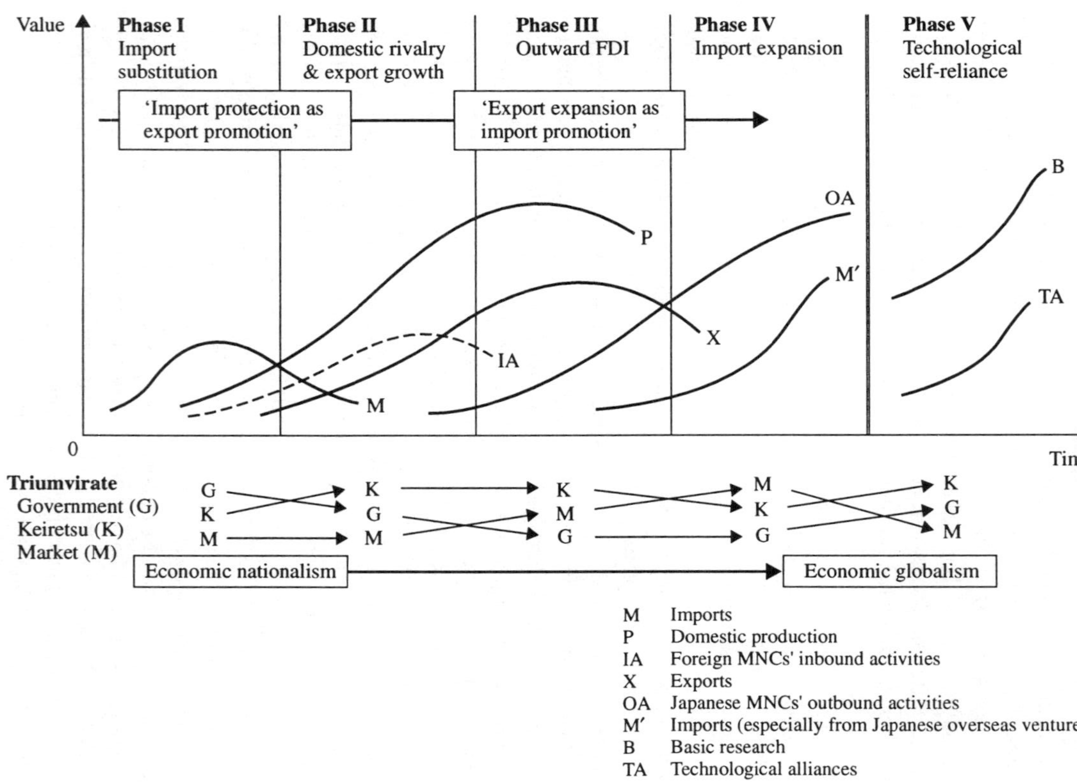

FIG 13.1. The paradox of 'import protection as import expansion' and the macro-organizational triumvirate

compression occurred in the pace of 'infant-industry' growth for a variety of reasons. Furthermore, in addition to importing and exporting, other forms of international business activity—for example, FDI (both their own and foreign)—came to play a number of key restructuring functions. Besides, management of the phase of decline in domestic output with the growth of transplanted production abroad (a late phase of industrialization) became no less critical than the phase of industrial fostering at home (an early phase of industrialization). And indeed, import expansion, a phenomenon observable late in the cycle, has become an equally important activity to be managed by both government and industry as is the initial stage of import substitution. In other words, a full cycle of imports → domestic production → exports → outward FDI → overseas production → imports has come into existence. This is a seeming paradox of 'import protection as import expansion'.

3. Fostered Growth and the Paradox of 'Import Protection as Import Expansion'

A full cycle of the developmental sequence from import substitution to import expansion is illustrated in Fig. 13.1. In contrast to Akamatsu's 'fundamental' model of industrial growth (which covers only a sequence of imports → exports), Fig. 13.1 includes the home-output-declining-cum-multinationalizing stage of an industry, which involves FDI and/or non-equity types of business involvement. In fact, the cycle is comprised of the phase of 'import protection as export promotion' *à la* Krugman plus the phase of 'export expansion as import promotion' *à la* Vernon.

This full life cycle of a developmental path can be chronologically divided into four phases: (1) import substitution via technological absorption, (2) domestic rivalry and export expansion, (3) outbound FDI, and (4) import expansion. What is worth noting here is that, as a given industry progresses through these phases, the role of government changes—indeed, dramatically so from economic nationalism to economic globalism (or regionalism) for that particular industry, and that various types of international commercial activity play phase-specific roles during the life cycle. These phenomena are examined below.

To explore further the trilogy of government, competitiveness, and globalization, it is necessary to understand how Japan has been using different forms of international business activity as macro-organizational instruments of economic growth—that is, as competitiveness (learning/productivity)-enhancing catalysts.

3.1. External Commercial Activities as Macro-Organizational Instruments

The concept of macro-organizational policy as distinct from that of macroeconomic policy was introduced by John Dunning (1992*a*: 7) in order to delineate the importance of organization and management of 'resource- (or assets-)

usage to (1) counteract market distorting behaviour and (2) help create and facilitate the efficient workings of markets'. In reviewing Michael Porter's book, *The Competitive Advantage of Nations* (1990), Dunning (1992*b*) also points out that transnational business activities may themselves affect the facets of Porter's 'diamond' as a distinctive exogenous variable in the same way as does the government's macro-organizational involvement.

It is exactly along the same line of reasoning that we wish to emphasize that transnational business activities themselves (such as exporting, importing, subcontracting, technology licensing, and inward and outward FDIs) can all be turned into strategic macro-organizational instruments of economic upgrading and the enhancement of competitiveness. Indeed, for that matter, the Japanese government and industry, often in such a close collaborative manner as described by outside observers as 'Japan, Inc.', have been the most active macro-organizational strategists. (Since Japan's competitive 'diamond' is already well examined in Porter's work, throughout this chapter we are focusing on the topic of how Japan has capitalized on external commercial activities as developmental devices.)

3.2. **The Government, the *keiretsu* (Hierarchical Networks), and the Market**

Indeed, Japan has been an active macro-organizational practitioner (a seeker of adaptive efficiency) *à la* Frederick List ever since the start of its economic and social modernization in the mid-nineteenth century.[3] Of course, in what form, how intensively, and how effectively such measures were adopted and employed differed over time, depending upon the particular internal and external socio-political economic environments. In this respect, Japan's propensity to use a macro-organizational approach is largely a product of history, a history of Japan as a late-industrializer. Its social structure (at the initiation of modernization in 1868 following more than two centuries' centralized feudalism) was such that the central government was given a special role to organize and govern Japan's catching-up effort.

In the history of Japan's managed industrialization, however, the market did play a considerable role in the early part of this century (especially up to the mid-1930s), during which, for example, inward FDI was accepted without any significant restrictions. Both GM and Ford established automobile assembly subsidiaries during this time. But the mindset of Japanese policy-makers has long been that 'the market is a good servant but a bad master'.[4] The market is basically neither goal-determining nor goal-pursuing; it is goal-neutral at best and sometimes even goal-hindering. In essence, the market is merely a resource-allocative institution, not a goal-setting institution.

Until recently, moreover, the Japanese policy-makers and captains of industry had long possessed a strong sense of being a 'follower' goose. They felt that Japan was disadvantaged by its lack of natural resources at home and the backwardness of the industrial knowledge of its corporations. Hence, they reasoned that the free-market approach alone would not work as a catching-up mechanism.

Furthermore, so far as the post-war experience is concerned, the Japanese bureaucrats had exercised controls on the Japanese economy during the war, and were then given by the Supreme Commander for Allied Powers (SCAP) the permission to continue to use their authority and expertise in order to orchestrate economic reconstruction and expansion. Thus, history did matter a lot for the role of the Japanese government as a practitioner of macro-organizational strategies. Yet, it should be stressed that macro-organizational policy in Japan has not only been pursued by the government. The private sector has also taken up the task of macro-organizational management by forming industrial groups, the *zaibatsu* ('hierarchies') in the pre-war days and the *keiretsu* ('hierarchical networks') in the post-war period.[5] In other words, macro-organizational tasks are carried out simultaneously and in close coordination between the bureaucrats and the private sector.

In the immediate post-war period, indeed, the Japanese economy was in a shambles, and there was no way for the market mechanism to work. New institutional arrangements had to be made to convert the economy from the wartime mode to a peacetime mode. Therefore, they strove to create a market-oriented yet managed economy to achieve the national goal of catching up with the West.

Obviously, the essence of catching-up is the absorption of advanced technologies from the West and the building-up of local technological capability. To this end, the traditional market mechanism needed to be supplemented by other organizational mechanisms. Here, an 'information-theoretic' framework of analysis (Stiglitz 1989) is most appropriate to understand the behaviour of Japanese policy-makers, since they were confronted with the twin problems of 'imperfect markets' and 'incomplete information'. In fact, the strategic approach adopted by the Japanese government and industry is now widely recognized among institutionalists (if not among liberal neoclassicists) as an effective and justifiable way of accomplishing the national task of catching-up.[6]

3.3. Development and Management of a Macro-Organizational Ecosystem

3.3.1. Phase I: Import Substitution via Technology Absorption

In its early stages of economic development, Japan found it necessary to import a large number of manufactured goods which were not as yet produced at home. The situation was again very similar after 1945, since many new technologies had been introduced in the West during the war. The government, indeed, did promote the first round of such manufactured imports to see if Japanese industry might be able to unlock the secrets of embodied technologies and manufacture the same products.

This strategy was a continuation of the 'technoprotectionism' pursued by the Japanese authorities since the Meiji Restoration of 1868. As Richard Samuels (1994) observes, this has been Japan's national developmental ideology, an ideology 'that technology is a fundamental element in national security, that it must be indigenized [*kokusanka*], diffused [*hakyu*], and nurtured [*ikusei*] in order to make a nation rich and strong' (Samuels 1994: p. x). This 'triple-note chord' of Japan's technological ideology springs from a pervasive anxiety and insecurity [*fuan*] that Japan as a nation constantly feels as a result of 'its special vulnerabilities in a Hobbesian world' (Samuels 1994: p. x).

In the pre-war days, Japan's Ministry of Foreign Affairs (through its network of overseas consulates) and its Ministry of Agricultural and Commercial Affairs (through its overseas business trainees programme and its overseas commercial 'museums' or exhibition facilities) served as the 'eyes and ears' of Japanese industry in collecting information on foreign products and technologies, and as promoters of whatever Japan was capable of exporting at that time (such as silk, marine products, textiles, and sundries) (Sugihara 1994). In many cases, preferential allocations of precious foreign exchange (which is usually scarce in any developing country) were made specifically for the purpose of importing manufactured 'samples'.

For example, back in the 1910s a number of automobiles and engines were imported for limited domestic use but also as prototypes for 'reverse engineering' and local reproduction (i.e. objects of learning-by-imitating). When Japan began to foster domestic automobile production in 1931 (a ban was imposed on imports of completed vehicles and knock-down sets in 1936), Toyota's managers were convinced that they would be able to 'copy foreign vehicles without violating patent laws' (Cusumano 1989: 60). The company 'began by copying a 21-cylinder, 60cc engine that Smith Motors in the United States made for 2-wheel and 3-wheel vehicles' (Cusumano 1989: 63). A number of specialists were dispatched to the United States and Europe to purchase the necessary machine tools and learn engine-casting. The company then

> began working on a car body design early in 1934 and used a 1934 Chrysler DeSoto . . . acquired in April 1934 as a model because [it] had the best body lines. Ford appeared to have the strongest frame and rear axle, so [they] used these components but took the front axle from a Chevrolet and added a free-floating suspension system for the axles to make sure the car would not fall over if an axle or axle shaft broke on a bumpy road . . . The result was a hybrid car, finished in May 1935, that had a Chrysler body and Ford and Chevrolet parts. (Cusumano 1989: 65)

Indeed, one of the advantages of being a latecomer is an opportunity to hybridize the existing superior forms of knowledge into an even more superior synthesis.

Similar stories were repeated after the Second World War. For example, when Masuru Ibuka, one of Sony's founders, visited an American officer's office in the late 1940s when Japan was still under allied occupation, he spotted an American-made tape recorder. Ibuka asked if he could borrow it. A few days later, the officer took the trouble of bringing the machine to Ibuka's workshop and demonstrated it. 'Everybody crowded around for the demonstration, and when it was over everybody was convinced that this would be a good project for the company to work on' (Morita 1986: 61). The rest is history. From then on, Sony went eventually to produce both magnetic tapes and miniaturized (transistorized) recording machines. These were among the most important milestone products for Sony's rise as the world's leading electronics manufacturer.

The typical imitative/learning endeavour by Japanese firms in those days may be summarized as follows:

1. importation of new products as models for reverse engineering and reproduction;
2. reproduction of a domestic version by combining the best features of different foreign models;
3. acquisition and study of related patent documents, if any, issued at home and abroad to see if a similar result can be obtained by using the information revealed in the patents (an effort often resulting in patent-document-based reproductions) and to see if any other alternative ways can be found to achieve the same result, a situation well illustrated by Japan's synthetic-fibre industry (Ozawa 1980);
4. short-term visits to factories and laboratories abroad to gain first-hand knowledge of production processes;
5. dispatching of promising company personnel/engineers to the West for study at some technical institutions of high learning (e.g. the Massachusetts Institute of Technology) and to have them monitor the latest manufacturing activities there;
6. securing of the necessary licensing agreements for the use of patents.

In this emulative learning process, the government served the role of a 'hidden' party to assist Japanese buyers of technology to gain bargaining advantages in their negotiation with the technology suppliers (licensers), especially when its import controls on technology were exercised throughout the 1950s and the 1960s (Ozaki 1972; Henderson 1973; Ozawa 1974; Peck 1976). Although the effectiveness of such a policy is now subject to debate, it is also accepted that, at least potentially 'governments can alter the nature of the market environment by intervention' (World Bank 1993: 293–4). 'By coordinating the actions of buyers of technology and trying to increase competition among sellers, governments can appropriate more of the surplus associated with the transfer of technology than they otherwise could' (World Bank 1993: 294; the idea is attributed to Joseph Stiglitz 1993).

It needs to be noted here that, in entering a new industry, Japanese manufacturers normally began with the low-end goods suitable for their learning process because of a relatively small technology gap for them to conquer. Those mature (standardized) goods already have large price-sensitive markets, and the needed technologies are readily available. Latecomers have a comparative advantage in price competition rather than in non-price competition. There is, furthermore, a natural order of emulative learning, from simple goods to more sophisticated goods. By such means, Japanese emulators were able to make numerous improvements on Western technologies. Early on, their adaptive technological progress was process-focused (rather than product-focused) and shop-floor-based.[7]

There is a considerable literature on Japanese development policies in the early post-war period. *Inter alia*, these include Johnson (1982); Komiya *et al.* (1988); Okimoto (1989); Johnson *et al.* (1989); and Okuno-Fujiwara (1991). It is worth noting that in 1955 the government introduced and implemented the Five-Year-Plan for Economic Independence, which was designed to make Japan 'independent' from economic aid from the USA and from the special procurements of US forces in Japan, and simultaneously to industrialize the economy. The plan specifically set forth four principal objectives—namely, modernization of industrial plant and equipment; promotion of international trade (which actually meant export promotion); an increase in self-sufficiency; and curtailment of consumption (Komiya *et al.* 1988). These objectives, especially the third and fourth ones, came to colour the post-war path of Japan's economic growth.

3.3.2. Phase II: Domestic Rivalry ('Reserved Competition') and Export Growth

Protection is usually said to breed inefficiency, since it reduces competition. In certain Japanese manufacturing industries, however, protected local production actually did *not* create growth-stunted infants. On the contrary—and paradoxically—protection ended up by generating more—rather than less—intense competition at home than might have occurred without protection. In fact, many protected industries soon grew to be more efficient and strongly export-focused; and exporting in turn stimulated further technological improvements because of the necessity to compete with more technologically advanced Western producers. The primary examples are Japan's automotive and computer industries. Why and how did certain types of protected Japanese manufacturing turn out to be such success stories? How did they manage to grow into efficient and export-competitive industries?

It is well known that a distinct feature of Japanese industry is the existence of a large number of fiercely competing firms in many manufacturing industries. This phenomenon is known as 'excessive competition' in Japan (Abegglen and Rapp 1970). Porter (1990) produced a list of estimated numbers of competitors in many of Japan's export-competitive sectors in the late 1980s; *inter alia*, 25 rivals in audio equipment, 9 rivals in automobiles, 15 rivals in cameras, as many as 112 rivals in machine tools, 16 rivals in personal computers, 34 rivals in semiconductors, 33 rivals in shipbuilding, and 10 rivals in VCRs. Many of these sectors such as cameras, audio equipment, shipbuilding, and videocassette recorders were not protected—but the very prevalence of such ferocious rivalry and overcrowdedness at home constituted 'natural protection' from any interlopers from the outside.

The existence of the *keiretsu* and other group-oriented modalities of economic activities is one important reason for multiple entries in any profitable sector, since inter-group rivalry induces an entry into a promising growth area, while it reduces the cost and risk of such an entry. For example, an entrant—say, a new producer of computers—may be able to secure relatively low-cost finance from its affiliated bank and an assured 'captive' market from its affiliates, at least initially, for its newly produced goods. In addition, the still-war-damaged environment meant that Japanese firms pursued mostly 'opportunist' and 'imitating' business strategies[8] by way of absorbing advanced Western technologies which were available from different alternative sources. Hence there was relatively easy entry to, and rivalry in, most new growth sectors.

Moreover, the early protection of markets such as automobiles and computers further encouraged new entrants because of the rents created under protection; this promoted further competition. Such intensified competition did contribute to technological progress, particularly when the MITI, the erstwhile guardian of Japanese industry, administered 'orderly' pricing practices and allowed the retention of protection rents as profits to be ploughed back into investment in new productive facilities as well as in R&D. Competitive energy was thus channelled into the non-price forms of rivalry which were focused on efforts to reduce costs, differentiate products, and develop new products and processes—hence dynamic technology-based competition. Under such protected, yet domestically competitive conditions, the winners naturally proved to be Japanese firms, simply because foreign firms were excluded from their struggle for survival. This unique institutional arrangement can be conceptualized as 'reserved competition' (Ozawa 1988, 1994):

Fostered domestic competition (FDC)		Suppressed foreign competition (SFC)		Net competitive effect (NCE)
[+]	+	[–]	=	NCE > 0

This describes the situation in which the competitive pressure created among a large number of local entrants in a fostered domestic market (+FDC) became much stronger in absolute terms than the reduction in competition due to the exclusion of foreign competition (–SFC). Hence the net competitive effect is positive (NCE > 0). This is perhaps the most distinctive macro-organizational feature created by the interactions between the government and the private sector.

The reserved competition paradigm is distinct from the European 'national-champion' model. In the former case, the basis for scale economies is established on a cross-border basis, while in the latter it is largely confined to the home base; they become national champions but not international champions (Ozawa 1988). Krugman's notion of 'import protection as export promotion' (1984) more appropriately matches the 'national-champion' paradigm, since he stresses the economies of scale obtainable under protection and exploited by a domestic firm.[9]

It should be emphasized here, however, that the concept of 'reserved competition' is only an *a posteriori* notion—that is to say, Japan's policy-makers—or, for that matter, Japanese industry—had no such clear-cut idea as is detailed above about the coincidental efficacy of their protectionist approach. It was coincidental because what really mattered was the structural dynamism of Japan's private sector. That sector happened to be highly responsive to protection and promotion in the early post-war period and was, above all, nurtured in the favourable growth environment of the Pax Americana (i.e. during the Golden Age of Capitalism, 1950–1974). In other words, the efficacy of reserved competition owed much more to this private-sector dynamism than to MITI's interventionism, although the latter was certainly a necessary component of this unique phenomenon in certain high value-added industries such as automobiles and computers.

As seen in those 'unprotected' (at least, not formally protected) industries such as cameras, televisions, audio equipment (transistor radios and hi-fi equipment), and calculators, an extremely high degree of entrepreneurship was demonstrated, resulting in a large number of rivals battering each other in each industry. In fact, as pointed out earlier, such a competitive market structure itself serves as a very strong 'natural' barrier not only to imports but also to foreign MNEs' entry as FDI investors (direct local producers) in those Japanese industries. And the continuous existence of closely knit *keiretsu* groups may hinder transnational businesses from the outside world. Some call these structural barriers 'private sector impediments' (Mason 1992).

In short, the upshot of reserved competition, whether officially reinforced or not, is a rapid build-up of productive capacity in a new industry—often in excess of domestic demand. In consequence there is a strong inducement for firms to export to gain scale economies. The larger the number of rivals relative to the size of the home market, the stronger their efforts to capture overseas markets. Indeed, second entrants—say, Honda relative to Toyota, and Sony relative to Matsushita—initially exhibited a much higher propensity to exploit overseas markets. But in the end such second entrants' challenge also forced established firms to be equally aggressive in overseas markets. In other words, the reserved-competition phenomenon proved to be 'export-energy-packing' competition.

In this phase of export expansion in the post-war period, such trade-promoting governmental agencies as Japan External Trade Organization (JETRO) and the Export–Import Bank of Japan played an important supportive role. JETRO was modelled on BETRO (British Export Trade Research Organization), which existed only briefly from 1947 to 1952. But JETRO, a Japanese clone, has grown into an effective supporting entity by adapting to the fast-changing needs of Japanese industry, and proving itself to be one of Japan's major 'institutional innovations in the organization of trade' (Ozawa and Sato 1989).

In addition, *keiretsu*-based general trading companies or *sogo shosha* were a big success factor for Japan's export expansion. Indeed, they are, again, Japan's unique institutional innovation in the organization of trade.

3.3.3. Phase III: Outward FDI and the 'Price-Knowledge-Flow' Mechanism

Japanese manufactured exports have often been likened to 'torrential rains' because an overseas market, once targeted, was soon flooded with made-in-Japan products. This has happened to many consumer-good markets, especially in the USA and Europe—but also in some developing countries. The ineluctable outcome is trade friction.

To ease new trade conflicts, Japanese manufacturers have set up local production via FDI in their core export markets—initially, by way of assembly operations, but later by more integrated forms of production. In the meantime, ironically, two developments, both of which were caused by the very success of the exports, took place and began to erode Japan's hard-won competitiveness. The first was a steady appreciation of the yen stemming from the ever-ballooning trade surpluses. The second was the rising labour costs at home. These twin effects then forced Japanese manufacturers to upgrade their products by way of R&D and product development. Sometimes this has resulted in the introduction of new varieties of products (as is the case with electronics goods); sometimes of improved versions of the existing products (as is the case with automobiles). In other words, a Schumpeterian phenomenon of 'creative destruction' occurred in the course of continuous product development.

Yet, older products do not need to be subjected to the process of 'creative destruction', since their production can be transplanted overseas as a substitute for exporting from home. In other words, a form of 'creative recycling' occurred. The more successful the product development and other innovating endeavours, the more willingly overseas production has been promoted. Besides, having started out with low-end goods, Japanese producers have been all the more motivated to shed them via FDI and move up the qualitative ladder of manufacturing. So far as the lines of old products are concerned, Japanese industry has become outward-FDI-focused by way of shifting production abroad. But the industry is then generating another FG pattern of industrial growth on higher value-added goods (such as parts, components, and machinery), which may be in the export-expansion phase as they are now increasingly exported in connection with their newly opened overseas ventures as inputs.

It should be noted that, in this process of industry/market recycling, former Japanese exports to the USA are rerouted through their overseas ventures and local affiliates. This development occurs because the US market remains relatively open, while the Japanese market is still import-inhibiting. Asian 'super-exporters' have long depended on the US market in pursuing their strategy of export-led growth (Krueger 1993).

The role of MITI during this third phase of industrial development is obviously no longer primarily devoted to assisting the private sector to develop competitiveness, but rather to mediate any trade friction the industry experiences overseas. MITI's role has then changed from a promoter/developer of an industry to a trade conflict mediator/negotiator *vis-à-vis* foreign governments. MITI is also performing a new role as a facilitator of outward FDI and Japanese MNEs' other business activities. Particularly, Japan's small and medium-sized firms are in need of assistance in finance and market information for the purpose of setting up overseas operations. As a result, there have emerged a number of government-supported programmes such as those administered, or participated in, by the Japan Overseas Development Corporation, the Japan–ASEAN investment funds, the Japan Overseas Economic Cooperation Fund, the Japan International Cooperation Agency, JETRO, and the Japan Export–Import Bank (Ozawa 1989). These governmental agencies are inducing host (especially, developing) countries to utilize the outward FDI needs of Japanese industry as inputs in the latter's development programs.

3.3.4. Phase IV: Import Expansion

As domestic production is transplanted to overseas countries, imports begin to rise from Japan's own foreign ventures in both finished and intermediate (parts) goods. This is exactly what is currently happening to the electrical and electronics goods sectors, as well as to the automotive industry—two representative industries where product development and differentiation have considerably advanced—and a vertical division of labour in production of intermediate goods has deepened. For example, roughly speaking, Japan's electrical and electronics goods industry now produces (or assembles) via FDI and subcontracting those technologically most standardized products such as electric household appliances (e.g. electric fans, washing machines, and switches) in China and Vietnam, intermediately standardized goods (e.g. colour TV sets, air-conditioners, microwave ovens, and computer keyboards) in ASEAN-4 (Thailand, Malaysia, Indonesia, and the Philippines), and relatively sophisticated goods such as personal computers and integrated circuits in the NIEs (especially, Taiwan and South Korea). Indeed, imports of standardized electrical and electronics goods, both finished and intermediate, from other Asian countries into Japan are sharply on the rise. These imports are mostly from Japanese overseas ventures and take the form of intra-firm trade.

There is a rising fear among Japanese politicians and businessmen of the hollowing-out effect of these overseas investments at both the economy and the industry levels. Yet at the individual firm level, fierce inter-enterprise competition leaves no choice. No firm can afford to keep high-cost production at home in the wake of the continued appreciation of the yen and rising wages. This is all the more true when its competitors are shifting production to lower-cost locations. One irony of this situation is that, while the fierce domestic rivalries once contributed to the growth of a new industry and its exports, they are now compelling industrial shedding at home by way of Japanese MNE-facilitated transplantation of production across borders and their own pulled-imports; thus this process creates a fear of hollowing-out.

This is the dynamics—and the flip side—of 'creative recycling'. It also reflects the 'price-knowledge-flow' mechanism *à la* Hume of a neo-mercantilist way of building up a domestic industry; the very effort and success of accumulating industrial knowledge at home eventually lead to the outflow of such knowledge abroad. So long as the Japanese firms are capable of generating new growth products one after another, this knowledge metabolic process can continue to the benefit of both the Japanese economy and the individual firms. Yet the rate of technological infusion (new product/process development) is most likely to become slower and slower than the rate of technological diffusion, now that Japan has, on the whole, caught up with the advanced West in industrial endeavours—and especially now that the yen has so dramatically appreciated and become overvalued. Hence, a strong possibility of hollowing-out exists.

3.3.5. Phase V: Technological Self-Reliance

The comparative-advantage-nurturing sequence described above traces out Japan's experiences as a late starter. Nowadays, Japanese industries are in either phase III or phase IV of their development. Labour-intensive light industries such as apparel, standardized electrical and electronics goods (e.g. refrigerators, air-conditioners, television sets, and low-end VCRs), toys, and sundries are in phase IV. Imports of these goods, especially from other Asian countries, are sharply on the rise. Automobiles, automotive-parts, and high-end electronics goods are in the midst of phase III, where their domestic production is reaching its zenith, while overseas production by Japanese subsidiaries is expanding rapidly. No industry is any longer in phase I or phase II. In other words, Japan has used up all the catching-up opportunities given by the 'lead-geese' countries since the end of the Second World War. Japan has no more new industry to snatch from the advanced Western nations.

In consequence, Japan is increasingly seeking new industrial knowledge by stepping up its own R&D programmes—particularly basic research. This new phase of technological self-reliance does not mean isolationism; on the contrary, Japanese industry is increasing its technological alliances with firms in the advanced West. To stay ahead technologically is of critical importance for Japan to prevent itself from hollowing-out and from being overtaken by the new Asian 'follower-geese'. But knowledge creation entails externalities and uncertainties. Consequently, the role of the government, notably MITI, is re-emerging as a macro-organizational facilitator of knowledge advancement and innovations at home (along the line of reasoning emphasized by Richard Lipsey in Chapter 2). At the same time the Japanese government is unlikely to play such a dominant or authoritarian role as it used to do in phase I back in the 1950s and the early 1960s. The prime sector in forging innovatory activity is likely to be the *keiretsu*, although the government's complementary inputs (such as investment in higher education and technical training and its support of basic research) are crucial. Currently, indeed, Japanese industry is in this new phase of knowledge intensification.[10]

In this regard, it is useful to look back and summarize how the triumvirate of macro-organizational coordinators, i.e. the government (G), the *keiretsu* (*K*), and the market (M), have played their respective roles as a particular Japanese industry has gone through the different phases of growth (cf., the bottom of Fig. 13.1).[11] Because systemic market failures characterized phase I (Import Substitution), the government played the dominant leadership role in identifying a promising industry to be transplanted onto the domestic soil—in collaboration with the private sector. The market was practically non-existent except for the market for imports. Hence, G, *K*, M was the prevailing order of ranking.

For phase II (Domestic Rivalry and Export Growth) the initiative was shifted to the private sector (the *keiretsu* and their affiliated institutions such as *keiretsu* banks and trading companies). The government's role became less direct and centred on indirect supportive measures such as favourable taxation and finance for industrial promotion and exports. Hence, the ranking was *K*, G, M, in that order. In contrast, phase III (Outward FDI) witnessed the important role of the market mechanism; here, rising wages at home and/or the rising value of home currency served as the 'push' factors for outward FDI. The *keiretsu* was able to reduce the transaction and coordination costs of FDI when it was *keiretsu*-organized and managed. The government's role became minimal and more indirect in management of outward industrial transplantation at a specific industry level, even thought the Ministry of Foreign Affairs and MITI often became involved in smoothing out any frictional problems associated with Japan's FDI abroad. The ranking was, therefore, *K*, M, G.

Phase IV essentially depicts the declining (increasingly comparatively disadvantaged) stage of a once-flourishing industry at home. Production facilities were transplanted abroad and intra-firm imports rose. The market was the driving mechanism for these phenomena, and the private sector capitalized on this trend by offshore production via FDI, OEM, licensing, subcontracting, and other forms of business affiliation. The ranking then became M, *K*, G.

Phase V is added to illustrate a new phase that applies to the entire Japanese industry rather than to a specific sector in decline. Here, now that many sectors of Japanese industry have, by and large, closed the technology gap *vis-à-vis* the USA and Europe, it must create new technologies on its own and join the ranks of technological lead geese—through the medium of basic research and strategic R&D alliances with the firms in the advanced West. The initiative for innovations is definitely on the part of the private sector, but the government's support in various forms is called for to maximize social gains. The ranking of *K*, G, M characterizes this new phase.

4. The 'Japanese-Disease' Syndrome: A Complication of the 'Dutch Disease'

Was the FG strategy a success? As a latecomer, Japanese industry did have an advantage in benchmarking the advanced countries, especially the USA as the 'lead goose' to follow, for the purpose of ascending the ladder of industrialization. The USA provided a flight map, as it were, for Japan. Japan first pursued its comparative advantage in labour-intensive, low-value-added industries such as textiles, toys, and sundries by exploiting an abundant 'natural asset', low-skilled labour. But it soon developed new advantages in more capital-intensive, scale-based heavy and chemical industries such as steel, ships, and synthetic fibre by capitalizing on mobilized savings and the 'created assets' mostly imported from the advanced West. From there, Japan moved on to the next stage of building an advantage in automobiles and electronic goods by introducing an innovation in organization of production, popularly known as 'lean' production (Womack, Jones, and Roos 1990; Abo 1994). It is currently in the stage of increasing its output of technology-intensive goods. Thus, Japan has moved up from low-tech, low-productivity sectors to high-tech, high-productivity sectors, step by step, as Japan's capacity to do so developed in terms of asset availability.[12]

So far as Japan's trade-oriented sector is concerned, therefore, the FG catching-up strategy has been carried out very effectively. In other words, this successful evolutionary progress has been attained in those industries which were initially disadvantaged but later, under the Japanese-style infant-industry strategy, developed into competitively (and comparatively) advantaged ones. In the meantime, Japanese industry has also ended up having a slew of still heavily regulated and protected industries, protected if not by outright tariffs and quotas but by the built-in bias of regulations and red tape against imports. The upshot is that a new industrial dualism has come to exist: a *highly multinationalized efficient* sector and a *highly secluded import-averse* sector, as illustrated in Fig. 13.2.

During the course of the dynamic infant-industry approach, there have evolved basically two sectors: one is the outer-focused (OF) sector and the other the inner-dependent (ID) sector. The ID sector is represented largely by the sheltered 'inefficient'[13] service industries such as distribution (wholesale and retailing), construction, finance, insurance, medical/health, legal services, after-sale consumer services (such as automobile repair) as well as by some inefficient manufacturing industries which are heavily domestic market focused (such as food and beverage and telecommunications). In the beginning, extensive protection and a web of regulations were applied to the entire economy.

Roughly speaking, the OF sector is under the purview of MITI, while the ID sector is under the supervision of a variety of inner-focused ministries: the Ministry of Health and Welfare, the Ministry of Posts and Telecommunications, the Ministry of Home Affairs, the Ministry of Finance, the Ministry of Labour, the Ministry of Transportation, and the Ministry of Agriculture, Forestry, and

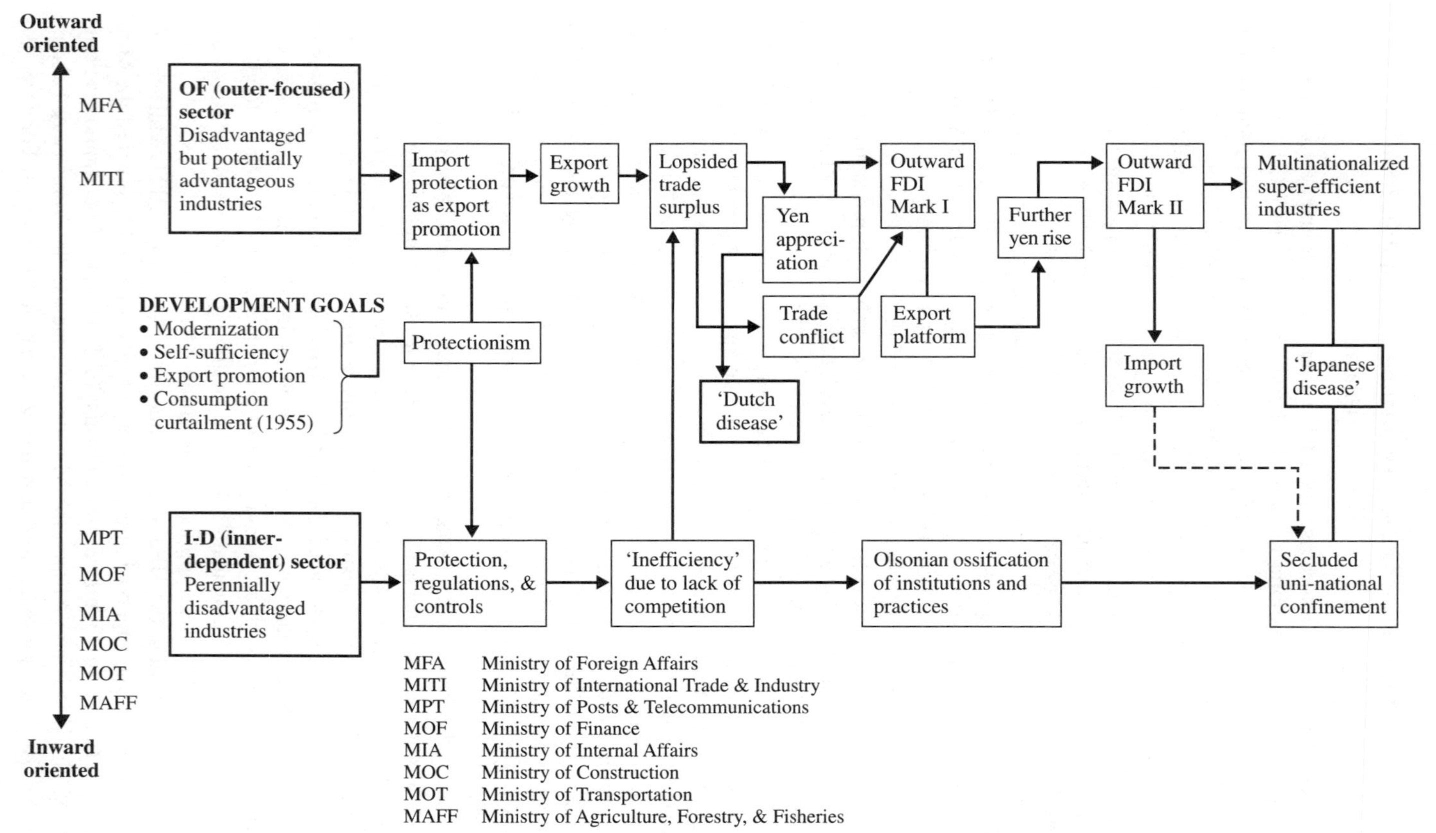

FIG 13.2. The 'Japanese-Disease' syndrome: An advanced complication of the 'Dutch Disease'

Fisheries, although some of them also have overlapping regulatory power over the OF sector in varying degrees and forms.

All these government ministries have been the dirigiste activists promoting the development of domestic industries under their jurisdictions, thus continuing the bureaucratic tradition established by the Japanese government after the Meiji Restoration of 1868. As Japan was a latecomer nation, government ministries and agencies were created, as Chalmers Johnson (1989) so aptly describes, not so much as 'civil servants' *per se*, as in the USA, but rather as 'task-oriented mobilization and development agencies' whose main functions were originally 'to guide Japan's rapid forced development in order to forestall incipient colonization by Western imperialists'. In other words, their current predispositions toward controls are path-dependent. In the terminology of Dunning (1992*a*), they were established specifically as macro-organizational institutions devoted to exercising 'the modality by which the resources and capabilities with their jurisdictions are created, upgraded, and allocated among different uses, and the efficiency at which they are deployed for any given use'.

As the scenario of 'import protection as export promotion' unfolded in the OF sector, its rising trade surplus began to cause a sharp appreciation of the yen and an ever-relentless competitive pressure on the ID sector; hence a 'Dutch disease' effect. However, instead of letting market forces rationalize the ID sector, the government held on to—and even reinforced through administrative guidance—its regulatory involvement further to protect the ID sector. This aggravated the structural gap between the two sectors in respect of their openness to the outside world—a gap which continues to be reflected in price discrepancies between home and foreign markets, especially at the retail level. This is the major symptom of the 'Japanese disease', an increasingly complicating case of the 'Dutch disease'. The OF sector kept raising productivity as it succeeded to become export-competitive and further exposed to the rigor of international competition in a sequence of cumulative causation, whereas the ID sector became even more secluded from such an effect (in terms of exchange rates). (In one sense, the OF industries have successfully taken off as 'flying geese', whereas the ID industries have been turned into 'domesticated geese' or 'fat ducks', so to speak.)

In fact, we would argue that one important reason Japan has been—and still is—able to maintain a low rate of unemployment by international standards, at least in official statistics, is not so much because many Japanese firms practise life-time employment but because the ID sector has been capable of absorbing excess supplies of workers in a disguised form of underemployment. In this respect, the 'inefficient' ID sector once did play an important macro-organizational role as a social safety net or a 'privatized' (yet indirectly subsidized via regulations) welfare programme. But whether such a welfare programme is cost-effective or efficiency-enhancing is debatable.

It should be noted that these two structurally differentiated sectors which have come into existence are not totally separate entities but interconnected in a variety of ways. Japan's automotive industry is in the OF sector, but its distribution and some of its suppliers of inputs are in the ID sector. Japan's automobile-makers established their own networks of exclusive dealerships as well as their own multi-layered systems of parts suppliers. And there is little doubt that their tight controls on distribution are one important hindrance to automobile imports. Even though one automobile-maker's exclusive dealership discriminates equally against all other compatriot competitors (such that some claim that it is not discriminatory to imports), the exclusive dealerships set up by all the major domestic producers as a whole surely become a barrier to imports.

Particularly as the result of their exclusive *keiretsu* sales arrangements, Japan's automobile-makers have been able to maintain relatively price-stable and profitable market conditions at home, which until recently has been enhanced by Japan's steady macro-economic growth environment (Itami 1994). The same situation applies to the consumer electrical and electronic goods sector. Thus, the *keiretsu* groups straddle both the OF and the ID sectors. And the OF portion of their business activities often benefits from the ID portion. This may probably explain, at least in part, why price duality occurs between home and abroad. As Ito and Maruyama (1991: 170) put it,

> The *keiretsu*, or whatever structures make possible vertical restraints and resale price maintenance, may segregate the Japanese market from the rest of the world. Then the pricing-to-the-market behavior [export prices are lowered relative to domestic prices in order to limit the effects of currency appreciations] becomes possible, and the Japanese manufacturers seem to exercise this power. In that sense, the distribution system is guilty of causing the price differential between Japan and abroad.

In addition to the *keiretsu*, the more protected the domestic market is, the easier it is for Japanese producers to discriminate by price against their home consumers. Price discrimination (such as pricing to market) is a 'hidden' form of creating subsidies—that is letting domestic consumers indirectly subsidize exports—and domestic producers. And the OF–ID dual structure provides such a mechanism.[14]

Returning to the OF sector, the incessant drive to product and process innovations, especially the widening spread of 'lean' or flexible production techniques from the automotive industry (i.e. Toyota's production system) to other assembly-based OF industries, especially electronics, further expanded Japan's manufactured exports, causing inevitable trade conflicts overseas. These assembly-based firms first resorted to setting up assembly foreign operations in their core export markets, North America and Europe. This move actually *increased* Japanese exports of parts and components, further ballooning Japan's trade surplus, all the more because the OF sector itself became less resource-using (hence less import-dependent) and higher value added (i.e. human-capital intensive), while the ID sector continued to hinder imports; the upshot was an intensified appreciation of the yen—hence an aggravation of the 'Japanese disease'.

Yet the ID sector-related government ministries continued to protect their own bureaucratic power and interests, resulting in what may be called an Olsonian rigidification of macro-organizational institutions and their practices (Olson 1982).

The super-yen that had started its ascent after the 1985 Plaza accord began to wipe out the price competitiveness of the OF manufacturers. In response, they had to transplant more price-sensitive segments of production involving low-end products and standardized parts and components to low-cost countries, mostly in Asia, via FDI, OEM, and subcontracting. Geographical proximity is critical for the purpose of reducing transaction costs related to delivery logistics, communications, and quality controls. Besides, many Asian economies began to grow rapidly, creating appropriate local markets for low-end products. Initially, Japanese overseas manufacturing was also targeted at Japan's former export markets in North America and Europe through the route of circular production and exporting. But with the rise in the value of the Japanese yen and the accompanying decline in the values of the dollar and other, especially Asian, currencies, Japan began to pull in more manufactured imports from its own overseas ventures. In other words, it is not really the ID sector but the initially export-competitive OF sector that is becoming increasingly more and more import-pulling; that is, a full unfolding of the paradox of 'import protection as import expansion' in the OF sector. Ever since 1985, in fact, the Japanese electronics industry has rapidly lost price competitiveness in many consumer electronics goods and has begun to import them in growing amounts—mostly from their own overseas ventures. It is now concentrating on development and production of higher value-added high-tech components at home.

In sum, ironically, many once export-competitive industries in the OF sector have grown import-compatible—and in fact, import-promoting at least in volume if not in value because of the appreciated yen. Yet this development has only recently begun, and its effect is not large enough to offset the import-aversion of the ID sector. This may provide one explanation of why the Japanese economy as a whole is unusually import-averse and has become even more so in the recent past. A recent study by Kiyoshi Kojima (1994, 1996) reveals a *declining* trend in the ratio of imports to GNP from ever since 1980; it declined from 13.3 per cent in 1980 down to 6.3 per cent in 1992. The ratio had gradually risen from 10.4 per cent in 1960 to 13.3 per cent in 1980 largely because Japan's heavy and chemical industrialization pulled in imported resources.

Kojima, therefore, advocates the promotion of imports of finished goods, particularly consumer goods, instead of imports of raw materials and intermediate producer goods, by arguing that the latter merely lead to more exports—hence a greater trade surplus—since they reduce production costs in manufacturing, especially now that the yen has appreciated so much. We would add that probably 100 per cent pass-throughs usually occur for intra-firm-imported intermediate products (parts and components) from Japanese manufacturers' overseas ventures.

The 'new-industrial-dualism' paradigm we have presented in this chapter is thus consistent with, and supportive of, Kojima's policy prescription. Super-yen-pulled imports are taking place mainly in the OF sector, resulting in greater export competitiveness, but such imports have so far been only reluctantly allowed into the ID sector, the sector which is still laden with many distribution-related regulations, and administrative guidance hinders imports.

4.1. The Possibility of Self-Immuno-Cure

Particularly after the collapse of Japan's bubble economy in 1990, its government became disarrayed. Interestingly enough, MITI, which used to be the most ardent nationalist in its zeal to build domestic industries, has ended up emerging as a self-claimed 'internationalist' or 'two-way facilitator of international exchanges'—an internationalist, at least by the traditional standard of Japanese ministries and compared to other ministries, even though it still retains some import-inhibiting regulations, notably the notorious Large-Scale Retail Store Law aimed at protecting the country's politically powerful constituency, small shopkeepers (i.e. the small-business sector) (Ozawa 1996). MITI, for example, is promoting manufactured imports and inward FDI through its agency, JETRO—and most recently (in 1994) promised to 'review' the retail law (but by March 2000).

This development demonstrates that, in this age of global capitalism, there is no longer such a thing as a successful *national* industry in an open economy. The more successful—i.e. the more able to compete in the world market—an industry becomes under the dynamic formula of 'infant-industry' protection, the more deeply it inevitably ends up getting involved with its foreign markets and competitors, going beyond exporting and transforming itself into a FDI operator. In other words, any successful industry cannot remain national; it ineluctably turns multinational. Fostering industrial growth is basically the same as fostering industrial knowledge. This seeming irony of *knowledge accumulation as knowledge diffusion* can then be called the 'price-knowledge-flow' mechanism as an analogy to David Hume's 'price-specie-flow' mechanism; even if a country tries to foster and accumulate knowledge at home under protection or special promotion, such knowledge, once accumulated, will be eventually drained out through transnational business activities. This analogy seems most appropriate; after all, Japan has long pursued neo-mercantilist policies.

No wonder, then, that the policy orientation of MITI, the OF sector overseer, has drastically altered and grown increasingly 'international' as a result of the enormously successful expansion of manufacturing (i.e. knowledge accumulation), notably in assembly-based industries where lean production techniques are innovated and effectively exploited. In contrast to this supercompetitive, multinationalized status of the OF sector, however, the ID sector still remains inner-oriented and import-averse—so rendered mostly by the institutional rigidification of the ministries and their administrative practices, as well as by Japan's distinct business culture.

Given the scarcity of land and natural resources in Japan, the Ministry of Agriculture, Forestry, and Fisheries has inevitably taken and continues to take a protectionist stance. Although the Japanese financial sector has been liberalized to a considerable extent, there are still many regulatory restrictions and bureaucratic self-preserving barriers. The national economy needs to be 'bounded' or 'encircled' to such an extent as necessary for effective macro (fiscal and monetary) stabilization (Pasinetti 1993). Japan's financial sector is, therefore, by nature not as open as the manufacturing sector, and the Ministry of Finance—along with its agent, the Bank of Japan—is thus still strongly inward-focused as opposed to MITI. The Ministry of Posts and Telecommunications, the Ministry of Construction, the Ministry of Health and Welfare, and other IP-sector-related agencies are basically domestic-service-focused and therefore do not have much orientation towards the outside world.

A big question, then, is: Will the 'Japanese disease' continue to get worse or will it be cured in some way? Here, we believe that there are some encouraging signs. Since the OF sector can no longer tolerate the debilitating effects of the disease (the ever-rising yen and the threat of sectoral hollowing-out), it is increasingly putting pressure, both politically and in terms of market connectedness (i.e. via its own imports), on the ID sector and its affiliated ministries to deregulate and rationalize/modernize. For example, imported food and beverage (liquor, beer, and soft drinks) have begun to be marketed at substantial discount prices. Coca Cola, Japan, and its bottlers are now confronted with much cheaper imports; imported Coke from the USA is cheaper than the one produced in Japan. Coca Cola, Japan, has lost its highly lucrative market long sheltered from imports! Toys 'R' US has revolutionalized the toy retailing system in Japan. It now offers 15,000 items at 10–15 per cent discounts in contrast to the typical small Japanese toy store with stocks between 1,000 and 2,000 (*Business Week* 1991). This is surely a boon to Japanese consumers, since they are given a much greater degree of freedom in their choice of different items at discount prices all at once for one-stop shopping.

Politicians and bureaucrats have certainly declined in social esteem. In April 1995 Japanese voters in Tokyo and Osaka elected two 'entertainers' as mayors for Japan's two largest cities by casting protest ballots—the elections interpreted as messages that the people want change in Japan's politics. The historic rise of the yen in 1995 is one key factor behind this development.

Although there is a long way to go, the ID sector has no doubt begun to be exposed to the international market forces that are gradually but inexorably penetrating into the sheltered Japanese markets. The new industrial dualism will sooner or later have to be removed. The macro-organizational institutions entrenched and ossified in the ID sector are now about to be rejuvenated by the same forces of international competition from which they were originally protected. The rationalization/modernization of the ID sector is in the long-term interest of Japanese industry, since it will enhance its overall structural efficiency and competitiveness—and, more importantly, it may be able to eliminate the burden of one external pressure, a super-yen, imposed on the highly competitive OF sector.

Will Japan, then, be a more open, more highly market-guided, and less government-involved economy? Yet, as cautioned by some observers, the Japanese government's role as a strategic promoter of knowledge creation will continue to be intensified so as to stay ahead of their competitors, especially ahead of Asia's catching-up economies in the context of the FG paradigm. For example, Laura Tyson (1991: 301) observes:

> There is no doubt that overt trade and investment barriers to the Japanese market have been largely eliminated. But government R&D subsidies continue to target activities and industries for promotion, and these subsidies continue to advantage Japanese producers in both domestic and global competition. In addition, structural barriers continue to persist in a variety of forms, including standards, testing, and certification procedures, procurement and bidding practices, and the pattern of cooperative business relationships that Japan's strategic industrial policy continues to foster. To many foreign producers, especially those competing with Japanese companies in activities that have been accorded strategic significance by the Japanese government, the Japanese market, while formally open, is effectively closed.

In other words, this implies a possibility that the OF sector itself—instead of the ID sector—becomes relatively more restrictive in permitting foreign MNEs' participation in Japan's high-tech industries, a need certainly much greater if the 'Japanese disease' continues to worsen and the yen remains at its overvalued level. Even if what Tyson says is true, this will not lead to the 'Japanese disease' so long as the ID sector is made open and Japan becomes more import-absorbent. A successful origination of a series of new technologies in Japan against the backdrop of the ever-integrating global economy will initiate a sequence of R&D → domestic production → exports → outward FDI → overseas production → imports—that is, Vernon's product-cycle type of transnational business activities.

5. Conclusions

The Japanese experience presents an interesting case of a mixture of success and failure of macro-organizational policies and their strengths and weaknesses. Perhaps Japan has been one of the most active macro-organizational strategists because of its erstwhile status as a latecomer. In general, it may be hypothesized that macro-organizational policies are more likely to be adopted by—and are more relevant for—a developing (catching-up) economy than an advanced (fully marketized) economy, because of the former's very need to supplement the as yet underdeveloped market mechanism. In this respect, Japan has accumulated a large amount of 'know-how' about the techniques of macro-organizational management. At least, certainly the government officials appear to think so—despite the problem of the 'Japanese disease'. And this is the very reason why MITI and the Ministry of Finance are eager to 'sell' developmental advice and ideas to the developing world, including the transition economies in Eastern and Central

Europe, especially in connection with Japan's ever-growing capacity to offer economic aid (*The Economist* (1995) calls this new brand of Japan's confidence 'nice new nationalism').

The evolutionary FG framework, as reformulated above, of 'import protection as import expansion' is useful in explaining how Japan has achieved its catch-up with the advanced West in a number of key industries and in understanding how Japan's strategies *vis-à-vis* developing countries, especially in Asia, have been formulated at both the government and industry levels. For both levels, a hierarchical perspective is germane. Now that Japan has joined the ranks of the advanced countries, a more horizontally (instead of vertically) oriented frame of references—in the place of a hierarchical one—is required in managing its relations harmoniously with other advanced countries. It remains to be seen if and how Japan can devise such a new policy framework.

NOTES

1. For a somewhat similar but more generic explanation of the relationship between MNE activity and the economic development of countries, see Dunning and Narula (1995).
2. Pekka Korhonen (1994) specifically identifies the FG paradigm as Japan's development ideology, especially for the post-Second-World-War period.
3. See Ch. 1 (by Dunning) for Frederick List's view of a latecomer's economic development.
4. This description of the market is used in Eatwell (1982) and also emphasized in Ozawa (1987) in the context of the Japanese experience.
5. The *keiretsu* is a much looser form of inter-firm affiliation than the *zaibatsu*, which centralized its administrative power in the hands of the family-owned parent holding company. There are six major bank-centred (*kinyu*) *keiretsu* groups: Mitsubishi, Mitsui, Sumitomo, Fuyo, Sanwa, and Dai-Ichi Kangyo. At the same time, there are many groups of closely affiliated manufacturers who are involved in a chain of vertically integrated operations, thereby forming so-called *kigyo* (industrial or corporate) groups; the best examples are the Toyota group and the Matsushita group. In this study, the concept of *keiretsu* is used in a very broad sense to cover the *kigyo* groups, as well as other much more loosely affiliated ones. So defined, Japan's manufacturing sector in particular is coordinated mostly by the *keiretsu* rather than the market.
6. Pranab Bardhan (1988: 62), for example, aptly observes: 'If managing the local acquisition of technology capability, more than factor accumulation or allocation, is at the core of industrialization, the catalytic role of strategic and selective intervention is imperative in information gathering in encountering indivisibilities in effective assimilation of new knowledge, in bargaining terms of technology agreements, in underwriting risks and raising credit, in providing marketing infrastructure, in coordinating rationalization in established industries, in minimizing the social costs of dislocation in industrial reorganization, and, in general, in sailing the uncharted waters of potential

dynamic comparative advantage, as the recent history of Japan and South Korea amply demonstrate.'

7. This point was emphasized by Moritani (1982). In reference to the Korean experience, Alice Amsden (1989) similarly points out that these are the features of latecomers' technological achievements.
8. Christopher Freeman (1974) introduced a taxonomy of strategic firm characteristics: offensive, defensive, imitative, dependent, traditional, and opportunist.
9. 'Firms with a secure home market, the argument runs, have a number of advantages; they are assured of the economies of large-scale production, of selling enough over time to move down the learning curve, of earning enough to recover the costs of R&D. While charging high prices in the domestic market, they can "incrementally price" and flood foreign markets with low cost products . . . By giving a domestic firm a privileged position in some one market, a country gives it *an advantage in scale over foreign rivals*. This scale advantage translates into lower marginal costs and higher market share even in unprotected markets' (Krugman 1984: 180–1; emphasis added). Under 'reserved competition' Japanese firms did not enjoy an advantage in scale over foreign rivals.
10. This means that in terms of the stages paradigm mentioned in n. 12, Japanese industry is in the Schumpeterian stage of knowledge-driven growth.
11. For a related analysis of the changing role of the market, hierarchies and governments in the advanced Western economies since the late nineteenth century, see Dunning (1993: ch. 12).
12. Elsewhere (Ozawa 1991) I have introduced an evolutionary-stages paradigm of growth and FDI. The structural transformation of Japanese industry and its outward investment can be divided into a sequence of four stages. Stage I (1950 to the mid-1960s): labour-intensive growth in textiles, sundries, and other low-wage goods (or 'Heckscher-Ohlin industries') soon accompanied by the 'elementary' (low-wage labour-seeking) type of FDI, especially in the neighbouring Asian countries. Stage II (the late 1950s to the early 1970s): heavy and chemical industrialization in such scale-based industries as steel, petrochemicals, and synthetic fibres ('non-differentiated Smithian industries') accompanied by the resource-seeking (later followed by 'house-cleaning') type of FDI. Stage III (the late 1960s to the present): growth of, and the rising trade surplus in, components-intensive, assembly-based industries (notably automobiles and electronics) or 'differentiated Smithian industries'—soon resulting in the 'export-substituting' and 'surplus-recycling' types of FDI. Stage IV (the early 1980s onwards): growth of mechatronics-based flexible manufacturing ('Schumpeterian industries') and high-yen-induced industrial restructuring resulting in the 'industrial shedding' and 'strategic-alliance-seeking' types of international business activities.
13. Some (so-called 'revisionists') argue that the Japanese distribution system is not inefficient, since the way it operates is what Japanese customers want. According to this group, for example, Japanese consumers prefer small neighbourhood stores for frequent shopping, since they lack large storage/refrigerator capacities at home and like fresh supplies. Moreover, a study made by Ito and Maruyama (1991: 170) concludes: 'Although the Japanese distribution system appears to be very different from its US counterpart, its performance, measured by value added, gross margin, operating expenses, and labor costs, is quite comparable with US performance. Hence, we do not have any evidence to conclude that the Japanese characteristics are symptoms of inefficiency.'

14. One of the most controversial regulations in the ID sector is the Large-Scale Retail Store Law, a barrier to the establishment of large-scale stores, especially discount stores. It is said that there are about five times more department stores per person in the USA than in Japan (Flath 1991). As Okuno-Fujiwara (1991: 294) put it: 'The system of the Large Stores Law is a system for insiders, where not only local stores and large stores who have already entered, but also large stores whose entry is temporarily blocked may benefit from the system. Consumers are the real losers, but there is no place where they can file their complaints'. As mentioned earlier, one of Japan's developmental objectives embedded in Japan's 5-Year-Plan for Economic Independence was 'curtailment of consumption'. Unfortunately, such an objective has been more or less institutionalized and petrified, despite Japan's economic growth and rising personal income.

REFERENCES

Abegglen, J. C., and Rapp, W. V. (1970), 'Japanese Managerial Behaviors and "Excessive Competition"', *The Developing Economies*, 8 (December), 427–44.

Abo, T. (1994), *Hybrid Factory: The Japanese Production System in the United States* (New York: Oxford University Press).

Akamatsu, K. (1935), 'Waga Kuni Yomo Kogyohin no Boeki Susei [The trend of Foreign Trade in Manufactured Woolen Goods in Japan]', *Shogyo Keizai Ronso* (Journal of Nagoya Higher Commercial School), vol. unknown, pp. 129 ff.

—— (1956), 'Waga Kuni Sangyo Hatten no Ganko Keitai, tokuni Kikai Kigu Kigyo ni tsuite [FG Formation in the Development of Industries in Japan: with Special Reference to the Machine Tool Industry]', *Hitotsubashi Ronso* (Journal of Hitotsubashi University), vol. unknown (November), pp. 68 ff.

—— (1957), 'Waga Kuni Keizai Hatten no Sogo Beshoho [Synthetic Dialectics of Industrial Development in Japan]', *Shogyo Keizai Ronso* (Journal of Nagoya Higher Commercial School), vol. unknown, pp. 179 ff.

—— (1961), 'A Theory of Unbalanced Growth in the World Economy', *Weltwirtschaftliches Archiv*, 86: 196–215.

—— (1962), 'A Historical Pattern of Economic Growth in Developing Countries', *The Developing Economies*, Preliminary Issue No. 1 (March–August), 1–23.

Amsden, A. H. (1989), *Asia's Next Giant: South Korea and Late Industrialization* (Oxford: Oxford University Press).

Bardhan, Pranab (1988), 'Alternative Approaches to Development Economics', in Hollis Chenery and T. N. Srinivasan (eds.), *Handbook of Development Economics* (Amsterdam: North Holland), 39–72.

Business Week (1991), 'Guess Who's Selling Barbies in Japan Now' (9 Dec.), 72–6.

Cusumano, M. A. (1989), *The Japanese Automobile Industry: Technology and Management at Nissan and Toyota* (Cambridge, Mass.: Harvard University Press).

Dunning, J. H. (1992*a*), 'Review Article: The Competitive Advantage of Countries and the Activities of Transnational Corporations', *Transnational Corporations*, 1 (February), 135–168.

Dunning, J. H. (1992*b*), 'The Global Economy, Domestic Governance, Strategies and Transnational Corporations: Interactions and Policy Implications', *Transnational Corporations*, 1 (December), 7–45.

—— (1993), *The Globalization of Business* (London: Routledge).

—— and Narula, R. (1996) (eds.), *Foreign Direct Investment and Governments: Catalysts for Change* (London: Routledge).

Eatwell, J. (1982), *Whatever Happened to Britain? The Economics of Decline* (London: British Broadcasting Corporation).

The Economist (1995), 'Japan: The New Nationalists' (14–20 Jan.), 19–21.

Flath, D. (1991), 'Comment: Motoshige Itoh, "The Japanese Distribution System and Access to the Japanese Market"', in Paul Krugman (ed.), *Trade with Japan: Has the Door Opened Wider?* (Chicago: University of Chicago Press).

Freeman, C. (1974), *The Economics of Industrial Innovation* (Harmondsworth, Middx.: Penguin).

Henderson, D. F. (1973), *Foreign Enterprise in Japan: Laws and Policies* (Chapel Hill, NC.: University of North Carolina Press).

Itami, H. (1994), *Nihon no Jidosha Sangyo: Naze Kyubureiki ga Kakkatta noka?* [Japan's Auto Industry: Why a Sudden Brake?] (Tokyo: NTT).

Ito, T., and Maruyama, M. (1991), 'Is the Japanese Distribution System Really Inefficient?', in P. Krugman (ed.), *Trade with Japan: Has the Door Opened Wider?* (Chicago: University of Chicago Press).

Johnson, C. (1982), *MITI and the Japanese Miracle: The Growth of Industrial Policy, 1925–1975* (Stanford: Stanford University Press).

—— (1989), 'MITI, MPT, and The Telecom Wars: How Japan Makes Policy for High Technology', in C. Johnson, L. Tyson, and J. Zysman (eds.), *Politics and Productivity: How Japan's Development Strategy Works* (New York: HarperBusiness).

—— Tyson, L., Zysman, J. (1989) (eds.), *Politics and Productivity: How Japan's Development Strategy Works* (New York: HarperBusiness).

Kojima, K. (1994), 'Nihon no Yunyu Izondo [Import Dependency of Japan]', *Sekai Keizai Hyoron* (May), 24–33.

—— (1996), *Kaiho Keizai Taikei* [Open-Economy Paradigm] (Tokyo: Bunshindo).

Komiya, R., Okuno, M., and Suzumura, K. (1988), *Industrial Policy of Japan* (Tokyo: Academic Press).

Korhonen, P. (1994), *Japan and the Pacific Free Trade Area* (London: Routledge).

Krueger, A. O. (1993), 'American Bilateral Trading Arrangements and East Asian Interests', in Takatoshi Ito and Anne O. Krueger (eds.), *Trade and Protectionism* (Chicago: University of Chicago Press).

Krugman, P. (1984), 'Import Protection as Export Promotion: International Competition in the Presence of Oligopoly and Economics of Scale', in H. Kierzkowski (ed.), *Monopolistic Competition and International Trade* (Oxford: Oxford University Press).

Linder, B. S. (1961), *An Essay on Trade and Transformation* (New York: John Wiley).

Mason, M. (1992), *American Multinationals and Japan* (Cambridge, Mass.: Harvard University Press).

Morita, A. (1986), *Made in Japan: Akio Morita and Sony* (New York: Dutton).

Moritani, M. (1982), *Japanese Technology: Getting the Best from the Least* (Tokyo: Simul Press).

Nau, H. R. (1994), 'Making United States Trade Policy Truly Strategic', *International Journal*, 49 (Summer), 509–35.

Nivola, P. S. (1993), *Regulating Unfair Trade* (Washington: Brookings Institution).

Okimoto, D. I. (1989), *Between MITI and the Market: Japanese Industrial Policy for High Technology* (Stanford, Calif.: Stanford University Press).

Okuno-Fujiwara, M. (1991), 'Industrial Policy in Japan: A Political Economy View', in P. Krugman (ed.), '*Trade with Japan: Has the Door Opened Wider?* (Chicago: University of Chicago Press).

Olson, M. (1982), *The Rise and Decline of Nations: Economic Growth, Stagnation and Social Rigidities* (New Haven, Conn.: Yale University Press).

Ozaki, R. S. (1972), *The Control of Imports and Foreign Capital in Japan* (New York: Praeger).

Ozawa, T. (1974), *Japan's Technological Challenge to the West, 1950–1974: Motivation and Accomplishment* (Cambridge, Mass.: MIT Press).

—— (1980), 'Government Control over Technology Acquisition and Firms' Entry into New Sectors', *Cambridge Journal of Economics*, 4 (June), 133–46.

—— (1987), 'Can the Market Alone Manage Structural Upgrading? A Challenge Posed by Economic Independence', in J. Dunning and M. Usui (eds.), *Structural Change, Economic Interdependence and World Development* (London: Macmillan).

—— (1988), 'Geo-informatics and a Dynamic Infant-Industry Paradigm: Japan and the Computer Industry' (Working Paper TP-3, the Americas Program, Stanford University, paper presented at the International Symposium of Technology Policy in the Americas at Stanford University, 1–3 December 1988).

—— (1989), 'Japan's Strategic Policy Towards Outward Direct Investment' (mimeo; Fort Collins: Colorado State University, July).

—— (1991), 'Japanese Multinationals and 1992', in B. Burgenmeier and J. L. Mucchielli (eds.), *Multinationals and Europe 1992: Strategies for the Future* (London: Routledge).

—— (1994), 'Japan's External Asymmetries and Assembly Industries: Lean Production as a Source of Competitive Advantage', *Transnational Corporations*, 3 (December), 25–51.

—— (1995), 'Dynamic Industrial Policy and Flexible Production: Toward A Techno-structural Evolutionary Paradigm of MITI's Role', *Revue d'Économie Industrielle*, 71: 39–59.

—— (1996), 'The New Economic Nationalism and the "Japanese Disease": The Conundrum of Managed Economic Growth', *Journal of Economic Issues*, 30: 483–91.

—— and Sato, M. (1989), 'JETRO, Japan's Adaptive Innovation in the Organization of Trade', *Journal of World Trade*, 23 (August), 15–24.

Pasinetti, L. L. (1993), *Structural Economic Dynamics: A Theory of the Economic Consequences of Human Learning* (Cambridge: Cambridge University Press).

Peck, M. J. (1976), 'Technology', in Hugh Patrick and Henry Rosovsky (eds.), *Asia's New Giants: How the Japanese Economy Works* (Washington: Brookings Institution).

Porter, M. E. (1990), *The Competitive Advantage of Nations* (New York: The Free Press).

Samuels, R. J. (1994), '*Rich Nation, Strong Army': National Security and the Technological Transformation of Japan* (Ithaca, NY: Cornell University Press).

Stiglitz, J. E. (1989), 'Markets, Market Failures, and Development', *American Economic Review*, 79: 197–203.

—— (1993), 'The Role of the State in Financial Markets', in *Proceedings of the World Bank Annual Conference on Development Economics* (Washington: World Bank), 19–54.

Sugihara, K. (1994), 'The Development of an Informational Infrastructure in Meiji Japan', in L. Bud-Frierman (ed.), *Information Acumen: The Understanding and Use of Knowledge in Modern Business* (London: Routledge).

Tyson, L. (1991), 'Comment [on Okuno-Fujiwara's Paper]', in P. Krugman (ed.), *Trade with Japan: Has the Door Opened Wider?* (Chicago: University of Chicago).

Vernon, R. (1966), 'International Investment and International Trade in the Product Cycle', *Quarterly Journal of Economics*, 80: 190–207.

Womack, J. P., Jones, D. T., and Roos, D. (1990), *The Machine that Changed the World* (New York: Macmillan).

World Bank (1993), *The East Asian Miracle: Economic Growth and Public Policy* (New York: Oxford University Press).

14

East Asia

Sanjaya Lall

1. **Introduction**

The role of the government in economic life is comprehensively reviewed by John Dunning in Chapter 1. This role in East Asia has been the subject of intense debate in the economic development literature. The intention in this chapter is not to go into the general debate, but to highlight the approach (or rather, the diverse range of approaches) of the leading East Asian NIEs to FDI as one aspect of their industrial strategy. This nevertheless leads to some consideration of the industrial policy debate, since the factors that attracted or kept out FDI in the NIEs were related to the creation of the specific ownership advantages of their national firms, and determined the form of their participation in trade. Our focus will be on the technological aspects of FDI policy, as it is here that the interaction between governments, international business, and competitiveness is most vividly revealed. The chapter focuses on the Four Tigers (Hong Kong, Singapore, Korea, and Taiwan).[1]

We begin with a few remarks on the industrial policy debate in Asia. For much of the 1970s and the early 1980s development economists regarded the NIEs of East Asia as market-driven economic systems that pursued practically free trade, open-door policies to FDI, and liberal resource allocation domestically. Their astounding economic success was then traced to the efficiency of free markets and private enterprise; by contrast, the sluggish performance of other developing countries was blamed on inefficient government intervention. This portrayal had a strong basis in theory. Neoclassical economics provided the framework and tools for explaining how free markets optimize resource allocation, and the development community assumed that static optimization led to dynamic growth of the sort witnessed in East Asia. The creation of new competitive advantages in response to signals given by free trade and driven by the accumulation of the primary factors of production, the transfer and costless absorption of new technologies and information by FDI and trade, and the development of institutions supporting industrialization by the private sector, were all taken for granted.

The result was a formidable case for *wholesale* and *rapid* liberalization in all developing countries regardless of their level of development: not the improvement of government interventions, not the improvement of markets and the setting-up of new institutions, but the wholesale rejection of the state as an organizer of economic activity. In the context of FDI policies, the case was for open-door policies to investment and technology flows in a liberal trade setting, letting market prices decide a country's comparative advantage and the reaction of MNEs to this advantage. No intervention was envisaged either in the flow of international investment or in the behaviour of investors, since free markets were assumed to be fully efficient. This approach drew explicitly or implicitly on the success of East Asia.

This interpretation of the East Asian experience has been strongly challenged, on both theoretical and empirical grounds. The theoretical presumption that static optimization led to faster sustained growth is not part of traditional neoclassical growth theory, which assumes diminishing returns to investment and a convergence of growth rates. It then becomes necessary to introduce productive factors that enjoy increasing returns. 'New' growth theory does this in the form of human capital and technology. Since these tend to have significant externalities, they can suffer from market failure: optimal levels of investment may then require non-market intervention. These interventions are generic in the sense that they do not favour particular activities over others; these are termed 'functional' or 'market friendly' in the current industrial policy literature, in contrast to 'selective' interventions where governments pick particular activities to encourage or discourage. Much of the current debate revolves around the desirability of selective interventions, since it is now accepted that functional interventions are widely needed in infrastructure, skill, and technology creation.

Nevertheless, as described by Lipsey in Chapter 2 of this volume, there are theoretical grounds for expecting other kinds of market failures in resource allocation. Capital market failures in developing countries are widely recognized (Stiglitz 1989), but failures in other markets can arise from several sources: externalities arising in industrial and technological activities, information market deficiencies, the need to coordinate interlinked investment decisions, risky and unpredictable learning processes (and the need to invest in learning the learning process itself), institutional gaps, and so on. These failures may call for selective interventions rather than functional ones. In particular, externalities and learning processes are likely to differ substantially between activities, and their exploitation or remedying is likely to call for different policy interventions geared to the circumstances (Lall 1994*b*). There is nothing in economic theory that says that functional interventions are better than selective ones. The recent trend to favour functional interventions has no theoretical basis if the relevant forms of market failure exist. The basis for rejecting selectivity must then lie in *empirical* reasoning: either the relevant market failures do not exist (or are trivial), or they are important but in practice cannot be remedied efficiently by governments.

On the empirical side, considerable evidence has been accumulated to show that selective interventions can be of vital significance for accelerating and deepening the process of industrial development, and that, under certain conditions, governments can and do intervene effectively. This does not contradict the failures of earlier interventions, since the conditions for efficient industrial policy differ from those under which classic import-substituting strategies were devised and implemented. Moreover, theory suggests that not all forms of industrial development require selective interventions—it is mainly entry into complex and difficult technologies that faces severe market failures and calls for policy support. Here selectivity may be needed not just in product and capital markets but also in factor markets such as education, technology, information, and institutional development normally considered the province of functional interventions. The essence of effective industrial policy seems to lie in selectivity in all these markets and in the integration of both factor and product market interventions around well-defined strategic goals.

The evidence shows clearly that for much of the past thirty years the governments of most Asian NIEs have intervened pervasively, over long periods, and often highly selectively, in factor and product markets (including FDI).[2] Each has aimed at differing levels of industrial deepening, local content, local ownership of industry, and indigenous mastery of complex technological functions. As a consequence, each has pursued a different strategy, with different functional and selective interventions. There have been been many routes to, and strategies for, economic success, and 'success' has been compatible with many ways of building up industry, ownership advantages, and international integration. In other words, there has been no unique 'East Asian model' but a variety of models with a variety of results from differing interventions. It is these *differences* that are of most analytical and policy interest.

2. **Policy Issues in International Investment**

Two broad interrelated policy issues arise for developing countries in the context of international investment.[3] The first is whether and how much FDI to allow in—that is, whether to exercise selectivity in letting in MNEs. The second is, having permitted FDI, whether to intervene in resource allocation by MNEs, in setting conditions for their operations, and in attracting more FDI or investments of higher 'quality'. A case can be made that both forms of intervention are justifiable if there is a perceived divergence between private and social returns from MNE activity in free markets. The first set of issues is determined by the costs and benefits of FDI to a developing host country as compared to alternative ways of accessing capital, technology, and skills. The second is determined by market failures in domestic (and foreign) markets which guide MNE activities and which may be altered to obtain larger social benefits for the host economy.

It is not clear that this market-failure framework is necessarily the best way of addressing issues of government strategy. As Professor Lipsey (1995) notes in a private communication:

> the only context in which I can understand the concept of 'market failure' is when there is a unique social optimum and the free market fails to achieve it (which, of course, it

always would if such an optimum existed in the real world rather than, as it does, just in the theorist's imagination). But we live in a world of acquired human capital in which there is no *effective* upper limit to the amounts and kinds of capital that can be acquired. (Of course, there are ultimate limits, but neither the developing or the developed countries are typically pressing on them . . .) In such a world, there are many possible equilibria and many possible skill and trade patterns . . . *What would a non-market-failing world produce by way of human capital and acquired comparative advantage?*

In other words, when government policies change the parameters within which market forces operate and markets clear (if they do), it becomes very difficult to apply static optimization analysis and determine deviations from an optimum that interventions should address. The strategies adopted by the East Asian NIEs have been very much of this kind, and the particular targets they have aimed at have changed the basic ground rules within which their markets functioned, and are functioning.

There remain many valid cases in which the static market failure analysis is valid, in that existing markets do not function well and can be improved. In principle, therefore, the analyst of policy must distinguish between interventions that are addressing static market failures and those that are changing the market parameters. In practice, this distinction is very difficult to apply. Many interventions would tend to span both categories—for instance, a policy to improve the functioning of the training market may improve the provision of skills in relation to existing demand and also create skills in anticipation of new technologies or of increasing the nature of activities undertaken within the economy. For present purposes, the distinction is probably not very important, and it is convenient to use the language of market failures as long as it is recognized that we are including larger strategic considerations.

To return to policies with respect to FDI, we noted that these may be directed to two sets of issues: the entry and extent of FDI, and the conditions under which foreign investors are allowed to operate in a host country. What are the relevant considerations?

2.1. Entry and Extent of FDI

The literature on international investment attributes the existence of MNEs to the presence of failures in the markets for the intangible assets that constitute their 'ownership advantages' (Dunning 1988). Without such advantages there would be no reason for MNEs to come into being: the essence of transnationalization is the internalization of imperfect intermediate markets. This, by itself, has no particular policy implications, though the structural market failures that account for the existence of MNEs may be exacerbated by their expansion (for instance, by increasing market concentration and the internalization of information markets). However, as long as the internalized markets of MNEs are considered 'efficient', not just for the firm, but also for host economies, there will be no divergence between private and social interests. It is only when there is such a divergence that the imposition of internalized markets of MNEs on those of the host economy may become economically undesirable.

Developing countries see many important benefits in gaining access to the internalized markets of MNEs, especially for technology and skills. MNEs are among the most powerful means available for transferring modern technologies to developing countries and overcoming obstacles to their utilization. By virtue of their internal reserves of capital, skills, technology, and information, they face fewer market failures than local firms in utilizing new technologies efficiently in developing economies. In most circumstances, therefore, it is reasonable to expect that their presence benefits local productivity and competitiveness. Moreover, since MNEs are at the forefront of innovation, their presence provides an effective means of keeping up with new technologies as they emerge. Their established brandnames, global marketing presence, and international flows of skills all add to their technological advantages.

What case can there be for exercising selectivity on FDI? Three reasons can be found in the development literature.

1. There is an important distinction between the transfer and utilization of production technologies and the transfer and development of more complex design, development, and innovative capabilities. Innovative activity by MNEs tends to be concentrated in a few developed countries, because of the location of management and decision-making centres, availability of advanced and specialized technical skills, large local markets, linkages with established suppliers and buyers, closeness to advanced science and technology institutions, and proximity to central decision-making. The upgrading of capabilities in developing countries to the levels needed for high-level technological activity generally involves high learning and other costs which foreign investors tend to be unwilling to take. In less developed economies MNEs may hold back the development of innovative capabilities while enhancing production capabilities; it is mainly the more advanced industrial countries that can attract and fully benefit from the transfer of innovative capabilities by MNEs (Dunning 1993: ch. 11). Thus a passive reliance on MNEs to upgrade and deepen technological capabilities may take a very long time to bear results.
2. The development of high-level capabilities in local firms may be more beneficial than a similar development within MNE affiliates. This would be the case where technological development by local firms leads to a greater spillover of benefits and linkages (to local suppliers and institutions) within the host economy.
3. A strong MNE presence in industry, while stimulating local competitors to be more efficient in their production, can inhibit them from deepening their technological capabilities. Because of the higher risks and longer learning periods involved in creating a design and development capability, local firms exposed to full MNE competition may prefer to import foreign

technologies proven and 'ready made' from overseas rather than invest in their own R&D capabilities.

There may, therefore, be deficiencies in technological deepening in relying *passively* on transfer of technology through MNEs, leading to a relatively static pattern of specialization as far as capability development is concerned. But it may be in the interests of the industrializing country to promote technological deepening. Technological deepening would allow countries to import and absorb new technologies more economically, enter into more advanced activities, keep abreast of new developments, develop new products and processes, and better utilize local resources and linkages. The argument for limiting reliance on internalized means of technology transfer to induce technological development is rather similar to the case for intervening to promote comparative advantage by fostering infant industries, and rests on the remedying of similar market failures in information, capital, technology, and other markets (of course, this is a clear case when the static market-failure approach seems most inadequate in dealing with policy issues, since interventions can take an economy into a completely new realm of competitive advantage in a dynamic sense).

The deepening of local technological capabilities is not an argument for the wholesale exclusion of FDI. On the contrary, it suggests a need for selectivity only in activities and at times that the local technological development is feasible and desirable. In circumstances where the host economy is not capable of economical technological deepening, or where the technology is so closely held or advanced that local development is not possible, a reliance on FDI would be fully justifiable. Moreover, in some cases technological deepening would be achieved not by keeping out MNEs but by inviting them and influencing their activities (see below). Technological deepening can itself become a major factor in attracting higher 'quality' and more FDI: if local innovative capabilities advance, it becomes in the interests of MNEs to transfer more complex activities and R&D itself to those countries.

If it is accepted that *some* interventions are needed to speed up technological development, then we can distinguish two broad strategies for promoting technological deepening:

1. One is actively to seek FDI, but to induce technological upgrading by active interventions in the decisions of foreign investors. Thus, the host country would attract MNEs and use a mixture of incentives, rules, and negotiations, combined with domestic supply-side measures, to induce them to enter activities with more complex technologies, invest in local technological capabilities, establish closer linkages with local technology institutions, and set up local R&D units.
2. The other is to adopt a more independent strategy, restricting technology import via FDI and promoting it in 'externalized' forms (such as licensing, joint ventures, or other means), with local firms retaining control and deepening and extending their technological capabilities.

The choice between the FDI and nationally led strategies of technological development must obviously depend on the country's political economy (some countries, for instance, are committed to open FDI policies or lack the tools of intervention or the local entrepreneurship to mount effective national technological strategies). It will also be influenced by the size and spread of the industrial sector (smaller economies with more specialized industries may prefer the FDI-led route, while larger ones with diverse sectors may prefer the national route). It must be noted, however, that the second strategy of indigenous technological development involves more than keeping down FDI and promoting local ownership or control. Local ownership *per se* may not ensure that deeper innovative capabilities would develop (Najmabadi and Lall 1995), if local firms choose to remain passively dependent on imports of foreign technology and skills, or if they have lower technical skills and managerial capabilities, and are more risk averse, than foreign affiliates. The development of deeper capabilities requires other *complementary* interventions to ensure that incentives exist for local firms to invest in such risky activity. The necessary skills and information have to be available, and capital markets have to be able and willing to finance the learning process. In some circumstances, it may be necessary for local firms to be promoted to sizes that enable them to internalize deficient capital and other markets.

2.2. Intervening in MNE Activities to Promote the Upgrading of Technological Advantages

Market deficiencies may make it necessary to strengthen a country's attractiveness to MNEs, guide MNEs into more complex activities, and develop factor markets that lead to upgrading in the quality of FDI. Given the basic preconditions for attracting foreign investors, for instance, governments may have to 'sell' their countries in international investment markets and target their promotion to particular home countries or firms to overcome deficiencies in information markets (Wells and Wint 1990).

In responding to free market forces, one would normally expect foreign investors to focus on activities that exploit the host country's given competitive advantages rather than those that could be developed with additional effort. In such cases, the upgrading of industrial activities has to wait for a gradual accumulation of production factors, and the reflection of this in relative factor prices. Even so, host countries with rising wages and growing stocks of capital may not necessarily attract FDI in complex and high-skill activities that involve heavy 'learning' costs and externalities. Intervention could then be used to promote the upgrading of FDI from simple, labour-intensive, and low-technology activities to more complex and demanding ones. Intervention could also be used to induce MNEs to deepen their technological activities within given activities, from final assembly and processing to adaptation, design, development, and innovation. Such

TABLE 14.1. FDI inflows, 1982–1992 ($US m.)

Country	1982–7	1988	1989	1990	1991	1992	1993
Hong Kong	1,014	2,627	1,077	1,728	538	1,918	1,667
Korea	253	871	758	715	1,116	550	n.a.
Singapore	1,605	3,655	2,773	5,263	4,395	5,635	6,830
Taiwan	306	959	1,604	1,330	1,271	879	917
Indonesia	282	576	682	1,093	1,482	1,774	2,004
Malaysia	844	719	1,668	2,332	3,998	4,469	4,351
Thailand	287	1,105	1,775	2,444	2,014	2,116	1,715
TOTAL	5,953	15,694	15,719	20,382	21,171	30,489	44,999

Note: n.a. = not available.
Source: UNCTAD (1994, 1995).

intervention would involve MNEs in creating new technological skills, setting up local R&D facilities, establishing closer links with local technology institutions, and strengthening local suppliers.

These are not hypothetical issues: they have guided policy-making in East Asia, and have led to striking differences in the pattern and effects of FDI in the NIEs. The analysis of this is taken up in the following section.

3. East Asian Strategies and Outcomes

The need for selective and other interventions to promote industrialization was widely (though not universally) recognized by the Asian NIEs. However, each government perceived different policy needs, identifying different market failures and adopting different solutions. Some chose to intervene very little in either the entry of MNEs or their subsequent activities; some to rely heavily on MNEs but to intervene in their operations; and some to reduce reliance on MNEs and to intervene intensively to promote local enterprises and indigenous technological capabilities. Unlike many other developing regions, each of these policies was undertaken in a common setting of strong export-orientation, private-sector primacy, well managed macro-economies, and strong, capable governments. However, these common factors, while providing the necessary conditions for industrial success, do not explain the nature and effects of the particular industrial and internationalization strategies followed by the different NIEs.[4]

Table 14.1 shows the recent data on values of FDI inflows and outflows in the leading Asian NIEs as well as the 'new NIEs'. It shows that the largest host countries of the NIEs are Singapore and Malaysia, which are relatively small economies by regional standards, while the large economies of Korea and Taiwan are fairly small recipients, with the amount of FDI inflows declining in 1992–3 and recovering somewhat hereafter. Hong Kong is a relatively large recipient but with stagnating inflows; Indonesia is on a rising trend, while Thailand seems

TABLE 14.2. Inward FDI as % of gross domestic investment, 1981–1994

Country	1981–5	1986–90	1991	1992	1993	1994
Hong Kong	6.5	13.6	2.3	7.7	7.1	8.2
Singapore	181	33.9	33.5	13.3	24.6	23.5
Korea	0.5	1.3	1.0	0.6	0.5	0.6
Taiwan	1.5	3.5	3.0	2.4	2.4	3.5
Indonesia	1.0	2.0	3.6	3.9	3.8	3.6
Thailand	3.2	5.9	4.9	4.8	3.5	1.1
Malaysia	10.8	10.6	23.8	26.0	22.5	16.1
Japan	0.1	—	0.2	0.3	—	0.1

Source: UNCTAD (1996: annex table 5).

to be stagnant or declining. In the 1990s the biggest destination for FDI in the region has not, in fact, been one of these NIEs but China, with inflows rising from $US3.5 billion in 1990 to an estimated $US27.5 billion in 1993. However, these figures are not shown in the table, since China lies outside the ambit of the present discussion.

The differing FDI reliance of the NIEs is further illustrated in Table 14.2, which shows the share of FDI in gross domestic capital formation in the region. It suggests that the countries which have developed the most diverse, deep, complex, and technologically dynamic industrial sectors (Korea, Taiwan, and Japan) had the least reliance on FDI. It is clearly not the lack of incomes, growth, or competitive potential that has led to this low reliance: it was their deliberate policies to restrict FDI inflows. Certainly, their industrial strategies, for most of the period in question, have been directed to the promotion of local enterprises and the development of indigenous technological capabilities, and selectivity on FDI was an important aspect of these strategies. Most of the other NIEs have had more modest technological ambitions and a lesser urge to promote local enterprises.

At the cost of some simplification, the above group of countries may be divided into four categories as far as FDI strategies are concerned:

1. Those that have followed passive open-door policies on MNEs and did not intervene in other ways selectively to promote industrial development (e.g. Hong Kong).
2. Those that have pursued active industrial policies and promoted local enterprises in certain activities, but adopted effectively open-door, non-interventionist policies in most export-oriented sectors (e.g. Thailand, Malaysia).
3. Those that have actively sought heavy MNE participation in manufacturing and did not seek to promote local industrialists, but intervened pervasively and selectively to guide and induce investors to upgrade their activities and increase local technological activity (e.g. Singapore).

4. Those that have selectively restricted FDI and sought to maximize reliance on externalized forms of technology transfer in the context of a comprehensive set of industrial policies to deepen the manufacturing sector, promote local linkages, and increase local innovative capabilities (e.g. Korea and Taiwan, and earlier Japan).

Let us describe briefly the important features of the industrial and FDI strategies of the NIEs.

3.1. Hong Kong

Hong Kong has the most liberal economic regime of the NIEs and has been able to combine free trade and substantial inward FDI with a dynamic indigenous industrial class which traditionally has been very successful in export markets. Hong Kong is, however, a very special case by virtue of its location, long entrepôt tradition, and established infrastructure of trade and finance, the presence of large British companies (the 'Hongs'), and the influx of entrepreneurs and trained textile and metalworking engineers and technicians (with considerable learning embodied in their skills) from mainland China. Its unique background has allowed it to launch into export-oriented light manufacturing under free trade, but it has started and stayed with light labour-intensive manufacturing industry, where the learning costs were relatively low and predictable. Hong Kong's success has been based on the development of operational and marketing capabilities, but there has been little industrial deepening and R&D growth. While there has been some 'natural' progression up the ladder of industrial complexity as product quality has been upgraded and new products added within existing areas of strength, this has been limited in relation to that experienced in other NIEs.

As wages and land costs have risen in Hong Kong, the colony has relocated its manufacturing to other countries, mainly mainland China, with a significant loss of industrial activity at home (during 1986–92 it lost about 35 per cent of its manufacturing employment, and the process is continuing (*Financial Times* 1993: 6)[5]). Its own manufactured exports (as opposed to re-exports) have been declining at around 10 per cent per annum since the mid-1980s, the only NIE to suffer this fate, and its manufacturing production is practically stagnant. Throughout its recent history, Hong Kong has sought not to 'use' MNEs in any deliberate sense, and increasingly its FDI structure has been specialized in activities geared to servicing the Chinese economy. Its impressive overseas investment performance, especially in China, is a reflection of its advanced entrepreneurial and limited technological capabilities rather than of broad industrial strengths. At the same time, the lack of a strong technology base is a cause for concern and the government is launching initiatives like the Hong Kong Industrial Technology Centre selectively to promote local high-technology companies (Clifford 1994: 69).

The Hong Kong economy is continuing to grow and prosper by moving into services, as it approaches its accession to China. However, the lessons of the Hong Kong 'miracle' for industrial development in general are ambiguous. In view of the colony's exceptional institutional history, location, and factor endowments, it is unlikely that its *laissez-faire* strategy would be sufficient by itself to launch a typical developing country on its style of industrial or export development. Furthermore, its lack of industrial policy has resulted in a lack of industrial deepening and the massive deindustrialization over time; most other developing countries would not choose this pattern of industrialization as the basis of long-term growth. Thus, the Hong Kong example does not establish a general case for fully liberal policies on trade or FDI.

3.2. **Singapore**

In contrast to Hong Kong, Singapore illustrates clearly the consequences of a more interventionist policy on FDI and industrial targeting combined with free trade. Singapore has half the population of Hong Kong, but has developed a far deeper industrial structure (in terms of the sophistication of production and exports) and has continued to sustain high rates of industrial and manufactured export growth despite having higher industrial wages. It has probably the world's highest reliance on MNEs, and has done extremely well from it; but, unlike Hong Kong, the government has pursued a policy of deliberately targeting industries and services for promotion, and has aggressively sought and used MNEs as the tool to achieve its objectives.

The Singaporean economy started its recent industrialization with a base of capabilities in entrepôt trading and ship servicing. After a brief period of import substitution, it moved into export-oriented industrialization, based overwhelmingly on investment by multinational enterprises. Unlike Hong Kong, there was a weak tradition of local entrepreneurship, with little influx of technical and entrepreneurial know-how from China. There then followed a decade or so of light industrial activity (garment and semiconductor assembly), after which the Singaporean government acted firmly to upgrade the economy's industrial structure. It intervened in foreign investments to guide MNEs to higher value-added activities, and evolved an education structure specifically designed to provide the high-level technical skills that would be needed in such activities (allowing liberal imports of expatriate skills where the domestic base was inadequate).[6] The government also set up a number of public enterprises to enter activities that were considered in the country's future interest and where foreign investment was considered unfeasible or undesirable; as a result, the public sector in Singapore accounts for a substantial proportion of GDP.

Within the areas in which MNEs operate, Singapore has specialized narrowly in high-skill activities and has drawn upon foreign investors for the basic technology. This has greatly reduced the need for local technological effort, and has permitted the economy to become efficient in very complex technologies without developing a large local R&D base. Over time, however, the Singaporean government has sought to increase indigenous R&D capabilities, and has mounted strong efforts to induce MNEs to establish laboratories there.[7] It has had some success in this, as seen below, but the level of R&D activity, at around 1 per cent of GDP, remains well below the 2.1 per cent achieved in Korea or the 1.7 per cent in Taiwan. Moreover, the Singapore government still finances around half of the total R&D expenditure, which is less than in Taiwan, (around 60 per cent), but far more than the 20 per cent achieved in Korea.

Let us consider just one case of industrial targeting by Singapore—namely its 1991 decision to promote a biotechnology industry (Carroll 1994). In 1988, the government set up an Institute of Molecular and Cell Biology (IMCB) to promote biotechnology research at the cost of $US13.8 million and with an annual funding of $US17.5 million. To nurture the industry further, in 1991 the government set up Singapore Bio-Innovation (SBI) Ltd., through which it invested $US41 million in twelve biotech start-up firms by 1994. The investment in IMCB appears to be paying off scientifically. An IMCB group is at the forefront of research on tyrosine phosphates (for cancer research), while another is sequencing the genomes of several fish species (which could serve as a reference vertebrate genome for the human genome project). IMCB laboratories' innovative assay systems have convinced the pharmaceutical multinational Glaxo to establish a $US31 million trust fund in a drug screening centre within IMCB, and to invest another $US30 million for a neurobiology laboratory focusing on gene research.

Encouraged by these successes, the government has expanded IMCB's research base by establishing the Bioscience Centre which provides facilities for research at the National University of Singapore and the Food Biotechnology Centre. The Bioprocessing Technology Unit, opened in 1990, seeks to improve purification, synthesis, and fermentation methods for commercial production. The laboratory has recently achieved large yields of TNF-[beta], which other companies, including Genzyme in the USA and Boehringer Mannheim in Germany, are keen to put into clinical cancer trials. The National University Medical Institute, being built near IMCB, and the National University Hospital, are modelled on the US National Institutes of Health.

One obstacle to Singapore's quest for scientific success has been its shortage of well-qualified scientists and engineers. To overcome this, the IMCB has recruited scientists from the West, offering research freedom, ample funding, and generous salaries, as well as other benefits for principal investigators. However, Singapore's own students represent the largest source of scientific talent at IMCB. Its two polytechnics are training technicians to fill the growing demand from biotechnology laboratories and industries. The government provides graduate students at IMCB a stipend of $US10,000 a year in addition to tuition fees to encourage this.

This form of selective intervention is typical of the government's hands-on approach to industrial and technological development. The strategy clearly identifies the complex of market failures that holds back entry into high-technology and high-skill activities that it has (correctly) identified as its future comparative advantage. It then goes about addressing each in a systematic (and well-funded) way. There is clearly more to be learned by other developing countries from this approach than from the Hong Kong one of leaving everything to free markets.

3.3. **Korea**

The larger NIEs Korea and Taiwan have treated FDI in very different ways from the above, and also from each other. Korea has gone the furthest in developing advanced innovative capabilities and deepening the industrial structure.[8] The Korean government always had a strong preference for indigenous enterprises, and has assigned FDI a secondary role to that of other forms of technology import. Its export drive has been led by local firms, and a series of interventions (often very selective in both product and factor markets) has allowed these firms to grow to large sizes, span a large range of activities, and invest in developing advanced technological capabilities. In contrast to Hong Kong and Singapore, the domestic market has not been exposed to free trade, and the process of liberalization has been gradual and tightly controlled by the government. The potentially deleterious effects of protection have been offset by strong incentives and pressures to export and face international competition in foreign markets.

In the 1970s Korea launched a massive and highly compressed drive to set up heavy and high-technology industry, relying primarily on capital-goods imports, technology licensing, and other technology transfer agreements to acquire technology.[9] It used reverse engineering, adaptation, and, increasingly, its own design and development efforts to build upon these forms of arm's-length technology imports to develop its own capabilities. Some of the costs of technology imports have been quite high: in the area of semiconductors, for instance, Korean companies have paid over $US1 billion a year for components and technology. However, as a result of these interventions, Korea has been able to use imported technology to feed into its domestic technology and to develop a large and independent innovative base (Najmabadi and Lall 1995). As noted, its R&D expenditures are now around 2 per cent of GDP, and over 80 per cent of this comes from private enterprises: this is by far the highest R&D investment in the developing world (and also in the developed world with the exception of a handful of technological leaders).

One of the pillars of Korean technological strategy, and one that marks it off from the other NIEs (but parallels earlier Japanese experience), has been the deliberate creation of large private conglomerates, the *chaebol*. Initially, the *chaebol* were handpicked from successful exporters and were given a range of subsidies and privileges, including the restriction of MNE entry, in return for pursuing the government's industrial strategy of setting up capital and technology intensive activities geared to export markets.[10] The rationale for fostering size was obvious. In view of deficient local markets for capital, skills, technology, and even infrastructure, large and diversified firms could internalize many of their functions and undertake the cost, risk, and long-term perspective needed to absorb very complex technologies (without a heavy reliance on FDI), further develop it by their own R&D,[11] set up world-scale facilities and market their products abroad by creating their own brand image and distribution networks. This was a costly and high-risk strategy, since the dangers of fostering giant firms in a relatively small economy are obvious. However, these costs were contained by the strict discipline imposed by the government in terms of export performance, vigorous competition between the *chaebol* (except in some cases when they were bidding for international contracts), and deliberate interventions to ensure rationalization of the industrial structure.

Since the technological strategy of Korea is of direct interest to its FDI and globalization philosophy, it is useful to describe its main features. The most important point to note is that, while FDI has been an important input into Korean industrialization, and MNEs were the ultimate source of much of the technology used by industry, the government used MNEs mainly to further the acquisition of technology by local firms. This was a very different approach from that adopted by Singapore. Throughout the last three decades the internalized markets of MNEs have not been allowed to weaken the deficient factor markets of the host economy, but have been tapped in such a way that local innovative capabilities have been strengthened. As these capabilities have grown, FDI has been allowed to play a larger role, but it has never become the main engine of technological or industrial development.

The Korean government has also undertaken various measures to encourage the diffusion of technology. From the start, the government has put pressures on the *chaebol* to establish vendor networks. Such pressures have been very effective and have led to a rapid expansion of localization of components among subcontractors. The government also enacted a law to promote subcontracting by the *chaebol*, designating parts and components that had to be procured through SMEs and not made in-house. By 1987 about 1,200 items had been so designated, involving 337 principal firms and some 2,200 subcontractors, mainly in the machinery, electrical, electronic, and shipbuilding fields. Generous financial and fiscal support has also been provided to subcontractors, to support their operations and process and product development. In addition, subcontractors have been exempted from stamp tax and were granted tax deductions for a certain percentage of their investments in laboratory and inspection equipment and for the whole of their expenses for technical consultancy. Subcontracting promotion councils have been set up by industrial sub-sector, and also within the Korea Federation of Small Business, to represent small firms' interests to the government, to arbitrate disputes with large firms, and to monitor the implementation of contracts entered into.

Apart from the array of direct interventions to support local enterprise to develop its technological capabilities without relying on MNEs, the Korean government has provided selective and functional support by creating general and technical skills. Korea today has the highest rate of university enrolment in the developing world, and produces (in absolute numbers) more engineers each year than India.[12] While much of higher education is privately financed in Korea, the government has been instrumental in setting up universities, guiding the curriculum in the directions needed by industrial policy (and involving private business in governing universities), and regulating the quality of the education.

3.4. **Taiwan**

Taiwan has pursued an export-oriented strategy since the 1960s while mounting a comprehensive strategy encompassing import protection, directed credit, selectivity towards foreign investors, support for indigenous skill and technology development, and strong export promotion.[13] While this is similar to the Korean strategy, there are many important differences. Taiwan has not promoted giant private conglomerates, nor has it attempted the intense drive into heavy industry that Korea has done. Taiwanese industry has been, and still is, dominated by SMEs, and, given the disadvantages to technological activity inherent in small size, these have been supported by a variety of inducements and institutional measures in upgrading their technologies (Taiwan has perhaps the developing world's most advanced system of technology support for small and medium enterprises).

As with Korea, Taiwan has used a variety of means to acquire foreign technology in support of domestic development, though with less nationalistic fervour. In the early years of industrialization, the Taiwanese government sought to attract FDI into activities in which domestic industry was weak, and used a variety of means (see below) to ensure that MNEs transferred their technology to local suppliers. 'Taiwan restricted the entry and activities of multinational companies in many ways, tightening controls as goals of technological upgrading and foreign equity investments were reached' (Brautigam 1995: 171). As with Korea, FDI has been directed at areas where local firms lacked technological capabilities. Where necessary, the government has itself entered into joint ventures —for instance, to get into technologically very difficult areas such as semiconductors and aerospace.[14] The government has also played an active role in helping SMEs to locate, purchase, diffuse, and adapt new foreign technologies.

There are currently around 700 thousand SMEs in Taiwan, accounting for 70 per cent of employment, 55 per cent of GNP, and 62 per cent of total manufactured exports. Programmes to promote subcontracting have therefore been of special significance to the country's industrial development. In 1981 the government set up the Medium and Small Business Administration to support SME development and to coordinate the several agencies that provided financial, management, accounting, technological, and marketing assistance to SMEs. Financial assistance was provided by a number of banks and institutions. Management and technology assistance was provided by the China Productivity Centre, the Industrial Technology Research Institute, and a number of industrial technology centres, and subsidized heavily.[15]

The 'Centre-Satellite Factory Promotion Programme' of the Ministry of Economic Affairs integrates smaller factories around a principal one. This programme involves vendor assistance and productivity raising efforts, and a rationalized sharing of tasks between participating enterprises. By 1989 there were sixty networks with 1,186 satellite factories in operation, mainly in the electronics industry. The normal X-inefficiency effects of such promotion policies for SMEs (as have been found, say, in India) have been contained by the high degree of export orientation of both the principals and the suppliers, as well as the high levels of education and training that has accompanied Taiwan's industrialization.

MNEs have also been induced to play an important role in promoting backward linkages. In the early years, the government applied minimum content requirements on foreign affiliates in industries such as automobiles and consumer electronics. Over time it has moved to more indirect measures to promote linkages—for example, by giving incentives for principal firms to use local subcontractors and by improving the technological and business capabilities of SMEs.

As Taiwan has sought to upgrade its industrial structure, local R&D has been encouraged by tax incentives, and skill levels improved through sustained investments in education and training. The purchase of local equipment and entry into 'linkage-intensive' activities has been encouraged by fiscal incentives. A science town has been set up in Hsinchu, with 13,000 researchers in two universities, six national laboratories (including the Industrial Technology Research Institute (ITRI)), and a huge technology institute, as well as some 150 companies specializing in electronics. The science town makes special efforts to attract start-up companies and provides them with prefabricated factory space, five year tax holidays, and generous grants. Since 1980 the government has invested $US500 million in Hsinchu. In 1993 the Taiwanese government also announced a three-year stimulus package which included $NT40 billion ($US1.5 billion) in loans to SMEs and $NT20 billion for high-technology enterprises.

The best-known example of institutional support for local technology development is Taiwan's ITRI, which conducts R&D in areas considered too risky for private firms, including electronics, advanced metals, chemicals, energy, and, most recently, aerospace. Taiwan's flourishing integrated circuit (IC) industry was initially spun off from the R&D efforts of the ITRI, and its Electronics Research and Service Organization (ERSO) accounts for two-thirds of the Institute's $US450 million annual budget. Some ITRI laboratories have set up as private companies, including Taiwan's most successful IC-makers. Among other support measures provided to SMEs, one of the most important has been to transfer 'production-ready technology' that the government has imported and adapted. Another is to encourage industry to contract research to universities; in recent years about one-half of the National Science Council's research grants (about $US200 million per year) fund such contracts, with enterprises providing matching funds.

This sketch of the policies of the four NIEs leads to the following conclusions:

- Selective as well as functional interventions have played a vital role in the pattern of industrial and technological development in all but one of the NIEs. The lack of selective promotion of industrial and technological deepening in Hong Kong has led to a shallow industrial structure and progressive deindustrialization, while the other NIEs have continued to expand their industrial sectors and exports.
- Governments have shown an ability to devise and implement interventions effectively, partly because export-orientation imposed a strict discipline on both industry and governments and partly because of the high levels of training, adequate remuneration, and political insulation of bureaucrats.
- The nature and impact of interventions have differed according to differing government objectives and political economies; however, the extent of industrial and technological deepening achieved has been strongly related to selective interventions to promote such deepening.
- FDI has been treated very differently by each of the four countries and so has played very different roles in their technological development. Those that have wished to promote *indigenous* technological deepening have had to intervene to restrict foreign entry and to guide their activities and maximize the spillovers. Those that have chosen to rely on MNEs but to upgrade within their global production structure have had to intervene in the FDI process to target investors, guide their resource allocation, and induce them to undertake more complex value-added activities than they would otherwise have done.
- The different approaches to FDI adopted by Korea and Taiwan as compared to Singapore partly reflect their economic endowments in addition to their political beliefs. The options and compulsions applicable to the larger economies, with greater scope for internal specialization and local content as well as better established indigenous enterprises, have been different from those open to a small island state with weak indigenous entrepreneurship and a tiny internal market. Given the need to spread technological development more widely, the former have had to take more direct steps to assist local firms.[16]

4. **Conclusions**

It has been argued in this chapter that *laissez-faire* policies towards industrial development and FDI have not been the norm in East Asia, and that there have been sound economic reasons for the interventions seen among the leading NIEs. These interventions have not always led to restrictions on MNE entry; on the contrary, in some cases they have entailed aggressively seeking out and attracting foreign investors. They have always required functional interventions to strengthen basic factor markets and institutions, in order to upgrade competitiveness and the 'quality' of FDI inflows. This has been the kind of intervention practised by Hong Kong. In other economies they have entailed extensive selective interventions to upgrade technologies and technological capabilities.

This chapter has identified two broad strategies of selective intervention —namely, the 'target-and-guide' strategy of Singapore and the 'restrict-and-exploit' strategy of Korea and Taiwan. The latter strategy has had sub-elements, with Korea mounting more detailed interventions than Taiwan in order to enter heavy and high-technology industry and set up its own giant firms with ownership advantages to rival those of traditional MNEs from the developed world.

Can the relative successes or failure of these governments be explained by their ability to devise and implement a systemic or holistic approach to overcoming market failures, and to go further to create new dynamic parameters within which markets operate?[17] Certainly each government had a very different 'vision' of the direction its economy should take and a very different political economy in which it designed policies for the private sector. At one extreme, Hong Kong has had no such vision, and has interfered as little as possible with enterprises, except to offer smaller enterprises subsidized technical support and export marketing assistance and information. At the other extreme, Korea has been driven by a vision of an advanced, diversified, and nationally owned industrial sector with an autonomous ability to undertake innovation and create its own MNEs. Singapore has had a vision of an advanced economy fully integrated into the global production system, exploiting its strategic location and highly skilled population to retain a leading position in production and services. Taiwan has vacillated between being like Korea and being less interventionist, but clearly its ambition has been to deepen and diversify the industrial and innovation base (see Wade 1990, 1993).

It is difficult to assess the extent to which these visions have been consciously held by policy-makers in these countries, and whether their policies for realizing them have been carefully thought out. There has been a lot of policy learning-by-doing, and the vision has probably developed over time as mistakes were made, successes achieved, and policy instruments perfected. There have been some common policy elements among the NIEs: stable macro-economic policies, well-functioning financial systems and infrastructure, a good base of skills, and the encouragement of entrepreneurial activity in a hard-working community, backed by efficient technology support systems to help small and medium-sized enterprises and exporters more generally. However, it is perhaps the differences between them that are more striking, and more interesting for policy purposes, than the similarities.

The main similarities among the Tigers in their attempts to become competitive (apart from a common regional effect that may have helped their growth and policy development) are in meeting market failures 'in the small'—that is, in remedying the kinds of static market deficiencies where market-failure analysis is most appropriate. This applies, for instance, to investing in physical infrastructure, a base of general skills, providing technical support, and export-market information. Their main differences are probably in meeting market failures 'in the large'—that is, in formulating the strategies that, given their initial starting positions, may help change the entire basis of their competitiveness. This is where the static optimization approach is least satisfactory, since it does not explain why Korea chose to go into D-Ram chips, steel, and automobiles, Taiwan into PCs, and Singapore into specific types of producer electronics or biotechnology (Lipsey 1995). These were choices made out of a large range of possibilities and were not addressing any static optimization failure—there was almost an act of will on the government's part to enter particular activities and make them reach world levels of efficiency. Once the choice had been made, the instruments used had to vary to match the particular objectives the government had chosen.

Both the similarities and the differences between the NIEs have been essential ingredients of their success. It is difficult here to assess whether there was something *unique* about their social, political, cultural, and institutional settings that may account for both the similarities and differences. The author would like to believe that, while there may have been some unique, irreproducible elements, there are enough economic lessons that, after making allowances for their administrative and political circumstances, other countries can apply. The differences between the Tigers themselves may sometimes have been greater than between them and other developing countries. Their experience, then, does offer important and relevant lessons to other regions, developed, developing, or in transition.

This chapter has not been able to explore the outward direct investment by these countries, though they are all active and aggressive overseas investors. Their different patterns of outward FDI, and their relationship with their industrial strategies and the development of different ownership advantages, have been explored elsewhere (Lall 1991). However, it is clear that their industrial policies shaped the ownership advantages of their own enterprises and allowed them to globalize in differing ways. There have been common elements that support Dunning's concept of the investment development path (Dunning and Narula 1996), in which economic development leads to a predictable evolution in a country's location, ownership, and internalization advantages: from a low base of local capabilities where there is little inward or outward FDI, through the growth of inward FDI followed by outward FDI and finally a balance. The Tigers each show such a path as their own capabilities have grown over time.

However, the impact of *different* strategies by the NIEs has strongly affected their development path. Their MNEs have, as a consequence, taken very different shapes and sizes. Hong Kong has spawned a large number of essentially 'low-tech' investors that are relocating labour-intensive operations in cheap wage areas, though many are also active in developed areas in services and real estate. At the other end, the Korean *chaebol* have become large multinationals, very similar in competence, technological abilities, and market reach to the established MNEs of the advanced countries, and are globalizing in a way inconceivable for the other Tigers. Thus the investment development path is overlaid by individual strategic differences.

To conclude, the East Asian NIEs provide a fascinating panorama of experience in industrial development, government intervention, and treatment of FDI. What is undeniable is that their governments have played a critical catalytic role in forming their competitive (or ownership) advantages in trade and industry, which has then determined their participation in the global economy. Their approach to FDI and globalization has been an integral part of a larger industrial strategy, and MNEs have been increasingly seen as a resource which could be exploited in the national interest (an important shift from earlier perceptions of MNEs).

There remains considerable debate about the effects of the selective industrial policies in East Asia. Furthermore, there remain doubts about the extent to which the ability to mount such interventions is present elsewhere. The conditions under which governments can exercise efficient intervention are certainly not found in many developing countries. The risk of government failure is so great in some cases that it may be better to suffer the consequences of market failure than to indulge in selectivity. In such cases, the government should confine itself to 'market-friendly' interventions and entrust free markets to guide fully resource allocation. However, government capabilities are not static or given in perpetuity; they can be improved, and there are various levels of selectivity in intervention. Is it possible to gear the level of selectivity to the capabilities of governments? Is it possible to raise these capabilities by specific actions and institutional mechanisms? These are large and important questions that need much more research.

NOTES

I am grateful to John Dunning for his comments on an earlier draft, and to the participants at the Carnegie Bosch conference for their discussion. After the conference Richard Lipsey provided several papers and valuable insights on the role of government policy in technology development, for which I am most thankful even though I have not been able to incorporate fully their thrust and implications.

1. For an analysis of industrial policy in the 'new NIEs' of Malaysia, Indonesia, and Thailand, see Lall (1995).
2. Of the vast literature that now exists on this subject, see Pack and Westphal (1986), Amsden (1989, 1994), Wade (1990), Westphal (1990), OED (1992), World Bank (1993), Chang (1994), Fishlow *et al.* (1994), Moreira (1994), Rodrik (1994), Lall (various).
3. This abstracts from traditional concerns about transfer pricing, bargaining, predatory conduct, and so on.
4. World Bank (1993) claims that good macro-management, export orientation, and 'market-friendly' interventions to strengthen human capital are sufficient to explain East Asian industrial success; but this fails to take into account the very marked differences in industrial policy objectives, instruments, and achievements in the region (Lall 1994*a*).

5. *Financial Times* (1993). Manufacturing employment declined from 45% to 23% of the total in 1980–92, and its contribution to GDP from 27% to 16%.
6. See Lim (1994) on industrial policy, and Selvaratnam (1994) on Singapore's interventions in education.
7. In the late 1980s Singapore established the National Technology Board (NTB) to attract functional headquarters of MNEs' R&D activities. The NTB will direct the expansion of an R&D infrastructure for new industries, such as agrotechnology, biotechnology, robotics, and automation. Singapore also established several government-support research centres, including the Singapore Science Park, the Institute of Molecular and Cell Biology, the Institute of Systems Science, and the Information Technology Institute. It is expected that a new university devoted to S&T will double Singapore's R&D expenditure to over half a billion dollars. Singapore's Technology Development Centre (TDC) helps local companies identify their technology requirements and design appropriate strategies for upgrading their operations. Since its establishment in 1989, the centre has sent its multi-disciplinary staff of consultants and engineers on over 300 plant visits, and provided more than 130 companies with various forms of assistance, including sourcing of foreign experts and equipment, and advice on process improvement and product development.
8. For a summary description see Lall (1994*b*). For details on Korea see Amsden (1989), Westphal (1990), Moreira (1994), Kim (1995) and Najmabadi and Lall (1995).
9. Korean strategy in technology development in electronics is analysed by Hobday (1995).
10. One interesting example is in the field of semiconductors (Hobday 1995). Samsung Electronics, the largest Korean producer of semiconductors, now a world leader in the production of DRAM chips, started in 1980 by licensing its technology from Micron Technology of the USA, then forming its own company in Silicon Valley in 1983 to gain access to US technology and skills. It developed its own 64 and 256 kilobit chips, but sustained heavy losses. In 1987 it joined the race for the 1 megabit chip directly in competition with Japanese leaders, and started mass production of chips in Korea; by 1988 the firm had invested $800 million in semiconductors but had failed to make profits. Thereafter prices and profits picked up, and, by 1989, its semiconductor sales reached $US1.4 billion. Samsung continued to invest heavily in technology development and soon reached world frontiers in design of 4, 16, and 64 megabit chips, beating most Western companies and coming just behind the leading Japanese firms. In 1989–90 Samsung undertook a patent swap with IBM and forged partnerships with Toshiba, NEC, Texas Instruments, Oki, and Corning. In 1992 it joined with Toshiba in developing flash memory chips and was the world's first company to produce a working model of the 64 megabit chip in 1992. By 1993 Samsung had invested $US3 billion in chip technology, and had taken fifteen years to catch up and establish an independent technological role in global terms. In 1995 it announced a £450 million consumer electronics plant in the UK, and a collaboration with NEC to set up a plant in Portugal to make memory chips for the European market. While there was little direct government involvement in all this, the fact that Samsung was able to undertake it at all is due to the earlier government strategy of creating such a large firm, protecting its domestic markets in a range of products, and giving it privileged access to finance.
11. On semiconductors alone, four leading South Korean *chaebol* spent Won 1.8 trillion on capital investment and Won 300 billion on R&D in 1989–90. Their size and

financial resources give them a clear advantage over similar companies in Taiwan, Hong Kong, and Singapore.

12. According to Unesco data, in 1992 Korea had 347.6 thousand engineering students enrolled in universities as compared to India's 201.3 thousand (in 1988).
13. For a comprehensive analysis, see Wade (1990). Also see Brautigam (1995) for a concise exposition of Taiwan's industrial policies and the role of selective interventions.
14. In an attempt to acquire semiconductor design and production capability, in 1974 the Taiwanese government formed the Electronics Research and Service Organization (ERSO) authorizing it to recruit a foreign partner to help develop and commercialize the technology. In 1976 ERSO opened the country's first model shop for wafer fabrication, and a year later signed a technology transfer agreement with RCA in integrated circuit design (Wade 1990: 103–4).
15. The government covers 50–70% of consultation fees for management and technical consultancy services for SMEs. In addition, the Medium and Small Business Administration has a $NT10 billion fund for SME promotion.
16. There was, nevertheless, a strong political commitment to promoting local capabilities. There are other large economies with sizeable industrial sectors, such as Mexico, that have chosen to remain highly dependent on imported technologies. As a consequence, R&D by enterprises in Mexico is around 0.02% of GDP as compared to 1.8% in Korea, when both have roughly equal values of manufacturing value added (Najmabadi and Lall 1995).
17. See the chapters by Dunning and Lipsey which have dealt with the analytical implications of such an approach.

REFERENCES

Amsden, A. (1989), *Asia's Next Giant: South Korea and Late Industrialization* (New York: Oxford University Press).

—— (1994), 'Why Isn't the Whole World Experimenting with the East Asian Model to Develop? Review of *The East Asian Miracle*', *World Development*, 22: 627–34.

Brautigam, D. (1995), 'The State as Agent: Industrial Development in Taiwan, 1952–1972', in H. Stein (ed.), *Asian Industrialization and Africa* (London: Macmillan), 145–82.

Carroll, A. M. (1994), 'Technology Development Experiences of Japan, Singapore, Korea, Taiwan, and Hong Kong', draft, Washington, DC.

Chang, H. J. (1994), *The Political Economy of Industrial Policy* (London: Macmillan).

Clifford, Mark (1994), 'Trading Up', *Far Eastern Economic Review* (26 May), 68–9.

Dunning, J. H. (1988), *Explaining International Production* (London: Unwin Hyman).

—— (1993), *Multinational Enterprises and the Global Economy* (Wokingham: Addison Wesley).

—— and Narula, R. (1996) (eds.), *Foreign Direct Investment and Governments: Catalysts For Change* (London: Routledge).

Financial Times (1993), 'Survey of Hong Kong' (4 May), 6.

Fishlow, A., Gwin, C., Haggard, S., Rodrik, D., and Wade, R., *Miracle or Design? Lessons from the East Asian Experience* (Washington: Overseas Development Council).

Hobday, M. G. (1995), *Innovation in East Asia: The Challenge to Japan* (Cheltenham: Edward Elgar).

Kim, K. S. (1995), 'The Korean Miracle (1962–80) Revisited: Myths and Realities in Strategies and Development', in H. Stein (ed.), *Asian Industrialization and Africa* (London: Macmillan), 87–144.

Lall, S. (1991), 'Direct Investment in S. E. Asia by the NIEs: Trends and Prospects', *Banca Nazionale del Lavoro Quarterly Review*, 179: 463–80.

—— (1992), 'Technological Capabilities and the Role of Government in Developing Countries', *Greek Economic Review*, 14: 1–36.

—— (1993), 'Policies for Building Technological Capabilities: Lessons from Asian Experience', *Asian Development Review*, 11: 72–103.

—— (1994*a*), '*The East Asian Miracle* Study: Does The Bell Toll for Industrial Strategy?', *World Development*, 22: 645–54.

—— (1994*b*), 'Industrial Policy: The Role of Government in Promoting Industrial and Technological Development', *UNCTAD Review 1994*, 65–89.

—— (1995) (ed.), *Journal of International Development*, special issue (September).

Lim, L. (1995), 'Foreign Investment, the State and Industrial Policy in Singapore', in H. Stein (ed.), *Asian Industrialization and Africa* (London: Macmillan), 205–38.

Lipsey, R. G. (1994), 'Markets, Technological Change and Economic Growth', *Pakistan Development Review*, 33: 327–52.

—— (1995), private letter to author.

—— and Carlaw, K., 'A Structuralist View of Innovation Policy', in P. Howitt (ed.), *Implications of Knowledge-Based Growth for Micro-Economic Policies* (Edmonton: University of Alberta Press).

Moreira, M. M. (1994), *Industrialization, Trade and Market Failures: The Role of Government Intervention in Brazil and the Republic of Korea* (London: Macmillan).

Najmabadi, F., and Lall, S. (1995), *Developing Industrial Technology: Lessons for Policy and Practice* (Washington: World Bank, Operations Evaluation Department).

Selvaratnam, V. (1994), *Innovations in Higher Education: Singapore at the Competitive Edge* (Washington: World Bank, Technical Paper No. 222).

OED (1992): Operations Evaluation Department, *World Bank Support for Industrialization in Korea, India and Indonesia* (Washington: World Bank, OED).

Pack, H., and Westphal, L. E. (1986), 'Industrial Strategy and Technological Change: Theory versus Reality', *Journal of Development Economics*, 22: 87–128.

Rodrik, D. (1994), 'Getting Interventions Right: How South Korea and Taiwan Grew Rich' (New York, Columbia University and NBER, paper presented to 20th Panel meeting of *Economic Policy*, October).

Stiglitz, J. E. (1989), 'Markets, Market Failures and Development', *American Economic Review Papers and Proceedings*, 79: 197–202.

UNCTAD (1994): United Nations Conference on Trade and Development, *World Investment Report 1994: Transnational Corporations, Employment and the Workplace* (Geneva: United Nations).

—— (1995), *World Investment Report 1995: Transnational Corporations and Competitiveness* (draft (Geneva: United Nations)).

—— (1996), *World Investment Report 1996* (Geneva: United Nations).

Wade, R. (1990), *Governing the Market: Economic Theory and the Role of Government in East Asian Industrialization* (Princeton: Princeton University Press).

—— (1993), 'Managing Trade: Taiwan and South Korea as Challenges to Economics and Political Science', *Comparative Politics*, 25: 147–67.

Wells, L. T., and Wint, A. G. (1990), *Marketing a Country: Promotion as a Tool for Attracting Foreign Investment* (Washington: International Finance Corporation).

Westphal, L. E. (1990), 'Industrial Policy in an Export-Propelled Economy: Lessons from South Korea's Experience', *Journal of Economic Perspectives*, 4: 41–59.

World Bank (1993), *The East Asian Miracle: Economic Growth and Public Policy* (New York: Oxford University Press).

15

Latin America

Claudio R. Frischtak

1. Introduction

The fundamental economic forces of the period starting with the first oil shock —intense competition and an accelerated rate of technical progress—have generated powerful undercurrents that have pushed firms to globalize (and simultaneously regionalize) their value-added activities; continuously restructure and internationalize their operations; and adopt radically new models of management and organization.

1.1. Structural Trends in World Industry

Since the 1970s, industry worldwide has been undergoing profound changes. The series of exogenous shocks that affected the world economy in the mid-1970s, starting with the steep rise in energy and raw-material prices, followed by inflationary pressures and high interest rates, subsequently led to the slowdown of economic growth, initially in the USA, eventually spreading to other OECD and industrializing countries.

The recession affected a broad spectrum of industries, though the production of capital goods and consumer durables was particularly badly hit. After 1985 export-oriented industries from other OECD countries, which had been partially sheltered from the recession by catering to the US market during the early part of the decade, taking advantage of an overvalued currency, became less cost competitive and profitable as major currencies appreciated *vis-à-vis* the dollar. By the end of the last decade, most industries in practically all OECD countries faced difficult restructuring decisions, and were forced to engage in broad reorganizational efforts to remain competitive.

Firms initially failed to realize the significance of the structural changes occurring in the world economy, and the nature of the 'new competition' unleashed by the Japanese and other East Asian followers, masked as they were by major 'one-time' shocks in 1973 and 1979.

The first such change was increasing competition among firms and nations. With the long post-war expansion over, and as rivalry from Japan and the NICs (mostly from South-East Asia, but some from Latin America) intensified, most firms were forced to redo their competitive calculus. Competition begot competition. Awakened from the Hicksian 'easy life' by the East Asian onslaught, and facing shrinking profits, US and European managers progressively changed their behaviour, became more quality conscious, and service-oriented. With no choice but to challenge rivals in order to survive, firms' aggressive tactics changed the nature of many industries; where tacit cooperation once prevailed, the norm became aggressive competition.

There was also an accelerated rate of technical progress. In an effort to move out of the long cycle of recession and frail recoveries that had characterized these economies since the 1970s, there was a renewed focus on technical progress as the means to gain a competitive advantage over rivals. Technology became the object of considerable attention of business managers and policy-makers alike; resources were redirected towards R&D as well as the more mundane, but equally important factors behind technical progress, such as training and quality-oriented programmes. The result was the rapid introduction of new or differentiated products (as cycles shortened), and a large and continuous improvement in production processes, and in the overall productivity of the firm.

Growing rivalry and accelerated technical change has led to the restructuring of whole industries and of the leading firms within them, not only reactively, but also on a preventive basis. Restructuring has progressively become a continuous activity, part of the normal competitive effort of firms.

1.2. **The Response of Industrial Firms**

Driven by the need to increase productivity, improve quality, establish closer relations with clients (thus becoming client- and service-driven), and earn innovation rents, firms moved to internationalize their operations. Throughout the 1970s, FDI, domestic output, and domestic investment grew at similar rates. Yet in the early 1980s, with firms facing growing competitive pressures, these rates of growth began to diverge. Since 1985, DFI has grown four times faster than GDP, twice as fast as domestic investment, and two-and-half times the rate of growth of exports.[1]

As markets become increasingly unified, firms must be able to reallocate capital in a flexible and timely way. Although capital mobility or reallocation is often achieved through M&As, in which weaker firms exit and stronger ones acquire the critical mass to compete in larger or more demanding markets, this process has increasingly a geographical dimension.[2] Direct foreign investment has been the most important instrument for the geographical expansion of capital.

Firms are not only internationalizing their operations but moving to globalize (or regionalize) their production and sourcing activities—thus the rapid expansion of manufactured exports, which has been growing one-and-a-half times as fast as domestic output, with a significant proportion of intra-firm nature. In fact, intra-firm trade of transnational corporations accounts for an estimated 25 per cent of worldwide trade (UN 1992).

In addition, a new pattern of production is emerging that is increasingly vertically disintegrated, horizontally specialized, with tighter universal standards of productivity, quality, and delivery time, among others. The production unit is less hierarchical, more compact, with fewer levels between top management and the shop floor. Such 'flatter' team-focused structures allow information to flow more freely among levels and within ranks.

Progressively, firms are also attempting to decentralize and make basic corporate functions (buying, selling, financing, developing, producing, and servicing) more effective by changing their mode of internal organization, with greater reliance on worker initiative and a less rigid division of labour. Groups or circles of workers (or 'associates') are being empowered to make shop-floor decisions on their own regarding the best way to run a production line or a specific machine, reduce costs at all stages of production, and improve quality. Middle strata (such as supervisors), as a result, are becoming increasingly irrelevant.

The fundamental objective of this new mode of organization is to improve firm performance by facilitating the flow of information both within the firm, and between the firm and its network of suppliers and clients; and by establishing new incentive regimes for labour, whose greater involvement and increased responsibilities would be matched by longer tenure, extensive training, and better compensation.

The dissemination of these organizational innovations has been accompanied by a less parochial perception by management and labour of the firm's environment, and a willingness to extend the firm's boundaries through alliances ranging from pure marketing/services agreements to technological joint ventures, co-production, and other forms of cooperation.

Firms are thus becoming integrated to domestic and international networks through which they access technology, tap information, source critical inputs, and sell their output. In parallel, they are establishing strategic alliances within their industry, cooperating to compete more effectively. 'Virtual proximity' with suppliers, clients, and even government, is guiding investment decisions, contractual relations, and cooperative ventures, and increasing the speed of response to market signals.[3]

1.3. The Response of States

The object of this chapter is to discuss the response of Latin American governments to the forces of globalization and increasing competition. In Section 2, the role of governments in industrializing and developing countries contexts is discussed. Section 3 attempts to assess the recent Latin American experience. It argues that the road to reform—in the sense of changes in the regulatory environment, trade regimes, and asset-ownership structures—has advanced to the point of irreversibility. Latin economies have become relatively open and increasingly competitive, in contrast to the situation of the 1960s and 1970s. To a large extent, the wedge of reform has been driven by the globalization process, although the realization that past policies had become historically dated (and, in many ways, highly distortionary) also played an important role. There is little question that one currently finds a much more hospitable environment to international business in most countries, particularly MNEs able to link countries effectively to trade, technology, and investment networks.

The road to macro-economic stability, on the other hand, has been far more difficult. There remain persistent problems of fiscal largesse, accommodating monetary policy, low savings (public and private), and excessive domestic absorption. Combined, they have led to renewed balance-of-payment crises in several Latin American countries. Short-term capital ('hot money'), which would be helpful to make the transition to macro-stability less painful, and which has been made abundant with globalization, has proved to be a poor basis to offset persistent current-account deficits, themselves a symptom of maladjustment. Financial systems have also become fragile in some countries, because of excessive and non-sustainable public-sector borrowing and a lack of confidence of private agents. Section 4 concludes the chapter with some brief remarks regarding the sustainability of this process.

2. The Role of the State in Industrializing Countries

Since the 1950s the state in most developing countries has attempted to emulate a Schumpeterian engine of growth.[4] State activities have been largely directed to mobilizing resources, and directly investing in productive activities or steering them to specific sectors. A complex array of regulatory controls, protective policies and promotional instruments has led to the emergence of industries and entire social segments—entrepreneurs and rentiers—dependent upon them. Though industrial growth has been the main object of policy, industrial investment has also been used as an instrument of employment creation, regional balance, and other equity-related purposes. The quest for industrialization in the context of post-war reconstruction, decolonization, and independence gave political impetus to this pattern of state action; while the predominance of import-substitution industrialization models in the development literature provided the intellectual underpinnings and the economic rationale for an activist state.[5]

For most industrializing countries, this model of the state functioning as the 'vanguard' of economic development has become historically dated, and for two very distinct reasons. First, the growth of an entrepreneurial class, the extension of markets, and the reduction of transaction costs—arguably outcomes of state activities at a time when its thrust was to bestow endowments and stimulate agents to enter emerging markets—has lessened the need for the state to steer private forces towards, or to become directly involved, in productive activities. Moreover, and in contrast to the state's earlier role of inducing entry and thereby market dynamism, policy and regulatory activism has become associated in many industrializing countries with the protection of entrenched incumbents from the challenges posed by new competition. Rent-seeking behaviour was stimulated and sanctioned by the instruments of protection, promotion, and regulation.

Increasingly the state became a captive of its own creations; and in this process it has reached its fiscal limits.

Secondly, a series of exogenous factors has contributed to the exhaustion of a paradigm of state action characterized by detailed regulations of productive activities. The rapid pace of technological progress, the globalization of economic relations, and the increase in the value of information, all signify that the competitive standing of firms (and countries) is now predicated on their ability to scan the horizon, and respond quickly to market and technological trends. It does not 'fit' with the rigidity of regulatory regimes, the slowness of response of implementing agencies, and the opaqueness of many of its instruments, at a time when markets are more open and competitive.

Just as the import-substitution model of industrialization conferred respectability to an activist state, its criticism called for, and became the justification of, other models of state action. Advocates of minimalist state intervention argued that its functions were to administer justice, establish property rights, and enforce contracts. Those searching for an alternative developmental state, inspired by the East Asian 'miracle' economies, perceived its functions more broadly—namely, an agent for 'crowding in' investment in areas commanding high social returns; a catalyst for cooperation among social groups; an arbiter of economic conflict; and a partner to foster competitiveness and economic development.

Does this mean the idea of a developmental state is no longer appropriate? Certainly not. Is the Schumpeterian variant on the way out? Possibly yes. What then, is the scope of state action? What are its roles? At the most basic level, the state is to provide a set of rules and market-supportive institutions to assign property rights, enforce contracts, and establish a stable economic environment, so that productive activity can flourish. Stability, predictability, and transparency of policies are the basis of sound government action in the economic sphere. Either a minimalist or developmentalist perspective would abide by these precepts. Beyond this, there are three fairly distinct sets of economic functions—investment, policy, and regulatory—that differentiate the modes of state action.

In terms of its investment functions, a development-oriented state would attempt, first, to complement or 'crowd in' private investment, by providing physical and other supportive infrastructure.[6] Secondly, it would target areas that present large externalities, where the private sector would normally underinvest—for example, basic education, preventive health care, and other segments of the social infrastructure. Thirdly, the state would be involved in the production of 'merit' goods—of which all individuals should consume a minimal amount according to broadly accepted social norms.

In terms of its policy functions, the developmental state (just as the minimalist state) is expected to provide a stable and predictable macro-economic environment. This entails an unwavering commitment to monetary stability, maintaining the public thrust in financial institutions, as well as an avoidance of sudden policy shifts (except when necessary to guarantee the foundations of the monetary regime).[7]

What should be the State's policy functions at the micro-economic level? The presence of well-informed agents contribute to the stability and efficiency of markets; thus the provision of information concerning government policies and programmes to financial and other markets is a key policy function of the state.

Industrial policy, in particular, is increasingly perceived as being grounded in the capture and dissemination of market-relevant information in the context of a cooperative relationship between private agents and governments.[8] The constitution of bodies where information is exchanged between the public and private sectors concerning their basic economic goals and objectives, how they intend to pursue them, and what are the areas of common interests and complementary actions, is possibly among the most important of the initiatives of the new developmental state. Within such bodies, private actors would commit to specific projects (and related performance targets), while the state would attempt to remove major obstacles to private-sector activity: regulatory and bureaucratic barriers to the integration of the economy into the global trade, investment, technology, and information networks; infrastructure bottlenecks; weaknesses in technology delivery systems;[9] gaps in education and training; and inadequate coordination between its agencies (which often ignore or work at cross purposes with each other) and producers.

3. The Challenge of Reform

In most Latin American economies, where governments have assumed an important role in the promotion and protection of economic activity, there has survived, until recently at any rate, a complex regulatory maze, incompatible with the level of development reached by these economies. In the early stages of industrialization, such regimes may have been an instrument supportive of economic development, by helping mobilize resources and attract agents into thin markets. Over time, however, they have become less effective. Eventually, the same mechanisms and rules that once stimulated investment and promoted entry have come to create new barriers to resource mobility and competition.

Driving those barriers were rules generally applied by privileging incumbents at the expense of entrants. Information asymmetries also played a role, with established producers having detailed knowledge of the unwritten norms, and the individuals that implemented them. Relatively rigid market configurations emerged, as rents accruing to incumbents became a strong disincentive for such firms to penetrate new, untested arenas. By constraining flexibility in resource allocation and use, and limiting competition, such barriers brought losses in efficiency, in both a static and an inter-temporal sense. Further, in so far as such barriers tended to favour incumbents, they contributed to increase the degree of income inequality and decrease social welfare (on the presumption that the marginal utility of money falls with income).

The object of reform—changing the set of rules that frame economic activity, and rearranging or removing altogether the institutions that implement them—is to increase the flexibility and speed with which economic agents redeploy resources in response to changes in global markets and technologies; to remove barriers to competition, factor mobility, and firm growth; and to simplify and increase the transparency of rules. Ultimately, the aim is to improve the efficiency with which the economy operates, and its distributional outcomes.

Reform, however, is not a trivial process. It involves changing or phasing out a number of instruments and mechanisms to which markets, institutions, and agents have adapted, and which have their own constituencies. As such, it tends to be slow, subject to institutional rigidies and backward sliding; and it is generally undertaken after difficult and protected negotiations.[10]

Three major areas which directly affect the ability of domestic economies to insert themselves into global networks have been the object of reform efforts since the early 1980s. These are: (i) the domestic regulatory arena, including the rules governing direct foreign investment and technology transfer; (ii) the asset-ownership structure of the economy; and (iii) the international trade regime. Most Latin American countries have acted to remove regulatory and trade barriers to integration into world markets, while changing—in some cases dramatically—the economy's ownership structure away from a predominance of state-owned entities in production of goods and services.

Evidence of deregulation attempts in Latin America is generally referred to specific country experiences (see below), in view of the variegated nature of the process of deregulation itself. Yet, a cross-country bird's-eye view of the scope of reform efforts in privatization and trade liberalization suggests how generalized the efforts at structural reform have been in the continent since the mid-1980s. Table 15.1 provides a glimpse of the privatization experience in seven major Latin countries; in fact, in the Latin American and Caribbean region, there were over 2,000 publicly owned enterprises privatized between 1985 and 1992 (see Edwards 1993).

Possibly, the efforts at trade liberalization have been more systematic and wide-ranging than any other structural reform. Even for countries, such as Bolivia and Chile, that started the process relatively early on, the post-1985 changes in the trade regime have been substantial. For most countries, in a matter of half a decade, as Table 15.2 shows, a complex array of non-tariff barriers were dismantled, while average tariff rates fell to less than 20 per cent. Although it may still be too early to assess the impact of trade liberalization, evidence suggests that overall it has led to an expansion of both inter- and intra-industry trade, larger investment flows, and significant reductions in inefficiency.[11]

3.1. The Argentine Situation

It is useful to describe the paradigmatic changes that Argentina has recently undergone in some detail to illustrate the depth of regulatory and other reforms.

TABLE 15.1. The privatization experience of Latin America, selected countries and years, 1984–1993

	Argentina	Bolivia	Brazil	Chile	Mexico	Peru	Venezuela
Programme objectives/ rationale	• By reorganizing, privatizing, or liquidating SOEs under economy and defence ministries • Increase private sector participation • Reduce resource flows from treasury to SOEs • Enhance efficiency	• Eliminate the government's role in production of goods and services in areas where the private sector has competence • Increase efficiency of investment • Avoid potential drain on treasury reserves	• Redirect role of the state away from private sector competence; reduce public debt • Expand privatized firms • Strengthen domestic capital markets	• Maximize government revenues in first round (1974) • Reduce size of government in second round (1984) • Spread ownership • Reduce importance of government	• Improve public-sector finances • Develop an efficient productive base	• Privatize all SOEs by mid-1995, selling to experienced operators who will quickly improve performance and inject new capital	• Transfer to private sector all SOEs without an evident public-policy objective • Salvage airline from bankruptcy • Expand and improve telephonic service (reform programme and privatization stalled in 1992/3.)
Privatization completed (end 1993)	• The government sold SOEs (totally or partially) in telecommunications, oil and gas (YPF), railways, airline, petrochemicals, real estate, electricity generation,	• Between May 1992 and December 1993 the government sold or liquidated more than 30 small commercial enterprises • Only three had	• In 1990–3 companies were privatized, including: • 8 in the steel sector • 9 in the petrochemicals and chemicals sector	• In first round (1974), 470 firms, or 82% of SOEs, were privatized, including banks and manufacturing enterprises	• Government ownership was reduced from 1,155 parastatal entities in 1984 to 220 by June 1992	• Twenty firms were privatized, including: • 5 mining enterprises • 4 petroleum subsidiaries • 2 banks • 1 airline	• In 1990–3, the government privatized 18 holdings, including: • 1 telephone company (CANTV) • 1 airline

	radio and TV, and water supply	fixed assets valued at more than $US9m	• 4 in the fertilizer sector	• In second round (1984), 80 firms were privatized, for a total of 96% of SOEs			• 3 banks • 5 sugar refineries
Proceeds (end 1993)	• $US11.1bn. in debt reduction ($US5.5bn. from telecom, $US0.9bn. from YPF), $US8bn. in cash ($US2.3bn. from telecom, $US3bn. from YPF)	• Minimal—the sale of the first 11 small enterprises generated about $US10m	• $US6.5bn, mostly paid with discounted federal domestic public debt instruments	• Not available	• 1984–9: $US1.6bn. in 191 sales • 1990: $US3.2bn. in 89 sales • 1991: $US10.8bn. in 66 sales • 1992: $US6.2bn. in 18 sales	• $US522m. in cash plus • $US715m. in investment commitments	• $US2.5bn. cash proceeds • $US1.9bn. for CANTV, whose sale included commitment to add 3.6m. lines—roughly $US6bn.—over 9 years
Use of proceeds	• $US11.1bn. for debt reduction and $US8bn. in cash contributions to the treasury	• Privatization law stipulates that all proceeds are to be used for social projects	• Principally for reduction of federal public debt; also for social programmes	• Not available	• Internal debt reduction	• Mostly for community projects	• About 50% for social projects, 10% for R&D, 15% for retraining, and less than 10% for privatization expenses

Source: Thobani (1994).

TABLE 15.2. Trade liberalization in Latin America, selected countries and years, 1985–1992 (%)

Country	Average tariff protection[a]		Average coverage of non-tariff barriers[b]	
	1985	1991–2	1985–7	1991–2
Bolivia	20.0	8.0	25.0	0.0
Chile	36.0	11.0	10.1	0.0
Costa Rica	92.0	16.0	0.8	0.0
Mexico	34.0	4.0	12.7	20.0
Uruguay	32.0	12.0	14.1	0.0
Argentina	28.0	15.0	31.9	8.0
Brazil	80.0	21.1	35.3	10.0
Colombia	83.0	6.7	73.2	1.0
Ecuador	50.0	18.0	59.3	n.a.
Guatemala	50.0	19.0	7.4	6.0
Paraguay	71.7	16.0	9.9	0.0
Peru	64.0	15.0	53.4	0.0
Venezuela	30.0	17.0	44.1	5.0

Note: n.a. = not available.

[a] Average total charges (tariffs plus paratariffs), unweighted.
[b] Unweighted.

Source: World Bank (1995*b*: table 6).

Since 1989 the government (then newly elected) has aggressively pursued a 'policy offensive' for attaining macro-stability, deregulation, privatization, and a more neutral incentive regime. Although the country is still somewhat distant from a balanced macro-regime, there is little question that the changes introduced by structural reform have taken root, and have become, in large measure, irreversible.

A major incentive-related initiative has been the deregulation of domestic markets for goods and services. By the end of the last decade, the Argentine economy was gripped by a regulatory maze which functioned as a barrier to competition by constraining the mobility of factors; segmenting markets; and distorting or impeding their operation, particularly in their price-setting and allocative role. Firms also faced a multiplicity of internal and external tax wedges—mostly inefficient, growth-inhibiting, but easy to collect tax 'handles'. Combined, they dampened efforts to improve efficiency and added to the costs of doing business in the country.

The State Reform and the Economic Emergency Laws of 1989 provided the legal basis not only for the macro-economic and fiscal programme, and for the trade reforms, but also for the encompassing Deregulation Decree 2284 of 1991. They allowed the government to intervene, change the legal status and organizational frame, and sell, liquidate, or dissolve any state entity, including public enterprises and regulatory agencies (see Rojo and Canosa 1992; Sguiglia and Delgado 1993).

In the period 1991–3, a number of markets were deregulated: these included port and transportation services for cargo (including mail) and passengers (road, air, sea, and river); the wholesale of fruits, vegetables, and other fresh food; the services of the medical and teaching professions; and the import and sale of pharmaceuticals, insurance, cement, and oil and gas. The removal of regulatory barriers in these activities was complemented and reinforced by the dissolution of ten key regulatory authorities (including the National Grain Board, the National Meat Board, and the Special Tobacco Fund), and the special funds that supported their functioning.

The deregulation programme stimulated the production and commercialization of non-tradable goods and services by lowering mobility and competition barriers. All legal norms (including price controls, and entry and operation restrictions) that interfered with the free functioning of markets (with the exception of natural monopolies or privatized activities) were removed, while the legislation curbing the exercise of monopoly power was strengthened. Most important, deregulation allowed Argentine firms far greater flexibility, thereby lowering their response time and moving them closer to their international competitors.[12]

The reduction of regulatory barriers to mobility and competition was reinforced through trade reform, with the removal of most remaining quantitative restrictions (QRs), and the reduction in tariff levels. While QRs were reduced to 7 per cent of domestic production coverage by late 1990 (automotive and electronics being important exceptions), the *ad valorem* tariff band was narrowed from 0–115 per cent to 0–24 per cent, with an average rate of about 18 per cent.

In February 1991 the government announced that specific duties would be converted to *ad valorem* tariffs, while the number of tariff rates were to be reduced to three (0, 11, and 22 per cent). Finally, most export restrictions were lifted, customs procedures simplified and related taxes unified, the production coverage of industrial export taxes reduced to 30 per cent, and the statistical tax on exports eliminated.

The forces of import competition and export rivalry elicited by the process of trade liberalization became a powerful instrument for the structural transformation of Argentine industry. They led to greater horizontal specialization (as firms focused on what they were able to do best), vertical disintegration (as parts and components became more accessible), and the exploitation of scale economies (in so far as, in an open economy, the market is—potentially—the world). With the consolidation of the MERCOSUR integration process, firms started to internalize in their entrepreneurial calculus both the opportunities opened by (fundamentally) the Brazilian market, and the competitive threat from, as well as the opportunities for cooperation with, Brazilian firms.

Trade (and the stability of the exchange rate) also became an important force for the modernization of Argentine economy. The relatively low tariffs on capital goods (which oscillated between 0 per cent and 5 per cent) and the absence of non-tariff barriers, facilitated the modernization and stimulated the technological upgrading of firms. As investment recovered, capital goods imports expanded at a fast rate; they grew by 31.9 per cent in the 1992/3 period, whereas overall imports expanded by 10.5 per cent. In addition, the share of capital goods imports in gross domestic investment more than doubled in 1991–3, reaching 34 per cent. As a matter of comparison, in 1985 that proportion was just 10 per cent for Argentina, while cross-industrializing country experience suggests that modernization efforts are generally accompanied by high rates of penetration of imported capital goods.

As noted earlier in this chapter, in most countries the major force for integration in the global economy and modernization of domestic productive structures are transnational corporations. This is being reflected in legislation and regulatory practice of Latin American countries. The regime regulating FDI in Argentina, for example, is quite open, and on the whole does not create artificial obstacles to the inflow of capital.[13] Foreign investors are not required to obtain prior approval for their investments, and the Foreign Investment Law and supplementary rules establish the principle of equal treatment, with Argentine and foreign investors enjoying the same rights and duties.[14]

This unrestricted policy, which also applies to 100 per cent foreign-owned companies, extends to investment in the manufacturing, mining, commercial, and service sectors, as well as to such areas as defence, telecommunications, power, gas, and insurance.[15] Investments may be made not just in foreign currency, but in capital goods as well as intangible assets (including those of technological nature); after a 30 per cent flat rate on income, investors may remit profits without withholdings.

Licensing, technical assistance, and other forms of disembodied technology flows continue to be governed by a legislation enacted in 1981 (Law 22,426).[16] According to this legislation, transactions between non-related parties can be contracted and paid for without government interference, and such transactions are required to be registered only for information purposes. This approach is consistent with Argentina's technology needs. Further, it is in line with most countries that have liberalized the technology importation regime, but stands in contrast to its major MERCOSUR partner (in which case, all technology contracts are still subject to government approval, if payments are beyond a specified threshold).

In the case of intra-firm transfers of technology, prior government approval is required. The absence of such approval does not invalidate the technology-transfer contract, but disallows payments to be deductible from taxable income, and makes it subject to the 27 per cent withholding tax, the maximum rate. If the transfer is approved, the withholding tax rates of royalties and other technology payments are 18 per cent, 24 per cent, and 27 per cent, with the 24 per cent rate applying in most cases. Such withholding taxes are not considered out of line with international experience: in Brazil, for example, a potential competitor for technology flows, they vary in the range of 25–35 per cent.

Finally, the intellectual property rights (IPR) regime is in a state of transition, with a recently approved (March 1995) legislation substituting Law 111 still being the object of negotiation. Argentina is a signatory of the 1883 Paris Convention for the Protection of Industrial Property (and subsequent amendments). As a result, Argentine legislation grants inventors the exclusive right to exploit their inventions for a period which varies from five to fifteen years (according to the merits of the invention). Patents registered abroad are also protected in Argentina if registered within twelve months of registration in the country of origin, in which case protection extends for ten years or up to the time the patent lapses in the country of origin, if earlier. The major exception to patent-rights legislation is the case of pharmaceutical products. This is an area where the country has developed an important domestic industry based on reverse engineering and some local innovation efforts.[17] Though the current legislation allows the enforcement of pharmaceutical patents only in the year 2003, an agreement between Congress and government found a middle ground, and enforcement will start within five years.

What therefore characterized Argentina's policy regime in the immediate aftermath of the 1989–91 reform? First, a fairly simple system of protection: few non-tariff barriers (covering 7 per cent of production), and a tariff structure with just three levels: zero for capital goods, 11 per cent for intermediates, and 22 per cent for final goods. In addition, quantitative export restrictions and related fees were removed.[18] Secondly, the absence of any major distortionary promotional policies, with the suspension of regional and sectoral fiscal incentives. And, thirdly, a post-reform regulatory environment characterized by the elimination of most (but not all) policy-generated barriers to domestic competition and mobility.

In sum, while Argentine trade reform signalled a commitment to an open economy, deregulation underscored the intention for an environment free of impediments to the entry and operation of firms. The key legislation established an unambiguous frame of reference that oriented economic agents with respect to the government's views and intentions on regulation. Finally, an aggressively pursued privatization programme has led to the sale of most industrial and infrastructure assets previously in the hands of the state, while stimulating a strong influx of foreign investment.

3.2. **Other Latin American Economies**

Most Latin American countries, in addition to Argentina, have moved far on the road of structural reform, including all major economies of the region: Brazil, Mexico, Colombia, Peru, and Chile, among others. Smaller economies have also made significant progress, including El Salvador, in Central America, Jamaica, in the Caribbean, and Uruguay.

Take, for example, the case of Brazil. Since the late 1980s this country has

TABLE 15.3. Brazil, evolution of tariff structure, 1987, 1990, 1993 (*ad valorem* tariff rates)

Statistic	1987	1990	July 1993
Average	51	32.2	14.2
Mode	30	40	20
Standard deviation	26	19.6	7.9
Amplitude	0–105	0–85	0–35

Source: Government of Brazil.

TABLE 15.4. Brazil, tariff levels by major product groups, 1990, 1994 (*ad valorem* tariff rates)

NBM chapters	1990	Sept. 1994
Cotton	30.6	13.9
Synthetic fibres	30.0	15.1
Garments and accessories	50.0	20.0
Iron and steel	21.9	11.2
Aluminium	22.5	12.3
Electric machinery	38.8	16.5
Automobiles	63.3	18.0
Furniture	41.8	17.8
Meat	18.5	10.0
Cereals	20.7	6.7
Beverages	75.1	19.7
Organic chemicals	24.3	6.3
Drugs	22.8	10.1

Source: CNI (National Confederation of Industry).

become an increasingly open and competitive economy. The 1988 tariff rationalization efforts have been followed by a comprehensive trade reform. Starting in March 1990, the process of trade liberalization has involved the immediate removal of explicit non-tariff barriers (the so-called Anexo C of Cacex) and the announcement of a time-bound decrease in the level and dispersion of tariffs (see Table 15.3). For an economy emerging from half a century of import-substitution policies, this represented a quantum change in government policies and had profound implications for the market strategies and productive behaviour of firms which were caught by the liberalization moves as the economy entered a recession.

A more detailed look by major product groups set out in Table 15.4 shows significant decreases in tariff levels in the 1990–4 period, affecting a fairly broad spectrum of tradables, intermediates, durables, and non-durables. It is particularly striking for tariff reductions in products which were vulnerable to import competition—namely, synthetic fibres, tools, electric machinery, automobiles, and

TABLE 15.5. Brazil, imports/domestic consumption, 1990–1992

Segment	1990	1991	1992
Electric power equipment	11.9	17.6	26.6
Electr. components for automobiles	6.1	9.9	15.1
Electric machinery	27.4	36.4	45.9
Engines and autoparts	7.5	11.2	18.8
Fertilizers	17.3	22.6	24.3

Source: BNDES (National Bank for Economic and Social Development).

toys, and which had as a result to undergo major restructuring efforts. Although the numbers displayed refer to nominal rates of protection, the overall reduction in the levels of variance (as indicated by data on standards deviation from Table 15.1) suggest that effective rates of protection must also have moved down substantially.

Although import response was initially slow, partly due to the 1990–2 recession, import levels increased significantly thereafter, growing at an annual average rate of 27.8 per cent in 1992–4, reaching an estimated $US33.2 billion in 1994. Still, the stagnation in the value of imports in 1991–2 concealed the threat they actually posed. First, immediately after 1990, as Table 15.5 shows, the ratio of imports to domestic consumption increased substantially in a number of industrial sectors, increasing the intensity of import competition. Secondly, firms were pressured not only by actual import penetration, but by the fact that customers could credibly invoke the threat of looking for alternative suppliers in order to obtain better purchasing terms.

While trade reform has been the aspect of structural change in Brazil which has received most attention (despite the recent clampdown on the surge of imports of consumer durables and automobiles for balance of payment reasons), there have also been decisive moves towards lifting remaining barriers to foreign investment (including those of constitutional nature), be they related to sectoral investment restrictions or the repatriation of profits and capital.[19] In addition the process of international technology transfer has been dramatically simplified, with far lower levels of government interference on the specifics of contracts signed between foreign suppliers of technology and domestic firms. Finally, most state-owned enterprises have been included in the privatizatization programme, which started in earnest in 1991 and has by the end of 1995 led to the sale of over $US10 billion of industrial assets.

Both Chile and Colombia are often cited for their strong macro-economic records. And, while Chile's reforms are well documented,[20] Colombian reforms are less well known. Yet, between 1990 and 1994, significant policy reforms in trade, foreign investment, exchange rate as well as capital, labour market, and competition were undertaken in the country.[21] In particular, the provision of infrastructure services, hitherto a monopoly of the state, became open to private-sector entry. The legal and constitutional reforms also focused on building up or strengthening market-supportive regulatory institutions: an autonomous Central Bank, a reformed Superintendency of Industry and Commerce put in charge of implementing competition and anti-trust policy, and consumer protection; a set of Public Utility Regulatory Commissions for telecommunications, water supply and sanitation, and electricity and gas, to foster competition and prevent monopolistic practices in these sectors; and a Superintendency of Public Services, to look after consumer rights in the area, and monitor financial and administrative practices of public utilities.

Another illustrative example of structural reform, this time from a small economy (with GDP estimated at $US8.8 billion), is that of El Salvador, in Central America.[22] Since the end of the civil war (1979–91), the government has moved fairly decisively to deregulate the economy, by introducing greater competition (through trade reform) and privatization of commercial banks and finance companies, by dismantling state agricultural marketing, and by selling state-owned assets. After more than a decade of stagnation, economic growth rebounded to 5.2 per cent in 1992–3 and 5.8 per cent in 1994, while inflation lowered from a high of 30 per cent in 1986 to 10 per cent in 1994. At the same time, the private sector took the lead in the economy, becoming responsible for 93 per cent of total employment and for over 90 per cent of GDP.

The new administration which took office in mid-1994 announced an economic programme to promote more rapid economic growth on a sustainable basis by an explicit recognition that for all economies, large and small, the challenge of globalization called for an increase in the country's outward orientation. That translated into making El Salvador a cost-competitive locus of global value-added activities, which was predicated on significant strides in the provision of infrastructure and other public services, while opening multiple channels of communications to improve public–private sector coordination. The bipartisan San Andres Pact of 31 May 1995 (entitled 'Development: The New Game of Peace of Peace') ratified these objectives through an explicit agreement to make El Salvador a more open and competitive economy (with a transparent schedule of tariff liberalization reducing the rates from 1–20 per cent in 1995 to 0–6 per cent in 1999; the enactment of competition law and the reform of consumer-protection law by the end of 1995; the privatization and introduction of competition in the provision of infrastructure services; the modernization of the financial system); and to generate a cooperative environment among government, business, and labour to ensure continuous productivity gains through training, information dissemination, technological upgrading, and more flexible labour-market arrangements.

4. The Challenge of Stability

Printing money, and controlling its volume, are activities classically regulated by the government. More than a 'veil', money becomes the anchor that allows the real economy to function without turbulence (except for the noise inherent in changes in technologies and markets). An essential function of government is thus to guarantee monetary stability.

The record in Latin America is mixed in this regard. In contrast to an earlier period when inflation was accepted as a 'price' countries had to pay for development, indulgence with macro-economic instability is now at its nadir. There is, to the contrary, very limited political support for fiscal largesse or monetary laxity. As recent elections in Brazil, Peru, and Argentina have shown, the relative importance attributed to a stable, low-inflation environment has changed dramatically in the last two decades.

Yet, even if Brazilians, Peruvians, Argentineans, and other Latins are voting for stability, they do not necessarily support the harsh austerity measures that accompany the pursuit of a low-inflation environment, the short-term effects of which are quite painful in terms of unemployment and domestic absorption. Policy persistence is critical for the country to remain in a path of low inflation. It is not enough for a country to run a budget surplus in a single year: fiscal discipline has to be accepted as the normal behaviour of governments. Moreover, coming out of high inflation requires building up a reputation by overshooting budget surplus targets. Thus the requirements of stability are far from trivial and explain the cleavage one observes between the dramatic progress in micro-economic reform, which is now regarded as irreversible in most Latin countries, and macro-economic adjustment, which in a number of countries is still tentative.

Although it is arguable that fiscal discipline is the fundamental requirement for economic stability, particularly for countries where the governments have systematically outspent its ability to raise revenues, private absorption must be equally in line with the potential of domestic productive capabilities and balance of payment limits. Monetary and exchange-rate policy are thus key additional macro-stability elements, the management of which can go astray, as the example of Mexico illustrates.[23]

A combination of loose monetary policy, excessive private spending, and overvalued exchange rates led to explosive current-account deficits financed by short-term capital, parked in the country to take advantage of large interest-rate differentials, and propitiated by the globalization of financial flows. While short-term reliance on 'hot money' might have been justified to finance on a non-inflationary basis excessive domestic absorption in the transition to macro-stability, it is, however, a shaky basis to anchor an adjustment programme, in view of its inherently unstable nature.

While the government expected a post-1994 election 'soft landing' (with the consequent 'corrective' fiscal, monetary, and exchange-rate policies implemented in its aftermath), a combination of lowering investors' confidence in the ability of the government to continue to sustain the peso and successful speculative attacks against the Central Bank (which lost over $US10 billion in the first three-quarters of 1994) instead brought about a crash reminiscent of the 1982 moratorium. The capital flight depleted the country's foreign-exchange reserves (which stood at $US6 billion by the end of 1994) and forced a major devaluation (and ensuing floating) of the peso. The difference this time was the decisive intervention of the US Treasury (an emergency package totalling $US52.8 billion in loans and guarantees was arranged by early 1995, including $US20 billion from the USA and $US17.8 billion from the International Monetary Fund (IMF))—without which there might have been a crisis of unheard-of proportions, as investors retreated from emerging markets, back to the USA and Germany, in the first place.

After the crisis of December 1994, Mexico is now attempting to regain macro-economic balance, particularly in terms of controlling its external accounts. The current recession, induced by a fastly shrinking rate of domestic absorption, and the fall in the value of the peso, is allowing the country to attain a surplus in the trade balance. With continued support from the US Treasury and multilateral institutions, it is unlikely that the December 1994 crisis will repeat itself in the near future, short of a major political upheaval, driven by the unravelling of the Partido Revolucionario Institucional and growing dissatisfaction with shrinking output and unemployment (which currently affects one-quarter of the population).

Among the other larger Latin American economies, Chile and Colombia appear to be most stable from a macro-economic standpoint, with the best managed fiscal, monetary, and exchange-rate policies. Chile, in particular, had an outstanding performance in 1995, with 8 per cent GDP growth (the twelfth consecutive year of positive growth), an 8 per cent rate of inflation (the lowest in thirty-five years), and a trade surplus of $US1.3 billion. High economic growth and low inflation rates are driven by sound policies (including a conservative posture towards short-term capital) and possibly the highest domestic savings rate in Latin America (equivalent to 27.5 per cent of GDP).

Brazil, on the other hand, is in the midst of its first successful stabilization plan since the mid-1960s, after a sequence of failed attempts during the early 1980s. The sustainability of the Brazilian stabilization attempt, which is approaching its second anniversary (monetary reform and the introduction of the Real came on 1 July 1994), will ultimately depend on a strenuous fiscal effort: the government should be targeting (and convincing the population of the importance of) a budgetary surplus for the second half of the 1990s, particularly in view of the fact that it is unlikely that the country will be able to rely on the elastic supply of capital that Mexico (and Argentina) did in the early 1990s. On the contrary, as a result of investors' fears after the Mexican débâcle, and a trade deficit engendered by excess absorption, the Central Bank lost nearly $US10 billion between July 1994 and March 1995—when foreign-exchange reserves (measured on an international liquidity basis, which takes into account medium-term receivables) shrank from $US43,090 million to $US33,742 million. Although the level of reserves have since recovered, reaching $US51.8 billion by the end of 1995, those sharp movements in such a brief period are a testimony of how integrated global financial markets have become. In any case, Brazilian adjustment will probably need to rely to a far greater extent on domestic savings, given the increased volatility of financial flows to emerging markets and investors' continued fears.

In a number of ways, the adjustment efforts of Argentina are the most impressive, in the sense that, defying expectations, the government has been able to improve its fiscal position, and, with the support of multilateral institutions and private banks (totalling over $US11 billion), shore up a frail financial system, avoiding a generalized run on the banks at the beginning of 1995. It could be argued that the ability of the economic team, combined with strong support in Congress, avoided the unravelling of the Cavallo stabilization plan.

It is worth recalling that, when the new government took over in 1989, it inherited public institutions that functioned under an incentive framework favouring spending but not raising revenues, and this led to a structural reliance on the inflation tax to sustain the fiscal deficit. As a result, the deficit became endogenous and thus explosive. By 1989 the state had become insolvent.[24]

To eliminate the fiscal deficits fuelling the inflationary spiral that gripped the economy at the end of the 1980s (in mid-1989, monthly inflation reached 200 per cent), the new government initiated profound changes in public finance that were remarkable for the scope and speed at which they were pursued. They included measures in the area of revenue mobilization—the base of value-added tax was expanded and inefficient taxes on exports and financial intermediation were removed, while tax administration was modernized. Expenditure reforms were also undertaken—the public administration was streamlined by reducing the total number of federal employees by over 103,000 (about 15 per cent of the total), and transferring another 284,000 positions (40 per cent of the total) to the provinces. At the same time, legislation suspending costly and distortionary fiscal subsidies was enacted.[25]

Equally important was the restructuring of government liabilities with domestic and foreign creditors, in particular through the sale of nearly all public enterprises at the national level and using part of the proceedings for debt retirement. In August 1993 a new two-year revenue-sharing agreement with the Provinces was announced as a first step towards strengthening the adjustment process at the provincial level. Finally, in September 1993 the social-security reform was approved, introducing an optional capitalized private-pension system.

Primary responsibility for price stability was shifted to the monetary authority. At the end of 1989 the Central Bank's quasi-fiscal deficit was eliminated through the forced conversion of short-term, high-interest deposits into long-term dollar bonds. The April 1991 Convertibility Law fixed the exchange rate at the equivalent of one peso to the US dollar; formally de-indexed contracts; facilitated a dual currency system; and required the monetary base to be fully backed by international reserves.

The price stability that followed the economic reforms of the early 1990s was accompanied by the remonetization of the economy, an increase in the supply of credit, and an expansion in real incomes. Combined, they brought about the resumption of economic growth, with the economy expanding at 8.9, 8.7, and 6 per cent in 1991, 1992, and 1993 respectively, and a further 4.6 per cent in 1994. The most dramatic result of the reforms was, however, a sharp decrease in the rate of inflation to single-digit levels in 1993, and, more generally, a dampening in the degree of volatility of the economy. In fact, as shown in Table 15.4, Argentina had the lowest rate of inflation in 1995 among all major Latin economies (1.5 per cent, compared to 8 per cent for Chile, 10 per cent for Peru, 15 per cent for Brazil, 19 per cent for Colombia, and 52 per cent in the case of Mexico). Still, despite the progress achieved on the macro-economic front (and the competence of the economic team), stability is far from assured, as the ripple effects of the Mexican crisis nearly led to a financial crisis of major proportions. In addition, rising unemployment (which jumped from 6.9 per cent in 1991 to 18.6 per cent at the end of the first half of 1995, according to the UN's Economic Commission for Latin America) has provided political impetus to the opposition, despite its inability to present a credible alternative stabilization plan.

The Argentine case thus underscores the key proposition of this chapter—namely, that, while trade, regulatory, and asset ownership-related reforms have taken hold and can be considered irreversible, at least from the current vantage-point, the same cannot be said about macro-economic adjustment and stability. The latter is a far more protracted and complex process than what was originally envisaged in the early 1980s after the onset of the debt crisis, and it is unlikely that a stable and sustainable macro-economic path can be achieved before another decade of persistent efforts.

5. Concluding Remarks

This chapter has argued that, with the exhaustion of the Schumpeterian state, which had spearheaded industrialization in developing countries since the 1950s, a novel mode of state action is required. In Latin America, the transition to a new mode of state action is predicated on a set of structural reforms of micro-economic nature, focused on trade liberalization, privatization, and changes in regulatory regimes, and on sustained macro-economic adjustment to a low inflation regime.

Although the reform process in Latin America has advanced considerably, it has taken hold, and to a great extent can be considered irreversible, on the micro-economic front. This does not preclude short-term reversals (as in the trade regime) and slow changes in the more controversial aspects of the regulatory regime (exemplified by the case of IPR, as countries adapt their current legislation and practice to the Uruguay Round TRIPS agreement and balance off pressure from the USA and, to a lesser extent, from the EU). In the macro-economic arena, and with the exception of Chile and possibly Colombia, there is still considerable ingrained instability that must be dealt with though persistent efforts in fiscal discipline, monetary restraint, and realistic exchange-rate policies.

NOTES

1. UN (1992: 51). Note as well that in 1990 the Asian region attracted 61% of DFI inflow to developing countries, whereas flows to developing countries and the Caribbean reached 32%.
2. The experience of the East Asian economies is telling, in this regard. The post-1985 revaluation of Japan's yen, and later on of South Korea's won and Taiwan's dollar, led to an intense search for new, lower-cost locations: Malaysia, and then Thailand, Indonesia, southern China, and, more recently, Vietnam. Although the rise of the yen against the dollar, in particular, took a respite from mid-1988 to mid-1990, since then and until recently Japan's currency has been gaining ground relentlessly. Exporters, such as of automobiles, electronics, and industrial machinery, faced with lower revenues and reduced cost competitiveness responded by, *inter alia*, accelerating the process of transferring overseas their production facilities and through greater efforts to procure components from local sources.
3. For a more detailed discussion on globalization and key trends in technical progress, how they redefine international competitiveness for the firm, and what are their implications for policy, see Dahlman (1994).
4. This section draws heavily on Frischtak (1995: ch. 1).
5. See Katz (1994) for a view on both the traditional and the 'new' development economics rationale for industrial-policy activism.
6. An econometric investigation on the determinants of real private investment presents strong evidence on the positive impact of public investments, with a 1% increase in the ratio of public investment to GDP expanding the private investment–GDP ratio by 0.257 percentage point, far outstripping the impact of other variables. See Serven and Solimano (1992*b*: Table 7.9).
7. The perception of uncertainty by investors (even if investors are risk neutral and their risks diversifiable) is a major obstacle for long-term economic growth. It is particularly critical in the context of adjustment programmes, where investment response has often proved to be unexpectedly slow and weak because of the incomplete credibility of policy reforms. On this point see Serven and Solimano (1992*a*).
8. Thus the notion of 'alliance capitalism' to denote a new phase of economic organization and a new role of the state in market economies, as a regulatory arbiter in the public interest, as a facilitator of markets, as a creator of key assets (such as an educated labour force), and as a partner to the private sector. See Dunning's conceptual and historical discussion in Chapter I of this volume.
9. In Chapter 14 Sanjaya Lall makes a strong argument that selective (in addition to functional) state interventions should be part of industrial policy, having for empirical reference the contemporary experiences of East Asian economies. In particular, technological deepening would be aided by a more active posture towards multinational enterprises, which would be steered to collaborate with local R&D institutions, strengthen local technological activities, and improve the capabilities of networks of supplier firms. See also World Bank (1993*b*) for a comprehensive assessment of the role of public policy in the East Asian 'miracle'.
10. Not infrequently, the agents favoured by certain rules argue that the decision to invest in a specific area was taken in response to implicit government guarantees and

directly under its orientation. How should the government therefore remove its support from an activity that was once a priority to the point that the state 'commanded' private investment and regulated its allocation? Government officials, on the other hand, responsible for the design and implementation of the old regime, saw as their responsibility assuring the survival of firms that undertook what were once priority projects.

11. For a more critical view of the impact of trade reforms, particularly on domestic engineering capabilities, see Katz (1994).
12. The evolution of freight and port costs, which fell considerably within a year or two after deregulation—by as much as 35–40%—illustrates the importance of regulatory reform to the integration of Argentine economy to world markets. The simplification of customs and other related bureaucratic procedures, with savings estimated at 1% of the FOB value of exports, have served to further facilitate integration. See Roja and Canosa (1992: 49, annex III).
13. 'Argentina . . . laws governing foreign investment are among the most liberal in the world. In general, Argentina encourages investments though a free-market policy and low income tax rates rather than through subsidies. Tax exemption for new investments, accelerated depreciation of fixed assets and tax reimbursement on exports are granted under identical conditions to nationals and foreigners' (Ernst & Young 1992: 1). The discussion on direct foreign investment draws heavily on this document.
14. A survey of multinational corporations published in the December 1991 edition of *Latin America* rated Argentina's foreign investment policy a 3.8 on a scale of 0 to 5, with 5 being the best. Chile with a rating of 4.3 was the only higher score on the survey. The average score was just below 3.2.
15. Registration with the Registry of Foreign Investment is optional (and easy to accomplish), though advisable if the government were to impose restrictions on access to or remittance of foreign exchange.
16. The rules regulating international technology transfer were initially drawn in Law 19,231 of 1971, the primary objective of which was to constrain the outflow of foreign exchange and stimulate labour-intensive activities. The provisions of this law were made more discriminatory by Law 20,794 of 1974, which increased the discretionary power of the state to regulate technology transfer. In 1967, Law 21,617 partially liberalized the process of acquisition of foreign technology, followed by Law 22,426, which eliminated most remaining barriers.
17. Argentina's pharmaceutical industry sales are in the order of $US3 billion, of which 56% are by domestic laboratories, the highest proportion in Latin America (other than Cuba).
18. Since July 1993 import duties have been 0% on industrial equipment and machinery (although some exceptions are taxed at 15–20%); 0–5% on raw materials; 5–10% on intermediate products, and 15–20% on finished goods.
19. In 1995 the Brazilian Congress approved overwhelmingly an amendment to the Constitution eliminating any distinction between national and foreign firms located in Brazil. The changes also allow free entry into mining, a sector which had been closed off to foreign-owned producers since 1988. For the first time in recent history, the law does not differentiate from either a regulatory or an incentive perspective national and foreign firms, as long as legally established in the country.
20. See, e.g., Bosworth *et al.* (1994).
21. See Montenegro (1995).

22. For a detailed discussion, see World Bank (1995*a*).
23. See the excellent (and prescient) discussion in Dornbush and Werner (1994).
24. For a detailed discussion, see World Bank (1993*a*).
25. In this regard, the government decided to replace the self-monitored tax deductions with a tax credit programme launched in November 1992 with Decree 2054/92. Under the decree, each beneficiary was fully audited for compliance against its original contract. Those passing the audit received non-transferable fiscal tax credits redeemable against taxes in the year of the tax collection. Those failing received a credit of sharply reduced value in proportion to their non-compliance and will be audited for back taxes. This criterion was applied on a sliding scale, according to which the greater the non-compliance the larger the number of tax credits forfeited. Phasing out tax expenditures to support Tierra del Fuego was also necessary for both fiscal and resource allocation reasons. The government progressively reduced the fiscal cost of the Tierra del Fuego regime, first by eliminating the domestic sales tax on electronic products in November 1991 and, with it, the value of the exemption for Tierra del Fuego producers. Secondly, tax rebates on exports from Tierra del Fuego to the mainland and abroad were virtually eliminated by the Decree 888 of June 1992. Finally, the government decided on the progressive elimination of the VAT exemption (Decree 1999/92). The major benefits for industries located in Tierra del Fuego will remain the exemption from import duties and the exemption from income tax, while the total fiscal cost of the Tierra del Fuego regime will by 1995 be reduced to a tenth of its original projected value.

REFERENCES

Bosworth, B. P., Dornbush, R., and Laban, R. (1994), *The Chilean Economy: Policy Lessons and Challenges* (Washington: Brookings Institution).

Dahlman, C. (1994), 'New Elements of International Competitiveness: Implications for Developing Economies', in C. Bradford Jr. (ed.), *The New Paradigm of Systemic Competitiveness: Towards More Integrated Policies in Latin America* (Paris: OECD Development Centre Documents).

Dornbush, R., and Werner, A. (1994), 'Mexico: Stabilization, Reform and No Growth', *Brookings Paper on Economic Activity*, 1: 253–315.

Edwards, S. (1993), *Latin America and the Caribbean: A Decade After the Debt Crisis* (Washington: World Bank).

Ernst & Young (1992) *Doing Business in Argentina* (Buenos Aires: Ernst & Young).

Frischtak, C. (1995), 'Introduction', in C. Frischtak (ed.), *Regulatory Policies and Reform: A Comparative Perspective* (Washington: World Bank, Private Sector Development Department, December).

Katz, J. (1994), 'Industrial Organization, International Competitiveness and Public Policy', in C. Bradford Jr. (ed.), *The New Paradigm of Systemic Competitiveness: Towards More Integrated Policies in Latin America* (Paris: OECD Development Centre Documents).

Montenegro, A. (1995), 'Economic Reforms in Colombia: Regulation and Deregulation, 1990–94' (Washington: World Bank, Economic Development Institute Working Papers).

Rojo, P. and Canosa, A. (1992), 'El Programa de Desregulación del Gobierno Argentino', *Boletín Informativo Techint*, 269: 29–46.

Sguiglia, E., and Delgado, R. (1993), 'Desregulación y Competitividad: Evaluación de la Experiencia Argentina', *Boletín Informativo Techint*, 276: 17–64.

Serven, L., and Solinamo, L. (1992*a*), 'Economic Adjustment and Investment Performance in Developing Countries: The Experience of the 1980s', in V. Corbo, S. Fisher, and S. Webb (eds.), *Adjustment Lending Revisited: Policies to Restore Growth* (Washington: World Bank).

—— —— (1992*b*), 'Private Investment and Macroeconomic Adjustment: A Survey', *The World Bank Economic Observer*, 7.

Thobani, M. (1994), 'The Privatization Experience of Latin America', in *Private Sector* (Washington: World Bank), 1: 9–12.

UN (1992): United Nations, *World Investment Report: Transnational Corporations as Engines of Growth* (New York: UN Centre on Transnational Corporations).

World Bank (1993*a*), *Argentina—From Insolvency to Growth* (Washington: World Bank).

—— (1993*b*), *The East Asian Miracle* (New York: Oxford University Press).

—— (1995*a*), *El Salvador: Meeting the Challenge of Globalization* (Washington: Report No. 14109-ES).

—— (1995*b*), *Labor and Economic Reforms in the Latin America and the Caribbean* (Washington: World Bank).

PART THREE

IMPLICATIONS FOR NATIONAL AND SUPRA-NATIONAL GOVERNANCE

16

Implications for National Governments

John M. Stopford

1. **Introduction**

In Chapter 2 of this volume Richard Lipsey raised two general arguments that affect any interpretation of the national case studies which are set out in Chapters 6 to 15. First, he argued that the dynamic of technological change has created pressure for some sovereign powers to be transferred to supra-national bodies, such as the WTO, the EU, and NAFTA. Secondly, he observed that other powers needed to be transferred to more local levels of authority. In Chapter 3 John Dunning, drawing upon some remarks of Michael Porter, adds further detail about the localizing tendencies for some parts of the value-creating investments increasingly made by multinational corporations. The forces of globalization, it would seem, are pulling apart the traditional roles and powers of sovereign governments. These observations are part of the general argument that John Dunning reviews in Chapter 1 and support his contention that national competitiveness is today much more a matter of a contest among created assets rather than of natural endowments. The national cases can help to answer the questions of who should be creating what kinds of assets, and where.

These questions suggest the need for theory to embrace notions of dynamic efficiency and go beyond the limitations of so much conventional theory that is based on ideas of static efficiency and static optimality in the allocation of resources. In many different ways and with different emphases, the national case studies provide rich detail for the development of a dynamic view of appropriate policy. Despite the wide variation in methodology and data, the descriptions of the countries place them in three loosely defined categories. The countries in each category share many common features, but the variety of policies deployed to deal with local social and political, as well as economic, structures defies any attempt to construct a general theory of dynamic optimality.[1]

This chapter starts from the proposition that guided my work some years ago with Susan Strange: that nations compete today more for the means to wealth as a route to power and less for territory as a means to wealth (Stopford and Strange, 1991). Wealth, for these purposes, is treated as both economic and (broadly defined) social wealth; it is not clear that the world is becoming more materialistic. Any attempt to define policies that build competitiveness without taking into account the social consensus about what is 'right', however rightness may be defined, is doomed to failure. Just as technological forces are spurring globalization of many forms, many social and political forces are tugging in the other direction.

The cross currents of contemporary market forces have fundamentally altered the ability of national authorities to 'control' the domestic economy and to respond adequately to external events. The national cases have painted a general picture in which governments are changing their priorities for defining how best they might foster competitiveness. From being prime movers in the drama—as, for example, in Sweden until very recently—some governments are beginning to see their role as orchestrators of the full range of national resources needed to gain the most from wealth-creating investments. For France, Michalet argues that a national government within the EU can no longer afford the independent command of all necessary resources and must therefore begin to adopt more collaborative protocols with its neighbours. Thus, after about 1983, France is seen to be moving away from its independent, Colbertist tradition of the power of the central state. Yet, while France considers an uncertain policy future, Lall has shown how many Asian states remain committed to policies of state-led investments in new resources.

Different responses to the same phenomenon of global competition are only to be expected, given national differences in history, social tradition, ambition, and capacity to absorb and deploy the new technologies and new demands on managerial capacity created by a globalizing economy. Some countries have been or still are aiming to change their comparative advantage by direct government intervention. These are countries in a state of 'catch-up', where the main issue is that of creating new advantages, typically by imitating those further ahead. Smaller economies, many of them in Asia, are in this category. So too have been countries like France and Japan, where catch-up has been a matter of policy in key industries.[2]

A second category is the resource-rich country, whose competitiveness essentially depends on adding value in a limited number of industries. Here, the primary concern is that of exploiting advantages. In some cases such as Canada, there is a similar sense of catch-up in that they are seeking to create new assets with which to displace processing facilities installed earlier in other countries. The turbulence of the competitive battle and the difficulty of maintaining advantage, even when richly endowed with natural resources, are vividly illustrated in the chapter on Australia. Though it enjoyed the highest *per capita* income in the world in 1900, Australia has since slipped down to fifteenth place in the league rankings.

The third category is that of defending competitiveness. Countries already at the leading edge of technology and competition face more complex policy issues. Competitive forces have required a shift in the focus of policy, away from industries and towards the individual enterprise. It is, after all, firms not states, that compete in world markets. Innovations in strategy change the 'rules' of competition and overturn many scale advantages to permit David to defeat Goliath (see, e.g., Baden-Fuller and Stopford 1994: 281).

Similarly, erstwhile leading nations that have grown rich can find the task of defending their competitiveness against the predatory attack of smaller newcomers extremely taxing. The chapter on Germany illustrates the policy dilemmas as governments struggle to balance the competing interests of many stakeholders, including trade unions, in the adjustment process. Chapters on other defenders also suggest the possibilities for innovation in policy. For example, the adoption of indirect policies aimed at creating a climate of innovation and reducing the risks for local firms that aspire to world leadership can assume great effectiveness.

The shift from prime mover towards orchestrator can raise new questions about the legitimacy of government, especially when the momentum of growth is lost, even temporarily. There are related issues of whether the nation state remains the appropriate unit of analysis for considering competitiveness in a world of simultaneous global/local forces. Moreover, changes in national policy and role can create frictions both domestically and in a nation's international dealings, raising the spectre of inconsistent actions and unintended outcomes. All these issues and worries are addressed towards the end of the chapter, where the contention is advanced that national authorities retain considerable powers but need to adjust how they are to be deployed to best advantage.

2. Creating New Sources of Competitiveness

Is it possible for governments to create new sources of advantage for firms operating within their jurisdiction? If so, how? Dunning and others have identified man-made or created assets as more important in today's competitive battles than the wealth of natural endowments. Some of the countries included in the catch-up category show that much progress has indeed been made to overturn disadvantages of the kind associated with the conventional tenets of comparative advantage.

To draw some general lessons from these examples, the nature of competitiveness as well as the role of national authorities in different social and cultural circumstances need at least some rough definition. Consider first the question of competitiveness. None of the authors of earlier chapters offers a clear definition of what it might mean for nations. The references to the annual World Competitiveness Report beg the question, because the data in those reports are an amalgam of opinion and multiple variables of questionable relevance and dubious weighting. Yet everyone has a reasonably clear view of what—in very general terms—is meant by the concept. A competitive nation is one whose economy is kept under control and is growing. But how? Dunning offers some helpful guidance for the role of macro-organizational policy to create a climate for progress that goes well beyond the normal scope of arguments about the role of industry policy. His concept is akin to that of a coordinated government as an orchestrator of resources of all kinds. But Dunning stops short of a full specification of how that role can be defined in specific circumstances.

The gap in the argument is understandable, for a full specification requires a level of dynamic theory that does not yet exist. Part of the problem can be attributed to the equally vexing question of what is meant by the competitiveness of a firm—an altogether different concept. Most economists' definitions of firm-level competitiveness are restricted to notions of scale and cost, though some include organizational capability as a specific source of advantage relative to competitors.

Earlier chapters have, however, hinted at the need to add two further dimensions of firm-level competitiveness. One is the ability of a firm to gain productive access to other firms' resources through contracts and local networks, as in the Japanese *keiretsu* structures and their Canadian equivalents. The other is the role and effectiveness of public policy in accelerating the speed at which new resources can be accumulated within firms and local networks.

These issues bind together the ideas of competitiveness at both national and firm level: the fate of each is conditioned by the fate of the other. It is this nexus of dynamic interdependence that seems to determine the major implications of global competition for national governments.

The search for new sources of competitiveness in post-war Japan illustrates the breadth of the concerns and the need to think in terms of the macro-organizational policy requirements discussed in earlier chapters. Initially, Japan was in the catch-up phase. Policy was aimed unambiguously and successfully at creating new advantage for heavy industries such as steel and industrial machinery where 'income elasticity of demand is high, technological progress is rapid, and labour productivity rises fast' (OECD 1972: 15). With hindsight, one can now see that such policies of intervention worked in part because the crucial economic factors of production could be clearly identified, fostered, and controlled. Industrial policy could be used as a complement to market forces: where short-term forces conflicted with longer-term possibilities, government could provide the means to fund the time gap. And, given the structure of the financial markets, government could provide effective 'administrative guidance' and gain the desired outcome with only modest expenditures of public money (Pepper *et al.* 1985: 71).

Such policy coordination has been regarded by many as an essential part of purposeful government, directly or indirectly. Johnson (1984) defined it as 'the government's explicit attempt to coordinate its . . . expenditures and to reform them using as a basic criterion the achievement of dynamic comparative advantage'.

The difference between those who seek to capture position in new sectors and those who defend existing territory can be seen in many of the US concerns about the meddling with market forces and the twin risks of both inefficiency and 'unfair' international competition. Using the much narrower notion of industrial policy, the US International Trade Commission (ITC) defined the effort in terms of industrial targeting: 'coordinated government actions taken to direct productive resources to help domestic producers in selected industries become more competitive. The[y] . . . can be incentives or restrictions, such as subsidies, tax incentives, import barriers or other market-distorting actions' (ITC 1983).[3] They found many examples of selective intervention and provided part of the base case for US complaints about the 'playing field' being tilted by 'unfair' subsidies (Tyson 1992). These complaints have been most vociferous when the subsidies have involved strategically important industries, especially those like semiconductors with important spillover effects for related industries (Borrus *et al.* 1986).

Such differences of view have led to quite contradictory interpretations of the astonishing growth of many Asian economies after the mid-1970s. Those who emphasize the efficiency of market signals and private enterprise look for evidence that supports the tenets of neoclassical economics, which provides a theoretical justification in terms of optimal resource allocation under conditions of free trade. Observers of this school tend to regard the Japanese experience as unique and to explain the later growth of other Asian nations in terms of the relative sluggishness of developed economies, constrained by inefficient government intervention.

Lipsey has provided one of many challenges to this view. The country cases also provide evidence of quite different means to create new dynamic efficiencies. The evidence seems to be favouring alternative interpretations about how nations might accumulate additional factors of production, can absorb new technologies and new information-processing demands, and simultaneously create new institutions capable of responding to the new demands of extensive industrialization.

The World Bank's study of the eight fastest-growth Asian economies (World Bank 1993) illustrates the problem of interpretation. The bank's central conclusion was that the 'rapid growth in each economy was primarily due to the application of a set of common, market-friendly economic polices' (World Bank 1993: p. vi). Of the three kinds of government intervention identified, the report concluded that promotion of specific industries was largely ineffectual;[4] that directed credit may have raised investment and generated some productivity spillovers in Japan and South Korea, but not elsewhere; and that only export-push policies were generally effective. In short, the discipline of international markets was regarded as the best bet for influencing how competitiveness can be created and maintained.

The Bank's interpretation of events has been strongly challenged, on both theoretical and empirical grounds (see, e.g., Lall 1994, and Chapter 14 in this volume). Neoclassical theory assumes diminishing returns to investment and a convergence of growth rates. To explain the evidence of sustainable growth, 'new' growth theory has had to introduce productive factors that enjoy increasing returns—human capital and technology. Because these typically have important externalities, they can suffer from market failure.

It is now widely accepted, even in the USA, that intervention is both needed and acceptable in education, efficient infrastructure, and the creation of technology. If intervention is 'functional' or generic, it is called 'market friendly'. The World Bank and others have set up a straw man by posing 'government intervention' as the only alternative to 'market-friendly policies plus export push' as a means to creating export-led growth. An important alternative is 'favourable initial conditions plus investment-led growth'. The causality of growth can run from high investment to high imports to high exports (Wade 1990: 47–8). Government industrial policies come into this picture as one important cause of high investment as well as a cause of the structure of that investment. To do so effectively requires policy to become a complement to market forces, otherwise the resistance to beneficial change is insuperable.

3. Alternative Ways of 'Catching Up'

Defining the role for policy under conditions of catch-up is perhaps easier than for conditions of defending leadership at the technological or competitive frontier. In the former case, the rules of the game are reasonably well known and the technical trajectory of advancement reasonably predictable. Policy can be constructed to complement market forces. In the latter case, alternative, more complex approaches are required to cope with technological volatility and firm-level innovations in corporate strategy.

All the cases of catch-up started under conditions of relative stability, leaving room for nations to take long-term approaches to imitating the advantages of the leaders. Thus France could rely on the Planning Commissariat, South Korea on its series of five-year plans, and Japan on MITI's indicative guidance. The effectiveness of the chosen policies depended critically on local circumstance. Thus, there was no single 'recipe' for Asian countries,[5] nor for France and Sweden (up to the early 1990s). In addition, the description of Canada suggests strong elements of a catch-up strategy for many years.

Most of the countries studied used the large-scale enterprise as the prime vehicle for catching up: only Singapore and Taiwan concentrated on smaller entities. In the main, the hope was to create scale to overcome initial competitive disadvantages. To this end, a battery of policy weapons was deployed to give the necessary incentives and to reduce the risks for entrepreneurs. In Sweden, tax policy up to 1991 discriminated against young, less-capital-intensive firms; generous R&D incentives were allocated, especially after 1967, to the larger firms; and high levels of government purchases of goods and services specified at international standards were further inducements to build scale with an outward orientation. In France, some of the large enterprises were state-owned; in other sectors the means of inducing world-class scale and standards were defined around the *grands projects*, such as the nuclear programme, high-speed trains (TGV), and aerospace. These projects were financed, as in South Korea, with soft loans and had other risk-reducing features.

The general approach taken by South Korea has resembled many of Japan's earlier catch-up practices. To manage its time-compressed entry into heavy industries and to promote advanced innovative capabilities, Korea relied heavily on capital-goods imports, technology licences, and large investments in depending indigenous technical capacity. Korea deliberately set out to create its own large private enterprises, the *chaebol* (for some useful discussion, see Amsden 1989). The *chaebol* were given generous government contracts and preferential access to capital.[6] They became the main vehicle for ensuring the continuance of the investments in technology, contributing over 80 per cent of the national R&D spending.[7]

By contrast, Taiwan has relied on small enterprises to build its catch-up advantages (for further details to complement Lall's description, see Wade 1990). Taiwan has one of the world's most advanced forms of technology support for small and medium-sized enterprises, with devices like the Ministry of Economic Affairs' 'Centre-Satellite Factory Programme' to harness smaller factories around a principal one. The normal inefficiencies that plague such promotion policies in many countries have been kept in check by the export orientation of suppliers and assemblers, plus high levels of technical education. In these latter respects, Taiwan's policies have resembled those of South Korea.

Singapore has not relied on the scale of the enterprises within its borders, but on the scale of the multinationals' systems that are attracted at the margin into the country. To avoid the familiar dangers of becoming a branch-plant economy, Singapore has targeted underlying technologies, such as biotechnology. Initially, the government set up an Institute of Molecular and Cell Biology and funded a string of new venture start-ups. Early success in cancer research attracted foreign investors like Glaxo. Encouraged by these successes, the Singapore government added other research 'building blocks' and increased the supply of trained manpower by recruiting foreign experts on three-year visits and investing in more science education. Such selective and sequentially reinforcing targeting goes far to offset the costs of the complex market failures that impede entry into new technology. Yet, it must be remembered that success that is modest by world standards can have an enormous impact in a small state; there is room for niche players in a few segments of the worldwide industry and sustainable success does not always require leadership.

Singapore has also invested heavily in creating an efficient infrastructure that will further attract financial-services enterprises as well as the regional headquarters operations of multinationals. Just as Canada has been described as concentrating on improving the quality of its domestic supplier networks to overcome the handicap of low scale relative to the USA, so Singapore is investing in improving the supplier network in the 'growth triangle' that includes parts of its neighbours.

Singapore is unusual in its preference for foreign entities as the vehicle for catch-up. All others have tended to discriminate against foreigners both in terms of trade and by placing heavy restrictions on inward flows of FDI. Japan's catch-up policies before the Plaza Accord in 1985 relied heavily on protection of this kind. In addition, Japan provided specific support for domestic entities, whether large or smaller ones in *kieretsu* relationships. Together, these policies and practices were the centrepiece of government-led investments in creating new resources and overturning the relationships implied by static comparative advantage.

To make such policies work over long periods of time, they have relied on a strong degree of social consensus. Social consensus is normally associated with Asian countries, but it is equally visible in the chapter on France. There, the élite's concern with technical priorities was allied with a strong sense of national pride in the effort to reduce the dependency on foreigners for the imports of strategically important goods. Despite the Treaty of Rome, France was for a long time concerned to resurrect the older traditions of Colbert and to create new industrial strength. The rallying cries of a 'France First' kind attracted broad support among the unions as well as society more generally.

Strong social and union support was also critical in Sweden, though with one important difference. Swedish unions could see the benefits in trade created by a strong policy of outward FDI on the part of the major producers: French unions regarded such outwardness with suspicion and, especially in the state enterprises, generally opposed foreign investments for fear of a loss of domestic jobs.

4. Followers can Become Leaders—with Difficulty

The evidence in this volume shows how the very strengths of a long-term perspective and explicit planning for domestic advantage can, over time, become disadvantages. In Sweden, for example, the support for large enterprise acted to stifle entrepreneurship and to diminish the flow of new ideas. When the pressures of global competition intensified in the early 1990s and caused many large Swedish firms to lose international competitiveness, this problem became serious and a matter of public debate. At the same time, central finances were weakening and the Krona was devalued. The earlier social consensus eroded as labour unions saw less benefit from outward FDI and inward FDI began to assume importance as a new source of both capital and jobs.

The turbulence described for Sweden is an example of the difficulty of the transition from being a successful imitator to being a leader needing to defend a hard-won position. France has the same concerns, though these have been ascribed more to the impact of regionalization within Europe than merely to the forces of globalization. The role of the state has begun to shift as parts of the central apparatus of control have been dismantled. State enterprises are being sold off, and FDI flows, both inward and outward, are increasing. Direct intervention is giving way to a form of 'guidance' akin to the role of the Japanese central bureaucracies, but with many internal frictions and inconsistencies. Because the old doctrine of national champions has yet to be replaced with anything more robust than a vague commitment to revitalizing Europe, the possibilities for fudge and compromise are legion (for additional details, see Minc 1994). The opening of the economy is being achieved at a 'high price'.

The social and union consensus has eroded, as Chirac's Administration found out during the national strikes in late 1995.

Similar turbulence is evident in Japan, as will be discussed below. Even South Korea is finding that it cannot maintain its momentum of catch-up without some encouragement of FDI flows in both directions. Moreover, there is acute public debate about the future role of the *chaebol*, as their power is now regarded by many as excessive. Like Sweden, Korea could suffer from a slow-down in innovation as a long-term result of its 'restrict-and-exploit' strategy. The turbulence of global competition is challenging the polices of even the most successful exponents of catch-up.

5. Exploiting Natural Endowments

Australia and Canada have natural endowments few other countries enjoy. Yet both have found policies of domestic protection inadequate for the task of creating sustainable wealth-creating resources capable of survival in the globalizing economy. For Australia, this has meant a far-reaching programme of micro-economic reforms.Tariff protection for manufacturing industry was sharply reduced in order to force enterprises into greater efficiencies. As Hill and McKern show in Chapter 7, the Australian government has always had an important role, particularly since 1940. They point out that the wage-fixing system, and attitudes towards protectionism and regulatory measures, are all symptoms of the acceptance of a strong role for government. For these reasons, according to Hill and McKern, reform in Australia had to be initiated by government, even as it was being forced upon the country by growing globalization.

The social consensus that underpinned the policies of strong federally controlled protection have eroded as relative living standards have fallen. Hardly surprisingly, as in France, opening the market has revealed deep divisions in vested interests. In Australia, the role of the unions is in transition. From national wage-fixing, the trend is now towards enterprise- and site-level bargaining. In order to create new capabilities, there is a growing realization that unions and management should collaborate, not compete, for the division of a diminishing cake. The path towards such reform is certainly not smooth, but its broad direction is towards according the enterprise and management a greater role in managing the exploitation of natural resources in a world of competition among created assets.

This theme of a greater reliance on firms and managers is emphasized in the description of Canada. Canada's transition, however, is complicated by the large role played—as in Singapore—by foreign firms and by the fact that globalization means regionalization with the USA. None the less, Rugman illustrates the shift away from a sense of national controlling power—symbolized by the abolition of the Foreign Investment Review Agency—towards policies of building specialized business and non-business infrastructures. As in Japan, there is a strong sense of the need to build robust networks of linked production. Government, it could be argued, is moving towards the role of orchestrator.

In Latin America there is a mixture of the resource-rich country and the poorer country beginning to face up to the need for policies of catch-up and imitation. For both groups of country, however, the picture is more one of clearing the decks for future action than of making significant progress in building new competitive advantages. Recent actions have been focused on deregulation; privatization in some sectors; some liberalization of trade and investment; and initial moves, some extremely tentative, to tackle the problems of labour reform and the inefficiencies of central bureaucracies. Above all, to restore investor confidence after the turmoil and the losses during the 1980s, there is a need to create stability: a platform on which growth can be built.

Claudio Frischtak observes, in Chapter 15, that the requirements for economic stability are far from trivial and explain the cleavage in Brazil and Argentina between the dramatic progress in micro-economic reform—which is regarded as irreversible in most Latin American countries—and macro-economic adjustment, which in many countries is still tentative. Whether the new model state action implied in the Latin American chapter will prove to be sufficient to enable new wealth creation is open to dispute. Competition from Asia is growing at an accelerating pace that continues to erode the benefits of natural resources, as the examples of Australia and Canada show so vividly.

6. **Defending Leadership**

The recent shifts for Sweden and France into the role of defending leadership highlight the difficulties of maintaining social consensus. Both opening previously protected economies and managing the adjustment of open economies to the turbulence of global competition carry high social costs. The conclusion of Rose Marie Ham and David Mowery in the US chapter is that it is extremely difficult to get such issues fully onto the political agenda. The authors further suggest that the failure of US government policy to address the growing inequality of declining living standards among a significant portion of the domestic population might well produce a domestic political response favouring protection or limiting the expansion of links between the US and foreign economic and R&D systems. They argue that such a response would have troubling implications for the future welfare of citizens of both the USA and the world.

A central feature of the difficulty is that of volatility. Unlike the world of catch-up, when others have set the rules, leaders have to work at the uncertain frontier. Japan found that its much vaunted twenty-year planning horizon could become a liability. The High Definition Television (HDTV) system was almost ready for the market when breakthroughs in digital technology made most of its analogue technology obsolete. MITI's Fifth Generation computer project has been abandoned with little to show for all the public funds expended. Adapting to two-year technology cycles is almost impossible in Japan's planning system. The price Japan has paid has been a lack of flexibility. Perhaps ironically, the USA itself provides evidence of the difficulty. Government-sponsored initiatives in micro-electronics, such as the SEMATECH consortium and trade agreements, have yielded little and may even have been counter-productive (Spencer and Grindley 1993).

Similarly, protective regulations, as in Japanese telecommunications, have served to slow down the pace of development and to leave the cushioned domestic players vulnerable to fleeter-footed competitors elsewhere. The developments of cross-border alliances and the creation of new resources through contract have contributed to the erosion of the effectiveness of Japan's version of 'infant-industry' nurturing. So too has the increasing uncertainty about both the form and the pace of technical leapfrogging. At the frontier, direct intervention can create outcomes that are the reverse of what they used to be.

The difficulty is that forecasting—the basis for determining policy—is extremely unreliable at the frontier of technology or competition. In the chapter on Germany, the Federal Government is accused of not having done its homework on the nature of the adjustment required and of being overly obsessed with the political power of the unions defending their own positions. 'Doing the homework' may, however, be impossible.

Contrast the position in Germany and the USA today with the conditions prevailing when Japan sought leadership in selected heavy industries. Then, the underlying technologies were advancing at a sedate pace. Subsequently, the increases in the volatility of those industries have served to support Lawrence's criticism of industry policy. 'The alleged US weaknesses may actually be strengths for an economy at the technological frontier operating in an uncertain environment. In contrast, the foreign adherence to long-range planning may better suit less developed countries with clear schedules of change in comparative advantage' (Lawrence 1984: 143).

Ham and Mowery agree with Lawrence when they say 'the US federal system of separation of powers is designed to maximize political access and pluralism, while limiting the ability of central government to respond to slow-acting economic trends that are harmful in the long run but not critical in the near term'. Contrary to their conclusions, however, the very inability of the Federal authorities to manage systematically the investments needed to create new assets of the type Dunning calls for in Chapter 1 may prove to be a blessing in disguise. What may appear ineffective in the short term may also provide the seeds for future competitiveness.

Orchestrating the development of an environment that encourages entrepreneurship and rapid responses to new opportunity seldom gains political plaudits. Yet such slow work can be the essence of an effective policy response to the pressures of globalization. How else can one interpret the remarkable resurgence of the US computer, microprocessor, and semiconductor industries? During the mid-1980s the US government was widely criticized for failure to act decisively to counter the Japanese threat. Yet the same firms that were being written off—Intel and many others—reached a new peak of international competitiveness in 1996. Their resurgence has helped, and been helped in turn, by the emergence of new software capability and a general sense of leadership in the nascent multimedia industry. Meanwhile, the Japanese firms that were once regarded as unstoppable juggernauts, strongly supported by their home institutions, continue to suffer from depressed margins.

Ozawa's claim that 'the Japanese government is in disarray' echoes the dilemma faced in France. Once the evolutionary, four-phase framework of 'import protection as import expansion' had lost its power and as the concept of a successful national industry became unworkable in an open-economy setting, so the Japanese authorities have had, perforce, to search for a new paradigm to guide their efforts. The old traditions still surface from time to time, but the sheer complexity of the contemporary challenges defies the creation of new policies that are clear and capable of being understood by all. Herein lie the seeds of future experimentation, perhaps.

The UK, another defender of past leadership, differs sharply from the US and Japanese experience, in that foreign firms have played a crucial role in the establishment of new capability and the regeneration of old ones. The automotive industry, for example, was trapped in a vicious downward spiral of declining locational attractiveness, declining FDI, and declining technical capabilities embodied in rigid union-dominated structures of work demarcation. It took the arrival of new inward investors—the Japanese—to show the alternative possibilities. The Japanese had the same impact on the UK consumer electronics industry, turning a trade deficit into a surplus.

The analysis presented in the UK chapter suggests that the UK government, like others, progressively shifted its priorities towards that of creating an enabling environment within which new entrepreneurship, for firms large and small, can flourish regardless of the nationality of their owners. Policies of privatization and deregulation set the scene for actions that are now far ahead of those anticipated in Latin America. This optimistic picture is marred by what was dubbed 'bounded prejudice'. Liberal, market-friendly policies give way to direct intervention when politically expedient.

The optimism is also reduced by the seeming failure of the UK authorities adequately to appreciate the urgency of the competition for resources that are only poorly provided for by the market mechanism. The UK is one of the very few developed countries that suffers from a declining share of national income being spent on R&D. Moreover, critical parts of the infrastructure and education, all necessary ingredients for continuing competitiveness, are the subject of national debate and concern.

Under these circumstances, it is perhaps not surprising that, of all the country case studies, the UK provides the sharpest sectoral differences. Where the benefits of the policies greatly outweigh the costs, as in the City and financial services, there is a beneficial spiral of growth and international competitiveness. By contrast, much of what is left of UK capacity in electronics is in foreign hands and restricted to limited activities in the total value chain. Between the two extremes are sectors where, as in automobile components, many of the critical resources are provided by other European rivals. EU-wide investments of this kind are seen to limit the benefits of agglomeration that underpin the success of, say, the City; only a part of the value chain is transferred and what is transferred is closely coordinated with other units located elsewhere throughout the rest of Europe. Adjustments that are favourable for Europe as a whole may not be to the advantage of a member state that is struggling to retain some leadership with old resources.

Common to all the cases of defenders is the growing attention being paid to the role of the enterprise. If governments cannot forecast the outcomes, let managers try. By the late 1980s, one observer could conclude that not only had Japan shifted away from industry as the unit of analysis, but also that 'MITI's policy is not simply the enhancement of basic R&D; it ultimately aims at increased international competitiveness of individual firms' (Ishiyama 1989: 262).

At the same time, most 'defender' governments appear to be concentrating more on those parts of the competitiveness agenda that change only slowly: the underlying technologies, the efficient infrastructures, the provision of mass education, and a set of policies that permit rapid adjustment to events as they happen. In these respects, governments may be seen to be adopting some of the 'clothes' of modern management. Yet there are differences, as the following sections of this chapter elaborate.

7. Globalization and Localization

All countries, irrespective of the category to which they belong, are responding to the paradox that contemporary global markets are being shaped by forces that have opposite effects simultaneously. Technological advances, for example, can both create global scale and destroy the benefits of large scale. How best to respond to the paradox at the national level depends crucially on the size of the national market and the quality of the institutional base.

In Chapter 5 in this volume, Stephen Kobrin claimed that we are on the verge of a qualitative transformation of the world economy in which the old 'rules' of international exchange will progressively be swept away. He advanced three arguments, each of which has some bearing on the analysis presented in each country study. First, the dramatic increases in the scale of technology in many industries—affecting costs, risks, and complexity—have made even the largest national markets too small to be meaningful units. He depicts a trend in the world economy by which national markets are becoming progressively more fused transnationally rather than being just linked across borders. Secondly, the explosion of international strategic alliances is the visible sign of a transformation in the modality of transactions away from the choice of markets or hierarchies (i.e.

trade or FDI) towards what he calls a 'postmodern network'. Thirdly, related to the second, is the fact that the emerging global economy is integrated through information systems and information technology rather than through hierarchical organization structures.

In a world of 'alliance capitalism', to use John Dunning's term, Kobrin's argument is that both the nation state and the firm diminish in their importance as principal agents in the organization of wealth-creating work. Like Lipsey, he regards the future as having more to do with building the network that transcends legal and spatial boundaries than with conventional notions of competitiveness in a closed economy.

Kobrin creates a scenario for a future that is dominated by scale and by ever-denser webs of transactions. Such a view needs to be modified drastically, for there are many other possibilities that can coexist with some advantages being held by the big battalions. Many alternative trends and possibilities are sketched in the national studies.

Consider first the impact of technology. Certainly, some technological advances increase the minimum economy of scale, but others reduce it. Technological advances in electronics and information-handling mean that many factories have much smaller minimum economies of scale than before. In some industries, the effective unit of scale has shifted from the factory, the focus of most industrial economic analysis, towards what is being termed *corporate* scale. While large firms can gain advantage by being able to command the resources needed to create and exploit critical technologies—the global reservation system of major airlines, rather than the scale of the individual plane—smaller firms can prosper in market niches when they can gain access to scale-diminishing operating technologies.

The double-edged sword of technology has made some sources of wealth creation more mobile, but others have become more deeply embedded in regional networks. Rising standards of education have made many technologies more readily absorbable in local economies and therefore more mobile as a source of competitiveness. When combined with deregulation, as for many capital markets, monetary flows have become more mobile and the financial industry more tightly linked across borders. It can also be argued that global competition and technological change of other forms have served to make other resources and other industries less mobile. A prime example is in the growing power of specialized networked infrastructures that are fuelling the growth of clusters of industries in regional economies that John Dunning discussed in Chapter 3.

These new 'clusters' differ fundamentally from the older industrial districts, because firms are no longer transferring the entire business to new locations. Instead they are choosing to separate the location of parts of their value chain and so have quite new dynamic impacts on the development of the associated local social systems needed to create durable efficiency and adaptability (Harrison 1992). Firms can increasingly relate to the special characteristics and resources of local environments. Thus a skill-intensive region might attract the design function of firms in many different industries as well as the highest added-value parts of the physical production. As high-skill areas tend to have the most discerning consumers, such regions tend also to attract the strategically important offices of the marketing department (see, e.g., Williamson and Hu 1994). In many cases, the requirements for density and frequency in the web of transactions means that the city and its immediate suburbs become the focus for the cluster.[8]

Just as Kobrin ignores the scale-diminishing edge of the technological sword, so he underestimates the demand for local variety in the global market place. The national studies hint strongly that the world is not becoming more homogeneous in all respects. Demand for goods and services that have individual or local character can be be often supplied today at economic cost by the new systems of production (for one industry study to this effect, see Baden-Fuller and Stopford 1991). These differences can become part of the distinctiveness of local clusters.

Alliance structures of association among firms are as seemingly paradoxical in their effect as technology. On the one hand, they have scale-building properties that lead some analysts to conclude that both the nation state and the firm diminish as principal agents in the organization of wealth-creating work as networks grow to transcend legal and spatial boundaries. On the other hand, the challenges of managing the networks efficiently and of maintaining flexibility suggest that there are limits to the complexity that can be accommodated.

Alliance structures, therefore, are not quite so robust in their creation of the postmodern network as Kobrin suggests. As with all other forms of organization, they have their weaknesses and are appropriate for only some forms of activity. Where they have proved inappropriate relative to the more traditional alternatives, they have collapsed. Moreover, many alliances are restricted geographically by firms' choices to transfer only part of their value chains to new locations and thus to create new international divisions of labour. These restrictions bolster the development of the regional clusters of high-density webs of transaction. They also pose new regulatory challenges, for many might be regarded as a re-emergence of the old cartels, albeit in new clothes. Germany, for example, is now studying how best it might adapt its regulations to the new competitive structures.

There is another issue in Kobrin's argument that requires further exploration, for it has implications for the general argument in this chapter. Kobrin is surely right to emphasize the importance of information systems and information technology rather than hierarchical organizations as the means of providing integration of effort in trust- and contract-based relationships. Yet, there is much behaviourial evidence to show that greater availability of information does by itself increase either common understanding or greater networking capability.

There is much evidence that the perspectives held by different societies and religions around the world remain as far apart as ever. Even in financial services —supposedly the most global of industries—the proportion of foreign stocks held in pension funds and most mutual funds remains low. Furthermore, governments serve the interests of the electorate and therefore of the societies they represent.

To take an economic perspective only and therefore presume some degree of convergence of what is deemed to be rationality limits the argument unnecessarily. If multinational enterprises have great managerial difficulty in creating common perspectives across nations and cultures for their employees—and there is growing evidence of the costs of managing this form of complexity[9]—how much more difficult for national authorities to make progress on this score.

All of these contradictory forces make forecasting about where best to concentrate the building of new competitive assets especially difficult, if not impossible. In response to such uncertainty, one firm, Royal Dutch/Shell, has developed a series of elaborate alternative scenarios on the politics of identity. In their view, the world might shift towards a setting of 'Barricades' in which national self-interest dominates and damaging 'beggar-thy-neighbour' trade policies become reintroduced in a descending spiral. The alternative is that cooperation across frontiers becomes a stronger political and social reality in a world of 'New Frontiers'. The difference between the two scenarios for the expected demand of oil by the end of the decade is enormous. Because they use scenarios, Shell does not suggest the probability of either eventuality—that would defeat the purpose of the thinking. Yet the fact that Shell sees both possibilities is just one instance of a corporation attempting to deal explicitly with the uncertainty. The key is to be able to create options that allow rapid responses to events as they occur, rather than gamble on a strategy.

7.1. **Macro-Regions**

Many of the national cases suggest that yesterday's formula for national policy has been broken by the advent of regional groupings such as the EU, and perhaps in the future by MERCOSUR. In part, the concentration and specialization of manufacturing that is taking place within such groupings helps to create the conditions of 'deep integration' that Lipsey and others have discussed. For the purposes of the argument here, such groupings are dubbed *macro*-regions to distinguish them from the *micro*-regions or local authorities discussed later.

The argument goes that the sheer weight of money and information flowing across national borders has inexorably weakened the powers of national authorities to control the domestic economy. As a former British Chancellor of the Exchequer claimed after leaving office, 'the ability of national governments to decide their exchange rate . . . and output [levels] has been savagely crippled by market forces'. This argument, in extreme form, suggests that the row over a common currency for Europe is little more than a rearguard action by politicians fearful of admitting they have already lost the game.

If this argument is true, the consequence is that the maintenance of financial stability—a critical role of the authorities in creating a climate for building and maintaining competitiveness—may be better discharged at a regional level. Thus Lipsey is one of those who argue that some sovereign powers should be ceded to regional authorities.

There are some clear benefits from accommodating the pressures for macro-regionalism. There is a need to discipline national governments and stop them from initiating stupid or overly self-interested policies. All the European cases agree that the EU has had a powerful—and perhaps beneficial—effect in limiting national excesses. There is also a need to regulate some activities at a regional level—as for European air transport and the need to reconsider competition policy in the light of the regional (as well as global) aspects of the new structures of alliance-based collaboration for competitiveness. If the efficiencies theoretically made possible by 'deep integration' at the macro-regional level actually exist, then nations must find better means to avoid the prisoner's-dilemma type of behaviour that satisfies no one.

Lipsey makes a further set of arguments for ceding some powers to supranational bodies like the WTO. These are couched in terms of dealing with the various forms of serious and persistent government failure. In particular, there are rigidities in government behaviour and limits to the administrative capability of national authorities when faced with some of the international complexities discussed above. He also points to the problems of social attitudes and the need to take an internationalist view for some matters. This last point was especially evident in the Swedish case when the early consensus about the benefits of internationalism wore away and was replaced by no more than factional argument.

7.2. **Micro-Regions**

These latter arguments about government failure can be turned on their head to make the case for micro-regions. To deal with the volatilities at the technical and competitive frontiers, enterprises need to react quickly to events. They can be assisted in this effort by working with localized authorities that understand their particular needs. It is partly in response to the inertia of national government that there is a countervailing trend towards 'micro-regionalization' and the development of what has been dubbed the 'region state' (Ohmae 1995).

The principal arguments in favour of ceding national powers to macro-regions are all to do with limiting the *negative* powers of the state. By contrast, the principal arguments in favour of the micro-region are to heighten the importance of the *positive* powers of public authorities so as to be able more readily to harness the dynamism of the markets.[10]

An investment-led climate for growth can perhaps be created most readily at the micro-regional level, as regional authorities learn to deploy national resources locally. To nurture clusters, work needs to be done to identify specific technologies that can reinforce the position of existing leaders, or that suit the skills of the workforce or even that satisfy a demand that is particularly sophisticated in the nation. Investment in the 'market-friendly' aspects of the underlying technologies can, as in Singapore, create a vital base for the building of firm-specific advantages by either local or foreign firms. The more these technologies cover the entire range of needed resources and cut across sectors represented in the cluster, the greater the leverage gained from the investment.

Many clusters, however, are incomplete in their structure. The 'holes' indicate where supplier and related industries are not well developed and can provide opportunities for new growth and perhaps even targeted intervention. The regulatory regime that permeates the cluster has to foster cooperation and mutual learning, and at the same time maintain the keen rivalry needed to provide the spur for rapid adjustment.

One key to developing clusters and to filling in the 'holes' is to pay particular attention to enhancing the capabilities of the smaller firm. Many of the specialist technologies that provide the 'glue' binding a cluster together are not very scale-intensive and seldom well developed within the large multinational. It is no accident that the successful policies in Taiwan are being carefully studied by MITI as part of the search for a way out of the 'confusion' referred to earlier. Where large firms have sufficient internal resource to fund capability developments, smaller firms can gain enormously when the transaction costs and the risks are reduced. As the high Yen forces more industrial capacity out of Japan, so the cost squeeze falls disproportionally on the smaller firms in the *keiretsu* networks. Public support to create a vital supplier network with multiple opportunities for new growth may become the centrepiece of a new economic structure that maintains the momentum of competitiveness.

Global competition is placing new demands on firms to develop multiple sources of advantage. Consequently, many leading firms are investing in developing new capabilities to manage growing internal variety of approach. The investments, in turn, are helping to reinforce the micro-regional trends; behaviour that is necessary to harness the resources of Silicon Valley is unlikely to be appropriate for success in the technological cluster around Tsukuba City in Japan.

These developments can put pressure on national authorities to relax their general policies and requirements for uniform structures and to permit more local variety. In Germany, the very strength of the educational system has been described as a growing constraint: it is slow to adapt to the new skill priorities. The debate there could lead to the Länder assuming some powers over local education tailored to the needs of the clusters such as that around Stuttgart. Similarly, the strength of the Japanese *keiretsu* system in terms of its ability to take a longer-term view of product and process developments than might be practical for an individual enterprise has been bought at the price of rigidity and a slow pace of evolution. Where the dynamics of a cluster require faster changes, cracks are appearing in the national system, permitting local variation.

8. Nation States are Alive and Well

Despite the pressures to move the focus of effective policy-making either to macro- or to micro-regions, the nation state retains and is even increasing its vitality. The national case studies are full of detail about how sovereign powers are being exercised. To claim, as does Ohmae in his advocacy of the region state (1995), that the nation state is a 'dinosaur waiting to die' is to ignore much evidence to the contrary.

One of the positive powers of national government is to foster a climate of expectations about progress and to create standards of behaviour. Most often these powers are effective when they work with the grain of industry thinking; government can act to accelerate the transfers of best practice across firms and across sector boundaries and perhaps offset some of the costs referred to earlier for the actions within firms. Public money can be used to reduce the 'barriers-to-entry' against new thinking. In Australia, as Hill and McKern emphasize, the increased competitiveness of local firms has seemed to be spurred less by increased domestic competition *per se* (the consequences of deregulation and the effect of initiatives such as the Button plans for pharmaceuticals and automobiles) and more by superior export orientation, induced in part by government investments in training (Ergas and Wright 1994). Equally important in spurring actions have been the constant political repetition at the political level of the sense of the country's destiny as being increasing attached to Asia and the need for an external orientation to achieve world-class standards.[11]

In many important respects nation states still define the boundaries of systems of wealth accumulation. Though often far removed from the tortuous decision procedures of central government and national politics, the region states are dependent upon national policy for much of their operating environment, and often public capital to create new resources. As Wade (1996) has pointed out, and as the earlier chapters have illustrated, the globalization trends are easily exaggerated.

Consider the following stylized facts. In most developed economies, about 90 per cent of production is for the domestic market, and about 90 per cent of consumption is locally produced. Domestic investment by domestic capital is financed mostly by domestic savings and far exceeds the size of FDI flows in all major markets. As suggested earlier, world stock markets are far from integrated, partly because few firms have a sufficiently strong global reputation to be traded actively on foreign markets: traders still prefer to trade those stocks they know best and to do so without exchange risk.

Managerial structures within the multinationals remain strongly biased towards the home country. Relatively few boards of directors have foreign nationals; most strategic decision-making remains concentrated at headquarters; and most R&D is undertaken at home rather than spread across the globe. Moreover, the emerging trade and investment patterns emphasize more of a focus on the macro-regions than the global market as a whole.

These are all manifestations of a world in which few resources have become mobile and where there is mobility it is easier to manage within a macro-region than more broadly. The sense of immobility is strengthened by the development of the micro-regions. These act as a magnet for further investment to allow the firms to capitalize on local learning effects. The caricature of the multinational as essentially 'footloose' following shifts in factor-cost advantage is far from the reality.

For so long as these sorts of conditions hold true, then the nation state will continue to play an important role in shaping how wealth is both created and distributed. Yet there are stresses and strains from the complexities of the adjustment process. It is not clear whether many governments can play the co-ordinating role in the macro-organizational scheme proposed by Dunning in Chapter 1 of this volume.

9. Is Consistency in the Adjustment Process Possible?

One reason for concern about the managerial capabilities of sovereign authorities is that the very nature of the countervailing shifts described earlier creates ambiguity and therefore muddle in the political response. On the domestic agenda, for example, it seems clear that policy can shift much faster than the acceptable pace of change at the level of social institutions. In Latin America, government policy at the macro-level has shifted dramatically in many countries towards market principles, but the effect of that shift has been blunted by considerable social resistance and the resilience of deeply entrenched social institutions.

Similarly, at the regional level in Europe, most attempts to create common social policy have so far been halted or so watered down that the policy guidelines are of only tenuous importance. Profound differences in the workings of local-government authorities make cooperation in the development of infrastructure hard, sometimes impossible, as the example of the Channel Tunnel illustrates. Moreover, the UK maintains its 'semi-detached' status in Europe as politicians and their electorates reconsider what a continental future really means and whether that future is welcome or not.

Such concerns are amplified and extended when one considers the implications of similar inconsistencies across borders. Not only within countries, but especially across countries, the pace of globalization is making visible the cracks in the 'architecture' of treaties and institutions, many of which could conveniently be kept out of the public eye. Global structural changes in finance, technology, knowledge, and politics have altered how governments approach the task of stimulating competitiveness and encouraging inward investment (Strange 1988). The risk now is twofold: that sovereign government will not readily concede any limitation or alteration of its direct powers; and that its actions will be inconsistent.

Like a rather tired and mangy old tiger, driven into a corner, government in a defender country may lash out in unpredictable and inconsistent ways.[12] In France, as suggested earlier, the strong EU-induced challenge to the 'Colbertist' model makes a return to actions of direct national intervention perfectly possible. Responding to the fact that the great majority of French people remain unconvinced of the benefits of internationalism, politicians may swallow their earlier rhetoric about the advantages of encouraging more inward investment and emphasize the alternative of domestically oriented employment-enhancing policies. Even though the consequences might be to reduce the attractiveness of France as an investment location, the political calculus could be to prefer short-term (and maybe cynical) expediency. So too in the UK, where 'bounded prejudice' can conceivably lead to wealth-destroying actions.

The analysis of contemporary conditions in the USA highlights the same difficulty of political calculations being made in response to opposing pressures. The resulting dilemma is 'resolved' by the drunk looking for his keys under the lamppost bathed in political light, even though far away from illumination about the real possibilities for building greater wealth and competitiveness. Domestic priorities may thus clash and the resulting inconsistencies work against progress for the nation as a whole.

10. **Conclusions**

Accelerating global competition seems entirely consistent with a nation state that is not only alive and well, but also flexing its muscles. How else can one explain the enormous range in the proportion of a nation's income that governments spend? At the high end of the scale, Singapore has nearly 70 per cent of its income spent by the government. Moreover, in many high-growth economies, governments are spending more not less. Yet, the appropriate role for sovereign government must necessarily differ according to the state of each nation.

All the evidence presented in earlier chapters is about a world in transition. There are countervailing trends at work *simultaneously* at global, macro-regional, national, and micro-regional levels. While the global capital market is rewriting the macro-economic rulebook, there are also subregional forces creating sources of new wealth.

To respond to all this complexity coherently and consistently over time is seemingly beyond the grasp of all but a few nations. When the country is no longer relatively small and relatively specialized, and especially when the need is to defend existing strengths, then the demands of Dunning's call for macro-organization are too stringent. The holistic view is possible as a matter of the perspective of the politicians and administrators, but the 'spider's web' of integrated policies and actions remains only a theoretical possibility.

The repetitive refrain in the country cases is that governments are in a state of crisis. With few exceptions, the old models have run out of power and replacements have yet to be found. This is a period of great experimentation in policy, and no doubt failures will become evident along the way.

The likely result of experimentation is that we will see a world of increasing divergence. Global competition is not producing the sort of convergence that was fashionable to forecast in the 1980s. National society and the need for local identity are but two of the reasons for both accepting and welcoming limits to a economy driven by scale alone.

A central feature of the experimentation is the shift away from government as the prime actor to government as the orchestrator of resources. This shift has placed the firm centre-stage in the process of wealth creation. The role of sovereign government remains importantly that of providing, to greater or lesser degree, the 'market-friendly' assets of general education, infrastructure, and general technology. But these are becoming commodities that by themselves do not create superior wealth. For these resources to become part of durable wealth creation, they have to be turned from generalities to specialties that are for others to emulate. That is the central message of the micro-regional developments.

To turn local dynamics into national advantage, there must be complementarity between public policies for competitiveness and private-investment policy. This seems to be an essential requirement for creating the 'favourable initial conditions' and for stimulating the stream of investments that provide the strongest response to the turbulence of the global market.

Precisely how complementarity can be established and fostered is a question that poses an enormous challenge both to theory and to policy-makers trying to come to grips with the new sources of competition. The needs for consistency and for broad consensus within the national polity fly in the face of established concepts and institutions. There is an urgent need for work on developing dynamic models that hold out some promise of illuminating the possibilities of unexpected consequences of policy in one domain (say, trade) directly affecting policy in another (say, employment and welfare). Better to invest in some flight simulators than risk the enormous expense of social failures.

NOTES

1. For the sake of brevity, I shall not attempt to attribute each point to every author that raised the thought in the national case studies. Instead, I shall use examples and trust that the others making similar points will forgive the omission.
2. There are many poor countries that have yet to begin any systematic attempt to catch up. These countries are omitted from this volume, though some of the issues about how the process might be initiated are alluded to in the chapter on Latin America.
3. There is another facet to industrial policy—dealing with declining industries. In Italy and other countries, governments can subsidize inefficient producers to stay in operation longer than would otherwise be the case. These issues are, however, beyond the scope of this chapter and are omitted.
4. Korean financial-services institutions were seen to have blunted development, because of constant government intervention.
5. For a complementary interpretation of the various Asian challenges to Japan's early leadership, see, e.g., Hobday (1995).

6. The extent of the business–government collaboration and the consequent temptation to cheat has only recently become evident. The corruption trials of late 1995 and early 1996 suggested that the problem was far greater than previously suspected.
7. South Korea spends around 2% of GDP on R&D, one of the highest rates in the world.
8. There is growth evidence from the development of East Asia that cities play a strategic role in fostering competitiveness. For example, Gipouloux (1996) claims that the trade among cities in the region is 100 times the density of trade among nation states.
9. There are considerable obstacles to the transfers of best practice and sometimes great cost. 'Best-in-class' benchmarking, as it is sometimes called, is one of the current management fashions, but one that is by no means universally affected. Managers, all too often, prefer to stick to the practices that they know from experience. Thus, even within the same firm, there are costs of transfer among scattered units. For some data, see Szulanski (1993).
10. For a review of these different powers, see Stopford and Strange (1991).
11. Perhaps ironically, since the Australian chapter was completed, the 1996 election showed just how fragile such achievements can be in the face of deep-seated social attitudes. The victorious Conservative party found they could gain political mileage from a society long suspicious of foreign investment. Several foreign takeovers became the subject of acrimonious debate, which has raised the possibility of a return to some form of controls on inward investment being reimposed.
12. I am indebted to Simon Nutall, recently retired from the European Commission, for this analogy.

REFERENCES

Amsden, A. H. (1989), *Asia's Next Giant: South Korea and Late Industrialization* (New York: Oxford University Press).

Baden-Fuller, C. W. F., and Stopford, J. M. (1991), 'Globalization Frustrated: The Case of White Goods', *Strategic Management Journal*, 12/7 (Oct.), 493–507.

—— —— (1994), *Rejuvenating the Mature Business* (Cambridge, Mass.: Harvard Business School Press).

Borrus, M., Tyson, L., and Zysman, J. (1986), 'Creating Advantage: How Government Policies Shape International Trade in the Semiconductor Industry', in P. Krugman (ed.), *Strategic Trade Policy and the New International Economics* (Cambridge, Mass.: MIT Press).

Ergas, H., and Wright, M. (1994), 'Internationalisation, Firm Conduct and Productivity', in P. Lowe and J. Dwyer (eds.), *International Integration of the Australian Economy* (Sydney: Reserve Bank of Australia), 51–105.

Gipouloux, F. (1996), *Role of Cities and Business Networks* (Paris: Seuil).

Harrison, B. (1992), 'Industrial Districts: Old Wine in New Bottles?', *Regional Studies*, 26/5: 469–83.

Hobday, M. G. (1995), *Innovation in East Asia: The Challenge to Japan* (Aldershot, Hants: Edward Elgar).

Ishiyama, Y. (1989), 'Industrial Policies of Japan and the United States—Their Mechanisms and International Implications', in K. Hiyashi (ed.), *The US–Japanese Economic Relationship: Can it be Improved?* (New York: New York University Press).

Johnson, C. (1984), 'Introduction: The Idea of Industrial Policy', in C. Johnson (ed.), *The Industrial Policy Debate* (San Francisco, Calif.: Institute for Contemporary Studies).

ITC (1983): International Trade Commission, *Foreign Industrial Targeting and its Effects on US Industries, Phase 1: Japan* (Washington: US Government Printing Office).

Lall, S. (1994), 'The East Asian Miracle Study: Does the Bell Toll for Industrial Strategy?', *World Development*, 22/4: 645–54.

Lawrence, R. Z. (1984), *Can America Compete?* (Washington: Brookings).

Minc, A. (1994), *La France de l'an 2000* (Paris: Éditions O. Jacob).

OECD (1972): Organization for Economic Cooperation and Development, *The Industrial Policy of Japan* (Paris: OECD).

Ohmae, K. (1995), *The End of the Nation State: The Rise of Regional Economies* (New York: The Free Press).

Pepper, T., Janow, M. E., and Wheeler, J. W. (1985), *The Competition: Dealing with Japan* (New York: Praeger).

Porter, M. E., *The Competitive Advantage of Nations* (New York: The Free Press).

Spencer, W. J., and Grindley, P. (1993), 'SEMATECH after Five Years: High-Technology Consortia and US Competitiveness', *California Management Review* (Summer), 9–32.

Stiglitz, J. E. (1989), 'Markets, Market Failures and Development', *American Economic Review Papers and Proceedings*, 79/2: 197–202.

Stopford, J. M., and Strange, S. (1991), *Rival States, Rival Firms* (Cambridge: Cambridge University Press).

Strange, S. (1988), *States and Markets* (London: Pinter).

Szulanski, G. (1993), 'Intra-Firm Transfer of Best Practice, Appropriate Capabilities, and Organizational Barriers to Appropriation' (INSEAD working paper).

Tyson, L. (1992), *Who's Bashing Whom? Trade Conflict in High-Technology Industries* (Washington: Institute for International Economics).

Wade, R. (1990), *Governing the Market: Economic Theory and the Role of Government in East Asian Industrialization* (Princeton: Princeton University Press).

—— (1996), 'Globalisation and its Limits', in S. Berger and R. Dore (eds.), *National Diversity and Global Capitalism* (Ithaca, NY: Cornell University Press).

Williamson, P., with Hu, Q. (1994), *Managing the Global Frontier: Strategies for Developing Markets* (London: Pitman).

World Bank (1993), *The East Asian Miracle: Economic Growth and Public Policy* (New York: Oxford University Press).

17

Should there be Multilateral Rules on Foreign Direct Investment?

Edward M. Graham

1. **Introduction**

The surge of foreign direct investment (FDI) in the late 1980s and first half of the 1990s and the associated expansion of the activities of multinational enterprises (MNEs) has left the world a somewhat different place than it was as recently as fifteen years ago. What has changed is that the 'globalization' of business, a term that had become a well-worn cliché by the early 1990s, has come to look more and more like a description of reality. MNEs account for a large share of business activities worldwide and are figuring significantly in the growth of the newly industrializing economies of the Far East (including China), the revitalization of industry in North America, and the deep integration of Europe. In addition, they conduct a substantial portion of world trade in non-agricultural goods and services. The formerly Communist nations of East Europe and the former Soviet Union all look to FDI as one means to upgrade their own economic performance; these are nations to which FDI was all but closed as recently as the late 1980s. The sources, destinations, and industrial composition of FDI have become much more diverse than was the case during the 1970s and earlier, when FDI was looked upon with suspicion.

All of this has resulted in much debate over whether the rules and institutions of the world's multilateral trading system should be augmented to cover more explicitly FDI and the international activities of MNEs. While there is no complete consensus on what the substance of new rules would be, there is a general feeling among specialists that at least three issues should be addressed.

First, the extent to which national governments should be allowed to engage in discriminatory treatment towards foreign controlled enterprises (including initial entry of these via FDI) needs clarification and, if possible, the establishment of international standards. In this regard, purists argue that the ideal standard is that there would be no such discrimination at all. This is probably unrealistic; national governments do, and probably always will, engage in discriminatory behaviour. What is needed is a set of standards to define the unacceptable limits of such behaviour.

Secondly, and more controversial, is whether there should be limits on the abilities of national governments to create and apply measures to foreign investors that have the potential to distort world allocation of resources—that is, that act in ways similar to international trade restrictive measures. Those investment measures that might be so covered include various performance requirements placed on direct investors (some such requirements are now already banned under the WTO Agreement on Trade Related Investment Measures). There is also some sentiment that subsidies to direct investment by host nations (i.e. 'investment incentives') should also be subject to international rules.

Thirdly, it is widely felt that a more effective international mechanism to resolve disputes between foreign direct investors and governments would be useful. The existing dispute settlement procedures under the WTO are conducted on a government-to-government basis, and there is a perceived need for procedures in which firms rather than governments would have standing. While such procedures do exist under the auspices of the International Centre for the Settlement of Investment Disputes (ICSID)—an agency within the World Bank—governments are neither bound by ICSID decisions nor required to submit disputes to ICSID procedures, and many firms would favour a stronger institutional setting for dispute settlement.

This debate, it should be noted, has occurred in a context of worldwide revision of national policies affecting FDI and MNEs. By and large, the global trend in this regard has been towards liberalization—that is, less regulation of MNEs and fewer restrictions on FDI. Indeed, in some areas—for example, the Far East —what were until quite recently restrictive policies towards FDI have been largely replaced by policies designed to encourage FDI. Accompanying this liberalization, however, has come much uncertainty with respect to what are the new rules. This is nowhere more apparent than in the Peoples' Republic of China. FDI is now encouraged where it would have been forbidden ten years ago. But with the new attitude towards FDI have come significant strings in the form of performance requirements on foreign investors and uncertainties with regard to what the standing of the foreign firms actually is in China. At least one rationale for multilateral rules on investment is, then, to establish some international standards for treatment that should be accorded to foreign-controlled firms as well as, perhaps, some international forum for resolution of disputes over such treatment.

It should be noted, however, that the trend is not universally towards nations liberalizing their policies towards FDI. In the USA, for example, it could be argued that the tide has flowed in the opposite direction. In particular, during a period of very high rates of FDI in the USA that lasted from roughly 1986 through 1991, numerous bills were introduced in the US Congress which aimed to place restrictions or conditions of various sorts on in-bound FDI and the activities of foreign-controlled enterprises operating in the USA.[1] Only one significant measure actually passed into US law—namely, the Exon-Florio provision of the Omnibus Trade Act of 1988. This was made, in slightly amended form, a permanent part of US law in 1991. Also, the administration of a number of US federal programmes, especially in the domain of support of high technology, has introduced measures that *de facto* discriminate against foreign-controlled firms. One possible argument for extended coverage of FDI under international rules would be for such rules to act as a counterweight against tendencies of countries to enact new laws or policies that discriminate against foreign investors.

The idea that FDI and MNEs should be subject to some sort of rules at the international level is, however, hardly a new one, nor is world commercial law devoid of such rules. Rather, there have been a number of efforts since the Second World War to create and/or extend such rules at an international level. Some of these have been pursued within regional arrangements or other institutions with limited international membership such as the OECD; others have been pursued under the institutions of the UN. Over the years, there has been a major debate as to whether the international regime should focus on regulating the conduct of MNEs themselves or should focus largely on setting standards for host-nation policy towards FDI and MNEs. Until quite recently, the developing nations, as a bloc, favoured the former approach while the developed nations preferred the latter approach (to the extent that these nations sought any international rules at all).

The next section of this chapter examines the history of efforts to create some sort of international regime regarding FDI and MNEs. The approach of this section is largely historical, but an effort is made, through the presentation, to detail what are some of the specific issues that are raised by the efforts. The third section of this chapter returns to the present context to examine the issue of where we might be going from here.

2. International Treatment of FDI from a Historic Perspective

While there does not exist any comprehensive international set of rules pertaining to FDI (or to the operations of MNEs) that are parallel to the rules governing international trade embodied in the WTO, there do exist a number of arrangements that partially cover FDI.[2] They are partial in the sense that they are either incomplete (not all issues are covered) or apply only to a limited subset of nations. These include certain of the 'new-issues' agreements administered by the WTO, and also certain rules and agreements struck in other bodies. In this section the histories of the most important of these arrangements are surveyed, including certain failed arrangements that are none the less of historic interest. The material is organized by the international organization or agreement in which they are codified, notably WTO (including its predecessor GATT), the OECD, the UN, and the 'Bretton Woods' institutions, the World Bank and the IMF. Following this, the investment-related provisions of the two important regional trading regimes, notably the EU and NAFTA are surveyed.

2.1. The WTO and GATT

Some coverage of investment issues was provided for in the Havana Charter of 1948, a failed treaty that, had it been ratified, would have supplanted the existing

GATT by enlarging the GATT rules and by creating an international organization (the International Trade Organization (ITO)) to administer the treaty had it been ratified. The Havana Charter would have created a much broader set of rules to govern international commerce than were contained in GATT. In particular, unlike GATT, the Havana Charter made provision both for international direct investment activities under Articles 11 and 12 and for competition policies (anti-trust policies) under chapter V. The ITO would thus have been granted some competence over both the policies and the actions of governments affecting international corporations and the conduct of corporations themselves.

The language of Articles 11 and 12, however, was rather weak and would not *per se* have provided for very strong international rules governing host nation policies and practices on FDI. For example, member nations of the ITO would have been exhorted 'to give due regard to the desirability of avoiding discrimination as between foreign investments'. But member nations under these articles would not have been *required* to make strong commitments on either non-discrimination or such matters as right of establishment or national treatment. The Havana Charter was silent on many issues of salience—for example, there would have been created no rules regarding the use of either investment incentives or performance requirements by host or home-nation governments. Likewise, the Havana Charter would have created no binding dispute-settlement procedure to arbitrate disputes between investors and governments, where such disputes could not be settled by the disputing parties. All of these elements, as argued in the introductory paragraphs of this chapter, have been proposed as necessary components of an international accord on investment. In other words, of the three general substantive issues that might be addressed by international rules on direct investment, only one (discrimination towards foreign investors) was touched upon by the Havana Charter, and the commitment to non-discrimination that nations would have entered into was exhortatory rather than binding.

Under chapter V, the Havana Charter would have given the ITO some powers to regulate the restrictive business practices of international corporations. Thus, the ITO would have had much more authority to regulate the activities of international firms than to regulate those actions of national governments that might have affected these firms. This asymmetry, indeed, represented a major problem that the business community, especially the USA, had with respect to the Havana Charter, and this doubtlessly contributed to the failure of the charter ever to be enacted. It should be noted, however, that the idea that there should be international rules pertaining to competition policy and its enforcement has in recent years been resurrected (see, e.g. Scherer 1994).

Thus, although the Havana Charter did provide for some rules on FDI, it really was not a model for what is now needed. It must be remembered that, from the perspective of the late 1940s, the globalization of business was neither as extensive nor as large an economic issue as it is today. Rather, at the time, the major concern was that the gains from more liberalized trade not be negated by restrictive business practices such as international cartels to fix prices or to restrict territories in which member firms could sell. Such cartels had figured significantly in world trade in the Great Depression years (for further details, see Edwards 1942 and Hexner 1945). Thus, the restrictive business practices provisions of the Havana Charter were meant primarily to deal with international trade issues rather than international investment issues *per se*.

The Havana Charter was never ratified, largely because of resistance from the US Congress. Details can be found in Diebold (1952) and Schott (1990). Thus, GATT became the major international instrument to guide world commerce. But, if the provisions of the Havana Charter pertaining to international investment were inadequate from today's perspective, those of GATT, as originally drafted, were totally useless, as they contained no provisions whatsoever to deal with international investment or competition issues. Furthermore, for almost forty years, until the Uruguay Round of multilateral trade negotiations that were begun in 1986, international investment and competition remained issues that GATT 'rounds' of multilateral trade negotiations (and other negotiations under the aegis of GATT) largely eschewed.

However, in 1981, drawing on a report of the Joint Development Committee of the IMF and the World Bank, the USA began formally to introduce host-government policies towards FDI and MNEs into GATT discussions. These efforts culminated in a decision taken at the Punta del Este meeting launching the Uruguay Round of multilateral trade negotiations to include discussions of trade-related investment measures (TRIMs).[3] In part the decision was taken so as to clarify some ambiguities left in the wake of the GATT FIRA decision (see below). The following mandate was established for the TRIMs exercise in the Ministerial Declaration of the Punta del Este meeting:

> Following an examination of the operation of the GATT articles related to the trade restrictive and distorting effects of investment measures, negotiations should elaborate, as appropriate, further provisions that may be necessary to avoid such adverse effects on trade.[4]

As just noted, the mandate was established in part to clarify the outcome of a dispute brought to GATT in 1982 by the USA over Canadian legislation that gave FIRA[5] authority to impose certain types of performance requirements on local subsidiaries of non-Canadian firms.[6] A GATT panel ruled that FIRA's imposition of local-content requirements was inconsistent with GATT article III.4 (national treatment) on the grounds that such requirements had the effect of discriminating against imported goods relative to locally produced substitutes, but noted that countries could in principle invoke article XVIII.C to justify these requirements. Canada accepted the panel's ruling, but developing countries maintained that the statement on article XVIII.C could be interpreted to mean that their own local-content requirements were consistent with GATT law, and that the FIRA ruling did not apply to them.

The TRIMs negotiations quickly became bogged down over two issues. The first was defining a TRIM, and the second was determining whether the negotiating mandate covered TRIMs only as a condition of entry for the firm or TRIMs as a condition for receipt of investment incentives as well. On the second issue, quite early on the Negotiating Committee on TRIMs decided that investment incentives *per se* should fall under the jurisdiction of the GATT Committee on Subsidies. The USA, however, interpreted this to mean that both committees were mandated to discuss TRIMs tied to investment incentives, while other nations held that this issue was reserved for the Committee on Subsidies. Given that investment incentive and performance requirements are often linked, the US position is intellectually defensible. However, the motivation for putting TRIMs tied to investment incentives into the subsidies negotiations doubtlessly was to kill any possibility of agreement in this domain. Indeed, only a very limited agreement on TRIMs tied to investment incentives emerged from the Uruguay Round.

With respect to the kinds of measures which should be considered as 'trade related' as conditions for entry, the USA proposed a list of eight types to be prohibited. Japan supported the USA on the first seven of these measures (as conditions for entry) and the EU gave its blessing to the first six. The Nordic group of nations also proposed a list, but one that was shorter and more specific. The eight generic measures proposed by the USA were:

1. local-content requirements
2. export-performance requirements
3. local-manufacturing requirements
4. trade-balancing requirements
5. production mandates
6. foreign-exchange restrictions (other than those consistent with existing GATT articles)
7. mandatory technology transfer
8. limits on equity participation and on remittances

However, when the Uruguay Round was completed in early 1994, only the first, fourth, and part of the sixth item on the list above appeared in the final TRIMs agreement. The negotiating committee had sought an agreement to which all nations could unanimously subscribe. Under this approach, 'hard-line' national governments resisting any discipline whatsoever on nations' abilities to impose TRIMs were able to prevail, such that all but what were perceived to be the most egregious of practices in clear violation of existing GATT articles were removed from the list. It would appear that this outcome did little more than codify the results of the FIRA decision and require nations to phase out those policies that were inconsistent with GATT under this decision.

Under the TRIMs agreement, nations must notify the WTO, within ninety days of the date that WTO entered into force, all TRIMs that are inconsistent with GATT. Developed nations will then have two years to phase these out; countries categorized as 'developing' or 'least developed' will have five and seven years respectively to phase out their inconsistent TRIMs. The phase-out period does not apply to TRIMs that were introduced within 180 days of the

WTO entering into force (such TRIMs must be ended immediately, subject to the exception immediately following). Countries are allowed to introduce new TRIMs during the relevant phase-out period if (and only if) these are necessary not to disadvantage existing investments currently subject to TRIMs. There is provision for the whole issue of TRIMs to be revisited before the year 2000 in order to determine if complementing provisions on investment policy or competition policy are warranted.

As noted, the Committee on Subsidies was charged with looking at investment incentives. In the end, a small step was taken—notably, subsidies contingent upon export performance or domestic sourcing were banned. Because export performance or domestic sourcing requirements themselves are banned under the TRIMs agreement, these categories of banned subsidies serve to reinforce this agreement.

The Uruguay Round also dealt with a number of additional issues that bear upon FDI. One of these was trade-related intellectual property (TRIPs) policies, which is of particular relevance because MNEs are often the conduit of technology transfer to developing nations. The ultimate objective of the industrial nations was to encourage developing nations to strengthen the substance of their patent and copyright laws and to tighten procedures for enforcing them. Many developing nations, especially a number of the Latin American NICs, had in fact been doing so unilaterally in order to create incentives for inward-technology transfer by multinational firms.

One objection raised by certain developing nations to the TRIPs exercise was the issue of overzealous enforcement of intellectual property rights. The overzealous-enforcement issue centres on the practice of the industrial nations to use border measures to block the imports of 'clone' products from developing nations on grounds that these violate patent or copyright laws when in fact no violation could be established in a legal proceeding.

Unlike in the TRIMs exercise, the developed-nation position largely prevailed in the negotiation of the TRIPs agreement. This doubtlessly resulted because sentiment in most of the larger and more rapidly growing developing nations was turning in the direction of greater legal protection for intellectual property under any circumstances. In these nations it has been recognized that foreign suppliers of advanced technology are increasingly unwilling to transfer the technology (or even in some cases to sell products embodying it) in the absence of strong intellectual property protection.

Some of the highlights of the TRIPs agreement are the following provisions:

1. A national treatment clause under which a nation must grant to the nationals of all WHO member nations treatment no less favourable than the nationals of that nation with respect to intellectual property.
2. A most favoured nation obligation under which any advantage a nation might grant to the nationals of another nation must be extended immediately to the nationals of all signing parties.

3. Detailed rules pertaining to each form of intellectual property protection (e.g. patents, copyrights, trademarks, service marks, etc.). There are also provisions pertaining to protection of trade secrets and industrial designs; integrated circuits are granted special protection. Additionally, there is a provision that prohibits any 'indication' on a product that would mislead a consumer with respect to the true origin of the product.
4. A provision to ban anti-competitive practices that might arise in licensing of intellectual property; the main provision calls for intergovernmental consultation where licensing practices might have an adverse effect on competition.
5. Enforcement and dispute settlement procedures. Minimum obligations of governments with respect to procedures for enforcement of intellectual property rights within their territories are established under this provision. Foreign holders of intellectual property rights must have access to these procedures.

Disputes under the TRIPs agreement are to be settled under the disputes settlements procedures of the WTO. Developed nations will have one year to accept the obligations of the TRIMs agreement and to bring their laws and practices into compliance with it. Developing nations would have from five years to do so, and least developed nations eleven years. Developing nations also are allowed five additional years (to bring the total to ten years) to implement laws and policies affecting pharmaceuticals and agricultural products into compliance with the TRIMs agreement.

A third area taken up in the Uruguay Round bearing upon international investment was the General Agreement on Trade in Services (GATS). In many service industries, it is difficult to disentangle 'international trade' from 'international investment'. For example, in insurance, international trade is generated when insurance policies to benefit individuals in one nation are written by a firm based in another nation. But, on practical grounds, such a transaction cannot take place unless the firm has offices and staff in place in the host as well as the home nation, and for legal reasons these offices and staff typically must be organized as a local subsidiary of the firm (and hence direct investment must take place). Indeed, in this industry, it is often difficult to determine exactly where, geographically speaking, the creation of the service takes place, and hence difficult (and possibly moot from any but a legal perspective) to disentangle 'local' provision of services by affiliates of multinationals from international trade in these services. For example, if an insurance policy is written by the US office of a German insurer to insure a party in the USA, this would be a sale associated with direct investment. But if an otherwise identical insurance policy were to be written for the same party by the company's home office in Germany, this would be considered to be an import of service into the USA from Germany. And, if the first policy were to be written by the US subsidiary but, in the event of a claim, the home office would pay, the policy would have aspects both of a sale associated with direct investment and an international trade in a service.

Similar statements can be made about other financial-services industries (e.g. banking, investment banking, and securities brokerage). In some services industries, international trade is virtually synonymous with FDI—for example, international hotel chains cannot exist without FDI.

Correspondingly, the GATS contains numerous provisions for services that are as much investment-related as trade-related. Part I of the basic agreement on services defines its scope, attempting to differentiate among (*a*) services provided in the territory of one signing party to consumers located in the territory of some other party, versus (*b*) services provided by affiliates of one party's nationals inside the territory of another signing party, versus (*c*) services provided by the nationals of one party within the territory of another party. The lattermost distinction comes into play in, for example, banking. If the banking service is provided by a subsidiary in country 2 of a bank domiciled in country 1, item (*b*) above is extant. But if the same service is provided in country 2 by a local branch of the same bank—again, it is domiciled in country 1—then item (*c*) is extant.

Parts II and III of GATS thus contain a number of provisions that might be placed in a more general investment accord. For example, the draft agreement contains an MFN obligation whereby each signing party 'shall accord immediately and unconditionally to services and service providers of any other party treatment no less favourable than that it accords to like services and services providers of any other country'. (Countries, however, may specify exceptions for MFN.) Part II provides for transparency requirements pertaining to relevant laws and regulations and a requirement that these laws and regulations be administered in an objective and impartial manner. Further provisions require that parties ensure that state-sanctioned exclusive service providers do not abuse their positions and that restrictive business practices be subject to consultations between parties with a view to their elimination. Finally, part II contains both general and security exemptions from obligations.

Part III pertains to market access and national treatment. Under GATS, however, these are not general obligations, but rather sector-specific ones that are specified in individual national schedules. Thus, for example, a foreign-controlled insurance company is not entitled under GATS to national treatment in any given nation unless the schedule of that nation lists the insurance sector. This approach, termed a 'positive-list' approach, is in fact anything but positive because the presumption is that a service activity is not entitled to the benefits brought on by a government's obligations unless that activity is actually listed. Under the market-access provisions, barriers to market access by non-national services providers would be reduced over time where such barriers exist—providing, of course, that the specific industry is listed. Also, the national treatment provision is of rather strange construction. Unlike the situation that would pertain to foreign investors under a general concept of national treatment, domestic suppliers and those of nationals of other nations are not necessarily accorded substantially the same treatment under national laws and regulations under GATS. Rather, nations are obliged not to modify conditions of competition in order to favour the domestic suppliers.

A number of annexes to the draft agreement spell out provisions pertaining to specific service sectors.

Overall, the Uruguay Round agreements introduce a number of new measures into international trade law that bear substantially upon direct foreign investment and the operations of multinational firms. Most of these constitute positive steps forward in that they are designed to liberalize the environment in which multinational firms operate. However, they fall far short of a comprehensive set of rules for international direct investment.

2.2. **The OECD**

During the 1960s the member nations of the OECD created two codes, the Code of Liberalization of Capital Movements and the Code of Liberalization of Current Invisible Operations, under which each nation pledges to remove barriers to inward or outward investment (including but not limited to direct investment), to allow free transfer of capital following liquidation of assets or the obtaining of finance in the form of long-term loans, and to allow current transactions (payments of dividends, interest payments, royalties, and so on). Although in principle OECD member nations have accepted these codes as binding, there is no mechanism in place by which they can actually be enforced and, indeed, they may be overridden by national law or policy. Under the first of these codes member nations are exhorted (but not required) to avoid introducing new exchange restrictions on capital movements or making existing regulations more restrictive.

In principle, OECD members agreed at the time of the adoption of Code on Capital Movements to accept the obligations therein *in toto*, albeit on a phase-in basis. However, member governments were allowed ‘to lodge reservations’ (article 2*b*) relating to article 2*a* obligations at such time as an item on List A of Annex A (capital-movement items) became applicable to them or when an item was added or an obligation extended to List A. Members could also lodge reservations at any time regarding items on List B of Annex A (transfer items). The reservations as lodged by member countries are contained in Annex B of the code, and a glance at this annex reveals that a number of countries (Australia, Austria, Finland, Greece, Ireland, Italy, Japan, New Zealand, Norway, Portugal, Spain, and the USA) have all listed at least some reservations with respect to inward direct investment. Many of these were sector-specific exceptions—that is, sectors in which FDI was prohibited or discouraged. In addition to the reservations lodged in this annex, under Article 3 all OECD nations could take actions affecting international capital flows deemed necessary for the maintenance of public order or public health, protection of essential national-security interests, or fulfilment of international obligations relating to peace and security without filing reservations. In addition to a reservation, an OECD member country can also lodge a ‘derogation’, the distinction being that the former is a long-term exception and the latter is in principle a temporary measure. The two codes also in principle bind each member country to a 'standstill' on new reservations and derogations—that is, an obligation not to enlarge its list of exceptions.[7]

Under OECD procedures, the practices of each member country are reviewed on a regular basis to determine if these obligations are being met. This review is conducted by the standing OECD Committee on Capital Movements and Invisible Transactions (CMIT). During a review, in principle any member country can demand that the country under review *or any other country* explain and justify any new measure that could be seen as in violation of code obligations. Also, the code calls for these governments to permit liquidation of non-resident-owned assets and the transfer of the assets or the proceeds of the liquidation, including capital gains thereon (articles 1*b* and 2*c*). How well the reviews have actually functioned is open to some debate. On the one hand, reviews are scheduled on a regular basis, and objections to individual countries' policies and practices are raised in the review sessions (but, because the record of the sessions is not made public, it is difficult to know how often this happens). On the other hand, it has been claimed by some individuals who have knowledge of what transpires in the reviews that certain OECD nations have never even made an effort to bring national policies into line with the obligations of the code, in spite of regular findings in the reviews that the country's policies are in violation of these obligations.

In addition to the two codes discussed above, which do not provide for full national treatment for foreign-controlled enterprises in member countries, the OECD in 1976 drafted a non-binding National Treatment Instrument (NTI). OECD nations choosing to adhere to the NTI (all currently do) must in principle grant national treatment to enterprises that are controlled by investors from another member country subject to reservations and derogations. A number of efforts have been mounted over the years to make the NTI binding and to make OECD countries subject to reviews similar to those conducted under the codes, but these foundered over specifics. In particular, a US-led effort to strengthen significantly the NTI failed in 1990 over the issue of whether these provisions would be binding on local governmental entities. The EU maintained that they should apply to the individual states of the USA and the provinces of Canada, a proposition to which neither the US nor Canadian government was willing to subscribe at the time.

The OECD Committee on International Investment and Multinational Enterprise (CIME) is the organ that debates how to strengthen the NTI.

Concurrently with the issuance of the Declaration on International Investment and Multinational Enterprise, the OECD nations in 1976 agreed to publish voluntary Guidelines for Multinational Enterprises that were seen as an alternative to the UN code then under negotiation (see below). These guidelines attempted to establish new norms with respect to disclosure requirements and procedures for plant closure. Otherwise, they served largely as an attempt to codify policies and practices that most OECD nations (and firms based in these nations) were already following. The USA indicated that it would accept the guidelines as a hortatory declaration only, one that had no standing in any actual situation involving US-based international firms.

In 1979 the OECD nations agreed to take limited steps to make investment incentives offered to multinational enterprises by member governments more transparent. This was in response to a nascent US effort to bring some discipline to bear on investment incentives and performance requirements (see discussion under World Bank and IMF below). The OECD issued declarations and related measures but, again, these were not binding on either member governments or firms.

In the autumn of 1994 the OECD secretariat began to prepare for an effort to create a 'multilateral agreement on investment' that would consolidate and strengthen existing codes and instruments. In June 1995 the annual meeting of OECD ministers endorsed this effort, and actual discussions among governments were scheduled to begin in September. At the time of this writing, these discussions were just beginning and no information was available on outcome.

2.3. **The UN**

As already noted, the 1976 OECD Guidelines were largely a response to negotiations taking place within the UN that were driven by a bloc of developing nations. At the time, thinking in most developing nations about the activities of MNEs was heavily influenced by leftist scholars who held that these entities were largely malevolent. As a consequence, attitudes and policies of the governments of most of these nations towards MNEs tended to be hostile.

Thus, during a period of time lasting roughly from the first oil crisis in 1974 until the debt crisis of 1982, these nations as a bloc (the 'Group of 77') sought within the UN to create a 'new international economic order' that would favour developing nations' interests over those of the industrialized nations along lines set out by leftist thinking. Two keystones of the 'new international economic order' were to be the negotiation of both a mandatory code of conduct for MNEs and a code to regulate restrictive business practices of these firms. Although negotiating committees were formed, none of the major industrial nations saw these as serious exercises and no international agreements have resulted. On the recommendations of the UN Economic and Social Council, the drafting of the code of conduct was begun in the mid-1970s. Originally the code was to cover only the conduct of firms. In 1980 it was agreed that the draft should be expanded to cover the conduct of governments as well.

A completed draft was presented to the UN Commission on Transnational Corporations in 1982, but no consensus could be found to implement the code at that time. In 1988 through 1990 there was an effort by certain developing nations and the UN Secretariat to revive the by-then moribund negotiations on this code, and a revised draft was submitted to the Economic and Social Council, which forwarded it to the General Assembly. In 1992 the General Assembly failed to reach a consensus on the code, and a special intra-governmental group was convened to suggest further action. This group recommended that an alternative to the code be found, which in effect terminated the whole exercise.

2.4. **The World Bank and the IMF**

In 1979 the USA opened discussions with a group of developing and industrialized nations within the context of the Joint Development Committee of the IMF and the International Bank for Reconstruction and Development—the World Bank—over possible discipline on host countries' use of measures to tilt the advantages of FDI to their national economies. The work of the Task Force on International Investment that was constituted to explore this issue was pursued in tandem with the OECD discussions on investment incentives and performance requirements that resulted in the 1979 agreement noted above. The measures considered by the Task Force included performance requirements on MNEs. The USA emphasized the distorting (and thus anti-developmental) effects of these requirements when they were made a condition for either entry by foreign firms or receipt of investment incentives. The result of these discussions was a report concluding that performance requirements could have distorting effects on both development and world trade. A number of academic works subsequently bolstered this conclusion; see, for example, Grossman (1984), Davidson *et al.* (1985), and Guisinger (1985), which is the published version of a study commissioned by the Development Committee. More recently there has appeared additional work on the possible distorting effects of investment incentives; see, for example, Moran (1990), Guisinger and Loree (1993), and UNCTAD (1995). Although neither the World Bank nor the IMF subsequently took any actions on these conclusions, the report of the Development Committee was an important impetus towards the launching of the TRIMs exercise in the Uruguay Round (see discussion above.)

Within the World Bank ICSID is designed to facilitate settlements of disputes between investor firms and host nations. Currently 130 nations are signatories to ICSID. However, ICSID has not been frequently used as a facility actually to settle investment disputes. During 1994, for example, only five cases were handled by ICSID. ICSID could become more active in the future if it is used, as envisaged, as the principle arbitral body for the settlement of investment disputes under the North American Free Trade Association, chapter 11, part B, dispute settlement mechanism (see discussion below).

Also within the World Bank there exists the Multilateral Investment Guarantee Agency (MIGA), an institution designed to supplement and perhaps eventually supplant national investment insurance programmes such as the Overseas Private Investment Corporation (OPIC) in the USA. Like its national counterparts, MIGA was designed to encourage FDI specifically in developing economies. But, to date, like ICSID, MIGA appears to be somewhat under-utilized. In 1994, although 147 countries were signatories to MIGA, only slightly more than 100 such contracts were outstanding, with contingent liabilities of about $US1 billion. However, the demand for MIGA guarantees has been rising; in 1992 there were 244 applications for these guarantees, and in 1994 the number of applications more than doubled, to 574. Much of the demand for guarantees is associated with investment in the formerly socialist nations.

MIGA also provides technical assistance to developing countries through its Foreign Investment Advisory Service (FIAS). In 1994 FIAS completed twenty-nine projects in twenty-six different countries.

2.5. **Regional Approaches to FDI**

In addition to multilateral institutions, certain regional international groupings have instituted rules pertaining to international investment and multinational enterprises. These are of importance because the rules implemented within these groupings have tended to have more 'bite' than those at a multilateral level. Indeed, many analysts believe that the correct models for a future global set of standards are better found in these regional groupings than in the multilateral organizations. The most significant of these groupings are the EU and NAFTA. Interestingly, there is almost no overlap between the rules of the two. Whereas the EU has built up a substantial body of law and policy in the areas of competition policy which can affect international investment and multinational enterprises, there is no law and policy in the EU directed towards international investment *per se*. By contrast, the NAFTA lacks any law and policy in the domain of competition policy but breaks new ground in creating rules directed explicitly towards FDI and how multinational firms operate.[8]

Also considered in this subsection are efforts within the nascent APEC to create standards for FDI.

2.5.1. The EU

That international cartels can pose a threat to gains from international trade liberalization was embodied in the Havana Charter, but, as we have seen, this was never enacted. However, this same concern was reflected in the language of the Treaty of Rome establishing the European Common Market, drafted in the middle 1950s, wherein articles 85 and 86 deal with cartels and monopolistic business practices (the latter, in the language of the article, 'abuse of a dominant firm position') and articles 92 and 93 deal with state aids to industry or regions that might distort competition or intra-European trade. Significantly, the European Commission was given powers to deal with these practices beyond those granted in almost any other domain. There are no other European-wide rules or policy pertaining to FDI or multinational enterprises *per se* in the Treaty of Rome, however, and it is an unsettled issue as to whether the European Commission has authority to implement such rules or to negotiate them in international fora.

Nonetheless, because articles 85 and 86 of the Treaty of Rome do give the European Commission rather broad powers to deal with cartels and abuse of dominant firm position, the Commission holds limited but significant power to regulate the European activities of MNEs. These powers, administered by Directorate General IV (DG IV) of the European Commission[9]—the Competition Directorate—have indeed been used on occasion to regulate MNEs, especially in the domain of mergers regulation. In fact, an early milestone in efforts by DG IV to apply articles 85 and 86 to mergers was the successful blockage in 1972 of an attempt by the Continental Can Company of the USA to attain a dominant position in the European industry via acquisition. In spite of this milestone, however, the EU was unable to achieve a mergers regulation until 21 December 1989.[10] Under the 1989 regulation, the European Commission (i.e. DG IV) can review a merger or acquisition involving two firms meeting certain minimum size criteria and criteria for minimum involvement in the EU. If these criteria are met, the Commission can, in principle, block a merger or acquisition involving one or more firms not domiciled in or controlled by nationals of the EU. And, in fact, the first blockage of a major merger did indeed involve a non-US firm; this was the proposed merger in 1992 of De Havilland, a Canadian-based aircraft firm under the control of the US aerospace giant Boeing, by Aerospatiale, the French partner in the European Airbus consortium.

In addition to power to regulate certain aspects of MNE conduct, the European Commission has limited powers over governments. The most important of these are powers to curb subsidies to enterprises (including state-owned enterprises) by national governments under articles 92 and 93 of the Treaty of Rome. In particular, article 92 states *inter alia* that 'any aid granted by a Member State in any form whatsoever which distorts or threatens to distort competition by favouring certain undertakings or the production of certain goods shall, in so far as it affects trade between Member States, be incompatible with the Common Market'. Any measure that is deemed to be 'incompatible with the Common Market' is, in principle, banned. This provision gives the Commission power to curb investment subsidies and other, subsidy-like investment incentives to multinational enterprises.

In practice, however, investment subsidies in Europe are rife and little has been done at the level of the EU to inhibit member countries from granting them. Article 92 allows for a number of exceptions to the principle articulated in the preceding paragraph (as do a number of other articles of the Treaty of Rome), and many investment subsidies fall into these exceptions. Relevant exceptions include aid to regions where the standard of living is considered to be abnormally low and aid 'to promote the execution of an important project of common European interest or to remedy a serious disturbance in the economy of a Member State'. In 1988–90 the total state aid in Europe averaged $US103 billion per year, of which about 40 per cent went to manufacturing industries.

During the 1990s the European Commission has attempted to toughen up its authority to monitor and regulate state aid to industry. Article 93 calls for the

Commission to 'keep under constant review' all systems of aid in the EU and empowers the Commission to order such aid to be abolished if it is deemed incompatible with the Common Market.[11] In particular, under the tenure of Sir Leon Brittan as Commissioner for Competition Policy, DG IV attempted to abolish subsidies to many manufacturing firms, going so far as to order repayment of the subsidies in some cases, including subsidies paid as investment incentives to some multinational enterprises. However, Member nations frequently questioned whether or not DG IV was overstepping its authority in doing so, and some of the cases were referred to the European Court of Justice. Karel van Miert, the EU commissioner in charge of competition policy at the time of writing (August 1996) has in principle continued with the policies of Brittan, but some observers believe that DG IV under van Miert has significantly softened its line.

2.5.2. NAFTA

In contrast to the law and policy of the EU, the treaty to establish a NAFTA among Canada, Mexico, and the USA does contain explicit provisions pertaining to direct investment.[12] Most of the provisions relating to investment are in chapter 11. These include:

(1) National treatment for investors from other NAFTA countries on the part of national, state, provincial, and local governments, whereby any such government must accord to investors (and investments of investors) from other NAFTA signing party nations treatment that is 'no less favorable than that it accords, in like circumstances, to its own investors with respect to the establishment, acquisition, expansion, management, conduct, operation, and sale or other disposition of investments' (article 1102.1).[13] Thus, national treatment in the context of NAFTA includes right of establishment.

(2) Most-favoured-nation and minimum-standard-of-treatment provisions (articles 1103–5), which are designed to ensure that any treatment accorded by a NAFTA government to investors and investments from NAFTA countries is no less favourable than treatment granted to investors and investments from non-NAFTA countries.

(3) Most new performance requirements on investments in NAFTA countries are banned, and old performance requirements must be phased out (article 1106). Also, most linking of performance requirements to receipt of subsidies is prohibited. These prohibitions apply to all investments and not just those of NAFTA investors.

(4) NAFTA investors can convert earnings, proceeds of sales, loan repayments, or other capital transactions into any foreign currency at prevailing market rates of exchange (article 1109).

(5) No NAFTA country can expropriate investments of NAFTA investors except for a public purpose, on a non-discriminatory basis, and in accordance with principles of due process of law. In the event of an expropriation, investors

must be paid at the fair market value of the investment and without delay (article 1110).

Under NAFTA chapter 11, a set of new procedures for the resolution of investment disputes is created (articles 1115–38). These go beyond any mechanism yet in place or proposed in any other agreement on international investment. Under these procedures, most investors (but not investments) may seek arbitration of a dispute against a signing party. In most other international dispute-settlement mechanisms (most notably, those of WTO), only governments have standing to use the mechanism, and hence an investor must be represented by a government in any proceeding to resolve a dispute utilizing such a mechanism, even if the government is not a direct party to the dispute. Under the NAFTA chapter 11 procedures, however, an investor can pursue a claim on its own behalf or on behalf of its investment against a NAFTA government if the investor can claim monetary loss or damages resulting from alleged breaches of chapter 11 obligations (or certain other obligations) by that government. An effort must first be made to solve the dispute by means of consultation and negotiation (article 1118). If these fail, the dispute can be submitted to binding arbitration under the rules of ICSID (see above) or the United Nations Commission on International Trade Law (UNCITRAL). Under either set of rules, a tribunal (i.e. arbitration panel) is empowered to order interim measures to protect the rights of the disputing investor and to order that an award be made to the investor in the form of monetary (but not punitive) demages and/or restitution of property with applicable interest. The tribunal cannot, however, order a government to revoke or rescind a measure deemed to be in violation of NAFTA obligations. Any award granted by the tribunal is without prejudice to any right that an investment might have to relief under domestic law.

Under NAFTA there are numerous exceptions allowed to signing parties to the chapter 11 obligations. These include general exceptions (e.g. a national-security exception) and country- and sector-specific ones, spelt out in the annexes to chapter 11. These are discussed in detail in Gestrin and Rugman (1993) and Graham and Wilkie (1994).

The environmental accord negotiated as a 'sidebar' to NAFTA includes a provision that no country will lower its environmental standards in order to attract a new investment undertaking.

In addition to these provisions, NAFTA contains provisions pertaining to competition policy and the regulation of state enterprises and state-sanctioned monopolies. Also, NAFTA contains a number of measures designed to liberalize trade in financial services which, *inter alia*, grant right of establishment to financial-services providers of one NAFTA country in the territories of others.

Somewhat offsetting the liberalizing provisions of NAFTA in the view of many are complex rules of origin. These prescribe complex and legalistic procedures for calculation of local content which, in the view of some analysts at least, act to favour incumbent firms over new entrants if the new entrants happen to be non-North American multinational firms.

At the time of writing (August 1996), NAFTA has been in effect for slightly more than a year and a half, and it is not possible to assess the effectiveness of the provisions pertaining to direct investment therein. However, in principle, in the direct-investment area, NAFTA seems to represent a significant net step forward.

2.5.3. APEC

The heads of state of the APEC nations, at their second meeting held in Bogor, Indonesia, in November 1994, agreed to a set of non-binding investment principles. Development of these principles had been recommended the previous year by the APEC Eminent Persons Group at the 1993 ministerial meeting of APEC held in Seattle. Also, substantially the same principles that were agreed to in Bogor had previously been developed by the Pacific Economic Cooperation Council (PECC), through its Trade Policy Forum, in the form of a model voluntary code for direct investment that was presented for consideration by governments at the Seattle meeting. At the APEC Heads of State meeting held just after the ministerial meeting in Seattle, the Committee on Trade and Investment (CTI) of APEC was charged with developing a set of non-binding investment principles to be considered at ministerial level the following year in Bogor.

The CTI subsequently created an experts' group on investment principles that met several times during 1994 in order to draft a set of such principles. It was agreed that the objective of these principles would be to facilitate, rather than to inhibit, FDI and technology transfer. The principles would be strictly non-binding and thus, *inter alia*, would not prejudice existing applicable international instruments, including bilateral investment treaties. At the CTI meetings there was considerable diversity expressed by the representatives of the various APEC nations with respect to what policy regimes towards FDI were desirable, and in the end many compromises were struck. As a result, the following principles were emphasized as ones to which APEC nations as host nations to direct investment might aspire rather than be bound:

1. *Transparency*: member countries would make all laws, regulations, administrative guidelines, and other instruments of policy (including those instruments by which policy is actually implemented) publicly available in a form that was readily accessible to the public.
2. *Non-discrimination between source economies*: member countries would extend to investors from any nation treatment in relation to the establishment, expansion, or operation of their (the investors') investments (e.g. subsidiaries) that is no less favourable than that accorded to investors from any other nation in like circumstances.
3. *National treatment*: with exceptions as provided for in domestic laws, regulations, and policies, member nations would accord to foreign investors

in relation to the establishment, expansion, operation, and protection of their investments treatment no less favourable that accorded in like situations to domestic investors.

4. *Investment incentives*: member nations would not relax health, safety, and/or environmental regulations as an incentive to encourage foreign investors to place investments within their economies.
5. *Performance requirements*: member countries would minimize the use of performance requirements (requirements placed by governments on foreign investors to meet certain specified objectives) as a means of achieving policy objectives in circumstances where these would distort or limit expansion of trade and investment.[14]
6. *Expropriation and compensation*: member nations would not expropriate foreign investments or take measures that have the effect of expropriation, except for a public purpose, on a non-discriminatory basis, and in accordance with the laws of the country and principles of international law. If an investment were to be appropriated, the investor would be adequately and effectively compensated.
7. *Repatriation and convertibility of funds*: member nations would allow the free and prompt transfer of funds related to FDI, such as repatriation of profits or dividends, royalties, loan payments and liquidations, in freely convertible currencies, subject to the laws of each country.
8. *Settlement of disputes*: member countries would accept that disputes arising in connection with a foreign investment would be settled promptly through consultations and negotiations between the parties to the dispute (the investor and the host-nation government) or, failing this, through procedures for arbitration in accordance with members' international commitments or through other arbitration procedures acceptable to both parties.
9. *Entry and sojourn of personnel*: member countries would permit the temporary entry and sojourn of key foreign technical and managerial personnel for the purpose of engaging in activities connected with the foreign investment, subject to relevant laws and regulations.
10. *Avoidance of double taxation*: member countries would seek to avoid double taxation of income related to FDI.
11. *Investor behaviour*: acceptance of foreign investment is facilitated when foreign investors abide by the host nation's laws, regulations, administrative guidelines, and policies.
12. *Removal of barriers to foreign capital*: member economies accept that regulatory and institutional barriers to the outflow of investment will be minimized.

The question might be legitimately asked, if these principles are not binding, of what value are they? Do they, for example, protect investors in any meaningful way from arbitrary or capricious actions by host or home governments? Given that governments are not bound by the principles, a violation of any of them could not be the subject of a challenge in the domestic courts of a nation held to be in violation, because they would have no standing in domestic law. Likewise, it is hard to conceive of a government being willing to enter into arbitration of a dispute involving alleged breach of one of the principles under the international rules established under ICSID or UNCITRAL. Thus, in a legalistic sense, the principles indeed provide no protection.

The principles could be of value, however, if governments in the APEC region felt inclined to bring national law and policy into conformity with the principles or even simply felt that in the *de facto* exercise of law and policy they should observe the spirit of the principles. Westerner lawyers might feel some discomfiture with the rather imprecise language of the principles. However, it should be noted that in many of the East Asian nations the legal tradition—as far as civil law goes, at least—is for the letter of the law to be somewhat loosely or even ambiguously stated but for the law to be interpreted according to rule of reason. Also, the East Asian approach to the settlement of disputes is to attempt to the maximum extent for these to be settled informally and in a fashion where neither party 'wins' or 'loses' but where both parties accept an outcome that is fair to both. Such an approach requires that there be a common understanding with respect to what is fair. The investment principles might thus help establish such an understanding in the domain of national policy towards direct investment.

Whether this last comes to pass, the APEC experience demonstrates two realities of 1995. The first is that a diverse group of nations, including some of the most dynamic of the newly industrializing nations, were willing to discuss some sort of international convention on direct investment embodying the principles that were recommended in the previous chapter. The second, alas, is that, while these nations are willing to talk about these principles, they are not yet prepared to bind themselves to them. At the end of the day, the APEC non-binding investment principles are nothing but a hortatory declaration, and in language that is often ambiguous as well. The principles represent the beginning of a dialogue, but not a satisfactory end product.

3. Where do We Go from Here?

At best, the current international policy regime affecting FDI and multinational enterprises consist of a mishmash of rules that are in principle binding upon governments (e.g. those of NAFTA), voluntary principles (e.g. those of APEC), and half-way measures (e.g. the TRIMs agreement of the WTO). Coverage is not universal in either a geographic sense or a substantive sense. The obvious question that can be posed is, what policy regime might be better?

There are at least three alternatives.

One alternative would be to do nothing. Proponents of this alternative argue that what really matters is policy at the level of national and sub-national governments and that, during the past decade, in most areas of the world the direction of policy change is towards liberalization.[15] International rules, it is argued, would imply nothing more than a more complex bureaucracy and the costs of additional international civil servants. Extreme advocates of the view argue that, in fact, an optimal set of policies might be achievable via 'policy competition' among nations where each nation seeks to maximize its own interests with respect to FDI.

This view, however, can be challenged. While the trend worldwide might indeed be towards liberalization of policies affecting FDI, many restrictions on direct investors remain in place, and often these restrictions work to the benefit of local special-interest groups (e.g. those firms seeking to protect local monopoly rents), and hence 'policy competition' might not necessarily be based upon each country maximizing overall national interests but rather be dominated in many countries by special-interest groups. Thus, it is argued, some sort of international rules to spell out rights and obligations of host and home governments would at least establish an international norm for proper policy. Additionally, if governments are required to specify explicitly what exceptions to those obligations are in place, international rules could also achieve some measure of transparency, often cited as an important objective in its own right.

It should be noted that the international business community itself seems to favour explicit international rules to 'policy competition' (see BIAC 1995).

Thus, remaining alternatives to reforming the international policy regime come down to how to implement an agreement to establish international rules. On this matter, there are a number of possibilities.

One alternative (call this alternative 2, alternative 1 being to do nothing) would be for a new agreement to be negotiated within the aegis of the WTO. Exactly what would be the substance of such an agreement is a topic that will doubtlessly fill quite a number of conferences during the coming several years, but many advocates of such an agreement point to chapter 11 of NAFTA (discussed above) as being an appropriate starting-point. Two reasons for creating such an agreement within the venue of the WTO are as follows. First, the WTO represents most of the nations of the world with a significant stake in FDI (one major exception is China, but China is likely to be admitted to the WTO sometime in the proximate future). Thus, a WTO-based agreement would involve all of the major nations involved in FDI, either as host or home nations. Secondly, substantive issues pertaining to FDI are increasingly linked to those pertaining to international trade and hence it is desirable that these two sets of issues be dealt with under the 'same roof'. The 'same roof' might also help with respect to enforcement of obligations under the agreement on investment—for example, if violation of obligations could be subject to trade or trade-related sanctions.

The main problem with alternative 2, however, derives from the very fact that the WTO is an organization with a very wide membership. The fear is that it might prove difficult, if not impossible, to achieve consensus on the substance of a WTO agreement on FDI. As noted above, the effort within APEC to develop a set of non-binding investment principles encountered the difficulty of there being no consensus on what should be the substance of these (even though the principles were non-binding, nations could not agree on what they were not committing themselves to!), and this difficulty would be likely to be magnified several-fold at the level of the WTO.

Thus, it has also been proposed that some sort of agreement on FDI be hammered out among a subset of nations holding something like a common view on what would be the substance of the agreement (let us call this alternative 3). In fact, as noted, such an exercise is being carried out within the OECD during 1996–7. The OECD Multilateral Agreement on Investment (MAI), if successfully completed, will not even necessarily be binding upon all OECD nations; rather each nation could decide whether or not to participate in the agreement. Also, non-OECD nations wishing to commit to the agreement would be free to do so.

However, problems have already appeared with respect to this approach. In a number of forums, representatives of nations that are not OECD members have expressed views ranging from discomfiture to out-and-out resentment over the negotiation of an agreement to which their governments are not party. Non-OECD nations have become both major hosts and sources of FDI in recent years, and the claim is that the interests of these nations are not represented in the OECD negotiations. Indeed, it is reported that at one meeting held at the headquarters of UNCTAD in late 1995, leaders of certain major developing nations indicated that they would not participate in an OECD MAI even if they found the substance of the agreement to their liking. The sentiment essentially was that it is no longer acceptable that the rich countries (i.e. the member nations of the OECD) force an international agreement upon the developing nations. Furthermore, although the substance of the OECD negotiations is meant at this time to be confidential, reports have leaked out that the commonality of views held by various member nations with respect to substantive issues might not be as strong as was initially believed.

There are also institutional issues that surround the MAI that could prove thorny. The big questions in this domain are, if an MAI is successfully concluded, how will it be administered and under what circumstances would new members be admitted? The OECD, unlike the WTO, is not an organization geared towards administering a multilateral agreement. Would the effort be made to transform the existing OECD secretariat into an administrative body? If so, how would OECD non-member nations that sought to participate in the MAI be handled? Would, instead, a separate administrative organization be created?

Which of these three alternatives is actually likely to prevail is a very open question. Alternative 2 would at first appear to have a commanding lead over the other two alternatives if for no other reason than that the OECD MAI negotiations are actually in progress. But it remains to be seen whether these negotiations can be brought to a satisfactory conclusion and, if so, how many countries (especially non-OECD member nations) would actually be willing to commit themselves to the agreement. Alternative 3 is likely to be widely discussed during

1996, because the issue of whether the substantive coverage of agreements under the WTO should be expanded to include FDI is likely to be one topic of the WTO meeting at ministerial level scheduled to take place in Singapore in December of this year. But whether anything concrete will actually emerge from this meeting is very much in doubt. One reason is that the OECD countries, or at least some significant subset of them, might urge that the WTO not enter into this domain until after completion (or termination) of the MAI negotiations. Alternative 1, of course, would prevail by default if neither alternative 2 nor 3 takes wing.

Which of the three alternatives is preferable? All three pose problems but, all things considered, the second alternative (WTO) wins by default. The first alternative is rejected by almost everyone except a small band of *laissez-faire* enthusiasts who honestly believe that there is a surrogate 'policy market' in which governments compete for FDI and, by competing, can arrive at an optimal mix of policies. This concept is rejected even by most multinational firms, even though the executives of these firms tend to believe in minimal government. These firms prefer international standards for governmental policies, in order to achieve consistency and predictability and, through a dispute settlement procedure, to have access to some form of recourse in the event that international standards are violated by a government (BIAC 1995). The third alternative is likely to produce an agreement to which only the OECD nations (or, more likely, some subset of these nations) commit themselves; it is unlikely that many, or indeed any, non-OECD nations would be willing to 'dock on' to an agreement where they were excluded from the negotiations that led to the creation of the agreement. But non-OECD nations figure importantly as both host and home nations to FDI, and an MAI without participation of these nations makes little sense. The second alternative has the advantage that such nations necessarily would be included in any arrangement that might be achieved under the WTO. The further advantage is that obligations entered into under a WTO arrangement could be made more enforceable via linkage to trade sanctions (and, without some possibility of sanctions on violation of obligations, an agreement on investment would be little more than hortatory). The main difficulty lies in whether nations are, at this time, willing to commit themselves to hard and binding international rules. On this, only time and further discussion will tell.

NOTES

1. These are covered in detail in Graham and Krugman (1995).
2. This section is adapted from Graham (1996: ch. 5).
3. An extensive treatment of the TRIMs exercise is contained in Graham and Krugman (1990).
4. GATT (1986).

5. FIRA was an agency of the government of Canada. It was later renamed Investment Canada.
6. Investment Canada as a separate agency of the Canadian government was dissolved in June 1993; part of the function of Investment Canada was transferred to the Ministry of Foreign Affairs and part to the Department of Industry and Science.
7. The codes also commit each member nation over time to 'roll back' its exceptions, i.e. to reduce these in number or scope. However, there has *de facto* been very little such reduction.
8. Provision is made in the NAFTA agreement for a future extension into competition policy.
9. Article 3 of the Treaty of Rome requires that 'the activities of the Community shall include . . . the institution of a system ensuring that competition in the common market is not distorted'.
10. This regulation actually entered into force in September 1990.
11. The relevant authority is also administered by DG IV. Under a 1972 treaty, the Commission can take measures against Austria if its policies are found to be incompatible with a free trade agreement with Austria.
12. A detailed analysis of the investment provisions of NAFTA is contained in Graham and Wilkie (1994). See also Gestrin and Rugman (1993).
13. Under NAFTA parlance, the term 'investment' generally would include a subsidiary or other legal affiliate of a multinational firm and 'investor' the parent organization of that subsidiary.
14. It should be noted that member nations of the WTO will be subject to the agreement on TRIMs, which will disallow the use of certain types of performance requirements such as domestic content or trade balancing requirements. Because most APEC member nations are WTO members, there is feeling that the APEC agreement represents a retrogression.
15. The extent of liberalization is documented in recent issues of the *World Investment Report* issued annually by UNCTAD; see especially UNCTAD (1994).

REFERENCES

BIAC (1995): Business and Industry Advisory Committee, 'Supplementary BIAC Recommendations for the OECD Multilateral Investment Agreement' (Paris: Organisation for Economic Cooperation and Development).

Davidson, C., Matusz, S., and Kreinen, M. (1985), 'Analysis of Performance Standards for Direct Foreign Investments', *Canadian Journal of Economics*, 18/4 (November), 876–90.

Diebold, W. (1952), *The End of ITO* (Princeton: International Finance Section, Dept. of Economics and Social Institutions, Princeton University).

Edwards, C. D. (1942), *Economic and Political Aspects of International Cartels* (Washington: US Government Printing Office).

GATT (1986): General Agreement on Tariffs and Trade, *Ministerial Declaration of the Punta del Este Meeting* (Geneva: General Agreement on Tariffs and Trade).

Gestrin, M., and Rugman, A. M. (1993), 'The NAFTA's Impact on the North American Investment Regime', *C. D. Howe Institute Commentary*, no. 42.

Graham, E. M. (1996), *Global Corporations and National Governments: Are Changes Needed in the International Economic and Political Order in Light of the Globalization of Business?* (Washington: Institute for International Economics).

—— and Krugman, Paul R. (1995), *Foreign Direct Investment in the United States* (3rd edn., Washington: Institute for International Economics).

—— —— (1990), 'TRIMs in the Uruguay Round', in Jeffrey J. Schott (ed.), *Completing the Uruguay Round: A Results-Oriented Approach to the GATT Negotiations* (Washington: Institute for International Economics).

—— and Wilkie, C. (1994), 'Multinationals and the Investment Provisions of the NAFTA', *International Trade Journal*, 8/4 (spring).

Grossman, G. M. (1984), 'The Theory of Domestic Content Protection and Content Preference', *Quarterly Journal of Economics*, 96/1 (Nov.), 583–603.

Guisinger, S. E. (1985), *Investment Incentives and Performance Requirements: Patterns of International Trade, Production, and Investment* (New York: Praeger Publishing).

—— and Loree, D. (1993), 'Policy and Non-Policy Determinants of US Foreign Direct Investment' (mimeo; The University of Texas at Dallas).

Hexner, E. (1945), *International Cartels* (Chapel Hill, NC: University of North Carolina Press).

Moran, T. H. (1990), 'The Impact of Trade Related Investment Measures (TRIMs) on Trade and Development: Theory, Evidence, and Policy Implications' (mimeo, Georgetown University School of Foreign Service).

OECD (1990): Organization for Economic Cooperation and Development, *Investment Incentives and Disincentives: Effects on International Direct Investment* (Paris: OECD).

Schott, J. J. (1990), 'US Policies Toward the GATT: Past, Present, Prospective', in R. Rode (ed.), *GATT and Conflict Management: A Transatlantic Strategy for a Stronger Regime* (Boulder, Colo.: Westview Press, published in cooperation with the Peace Research Institute, Frankfurt).

Scherer, F. M. (1994), *Competition Policies for an Integrated World Economy* (Washington: Brookings Institution).

UNCTAD (1994): United Nations Conference on Trade and Development, *World Investment Report 1994: Transnational Corporations, Employment and the Workplace* (Geneva: United Nations).

—— (1995), *World Investment Report 1995: Transnational Corporations and Competitiveness* (Geneva: United Nations).

INDEX